GREENBOOK®
Guide to the
PRECIOUS MOMENTS®
Collection
by Enesco

13th Edition

1999

The Most Respected Guides to Popular Collectibles
& Their After Market Values

P.O. Box 645
Pacific Grove, CA   93950
831.656.9000
FAX 831.656.9004
www.greenbooks.com

ISBN   0-923628-64-9

Printed in the United States.

The GREENBOOK would like to thank -

SAM BUTCHER.

PRECIOUS MOMENTS, INC., for assisting in the compilation of the factual information contained in this Guide.

ENESCO, for assisting in the compilation of the factual information contained in this Guide.

THE PRECIOUS MOMENTS CHAPEL, for assisting in the compilation of the factual information contained in this Guide.

KRISTI SCHULT, of PRECIOUS MOMENTS Collectible Treasures.

LORI HOLLE, PM Enterprises, Lincoln, NE, secondary market specialist.

The DEALERS, COLLECTORS and PUBLICATIONS across the country who take their valuable time to supply us with information including secondary market status and prices.

⁴ Editor & Publisher Louise Patterson Langenfeld

Louise Patterson Langenfeld is unique in collectible annals, for she grew up immersed in collectibles. Her father developed the BRADEX, the first comprehensive listing of collector plates and their secondary market values, for the world renowned BRADFORD EXCHANGE. A graduate of Michigan State University, during summers and school breaks, Louise helped her Dad with his successful limited edition plate publishing business. Louise attended many South Bend Conventions, greeting and getting to know collectors in the exhibit.

After graduation, Louise gained a thorough education in retailing, working for New York Department Stores Abraham & Strauss. In the early eighties, she joined her father full time.

In 1985, they realized that there was no comprehensive, complete guide to one of the most popular new products, Enesco's Precious Moments Collection. Encouraged by her Dad, Louise proudly published the first GREENBOOK Guide to the Enesco Precious Moments Collection in 1986.

Louise can muddle through the most confusing complexity of information, reducing it to comprehensible components. Collectors appreciate her clear thinking and ability to discern the important facets of a collection. GREENBOOK Guides, deceptively simple in appearance, are chock-full of every fact any collector seeks. Every new Guide enjoys ever growing audiences, and imitators. Like the words Kleenex or Xerox have come to represent facial tissues and photocopies, GREENBOOK has come to mean secondary market price guide to many. GREENBOOK Guides are vastly different, collectors learn, for no detail is overlooked, and pricing is based on research, not fiction.

GREENBOOK is Louise. Her vision and concern for the collector is legend. As collectors' tastes and interests change, Louise is at the forefront, documenting and reflecting current enthusiasms. Her innovation and understanding of the collectible marketplace led GREENBOOK to be the first to document the Enesco Cherished Teddies Collection, and, more recently, Ty Beanie Babies. When a new product becomes hot, collectors, retailers, secondary market dealers and even makers turn to GREENBOOK, urging publication of the definitive GREENBOOK Guide.

1997 saw the launch of the very first GREENBOOK Guide on CD-Rom. Computer-savvy collectors are delighted, for this innovative product makes everything much easier, from insurance documentation to shopping Wishlists.

Louise's husband, Nick Langenfeld, joined GREENBOOK in 1996 to bear the administrative load leaving Louise free to develop even more Guides. And to enjoy some leisure time watching their 10-year-old daughter, Ally, compete on her horse, Bubble Bath.

Table Of Contents

GREENBOOK is the most respected publisher of guidebooks to contemporary collectibles. We know the collection and the collector intimately, and have developed innovative features that ease tracking your collection. The complexities of the Precious Moments Collection led us to create exclusive features that have become the norm. GREENBOOK ARTCHARTS, up-to-the-minute GREENBOOK TruMarket secondary market values and easy-to-use QUIKREFERENCE lists make the hobby of collecting more enjoyable. Collectors turn to our Guides every day to verify a fact, check a detail or test their in-depth knowledge.

Many have imitated us, but no other book even comes close. We are the original and genuine GREENBOOK Guide and we're proud to be the only publisher that devotes itself entirely to publishing guides. Like the Wall Street Journal, GREENBOOK reports activity only, leaving buying and selling to others, ensuring an impartial foundation. This is the Guide trusted by insurance companies.

Please take a few moments to familiarize yourself with how to use the Guide. The Introduction on page 8, The Glossary on page 18 and the How To Read A Listing on page 186 are all important.

Your comments and suggestions are always welcome.

You can reach us –

by mail: P.O. Box 645
                  Pacific Grove, CA   93950

by phone: 831.656.9000 9AM to 5PM Pacific Time

by fax: 831.656.9004

on the web: www.greenbooks.com

Many thanks.

GREENBOOK Guide to
Cherished Teddies™

GREENBOOK Guide to
Department 56® Villages including
The Original Snow Village® and
The Heritage Village Collection®

GREENBOOK Guide to
Department 56® Snowbabies™

GREENBOOK Guide to
Hallmark Keepsake Ornaments

GREENBOOK Guide to
Kiddie Car Classics

GREENBOOK Guide to
the Walt Disney Classics Collection

GREENBOOK Guide to
Harbour Lights

COMING IN 1999:

GREENBOOK Guide to
Boyds Bears

GREENBOOK Guide to
Harmony Kingdom

GREENBOOK Guide to
Christopher Radko Ornaments

GREENBOOK Guide to
Shelia's Collectibles

Introduction

The GREENBOOK provides information about The Enesco PRECIOUS MOMENTS Collection in the form of GREENBOOK TRUMARKET VALUES plus factual information describing each piece.

The factual information is compiled by the GREENBOOK with assistance from Enesco. It appears in the Guide in many different forms making it possible for a new collector as well as the experienced collector to identify the pieces in their collection or the pieces they wish to buy or sell. The inclusion of GREENBOOK TRUMARKET VALUES make it possible to determine the value of each piece.

The current value is important for insurance purposes as well as buying and selling.

The GREENBOOK also affords collectors an opportunity to become familiar with the entire PRECIOUS MOMENTS Collection—not just the pieces that are currently available at Suggested Retail and displayed in stores. Current, Retired, Suspended, Discontinued, Annuals, Two Year Collectibles, Limited Editions, and earlier marks of each piece are included.

THE GREENBOOK ARTCHART

The GREENBOOK's exclusive ARTCHART contains authorized reproductions of 1159 line drawings. In addition, it lists the Enesco Item Number for the figurine, plate, bell, musical, ornament, doll, thimble, frame, candle climber, box, night light, egg, plaque, wreath, medallion, stocking hanger, tree topper, wall hanging and limoges box derived from each drawing. It is noted, also, if each piece is a Dated Annual, an Annual that is not dated, a Two Year Collectible, a Limited Edition, Retired, Suspended, or has a special Inspirational Title.

The ARTCHART, presented in alphabetical order by Inspirational Title, is designed to provide a graphic illustration of how individual pieces relate to each other and to the entire Collection as well as add to the fun of collecting PRECIOUS MOMENTS.

GREENBOOK QUIKREFERENCE SECTION

Many times certain pieces become important as part of a group. PRECIOUS MOMENTS groups that have become important are included in the QUIKREFERENCE SECTION in the form of lists and outlines.

GREENBOOK LISTINGS

The GREENBOOK LISTINGS are where specific factual information as well as GREENBOOK TRUMARKET VALUES for each collectible can be found.

The factual information includes:

- Inspirational Title
- Description
- Type of Product (Figurine, Plate, Bell ...)
- Enesco Item Number
- Year of Issue
- Edition Size
- Issue Price or Suggested Retail Price when first issued, as well as each year the Annual Production Symbol or Mark is/was changed
- Size
- Certification
- If it is Individually Numbered

- If it is part of a Collection, Set or Series and it's placement in the Series
- Annual Production Symbol
- Errors and Variations

GREENBOOK Listings are in Enesco Item Number order. Enesco Item Numbers can be found on the understamp of most pieces produced from 1982 to the present. If you don't know the Enesco Item Number, but you do know the Inspirational Title, use the ARTCHART to obtain the Enesco Item Number.

ANNUAL PRODUCTION SYMBOLS/aka MARKS

Since mid-1981 Enesco has indicated when PRECIOUS MOMENTS collectibles were produced by including an Annual Production Symbol as part of the understamp. Pieces crafted prior to 1981 have no Annual Production Symbol and have become known as "No Marks."

The GREENBOOK lists the year of issue, issue price (suggested retail) and a GREENBOOK TRUMARKET VALUE for each change in Annual Production Symbol.

Knowing issue prices for each PRECIOUS MOMENTS collectible when it was first produced as well as the current issue price or suggested retail can also be important when investment performance is evaluated. Many PRECIOUS MOMENTS collectibles have been produced for years and collectors who purchased earlier production pieces are enjoying an increase in value even though the piece is still current.

A very common error made by collectors is to mistake the copyright date for the year of issue because the copyright date appears on the understamp written out as ©19XX. In order to determine what year your piece was produced, you must refer to the Annual Production Symbol, not the © date.

MARKET STATUS

In order to make room in the Collection for new introductions, Enesco periodically retires and suspends individual pieces.

The definition of Retired and Suspended are as follows:

Retired: A figurine or collectible that has been permanently removed from production and the molds destroyed.

Suspended: A figurine or collectible that has been removed from production for an unspecified period of time. A piece designated as Suspended cannot be moved to Retired status without first being "Re-introduced" to the Collection. There is no time limit on how long a collectible may be Suspended from the Collection.

Don't forget, an item can be limited in many ways: by number, by time, by audience eligible to buy it (like Members Only pieces) and by an Event Only piece (like the Turn Back The Clock Celebrations).

Factors other than availability that affect secondary market prices include condition and general appeal.

Because there are so many factors based on individual judgements, and because prices can vary from one section of the country to another, GREENBOOK TRUMARKET VALUES **are never an absolute number**. Use them as a benchmark.

Most Secondary Market transactions are fairly straightforward. If you are selling to a dealer, expect to realize about 50 to 75%, or the wholesale price of the piece. If you are buying, expect to pay 75% to 100%+ of the TRUMARKET Value. If you are trading with another collector, assign 100% value to your pieces and their pieces. Insure all pieces for 100% of the TRUMARKET Value. This is a thumbnail of how GREENBOOK TRUMARKET VALUES provide dealers, collectors, retailers and insurance agents with benchmark points to go by.

Three questions that come up frequently in regard to their effect on GREENBOOK TRUMARKET VALUES are 1) boxes, 2) Sam Butcher's signature on the piece, and 3) variations:

1) GREENBOOK TRUMARKET VALUES are for pieces "Mint in Box." In general, the newer the piece the more important it is to have the box. On hard-to-find, scarce, older pieces, not having a box usually does not subtract significantly from the GREENBOOK TRUMARKET VALUE. On the other hand, pieces that are easier to come by are a tough sell without the box, because one with a box can always be found.

2) In the past we've said Sam Butcher signing a piece does not add appreciably to its GREENBOOK TRUMARKET VALUE, but that it does vary with the rarity of the piece. In our experience, many collectors expect that a Sam Butcher signature will add hundreds or even thousands to the value of a piece. To date, a Sam Butcher signature has added in the range of $25 to $75 to the market price, depending on the piece.

3) As with all things made by human hands, PRECIOUS MOMENTS porcelains exist with variations. Some differences occur naturally as a result of firing and painting. There are also pieces with variations caused by production changes or human error. In general, an error must be highly visible or be an announced production change before secondary market prices are affected appreciably. GREENBOOK makes note of what we have come to call "Classic Variations." Classic Variations are actively traded on the secondary market and often have a name! Examples of Classic Variations include "Smiley," "No 'e' Bible," "CROWNS" ...

History of the Precious Moments Collection

by Kristi Schult

Sam Butcher, the artist and creator of Precious Moments, first began his career as a "chalk board minister," using illustrations to teach young children about God. He accepted a job as an artist at the International Child Evangelism Fellowship in Grand Rapids, Michigan and for 10 years, his work was seen by millions of viewers on the program "Tree Top House." He only intended for his drawings of teardrop-eyed children to encourage and comfort family and friends.

In 1974, Sam partnered with a friend, William Biel, to start the "Jonathan & David" inspirational greeting card business that featured the teardrop-eyed children he had been drawing for family and friends. He called them "Precious Moments" because they spread love, caring and sharing in everyday situations. The Card Company was the first step toward success for the artist and his Precious Moments illustrations.

It was in 1978 that Enesco Corporation President Eugene Freedman first saw Sam's simple drawings on a small line of greeting cards and posters. One of them was a poster of two little boys with big, soulful eyes. One carried a fishing pole, the other a can of worms; it was titled "I Will Make You Fishers Of Men." He envisioned the drawings being transformed into three-dimensional figurines. When Gene called Sam and Bill, they were initially reluctant to talk to him, as they were hoping to have the artwork made into porcelain themselves. They were uncertain that anyone else could really share their commitment to creating artworks that conveyed the messages of devotion and inspiration. Fortunately for them, Gene was persistent.

Mr. Freedman took the artwork to Japan to his friend, Master Sculptor Yasuhei Fujioka, and with his creative genius, Fujioka-san transformed the illustrations into figurines. Sam was overcome with happiness when he saw the first Precious Moments figurine.

In the fall of 1978, the first 21 porcelain bisque figurines, each one handcrafted and individually painted, were introduced on the market. The first response from people who bought the figurines was very personal and moving. Thus the children with soulful expressions and inspirational titles soon became a phenomenon in the collectibles industry. The Precious Moments Collection by Enesco is now the number one collectible in the country and numbers more than 1,500 subjects for every occasion and every sentiment.

Over the past 20 years, Sam has continued to create hundreds of illustrations that reflect his faith, love, and compassion, as well as personal situations in his life. From Sam's sketchpad to the final Precious Moments figurine, each subject is truly a work of art. The drawings are sent to the Precious Moments Design Studio in Nagoya, Japan, where a team of highly skilled artisans translates the art into a finely sculptured clay model.

It requires five to seven days to produce a single Precious Moments figurine. Each artisan is extensively trained from the sculptor to the painter, who takes three years to master the famous teardrop eyes — considered to be the most important and most difficult element of the figurine. It's this attention to detail and quality that has kept the Precious Moments Collection so highly valued by collectors and so true to Sam's original artwork.

Each year, Sam Butcher and Enesco announce several pieces that have been retired, meaning they will never be produced again in the same form. The retired pieces, which make room in the Collection for more introductions, become highly sought after by collectors.

In 1989, Sam began what he calls his life's work — the Precious Moments Chapel located on hundreds of acres of rolling hills and farmland in Carthage, Missouri. The Chapel, featuring a Precious Moments version of Michelangelo's "Creation" along with many other drawings, statues, fountains, wedding chapel and attractions, draws more than one million visitors each year. You can read all about the Chapel at their Website http://www.preciousmoments.com.

The three founding "fathers" of the Collection, Sam, Gene, and Fujioko-san, are loyal to the integrity of the Collection and their belief in living the Precious Moments motto of "Loving, Caring, and Sharing." Whatever the occasion, the Precious Moments Collection expresses a heartfelt sentiment without saying a word. Collectors have found joy in both giving and receiving Precious Moments figurines.

Introducing GREENBOOK Historian Kristi Schult ¹³

Founder, "Precious Moments" Collectible Treasures Website

I was born in Little Rock, AR but grew up in Houma, LA. I joined the Air Force in 1984 and my first duty station was Hawaii. I met my husband, Roger, there and we lived in Hawaii for almost 12 years. I am the mother of three children, Brandyn (age 11), Ryan (age 6), and Haley (age 4). Both Roger and I worked our way through 5 years of night school to earn our college degrees. Roger is still on active duty but I left the Air Force in 1990 and began working as a government contractor. We were in Hawaii when I first brought the site on-line and we moved to Germany in January 1997. I work full-time as a Project Manager/Senior Systems Engineer for SAIC, I am the Webmaster for both my PMCT Website and the Precious Moments Company Website, and I'm the Greenbook Precious Moments Historian.

I started collecting Precious Moments in 1984 and I've been totally immersed ever since. In September 1996 I began the *"Precious Moments"* Collectible Treasures Website because living in Hawaii made it hard to get retired and suspended pieces. I began surfing the net and discovered that there was not much being offered for collectors of PRECIOUS MOMENTS ® figurines. Several collectors approached me about starting up a website but Terry Shuffler from Dreams & Rainbows encouraged me to make it happen. I am very grateful to Terry for all of her support and between the two of us we are creating something wonderful.

My website is totally non-profit so the sponsors and collectors make it possible for us to be a success. I'd like to thank each of my sponsors for their support and the following people who are the "staff" of my website: Patty Swatzell, Mary Ann DeTerra, Sandy McCowan, Illene Gagel, Karen Watson and Diane McBride. We have been at the Licensee Show for the past 2 years and will be there again in 1999.

Enesco worked very hard in 1998 to put the excitement back into the Precious Moments Collection. The hunt for those new Limited Editions, the retirements and re-introductions brought many collectors back into the Precious Moments family. Everyone likes to speak of the "good old days" of Precious Moments and I believe the 20th Anniversary of Precious Moments saw a return to those days.

In addition, the Precious Moments Care-A-Van traveling across the country brought the world of Precious Moments to everyone. The Care-A-Van helped the new collectors understand the history of the Collection and rejuvenated the experienced collectors. How would you have liked to win one of the "How Can Three Work Together, Except They Agree" figurines during the silent auctions?

The introduction of Tender Tails has spawned a Collection within a Collection and a whole new group of collectors. Young and old have been hunting down the Limited Edition Tails, Errored Tails, Exclusives, and of course the Local Club Convention Gorilla. The new Fun Club will excite these collectors as it introduces new Club Member Exclusives into the Tender Tail collection.

Last but definitely not least are the beautiful figurines that Sam has created for the Millenium.

I do hope that everyone is ready for a wonderful year ahead and remember, 1999 is the 10th Anniversary of the Precious Moments Chapel so be prepared for exciting events. I welcome you to explore the Internet with us!

14

The ONLY Official Precious Moments Online Club!

**WHY SHOULD YOU JOIN.....
PRECIOUS MOMENTS COLLECTIBLE TREASURES?**

THE ONLY Precious Moments Approved Website!

We are a PRECIOUS MOMENTS © LICENSEE.

Solely devoted to PRECIOUS MOMENTS© figurines and dolls.

Members have exclusive Bulletin Boards that are Password Protected so they can share exclusive information.

Precious Moments Collectible Treasures has areas to buy, sell and trade your pieces. As well as an exclusive Auction Board. We are dedicated to bringing together people from all over the world to share information about their collections!

Precious Moments Collectible Treasures has been in existence since September 10, 1996.

Email for info: kristi@preciousmom.com

http://www.preciousmom.com

Insuring Your Collection

by Peter George

Whether it is a clink, a crack, or a crash, there are very few sounds that will strike fear into the heart of a collector like these will. The first thought is "no, it couldn't have happened!" Then you see it ... it's over ... it's gone. One of the most cherished pieces you own has been broken. What are you going to do? How can you ever replace it?

Of course you can never replace the sentimentality of that very piece if it was a gift or commemorates a special occasion, but replacing the physical piece is relatively easy. But, you must take the proper precautions before anything happens.

Many collectors do not see the need to have a separate rider with their insurance company just to cover their collections. Others have such a vast number of pieces that they would not dare have them uninsured any more than they would not have their car, home, or other highly valuable object insured.

When or if you do look into insuring your collection, meet with the agent so you can show him photos and your GREENBOOK. This will help him understand what it is you are talking about. Remember, most agents have never heard of many of the collections we all consider to be common knowledge. Many collectors have had good luck using the analogy of baseball cards or coins to assist the agents in understanding the product.

Discuss with the agent the manner in which the pieces are limited or retire and are traded. Don't forget to include the subjects of Swap 'N Sells and Room Hops. If you will be bringing collectibles to other locations to sell them, will they be covered?

What happens if a piece is merely chipped? Is the piece insured if you break it? What if just the box gets damaged? Ask these and every other question you can think of that pertains to how you collect and how you think you may collect in the future. When the agent says that you are covered or will be covered for a particular circumstance, ask where in the policy it is stated. This will confirm that the agent understands your needs and that you are covered in case of a loss. Many insurance companies have a "fine arts" rider that will be useful for covering collectibles, and other companies are now offering "collectible riders."

Once you are covered, you will be responsible for updating the values of the insured items. Do this once a year or sooner if a piece experiences a substantial increase in value. A good time to do this is when your annual payment is due, in January, your birthday, or any date that you will easily remember.

The more evidence you have of your collection, the better it will be if you need to make a claim. Take photos or videotape your collection. If using a camcorder, take advantage of its audio capabilities and elaborate about the article you are taping. Keep records including when and where you purchased or received it, original cost and current value. If you have numbered limited editions, record the numbers. Photograph the pieces in your collection individually as well as in their setting in your home. Make duplicates of the photos or video. Keep one set in the house for reference and one off-site, perhaps in a safe deposit box. Keep receipts with the second set, if possible.

If you do insure your collection, we hope it is a precaution that will never have to be called upon. If you are unfortunate and have to turn to this solution, however, it's best to have done your homework ahead of time, not when it's too late.

Publisher's Note:
Peter George is the publisher of the Village Chronicle magazine and GREENBOOK's Historian for Department 56 Collectibles. Considered an expert on contemporary collectibles, Peter is often the guest speaker at conventions and clubs all over the United States. The topic of insuring collections is a favorite as he has many colorful stories to tell about collectors he's met who have literally taken the lemon and made lemonade. Pieces damaged in a real fire are used as part of a blazing scene in their Village or broken pieces are used to create an area under demolition. If you'd like to chat with Peter you can reach him at www.villagechronicle.com.

ADDITIONAL OFFERINGS - An item that is offered in conjunction with a Members Only Figurine offering using the same redemption form. They are exclusive to Members of either the Collectors' Club or Birthday Club.

ANNUALS (Not Dated) - Items released for only one year or introduced once a year. An example of this is the Event figurines that are released each year, a series like the Four Seasons figurines or the Easter Seals pieces.

ANNUALS (Dated) - Items released once a year that have a date on them. An example of this is the Christmas figurines and ornaments released every year with the date showing on them (i.e. 1998, 1999, etc.).

ART PLAS - A state of the art cold cast process used for producing PRECIOUS MOMENTS items requiring resiliency and minute detail. This process is used in many giftware items.

AUTHORIZED DEALER - A retail store that is authorized by Enesco to sell the PRECIOUS MOMENTS Collection and to act as an official redemption center for all Members Only forms.

BABY CLASSICS - This Series was introduced in 1996 and is a "baby" version of some of the classic figurines in the PRECIOUS MOMENTS Collection. An example of this is the Baby Classic "God Loveth A Cheerful Giver" which features a baby girl sitting on the ground with two puppies.

CATALOG EXCLUSIVE - An item that is offered exclusively through a gift catalog. Participating retail stores mail these catalogs to their customers or people in their immediate area. These select retail stores are members of the organizations that print the catalogs. These organizations include Gift Creations Concepts (aka GCC), Ideation, Palmer Marketing, Retail Resource, and Parkwest/NALED (National Association Of Limited Edition Dealers). An example of this would be the "Happiness To The Core" figurine, available in 1997 exclusively to participating catalog stores.

CENTURY CIRCLE RETAILER - The highest designation by Enesco that a PRECIOUS MOMENTS retail store can attain. These retailers receive early shipments of new pieces and bonus allocations of dated and retired pieces. In addition, and, perhaps most importantly, they receive exclusive limited editions, annual ornaments and event pieces.

CHAPEL EXCLUSIVE - A very special collection within the Enesco PRECIOUS MOMENTS Collection of items produced by special agreement between Sam Butcher and Enesco and sold only by the PRECIOUS MOMENTS Chapel in Carthage, Missouri. An example of this would be the figurine titled "He Is My Inspiration."

COLLECTION WITHIN A COLLECTION - The term used to describe concentrating your collecting efforts on a segment of the PRECIOUS MOMENTS Collection. For example, you may concentrate on just Angels, Clowns, Limited Editions, Sammy's Circus, Sugar Town, Country Lane, etc.

Glossary

COUNTRY OF ORIGIN STICKER/MARKING - It is a federal trade law that all items produced outside of the United States have a Country of Origin sticker. Point of interest, if you ever come across an item that has the Country of Origin permanently on the bottom of the item, it was originally produced and shipped to Canada. Their laws are different from the United States and say the Country of Origin must be permanently marked on the item.

CRUISE MEDALLIONS AND FIGURINES - Special pieces given as gifts to those on the 1993, 1995 and 1998 Precious Moments Cruises.

DAMAGED BOX - A Secondary Market term used when a collectible item's original box is in poor or "damaged" condition, thus usually diminishing the value of the item.

DISTINGUISHED SERVICE RETAILER (DSR) - Recognition given a retail store by Enesco. This recognition is achieved by offering a high level of goods and services to the collector. DSRs receive early shipments of new pieces, exclusive products, bonus allocations of dated and retired pieces and more. DSRs are required to hold an annual PRECIOUS MOMENTS Event.

EASTER SEAL FIGURINES - A series of figurines that started in 1987 with Enesco's commitment to the National Easter Seal Society. One 5" figurine is produced each year and limited to the year of introduction — the 5" for 1999 is "Heaven Bless You Easter Seal." Enesco also produces a 9" figurine each year since 1988 which is a Limited Edition. The 9" for 1999 is "We Are All Precious In His Sight." All proceeds from these figurines benefit the Easter Seal Society. Enesco presented a check for $4,204,504.00 to Easter Seals on behalf of PRECIOUS MOMENTS Collectors and Retailers during the 1997 Easter Seal Telethon.

ENHANCEMENTS - These are accessory pieces in the *Sugar Town* Collection that add to the scenery such as trees, roads, bridges, mailboxes and signs.

INSPIRATIONAL TITLE - A part of the appeal of the PRECIOUS MOMENTS subjects is their Inspirational Title. These titles are located on the base of each figurine. Some figurines may have the same or similar title. (As illustrated by the GREENBOOK ARTCHART). Because certain messages mean a great deal to Sam he will use the message for a variety of subjects.

INSTANT GRATIFICATION PROGRAM - A program where a PRECIOUS MOMENTS Authorized Dealer carries the Enesco PRECIOUS MOMENTS Collectors' Club and Birthday Club kits in stock. A renewing Club Member can take their renewal slip into one of their participating stores and pick up their kit right then, instantly! If a prospective Club Member would like to join either Club for the first time, they can fill out a Membership Application at the participating store and pick up their New Membership kit immediately as well!

LIMITED EDITION - Pieces limited to an announced specific number. An example of this would be the Candy doll limited to 12,000 pieces.

LITTLE MOMENTS - This line of figurines was introduced in 1997 to be a more affordable gift giving item. The Little Moments do not have Annual Production Symbols and retail between $20 and $25. They are approximately 3 - 4 inches tall.

MARK OF QUALITY - A series of numbers and letters placed on the base of a PRECIOUS MOMENTS piece that denotes the production facility and artisan that crafted it.

MEMBERS ONLY FIGURINE - This type of figurine is offered exclusively to Members of Enesco's PRECIOUS MOMENTS Collectors' Club or Birthday Club. A form offering the exclusive figurine is mailed directly to the Club Member from Club Headquarters. The Member then must turn the form in to a PRECIOUS MOMENTS Authorized Dealer. Usually, two Members Only figurines are offered each year.

MINT IN BOX (MIB) - This is a Secondary Market term used when a collectible item's original box is in "good as new" or "mint" condition. GREENBOOK TruMarket Values are for items "Mint In Box."

NO BOX - This is another Secondary Market term used when a collectible item's original box is missing. This will affect the value of the item for most collectibles on the Secondary Market.

NO MARK (NM) - The term used to describe the fact that no Annual Production Symbols/Marks were placed on the base of the pieces crafted prior to mid-1981.

ONGOING - A PRECIOUS MOMENTS piece that is still in production and generally available in retail stores at issue price in the current Annual Production Symbol.

"ORIGINAL 21" - The term used to describe the first 21 figurines that debuted in 1978.

PORCELAIN BISQUE - The hard and nonabsorbent material used to make PRECIOUS MOMENTS figurines. This is a kind of ceramic made primarily with kaolin (a pure form of clay) that is fired at extremely high temperatures.

PRECIOUS MOMENTS BIRTHDAY CLUB - A Club introduced in 1986 dedicated to the young and the young at heart. Benefits include a Symbol Of Membership figurine, birthday card, membership certificate, subscription to the GOOD NEWS PARADE, and the opportunity to purchase Members Only items.

PRECIOUS MOMENTS COLLECTORS' CLUB - In 1981, responding to collectors' enthusiasm, Enesco President Eugene Freedman offered to underwrite the cost of creating a Club with the provision that it be the finest of its kind and offer members the most benefits and the best value in appreciation for their interest. Club benefits include a Symbol Of Membership figurine, a subscription to the official publication, the GOODNEWSLETTER, and the opportunity to purchase Members Only items.

Glossary

PRIMARY MARKET - Items available from retailers at issue price or suggested retail price.

PRODUCTION MARK/aka ANNUAL PRODUCTION SYMBOL/aka YEAR MARK - A symbol that is incised on the base of a PRECIOUS MOMENTS figurine that indicates the year a figurine is/was crafted. The first symbol appeared in mid-1981 and was a Triangle. These markings change with the calendar year.

RE-INTRODUCED - A Suspended figurine that has been changed and re-introduced into the Collection. The changes can be anything from a color change to a sculpting change. An example of a color change is E-1377A "He Leadeth Me" figurine that was re-introduced for one day only on November 21, 1998. An example of a figurine that had design changes is E-1381R "Jesus Is The Answer." When this figurine returned from suspension the boy was leaning over the globe more, the ribbon was off the base of the globe and there was a hot water bottle on top of the globe. Once a suspended figurine has been re-introduced then subsequently retired the original suspended figurine is considered retired as well.

REDEMPTION FORM - A three part form mailed to all Members of the Club which enables the collector to redeem the form at an Authorized Dealer for the current Members Only offering.

REGIONAL EVENT FIGURINE/ORNAMENT - An item that is created and produced exclusively for Regional Events held around the country.

RETIREMENT - A figurine or collectible that has been permanently removed from production and the molds destroyed. It is regarded as an honor for a figurine to be chosen for Retired status. Pieces are Retired from time to time to make room in the Collection for new introductions. (Note: Limited Editions and Annual pieces that are no longer in production are termed "Closed.")

SECONDARY MARKET - Once an item is not generally available from a retailer at issue price and the only way to get it is from someone who owns it. The item may now be obtained through a Secondary Market Dealer or fellow collector. Pieces are sold through classified ads, collector newsletters, Internet sites, at Swap 'N Sell events...

SIGNATURE STORE - A retailer dedicated to carrying a high volume of PRECIOUS MOMENTS giftware including exclusive promotional items.

SPECIAL EVENT FIGURINE/ORNAMENT - An item that is created and produced exclusively for sale by the Distinguished Service Retailers at their Enesco approved events. Many stores hold Spring Celebration events around March or April and Holiday Preview events in late October or November. The 1998 Jungle Jamboree Event figurine was titled "Life Can Be A Jungle" and was offered during the one day event held on October 31, 1998.

SPRING CATALOG - Beginning in 1993, Enesco introduced a new program featuring an exclusive figurine for retailers who purchased and distributed a Spring PRECIOUS MOMENTS Catalog. The 1993 figurine was titled "Happiness Is At Our Fingertips."

SUSPENDED - A figurine or collectible that has been removed from production for an unspecified period of time. A piece designated as Suspended cannot be moved to Retired status without first being "re-introduced" to the Collection. There is no time limit on how long a collectible may be Suspended from the Collection. Once a suspended figurine has been re-introduced then subsequently retired the original suspended figurine is considered retired.

SYMBOL OF MEMBERSHIP - This is the gift to members of the Collector Clubs upon joining or renewing their membership. For example, the 1999 Symbol Of Membership for the Precious Moments Collectors' Club is "Wishing You A World Of Peace."

TWO YEAR COLLECTIBLES - These are items that have been released only for a period of two years.

VARIATIONS/aka ERRORS - As with all things make by human hands, PRECIOUS MOMENTS porcelains exist with variations. Some differences occur naturally as a result of firing and painting. There are also pieces with variations caused by production changes or human error. In general, an error must be highly visible or be an announced production change before secondary market prices are affected appreciably. An example of this would be the variation on "Nobody's Perfect." This figurine was first produced showing the dunce boy smiling. Sam decided that this figurine should be changed to have a more serious expression so his mouth was changed to a circular shape. The smiling piece is what GREENBOOK calls a "Classic Variation" and is commonly referred to as "Smiley" or the "Smiling Dunce."

QUIKREFERENCE SECTION

including

LISTS OF:

OUTLINES OF HOW THEY ALL FIT TOGETHER:

COLLECTIONS WITHIN THE COLLECTION:

LIMITED EDITIONS

MISCELLANEOUS

No Item # .. Figurine .... 20 ...... How Can Three Work Together Except They Agree
E-0538 .... Plate .... 15,000 ...... Wee Three Kings
E-2347 .... Plate .... 15,000 ...... Let Heaven And Nature Sing
E-2847 .... Plate .... 15,000 ...... Love Is Kind
E-2848 .... Plate .... 15,000 ...... Loving Thy Neighbor
E-5215 .... Plate .... 15,000 ...... Love One Another
E-5217 .... Plate .... 15,000 ...... Mother Sew Dear
E-5395 .... Plate .... 15,000 ...... Unto Us A Child Is Born
E-5646 .... Plate .... 15,000 ...... Come Let Us Adore Him
E-7173 .... Plate .... 15,000 ...... The Purr-fect Grandma
E-7174 .... Plate .... 15,000 ...... Make A Joyful Noise
E-7267B ..... Doll .... 5,000 ...... Cubby
E-7267G .... Doll .... 5,000 ...... Tammy
E-9256 .... Plate .... 15,000 ...... The Hand That Rocks The Future
E-9257 .... Plate .... 15,000 ...... I Believe In Miracles
12491 .... Doll .... 12,500 ...... Angie, The Angel Of Mercy
100455 ...... Doll .... 12,000 ...... Bong Bong
100463 ...... Doll .... 12,000 ...... Candy
102253 ...... Doll .... 7,500 ...... Connie
261106S .... Figurine .... 1,500 ...... Hogs And Kisses
307084 ...... Figurine .... 12,000 ...... Bringing In The Sheaves
456225 ...... Figurine .... 20 ...... God Loveth A Cheerful Giver (9")

LARGE (APPROX 9") EASTER SEAL FIGURINES

104531 ...... Figurine .... 1,000 ...... Jesus Loves Me (1988)
520322 ...... Figurine .... 1,500 ...... Make A Joyful Noise (1989)
523283 ...... Figurine .... 2,000 ...... You Have Touched So Many Hearts (1990)
523879 ...... Figurine .... 2,000 ...... We Are God's Workmanship (1991)
526010 ...... Figurine .... 2,000 ...... You Are Such A Purr-fect Friend (1992)
529680 ...... Figurine .... 2,000 ...... Gather Your Dreams (1993)
531243 ...... Figurine .... 2,000 ...... You Are The Rose Of His Creation (1994)
526886 ...... Figurine .... 2,000 ...... He's Got The Whole World In His Hands (1995)
152277 ...... Figurine .... 2,000 ...... He Loves Me (1996)
192376 ...... Figurine .... 2,000 ...... Love Is Universal (1997)
272981 ...... Figurine .... 2,000 ...... Love Grows Here (1998)
475068 ...... Figurine .... 2,500 ...... We Are All Precious In His Sight (1999)

(For Century Circle Limited Editions, See Below.)

CENTURY CIRCLE EXCLUSIVES

LIMITED EDITIONS

139475 ...... Figurine .... 15,000 ...... Love Makes The World Go 'Round
177091 ...... Ornament .... 15,000 ...... Peace On Earth
175277 ...... Figurine .... 15,000 ...... God's Love Is Reflected In You
261629 ...... Figurine .... 15,000 ...... In God's Beautiful Garden Of Love
150312 ...... Figurine .... 15,000 ...... Even The Heavens Shall Praise Him

CENTURY CIRCLE EXCLUSIVES CONTINUED

EVENT PIECES

184217 ...... Annual Figurine .... May The Sun Always Shine On You (1996)
526061 ...... Annual Figurine .... The Pearl Of Great Price (1997)
325503 ...... Annual Figurine .... Marvelous Grace (1998)

FALL EXCLUSIVES

184209 ...... Annual Ornament .... Love Makes The World Go 'Round (1996)
261599 ...... Annual Ornament .... In God's Beautiful Garden Of Love (1997)
475084 ...... Annual Ornament .... Even The Heavens Shall Praise Him (1998)

THE "ORIGINAL 21"

E-1372B ..... Figurine ...... Jesus Loves Me
E-1372G .... Figurine ...... Jesus Loves Me
E-1373B ..... Figurine ...... Smile, God Loves You
E-1373G .... Figurine ...... Jesus Is The Light
E-1374B ..... Figurine ...... Praise The Lord Anyhow
E-1374G .... Figurine ...... Make A Joyful Noise
E-1375A ..... Figurine ...... Love Lifted Me
E-1375B ..... Figurine ...... Prayer Changes Things
E-1376 .... Figurine ...... Love One Another
E-1377A ..... Figurine ...... He Leadeth Me
E-1377B ..... Figurine ...... He Careth For You
E-1378 .... Figurine ...... God Loveth A Cheerful Giver
E-1379A ..... Figurine ...... Love Is Kind
E-1379B ..... Figurine ...... God Understands
E-1380B ..... Figurine ...... O, How I Love Jesus
E-1380G .... Figurine ...... His Burden Is Light
E-1381 .... Figurine ...... Jesus Is The Answer
E-2010 .... Figurine ...... We Have Seen His Star
E-2011 .... Figurine ...... Come Let Us Adore Him
E-2012 .... Figurine ...... Jesus Is Born
E-2013 .... Figurine ...... Unto Us A Child Is Born

TWO YEAR COLLECTIBLES

408735	Musical Jack-in-the-Box	1990, 1991	The Voice Of Spring
408743	Musical Jack-in-the-Box	1990, 1991	Summer's Joy
408751	Musical Jack-in-the-Box	1990, 1991	Autumn's Praise
408778	Musical Jack-in-the-Box	1990, 1991	Winter's Song
408786	Doll	1990, 1991	The Voice Of Spring
408794	Doll	1990, 1991	Summer's Joy
408808	Doll	1990, 1991	Autumn's Praise
408816	Doll	1990, 1991	Winter's Song
417777	Musical Jack-in-the-Box	1991, 1992	May You Have An Old Fashioned Christmas
417785	Doll	1991, 1992	May You Have An Old Fashioned Christmas
422282	Musical Jack-in-the-Box	1991, 1992	You Have Touched So Many Hearts
427527	Doll	1991, 1992	You Have Touched So Many Hearts

RETIRED —

"A figurine or collectible that has been permanently removed from production and the molds destroyed. It is regarded as an honor for a figurine to be chosen for Retired status. Pieces are Retired from time to time to make room in the Collection for new introductions." - ENESCO

E-0504	Figurine	1990	Christmastime Is For Sharing
E-0506	Figurine	1989	Surrounded With Joy
E-0519	Musical	1986	Sharing Our Season Together
E-0525	Figurine	1989	You Can't Run Away From God
E-0530	Figurine	1987	His Eye Is On The Sparrow
E-0532	Ornament	1986	Let Heaven And Nature Sing
E-0534	Ornament	1989	To Thee With Love
E-1372B	Figurine	1998	Jesus Loves Me
E-1373B	Figurine	1984	Smile God Loves You
E-1373G	Figurine	1988	Jesus Is The Light
E-1374B	Figurine	1982	Praise The Lord Anyhow
E-1375A	Figurine	1993	Love Lifted Me
E-1377A	Figurine	1998	He Leadeth Me
E-1377R	Figurine	1998	He Leadeth Me
E-1378	Figurine	1981	God Loveth A Cheerful Giver
E-1379A	Figurine	1998	Love Is Kind
E-1379R	Figurine	1998	Love Is Kind
E-1380G	Figurine	1984	His Burden Is Light
E-1380B	Figurine	1984	O, How I Love Jesus
E-1381R	Figurine	1996	Jesus Is The Answer
E-1381	Figurine	1996	Jesus Is The Answer
E-2011	Figurine	1981	Come Let Us Adore Him
E-2351	Figurine	1987	Holy Smokes
E-2353	Figurine	1986	O Come All Ye Faithful
E-2368	Ornament	1984	The First Noel
E-2369	Ornament	1986	Dropping In For Christmas
E-2371	Ornament	1988	Unicorn
E-2374	Figurine	1993	Bundles Of Joy
E-2375	Figurine	1991	Dropping Over For Christmas
E-2376	Ornament	1985	Dropping Over For Christmas
E-2805	Figurine	1985	Wishing You A Season Filled With Joy
E-2806	Musical	1984	Christmas Is A Time To Share
E-2822	Figurine	1988	This Is Your Day To Shine
E-2841	Figurine	1986	Baby's First Picture
E-2850	Doll	1985	Mother Sew Dear
E-3107	Figurine	1985	Blessed Are The Peacemakers
E-3110B	Figurine	1993	Loving Is Sharing
E-3111	Figurine	1985	Be Not Weary In Well Doing
E-3112	Figurine	1983	God's Speed
E-3116	Figurine	1994	Thee I Love
E-3118	Figurine	1983	Eggs Over Easy
E-5211	Bell	1984	God Understands
E-5377	Figurine	1987	Love Is Kind
E-5388	Ornament	1987	Joy To The World
E-5645	Musical	1988	Rejoice O Earth
E-6120	Ornament	1984	We Have Seen His Star
E-7156	Figurine	1992	I Believe In Miracles
E-7156R	Figurine	1992	I Believe In Miracles
E-7157	Figurine	1986	There Is Joy In Serving Jesus

E-7185 .... Musical .... 1985 ...... Love Is Sharing
E-9254 .... Figurine .... 1994 ...... Praise The Lord Anyhow
E-9268 .... Figurine .... 1990 ...... Nobody's Perfect!
E-9273 .... Figurine .... 1987 ...... Let Love Reign
E-9274 .... Figurine .... 1986 ...... Taste And See That The Lord Is Good
12262 .... Figurine .... 1997 ...... I Get A Bang Out Of You
12319 .... Figurine .... 1998 ...... God Bless Our Home
12459 .... Figurine .... 1989 ...... Waddle I Do Without You
12467 .... Figurine .... 1988 ...... The Lord Will Carry You Through
15504 .... Musical .... 1989 ...... God Sent You Just In Time
100102 ...... Figurine .... 1990 ...... Make Me A Blessing
100129 ...... Figurine .... 1988 ...... Lord Keep Me On My Toes
100188 ...... Figurine .... 1993 ...... I'm A Possibility
100196 ...... Figurine .... 1991 ...... The Spirit Is Willing But The Flesh Is Weak
100226 ...... Figurine .... 1995 ...... The Lord Giveth And The Lord Taketh Away
100269 ...... Figurine .... 1989 ...... Help Lord, I'm In A Spot
100528 ...... Figurine .... 1991 ...... Scent From Above
101702 ...... Musical .... 1992 ...... Our First Christmas Together
101842 ...... Figurine .... 1991 ...... Smile Along The Way
101850 ...... Figurine .... 1992 ...... Lord, Help Us Keep Our Act Together
102423 ...... Ornament .... 1990 ...... Lord, Keep Me On My Toes
104035 ...... Figurine .... 1997 ...... Cheers To The Leader
105945 ...... Figurine .... 1993 ...... Showers Of Blessings
106798 ...... Figurine .... 1995 ...... Puppy Love Is From Above
106844 ...... Figurine .... 1997 ...... Sew In Love
109584 ...... Figurine .... 1992 ...... Happiness Divine
109762 ...... Figurines .... 1995 ...... We Gather Together To Ask The Lord's Blessing
112356 ...... Ornament .... 1997 ...... You Have Touched So Many Hearts
112402 ...... Musical .... 1993 ...... I'm Sending You A White Christmas
113980 ...... Ornament .... 1991 ...... Rejoice O Earth
142751 ...... Figurine .... 1998 ...... Making A Trail To Bethlehem
183857 ...... Figurine .... 1998 ...... Color Your World With Thanksgiving
307009 ...... Figurine .... 1998 ...... Charity Begins In The Heart
520632 ...... Figurine .... 1995 ...... A Friend Is Someone Who Cares
520640 ...... Figurine .... 1991 ...... I'm So Glad You Fluttered Into My Life
520675 ...... Figurine .... 1998 ...... Your Love Is So Uplifting
520683 ...... Figurine .... 1992 ...... Sending You Showers Of Blessings
520772 ...... Figurine .... 1990 ...... Many Moons In Same Canoe, Blessum You
520799 ...... Figurine .... 1992 ...... Someday My Love
521299 ...... Figurine .... 1995 ...... Hug One Another
521396 ...... Figurine .... 1993 ...... Faith Is A Victory
521418 ...... Figurine .... 1996 ...... I'll Never Stop Loving You
521450 ...... Figurine .... 1997 ...... Lord, Help Me Stick To My Job
521566 ...... Ornament .... 1992 ...... Glide Through The Holidays
521590 ...... Ornament .... 1994 ...... Don't Let The Holidays Get You Down
521779 ...... Figurine .... 1996 ...... Sweep All Your Worries Away
522023 ...... Figurine .... 1998 ...... May Your Life Be Blessed With Touchdowns
522058 ...... Figurine .... 1997 ...... Now I Lay Me Down To Sleep
522112 ...... Figurine .... 1993 ...... Don't Let The Holidays Get You Down
522260 ...... Figurine .... 1994 ...... To Be With You Is Uplifting
522317 ...... Figurine .... 1997 ...... Merry Christmas, Deer
522333 ...... Figurine .... 1998 ...... Sweeter As The Years Go By
522937 ...... Ornament .... 1995 ...... Friends Never Drift Apart
523623 ...... Figurine .... 1995 ...... I'm So Glad That God Blessed Me With A Friend Like You
523631 ...... Figurine .... 1996 ...... I Will Always Be Thinking Of You

523747 ...... Figurine .... 1994 ...... Blessings From Above
524085 ...... Figurine .... 1996 ...... My Warmest Thoughts Are You
524131 ...... Ornament .... 1997 ...... Good Friends Are For Always
524271 ...... Figurine .... 1994 ...... Friendship Grows When You Plant A Seed
524352 ...... Figurine .... 1997 ...... What The World Needs Now
524441 ...... Figurine .... 1996 ...... Sealed With A Kiss
524468 ...... Figurine .... 1997 ...... A Special Chime For Jesus
524476 ...... Figurine .... 1996 ...... God Cared Enough To Send His Best
524921 ...... Figurine .... 1996 ...... Angels We Have Heard On High
525898 ...... Figurine .... 1996 ...... Ring Those Christmas Bells
526150 ...... Figurine .... 1997 ...... Friends To The Very End
527270 ...... Figurine .... 1996 ...... Let's Be Friends
527335 ...... Figurine .... 1998 ...... Bless-um You
527378 ...... Figurine .... 1997 ...... You Are My Favorite Star
527599 ...... Figurine .... 1995 ...... Bringing You A Merry Christmas
527769 ...... Figurine .... 1998 ...... I Only Have Arms For You
529966 ...... Figurine .... 1997 ...... Ring Out The Good News
531073 ...... Figurine .... 1996 ...... Money's Not The Only Green Thing Worth Saving
531693 ...... Figurine .... 1998 ...... You Deserve A Halo–Thank You
531952 ...... Figurine .... 1998 ...... Dropping In For The Holidays
532010 ...... Figurine .... 1996 ...... Sending You Oceans Of Love

SUSPENDED —

"A figurine or collectible that has been removed from production for an unspeci-fied period of time. A piece designated as Suspended cannot be moved to Retired Status without first being "Re-introduced" to the Collection. There is no time limit on how long a collectible may be Suspended from the Collection." - ENESCO

E-0501 .... Figurine .... 1986 ...... Sharing Our Season Together
E-0502 .... Figurine .... 1986 ...... Jesus Is The Light That Shines
E-0503 .... Figurine .... 1986 ...... Blessings From My House To Yours
E-0507 .... Figurine .... 1987 ...... God Sent His Son
E-0508 .... Figurine .... 1986 ...... Prepare Ye The Way Of The Lord
E-0509 .... Figurine .... 1987 ...... Bringing God's Blessing To You
E-0511 .... Figurine .... 1993 ...... Tubby's First Christmas
E-0512 .... Figurine .... 1990 ...... It's A Perfect Boy
E-0515 .... Ornament .... 1988 ...... To A Special Dad
E-0517 .... Ornament .... 1990 ...... The Perfect Grandpa
E-0520 .... Musical .... 1986 ...... Wee Three Kings
E-0521 .... Frame .... 1987 ...... Blessed Are The Pure In Heart
E-0526 .... Figurine .... 1985 ...... He Upholdeth Those Who Call
E-0531 .... Ornament .... 1986 ...... O Come All Ye Faithful
E-0533 .... Ornament .... 1988 ...... Tell Me The Story Of Jesus
E-0535 .... Ornament .... 1986 ...... Love Is Patient
E-0536 .... Ornament .... 1986 ...... Love Is Patient
E-0537 .... Ornament .... 1985 ...... Jesus Is The Light That Shines
E-0539 .... Doll .... 1988 ...... Katie Lynne
E-1375B ..... Figurine .... 1984 ...... Prayer Changes Things
E-1377B ..... Figurine .... 1984 ...... He Careth For You
E-1379B ..... Figurine .... 1984 ...... God Understands
E-2010 .... Figurine .... 1984 ...... We Have Seen His Star
E-2012 .... Figurine .... 1984 ...... Jesus Is Born

E-2013 .... Figurine .... 1984 ...... Unto Us A Child Is Born
E-2343 .... Ornament .... 1988 ...... Joy To The World
E-2344 .... Cndl Clmb ...... 1985 ...... Joy To The World
E-2345 .... Figurine .... 1984 ...... May Your Christmas Be Cozy
E-2346 .... Musical .... 1989 ...... Let Heaven And Nature Sing
E-2348 .... Figurine .... 1988 ...... May Your Christmas Be Warm
E-2349 .... Figurine .... 1985 ...... Tell Me The Story Of Jesus
E-2350 .... Figurine .... 1984 ...... Dropping In For Christmas
E-2352 .... Musical .... 1984 ...... O Come All Ye Faithful
E-2355 .... Musical .... 1984 ...... I'll Play My Drum For Him
E-2356 .... Figurine .... 1985 ...... I'll Play My Drum For Him
E-2361 .... Figurine .... 1986 ...... Christmas Joy From Head To Toe
E-2362 .... Ornament .... 1988 ...... Baby's First Christmas
E-2364 .... Figurine .... 1989 ...... Goat
E-2365 .... Figurine .... 1984 ...... The First Noel
E-2366 .... Figurine .... 1984 ...... The First Noel
E-2367 .... Ornament .... 1984 ...... The First Noel
E-2372 .... Ornament .... 1985 ...... Baby's First Christmas
E-2377 .... Figurine .... 1985 ...... Our First Christmas Together
E-2378 .... Plate .... 1985 ...... Our First Christmas Together
E-2381 .... Ornament .... 1984 ...... Mouse With Cheese
E-2385 .... Ornament .... 1991 ...... Our First Christmas Together
E-2386 .... Ornaments ...... 1984 ...... Camel, Donkey, Cow
E-2801 .... Figurine .... 1984 ...... Jesus Is Born
E-2802 .... Figurine .... 1984 ...... Christmas Is A Time To Share
E-2803 .... Figurine .... 1984 ...... Crown Him Lord Of All
E-2804 .... Figurine .... 1984 ...... Peace On Earth
E-2807 .... Musical .... 1984 ...... Crown Him Lord Of All
E-2808 .... Musical .... 1984 ...... Unto Us A Child Is Born
E-2809 .... Musical .... 1985 ...... Jesus Is Born
E-2810 .... Musical .... 1993 ...... Come Let Us Adore Him
E-2821 .... Figurine .... 1996 ...... You Have Touched So Many Hearts
E-2823 .... Figurine .... 1987 ...... To God Be The Glory
E-2826 .... Figurine .... 1986 ...... May Your Birthday Be A Blessing
E-2827 .... Figurine .... 1986 ...... I Get A Kick Out Of You
E-2834 .... Figurine .... 1991 ...... Sharing Our Joy Together
E-2840 .... Figurine .... 1988 ...... Baby's First Step
E-2851 .... Doll .... 1989 ...... Kristy
E-2852 .... Figurines .... 1996 ...... Baby Figurines
E-2852A ..... Figurine .... 1996 ...... Baby Figurine (Baby Boy Standing)
E-2852B ..... Figurine .... 1996 ...... Baby Figurine (Baby Girl with Bow in Hair)
E-2852C ..... Figurine .... 1996 ...... Baby Figurine (Baby Boy Sitting)
E-2852D .... Figurine .... 1996 ...... Baby Figurine (Baby Girl Clapping Hands)
E-2852E ..... Figurine .... 1996 ...... Baby Figurine (Baby Boy Crawling)
E-2852F ..... Figurine .... 1996 ...... Baby Figurine (Baby Girl Lying Down)
E-2855 .... Figurine .... 1996 ...... God Blessed Our Years Together With So Much Love & Happiness (5)
E-2856 .... Figurine .... 1996 ...... God Blessed Our Years Together With So Much Love & Happiness (10)
E-2859 .... Figurine .... 1996 ...... God Blessed Our Years Together With So Much Love & Happiness (40)
E-3104 .... Figurine .... 1991 ...... Blessed Are The Pure In Heart
E-3105 .... Figurine .... 1984 ...... He Watches Over Us All
E-3108 .... Figurine .... 1984 ...... The Hand That Rocks The Future
E-3119 .... Figurine .... 1984 ...... It's What's Inside That Counts

E-3120	Figurine	1986	To Thee With Love
E-4720	Figurine	1987	The Lord Bless You And Keep You
E-4722	Figurine	1985	Love Cannot Break A True Friendship
E-4723	Figurine	1984	Peace Amid The Storm
E-4725	Figurine	1984	Peace On Earth
E-4726	Musical	1984	Peace On Earth
E-5200	Figurine	1984	Bear Ye One Another's Burdens
E-5201	Figurine	1984	Love Lifted Me
E-5202	Figurine	1984	Thank You For Coming To My Ade
E-5203	Figurine	1984	Let Not The Sun Go Down Upon Your Wrath
E-5205	Musical	1985	My Guardian Angel
E-5206	Musical	1988	My Guardian Angel
E-5207	Night Light	1984	My Guardian Angel
E-5208	Bell	1985	Jesus Loves Me
E-5209	Bell	1985	Jesus Loves Me
E-5210	Bell	1984	Prayer Changes Things
E-5213	Figurine	1989	God Is Love
E-5214	Figurine	1984	Prayer Changes Things
E-5216	Plate	1987	The Lord Bless You And Keep You
E-5376	Figurine	1986	May Your Christmas Be Blessed
E-5378	Figurine	1989	Joy To The World
E-5380	Figurine	1986	A Monarch Is Born
E-5381	Figurine	1987	His Name Is Jesus
E-5382	Figurines	1986	For God So Loved The World
E-5385	Figurine	1986	Oh Worship The Lord
E-5386	Figurine	1986	Oh Worship The Lord
E-5389	Ornament	1986	Peace On Earth
E-5390	Ornament	1989	May God Bless You With A Perfect Holiday Season
E-5391	Ornament	1989	Love Is Kind
E-5394	Musical	1986	Wishing You A Merry Christmas
E-5397	Doll	1991	Timmy
E-5619	Figurine	1985	Come Let Us Adore Him
E-5620	Bell	1985	We Have Seen His Star
E-5623	Bell	1984	Jesus Is Born
E-5627	Ornament	1985	But Love Goes On Forever
E-5628	Ornament	1985	But Love Goes On Forever
E-5630	Ornament	1985	Unto Us A Child Is Born
E-5631	Ornament	1985	Baby's First Christmas
E-5632	Ornament	1985	Baby's First Christmas
E-5633	Ornaments	1984	Come Let Us Adore Him
E-5634	Ornaments	1984	Wee Three Kings
E-5639	Figurine	1985	Isn't He Wonderful
E-5640	Figurine	1985	Isn't He Wonderful
E-5641	Figurine	1985	They Followed The Star
E-5642	Musical	1985	Silent Knight
E-6118	Cndl Clmb	1988	But Love Goes On Forever
E-6214B	Doll	1985	Mikey
E-6214G	Doll	1985	Debbie
E-6613	Figurine	1987	God Sends The Gift Of His Love
E-6901	Plaque	1986	Collection Plaque
E-7153	Figurine	1986	God Is Love, Dear Valentine
E-7154	Figurine	1986	God Is Love, Dear Valentine
E-7155	Figurine	1984	Thanking Him For You
E-7159	Figurine	1985	Lord Give Me Patience
E-7160	Figurine	1986	The Perfect Grandpa

E-7161	Figurine	1984	His Sheep Am I
E-7162	Figurine	1984	Love Is Sharing
E-7163	Figurine	1984	God Is Watching Over You
E-7164	Figurine	1984	Bless This House
E-7165	Figurine	1987	Let The Whole World Know
E-7166	Frame	1993	The Lord Bless You And Keep You
E-7167	Box	1985	The Lord Bless You And Keep You
E-7168	Frame	1984	My Guardian Angel
E-7169	Frame	1984	My Guardian Angel
E-7170	Frame	1985	Jesus Loves Me
E-7171	Frame	1985	Jesus Loves Me
E-7172	Plate	1985	Rejoicing With You
E-7175	Bell	1985	The Lord Bless You And Keep You
E-7176	Bell	1985	The Lord Bless You And Keep You
E-7177	Frame	1987	The Lord Bless You And Keep You
E-7178	Frame	1987	The Lord Bless You And Keep You
E-7179	Bell	1993	The Lord Bless You And Keep You
E-7181	Bell	1988	Mother Sew Dear
E-7183	Bell	1988	The Purr-fect Grandma
E-7184	Musical	1993	The Purr-fect Grandma
E-7186	Musical	1986	Let The Whole World Know
E-7241	Frame	1986	Mother Sew Dear
E-7242	Frame	1988	The Purr-fect Grandma
E-9251	Figurine	1985	Love Is Patient
E-9252	Figurine	1989	Forgiving Is Forgetting
E-9253	Figurine	1985	The End Is In Sight
E-9259	Figurine	1990	We're In It Together
E-9260	Figurine	1987	God's Promises Are Sure
E-9261	Figurine	1986	Seek Ye The Lord
E-9262	Figurine	1986	Seek Ye The Lord
E-9263	Figurine	1985	How Can Two Walk Together Except They Agree
E-9266	Box	1988	I'm Falling For Somebunny
E-9266	Box	1988	Our Love Is Heaven Scent
E-9267	Figurines	1991	Animal Collection
E-9267A	Figurine	1991	Teddy Bear
E-9267B	Figurine	1991	Dog
E-9267C	Figurine	1991	Bunny
E-9267D	Figurine	1991	Cat
E-9267E	Figurine	1991	Lamb
E-9267F	Figurine	1991	Pig
E-9275	Plate	1984	Jesus Loves Me
E-9276	Plate	1984	Jesus Loves Me
E-9280	Box	1985	Jesus Loves Me
E-9281	Box	1985	Jesus Loves Me
E-9282	Figurines	1990	To Somebunny Special You're Worth Your Weight In Gold Especially For Ewe
E-9282A	Figurine	1990	To Somebunny Special
E-9282B	Figurine	1990	You're Worth Your Weight In Gold
E-9282C	Figurine	1990	Especially For Ewe
E-9283A	Box	1984	Forever Friends - Dog
E-9283B	Box	1984	Forever Friends - Cat
E-9285	Figurine	1985	If God Be For Us, Who Can Be Against Us
E-9287	Figurine	1986	Peace On Earth
E-9288	Figurine	1986	Sending You A Rainbow

E-9289	Figurine	1987	Trust In The Lord
12009	Figurine	1991	Love Covers All
12017	Frame	1987	Loving You
12025	Frame	1987	Loving You
12033	Frame	1987	God's Precious Gift
12041	Frame	1992	God's Precious Gift
12149	Figurine	1989	Part Of Me Wants To Be Good
12157	Figurine	1990	This Is The Day Which The Lord Has Made
12165	Musical	1989	Lord, Keep My Life In Tune
12173	Figurine	1990	There's A Song In My Heart
12203	Figurine	1986	Get Into The Habit Of Prayer
12211	Figurine	1987	Baby's First Haircut
12238	Figurines	1996	Clown Figurines
12238A	Figurine	1996	Clown Figurine (Boy Balancing Ball)
12238B	Figurine	1996	Clown Figurine (Girl Holding Balloon)
12238C	Figurine	1996	Clown Figurine (Boy Bending over Ball)
12238D	Figurine	1996	Clown Figurine (Girl with Flower Pot)
12254	Thimble	1990	Love Covers All
12270	Figurine	1998	Lord Keep Me On The Ball
12297	Figurine	1987	It Is Better To Give Than To Receive
12335	Figurine	1988	You Can Fly
12343	Figurine	1986	Jesus Is Coming Soon
12351	Figurine	1988	Halo, And Merry Christmas
12378	Figurine	1990	Happiness Is The Lord
12386	Figurine	1990	Lord Give Me A Song
12394	Figurine	1990	He Is My Song
12408	Musical	1987	We Saw A Star
12416	Ornament	1998	Have A Heavenly Christmas
12424	Doll	1986	Aaron
12432	Doll	1986	Bethany
12475	Doll	1986	P.D.
12483	Doll	1986	Trish
12580	Musical	1990	Lord Keep My Life In Tune
15482	Figurine	1994	May Your Christmas Be Delightful
15776	Figurine	1992	May You Have The Sweetest Christmas
15784	Figurine	1992	The Story Of God's Love
15792	Figurine	1992	Tell Me A Story
15806	Figurine	1992	God Gave His Best
15814	Musical	1992	Silent Night
15822	Ornament	1989	May Your Christmas Be Happy
15830	Ornament	1989	Happiness Is The Lord
15849	Ornament	1993	May Your Christmas Be Delightful
15857	Ornament	1993	Honk If You Love Jesus
16012	Figurine	1989	Baby's First Trip
16020	Night Light	1989	God Bless You With Rainbows
100021	Figurine	1988	To My Favorite Paw
100056	Figurine	1991	Sending My Love
100145	Figurine	1990	God Bless The Day We Found You (Daughter)
100153	Figurine	1990	God Bless The Day We Found You (Son)
100161	Figurine	1990	Serving The Lord (Girl)
100285	Musical	1993	Heaven Bless You
100293	Figurine	1990	Serving The Lord (Boy)
100544	Figurine	1989	Brotherly Love
100625	Thimble	1989	God Is Love, Dear Valentine
100633	Thimble	1991	The Lord Bless You And Keep You

100668	Thimbles	1988	Clown Thimbles
102288	Ornament	1993	Shepherd Of Love
102296	Figurines	1992	Mini Animal Figurines
102369	Figurine	1992	Wedding Arch
102415	Ornament	1989	It's A Perfect Boy
102431	Ornament	1988	Serve With A Smile
102458	Ornament	1988	Serve With A Smile
102474	Ornament	1991	Rocking Horse
102490	Figurine	1988	Sharing Our Christmas Together
102962	Figurine	1989	It's The Birthday Of A King
104027	Figurine	1990	Love Is The Glue That Mends
104396	Figurine	1990	Happy Days Are Here Again
104418	Figurine	1993	Friends To The End
104817	Figurine	1998	A Tub Full Of Love
104825	Figurine	1990	Sitting Pretty
105635	Figurine	1991	Have I Got News For You
105643	Figurine	1991	Something's Missing When You're Not Around
105813	Figurine	1990	To Tell The Tooth You're Special
105953	Figurine	1993	Brighten Someone's Day
106151	Figurine	1991	We're Pulling For You
106216	Figurine	1990	Lord Help Me Make The Grade
106836	Figurine	1993	Happy Birthday Poppy
109487	Figurine	1991	Believe The Impossible
109746	Musical	1993	Peace On Earth
109754	Figurine	1994	Wishing You A Yummy Christmas
111120	Ornament	1990	I'm A Possibility
111163	Figurine	1996	'Tis The Season
111333	Figurine	1991	O Come Let Us Adore Him
112372	Ornament	1992	I'm Sending You A White Christmas
112577	Musical	1996	You Have Touched So Many Hearts
113964	Ornament	1993	Smile Along The Way
113972	Ornament	1991	God Sent You Just In Time
113999	Ornament	1991	Cheers To The Leader
114006	Ornament	1991	My Love Will Never Let You Go
115274	Figurine	1996	Some Bunny's Sleeping
115290	Figurine	1991	Our First Christmas Together
429570	Musical Doll	1994	The Eyes Of The Lord Are Upon You
429589	Musical Doll	1994	The Eyes Of The Lord Are Upon You
520357	Figurine	1993	Jesus The Savior Is Born
520535	Figurine	1996	The Lord Turned My Life Around
520543	Figurine	1996	In The Spotlight Of His Grace
520551	Figurine	1996	Lord, Turn My Life Around
520659	Figurine	1996	Wishing You A Happy Bear Hug
520691	Musical	1993	Lord, Keep My Life In Balance
520705	Figurine	1994	Baby's First Pet
520721	Figurine	1996	Just A Line To Wish You A Happy Day
520756	Figurine	1993	Jesus Is The Only Way
520802	Figurine	1991	My Days Are Blue Without You
520810	Figurine	1991	We Need A Good Friend Through The Ruff Times
520853	Figurine	1991	I Belong To The Lord
521043	Figurine	1993	To My Favorite Fan
521205	Figurine	1993	Hope You're Up And On The Trail Again
521272	Figurine	1994	Take Heed When You Stand
521280	Figurine	1994	Happy Trip
521302	Ornament	1994	May All Your Christmases Be White

521310	Figurine	1993	Yield Not To Temptation
521434	Figurine	1993	To A Very Special Mom And Dad
521485	Figurine	1996	There's A Light At The End Of The Tunnel
521574	Ornament	1994	Dashing Through The Snow
521671	Figurine	1996	Hope You're Over The Hump
521698	Figurine	1996	Thumb-Body Loves You
521841	Figurine	1996	Love Is From Above
521868	Figurine	1991	The Greatest Of These Is Love
521949	Figurine	1993	Wishing You A Cozy Season
521957	Figurine	1993	High Hopes
522031	Figurine	1993	Thank The Lord For Everything
522082	Figurine	1996	May Your World Be Trimmed With Joy
522104	Figurine	1994	It's No Yolk When I Say I Love You
522201	Figurine	1996	Bon Voyage
522244	Musical	1994	Do Not Open Till Christmas
522252	Figurine	1993	He Is The Star Of The Morning
522287	Figurine	1996	Thinking Of You Is What I Really Like To Do
522856	Figurine	1992	Have A Beary Merry Christmas
522910	Ornament	1996	Make A Joyful Noise
522953	Ornament	1994	I Believe In The Old Rugged Cross
522988	Figurine	1993	Isn't He Precious
522996	Figurine	1993	Some Bunnies Sleeping
523097	Figurine	1993	Jesus Is The Sweetest Name I Know
523224	Ornament	1994	Happy Trails Is Trusting Jesus
523763	Figurine	1994	I Can't Spell Success Without You
524484	Figurines	1994	Not A Creature Was Stirring
524875	Figurine	1993	Happy Birthday Dear Jesus
524883	Figurine	1992	Christmas Fireplace
526568	Figurine	1992	Bless Those Who Serve Their Country (Navy)
526576	Figurine	1992	Bless Those Who Serve Their Country (Army)
526584	Figurine	1992	Bless Those Who Serve Their Country (Air Force)
526959	Figurine	1994	We Have Come From Afar
527165	Ornament	1993	The Good Lord Always Delivers
527289	Figurine	1992	Bless Those Who Serve Their Country (Girl Soldier)
527297	Figurine	1992	Bless Those Who Serve Their Country (Soldier)
527343	Figurine	1996	Happy Birdie
527521	Figurine	1992	Bless Those Who Serve Their Country (Marine)
527580	Figurine	1996	Tied Up For The Holidays
527661	Figurine	1996	You Have Touched So Many Hearts
604208	Figurine	1998	A Poppy For You

RE-INTRODUCED

1987	I Believe In Miracles	**E-7156** as	*E-7156R*
1992	Jesus Is The Answer	**E-1381** as	*E-1381R*
1995	God Bless The Day We Found You	**100145** as	*100145R*
	God Bless The Day We Found You	**100153** as	*100153R*
1997	Peace On Earth	**E-9287** as	
	And A Child Shall Lead Them	*E-9287R*	
1998	Have A Heavenly Christmas	**12416** as	
	Have A Heavenly Journey	*12416R*	
	Love Is Kind	**E-1379A** as	*E-1379R*
	He Leadeth Me	**E-1377A** as	*E-1377R*

MOVED FROM SUSPENDED LIST TO RETIRED LIST

E-1377A . He Leadeth Me
- E-1377A *Suspended* in 1984.
- E-1377A *Re-introduced* 11/21/98 as E-1377R for Turn Back The Clock II
- Both E-1377A and E-1377R *Retired* immediately after the Event.

E-1379A . Love Is Kind
- E-1379A *Suspended* in 1984.
- E-1379A *Re-introduced* 6/6/98 as E-1379R for Turn Back The Clock I
- Both E-1379A and E-1379R *Retired* immediately after the Event.

E-1381 ... Jesus Is The Answer
- E-1381 *Suspended* in 1984.
- E-1381 *Re-introduced* in 1992 as E-1381R.
- E-1381R *Retired* in 1996.
- By definition, GREENBOOK considers E-1381 to be Retired as well.

E-7156 ... I Believe In Miracles
- E-7156 *Suspended* in 1985.
- E-7156 *Re-introduced* in 1987 as E-7156R.
- Both E-7156 & E-7156R *Retired* in 1992.

DATED ANNUALS

E-0505	Plate	1983	Christmastime Is For Sharing
E-0513	Ornament	1983	Surround Us With Joy
E-0518	Ornament	1983	Blessed Are The Pure In Heart
E-0522	Bell	1983	Surrounded With Joy
E-2357	Plate	1982	I'll Play My Drum For Him
E-2358	Bell	1982	I'll Play My Drum For Him (prototypes dated)
E-2359	Ornament	1982	I'll Play My Drum For Him
E-5383	Figurine	1984	Wishing You A Merry Christmas
E-5387	Ornament	1984	Wishing You A Merry Christmas
E-5392	Ornament	1984	Blessed Are The Pure In Heart
E-5393	Bell	1984	Wishing You A Merry Christmas
E-5396	Plate	1984	The Wonder Of Christmas
E-5622	Bell	1981	Let The Heavens Rejoice
E-5629	Ornament	1981	Let The Heavens Rejoice
12416R	Figurine	1998	Have A Heavenly Journey
15237	Plate	1985	Tell Me The Story Of Jesus
15539	Figurine	1985	Baby's First Christmas
15547	Figurine	1985	Baby's First Christmas
15768	Ornament	1985	God Sent His Love
15865	Thimble	1985	God Sent His Love
15873	Bell	1985	God Sent His Love
15881	Figurine	1985	God Sent His Love
15903	Ornament	1985	Baby's First Christmas
15911	Ornament	1985	Baby's First Christmas
101834	Plate	1986	I'm Sending You A White Christmas
102318	Bell	1986	Wishing You A Cozy Christmas
102326	Ornament	1986	Wishing You A Cozy Christmas
102334	Thimble	1986	Wishing You A Cozy Christmas
102342	Figurine	1986	Wishing You A Cozy Christmas
102350	Ornament	1986	Our First Christmas Together

102466 ...... Ornament .... 1986 ...... Reindeer Ornament
102504 ...... Ornament .... 1986 ...... Baby's First Christmas
102512 ...... Ornament .... 1986 ...... Baby's First Christmas
102954 ...... Plate .... 1987 ...... My Peace I Give Unto Thee
104515 ...... Ornament .... 1987 ...... Bear The Good News Of Christmas
109401 ...... Ornament .... 1987 ...... Baby's First Christmas
109428 ...... Ornament .... 1987 ...... Baby's First Christmas
109770 ...... Ornament .... 1987 ...... Love Is The Best Gift Of All
109835 ...... Bell .... 1987 ...... Love Is The Best Gift Of All
109843 ...... Thimble .... 1987 ...... Love Is The Best Gift Of All
110930 ...... Figurine .... 1987 ...... Love Is The Best Gift Of All
112399 ...... Ornament .... 1987 ...... Our First Christmas Together
115282 ...... Ornament .... 1988 ...... Baby's First Christmas
115304 ...... Bell .... 1988 ...... Time To Wish You A Merry Christmas
115312 ...... Thimble .... 1988 ...... Time To Wish You A Merry Christmas
115320 ...... Ornament .... 1988 ...... Time To Wish You A Merry Christmas
115339 ...... Figurine .... 1988 ...... Time To Wish You A Merry Christmas
127019 ...... Figurine .... 1995 ...... Love Blooms Eternal
128295A .... Ornament .... 1994 ...... An Event Showered With Love (WI)
128295C .... Ornament .... 1994 ...... An Event Showered With Love (TX)
128295D ... Ornament .... 1994 ...... An Event Showered With Love (CA)
128708 ...... Ornament .... 1996 ...... Owl Be Home For Christmas
129151 ...... Plate .... 1995 ...... He Hath Made Everything Beautiful In His Time
142654 ...... Figurine .... 1995 ...... He Covers The Earth With His Beauty
142662 ...... Ornament .... 1995 ...... He Covers The Earth With His Beauty
142670 ...... Plate .... 1995 ...... He Covers The Earth With His Beauty
142689 ...... Ornament .... 1995 ...... He Covers The Earth With His Beauty
142700 ...... Ornament .... 1995 ...... Our First Christmas Together
142719 ...... Ornament .... 1995 ...... Baby's First Christmas
142727 ...... Ornament .... 1995 ...... Baby's First Christmas
150134 ...... Ornament .... 1995 ...... Merry Chrismoose
160334 ...... Ornament .... 1995 ...... An Event Filled With Sunshine And Smiles (IL)
160334A .... Ornament .... 1995 ...... An Event Filled With Sunshine And Smiles (OH)
160334B .... Ornament .... 1995 ...... An Event Filled With Sunshine And Smiles (CA)
160334C .... Ornament .... 1995 ...... An Event Filled With Sunshine And Smiles (NJ)
160334D ... Ornament .... 1995 ...... An Event Filled With Sunshine And Smiles (MO)
160334E .... Ornament .... 1995 ...... An Event Filled With Sunshine And Smiles (MD)
160334F .... Ornament .... 1995 ...... An Event Filled With Sunshine And Smiles (FL)
160334G ... Ornament .... 1995 ...... An Event Filled With Sunshine And Smiles (OH)
160334H ... Ornament .... 1995 ...... An Event Filled With Sunshine And Smiles (Canada)
163716 ...... Plate .... 1996 ...... Of All The Mothers I Have Known,
                                             There's None As Precious As My Own
163732 ...... Figurine .... 1996 ...... Standing In The Presence Of The Lord
183342 ...... Figurine .... 1996 ...... Peace On Earth...Anyway
183350 ...... Ornament .... 1996 ...... Peace On Earth...Anyway
183369 ...... Ornament .... 1996 ...... Peace On Earth...Anyway
183377 ...... Plate .... 1996 ...... Peace On Earth...Anyway
183911 ...... Ornament .... 1996 ...... Our First Christmas Together
183938 ...... Ornament .... 1996 ...... Baby's First Christmas
183946 ...... Ornament .... 1996 ...... Baby's First Christmas
212563 ...... Figurine .... 1996 ...... Your Precious Spirit Comes Shining Through (TN)
212563A .... Figurine .... 1996 ...... Your Precious Spirit Comes Shining Through (IN)
212563B .... Figurine .... 1996 ...... Your Precious Spirit Comes Shining Through (MN)
260916 ...... Figurine .... 1997 ...... Lead Me To Calvary
270741 ...... Figurine .... 1997 ...... A Festival Of Precious Moments (CA)

270741A .... Figurine .... 1997 ...... A Festival Of Precious Moments (OH)
270741B .... Figurine .... 1997 ...... A Festival Of Precious Moments (TX)
270741C .... Figurine .... 1997 ...... A Festival Of Precious Moments (PA)
272671 ...... Figurine .... 1997 ...... Cane You Join Us For A Merry Christmas
272698 ...... Ornament .... 1997 ...... Cane You Join Us For A Merry Christmas
272701 ...... Plate .... 1997 ...... Cane You Join Us For A Merry Christmas
272728 ...... Ornament .... 1997 ...... Cane You Join Us For A Merry Christmas
272736 ...... Ornament .... 1997 ...... Our First Christmas Togetner
272744 ...... Ornament .... 1997 ...... Baby's First Christmas (Girl)
272752 ...... Ornament .... 1997 ...... Baby's First Christmas (Boy)
272760 ...... Ornament .... 1997 ...... Slow Down For The Holidays
272949 ...... Ornament .... 1997 ...... Pack Up Your Trunk For The Holidays
306835 ...... Figurine .... 1997 ...... He Shall Cover You With His Wings
455601 ...... Figurine .... 1998 ...... I'm Sending You A Merry Christmas
455628 ...... Ornament .... 1998 ...... I'm Sending You A Merry Christmas
455636 ...... Ornament .... 1998 ...... Our First Christmas Together
455644 ...... Ornament .... 1998 ...... Baby's First Christmas - (Girl)
455652 ...... Ornament .... 1998 ...... Baby's First Christmas - (Boy)
455660 ...... Ornament .... 1998 ...... I'll Be Dog-ged It's That Season Again
469327 ...... Plate .... 1998 ...... I'm Sending You A Merry Christmas
520233 ...... Ornament .... 1988 ...... Our First Christmas Together
520241 ...... Ornament .... 1988 ...... Baby's First Christmas
520276 ...... Ornament .... 1988 ...... You Are My Gift Come True
520284 ...... Plate .... 1988 ...... Merry Christmas, Deer
520292 ...... Ornament .... 1988 ...... Hang On For The Holly Days
520403 ...... Ornament .... 1995 ...... Hippo Holidays
520411 ...... Ornament .... 1992 ...... I'm Nuts About You
520438 ...... Ornament .... 1991 ...... Sno-Bunny Falls For You Like I Do
520462 ...... Ornament .... 1989 ...... Christmas Is Ruff Without You
520489 ...... Ornament .... 1993 ...... Slow Down And Enjoy The Holidays
520497 ...... Ornament .... 1990 ...... Wishing You A Purr-fect Holiday
521558 ...... Ornament .... 1989 ...... Our First Christmas Together
522546 ...... Figurine .... 1989 ...... Oh Holy Night
522554 ...... Thimble .... 1989 ...... Oh Holy Night
522821 ...... Bell .... 1989 ...... Oh Holy Night
522848 ...... Ornament .... 1989 ...... Oh Holy Night
522945 ...... Ornament .... 1991 ...... Our First Christmas Together
523003 ...... Plate .... 1989 ...... May Your Christmas Be A Happy Home
523062 ...... Ornament .... 1989 ...... Peace On Earth
523194 ...... Ornament .... 1989 ...... Baby's First Christmas
523208 ...... Ornament .... 1989 ...... Baby's First Christmas
523534 ...... Egg .... 1991 ...... I Will Cherish The Old Rugged Cross
523704 ...... Ornament .... 1990 ...... May Your Christmas Be A Happy Home
523771 ...... Ornament .... 1990 ...... Baby's First Christmas
523798 ...... Ornament .... 1990 ...... Baby's First Christmas
523801 ...... Plate .... 1990 ...... Wishing You A Yummy Christmas
523828 ...... Bell .... 1990 ...... Once Upon A Holy Night
523836 ...... Figurine .... 1990 ...... Once Upon A Holy Night
523844 ...... Thimble .... 1990 ...... Once Upon A Holy Night
523852 ...... Ornament .... 1990 ...... Once Upon A Holy Night
523860 ...... Plate .... 1991 ...... Blessings From Me To Thee
524166 ...... Figurine .... 1991 ...... May Your Christmas Be Merry
524174 ...... Ornament .... 1991 ...... May Your Christmas Be Merry
524182 ...... Bell .... 1991 ...... May Your Christmas Be Merry
524190 ...... Thimble .... 1991 ...... May Your Christmas Be Merry

525324	Ornament	1990	Our First Christmas Together
525960	Egg	1992	We Are God's Workmanship
526940	Ornament	1991	May Your Christmas Be Merry
527084	Ornament	1991	Baby's First Christmas
527092	Ornament	1991	Baby's First Christmas
527475	Ornament	1992	Baby's First Christmas
527483	Ornament	1992	Baby's First Christmas
527688	Figurine	1992	But The Greatest Of These Is Love
527696	Ornament	1992	But The Greatest Of These Is Love
527718	Thimble	1992	But The Greatest Of These Is Love
527726	Bell	1992	But The Greatest Of These Is Love
527734	Ornament	1992	But The Greatest Of These Is Love
527742	Plate	1992	But The Greatest Of These Is Love
528617	Egg	1993	Make A Joyful Noise
528870	Ornament	1992	Our First Christmas Together
529095	Egg	1994	A Reflection Of His Love
529206	Ornament	1994	Our First Christmas Together
530166	Figurine	1993	Wishing You The Sweetest Christmas
530174	Bell	1993	Wishing You The Sweetest Christmas
530182	Thimble	1993	Wishing You The Sweetest Christmas
530190	Ornament	1993	Wishing You The Sweetest Christmas
530204	Plate	1993	Wishing You The Sweetest Christmas
530212	Ornament	1993	Wishing You The Sweetest Christmas
530255	Ornament	1994	Baby's First Christmas
530263	Ornament	1994	Baby's First Christmas
530387	Ornament	1994	You're As Pretty As A Christmas Tree
530395	Ornament	1994	You're As Pretty As A Christmas Tree
530409	Plate	1994	You're As Pretty As A Christmas Tree
530425	Figurine	1994	You're As Pretty As A Christmas Tree
530506	Ornament	1993	Our First Christmas Together
530859	Ornament	1993	Baby's First Christmas
530867	Ornament	1993	Baby's First Christmas
530972	Ornament	1994	You Are Always In My Heart
531200	Ornament	1996	Wishing You A Bear-ie Merry Christmas
531359	Plate	1994	Bring The Little Ones To Jesus
531766	Plate	1994	Thinking Of You Is What I Really Like To Do
604216	Bell	1994	You're As Pretty As A Christmas Tree

ANNUALS (NOT DATED)

E-2838	Figurine	1987	This Is The Day Which The Lord Hath Made
12068	Figurine	1985	The Voice Of Spring
12076	Figurine	1985	Summer's Joy
12084	Figurine	1986	Autumn's Praise
12092	Figurine	1986	Winter's Song
12106	Plate	1985	The Voice Of Spring
12114	Plate	1985	Summer's Joy
12122	Plate	1986	Autumn's Praise
12130	Plate	1986	Winter's Song
100536	Figurine	1987	I Picked A Very Special Mom
100641	Thimbles	1986	Four Seasons
102903	Figurine	1987	We Are All Precious In His Sight
102938	Figurine	1986	God Bless America
107999	Figurine	1987	He Walks With Me

114022	Figurine	1988	The Good Lord Has Blessed Us Tenfold
115231	Figurine	1988	You Are My Main Event
115479	Figurine	1988	Blessed Are They That Overcome
136271	Figurine	1995	You Will Always Be Our Hero
163864	Figurine	1996	Hallelujah Hoedown
183814S	Figurine	1996	The Most Precious Gift Of All
184209	Ornament	1996	Love Makes The World Go 'Round
184217	Figurine	1996	May The Sun Always Shine On You
192368	Figurine	1997	Give Ability A Chance
204870	Figurine	1996	The Lord Is Our Chief Inspiration
212520	Ornament	1996	The Most Precious Gift Of Them All
261351	Figurine	1997	We're So Hoppy You're Here
261378	Figurine	1997	Happiness To The Core
261599	Ornament	1997	In God's Beautiful Garden Of Love
272957"S"	Figurine	1997	My Love Will Keep You Warm
272965	Ornament	1997	My Love Will Keep You Warm
306843	Figurine	1998	20 Years And The Vision's Still The Same
312444	Figurine	1997	Holiday Wishes, Sweetie Pie
325457	Figurine	1998	Life Can Be A Jungle
325465	Figurine	1998	Mom You Always Make Our House A Home
325481	Figurine	1998	Home Is Where The Heart Is
325503	Figurine	1998	Marvelous Grace
451312	Ornament	1998	20 Years And The Vision's Still The Same
455970	Figurines	1998	Flight Into Egypt
455989	Ornament	1998	My True Love Gave To Me
455997	Ornament	1998	We're Two Of A Kind
456004	Ornament	1998	Saying 'Oui' To Our Love
456012	Ornament	1998	Ringing In The Season
456217	Figurines	1998	Sugar Town Post Office Collector Set
456268	Ornament	1998	How Can Two Work Together Except They Agree
456276	Figurine	1998	You Have Mastered The Art Of Caring
456314	Figurine	1999	Heaven Bless You Easter Seal
475084	Ornament	1998	Even The Heavens Shall Praise Him
488259	Figurine	1998	Hope Is Revealed Through God's Word
520470	Ornament	1994	Take A Bow 'Cuz You're My Christmas Star
520861	Figurine	1989	Sharing Begins In The Heart
522325	Figurine	1998	Somebody Cares
521329	Figurine	1996	Have I Toad You Lately That I Love You
522376	Figurine	1989	His Love Will Shine On You
523291	Wall Hanging	1994	Blessed Are The Merciful
523313	Wall Hanging	1993	Blessed Are The Meek
523321	Wall Hanging	1993	Blessed Are The Ones Who Hunger
523348	Wall Hanging	1994	Blessed Are The Peacemakers
523380	Wall Hanging	1992	Blessed Are The Ones Who Mourn
523399	Wall Hanging	1995	Blessed Are The Pure In Heart
523437	Wall Hanging	1992	Blessed Are The Humble
523526	Figurine	1990	I'm A Precious Moments Fan
523593	Figurine	1993	The Lord Will Provide
524158	Figurine	1994	Lord, Teach Us To Pray
524263	Figurine	1991	He Loves Me
524379	Figurine	1994	So Glad I Picked You As A Friend
524387	Figurine	1995	Take Time To Smell The Flowers
524522	Figurine	1990	Always In His Care
525049	Figurine	1990	Good Friends Are Forever
525057	Ornament	1990	Bundles Of Joy

526061 ...... Figurine .... 1997 ...... The Pearl Of Great Price
526185 ...... Figurine .... 1992 ...... You Are My Happiness
526827 ...... Figurine .... 1996 ...... You Can Always Count On Me
527114 ...... Figurine .... 1991 ...... Sharing A Gift Of Love
527122 ...... Figurine .... 1991 ...... You Can Always Bring A Friend
527173 ...... Figurine .... 1992 ...... A Universal Love
527319 ...... Figurine .... 1992 ...... An Event Worth Wading For
527564 ...... Figurine .... 1992 ...... God Bless The USA
527777 ...... Figurine .... 1992 ...... This Land Is Our Land
528080 ...... Figurine .... 1995 ...... Follow Your Heart
528609 ...... Figurine .... 1995 ...... Sending My Love Your Way
528862 ...... Figurine .... 1993 ...... America, You're Beautiful
529648 ...... Ornament .... 1992 ...... The Magic Starts With You
529931 ...... Figurine .... 1993 ...... Happiness Is At Our Fingertips
529974 ...... Ornament .... 1993 ...... An Event For All Seasons
529982 ...... Figurine .... 1994 ...... Memories Are Made Of This
530026 ...... Figurine .... 1993 ...... You're My Number One Friend
530158 ...... Figurine .... 1993 ...... An Event For All Seasons
530786 ...... Figurine .... 1993 ...... 15 Happy Years Together, What A Tweet!
530840 ...... Ornament .... 1993 ...... 15 Years, Tweet Music Together
531111 ...... Figurine .... 1994 ...... It Is No Secret What God Can Do
531588 ...... Figurine .... 1998 ...... You Make Such A Lovely Pair
531634S .... Figurine .... 1996 ...... Who's Gonna Fill Your Shoes?
532061"S" . Figurine .... 1997 ...... Who's Gonna Fill Your Shoes?
617334 ...... Tree Topper .... 1990 ...... Rejoice O Earth

REGIONAL EVENT PIECES

1994   An Event Showered With Love *Ornament*
128295A ....Wisconsin
128295C ....Texas
128295D ....California

1995   An Event Filled With Sunshine And Smiles *Ornament*
160334 ....Illinois
160334A ....Ohio
160334B ....California
160334C ....New Jersey
160334D ....Missouri
160334E ....Maryland
160334F ....Florida
160334G ....Ohio
160334H ....Canada

1996   Your Precious Spirit Comes Shining Through *Figurine*
212563 ....Tennessee
212563A ....Indiana
212563B ....Minnesota

1997   A Festival Of Precious Moments *Figurine*
270741 ....California
270741A ....Ohio
270741B ....Texas
270741C ....Pennsylvania

CHRISTMAS

COMPLETED CHRISTMAS ANNUAL SERIES & GROUPINGS:

JOY OF CHRISTMAS ANNUAL PLATE SERIES   (Series of 4, Dated)
E-2357 .... 1982 ....I'll Play My Drum For Him
E-0505 .... 1983 ....Christmastime Is For Sharing
E-5396 .... 1984 ....The Wonder Of Christmas
15237 .... 1985 ....Tell Me The Story Of Jesus

CHRISTMAS LOVE ANNUAL PLATE SERIES   (Series of 4, Dated)
101834 ...... 1986 ....I'm Sending You A White Christmas
102954 ...... 1987 ....My Peace I Give To Thee
520284 ...... 1988 ....Merry Christmas, Deer
523003 ...... 1989 ....May Your Christmas Be A Happy Home

CHRISTMAS BLESSINGS ANNUAL PLATE SERIES   (Series of 4, Dated)
523801 ...... 1990 ....Wishing You A Yummy Christmas
523860 ...... 1991 ....Blessings From Me To Thee
527742 ...... 1992 ....But The Greatest Of These Is Love
530204 ...... 1993 ....Wishing You The Sweetest Christmas

ANNUAL CHRISTMAS BELLS 1981 - 1994   (Dated)
Traditional:
E-5622 .... 1981 ....Let The Heavens Rejoice
E-2358 .... 1982 ....I'll Play My Drum For Him
E-0522 .... 1983 ....Surrounded With Joy
E-5393 .... 1984 ....Wishing You A Merry Christmas
15873 .... 1985 ....God Sent His Love
102318 ...... 1986 ....Wishing You A Cozy Christmas
109835 ...... 1987 ....Love Is The Best Gift Of All
115304 ...... 1988 ....Time To Wish You A Merry Christmas
522821 ...... 1989 ....Oh Holy Night
523828 ...... 1990 ....Once Upon A Holy Night
524182 ...... 1991 ....May Your Christmas Be Merry
527726 ...... 1992 ....But The Greatest Of These Is Love
530174 ...... 1993 ....Wishing You The Sweetest Christmas

Restyled:
604216 ...... 1994 ....You're As Pretty As A Christmas Tree

ANNUAL CHRISTMAS THIMBLES 1985 - 1993   (Dated)
15865 .... 1985 ....God Sent His Love
102334 ...... 1986 ....Wishing You A Cozy Christmas
109843 ...... 1987 ....Love Is The Best Gift Of All
115312 ...... 1988 ....Time To Wish You A Merry Christmas
522554 ...... 1989 ....Oh Holy Night
523844 ...... 1990 ....Once Upon A Holy Night
524190 ...... 1991 ....May Your Christmas Be Merry
527718 ...... 1992 ....But The Greatest Of These Is Love
530182 ...... 1993 ....Wishing You The Sweetest Christmas

COMPLETED CHRISTMAS ANNUAL SERIES & GROUPINGS (CONT.):

ANNUAL BIRTHDAY COLLECTION ORNAMENTS (Dated)

102466	1986	Reindeer
104515	1987	Bear The Good News Of Christmas
520292	1988	Hang On For The Holly Days
520462	1989	Christmas Is Ruff Without You
520497	1990	Wishing You A Purr-fect Holiday
520438	1991	Sno-Bunny Falls For You Like I Do
520411	1992	I'm Nuts About You
520489	1993	Slow Down And Enjoy The Holidays
530972	1994	You Are Always In My Heart
520403	1995	Hippo Holidays
128708	1996	Owl Be Home For Christmas
272760	1997	Slow Down For The Holidays

ANNUAL MASTERPIECE ORNAMENT SERIES (BALL ORNAMENTS) (Dated)

523062	1989	Peace On Earth
523704	1990	May Your Christmas Be A Happy Home
526940	1991	May Your Christmas Be Merry
527734	1992	But The Greatest Of These Is Love
530190	1993	Wishing You The Sweetest Christmas
530387	1994	You're As Pretty As A Christmas Tree
142689	1995	He Covers The Earth With His Beauty
183350	1996	Peace On Earth...Anyway
272728	1997	Cane You Join Us For A Merry Christmas

DSR OPEN HOUSE ORNAMENTS/HOLIDAY PREVIEW

529648	1992	The Magic Starts With You
529974	1993	An Event For All Seasons
520470	1994	Take A Bow 'Cuz You're My Christmas Star
150134	1995	Merry Chrismoose
531200	1996	Wishing You A Bear-ie Merry Christmas
272949	1997	Pack Up Your Trunk For The Holidays

ONGOING CHRISTMAS ANNUAL SERIES AND GROUPINGS:

ANNUAL CHRISTMAS FIGURINES (Dated)

E-5383	1984	Wishing You A Merry Christmas
15539	1985	Baby's First Christmas (Boy)
15547	1985	Baby's First Christmas (Girl)
15881	1985	God Sent His Love
102342	1986	Wishing You A Cozy Christmas
110930	1987	Love Is The Best Gift Of All
115339	1988	Time To Wish You A Merry Christmas
522546	1989	Oh Holy Night
523836	1990	Once Upon A Holy Night
524166	1991	May Your Christmas Be Merry
527688	1992	But The Greatest Of These Is Love
530166	1993	Wishing You The Sweetest Christmas
530425	1994	You're As Pretty As A Christmas Tree
142654	1995	He Covers The Earth With His Beauty
183342	1996	Peace On Earth...Anyway
272671	1997	Cane You Join Us For A Merry Christmas
455601	1998	I'm Sending You A Merry Christmas

ANNUAL CHRISTMAS PLATES (Dated)

530409 ...... 1994 .... You're As Pretty As A Christmas Tree
142670 ...... 1995 .... He Covers The Earth With His Beauty
183377 ...... 1996 .... Peace On Earth...Anyway
272701 ...... 1997 .... Cane You Join Us For A Merry Christmas
469327 ...... 1998 .... I'm Sending You A Merry Christmas

ANNUAL CHRISTMAS ORNAMENTS (Dated)

E-5629 .... 1981 .... Let The Heavens Rejoice
E-2359 .... 1982 .... I'll Play My Drum For Him
E-0513 .... 1983 .... Surround Us With Joy
E-5387 .... 1984 .... Wishing You A Merry Christmas
15768 .... 1985 .... God Sent His Love
102326 ...... 1986 .... Wishing You A Cozy Christmas
109770 ...... 1987 .... Love Is The Best Gift Of All
115320 ...... 1988 .... Time To Wish You A Merry Christmas
520276 ...... 1988 .... You Are My Gift Come True
522848 ...... 1989 .... Oh Holy Night
523852 ...... 1990 .... Once Upon A Holy Night
524174 ...... 1991 .... May Your Christmas Be Merry
527696 ...... 1992 .... But The Greatest Of These Is Love
530212 ...... 1993 .... Wishing You The Sweetest Christmas
530395 ...... 1994 .... You're As Pretty As A Christmas Tree
142662 ...... 1995 .... He Covers The Earth With His Beauty
183369 ...... 1996 .... Peace On Earth...Anyway
272698 ...... 1997 .... Cane You Join Us For A Merry Christmas
455628 ...... 1998 .... I'm Sending You A Merry Christmas

ANNUAL "BABY'S FIRST CHRISTMAS" ORNAMENTS – UNISEX (Dated)

E-0518 .... 1983 .... Blessed Are The Pure In Heart
E-5392 .... 1984 .... Blessed Are The Pure In Heart

ANNUAL "BABY'S FIRST CHRISTMAS" ORNAMENTS – GIRL (Dated)

15911 .... 1985 .... Baby's First Christmas
102504 ...... 1986 .... Baby's First Christmas
109401 ...... 1987 .... Baby's First Christmas
520241 ...... 1988 .... Baby's First Christmas
523208 ...... 1989 .... Baby's First Christmas
523771 ...... 1990 .... Baby's First Christmas
527092 ...... 1991 .... Baby's First Christmas
527475 ...... 1992 .... Baby's First Christmas
530867 ...... 1993 .... Baby's First Christmas
530255 ...... 1994 .... Baby's First Christmas
142719 ...... 1995 .... Baby's First Christmas
183938 ...... 1996 .... Baby's First Christmas
272744 ...... 1997 .... Baby's First Christmas
455644 ...... 1998 .... Baby's First Christmas

ONGOING CHRISTMAS ANNUAL SERIES AND GROUPINGS (CONT.):

ANNUAL "BABY'S FIRST CHRISTMAS" ORNAMENTS – BOY   (Dated)
15903 .... 1985 .... Baby's First Christmas
102512 ...... 1986 .... Baby's First Christmas
109428 ...... 1987 .... Baby's First Christmas
115282 ...... 1988 .... Baby's First Christmas
523194 ...... 1989 .... Baby's First Christmas
523798 ...... 1990 .... Baby's First Christmas
527084 ...... 1991 .... Baby's First Christmas
527483 ...... 1992 .... Baby's First Christmas
530859 ...... 1993 .... Baby's First Christmas
530263 ...... 1994 .... Baby's First Christmas
142727 ...... 1995 .... Baby's First Christmas
183946 ...... 1996 .... Baby's First Christmas
272752 ...... 1997 .... Baby's First Christmas
455652 ...... 1998 .... Baby's First Christmas

ANNUAL "OUR FIRST CHRISTMAS TOGETHER" ORNAMENTS   (Dated)
102350 ...... 1986 .... Our First Christmas Together
112399 ...... 1987 .... Our First Christmas Together
520233 ...... 1988 .... Our First Christmas Together
521558 ...... 1989 .... Our First Christmas Together
525324 ...... 1990 .... Our First Christmas Together
522945 ...... 1991 .... Our First Christmas Together
528870 ...... 1992 .... Our First Christmas Together
530506 ...... 1993 .... Our First Christmas Together
529206 ...... 1994 .... Our First Christmas Together
142700 ...... 1995 .... Our First Christmas Together
183911 ...... 1996 .... Our First Christmas Together
272736 ...... 1997 .... Our First Christmas Together
455636 ...... 1998 .... Our First Christmas Together

COMPLETED FOUR SEASONS ANNUAL GROUPINGS

THE FOUR SEASONS ANNUAL PLATES   (Set of 4, Unnumbered Certificate)
12106 .... 1985 .... The Voice Of Spring
12114 .... 1985 .... Summer's Joy
12122 .... 1986 .... Autumn's Praise
12130 .... 1986 .... Winter's Song

THE FOUR SEASONS ANNUAL FIGURINES   (Set of 4, Unnumbered Certificate)
12068 .... 1985 .... The Voice Of Spring
12076 .... 1985 .... Summer's Joy
12084 .... 1986 .... Autumn's Praise
12092 .... 1986 .... Winter's Song

THE FOUR SEASONS ANNUAL THIMBLES   (Set of 4)
100641 ...... 1986 .... Four Seasons Thimbles

COMPLETED ANNUAL GROUPINGS

ANNUAL EGGS   (Dated)
523534 ...... 1991 ....I Will Cherish The Old Rugged Cross
525960 ...... 1992 ....We Are God's Workmanship
528617 ...... 1993 ....Make A Joyful Noise
529095 ...... 1994 ....A Reflection Of His Love

NATIONAL DAY OF PRAYER FIGURINES
527564 ...... 1992 ....God Bless The USA
528862 ...... 1993 ....America, You're Beautiful
524158 ...... 1994 ....Lord, Teach Us To Pray

CHAPEL WINDOW COLLECTION - BEATITUDE SERIES   (Announced Series of 7)
523437 ...... 1992 ....Blessed Are The Humble
523380 ...... 1992 ....Blessed Are The Ones Who Mourn
523313 ...... 1993 ....Blessed Are The Meek
523321 ...... 1993 ....Blessed Are The Ones Who Hunger
523291 ...... 1994 ....Blessed Are The Merciful
523399 ...... 1994 ....Blessed Are The Pure In Heart
523348 ...... 1995 ....Blessed Are The Peacemakers

MOTHER'S DAY ANNUAL PLATE SERIES   (Dated)
531766 ...... 1994 ....Thinking Of You Is What I Really Like To Do
129151 ...... 1995 ....He Hath Made Everything Beautiful In His Time
163716 ...... 1996 ....Of All The Mothers I Have Known, There's None As
                                    Precious As My Own

SPECIAL EVENTS FIGURINES/SPRING CELEBRATION
115231 ...... 1988 ....You Are My Main Event
520861 ...... 1989 ....Sharing Begins In The Heart
523526 ...... 1990 ....I'm A PRECIOUS MOMENTS Fan
525049 ...... 1990 ....Good Friends Are Forever (Rosebud Understamp)
527122 ...... 1991 ....You Can Always Bring A Friend
527319 ...... 1992 ....An Event Worth Wading For
530158 ...... 1993 ....An Event For All Seasons
529982 ...... 1994 ....Memories Are Made Of This
528080 ...... 1995 ....Follow Your Heart
163864 ...... 1996 ....Hallelujah Hoedown
261351 ...... 1997 ....We're So Hoppy You're Here

CROSS FIGURINE SERIES   (Dated)
127019 ...... 1995 ....Love Blooms Eternal
163732 ...... 1996 ....Standing In The Presence Of The Lord
260916 ...... 1997 ....Lead Me To Calvary
306835 ...... 1998 ....He Shall Cover You With His Wings

ONGOING ANNUAL GROUPINGS

SPECIAL EASTER SEAL FIGURINES

107999 ...... 1987 .... He Walks With Me
115479 ...... 1988 .... Blessed Are They That Overcome
522376 ...... 1989 .... His Love Will Shine On You
524522 ...... 1990 .... Always In His Care
527114 ...... 1991 .... Sharing A Gift Of Love
527173 ...... 1992 .... A Universal Love
530026 ...... 1993 .... You're My Number One Friend
531111 ...... 1994 .... It Is No Secret What God Can Do
524387 ...... 1995 .... Take Time To Smell The Flowers
526827 ...... 1996 .... You Can Always Count On Me
192368 ...... 1997 .... Give Ability A Chance
522325 ...... 1998 .... Somebody Cares
456314 ...... 1999 .... Heaven Bless You Easter Seal

SPRING CATALOG FIGURINES

529931 ...... 1993 .... Happiness Is At Our Fingertips
524379 ...... 1994 .... So Glad I Picked You As A Friend
528609 ...... 1995 .... Sending My Love Your Way
521329 ...... 1996 .... Have I Toad You Lately That I Love You
261378 ...... 1997 .... Happiness To The Core
325481 ...... 1998 .... Home Is Where The Heart Is

COMPLETED SERIES

MOTHER'S LOVE PLATE SERIES   (Series of 4, Individually Numbered)

E-5217 .... Mother Sew Dear
E-7173 .... The Purr-fect Grandma
E-9256 .... The Hand That Rocks The Future
E-2848 .... Loving Thy Neighbor

INSPIRED THOUGHTS PLATE SERIES   (Series of 4, Individually Numbered)

E-5215 .... Love One Another
E-7174 .... Make A Joyful Noise
E-9257 .... I Believe In Miracles
E-2847 .... Love Is Kind

CHRISTMAS COLLECTION PLATE SERIES   (Series of 4, Individually Numbered)

E-5646 .... Come Let Us Adore Him
E-2347 .... Let Heaven And Nature Sing
E-0538 .... Wee Three Kings
E-5395 .... Unto Us A Child Is Born

BRIDAL SERIES   (Series of 8)

E-2831 .... Bridesmaid
E-2836 .... Groomsman
E-2835 .... Flower Girl
E-2833 .... Ringbearer
E-2845 .... Junior Bridesmaid
E-2837 .... Groom
E-2846 .... Bride
E-2838 .... This Is The Day Which The Lord Hath Made

HEAVENLY HALOS SERIES   (Series of 4)
E-9260 .... God's Promises Are Sure
E-9274 .... Taste And See That The Lord Is Good
E-9288 .... Sending You A Rainbow
E-9289 .... Trust In The Lord

CLOWN SERIES   (Series of 4)
12262 .... I Get A Bang Out Of You
12459 .... Waddle I Do Without You
12467 .... The Lord Will Carry You Through
12270 .... Lord Keep Me On The Ball

REJOICE IN THE LORD BAND SERIES   (Series of 6)
12165 .... Lord, Keep My Life In Tune
12173 .... There's A Song In My Heart
12378 .... Happiness Is The Lord
12386 .... Lord Give Me A Song
12394 .... He Is My Song
12580 .... Lord, Keep My Life In Tune

BLESS THOSE WHO SERVE THEIR COUNTRY   (Series of 6)
526568 ...... Navy
526576 ...... Army
526584 ...... Air Force
527521 ...... Marine
527289 ...... Girl Soldier
527297 ...... African-American Soldier

CALENDAR GIRL SERIES   (Series of 12)
109983 ...... January Girl
109991 ...... February Girl
110019 ...... March Girl
110027 ...... April Girl
110035 ...... May Girl
110043 ...... June Girl
110051 ...... July Girl
110078 ...... August Girl
110086 ...... September Girl
110094 ...... October Girl
110108 ...... November Girl
110116 ...... December Girl

"BABY'S FIRST" SERIES   (Series of 8)
E-2840 .... Baby's First Step
E-2841 .... Baby's First Picture
12211 .... Baby's First Haircut
16012 .... Baby's First Trip
520705 ...... Baby's First Pet
524077 ...... Baby's First Meal
527238 ...... Baby's First Word
524069 ...... Baby's First Birthday

COMPLETED SERIES CONT.

THE FAMILY CHRISTMAS SCENE SERIES   (Series of 7)
15776 .... May You Have The Sweetest Christmas
15784 .... The Story Of God's Love
15792 .... Tell Me A Story
15806 .... God Gave His Best
15814 .... Silent Night
522856 ...... Have A Beary Merry Christmas
524883 ...... Christmas Fireplace

GROWING IN GRACE SERIES   (Series of 17)
136204 ...... It's A Girl
136190 ...... Age 1
136212 ...... Age 2
136220 ...... Age 3
136239 ...... Age 4
136247 ...... Age 5
136255 ...... Age 6
163740 ...... Age 7
163759 ...... Age 8
183865 ...... Age 9
183873 ...... Age 10
260924 ...... Age 11
260932 ...... Age 12
272647 ...... Age 13
272655 ...... Age 14
272663 ...... Age 15
136263 ...... Age 16

THE GOOD SAMARITAN SERIES
603864 ...... Nothing Can Dampen The Spirit Of Caring

GROWING IN GOD'S GARDEN OF LOVE
163856 ...... Sowing Seeds Of Kindness
176958 ...... Some Plant, Some Water, But God Giveth The Increase
184268 ...... A Bouquet From God's Garden Of Love

YOU ARE ALWAYS THERE FOR ME
163600 ...... (Mother & Daughter)
163627 ...... (Father & Son)
163635 ...... (Sisters)
163597 ...... (Father & Daughter)
163619 ...... (Mother & Son)

ONGOING SERIES

THE BIRTHDAY CIRCUS TRAIN SERIES
15938 .... May Your Birthday Be Warm (Baby)
15946 .... Happy Birthday Little Lamb (Age 1)
15962 .... God Bless You On Your Birthday (Age 2)
15954 .... Heaven Bless Your Special Day (Age 3)
15970 .... May Your Birthday Be Gigantic (Age 4)
15989 .... This Day Is Something To Roar About (Age 5)
15997 .... Keep Looking Up (Age 6)
109479 ...... Wishing You Grrr-eatness (Age 7)
109460 ...... Isn't Eight Just Great (Age 8)
521833 ...... Being Nine Is Just Divine (Age 9)
521825 ...... May Your Birthday Be Mammoth (Age 10)
488003 ...... Take Your Time It's Your Birthday (Age 11)
16004 .... Bless The Days Of Our Youth

ALWAYS VICTORIAN SERIES   (Announced Series of 3)
307009 ...... Charity Begins In The Heart
488259 ...... Hope Is Revealed Through God's Word

COUNTRY LANE COLLECTION
261106 ...... Hogs And Kisses
307017 ...... You're Just As Sweet As Pie
307025 ...... Oh Taste And See That The Lord Is Good
307033 ...... Fork Over Those Blessings
307041 ...... Nobody Likes To Be Dumped
307068 ...... I'll Never Tire Of You
307076 ...... Peas Pass The Carrots
307084 ...... Bringing In The Sheaves

BABY CLASSICS

272422 ...... Good Friends Are Forever
272434 ...... We Are God's Workmanship
272450 ...... Make A Joyful Noise
272469 ...... I Believe In Miracles
272477 ...... God Loveth A Cheerful Giver
272485 ...... You Have Touched So Many Hearts
272493 ...... Love Is Sharing
272507 ...... Love One Another
306916 ...... Friendship Hits The Spot
306932 ...... Loving You Dear Valentine
306940 ...... He Cleansed My Soul

LITTLE MOMENTS

139491 .... Where Would I Be Without You
139505 .... All Things Grow With Love
139513 .... You're The Berry Best
139521 .... You Make The World A Sweeter Place
139548 .... You're Forever In My Heart
139556 .... Birthday Wishes With Hugs And Kisses
139564 .... You Make My Spirit Soar
261173 .... Bless Your Little Tutu
261203 .... Birthstone January
261211 .... Birthstone May
261238 .... Birthstone September
261246 .... Birthstone February
261254 .... Birthstone June
261262 .... Birthstone October
261270 .... Birthstone March
261289 .... Birthstone July
261297 .... Birthstone November
261300 .... Birthstone April
261319 .... Birthstone August
261327 .... Birthstone December
272612 .... You Will Always Be A Winner To Me (Boy)
272639 .... It's Ruff To Always Be Cheery
283460 .... You Will Always Be A Winner To Me (Girl)
312444 .... Holiday Wishes, Sweetie Pie
320560 .... You're Just Perfect In My Book
320579 .... Loving Is Caring
320595 .... Loving Is Caring
320625 .... You Set My Heart Ablaze
320668 .... Just The Facts... You're Terrific
320706 .... You Have Such A Special Way Of Caring Each And Every Day
320714 .... What Would I Do Without You
456373 .... You Are A Duchess To Me (Holland)
456381 .... Life Is A Fiesta (Spain)
456403 .... Don't Rome Too Far From Home (Italy)
456411 .... You Can't Beat The Red, White And Blue (United States)
456446 .... Love's Russian Into My Heart (Russia)
456454 .... Hola, Amigo (Mexico)
456462 .... Afri-Can Be There For You, I Will Be (Kenya)
456470 .... I'd Travel The Highlands To Be With You (Scotland)
456896 .... Sure Would Love To Squeeze You (Germany)
456918 .... You Are My Amour (France)
456926 .... Our Friendship Is Always In Bloom (Japan)
456934 .... My Love Will Stand Guard Over You (England)

SPECIAL DATED CRUISE MEDALLIONS & FIGURINES

529079 .... 1993 .. Friends Never Drift Apart .... Cruise Medallion
529087 .... 1993 .. 15 Years Tweet Music Together .... After-Cruise Orlando Event Medallion
150061 .... 1995 .. Sailabration .... Cruise Figurine
325511 .... 1998 .. Our Future Is Looking Much Brighter .... Cruise Figurine

9 PIECE NATIVITY GROUP

E-2800 .... Come Let Us Adore Him *(Discontinued)*
104000 ...... Come Let Us Adore Him

3 PIECE NATIVITY STARTER SET WITH BOOKLET

142735 ...... Come Let Us Adore Him

ONGOING ADDITIONS

E-2360 .... I'll Play My Drum For Him
E-2363 .... Camel
E-5379 .... Isn't He Precious
E-5621 .... Donkey
E-5624 .... They Followed The Star
E-5635 .... Wee Three Kings
E-5636 .... Rejoice O Earth
E-5637 .... The Heavenly Light
E-5638 .... Cow
E-5644 .... Two Section Wall
15490 .... Honk If You Love Jesus
183954 ...... Shepherd With Lambs
183962 ...... Shepherd With Lambs
184012 ...... All Sing His Praises
272582 ...... Enhancement Set For Large Nativity
272787 ...... And You Shall See A Star
283428 ...... Lighted Inn
292753 ...... Wishing Well
455954 ...... The Light Of The World Is Jesus
527750 ...... Wishing You A Comfy Christmas
528072 ...... Nativity Cart

COMPLEMENTARY PIECE

455970 ...... Flight Into Egypt

RETIRED ADDITIONS

142751 ...... Making A Trail To Bethlehem
529966 ...... Ring Out The Good News

SUSPENDED ADDITIONS

E-0511 .... Tubby's First Christmas
E-0512 .... It's A Perfect Boy
E-2364 .... Goat
E-2365 .... The First Noel
E-2366 .... The First Noel
E-5378 .... Joy To The World
E-5639 .... Isn't He Wonderful
E-5640 .... Isn't He Wonderful
E-5641 .... They Follow The Star
102962 ...... It's The Birthday Of A King
105635 ...... Have I Got News For You
115274 ...... Some Bunny's Sleeping
520357 ...... Jesus The Savior Is Born
523097 ...... Jesus Is The Sweetest Name I Know
524875 ...... Happy Birthday Dear Jesus
526959 ...... We Have Come From Afar

11 PIECE MINIATURE NATIVITY

E-2395 .... Come Let Us Adore Him

3 PIECE MINIATURE NATIVITY STARTER SET WITH BOOKLET

142743 ...... Come Let Us Adore Him

ONGOING MINI ADDITIONS

E-2387 .... House Set And Palm Tree
E-5384 .... I'll Play My Drum For Him
102261 ...... Shepherd Of Love
108243 ...... They Followed The Star
184004 ...... Making A Trail To Bethlehem
213616 ...... Shepherd With Sheep
213624 ...... Wee Three Kings
279323 ...... Animal Additions
283436 ...... Mini-nativity Wall
283444 ...... For An Angel You're So Down To Earth
291293 ...... Cats With Kitten
455962 ...... Hang On To That Holiday Feeling
520268 ...... Rejoice O Earth
525278 ...... Tubby's First Christmas
525286 ...... It's A Perfect Boy
528137 ...... Have I Got News For You
530492 ...... Happy Birthday Jesus
530913 ...... We Have Come From Afar

SUSPENDED MINI NATIVITY ADDITIONS

E-5385 .... Oh Worship The Lord
E-5386 .... Oh Worship The Lord
102296 ...... Mini Animal Figurines
522988 ...... Isn't He Precious
522996 ...... Some Bunnies Sleeping

MISCELLANEOUS NATIVITY

SET OF 4 NATIVITY (9")

111333 ...... O Come Let Us Adore Him

"DEALERS ONLY" SET OF 9 NATIVITY

104523 ...... Nativity

DELUXE 4 PIECE NATIVITY

E-5382 .... For God So Loved The World

THE CLUBS

"Symbols Of Membership" are received with enrollment in the Clubs. Charter Members who renew receive **"Symbols Of Charter Membership."** All Members have the option to purchase **"Membership Pieces"** that are crafted exclusively for Club Members.

The Enesco PRECIOUS MOMENTS Collectors' Club is on a calendar year basis. Collectors renewing or joining by December 31 receive that year's Symbol Of Membership. Order forms for the Membership Pieces must be taken to an authorized Enesco PRECIOUS MOMENTS Retailer.

The 1999 Enesco PRECIOUS MOMENTS COLLECTOR'S CLUB membership fees are: 1 year $28.00 and 2 year $54.00.

To join, please copy the Membership Application on page 56 and send to the address below or call 1.800.NEAR YOU. (1.800.632.7968).

Enesco Collector Clubs
PO Box 219
Itasca, IL   60143-0219

The Enesco PRECIOUS MOMENTS Birthday Club's year has run from July 1 to June 30. Collectors who renewed or joined before June 30 received that year's Symbol Of Membership. The Birthday Club is changing on January 1, 1999 to the Fun Club. The Fun Club will be on a calendar year basis. Please see page 59 for an outline of 1999 Club benefits.

THE ENESCO PRECIOUS MOMENTS COLLECTORS' CLUB

SYMBOLS OF CHARTER MEMBERSHIP

E-0001 .... 1981 .... But Love Goes On Forever
E-0102 .... 1982 .... But Love Goes On Forever
E-0103 .... 1983 .... Let Us Call The Club To Order
E-0104 .... 1984 .... Join In On The Blessings
E-0105 .... 1985 .... Seek And Ye Shall Find
E-0106 .... 1986 .... Birds Of A Feather Collect Together
E-0107 .... 1987 .... Sharing Is Universal
E-0108 .... 1988 .... A Growing Love
C-0109 ...... 1989 .... Always Room For One More
C-0110 ...... 1990 .... My Happiness
C-0111 ...... 1991 .... Sharing The Good News Together
C-0112 ...... 1992 .... The Club That's Out Of This World
C-0113 ...... 1993 .... Loving, Caring & Sharing Along The Way
C-0114 ...... 1994 .... You Are The End Of My Rainbow
C-0115 ...... 1995 .... You're The Sweetest Cookie In The Batch
C-0116 ...... 1996 .... You're As Pretty As A Picture
C-0117 ...... 1997 .... A Special Toast To Precious Moments
C-0118 ...... 1998 .... Focusing In On Those Precious Moments
C-0119 ...... 1999 .... Wishing You A World Of Peace

SYMBOLS OF MEMBERSHIP

E-0202 .... 1982 .... But Love Goes On Forever
E-0303 .... 1983 .... Let Us Call The Club To Order
E-0404 .... 1984 .... Join In On The Blessings
E-0005 .... 1985 .... Seek And Ye Shall Find
E-0006 .... 1986 .... Birds Of A Feather Collect Together
E-0007 .... 1987 .... Sharing Is Universal
E-0008 .... 1988 .... A Growing Love
C-0009 ...... 1989 .... Always Room For One More
C-0010 ...... 1990 .... My Happiness
C-0011 ...... 1991 .... Sharing The Good News Together
C-0012 ...... 1992 .... The Club That's Out Of This World
C-0013 ...... 1993 .... Loving, Caring & Sharing Along The Way
C-0014 ...... 1994 .... You Are The End Of My Rainbow
C-0015 ...... 1995 .... You're The Sweetest Cookie In The Batch
C-0016 ...... 1996 .... You're As Pretty As A Picture
C-0017 ...... 1997 .... A Special Toast To Precious Moments
C-0018 ...... 1998 .... Focusing In On those Precious Moments
C-0019 ...... 1999 .... Wishing You A World Of Peace

SHARING SEASON ORNAMENTS

PM-864 ...... 1986 .... Birds Of A Feather Collect Together
520349 ...... 1988 .... A Growing Love
522961 ...... 1989 .... Always Room For One More
PM-904 ...... 1990 .... My Happiness
PM-037 ...... 1991 .... Sharing The Good News Together
PM-038 ...... 1992 .... The Club That's Out Of This World

MEMBERS ONLY ORNAMENT

PM-040 1993   Loving, Caring & Sharing
PM-041 1994   You Are The End Of My Rainbow

MEMBERSHIP PIECES

PM-811 ...... Hello Lord, It's Me Again
PM-821 ...... Smile, God Loves You
PM-822 ...... Put On A Happy Face
PM-831 ...... Dawn's Early Light
PM-841 ...... God's Ray Of Mercy
PM-842 ...... Trust In The Lord To The Finish
PM-851 ...... The Lord Is My Shepherd
PM-852 ...... I Love To Tell The Story
PM-861 ...... Grandma's Prayer
PM-862 ...... I'm Following Jesus
PM-871 ...... Feed My Sheep
PM-872 ...... In His Time
PM-873 ...... Loving You Dear Valentine
PM-874 ...... Loving You Dear Valentine
PM-881 ...... God Bless You For Touching My Life
PM-882 ...... You Just Cannot Chuck A Good Friendship
PM-890 ...... Beatitude Ornament Series (Set of 7)

	Individually, the seven Beatitude Ornaments are:
PM-190	Blessed are the Poor in Spirit, for Theirs is The Kingdom of Heaven
PM-290	Blessed are They that Mourn, for They Shall be Comforted
PM-390	Blessed are the Meek, for They Shall Inherit the Earth
PM-490	Blessed are They that Hunger and Thirst for Righteousness, for They Shall be Filled
PM-590	Blessed are the Merciful, for They Shall Obtain Mercy
PM-690	Blessed are the Pure in Heart, for They Shall See God
PM-790	Blessed are the Peacemakers, for they will be Called Sons of God

PM-891 ...... You Will Always Be My Choice
PM-892 ...... Mow Power To Ya
PM-901 ...... Ten Years And Still Going Strong
PM-902 ...... You Are A Blessing To Me
PM-911 ...... One Step At A Time
PM-912 ...... Lord Keep Me In Teepee Top Shape
PM-921 ...... Only Love Can Make A Home
PM-922 ...... Sowing The Seeds Of Love
PM-931 ...... His Little Treasure
PM-932 ...... Loving
PM-941 ...... Caring
PM-942 ...... Sharing
PM-951 ...... You're One In A Million To Me
PM-952 ...... Always Take Time To Pray
PM-961 ...... Teach Us To Love One Another
PM-962 ...... Our Club Is Soda-licious
PM-971 ...... You Will Always Be A Treasure To Me
PM-972 ...... Blessed Are The Merciful
PM-981 ...... Happy Trails
PM-982 ...... Lord Please Don't Put Me On Hold
PM-983 ...... How Can Two Work Together Except They Agree
PM-991 ...... Jumping For Joy
PM-992 ...... God Speed

SPECIAL & COMMEMORATIVE PIECES

*Last minute information not included in the Listings. See page 57 for photo.

12440 .... God Bless Our Years Together (10th Anniversary)
127817 ...... A Perfect Display Of 15 Happy Years (15th Anniversary)
527386 ...... This Land Is Our Land
PMB034 ..... Precious Moments Last Forever & You Fill The Pages Of My Life
N/A .... He Watches Over Us All (Millennium)*

FREQUENT BUYER PROGRAM

283541 ..... Rejoice In The Victory .... Level 1 — 300 points
283584 ..... God Bless You With Bouquets Of Victory .... Level 2 — 500 points
283592 ..... Faith Is The Victory .... Level 3 — 1000 Points

Wish upon a star with us!

"Wishing You A World
Of Peace"
1999 Membership Figurine

When you join The Enesco *Precious Moments*
Collectors' Club® you'll receive the 1999
Membership Figurine, *"Wishing You a World
of Peace,"* along with these star-filled
membership benefits:

- The opportunity to acquire Members' Only
  Figurines designed by artist Sam Butcher
  exclusively for *Club* members.
- The <u>Greenbook Guide</u>, the complete source
  to the **Precious Moments** collection.
- Subscription to the GOODNEWSLETTER,
  the official quarterly publication to
  keep you updated on all the latest
  Precious Moments news.
- A charming bisque photo frame.
- Fun-filled, *Club*-sponsored events.

"God Speed"
1999 Members'
Only Figurine
(#PM992)

Join today and capture a star-filled year of membership benefits...and have your wishes come true!

"Jumping For Joy"
1999 Members' Only Figurine
(#PM991)

Members' Only Millennium Exclusive

Our exclusive limited edition millennium piece, "He Watches Over Us All," is soaring to new heights. These four little angels will be watching over you.

MEMBERSHIP APPLICATION

❏ Yes! Please send my **Precious Moments** Star-Filled Package for $28.00 U.S.

Indicate form of payment enclosed:

❏ Check or money order payable to: The Enesco *Precious Moments Collectors' Club*

❏ Charge to my: ❏ Visa ❏ MasterCard ❏ Discover

Account # _____

Exp. Mo. _____ Yr. _____ Authorized Signature _____
(required if using credit card)

Must be valid for three months from the date the order form is sent to *Club* Headquarters.
(Note: Canadian residents may call (905) 673-9200 or 1-800-263-7095)

NEW MEMBER Name _____

Address _____

City _____ State _____ Zip Code _____

Country _____ Postal Code _____

Phone #: Daytime (_____) _____ Evening (_____) _____

E-mail Address _____

My Favorite Retailer _____

Retailer City _____ State _____

GK

GIFT MEMBERSHIP APPLICATION

Gift Recipient's Name _____

Address _____

City _____ State _____ Zip Code _____

Country _____ Postal Code _____

Phone #: Daytime (_____) _____ Evening (_____) _____

Gift Recipient's E-mail Address _____

Gift Recipient's Favorite Retailer _____

Retailer City _____ State _____

As the giver of the gift membership, do you wish to be notified when this subscription is due for renewal? Yes ❏ No ❏ GK

I understand that I will receive The Enesco *Precious Moments Collectors' Club* Membership Kit with my Membership Figurine within 14 days following processing of this application.

Application expires December 31, 1999

A renewal notice will be mailed 6 wks. prior to membership expiration.
The Enesco **Precious Moments** *Collectors' Club* is sponsored by Collector Appreciation, Inc.

Visit us at our web site: **www.enesco.com**

THE ENESCO PRECIOUS MOMENTS BIRTHDAY CLUB

SYMBOLS OF CHARTER MEMBERSHIP

B-0001 .... 1986 .... Our Club Can't Be Beat
B-0102 .... 1987 .... A Smile's The Cymbal Of Joy
B-0103 .... 1988 .... The Sweetest Club Around
B-0104 .... 1989 .... Have A Beary Special Birthday
B-0105 .... 1990 .... Our Club Is A Tough Act To Follow
B-0106 .... 1991 .... Jest To Let You Know You're Tops
B-0107 .... 1992 .... All Aboard For Birthday Club Fun
B-0108 .... 1993 .... Happiness Is Belonging
B-0109 .... 1994 .... Can't Get Enough Of Our Club
B-0110 .... 1995 .... Hoppy Birthday
B-0111 .... 1996 .... Scootin' By Just To Say Hi
B-0112 .... 1997 .... The Fun Starts Here

SYMBOLS OF MEMBERSHIP

B-0002 .... 1987 .... A Smile's The Cymbal Of Joy
B-0003 .... 1988 .... The Sweetest Club Around
B-0004 .... 1989 .... Have A Beary Special Birthday
B-0005 .... 1990 .... Our Club Is A Tough Act To Follow
B-0006 .... 1991 .... Jest To Let You Know You're Tops
B-0007 .... 1992 .... All Aboard For Birthday Club Fun
B-0008 .... 1993 .... Happiness Is Belonging
B-0009 .... 1994 .... Can't Get Enough Of Our Club
B-0010 .... 1995 .... Hoppy Birthday
B-0011 .... 1996 .... Scootin' By Just To Say Hi
B-0012 .... 1997 .... The Fun Starts Here

MEMBERSHIP PIECES

BC-861 ...... Fishing For Friends
BC-871 ...... Hi Sugar!
BC-881 ...... Somebunny Cares
BC-891 ...... Can't Bee Hive Myself Without You
BC-901 ...... Collecting Makes Good Scents
BC-902 ...... I'm Nuts Over My Collection
BC-911 ...... Love Pacifies
BC-912 ...... True Blue Friends
BC-921 ...... Every Man's House Is His Castle
BC-922 ...... I Got You Under My Skin
BC-931 ...... Put A Little Punch In Your Birthday
BC-932 ...... Owl Always Be Your Friend
BC-941 ...... God Bless Our Home
BC-942 ...... Yer A Pel-I-Can Count On
BC-951 ...... Making A Point To Say You're Special
BC-952 ...... 10 Wonderful Years Of
                    Wishes
BC-961 ...... There's A Spot In My
                    Heart For You
BC-962 ...... You're First In My Heart
BC-971 ...... Hare's To The Birthday
                    Club
BC-972 ...... Holy Tweet
BC-981 ...... Slide Into The Celebration

THE FUN CLUB

1999 CLUB BENEFITS

- Club Year: January 1, 1999 through December 31, 1999.
- All Members whether new or renewing will have Charter Status.

Membership Kit:
- Unique Clubhouse Kit with carrying handle.
- Symbol Of Charter Membership Figurine–*You Are My Mane Inspiration*.
- Special storybook about the true meaning of friendship.
- Huggable fabric kitten named *Boots* that can be personalized using the attached pen.
- Membership card holder which can clip to backpacks.

Additional Benefits:
- Fun Club newsletter four times a year.
- Three Members Only Offerings:
    1. *Buttercup*, a porcelain bisque lamb.
    2. *Chester*, a white Tender Tail pig.
    3. An additional Tender Tail offering to be announced.
- Early renewal gift of a Tender Tail gorilla for those who renew before December 31, 1999.
- Exclusive phone line for Original Charter Members of the Precious Moments Birthday Club.
- Website games and family-centered activities offered throughout the year.

One year membership is $24.00.
Two year membership is $44.00.

To join, please call 1.800.NEAR YOU.

PRECIOUS MOMENTS CHAPEL & VISITOR'S COMPLEX

480 Chapel Road
Carthage, MO   64836
800-543-7975
www.preciousmoments.com

The Precious Moments Chapel is located in the hills of the Ozarks in Carthage, Missouri. It was designed by artist Sam Butcher and was inspired by his desire to pay tribute to the Lord. Sam has always said that the Chapel and what it represents is his life's commitment ... it will always be a dream in progress. The Chapel opened in June of 1989 and has become a place of inspiration and comfort to the thousands of guests who visit yearly.

The Precious Moments Chapel is more than a quiet center of solitude and hope ... it is the center of a family oriented complex that will make your visit to Southwest Missouri a memory of a lifetime! The Chapel is located north of I-44 near the intersection of HH and 71A highways.

CHAPEL EXCLUSIVES

FIGURINES

1991	523038	He Is My Inspiration
1992	523011	There's A Christian Welcome Here
1993	527106	He Is Not Here For He Is Risen As He Said
1993	531677	Surrounded With Joy
1994	531928	Death Can't Keep Him In The Ground
1994	603503	On The Hill Overlooking The Quiet Blue Stream ...
1994	604151	A King Is Born
1995	129259	Grandpa's Island
1995	129267	Lighting The Way To A Happy Holiday
1996	135992	Heaven Must Have Sent You
1996	163872	His Presence Is Felt In The Chapel
1996	204862	The Lord Is Our Chief Inspiration (6")
1996	204870	The Lord Is Our Chief Inspiration (10")
1996	204889	Coleenia
1997	212547	This World Is Not My Home (I'm Just A Passin' Thru)
1997	261602	Crown Him Lord Of All
1997	271586	Seeds Of Love From The Chapel
1998	354406	A Prayer Warrior's Faith Can Move Mountains (5")
1998	354414	A Prayer Warrior's Faith Can Move Mountains (9")
1998	384844	Fountain Of Angels
1998	475092	Toy Maker

SHEPHERD OF THE HILLS FIGURINE EXCLUSIVE

1998	543722	Feed My Lambs

ORNAMENTS

1992 .... 528021 .... There's A Christian Welcome Here
1993 .... 531685 .... Surrounded With Joy
1994 .... 532088 .... A King Is Born
1995 .... 129275 .... Lighting The Way To A Happy Holiday
1996 .... 163880 .... His Presence Is Felt In The Chapel
1997 .... 261610 .... Crown Him Lord Of All
1998 .... 475106 .... Toy Maker

CHAPEL WINDOW BEATITUDE SERIES WALL HANGINGS

1992 .... 523437 .... Blessed Are The Humble
1992 .... 523380 .... Blessed Are The Ones Who Mourn
1993 .... 523313 .... Blessed Are The Meek
1993 .... 523321 .... Blessed Are The Ones Who Hunger
1994 .... 523291 .... Blessed Are The Merciful
1995 .... 523348 .... Blessed Are The Peacemakers
1994 .... 523399 .... Blessed Are The Pure In Heart

23RD PSALM FIGURINES

1st .... 523402 .... The Lord Is My Shepherd, I Shall Not Want
2nd .... 523305 .... He Leads Me Beside The Still Waters
3rd .... 523364 .... He Restoreth My Soul…
4th .... 523356 .... Yea, Though I Walk Through The Valley Of The Shadow Of Death
5th .... 523372 .... Though Preparest A Table Before Me…
6th .... 523429 .... Thou Annointest My Head With Oil…
7th .... 523410 .... Surely Goodness And Mercy Shall Follow Me…

RETIRED CHAPEL EXCLUSIVES

603503 ...... Figurine .... 1997 ...... On The Hill Overlooking The Quiet Blue Stream
604151 ...... Figurine .... 1995 ...... A King Is Born
532088 ...... Ornament .... 1995 ...... A King Is Born

SUSPENDED CHAPEL EXCLUSIVES

163880 ...... Ornament .... 1997 ...... His Presence Is Felt In The Chapel
523011 ...... Figurine .... 1995 ...... There's A Christian Welcome Here

In SUGAR TOWN every building, person, accessory, and ornament is part of a story related to the life of artist Sam Butcher. The name itself honors Dr. Sam Sugar, the family doctor who assisted in the birth of Sam Butcher on New Year's Day 1939. All SUGAR TOWN buildings are lighted. The figurines are on a slightly smaller scale than most in the Collection. All Ongoing Sugar Town pieces were retired December 31, 1997. In 1998, a Special Collector's 7 piece set featuring a lighted Post Office was available as an Annual. This set completed the Village. The announced set of 7 has a surprise 8th piece–a "Thank You For Visiting Sugar Town" sign.

BREAKDOWN OF SUGAR TOWN VIGNETTES

(All pieces are Retired, a * denotes pieces that were Annuals.)

1992:

Chapel Night Light 529621
Aunt Ruth & Aunt Dorothy .. 529486
Philip 529494
Grandfather 529516
Sam Butcher* 529567
Evergreen Tree 528684
Nativity 529508

1993:

House Night Light 529605
Sammy 528668
Dusty 529435
Katy Lynne 529524
Sam Butcher* 529842
Sam's Car 529443
Fence 529796

1994:

Doctor's Office Night Light 529869
Stork With Baby Sam* 529788
Leon And Evelyn Mae 529818
Jan 529826
Dr. Sam Sugar 529850
Free Christmas Puppies 528064
Lamp Post 529559
Mailbox 531847
Curved Sidewalk 533149
Straight Sidewalk 533157
Sugar And Her Dog House .. 533165
Single Tree 533173
Double Tree 533181
Cobble Stone Bridge 533203

1995:

Train Station Night Light 150150
Sam* 150169
Tammy And Debbie 531812
Donny 531871
Railroad Crossing Sign 150177
Luggage Cart 150185
Bus Stop Sign 150207
Fire Hydrant 150215
Bird Bath 150223
Park Bench 529540
Street Sign 532185

1996:

Warming Hut Night Light 192341
Mazie 184055
Leroy 184071
Hank And Sharon 184098
Skating Sign* 184020
Lighted Tree 184039
Skating Pond 184047
Cocoa 184063
Flag Pole 184136
Hot Cocoa Stand 184144
Bonfire 184152

1997:

Schoolhouse Night Light 272795
Aunt Cleo 272817
Aunt Bulah & Uncle Sam 272825
Heather 272833
Chuck* 272809
Merry-go-round 272841
Bike Rack 272906
Garbage Can 272914
Bunnies Carolling 531804

1998:

Post Office Set of 7* 456217
    Post Office Night Light
    Mail Truck
    Girl Mailing Snowballs
    Boy with Snow Cone
    Girl with Goose
    Girl Pushing Sleigh
    Girl with String of Lights

SUGAR TOWN ALSO INCLUDED THESE ANNUAL BRIGHTEN-UP ORNAMENTS & TRAIN CARS:

Sugar Town Chapel 1993 530484
Sam's House 1994 530468
Dr. Sugar's Office 1995 530441
Train Station 1996 184101

1996 Passenger Car 192406
1997 Cargo Car 273007

THE FOLLOWING COLLECTOR'S SETS WERE ALSO AVAILABLE:

- #152269 Train Station Enhancement 5 Piece Collector's Set
  (Includes Street Sign, Bus Stop Sign, Park Bench, Fire Hydrant and Bird Bath.)

- #272930 Skating Pond 6 Piece Collector's Set
  (Includes Hank And Sharon, Lighted Warming Hut, Mazie, Cocoa, Skating Pond & Leroy.)

- #184128 Skating Pond 7 Piece Collector's Set *(Adds Skating Sign to 6 Piece Set.)*

- #184160 Skating Pond Enhancement 3 Piece Collector's Set
  (Includes Flag Pole, Bonfire and Hot Cocoa Stand.)

- #184179 Train Station 5 Piece Collector's Set
  (Includes Railroad Crossing Sign, Train Station Night Light, Tammy And Debbie, Luggage Cart and Donny.)

- #150193 Train Station 6 Piece Collector's Set *(Adds Sam to 5 Piece Set.)*

- #184187 Doctor's Office 6 Piece Collector's Set
  (Includes Doctor's Office Night Light, Dr. Sam Sugar, Leon And Evelyn Mae, Jan, Free Christmas Puppies and Sugar And Her Doghouse.)

- #529281 Doctor's Office 7 Piece Collector's Set
  (Adds Stork w/Baby Sam to 6 Piece Set.)

- #184195 Sam's House 6 Piece Collector's Set
  (Includes Sammy, Sugar Town Fence, Sam's House, Dusty, Katy Lynne and Sam's Car.)

- #531774 Sam's House 7 Piece Collector's Set
  (Adds Sam Butcher with Sugar Town Population Sign to the 6 Piece Set.)

- #212725 Sugar Town Accessories 8 Piece Set
  (Includes 3 Trees, 2 Bushes, Fence, Wreath & Garland.)

- #272876 Schoolhouse 6 Piece Collector's Set
  (Includes Schoolhouse, Heather, Merry-go-round, Chuck, Aunt Cleo, and Aunt Bulah and Uncle Sam.)

- #273015 Schoolhouse 3 Piece Enhancement Set
  (Includes Bike Rack, Bunnies Caroling and Garbage Can.)

The Noah's Ark Story

TWO BY TWO

530123 ...... Bunnies
127809 ...... Congratulations, You Earned Your Stripes (Zebras)
530131 ...... Elephants
530115 ...... Giraffes
163694 ...... I'd Goat Anywhere With You (Goats)
531375 ...... Llamas
530042 ...... Noah, His Wife & Ark
530085 ...... Pigs
230077 ...... Sheep

Also available:
530948 ...... 8 Piece Collector's Set (Includes all but the Llamas, Zebras & Goats)

SAMMY'S CIRCUS

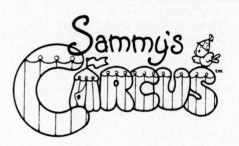

DATED ANNUAL
529222 ...... 1994 .... Sammy

SUSPENDED
163708 ...... 1996 .... Jennifer
528099 ...... 1996 .... Markie
528196 ...... 1996 .... Circus Tent
529168 ...... 1996 .... Jordan
529176 ...... 1996 .... Dusty
529184 ...... 1996 .... Katie
529192 ...... 1996 .... Tippy
529214 ...... 1996 .... Collin

The GREENBOOK ARTCHART contains authorized reproduction of 1159 line drawings. In addition, it lists the Enesco Item Number for the figurine, plate, bell, musical, ornament, doll, thimble, frame, candle climber, box, night light, egg, plaque, wreath, medallion, stocking hanger, tree topper, wall hanging and limoges box derived from each drawing. It is noted, also, if each piece is a Dated Annual, an Annual that is not dated, a Two Year Collectible, a Limited Edition, Retired, Suspended or has a special Inspirational Title.

The ARTCHART, presented in Alphabetical order by Inspirational Title, is designed to provide a graphic illustration of how individual pieces relate to each other and to the entire Collection as well as add to the fun of collecting PRECIOUS MOMENTS.

Although the following pieces are derived from the same art, they have Special Inspirational Titles.

THESE TITLES:		CAN BE FOUND UNDER:
BABY'S FIRST CHRISTMAS	531, 532	JESUS LOVES ME
BLESSINGS FROM ME TO THEE	167	BLESSINGS FROM MY HOUSE TO YOURS
CHRISTMAS IS SOMETHING TO ROAR ABOUT	983	THIS DAY IS SOMETHING TO ROAR ABOUT
CHRISTMAS KEEPS LOOKING UP	556	KEEP LOOKING UP
COLLECTION PLAQUE	184	BUT LOVE GOES ON FOREVER
DASHING THROUGH THE SNOW	518	JANUARY GIRL
FOUR SEASONS THIMBLES	968	THE VOICE OF SPRING
GLIDE THROUGH THE HOLIDAYS	384	HAPPY TRIP
GOD BLESS YOU THIS CHRISTMAS	321	GOD BLESS YOU ON YOUR BIRTHDAY
HAPPINESS IS THE LORD	213	CLOWN FIGURINES
HAPPY TRAILS IS TRUSTING JESUS	444	HOPE YOU'RE UP AND ON THE TRAIL AGAIN
HAVE A HEAVENLY JOURNEY	389	HAVE A HEAVENLY CHRISTMAS
HEAVEN BLESS YOUR SPECIAL CHRISTMAS	417	HEAVEN BLESS YOUR SPECIAL DAY
I WILL CHERISH THE OLD RUGGED CROSS	458	I BELIEVE IN THE OLD RUGGED CROSS
LOVING YOU	333, 334	GOD IS LOVE, DEAR VALENTINE
MAY YOUR CHRISTMAS BE GIGANTIC	667	MAY YOUR BIRTHDAY BE GIGANTIC
MAY YOUR CHRISTMAS BE HAPPY	210	CLOWN FIGURINE
MAY YOUR CHRISTMAS BE WARM - BABY	669	MAY YOUR BIRTHDAY BE WARM
MERRY CHRISTMAS, LITTLE LAMB	378	HAPPY BIRTHDAY LITTLE LAMB
MY GUARDIAN ANGEL(S)	184	BUT LOVE GOES ON FOREVER
MY PEACE I GIVE UNTO THEE	773	PEACE ON EARTH
OUR FIRST CHRISTMAS TOGETHER	942	THE LORD BLESS YOU AND KEEP YOU
OUR FIRST CHRISTMAS TOGETHER	418	HEAVEN BLESS YOUR TOGETHERNESS
OUR FIRST CHRISTMAS TOGETHER	1084	WISHING YOU ROADS OF HAPPINESS
OUR LOVE IS HEAVEN SCENT	489	I'M FALLING FOR SOMEBUNNY
PRAYER CHANGES THINGS	922	THANKING HIM FOR YOU
PRECIOUS MOMENTS LAST FOREVER	184	BUT LOVE GOES ON FOREVER
RETAILER'S DOME	184	BUT LOVE GOES ON FOREVER
SERVE WITH A SMILE	842, 843	SERVING THE LORD
SHARE IN THE WARMTH OF CHRISTMAS	239	DECEMBER GIRL
SOME BUNNIES SLEEPING	880	SOME BUNNY'S SLEEPING
SURROUND US WITH JOY	901	SURROUNDED WITH JOY
SWEET SIXTEEN BY PRECIOUS MOMENTS	749	OUR CLUB IS SODA-LICIOUS
THE LORD BLESS YOU AND KEEP YOU	171	BRIDE
THE MOST PRECIOUS GIFT OF THEM ALL	960	THE MOST PRECIOUS GIFT OF ALL
TRUST AND OBEY	506	IT IS BETTER TO GIVE THAN TO RECEIVE
UNTO US A CHILD IS BORN	523	JESUS IS BORN
YOU'RE "A" NUMBER ONE IN MY BOOK, TEACHER	623	LOVE NEVER FAILS

AC#	TITLE	FIG	PLATE	BELL	MUSIC	ORN	DOLL	THMBL	FRAME	OTHER
1	10 Wonderful Years Of Wishes	BC-952								
2	15 Happy Years Together, What A Tweet!	530786Ⓐ								
3	15 Years, Tweet Music Together					530840Ⓐ				
4	15 Years, Tweet Music Together									529087Ⓓ Medallion
5	20 Years And The Vision's Still The Same	306843Ⓐ					451312Ⓐ				
6	A Bouquet From God's Garden Of Love	184268								
7	A Festival Of Precious Moments	270741Ⓓ 270741AⒹ 270741BⓄ								
8	A Friend Is Someone Who Cares	520632Ⓑ								
9	A Growing Love	E-0108 E-0008					520349			
10	A King Is Born	604151Ⓑ					532088Ⓑ			
11	A Monarch Is Born	E-5380Ⓢ								
12	A Perfect Display Of 15 Happy Years	127817								177083 Medallion
13	A Poppy For You	604208Ⓢ								
14	A Prayer Warrior's Faith Can Move Mountains	354406 354414Ⓐ								
15	A Prince Of A Guy	526037								
16	A Reflection Of His Love	522279								529095Ⓓ Egg
17	A Silver Celebration To Share	163813								
18	A Smile's The Cymbal Of Joy	B-0102 B-0002								

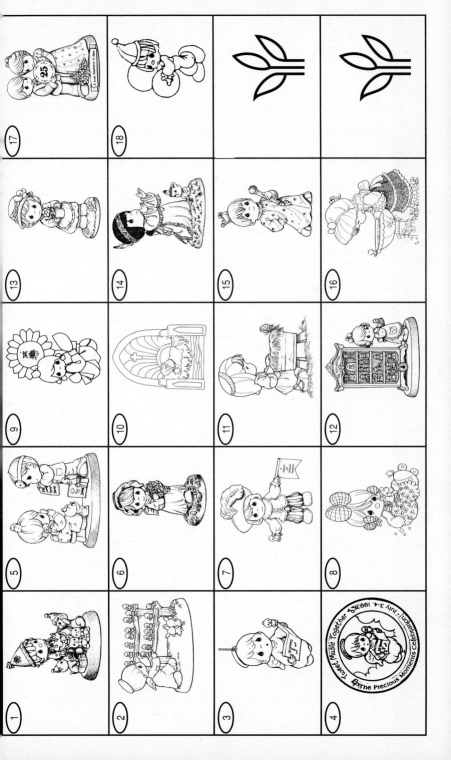

AC#	TITLE	FIG	PLATE	BELL	MUSIC	ORN	DOLL	THMBL	FRAME	OTHER
19	A Special Chime For Jesus	524468Ⓑ								
20	A Special Delivery	521493								
21	A Special Toast To Precious Moments	C-0117								
		C-0017								
22	A Tub Full Of Love	104817Ⓢ								
23	A Tub Full Of Love	112313								
24	A Universal Love	527173Ⓐ								
25	A Very Special Bond	488240								
26	A Year Of Blessings	163783								
27	Aaron						12424Ⓢ			
28	African Be There For You, I Will Be (Kenya)	456462								
29	Age 1	136190								
30	Age 10	183873								
31	Age 11	260924								
32	Age 12	260932								
33	Age 13	272647								
34	Age 14	272655								
35	Age 15	272663								
36	Age 2	136212								
37	Age 3	136220								
38	Age 4	136239								

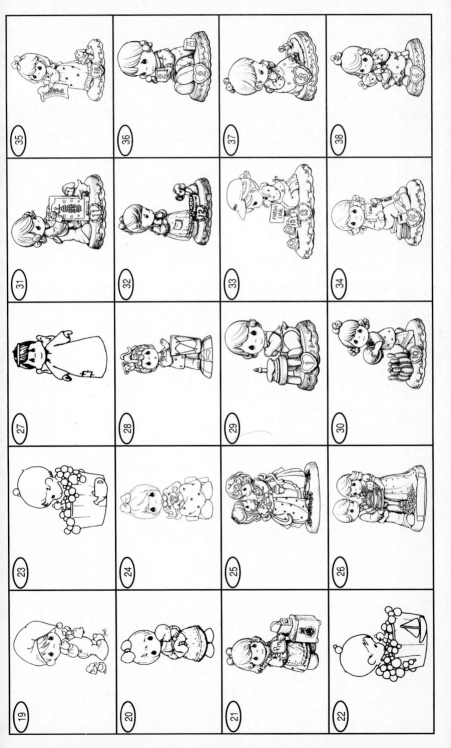

AC#	TITLE	FIG	PLATE	BELL	MUSIC	ORN	DOLL	THMBL	FRAME	OTHER
39	Age 5	136247								
40	Age 6	136255								
41	Age 7	163740								
42	Age 8	163759								
43	Age 9	183865								
44	Alaska Once More, How's Yer Christmas?	455784								
45	All Aboard For Birthday Club Fun	B-0107								
		B-0007								
46	All Sing His Praises	184012								
47	All Things Grow With Love	139505								
48	Always In His Care	524522Ⓐ								
49	Always Listen To Your Heart	488356								
50	Always Room For One More	C-0109					522961				
		C-0009								
51	Always Take Time To Pray	PM-952								
52	America, You're Beautiful	528862Ⓐ								
53	An Event Filled With Sunshine And Smiles					160334Ⓓ				
						160334				
						(A - H)Ⓓ				
54	An Event For All Seasons	530158Ⓐ					529974Ⓐ				
55	An Event Showered With Love					128295AⓄ				
						128295CⓄ				
						128295DⓄ				
56	An Event Worth Wading For	527319Ⓐ								

Ⓢ = Suspended　　Ⓛ = Limited Edition　　Ⓒ = Two Year Collectible　　Ⓓ = Dated Annual　　Ⓐ = Annual

Ⓡ = Retired

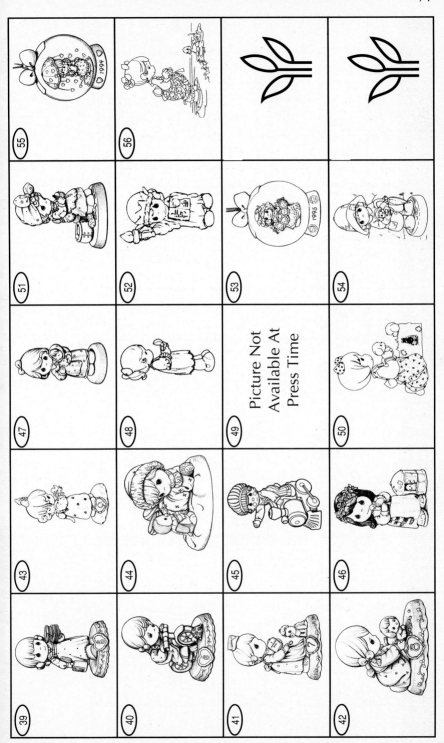

71

AC#	TITLE	FIG	PLATE	BELL	MUSIC	ORN	DOLL	THMBL	FRAME	OTHER
57	AND A CHILD SHALL LEAD THEM	E-9287R								
58	AND YOU SHALL SEE A STAR	272787								
59	ANGEL OF MERCY	102482				102407				
60	ANGELS ON EARTH	183776								
61	ANGELS WE HAVE HEARD ON HIGH	524921Ⓡ								
62	ANGIE, THE ANGEL OF MERCY						12491Ⓛ			
63	ANIMAL ADDITIONS	279323								
64	ANIMAL COLLECTION	E-9267Ⓢ								
65	ANIMAL COLLECTION A	E-9267/AⓈ								
66	ANIMAL COLLECTION B	E-9267/BⓈ								
67	ANIMAL COLLECTION C	E-9267/CⓈ								
68	ANIMAL COLLECTION D	E-9267/DⓈ								
69	ANIMAL COLLECTION E	E-9267/EⓈ								
70	ANIMAL COLLECTION F	E-9267/FⓈ								
71	ANOTHER YEAR AND MORE GREY HARES	128686								
72	APRIL									335576 Limoges Box
73	APRIL GIRL	110027								
74	AUGUST									335614 Limoges Box
75	AUGUST GIRL	110078								
76	AUNT BULAH AND UNCLE SAM	272825Ⓡ								

Ⓢ = Suspended   Ⓛ = Limited Edition   Ⓡ = Retired   ② = Two Year Collectible   Ⓓ = Dated Annual   Ⓐ = Annual

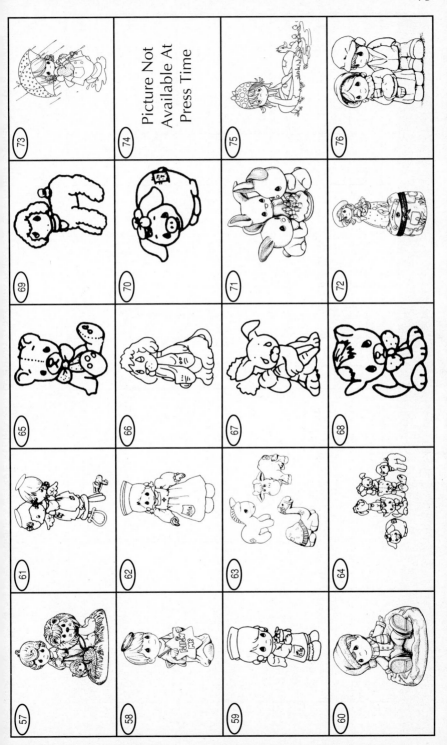

73

73

74 Picture Not Available At Press Time

75

76

69

70

71

72

65

66

67

68

61

62

63

64

57

58

59

60

AC#	TITLE	FIG	PLATE	BELL	MUSIC	ORN	DOLL	THMBL	FRAME	OTHER
77	Aunt Cleo	272817Ⓡ								
78	Aunt Ruth & Aunt Dorothy	529486Ⓡ								
79	Autumn's Praise	12084Ⓐ	12122Ⓐ		408751②		408808②			
80	Baby Figurine	E-2852/AⓈ								
81	Baby Figurine	E-2852/BⓈ								
82	Baby Figurine	E-2852/CⓈ								
83	Baby Figurine	E-2852/DⓈ								
84	Baby Figurine	E-2852/EⓈ								
85	Baby Figurine	E-2852/FⓈ								
86	Baby Figurines	E-2852Ⓢ								
87	Baby Girl Personalized	163651G								
	*Baby Boy Personalized	*163651B								
88	Baby's First Birthday	524069								
89	Baby's First Christmas					E-2362Ⓢ				
90	Baby's First Christmas					E-2372Ⓢ				
91	Baby's First Christmas	15539Ⓓ				15903Ⓓ				
92	Baby's First Christmas	15547Ⓓ				15911Ⓓ				
93	Baby's First Christmas					102504Ⓓ				
94	Baby's First Christmas					102512Ⓓ				
95	Baby's First Christmas					109401Ⓓ				
96	Baby's First Christmas					109428Ⓓ				

Ⓢ = Suspended   Ⓛ = Limited Edition   Ⓡ = Retired   ② = Two Year Collectible   Ⓓ = Dated Annual   Ⓐ = Annual

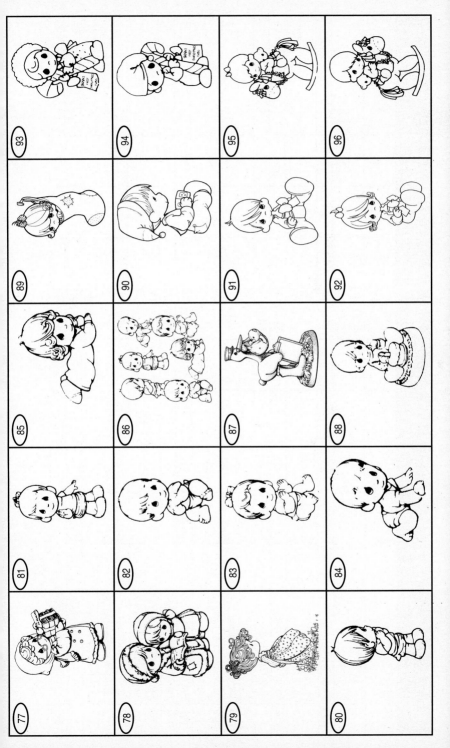

75

AC#	TITLE	FIG	PLATE	BELL	MUSIC	ORN	DOLL	THMBL	FRAME	OTHER
97	Baby's First Christmas					115282Ⓓ				
						523194Ⓓ				
98	Baby's First Christmas					520241Ⓓ				
						523208Ⓓ				
99	Baby's First Christmas					523771Ⓓ				
100	Baby's First Christmas					523798Ⓓ				
101	Baby's First Christmas					527084Ⓓ				
102	Baby's First Christmas					527092Ⓓ				
103	Baby's First Christmas					530859Ⓓ				
104	Baby's First Christmas					530867Ⓓ				
105	Baby's First Christmas					530263Ⓓ				
106	Baby's First Christmas					530255Ⓓ				
107	Baby's First Christmas					142727Ⓓ				
108	Baby's First Christmas					142719Ⓓ				
109	Baby's First Christmas (Boy)					527483Ⓓ				
110	Baby's First Christmas (Boy)					183946Ⓓ				
111	Baby's First Christmas (Boy)					272752Ⓓ				
112	Baby's First Christmas - (Boy)					455652Ⓓ				
113	Baby's First Christmas (Girl)					527475Ⓓ				
114	Baby's First Christmas (Girl)					183938Ⓓ				
115	Baby's First Christmas (Girl)					272744Ⓓ				
116	Baby's First Christmas - (Girl)					455644Ⓓ				

Ⓢ = Suspended　Ⓛ = Limited Edition　Ⓡ = Retired　② = Two Year Collectible　Ⓓ = Dated Annual　Ⓐ = Annual

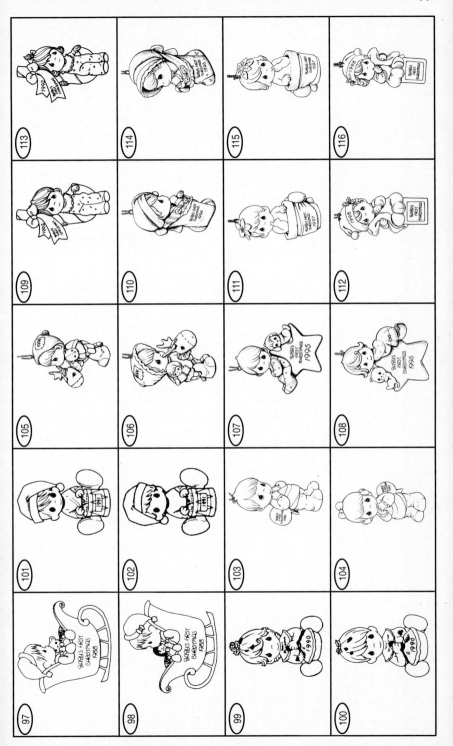

78

AC#	TITLE	FIG	PLATE	BELL	MUSIC	ORN	DOLL	THMBL	FRAME	OTHER
117	Baby's First Haircut	12211Ⓢ								
118	Baby's First Meal	524077								
119	Baby's First Pet	520705Ⓢ								
120	Baby's First Picture	E-2841Ⓡ								
121	Baby's First Step	E-2840Ⓢ								
122	Baby's First Trip	16012Ⓢ								
123	Baby's First Word	527238								
124	Be Not Weary In Well Doing	E-3111Ⓡ								
125	Bear The Good News Of Christmas					104515Ⓓ				
126	Bear Ye One Another's Burdens	E-5200Ⓢ								
127	Beautitude Ornament Series					PM-890				
128	Being Nine Is Just Divine	521833								
129	Believe It Or Knot I Luv You	487910								
130	Believe The Impossible	109487Ⓢ								
131	Bethany						12432Ⓢ			
132	Bike Rack	272906Ⓡ								
133	Bird Bath	150223Ⓡ								
134	Birds Of A Feather Collect Together	E-0106				PM-864				
		E-0006								
135	Birthday Personalized	163686								
136	Birthday Wishes With Hugs And Kisses	139556								

Ⓢ = Suspended   Ⓛ = Limited Edition   Ⓡ = Retired   ② = Two Year Collectible   Ⓓ = Dated Annual   Ⓐ = Annual

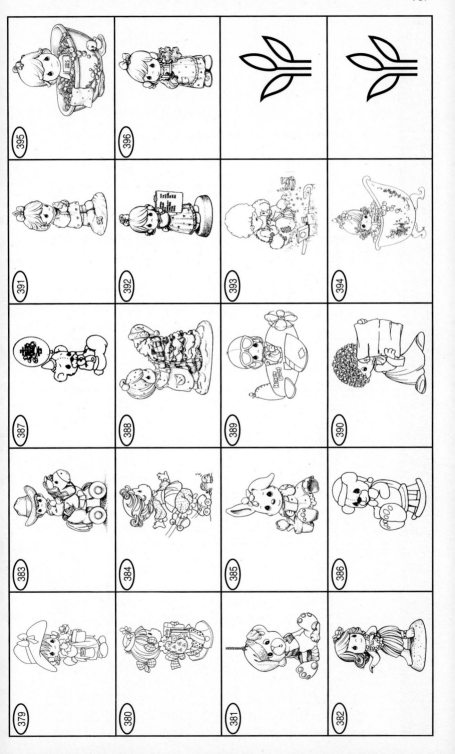

AC#	TITLE	FIG	PLATE	BELL	MUSIC	ORN	DOLL	THMBL	FRAME	OTHER
397	He Hath Made Everything Beautiful In His Time		129151Ⓓ							
398	He Is My Inspiration	523038								
399	He Is My Song	12394Ⓢ								
400	He Is Not Here For He Is Risen As He Said	527106								
401	He Is Our Shelter From The Storm	523550								
402	He Is The Star Of The Morning	522252Ⓢ								
403	He Leadeth Me	E-1377AⓇ								
		E-1377RⓇ								
404	He Leads Me Beside The Still Waters	523305Ⓛ								
405	He Loves Me	524263Ⓐ								
406	He Loves Me	152277Ⓛ								
407	He Restoreth My Soul...	523364Ⓛ								
408	He Shall Cover You With His Wings	306835Ⓓ								
409	He Upholdeth Those Who Call	E-0526Ⓢ								
410	He Walks With Me	107999Ⓐ								
411	He Watches Over Us All	E-3105Ⓢ								
412	He's Got The Whole World In His Hands	526886Ⓛ								
413	He's The Healer Of Broken Hearts	100080								
414	Heather	272833Ⓡ								
415	Heaven Bless You	520934			100285Ⓢ					
416	Heaven Bless You Easter Seal	456314Ⓐ								

Ⓢ = Suspended   Ⓛ = Limited Edition   Ⓡ = Retired   ② = Two Year Collectible   Ⓓ = Dated Annual   Ⓐ = Annual

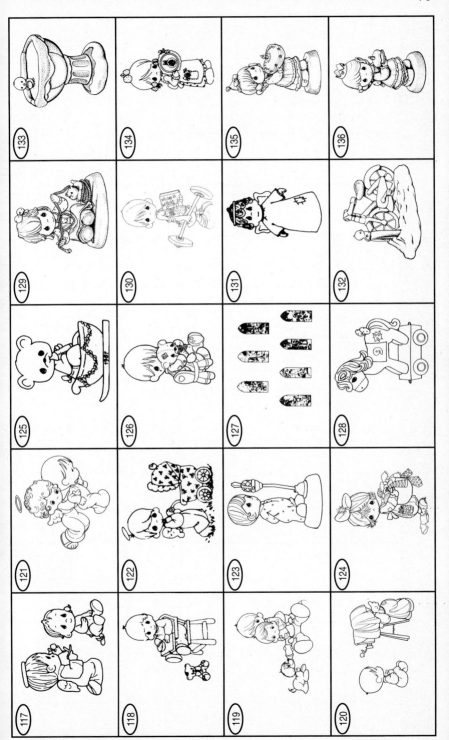

AC#	TITLE	FIG	PLATE	BELL	MUSIC	ORN	DOLL	THMBL	FRAME	OTHER
137	Birthstone April	261300								
	Birthstone August	261319								
	Birthstone December	261327								
138	Birthstone February	261246								
	Birthstone June	261254								
	Birthstone October	261262								
139	Birthstone January	261203								
	Birthstone May	261211								
	Birthstone September	261238								
140	Birthstone March	261270								
	Birthstone July	261289								
	Birthstone November	261297								
141	Bisque Ornament Holder									603171 Ornament Holder
142	Bless The Days Of Our Youth	16004								
143	Bless This House	E-7164Ⓢ								
144	Bless Those Who Serve Their Country– African-American Soldier	527297Ⓢ								
145	Bless Those Who Serve Their Country– Air Force	526584Ⓢ								
146	Bless Those Who Serve Their Country– Army	526576Ⓢ								
147	Bless Those Who Serve Their Country– Girl Soldier	527289Ⓢ								

Ⓢ = Suspended　　　Ⓛ = Limited Edition　　　Ⓡ = Retired　　　② = Two Year Collectible　　　Ⓓ = Dated Annual　　　Ⓐ = Annual

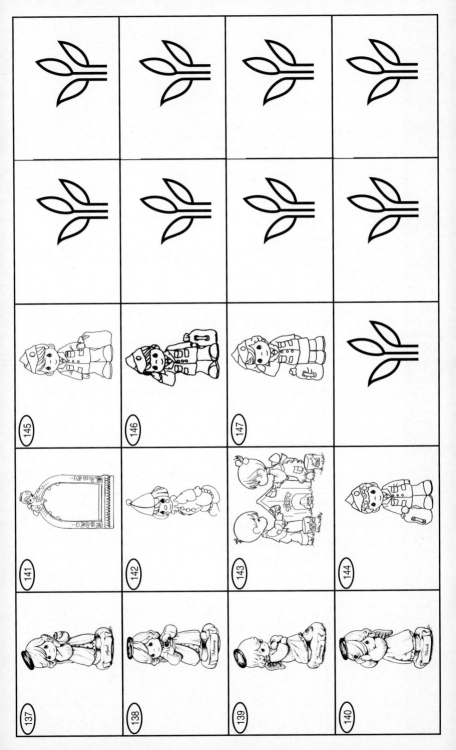

AC#	TITLE	FIG	PLATE	BELL	MUSIC	ORN	DOLL	THMBL	FRAME	OTHER
148	Bless Those Who Serve Their Country– Marine	527521Ⓢ								
149	Bless Those Who Serve Their Country– Navy	526568Ⓢ								
150	Bless You Two	E-9255								
151	Bless Your Little Tutu	261173								
152	Bless Your Soul	531162								
153	Bless-um You	527335Ⓡ								
154	Blessed Are The Humble									523437Ⓐ Wall Hanging
155	Blessed Are The Meek									523313Ⓐ Wall Hanging
156	Blessed Are The Merciful									523291Ⓐ Wall Hanging
157	Blessed Are The Merciful	PM-972								
158	Blessed Are The Ones Who Hunger									523321Ⓐ Wall Hanging
159	Blessed Are The Ones Who Mourn									523380Ⓐ Wall Hanging
160	Blessed Are The Peacemakers	E-3107Ⓡ								
161	Blessed Are The Peacemakers									523348Ⓐ Wall Hanging
162	Blessed Are The Pure In Heart	E-3104Ⓢ				E-0518Ⓓ E-5392Ⓓ			E-0521Ⓢ	
163	Blessed Are The Pure In Heart									523399Ⓐ Wall Hanging
164	Blessed Are They That Overcome	115479Ⓐ								
165	Blessed Are Thou Amongst Women	261556								
166	Blessings From Above	523747Ⓡ								
167	Blessings From My House To Yours	E-0503Ⓢ	*523860Ⓓ							
	*Blessings From Me To Thee									

Ⓢ = Suspended Ⓛ = Limited Edition Ⓡ = Retired ② = Two Year Collectible Ⓓ = Dated Annual Ⓐ = Annual

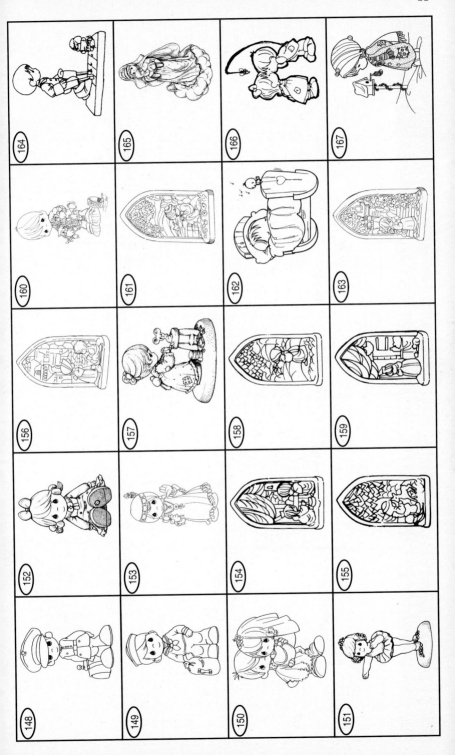

AC#	TITLE	FIG	PLATE	BELL	MUSIC	ORN	DOLL	THMBL	FRAME	OTHER
168	Bon Voyage!	522201⑤								
169	Bonfire	184152®								
170	Bong Bong						100455Ⓛ			
171	Bride	E-2846								
	*The Lord Bless You And Keep You							*100633⑤		
172	Bridesmaid	E-2831								
173	Brighten Someone's Day	105953⑤								
174	Bring The Little Ones To Jesus	527556	531359Ⓛ							
175	Bringing God's Blessing To You	E-0509⑤								
176	Bringing In The Sheaves				307084Ⓛ					
177	Bringing You A Merry Christmas	527599®								
178	Bringing You A Merry Christmas					528226				
179	Brotherly Love	100544⑤								
180	Bundles Of Joy	E-2374®								
181	Bunnies	530123				525057Ⓐ				
182	Bunnies Caroling	531804®								
183	Bus Stop Sign	150207®								
184	But Love Goes On Forever	E-3115			*E-5205⑤	E-5627⑤				E-6118⑤ Candle Climber
	*My Guardian Angel(s)	E-0001			*E-5206⑤	E-5628⑤				E-0102 Plaque
	***Collection Plaque									E-0202 Plaque
	***Retailer's Dome	***E-7350								*E-5207⑤ Night Light
	****Precious Moments Last Forever									**E-6901⑤ Plaque
										****12246Ⓐ Medallion

⑤ – Suspended   Ⓛ = Limited Edition   ® = Retired   Ⓒ = Two Year Collectible   Ⓐ = ...

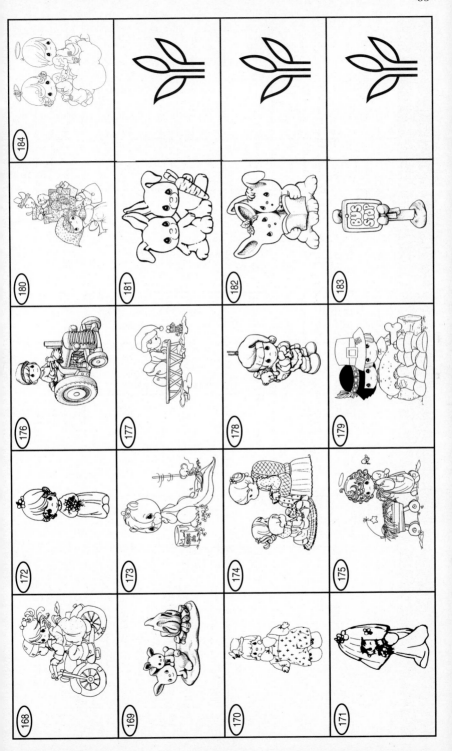

AC#	TITLE	FIG	PLATE	BELL	MUSIC	ORN	DOLL	THMBL	FRAME	OTHER
185	But The Greatest Of These Is Love	527688Ⓓ	527442Ⓓ	527726Ⓓ		527696Ⓓ 527734Ⓓ		527718Ⓓ		
186	Camel	E-2363								
187	Camel, Donkey, And Cow					E-2386Ⓢ				
188	Can't Be Without You	524492								
189	Can't Bee Hive Myself Without You	BC-891								
190	Can't Get Enough Of Our Club	B-0109 B-0009								
191	Candy						100463ⓁⒺ			
192	Cane You Join Us For A Merry Christmas	272671Ⓓ	272701Ⓓ			272698Ⓓ 272728Ⓓ				
193	Cargo Car									273007Ⓓ Train
194	Caring	PM-941								
195	Cats With Kitten	291293								
196	Caught Up In Sweet Thoughts Of You	521973								
197	Chapel Night Light									529621Ⓡ Night Light
198	Chapel Ornament					530484Ⓐ				
199	Charity Begins In The Heart	307009Ⓡ								
200	Cheers To The Leader	104035Ⓡ				113999Ⓢ				
201	Christmas Fireplace	524883Ⓢ								
202	Christmas Is A Time To Share	E-2802Ⓢ			E-2806Ⓡ					
203	Christmas Is Ruff Without You					520462Ⓓ				
204	Christmas Joy From Head To Toe	E-2361Ⓢ								

Ⓢ = Suspended   ⓁⒺ = Limited Edition   Ⓡ = Retired   ② = Two Year Collectible   Ⓓ = Dated Annual   Ⓐ = Annual

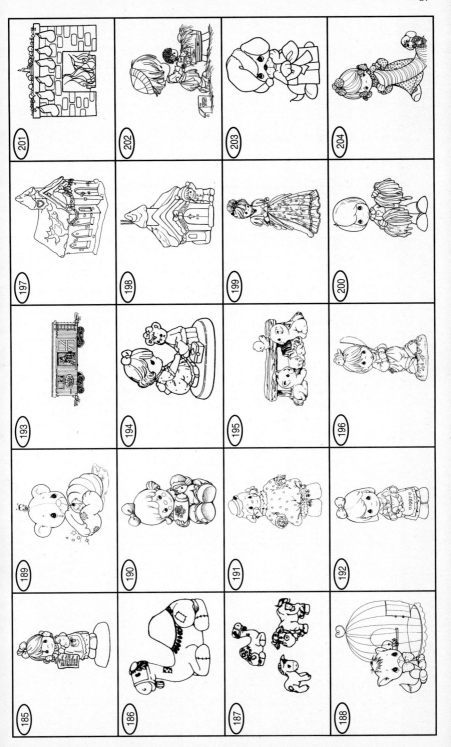

AC#	TITLE	FIG	PLATE	BELL	MUSIC	ORN	DOLL	THMBL	FRAME	OTHER
205	Christmas Personalization					150231				
206	Christmastime Is For Sharing	E-0504®	E-0505Ⓓ							
207	Chuck	272809Ⓓ								
208	Circus Tent									528196Ⓢ Night Light
209	Clown Figurine	12238/AⓈ								
210	Clown Figurine	12238/BⓈ								
	*May Your Christmas Be Happy					*15822Ⓢ				
211	Clown Figurine	12238/CⓈ								
	*Happiness Is The Lord					*15830Ⓢ				
212	Clown Figurine	12238/DⓈ								
213	Clown Figurines	12238Ⓢ								
	*Clown Thimbles							*100668Ⓢ		
214	Cobblestone Bridge	533203®								
215	Cocoa	184063®								
216	Coleenia	204889								
217	Collecting Makes Good Scents	BC-901								
218	Collin	529214Ⓢ								
219	Color Your World With Thanksgiving	183857®								
220	Come Let Us Adore Him	E-2011®								
221	Come Let Us Adore Him	E-2395	E-5646Ⓛ		E-2810Ⓢ	E-5633Ⓢ				
		E-2800								
222	Come Let Us Adore Him	E-5619Ⓢ								
223	Come Let Us Adore Him	104000								

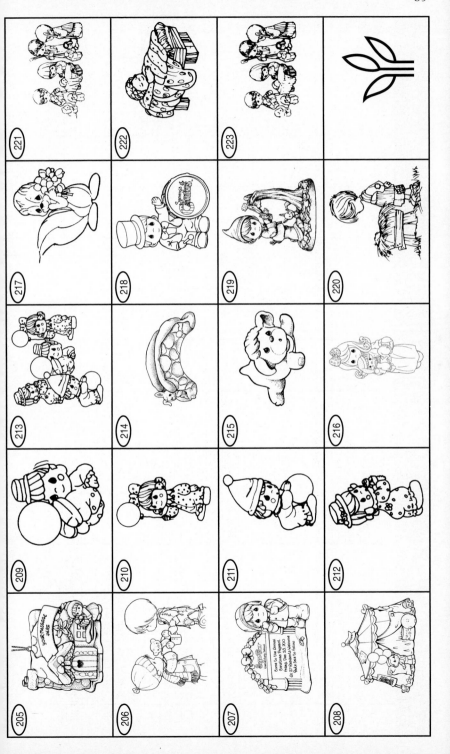

AC#	TITLE	FIG	PLATE	BELL	MUSIC	ORN	DOLL	THMBL	FRAME	OTHER
224	Come Let Us Adore Him	142735								
		142743								
225	Confirmed In The Lord	488178								
226	Congratulations, Princess	106208								
227	Congratulations, You Earned Your Stripes	127809								
228	Connie						102253Ⓛ			
229	Cow	E-5638								
230	Crown Him Lord Of All	E-2803Ⓢ			E-2807Ⓢ					
231	Crown Him Lord Of All	261602				261610				
232	Cubby						E-7267BⓁ			
233	Curved Sidewalk	533149Ⓡ								
234	Dawn's Early Light	PM-831								
235	"Dealers Only" Nativity	104523								
236	Death Can't Keep Him In The Ground	531928								
237	Debbie						E-6214GⓈ			
238	December									335673 Limoges Box
239	December Girl	110116								
	*Share In The Warmth Of Christmas					*527211				
240	Do Not Open Till Christmas				522244Ⓢ					
241	Doctor's Office Night Light									529869Ⓡ Night Light
242	Don't Let The Holidays Get You Down	522112Ⓡ				521590Ⓡ				
243	Don't Roam Too Far From Home (Italy)	456403								

91

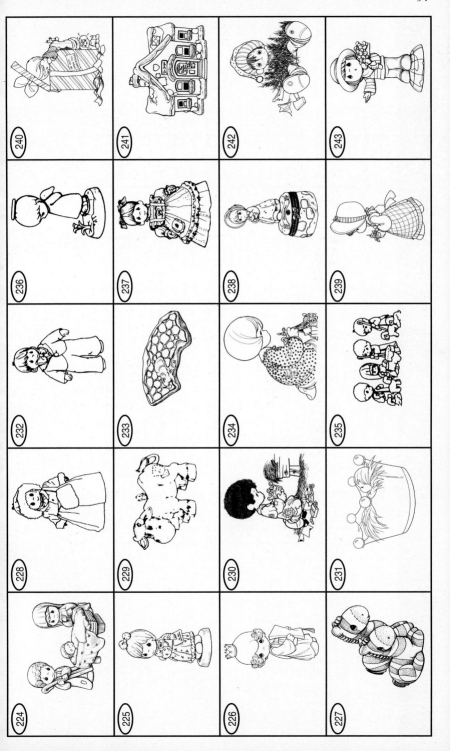

AC#	TITLE	FIG	PLATE	BELL	MUSIC	ORN	DOLL	THMBL	FRAME	OTHER
244	Donkey	E-5621								
245	Donny	531871Ⓡ								
246	Double Tree	533181Ⓡ								
247	Dr. Sam Sugar	529850Ⓡ								
248	Dr. Sugar's Office Ornament					530441Ⓐ				
249	Dreams Really Do Come True	128309								
250	Dropping In For Christmas	E-2350Ⓢ								
251	Dropping In For The Holidays	531952Ⓡ				E-2369Ⓡ				
252	Dropping Over For Christmas	E-2375Ⓡ				E-2376Ⓡ				
253	Dusty	529435Ⓡ								
254	Dusty	529176Ⓢ								
255	Each Hour Is Precious With You	163791								
256	Easter's On Its Way	521892								
257	Eggs Over Easy	E-3118Ⓡ								
258	Eggspecially For You	520667								
259	Elephants	530131								
260	Enhancement Set For Large Nativity	272582								
261	Enter His Court With Thanksgiving	521221								
262	Especially For Ewe	E-9282Ⓢ								
		E-9282CⓈ								
263	Even The Heavens Shall Praise Him	150312ⓁⒹ								

Ⓢ = Suspended Ⓛ = Limited Edition Ⓡ = Retired ② = Two Year Collectible Ⓓ = Dated Annual Ⓐ = Annual

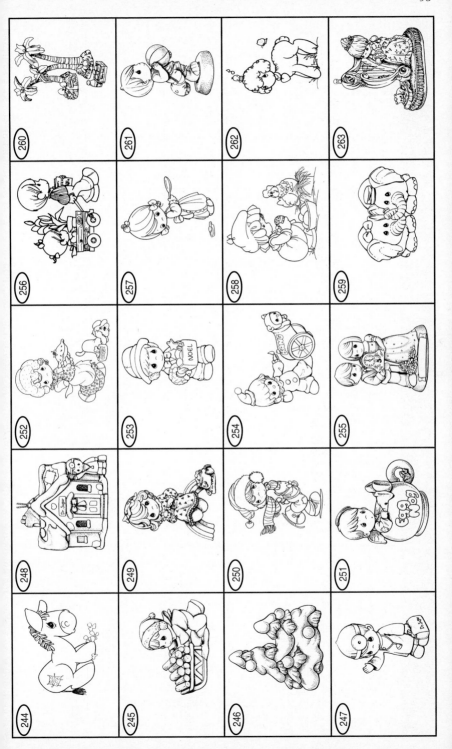

AC#	TITLE	FIG	PLATE	BELL	MUSIC	ORN	DOLL	THMBL	FRAME	OTHER
264	Even The Heavens Shall Praise Him					475084Ⓐ				
265	Evergreen Tree	528684Ⓡ								
266	Every Man's House Is His Castle	BC-921								
267	Faith Is A Victory	521396Ⓡ								
268	Faith Is The Victory	283592								
269	Faith Takes The Plunge	111155								
270	February									335541 Limoges Box
271	February Girl	109991								
272	Feed My Lambs	453722								
273	Feed My Sheep	PM-871								
274	Fence	529796Ⓡ								
275	Fire Hydrant	150215Ⓡ								
276	Fishing For Friends	BC-861								
277	Flag Pole	184136Ⓡ								
278	Flight Into Egypt	455970								
279	Flower Girl	E-2835								
280	Focusing In On Those Precious Moments	C-0018								
		C-0118								
281	Follow Your Heart	528080Ⓐ								
282	For An Angel You're So Down To Earth	283444								
283	For God So Loved The World	E-5382Ⓢ								

Ⓢ = Suspended   Ⓛ = Limited Edition   Ⓡ = Retired   ② = Two Year Collectible   Ⓓ = Dated Annual   Ⓐ = Annual

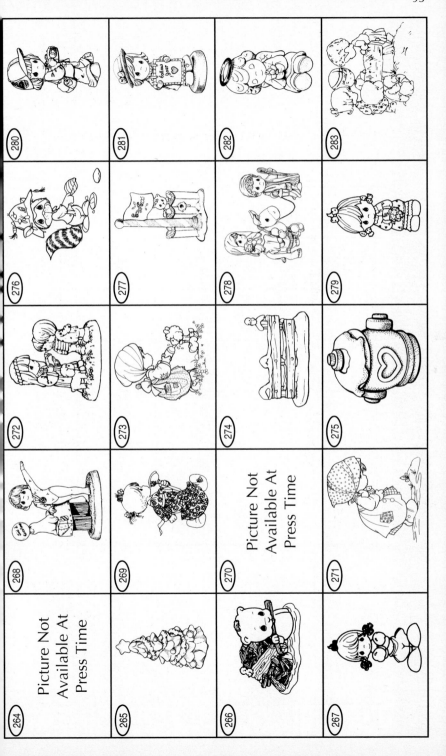

AC#	TITLE	FIG	PLATE	BELL	MUSIC	ORN	DOLL	THMBL	FRAME	OTHER
284	For The Sweetest Tu-lips In Town	306959								
285	Forever Friends									E-9283/A⑤ Box E-9283/B⑤ Box
286	Forgiving Is Forgetting	E-9252⑤								
287	Fork Over Those Blessings	307033								
288	Fountain Of Angels	384844								
289	Free Christmas Puppies	528064®								
290	Friends Are Forever, Sew Bee It	455903								
291	Friends From The Very Beginning	261068								
292	Friends Never Drift Apart	100250				522937®				
293	Friends Never Drift Apart									529079⑨ Medallion
294	Friends To The End	104418⑤								
295	Friends To The Very End	526150®								
296	Friendship Grows When You Plant A Seed	524271®								
297	Friendship Hits The Spot	520748								
298	Friendship Hits The Spot	306916								
299	From The Time I Spotted You I Knew (Know)* We'd Be Friends	260940								
300	Garbage Can	272914®								
301	Gather Your Dreams	529680⑪								
302	Get Into The Habit Of Prayer	12203⑤								
303	Giraffes	530115								

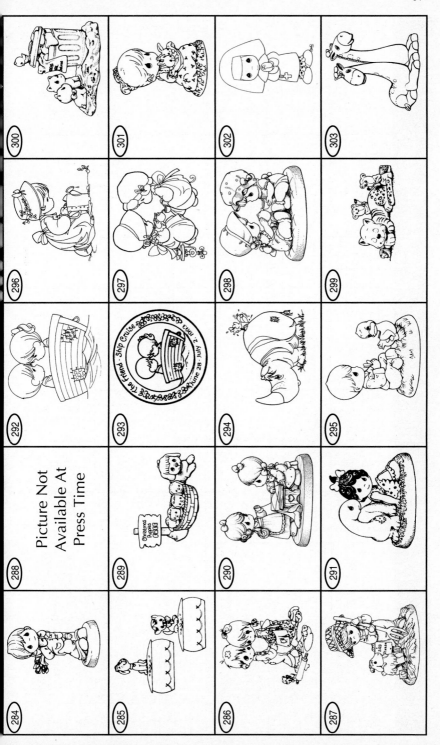

AC#	TITLE	FIG	PLATE	BELL	MUSIC	ORN	DOLL	THMBL	FRAME	OTHER
304	GIVE ABILITY A CHANCE	192368Ⓐ								
305	GOAT	E-2364Ⓢ								
306	GOD BLESS AMERICA	102938Ⓐ								
307	GOD BLESS OUR FAMILY	100498								
308	GOD BLESS OUR FAMILY	100501								
309	GOD BLESS OUR HOME	12319Ⓡ								
310	GOD BLESS OUR HOME	BC-941								
311	GOD BLESS OUR YEARS TOGETHER	12440								
312	GOD BLESS THE BRIDE	E-2832								
313	GOD BLESS THE DAY WE FOUND YOU	100145Ⓢ								
314	GOD BLESS THE DAY WE FOUND YOU	100153Ⓢ								
315	GOD BLESS THE DAY WE FOUND YOU	100153R								
316	GOD BLESS THE DAY WE FOUND YOU	100145R								
317	GOD BLESS THE USA	527564Ⓐ								
318	GOD BLESS YOU FOR TOUCHING MY LIFE	PM-881								
319	GOD BLESS YOU GRADUATE	106194								
320	GOD BLESS YOU ON YOUR BIRTHDAY	15962								
	*GOD BLESS YOU THIS CHRISTMAS					*521094				
321	GOD BLESS YOU WITH BOUQUETS OF VICTORY	283584								
322	GOD BLESS YOU WITH RAINBOWS									16020Ⓢ Night Light
323	GOD BLESSED OUR YEAR* TOGETHER WITH SO MUCH LOVE & HAPPINESS	E-2854								

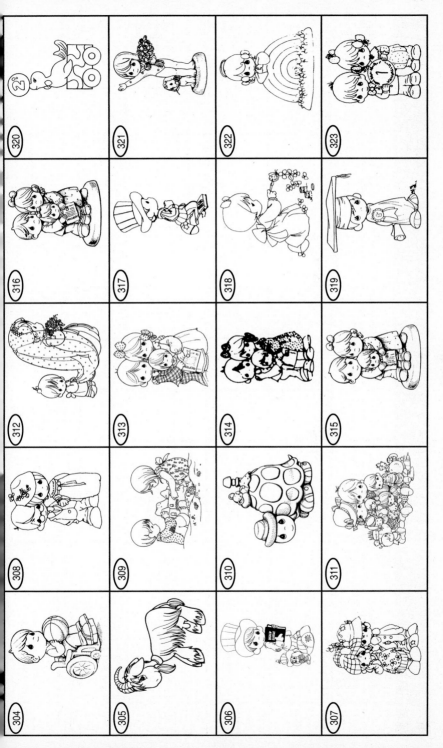

AC#	TITLE	FIG	PLATE	BELL	MUSIC	ORN	DOLL	THMBL	FRAME	OTHER
324	God Blessed Our Years Together With So Much Love & Happiness	E-2853								
325	God Blessed Our Years Together With So Much Love & Happiness	E-2855Ⓢ								
326	God Blessed Our Years Together With So Much Love & Happiness	E-2856Ⓢ								
327	God Blessed Our Years Together With So Much Love & Happiness	E-2857								
328	God Blessed Our Years Together With So Much Love & Happiness	E-2859Ⓢ								
329	God Blessed Our Years Together With So Much Love & Happiness	E-2860								
330	God Cared Enough To Send His Best	524476Ⓡ								
331	God Gave His Best	15806Ⓢ								
332	God Is Love	E-5213Ⓢ								
333	God Is Love, Dear Valentine *Loving You	E-7153Ⓢ								
334	God Is Love, Dear Valentine *Loving You	E-7154Ⓢ						100062Ⓢ	*12017Ⓢ	
335	God Is Love Dear Valentine	523518							*12025Ⓢ	
336	God Is Watching Over You	E-7163Ⓢ								
337	God Loveth A Cheerful Giver	E-1378Ⓡ / 456225Ⓛ								No Item # Limoges Box
338	God Loveth A Cheerful Giver	272477								

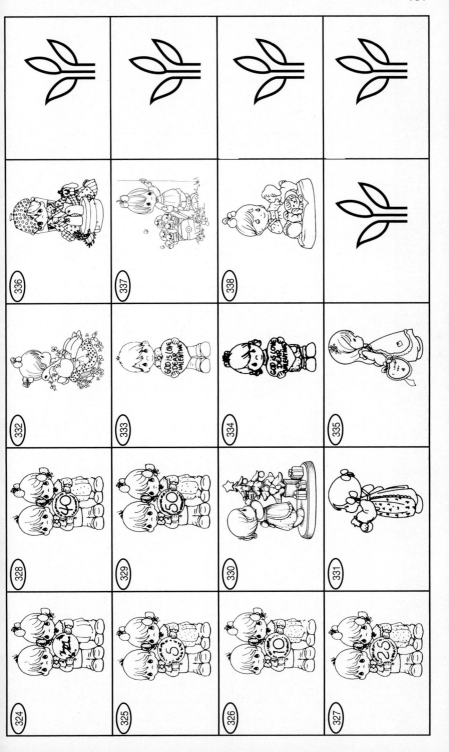

AC#	TITLE	FIG	PLATE	BELL	MUSIC	ORN	DOLL	THMBL	FRAME	OTHER
339	God Sends The Gift Of His Love	E-6613Ⓢ								
340	God Sent His Love	15881Ⓓ		15873Ⓓ		15768Ⓓ		15865Ⓓ		
341	God Sent His Son	E-0507Ⓢ								
342	God Sent You Just In Time				15504Ⓑ	113972Ⓢ				
343	God Understands	E-1379BⓈ		E-5211Ⓑ						
344	God's Love Is Reflected In You	175277Ⓛ								
345	God's Precious Gift								12033Ⓢ	
346	God's Precious Gift								12041Ⓢ	
347	God's Precious Gift					183881				
348	God's Promises Are Sure	E-9260Ⓢ								
349	God's Ray Of Mercy	PM-841								
350	God's Speed	E-3112Ⓑ								
351	God Speed	PM-992								
352	Going Home	525979								
353	Good Friends Are For Always	524123				524131Ⓑ				
354	Good Friends Are Forever	521817								
		525049Ⓐ								
355	Good Friends Are Forever	272422								
356	Good News Is So Uplifting	523615								
357	Grandfather	529516Ⓑ								
358	Grandma's Prayer	PM-861								

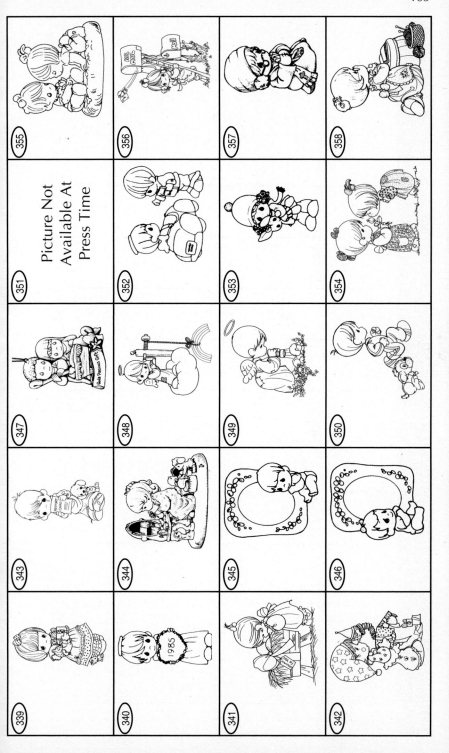

104

AC#	TITLE	FIG	PLATE	BELL	MUSIC	ORN	DOLL	THMBL	FRAME	OTHER
359	Grandpa's Island	129259								
360	Groom	E-2837								
361	Groomsman	E-2836								
362	Hallelujah Country	105821								
363	Hallelujah For The Cross	532002								
364	Hallelujah Hoedown	163864Ⓐ								
365	Halo, And Merry Christmas	12351Ⓢ								
366	Hang On For The Holly Days					520292Ⓓ				
367	Hang On To That Holiday Feeling	455962								
368	Hank And Sharon	184098Ⓡ								
369	Happiness Divine	109584Ⓡ								
370	Happiness Is At Our Fingertips	529931Ⓐ								
371	Happiness Is Belonging	B-0108								
		B-0008								
372	Happiness Is The Lord	12378Ⓢ								
373	Happiness To The Core	261378Ⓐ								
374	Happy Birdie	527343Ⓢ								
375	Happy Birthday Dear Jesus	524875Ⓢ								
376	Happy Birthday Jesus	530492								
377	Happy Birthday Jesus	272523								
378	Happy Birthday Little Lamb	15946								
	*Merry Christmas, Little Lamb					*521078				

Ⓢ = Suspended   Ⓔ = Limited Edition   Ⓡ = Retired   ② = Two Year Collectible   Ⓓ = Dated Annual   Ⓐ = Annual

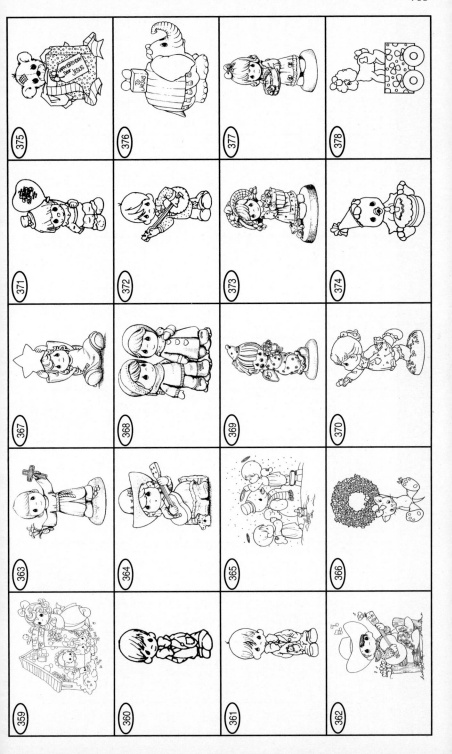

AC#	TITLE	FIG	PLATE	BELL	MUSIC	ORN	DOLL	THMBL	FRAME	OTHER
379	Happy Birthday Poppy	106836Ⓢ								
380	Happy Days Are Here Again	104396Ⓢ								
381	Happy Holi-daze					520454				
382	Happy Hula Days	128694								
383	Happy Trails	PM-981								
384	Happy Trip	521280Ⓢ								
	*Glide Through The Holidays					*521566Ⓡ				
385	Hare's To The Birthday Club	BC-971								
386	Have A Beary Merry Christmas	522856Ⓢ								
387	Have A Beary Special Birthday	B-0104 B-0004								
388	Have A Cozy Country Christmas	455873								
389	Have A Heavenly Christmas					12416Ⓢ				
	*Have A Heavenly Journey	*12416RⓇ								
390	Have I Got News For You	105635Ⓢ 528137								
391	Have I Toad You Lately That I Love You	521329Ⓐ								
392	Have You Any Room For Jesus	261130								
393	He Careth For You	E-1377BⓈ								
394	He Cleansed My Soul	100277				112380				
395	He Cleansed My Soul	306940								
396	He Covers The Earth With His Beauty	142654Ⓓ	142670Ⓓ			142662Ⓓ 142689Ⓓ				

Ⓢ = Suspended   Ⓛ = Limited Edition   Ⓡ = Retired   ② = Two Year Collectible   Ⓓ = Dated Annual   Ⓐ = Annual

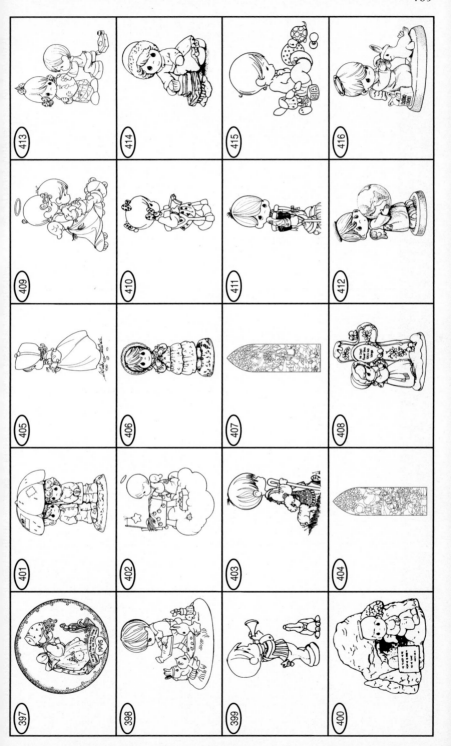

110

AC#	TITLE	FIG	PLATE	BELL	MUSIC	ORN	DOLL	THMBL	FRAME	OTHER
417	HEAVEN BLESS YOUR SPECIAL DAY	15954								
	*HEAVEN BLESS YOUR SPECIAL CHRISTMAS					*521086				
418	HEAVEN BLESS YOUR TOGETHERNESS	106755				522945Ⓓ				
	*OUR FIRST CHRISTMAS TOGETHER					*528870Ⓓ				
419	HEAVEN MUST HAVE SENT YOU	135992								
420	HEAVEN MUST HAVE SENT YOU	521388								
421	HELLO LORD, IT'S ME AGAIN	PM-811								
422	HELLO WORLD!	521175								
423	HELP LORD, I'M IN A SPOT	100269Ⓡ								
424	HI SUGAR!	BC-871								
425	HIGH HOPES	521957Ⓢ								
426	HIPPO HOLIDAYS					520403Ⓓ				
427	HIS BURDEN IS LIGHT	E-1380GⓇ								488429 Limoges Box
428	HIS EYE IS ON THE SPARROW	E-0530Ⓡ								
429	HIS LITTLE TREASURE	PM-931								
430	HIS LOVE WILL SHINE ON YOU	522376Ⓐ								
431	HIS LOVE WILL UPHOLD THE WORLD	531309								
432	HIS NAME IS JESUS	E-5381Ⓢ								
433	HIS PRESENCE IS FELT IN THE CHAPEL	163872				163880Ⓢ				
434	HIS SHEEP AM I	E-7161Ⓢ								
435	HOGS AND KISSES	261106								
		261106SⒺ								
436	HOLA, AMIGO (MEXICO)	456454								

Ⓢ = Suspended   Ⓛ = Limited Edition   Ⓡ = Retired   ② = Two Year Collectible   Ⓓ = Dated Annual   Ⓐ = Annual

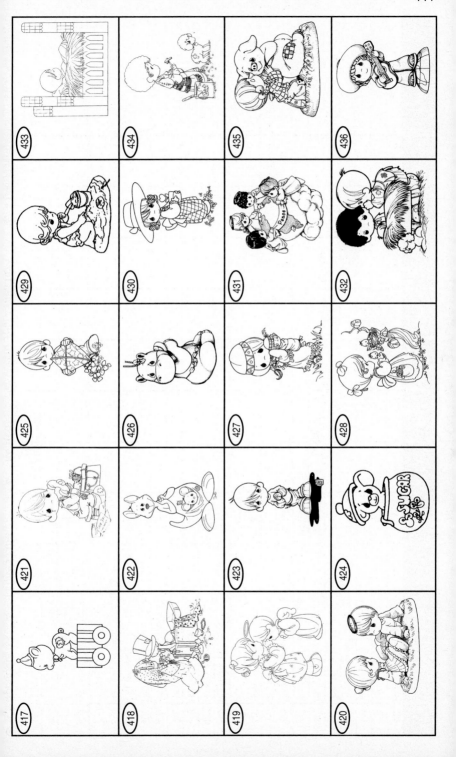

AC#	TITLE	FIG	PLATE	BELL	MUSIC	ORN	DOLL	THMBL	FRAME	OTHER
437	Holiday Wishes, Sweetie Pie	312444Ⓐ								
438	Holy Smokes	E-2351Ⓡ								
439	Holy Tweet	BC-972								
440	Home Is Where The Heart Is	325481Ⓐ								
441	Honk If You Love Jesus	15490				15857Ⓢ				
442	Hope Is Revealed Through God's Word	488259Ⓐ								
443	Hope You're Over The Hump	521671Ⓢ								
444	Hope You're Up And On The Trail Again	521205Ⓢ								
	*Happy Trails Is Trusting Jesus					*523224Ⓢ				
445	Hoppy Birthday	B-0110								
		B-0010								
446	Hoppy Easter Friend	521906								
447	Hot Cocoa Stand	184144Ⓡ								
448	House Night Light									529605Ⓡ Night Light
449	House Set And Palm Tree	E-2387								
450	How Can I Ever Forget You	526924								
451	How Can Three Work Together Except They Agree	NoneⓁ								
452	How Can Two Walk Together Except They Agree	E-9263Ⓢ								
453	How Can Two Work Together Except They Agree	PM-983				456268Ⓐ				
454	Hug One Another	521299Ⓡ								
455	I Believe In Miracles	E-7156Ⓡ	E-9257Ⓛ							

Ⓢ = Suspended   Ⓛ = Limited Edition   Ⓡ = Retired   ② = Two Year Collectible   Ⓓ = Dated Annual   Ⓐ = Annual

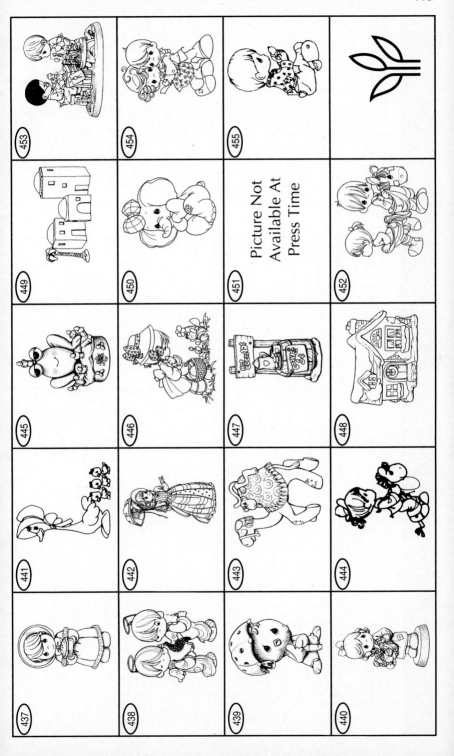

453

454

455

449

450

451 Picture Not Available At Press Time

452

445

446

447

448

441

442

443

444

437

438

439

440

AC#	TITLE	FIG	PLATE	BELL	MUSIC	ORN	DOLL	THMBL	FRAME	OTHER
456	I Believe In Miracles	E-7156R®								
457	I Believe In Miracles	272469								
458	I Believe In The Old Rugged Cross	103632				522953Ⓢ				
	*I Will Cherish The Old Rugged Cross									*523534Ⓓ Egg
459	I Belong To The Lord	520853Ⓢ								
460	I Can't Bear To Let You Go	532037								
461	I Can't Spell Success Without You	523763Ⓢ								
462	I Get A Bang Out Of You	12622®								
463	I Get A Kick Out Of You	E-2827Ⓢ								
464	I Give You My Love Forever True	129100								
465	I Got You Under My Skin	BC-922								
466	I Haven't Seen Much Of You Lately	531057								
467	I Love To Tell The Story	PM-852								
468	I Now Pronounce You Man And Wife	455938								
469	I Only Have Arms For You	527769®								
470	I Only Have Ice For You	530956								
471	I Picked A Special Mom	100536Ⓐ								
472	I Saw Mommy Kissing Santa Claus	455822								
473	I Still Do	530999								
474	I Still Do	531006								
475	I Think You're Just Divine	272558								

Ⓢ = Suspended   Ⓛ = Limited Edition   Ⓡ = Retired   ② = Two Year Collectible   Ⓓ = Dated Annual   Ⓐ = Annual

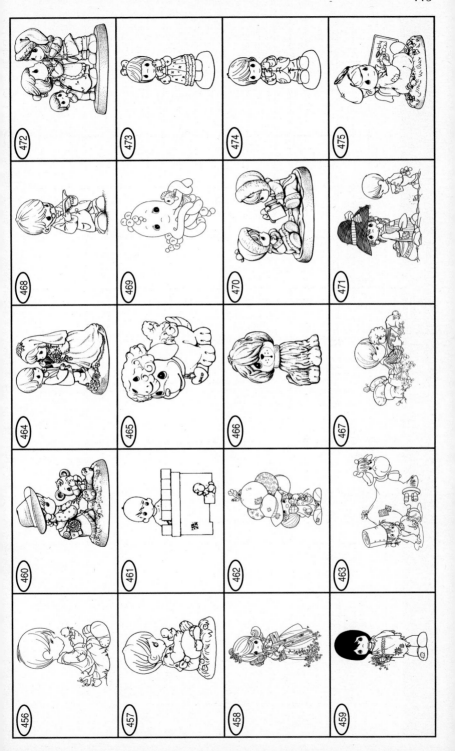

AC#	TITLE	FIG	PLATE	BELL	MUSIC	ORN	DOLL	THMBL	FRAME	OTHER
476	I Will Always Be Thinking Of You	523631Ⓡ								
477	I Would Be Lost Without You	526142								
478	I Would Be Sunk Without You	102970								
479	I'd Goat Anywhere With You	163694								
480	I'd Travel The Highlands To Be With You (Scotland)	456470								
481	I'll Be Dog-ged It's That Season Again					455660Ⓓ				
482	I'll Give Him My Heart	150088								
483	I'll Never Stop Loving You	521418Ⓡ								
484	I'll Never Tire Of You	307068								
485	I'll Play My Drum For Him	E-2356Ⓢ	E-2357Ⓓ	E-2358	E-2355Ⓢ	E-2359Ⓓ				
		E-2360								
		E-5384								
486	I'm A Possibility	100188Ⓡ				111120Ⓢ				
487	I'm A Precious Moments Fan	523526Ⓐ								
488	I'm Dreaming Of A White Christmas	272590								
489	I'm Falling For Somebunny									E-9266Ⓢ Box
	*Our Love Is Heaven Scent									*E-9266Ⓢ Box
490	I'm Following Jesus	PM-862								
491	I'm Just Nutty About The Holidays					455776				
492	I'm Nuts About You					520411Ⓓ				
493	I'm Nuts Over My Collection	BC-902								
494	I'm Sending You A Merry Christmas	455601Ⓓ	469327Ⓓ			455628Ⓓ				
495	I'm Sending You A White Christmas	E-2829	101834Ⓓ		112402Ⓡ	112372Ⓢ				

Ⓢ = Suspended   Ⓛ = Limited Edition   Ⓡ = Retired   ② = Two Year Collectible   Ⓓ = Dated Annual   Ⓐ = Annual

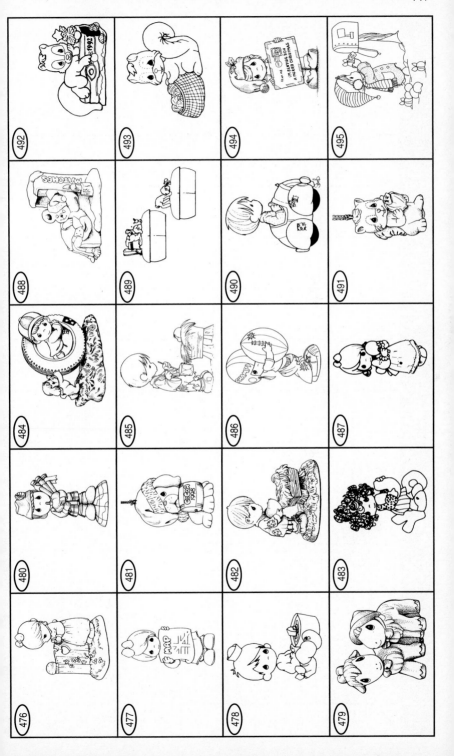

AC#	TITLE	FIG	PLATE	BELL	MUSIC	ORN	DOLL	THMBL	FRAME	OTHER
496	I'm So Glad That God Blessed Me With A Friend Like You	523623®								
497	I'm So Glad You Fluttered Into My Life	520640®								
498	If God Be For Us, Who Can Be Against Us	E-9285⑤								
499	In God's Beautiful Garden Of Love	261629⑭				261599Ⓐ				
500	In His Time	PM-872								
501	In The Spotlight Of His Grace	520543⑤								
502	Isn't Eight Just Great	109460								
503	Isn't He Precious	E-5379 529988⑤								
504	Isn't He Wonderful	E-5639⑤								
505	Isn't He Wonderful	E-5640⑤								
506	It Is Better To Give Than To Receive *Trust And Obey	12297⑤				*102377				
507	It Is No Secret What God Can Do	531111Ⓐ								
508	It May Be Greener, But It's Just As Hard To Cut	163899								
509	It's A Girl	136204								
510	It's A Perfect Boy	E-0512⑤ 525286				102415⑤				
511	It's No Yolk When I Say I Love You	522104⑤								
512	It's Ruff To Always Be Cheery	272639								
513	It's So Uplifting To Have A Friend Like You	524905				528846				
514	It's The Birthday Of A King	102962⑤								

Ⓢ = Suspended   ⓁⒺ = Limited Edition   Ⓡ = Retired   ② = Two Year Collectible   Ⓓ = Dated Annual   Ⓐ = Annual

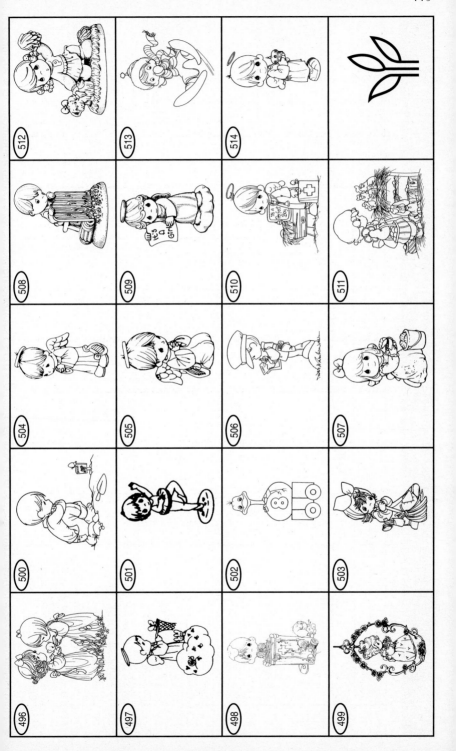

120

AC#	TITLE	FIG	PLATE	BELL	MUSIC	ORN	DOLL	THMBL	FRAME	OTHER
515	IT'S WHAT'S INSIDE THAT COUNTS	E-3119⑤								
516	JAN	529826®								
517	JANUARY									335533 Limoges Box
518	JANUARY GIRL	109983								
	*DASHING THROUGH THE SNOW					*521574Ⓐ				
519	JENNIFER	163708⑤								
520	JEST TO LET YOU KNOW YOU'RE TOPS	B-0106								
		B-0006								
521	JESUS IS BORN	E-2012⑤			E-2809⑤					
522	JESUS IS BORN	E-2801⑤								
523	JESUS IS BORN			E-5623⑤						
	*UNTO US A CHILD IS BORN					*E-5630⑤				
524	JESUS IS COMING SOON	12343⑤								
525	JESUS IS THE ANSWER	E-1381®								
526	JESUS IS THE ANSWER	E-1381R®								
527	JESUS IS THE LIGHT	E-1373G®								488437 Limoges Box
528	JESUS IS THE LIGHT THAT SHINES	E-0502⑤				E-0537⑤				
529	JESUS IS THE ONLY WAY	520756⑤								
530	JESUS IS THE SWEETEST NAME I KNOW	523097⑤								
531	JESUS LOVES ME	E-1372B®	E-9275⑤	E-5208⑤					E-7170⑤	E-9280⑤ Box
		E-9278								488399 Limoges Box
	*BABY'S FIRST CHRISTMAS					*E-5631⑤				
532	JESUS LOVES ME	E-1372G	E-9276⑤	E-5209⑤					E-7171⑤	E-9281⑤ Box
		E-9279								488380 Limoges Box
	*BABY'S FIRST CHRISTMAS	104531Ⓛ				*E-5632⑤				

⑤ = Suspended Ⓛ = Limited Edition ® = Retired ② = Two Year Collectible Ⓓ = Dated Annual Ⓐ = Annual

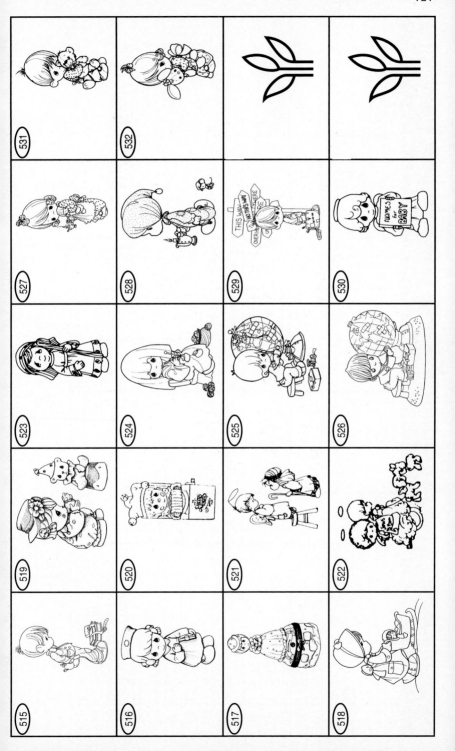

122

AC#	TITLE	FIG	PLATE	BELL	MUSIC	ORN	DOLL	THMBL	FRAME	OTHER
533	Jesus The Savior Is Born	520357Ⓢ								
534	Join In On The Blessings	E-0104								
		E-0404								
535	Jordan	529168Ⓢ								
536	Joy From Head To Mistletoe					150126				
537	Joy On Arrival	523178								
538	Joy To The World					E-2343Ⓢ				E-2344Ⓢ Candle Climber
539	Joy To The World	E-5378Ⓢ				E-5388Ⓡ				
540	Joy To The World					150320				
541	Joy To The World					153338				
542	Joy To The World					272566				
543	July									335606 Limoges Box
544	July Girl	110051								
545	Jumping For Joy	PM-991								
546	June									335592 Limoges Box
547	June Girl	110043								
548	Junior Bridesmaid	E-2845								
549	Just A Line To Say You're Special	522864								
550	Just A Line To Wish You A Happy Day	520721Ⓢ								
551	Just Poppin' In To Say Halo!	523755								
552	Just The Facts… You're Terrific	320668								

Ⓢ = Suspended   Ⓔ = Limited Edition   Ⓡ = Retired   ② = Two Year Collectible   Ⓓ = Dated Annual   Ⓐ = Annual

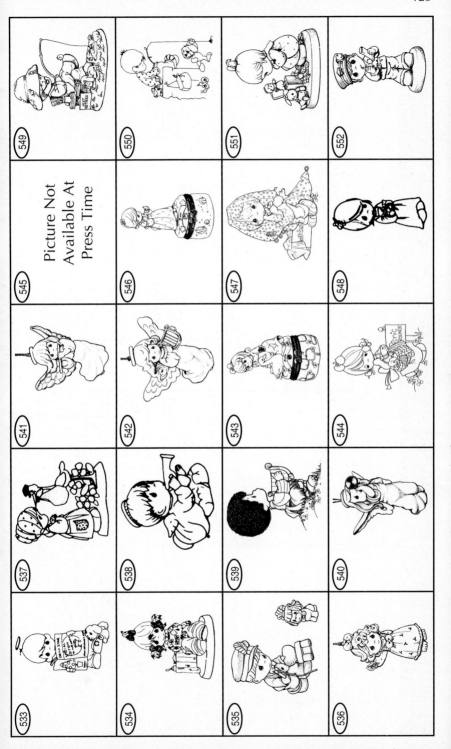

549
550
551
552
545 Picture Not Available At Press Time
546
547
548
541
542
543
544
537
538
539
540
533
534
535
536

AC#	TITLE	FIG	PLATE	BELL	MUSIC	ORN	DOLL	THMBL	FRAME	OTHER
553	KATIE	529184⑤								
554	KATIE LYNNE						E-0539⑤			
555	KATY LYNNE	529524®								
556	KEEP LOOKING UP	15997								
	*CHRISTMAS KEEPS LOOKING UP					*521124				
557	KRISTY						E-2851⑤			
558	LAMP POST	529559®								
559	LEAD ME TO CALVARY	260916Ⓓ								
560	LEON AND EVELYN MAE	529818®								
561	LEROY	184071®								
562	LET HEAVEN AND NATURE SING		E-2347Ⓐ		E-2346⑤	E-0532®				
563	LET LOVE REIGN	E-9273®								
564	LET NOT THE SUN GO DOWN UPON YOUR WRATH	E-5203⑤								
565	LET THE HEAVENS REJOICE			E-5622Ⓓ		E-5629Ⓓ				
566	LET THE WHOLE WORLD KNOW	E-7165⑤			E-7186⑤					
567	LET US CALL THE CLUB TO ORDER	E-0103								
		E-0303								
568	LET'S BE FRIENDS	527270®								
569	LET'S KEEP IN TOUCH				102520					
570	LET'S KEEP OUR EYES ON THE GOAL	549975								
571	LET'S PUT THE PIECES TOGETHER	525928								
572	LETTUCE PRAY	261122								

⑤ = Suspended   Ⓛ = Limited Edition   ® = Retired   ② = Two Year Collectible   Ⓓ = Dated Annual   Ⓐ = Annual

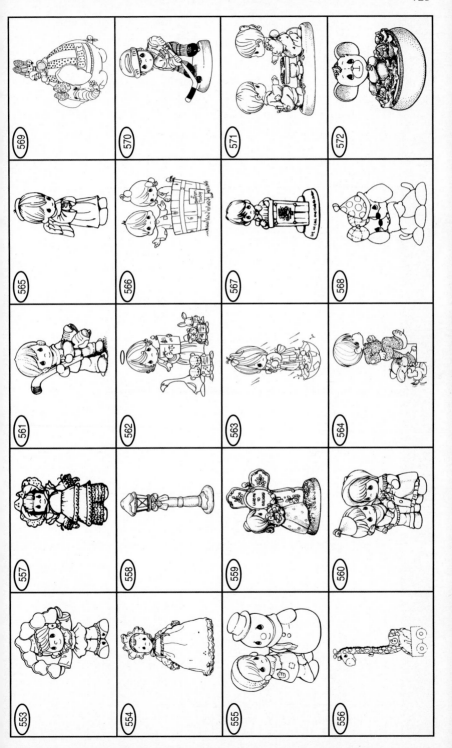

AC#	TITLE	FIG	PLATE	BELL	MUSIC	ORN	DOLL	THMBL	FRAME	OTHER
573	Life Can Be A Jungle	325457Ⓐ								
574	Life Is A Fiesta (Spain)	456381								
575	Lighted Inn									283428 Night Light
576	Lighted School House									272795Ⓡ Night Light
577	Lighted Tree									184039Ⓡ Night Light
578	Lighting The Way To A Happy Holiday	129267				129275				
579	Llamas	531375								
580	Lord Give Me A Song	12386Ⓢ								
581	Lord Give Me Patience	E-7159Ⓢ								
582	Lord Help Me Make The Grade	106216Ⓢ								
583	Lord, Help Me Stick To My Job	521450Ⓡ								
584	Lord Help Me To Stay On Course	532096								
585	Lord, Help Us Keep Our Act Together	101850Ⓡ								
586	Lord I'm Coming Home	100110								
587	Lord, Keep Me In Teepee Top Shape	PM-912								
588	Lord Keep Me On My Toes	100129Ⓡ				102423Ⓡ				
589	Lord Keep Me On My Toes					525332				
590	Lord Keep Me On The Ball	12270Ⓢ								
591	Lord, Keep My Life In Balance				520691Ⓢ					
592	Lord, Keep My Life In Tune				12165Ⓢ					

Ⓢ = Suspended   Ⓔ = Limited Edition   Ⓡ = Retired   ② = Two Year Collectible   Ⓓ = Dated Annual   Ⓐ = Annual

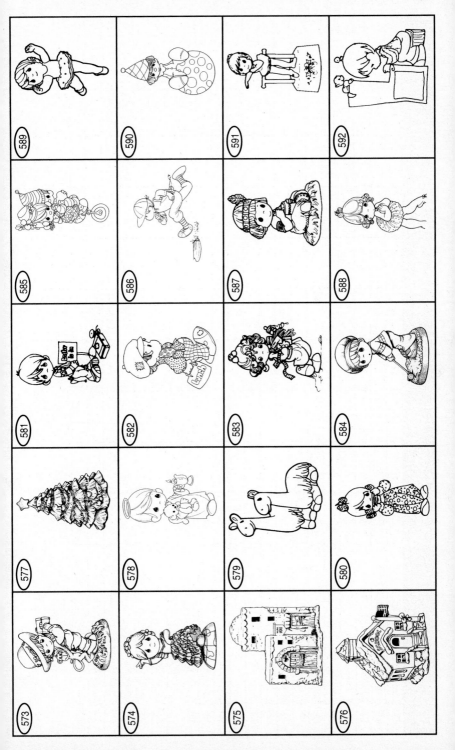

AC#	TITLE	FIG	PLATE	BELL	MUSIC	ORN	DOLL	THMBL	FRAME	OTHER
593	Lord Keep My Life In Tune				12580Ⓢ					
594	Lord Please Don't Put Me On Hold	PM-982								
595	Lord, Spare Me	521191								
596	Lord Speak To Me	531987								
597	Lord, Teach Us To Pray	524158Ⓐ								
598	Lord, Turn My Life Around	520551Ⓢ								
599	Love Beareth All Things	E-7158								
600	Love Blooms Eternal	127019Ⓓ								
601	Love Cannot Break A True Friendship	E-4722Ⓢ								
602	Love Covers All	12009Ⓢ						12254Ⓢ		
603	Love Grows Here	272981Ⓛ								
604	Love Is Color Blind	524204								
605	Love Is From Above	521841Ⓢ								
606	Love Is Kind	E-1379AⓇ E-1379RⓇ								
607	Love Is Kind		E-2847Ⓛ							
608	Love Is Kind	E-5377Ⓡ								
609	Love Is Kind					E-5391Ⓢ				
610	Love Is Patient					E-0535Ⓢ				
611	Love Is Patient					E-0536Ⓢ				
612	Love Is Patient	E-9251Ⓢ								

Ⓢ = Suspended   Ⓛ = Limited Edition   Ⓡ = Retired   ② = Two Year Collectible   Ⓓ = Dated Annual   Ⓐ = Annual

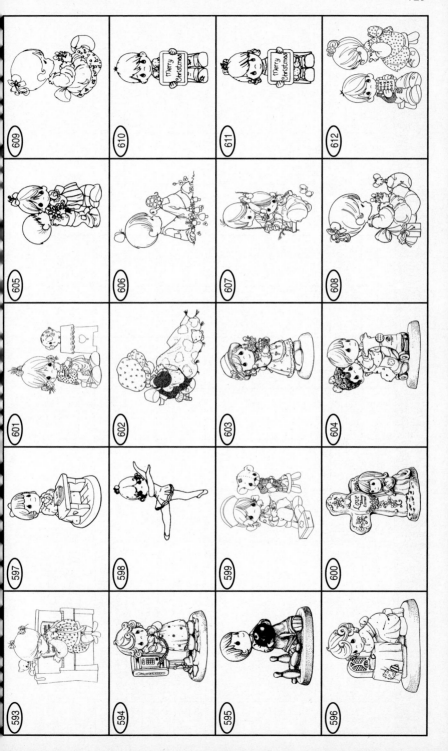

1

130

AC#	TITLE	FIG	PLATE	BELL	MUSIC	ORN	DOLL	THMBL	FRAME	OTHER
613	Love Is Sharing	E-7162Ⓢ			E-7185Ⓑ					
614	Love Is Sharing	272493								
615	Love Is The Best Gift Of All	110930Ⓓ		109835Ⓓ		109770Ⓓ		109843Ⓓ		
616	Love Is The Glue That Mends	104027Ⓢ								
617	Love Is The Key	482242S								
618	Love Is Universal	192376Ⓓ								
619	Love Letters In The Sand	129488								
620	Love Lifted Me	E-1375AⒷ								
621	Love Lifted Me	E-5201Ⓢ								
622	Love Makes The World Go 'round	139475Ⓓ				184209Ⓐ				
623	Love Never Fails	12300								
	*You're "A" Number One In My Book, Teacher					*150142				
624	Love Never Leaves A Mother's Arms	523941								
625	Love One Another	E-1376	E-5215Ⓓ			522929				488410 Limoges Box
626	Love One Another	272507								
627	Love Pacifies	BC-911								
628	Love Rescued Me	102393				102385				
629	Love Vows To Always Bloom	129097								
630	Love's Russian Into My Heart (Russia)	456446								
631	Loving	PM-932								
632	Loving, Caring And Sharing Along The Way	C-0113								
	*Loving, Caring And Sharing	C-0013				*PM-040				

629	625	621	617 Picture Not Available At Press Time
630	626	622	618
631	627	623	619
632	628	624	620

613	614	615	616

AC#	TITLE	FIG	PLATE	BELL	MUSIC	ORN	DOLL	THMBL	FRAME	OTHER
633	Loving Is Caring	320579								
634	Loving Is Caring	320595								
635	Loving Is Sharing	E-3110B®								
636	Loving Is Sharing	E-3110G								
637	Loving Thy Neighbor		E-2848®							
638	Loving You Dear Valentine	PM-873								
639	Loving You Dear Valentine	PM-874								
640	Loving You Dear Valentine	306932								
641	Luggage Cart	150185®								
642	Luke 2:10 - 11	532916								
643	Mailbox	531847®								
644	Make A Joyful Noise	E-1374G 520322®	E-7174®			522910©				528617® Egg 488402 Limoges Box
645	Make A Joyful Noise	272450								
646	Make Me A Blessing	100102®								
647	Making A Point To Say You're Special	BC-951								
648	Making A Trail To Bethlehem	142751® 184004								
649	Making Spirits Bright	150118								
650	Many Moons In Same Canoe, Blessum You	520772®								
651	Many Years Of Blessing You	384887								
652	March									335568 Limoges Box

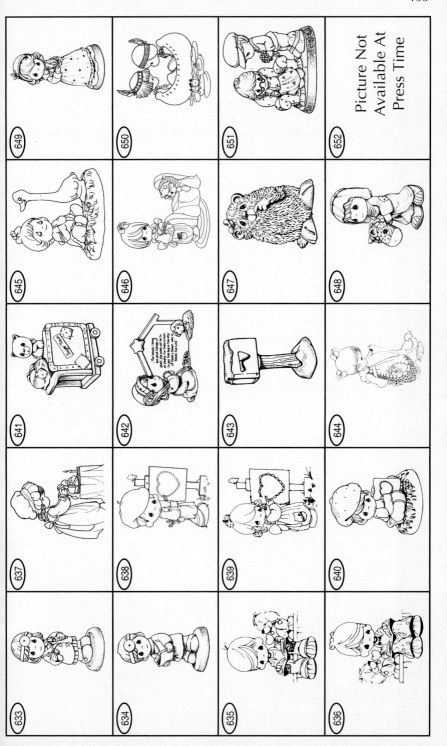

649

650

651

652 Picture Not Available At Press Time

645

646

647

648

641

642

643

644

637

638

639

640

633

634

635

636

AC#	TITLE	FIG	PLATE	BELL	MUSIC	ORN	DOLL	THMBL	FRAME	OTHER
653	March Girl	110019								
654	Marching To The Beat Of Freedom's Drum	521981								
655	Markie	528099⑤								
656	Marvelous Grace	325503Ⓐ								
657	May									335584 Limoges Box
658	May All Your Christmases Be White					521302⑤				
659	May Girl	110035								
660	May God Bless You With A Perfect Season					E-5390⑤				
661	May Only Good Things Come Your Way	524425								
662	May The Sun Always Shine On You	184217Ⓐ								
663	May You Have An Old Fashioned Christmas				417777②		417785②			
664	May You Have The Sweetest Christmas	15776⑤								
665	May Your Birthday Be A Blessing	E-2826⑤								
666	May Your Birthday Be A Blessing	524301								
667	May Your Birthday Be Gigantic	15970								
	*May Your Christmas Be Gigantic					*521108				
668	May Your Birthday Be Mammoth	521825								
669	May Your Birthday Be Warm	15938								
	*May Your Christmas Be Warm - Baby					*470279				
670	May Your Christmas Be A Happy Home		523003Ⓓ							
671	May Your Christmas Be Blessed	E-5376⑤				523704Ⓓ				
672	May Your Christmas Be Cozy	E-2345⑤								

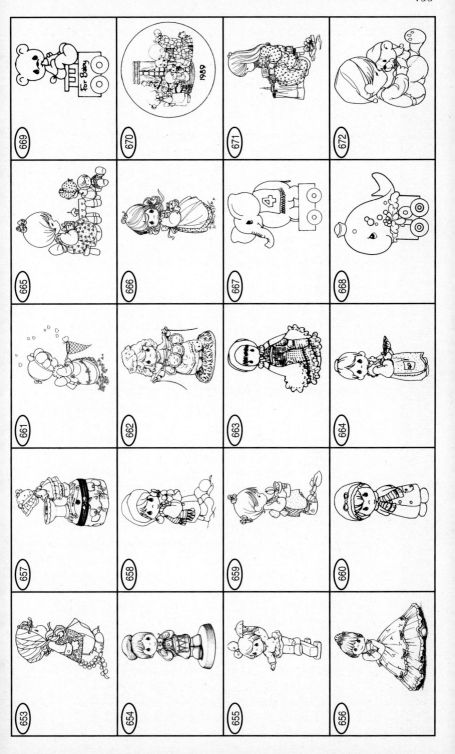

AC#	TITLE	FIG	PLATE	BELL	MUSIC	ORN	DOLL	THMBL	FRAME	OTHER
673	May Your Christmas Be Delightful	15482Ⓢ				15849Ⓢ				
674	May Your Christmas Be Delightful	604135								
675	May Your Christmas Be Merry	524166Ⓓ		524182Ⓓ		524174Ⓓ		524190Ⓓ		
						526940Ⓓ				
676	May Your Christmas Be Warm	E-2348Ⓢ								
677	May Your Every Wish Come True	524298								
678	May Your Future Be Blessed	525316								
679	May Your Life Be Blessed With Touchdowns	522023Ⓡ								
680	May Your World Be Trimmed With Joy	522082Ⓢ								
681	Mazie	184055Ⓡ								
682	Memories Are Made Of This	529982Ⓐ								
683	Meowie Christmas	109800								
684	Merry Chrismoose					150134Ⓓ				
685	Merry Christmas, Deer	523317Ⓡ	520284Ⓓ							
686	Merry-go-round	272841Ⓡ								
687	Mikey						E-6214BⓈ			
688	Mini Animal Figurines	102296Ⓢ								
689	Mini-nativity Wall	283436								
690	Missum You	306991								
691	Mom You Always Make Our House A Home	325465Ⓐ								
692	Mom, You're My Special-tea	325473								

Ⓢ = Suspended   Ⓛ = Limited Edition   Ⓡ = Retired   ② = Two Year Collectible   Ⓓ = Dated Annual   Ⓐ = Annual

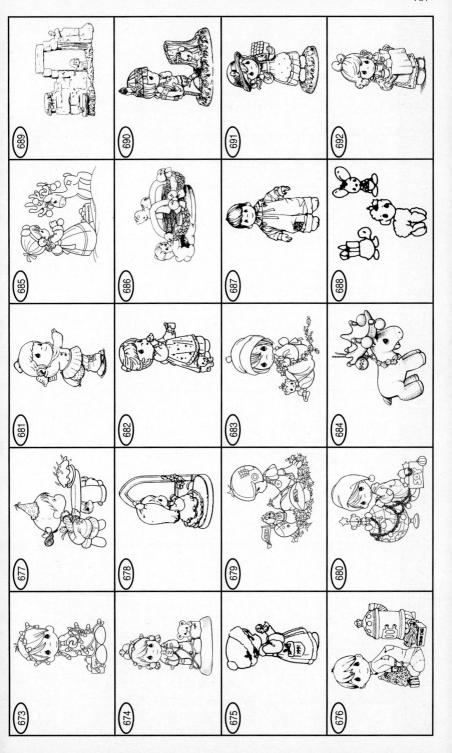

AC#	TITLE	FIG	PLATE	BELL	MUSIC	ORN	DOLL	THMBL	FRAME	OTHER
693	Mom, You've Given Me So Much	488046								
694	Mommy, I Love You	109975								
695	Mommy, I Love You	112143								
696	Money's Not The Only Green Thing Worth Saving	531073®								
697	Mornin' Pumpkin	455687								
698	Mother Sew Dear	E-3106	E-5217Ⓛ	E-7181Ⓢ	E-7182	E-0514	E-2850®	13293	E-7241Ⓢ	
699	Mouse With Cheese					E-2381Ⓢ				
700	Mow Power To Ya	PM-892								
701	My Days Are Blue Without You	520802Ⓢ								
702	My Guardian Angel								E-7168Ⓢ	
703	My Guardian Angel								E-7169Ⓢ	
704	My Happiness	C-0110 C-0010				PM-904				
705	My Heart Is Exposed With Love	520624								
706	My Love Blooms For You	521728								
707	My Love Will Keep You Warm	272957'SⒶ				272965Ⓐ				
708	My Love Will Keep You Warm	272957								
709	My Love Will Never Let You Go	103497				114006Ⓢ				
710	My Love Will Stand Guard Over You (England)	456934								
711	My True Love Gave To Me	529273								
712	My True Love Gave To Me					455989Ⓐ				

Ⓢ = Suspended   Ⓛ = Limited Edition   ® = Retired   Ⓣ = Two Year Collectible   Ⓐ = Dated Annual

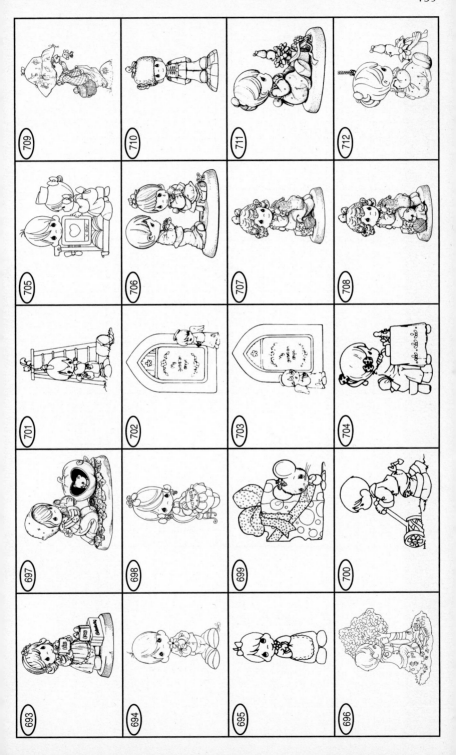

140

AC#	TITLE	FIG	PLATE	BELL	MUSIC	ORN	DOLL	THMBL	FRAME	OTHER
713	My Universe Is You	487902								
714	My Warmest Thoughts Are You	524085Ⓡ								
715	My World's Upside Down Without You	531014								
716	Nativity	529508Ⓡ								
717	Nativity Cart	528072								
718	No Tears Past The Gate	101826								
719	Noah, His Wife & Ark									530042 Night Light
720	Nobody Likes To Be Dumped	307041								
721	Nobody's Perfect!	E-9268Ⓡ								
722	Not A Creature Was Stirring	524484Ⓢ								
723	Nothing Can Dampen The Spirit Of Caring	603864								
724	November									335665 Limoges Box
725	November Girl	110108								
726	Now I Lay Me Down To Sleep	522058Ⓡ								
727	O Come All Ye Faithful	E-2353Ⓡ			E-2352Ⓢ					
728	O Come Let Us Adore Him	111333Ⓢ				E-0531Ⓢ				
729	O, How I Love Jesus	E-1380BⓇ								
730	October									335657 Limoges Box
731	October Girl	110094								
732	Of All The Mothers I Have Known, There's None As Precious As My Own		163716Ⓓ							

Ⓢ = Suspended   Ⓛ = Limited Edition   Ⓡ = Retired   Ⓨ = Two Year Collectible   Ⓓ = Dated Annual   Ⓐ = Annual

AC#	TITLE	FIG	PLATE	BELL	MUSIC	ORN	DOLL	THMBL	FRAME	OTHER
733	Oh Holy Night	522546Ⓓ		522821Ⓓ		522848Ⓓ		522554Ⓓ		
734	Oh Taste And See That The Lord Is Good	307025								
735	Oh What Fun It Is To Ride	109819								
736	Oh Worship The Lord	E-5385Ⓢ								
737	Oh Worship The Lord	E-5386Ⓢ								
738	Oinky Birthday	524506								
739	On My Way To A Perfect Day	522872								
740	On The Hill Overlooking The Quiet Blue Stream	603503Ⓡ								
741	Once Upon A Holy Night	523836Ⓓ		523828Ⓓ		523852Ⓓ		523844Ⓓ		
742	One Step At A Time	PM-911								
743	Only Love Can Make A Home	PM-921								
744	Only One Life To Offer	325309								
745	Onward Christian Soldiers	E-0523								
746	Onward Christmas Soldiers					527327				
747	Our Club Can't Be Beat	B-0001								
748	Our Club Is A Tough Act To Follow	B-0105 B-0005								
749	Our Club Is Soda-licious	PM-962								
	*Sweet Sixteen By Precious Moments					*266841				
750	Our First Christmas Together	E-2377Ⓢ	E-2378Ⓢ							
751	Our First Christmas Together				101702Ⓡ	102350Ⓓ 112399Ⓓ 520233Ⓓ				

Ⓢ = Suspended Ⓔ = Limited Edition Ⓡ = Retired ② = Two Year Collectible Ⓓ = Dated Annual Ⓐ = Annual

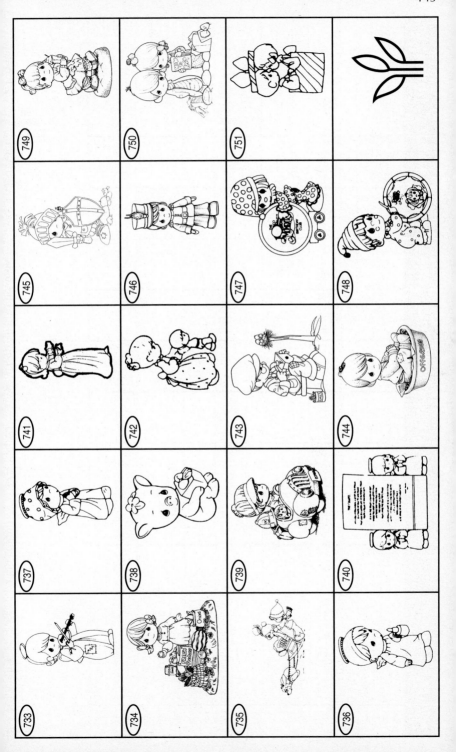

144

AC#	TITLE	FIG	PLATE	BELL	MUSIC	ORN	DOLL	THMBL	FRAME	OTHER
752	Our First Christmas Together	115290Ⓢ								
753	Our First Christmas Together					530506Ⓓ				
754	Our First Christmas Together					529206Ⓓ				
755	Our First Christmas Together					142700Ⓓ				
756	Our First Christmas Together					183911Ⓓ				
757	Our First Christmas Together					272736Ⓓ				
758	Our First Christmas Together					455636Ⓓ				
759	Our Friendship Is Always In Bloom (Japan)	456926								
760	Our Friendship Is Soda-licious	524336								
761	Our Future Is Looking Much Brighter	325511Ⓓ								
762	Owl Always Be Your Friend	BC-932								
763	Owl Be Home For Christmas					128708Ⓓ				
764	P.D.						12475Ⓢ			
765	Pack Your Trunk For The Holidays					272949Ⓓ				
766	Park Bench	529540Ⓡ								
767	Part Of Me Wants To Be Good	12149Ⓢ								
768	Peace Amid The Storm	E-4723Ⓢ								
769	Peace On Earth	E-2804Ⓢ								
770	Peace On Earth	E-4725Ⓢ			E-4726Ⓢ					
771	Peace On Earth	E-9287Ⓢ								

Ⓢ = Suspended　　Ⓛ = Limited Edition　　Ⓡ = Retired　　② = Two Year Collectible　　Ⓓ = Dated Annual　　Ⓐ = Annual

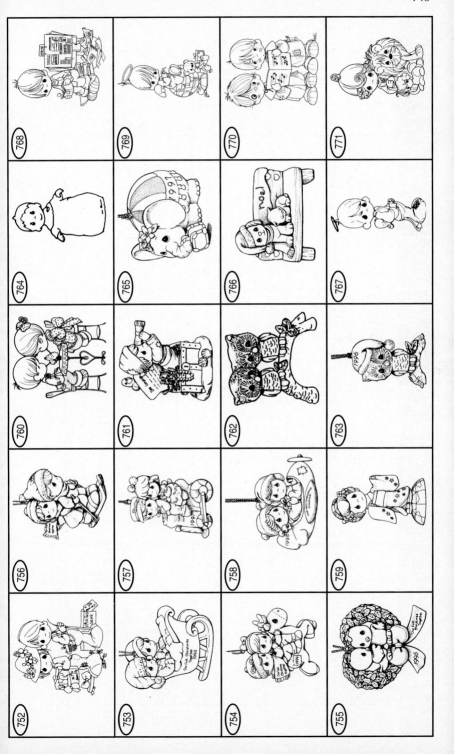

AC#	TITLE	FIG	PLATE	BELL	MUSIC	ORN	DOLL	THMBL	FRAME	OTHER
772	PEACE ON EARTH					E-5389Ⓢ				
773	PEACE ON EARTH				109746Ⓢ	523062Ⓓ				
774	*MY PEACE I GIVE UNTO THEE		*102954Ⓓ			177091Ⓛ				
775	PEACE ON EARTH...ANYWAY	183342Ⓓ	183377Ⓓ			183350Ⓓ 183369Ⓓ				
776	PEAS ON EARTH	455768								
777	PEAS PASS THE CARROTS	307076								
778	PERFECT HARMONY	521914								
779	PHILIP	529494Ⓡ								
780	PIGS	530085								
781	PIZZA ON EARTH	521884								
782	POTTY TIME	531022								
783	PRAISE GOD FROM WHOM ALL BLESSINGS FLOW	455695								
784	PRAISE THE LORD AND DOSIE-DO	455733								
785	PRAISE THE LORD ANYHOW	E-1374BⓇ								
786	PRAISE THE LORD ANYHOW	E-9254Ⓡ								
787	PRAYER CHANGES THINGS	E-1375BⓈ								
788	PRAYER CHANGES THINGS	E-5214Ⓢ								
789	PRECIOUS MEMORIES	E-2828								
790	PRECIOUS MEMORIES	106763								
791	PRECIOUS MOMENTS TO REMEMBER	163848								

Ⓢ = Suspended   Ⓔ = Limited Edition   Ⓡ = Retired   ② – Two Year Collectible   Ⓓ – Dated Annual   Ⓐ – Annual

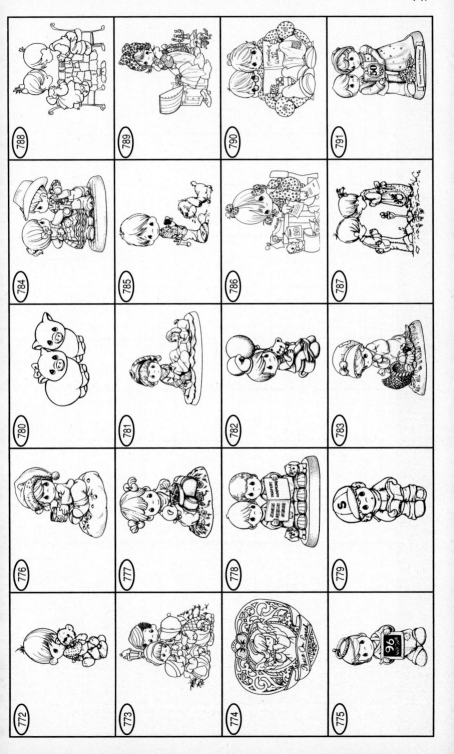

148

AC#	TITLE	FIG	PLATE	BELL	MUSIC	ORN	DOLL	THMBL	FRAME	OTHER
792	Prepare Ye The Way Of The Lord	E-0508Ⓢ								
793	Press On	E-9265								
794	Pretty As A Princess	526053				272892				
795	Puppies With Sled									
796	Puppy Love	520764								
797	Puppy Love Is From Above	106798Ⓡ								
798	Put A Little Punch In Your Birthday	BC-931								
799	Put On A Happy Face	PM-822								
800	Railroad Crossing Sign	150177Ⓡ								
801	Reindeer					102466Ⓓ				
802	Rejoice In The Victory	283541								
803	Rejoice O Earth	E-5636			E-5645Ⓡ	113980Ⓡ				
		520268								
804	Rejoice, O Earth									617334Ⓓ Musical Tree Topper
805	Rejoicing With You	E-4724	E-7172Ⓢ							
806	Retailer's Wreath									111465 Wreath
807	Retailer's Wreath Bell			112348						
808	Ring Out The Good News	529966Ⓡ								
809	Ring Those Christmas Bells	525898Ⓡ								
810	Ringbearer	E-2833								
811	Ringing In The Season					456012Ⓓ				

Ⓢ – Suspended   Ⓔ – Limited Edition   Ⓡ – Retired   ② – Two Year Collectible   Ⓓ – Dated Annual   Ⓐ – Annual

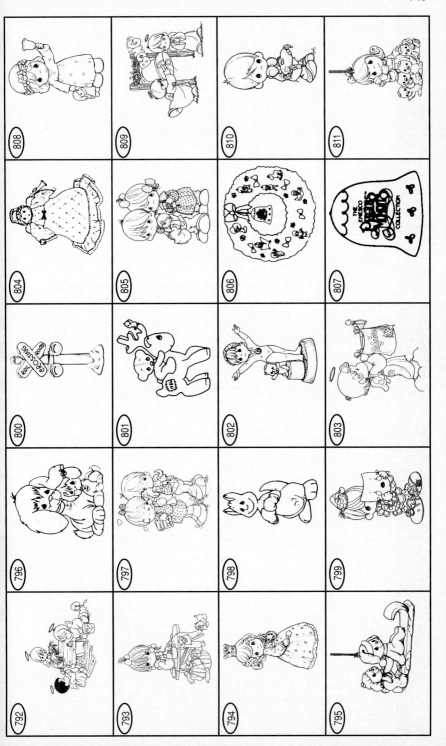

150

AC#	TITLE	FIG	PLATE	BELL	MUSIC	ORN	DOLL	THMBL	FRAME	OTHER
812	Rocking Horse					102474⑤				
813	Safe In The Arms Of Jesus	521922								
814	Sailabration	150061Ⓓ								
815	Sam	150169Ⓐ								
816	Sam Butcher	529567Ⓓ								
817	Sam Butcher	529842Ⓐ								
818	Sam's Car	529443Ⓑ								
819	Sam's House Ornament					530468Ⓐ				
820	Sammy	528668Ⓑ								
821	Sammy	529222Ⓓ								
822	Say I Do	261149								
823	Saying "Oui" To Our Love					456004Ⓐ				
824	Scent From Above	100528Ⓑ								
825	Scootin' By Just To Say Hi	B-0111 B-0011								
826	Sealed With A Kiss	524441Ⓑ								
827	Seeds Of Love From The Chapel	271586								
828	Seek And Ye Shall Find	E-0105 E-0005								
829	Seek Ye The Lord	E-9261⑤								
830	Seek Ye The Lord	E-9262⑤								
831	Sending My Love	100056⑤								

151

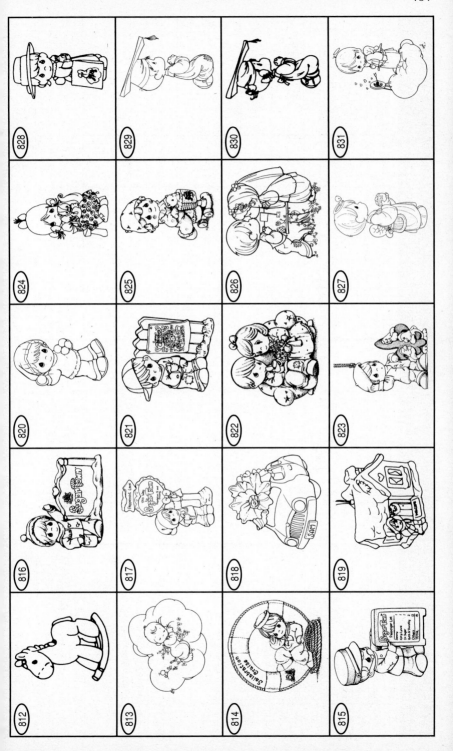

AC#	TITLE	FIG	PLATE	BELL	MUSIC	ORN	DOLL	THMBL	FRAME	OTHER
832	Sending My Love Your Way	528609Ⓐ								
833	Sending You A Rainbow	E-9288Ⓢ								
834	Sending You A White Christmas					528218				
835	Sending You My Love	109967								
836	Sending You Oceans Of Love	532010Ⓡ								
837	Sending You Showers Of Blessings	520683Ⓡ								
838	September									335622 Limoges Box
839	September Girl	110086								
840	Serenity Prayer Boy	530700								
841	Serenity Prayer Girl	530697								
842	Serving The Lord	100161Ⓢ								
	*Serve With A Smile					*102458Ⓢ				
843	Serving The Lord	100293Ⓢ								
	*Serve With A Smile					*102431Ⓢ				
844	Sew In Love	106844Ⓡ								
845	Sharing	PM-942								
846	Sharing A Gift Of Love	527114Ⓐ								
847	Sharing Begins In The Heart	520861Ⓐ								
848	Sharing Is Universal	E-0107								
		E-0007								
849	Sharing Our Christmas Together	102490Ⓢ								
850	Sharing Our Christmas Together	531944								
851	Sharing Our Joy Together	E-2834Ⓢ								

Ⓢ = Suspended   Ⓔ = Limited Edition   Ⓡ = Retired   ② = Two Year Collectible   Ⓓ = Dated Annual   Ⓐ = Annual

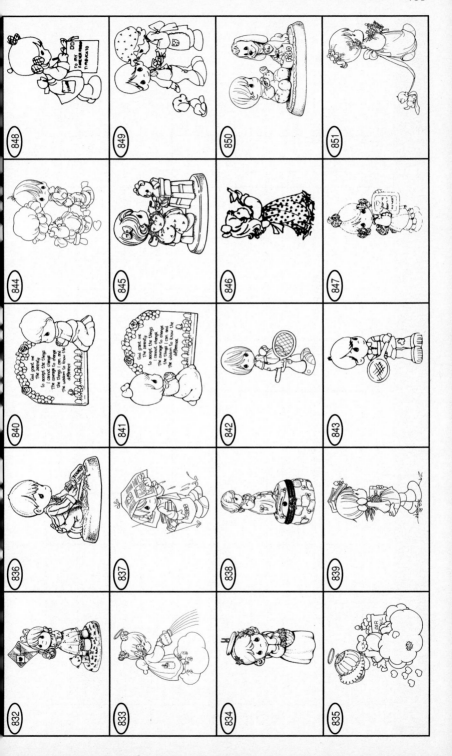

AC#	TITLE	FIG	PLATE	BELL	MUSIC	ORN	DOLL	THMBL	FRAME	OTHER
852	Sharing Our Season Together	E-0501Ⓢ			E-0519Ⓡ					
853	Sharing Sweet Moments Together	526487								
854	Sharing The Gift Of Forty Precious Years	163821								
855	Sharing The Good News Together	C-0111				PM-037				
		C-0011								
856	Sharing The Light Of Love	272531								
857	Sheep	530077								
858	Shepherd Of Love	102261				102288Ⓢ				
859	Shepherd With Lambs	183954								
860	Shepherd With Lambs	183962								
861	Shepherd With Sheep	213616								
862	Shoot For The Stars And You'll Never Strike Out	521701								
863	Showers Of Blessings	105945Ⓡ								
864	Silent Knight				E-5642Ⓢ					
865	Silent Night				15814Ⓢ					
866	Sing In Excelsis Deo									183830 Tree Topper
867	Single Tree	533173Ⓡ								
868	Sitting Pretty	104825Ⓢ								
869	Skating Pond	184047Ⓡ								
870	Skating Sign	184020Ⓐ								
871	Slide Into The Celebration	BC-981								

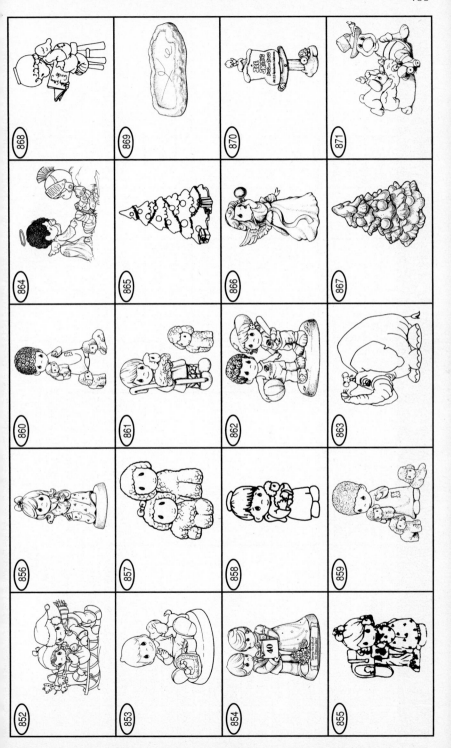

AC#	TITLE	FIG	PLATE	BELL	MUSIC	ORN	DOLL	THMBL	FRAME	OTHER
872	Slow Down And Enjoy The Holidays					520489Ⓓ				
873	Slow Down For The Holidays					272760Ⓓ				
874	Smile Along The Way	101842Ⓡ				113964Ⓢ				
875	Smile, God Loves You	E-1373BⓇ								
876	Smile, God Loves You	PM-821								
877	Sno-bunny Falls For You Like I Do					520438Ⓓ				
878	Snowbunny Loves You Like I Do	183792								
879	So Glad I Picked You As A Friend	524379Ⓐ								
880	Some Bunny's Sleeping	115274Ⓢ								
	Some Bunnies Sleeping	522996Ⓢ								
881	Some Plant, Some Water, But God Giveth The Increase	176958								
882	Somebody Cares	522325Ⓐ								
883	Somebunny Cares	BC-881								
884	Someday My Love	520799Ⓡ								
885	Something Precious From Above	524360								
886	Something's Missing When You're Not Around	105643Ⓢ								
887	Sometimes You're Next To Impossible	530964								
888	Soot Yourself To A Merry Christmas	150096								
889	Sowing Seeds Of Kindness	163856								
890	Sowing The Seeds Of Love	PM-922								
891	Standing In The Presence Of The Lord	163732Ⓓ								

Ⓢ = Suspended   Ⓔ = Limited Edition   Ⓡ = Retired   ② = Two Year Collectible   Ⓓ = Dated Annual   Ⓐ = Annual

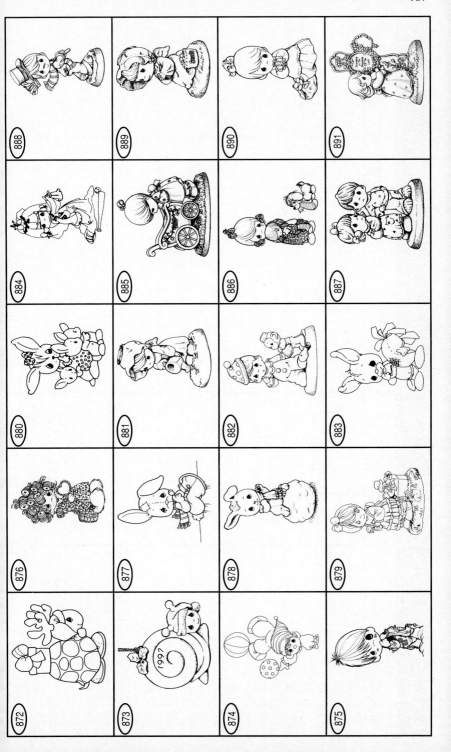

AC#	TITLE	FIG	PLATE	BELL	MUSIC	ORN	DOLL	THMBL	FRAME	OTHER
892	Stork With Baby Sam	529788Ⓐ								
893	Straight Sidewalk	533157Ⓑ								
894	Street Sign	532185Ⓑ								
895	Sugar And Her Dog House	533165Ⓑ								
896	Sugar Town Post Office 7* Piece Collector Set	456217Ⓐ								
897	Sugar Town Square Clock	532908Ⓑ								
898	Summer's Joy	12076Ⓐ	12114Ⓐ		408743②		408794②			
899	Sure Would Love To Squeeze You (Germany)	456896								
900	Surely Goodness And Mercy Shall Follow Me...	523410Ⓔ								
901	Surrounded With Joy *Surround Us With Joy	E-0506Ⓑ		E-0522Ⓓ		*E-0513Ⓓ				
902	Surrounded With Joy	531677				531685				
903	Sweep All Your Worries Away	521779Ⓑ								
904	Sweet Sixteen / Age 16	136263								
905	Sweeter As The Years Go By	522333Ⓑ								
906	Take A Bow 'cuz You're My Christmas Star					520470Ⓐ				
907	Take Heed When You Stand	521272Ⓢ								
908	Take It To The Lord In Prayer	163767								
909	Take Time To Smell The Flowers	524387Ⓐ								
910	Take Your Time It's Your Birthday	488003								
911	Tammy						E-7267GⒼ			

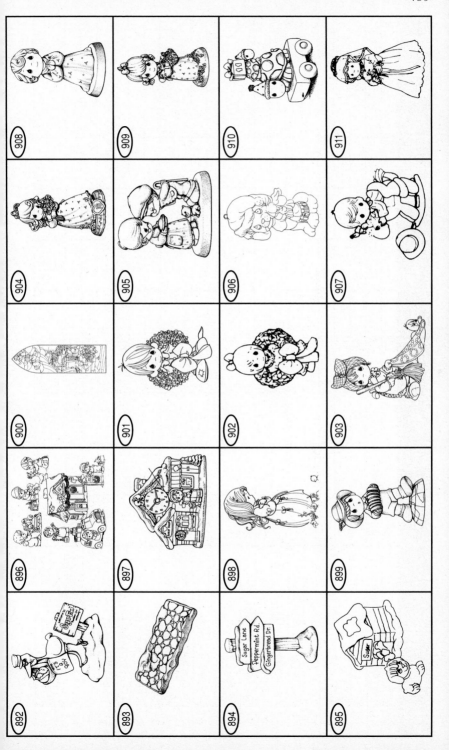

AC#	TITLE	FIG	PLATE	BELL	MUSIC	ORN	DOLL	THMBL	FRAME	OTHER
912	Tammy And Debbie	531812®								
913	Taste And See That The Lord Is Good	E-9274®								
914	Teach Us To Love One Another	PM-961								
915	Tell It To Jesus	521477								
916	Tell Me A Story	15792Ⓢ								
917	Tell Me The Story Of Jesus	E-2349Ⓢ	15237Ⓓ			E-0533Ⓢ				
918	Ten Years And Still Going Strong	PM-901								
919	Ten Years Heart To Heart	163805								
920	Thank You For Coming To My Ade	E-5202Ⓢ								
921	Thank You Lord For Everything	522031Ⓢ								
922	Thanking Him For You	E-7155Ⓢ								
	*Prayer Changes Things			*E-5210Ⓢ						
923	That's What Friends Are For	521183								
924	The Club That's Out Of This World	C-0112				PM-038				
		C-0012								
925	The End Is In Sight	E-9253Ⓢ								
926	The Eyes Of The Lord Are Upon You				429570Ⓢ					
927	The Eyes Of The Lord Are Upon You				429589Ⓢ					
928	The First Noel	E-2365Ⓢ				E-2367Ⓢ				
929	The First Noel	E-2366Ⓢ				E-2368®				
930	The Fruit Of The Spirit Is Love	521213								
931	The Fun Starts Here	B-0012								
		B-0112								

Ⓢ = Suspended   Ⓛ = Limited Edition   ® = Retired   Ⓓ = Two Year Collectible   Ⓐ = Annual   Ⓐ = Dated Annual

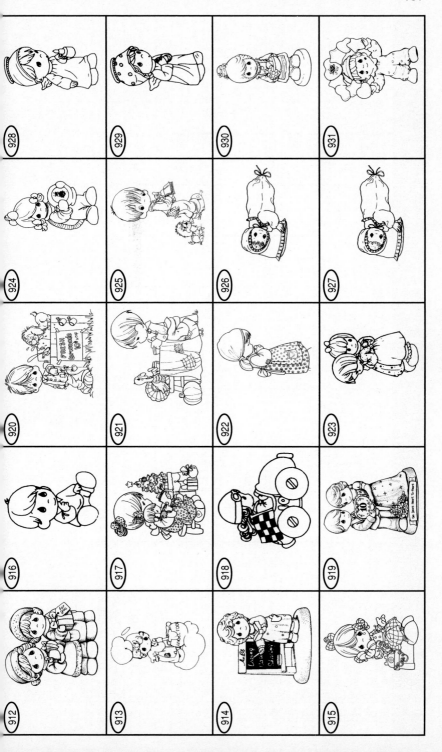

AC#	TITLE	FIG	PLATE	BELL	MUSIC	ORN	DOLL	THMBL	FRAME	OTHER
932	THE GOOD LORD ALWAYS DELIVERS	523453				527165⑤				
933	THE GOOD LORD HAS BLESSED US TENFOLD	114022Ⓐ								
934	THE GOOD LORD WILL ALWAYS UPHOLD US	325325								
935	THE GREATEST GIFT IS A FRIEND	109231								
936	THE GREATEST OF THESE IS LOVE	521868⑤								
937	THE HAND THAT ROCKS THE FUTURE	E-3108⑤	E-9256Ⓔ		E-5204					
938	THE HEAVENLY LIGHT	E-5637								
939	THE JOY OF THE LORD IS MY STRENGTH	100137								
940	THE LIGHT OF THE WORLD IS JESUS				521507					
941	THE LIGHT OF THE WORLD IS JESUS	455954								
942	THE LORD BLESS YOU AND KEEP YOU	E-3114	E-5216⑤	E-7179⑤	E-7180				E-7166⑤	E-7167⑤ Box
	*OUR FIRST CHRISTMAS TOGETHER					*E-2385⑤				
943	THE LORD BLESS YOU AND KEEP YOU	E-4720⑤		E-7175⑤					E-7177⑤	
944	THE LORD BLESS YOU AND KEEP YOU	E-4721		E-7176⑤					E-7178⑤	
945	THE LORD BLESS YOU AND KEEP YOU	532118								
946	THE LORD BLESS YOU AND KEEP YOU	532126								
947	THE LORD BLESS YOU AND KEEP YOU	532134								
948	THE LORD GIVETH AND THE LORD TAKETH AWAY	100226Ⓑ								
949	THE LORD IS COUNTING ON YOU	531707								
950	THE LORD IS MY SHEPHERD	PM-851								
951	THE LORD IS MY SHEPHERD, I SHALL NOT WANT	523402Ⓔ								

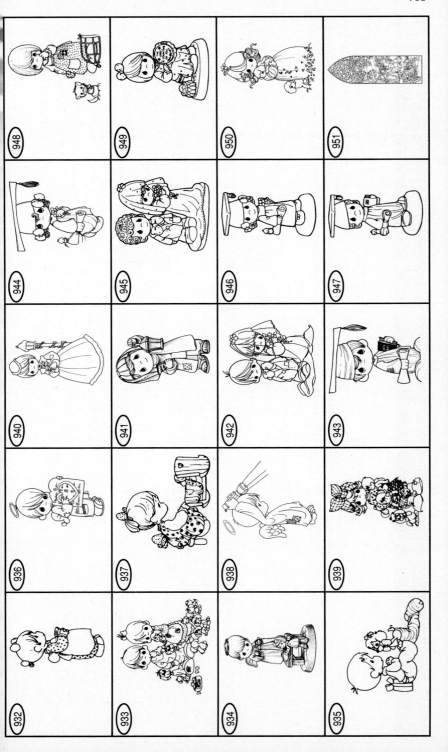

163

AC#	TITLE	FIG	PLATE	BELL	MUSIC	ORN	DOLL	THMBL	FRAME	OTHER
952	THE LORD IS OUR CHIEF INSPIRATION	204862 204870Ⓐ								
953	THE LORD IS THE HOPE OF OUR FUTURE	261564								
954	THE LORD IS WITH YOU	526835								
955	THE LORD IS YOUR LIGHT TO HAPPINESS	520837								
956	THE LORD TURNED MY LIFE AROUND	520535Ⓢ								
957	THE LORD WILL CARRY YOU THROUGH	12467Ⓑ								
958	THE LORD WILL PROVIDE	523593Ⓐ								
959	THE MAGIC STARTS WITH YOU					529648Ⓐ				
960	THE MOST PRECIOUS GIFT OF ALL	183814'SⓈⒶ								
	*THE MOST PRECIOUS GIFT OF THEM ALL	183814				*212520Ⓐ				
961	THE PEARL OF GREAT PRICE	526061Ⓐ								
962	THE PERFECT GRANDPA	E-7160Ⓢ				E-0517Ⓢ				
963	THE PURR-FECT GRANDMA	E-3109	E-7173Ⓓ	E-7183Ⓢ	E-7184Ⓢ	E-0516		13307	E-7242Ⓢ	
964	THE SPIRIT IS WILLING BUT THE FLESH IS WEAK	100196Ⓑ								
965	THE STORY OF GOD'S LOVE	15784Ⓢ								
966	THE SUN IS ALWAYS SHINING SOMEWHERE	163775								
967	THE SWEETEST CLUB AROUND	B-0103 B-0003								
968	THE VOICE OF SPRING	12068Ⓐ	12106Ⓐ		408735②		408786②			
	*FOUR SEASONS THIMBLES							*100641Ⓐ		
969	THE WONDER OF CHRISTMAS		E-5396Ⓓ							
970	THEE I LOVE	E-3116Ⓑ								
971	THERE ARE TWO SIDES TO EVERY STORY	325368								

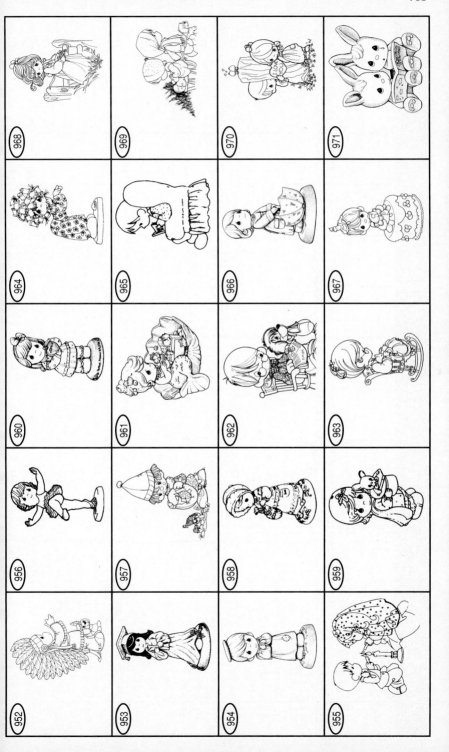

AC#	TITLE	FIG	PLATE	BELL	MUSIC	ORN	DOLL	THMBL	FRAME	OTHER
972	There Is Joy In Serving Jesus	E-7157®								
973	There Is No Greater Treasure Than To Have A Friend Like You	521000								
974	There Shall Be Showers Of Blessings	522090								
975	There's A Christian Welcome Here	523011Ⓢ				528021				
976	There's A Light At The End Of The Tunnel	521485Ⓢ								
977	There's A Song In My Heart	12173Ⓢ								
978	There's A Spot In My Heart For You	BC-961								
979	They Followed The Star	E-5624								
		108243								
980	They Followed The Star	E-5641Ⓢ								
981	Thinking Of You Is What I Really Like To Do	522287Ⓢ	531766Ⓓ							
982	This Day Has Been Made In Heaven	523496			523682					
983	This Day Is Something To Roar About *Christmas Is Something To Roar About	15989				*521116				
984	This Is The Day (Which) The Lord Has Made	12157Ⓢ								
985	This Is The Day Which The Lord Hath Made	E-2838Ⓐ								
986	This Is Your Day To Shine	E-2822®								
987	This Land Is Our Land	527386								
988	This Land Is Our Land	527777Ⓐ								
989	This Too Shall Pass	114014								
990	This World Is Not My Home (I'm Just A Passin' Thru)	212547								

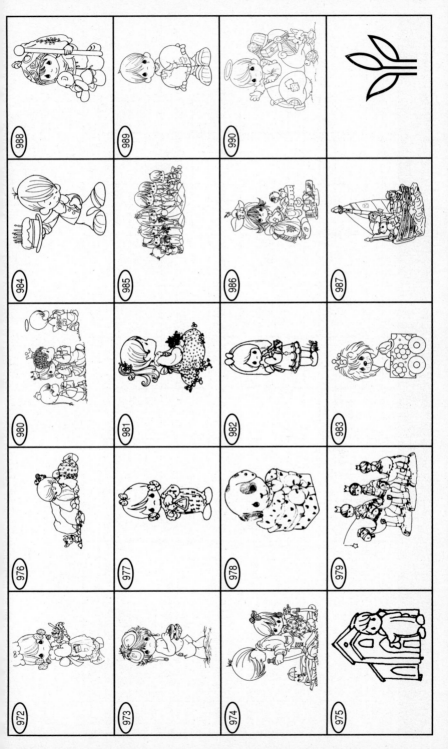

AC#	TITLE	FIG	PLATE	BELL	MUSIC	ORN	DOLL	THMBL	FRAME	OTHER
991	Thou Annointest My Head With Oil....	523429Ⓛ								
992	Thou Art Mine	E-3113								
993	Thou Preparest A Table Before Me...	523372Ⓛ								
994	Thumb-body Loves You	521698Ⓢ								
995	Tied Up For The Holidays	527580Ⓢ								
996	Time For A Holy Holiday	455849								
997	Time Heals	523739								
998	Time To Wish You A Merry Christmas	115339Ⓓ		115304Ⓓ		115320Ⓓ		115312Ⓓ		
999	Timmy						E-5397Ⓢ			
1000	Tippy	529192Ⓢ								
1001	'Tis The Season	111163Ⓢ								
1002	To A Special Dad	E-5212				E-0515Ⓢ				
1003	To A Special Mum	521965								
1004	To A Very Special Mom	E-2824								
1005	To A Very Special Mom And Dad	521434Ⓢ								
1006	To A Very Special Sister	E-2825								
1007	To A Very Special Sister	528633								
1008	To Be With You Is Uplifting	522260Ⓡ								
1009	To God Be The Glory	E-2823Ⓢ								
1010	To My Deer Friend	100048								

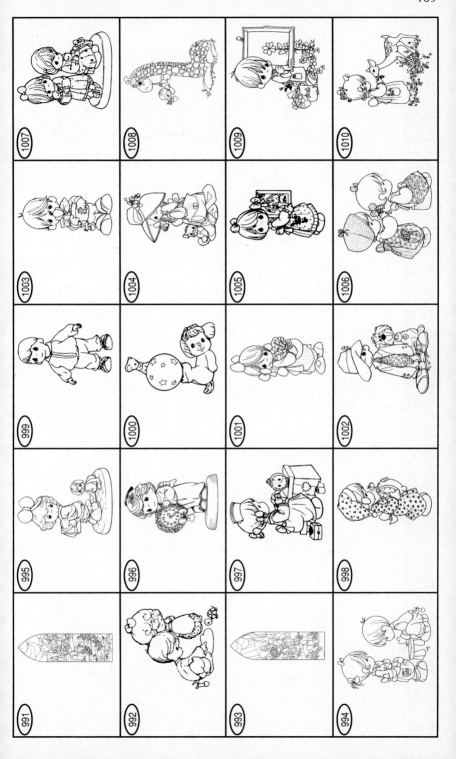

AC#	TITLE	FIG	PLATE	BELL	MUSIC	ORN	DOLL	THMBL	FRAME	OTHER
1011	To My Favorite Fan	521043Ⓢ								
1012	To My Favorite Paw	100021Ⓢ								
1013	To My Forever Friend	100072				113956				
1014	To Somebunny Special	E-9282Ⓢ								
		E-9282AⓈ								
1015	To Tell The Tooth You're Special	105813Ⓢ								
1016	To The Apple Of God's Eye	522015								
1017	To Thee With Love	E-3120Ⓢ				E-0534Ⓡ				
1018	Toy Maker	475092								
1019	Toy Maker					475106				
1020	Train Station Night Light									150150Ⓡ Night Light
1021	Train Station Ornament					184101Ⓐ				
1022	Trish						12483Ⓢ			
1023	True Blue Friends	BC-912								
1024	Trust In The Lord	E-9289Ⓢ								
1025	Trust In The Lord To The Finish	PM-842								
1026	Tubby's First Christmas	E-0511Ⓢ								
		525278								
1027	Two Section Wall	E-5644								
1028	Unicorn					E-2371Ⓡ				
1029	Unto Us A Child Is Born	E-2013Ⓢ			E-2808Ⓢ					
1030	Unto Us A Child Is Born		E-5395Ⓔ							

Ⓢ = Suspended Ⓔ = Limited Edition Ⓡ = Retired ② = Two Year Collectible Ⓓ = Dated Annual Ⓐ = Annual

172

AC#	TITLE	FIG	PLATE	BELL	MUSIC	ORN	DOLL	THMBL	FRAME	OTHER
1031	Vaya Con Dios (To Go With God)	531146								
1032	Waddle I Do Without You	12459®Ⓡ				112364				
1033	Walk In The Sonshine	524212								
1034	Walking By Faith	E-3117								
1035	Warming Hut Night Light									192341Ⓓ Night Light
1036	Water-melancholy Day Without You	521515								
1037	We All Have Our Bad Hair Days	261157								
1038	We Are All Precious In His Sight	102903Ⓐ 475068Ⓛ								
1039	We Are God's Workmanship	E-9258 523879Ⓛ								525960Ⓓ Egg
1040	We Are God's Workmanship	272434								
1041	We Belong To The Lord	103004								
1042	We Gather Together To Ask The Lord's Blessing	109762®Ⓡ								
1043	We Have Come From Afar	526959Ⓢ 530913								
1044	We Have Seen His Star	E-2010Ⓢ		E-5620Ⓢ		E-6120®Ⓡ				
1045	We Need A Good Friend Through The Ruff Times	520810Ⓢ								
1046	We Saw A Star				12408Ⓢ					
1047	We're Going To Miss You	524913								
1048	We're In It Together	E-9259Ⓢ								
1049	We're Pulling For You	106151Ⓢ								

Ⓢ = Suspended   Ⓛ = Limited Edition   Ⓡ = Retired   ② = Two Year Collectible   Ⓓ = Dated Annual   Ⓐ = Annual

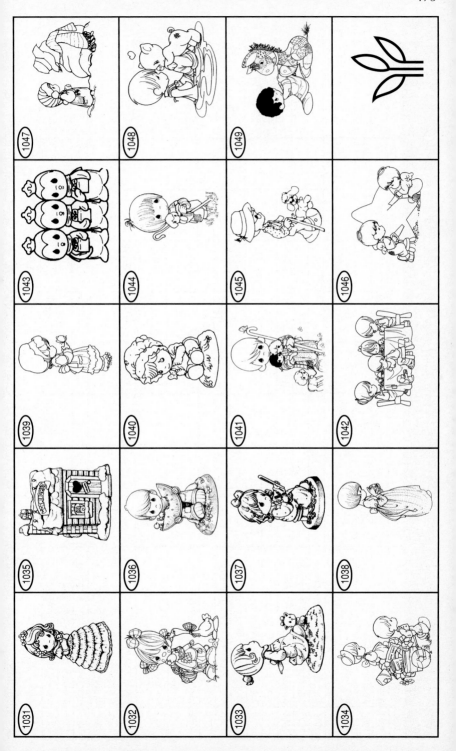

AC#	TITLE	FIG	PLATE	BELL	MUSIC	ORN	DOLL	THMBL	FRAME	OTHER
1050	We're So Hoppy You're Here	261351Ⓐ								
1051	We're Two Of A Kind					455997Ⓐ				
1052	Wedding Arch	102369Ⓢ								
1053	Wee Three Kings	E-5635	E-0538ⓁⒺ		E-0520Ⓢ	E-5634Ⓢ				
		213624								
1054	Well, Blow Me Down It's Yer Birthday	325538								
1055	What A Difference You've Made In My Life	531138								
1056	What Better To Give Than Yourself	487988								
1057	What The World Needs Is Love	531065								
1058	What The World Needs Now	524352Ⓡ								
1059	What Would I Do Without You	320714								
1060	When The Skating's Ruff, Try Prayer					183903				
1061	Where Would I Be Without You	139491								
1062	Who's Gonna Fill Your Shoes?	532061								
		532061'S'Ⓐ								
1063	Who's Gonna Fill Your Shoes?	531634					408816②			
		531634SⒶ								
1064	Winter's Song	12092Ⓐ	12130Ⓐ		408778②					
1065	Wishing Well	292753								
1066	Wishing You A Basket Full Of Blessings	109924								
1067	Wishing You A Bear-ie Merry Christmas					531200Ⓓ				
1068	Wishing You A Comfy Christmas	527750								
1069	Wishing You A Cozy Christmas	102342Ⓓ		102318Ⓓ		102326Ⓓ		102334Ⓓ		

Ⓢ = Suspended   ⓁⒺ = Limited Edition   Ⓡ = Retired   ② = Two Year Collectible   Ⓓ = Dated Annual   Ⓐ = Annual

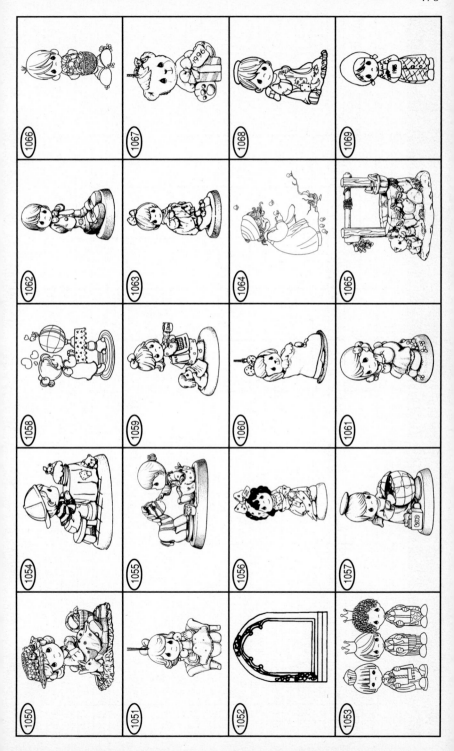

AC#	TITLE	FIG	PLATE	BELL	MUSIC	ORN	DOLL	THMBL	FRAME	OTHER
1070	Wishing You A Cozy Season	521949Ⓢ								
1071	Wishing You A Happy Bear Hug	520659Ⓢ								
1072	Wishing You A Happy Easter	109886								
1073	Wishing You A Ho Ho Ho	527629								
1074	Wishing You A Merry Christmas	E-5383Ⓓ		E-5393Ⓓ		E-5387Ⓓ				
1075	Wishing You A Merry Christmas				E-5394Ⓢ					
1076	Wishing You A Perfect Choice	520845								
1077	Wishing You A Purr-fect Holiday					520497Ⓓ				
1078	Wishing You A Season Filled With Joy	E-2805Ⓡ								
1079	Wishing You A Very Successful Season	522120								
1080	Wishing You A World Of Peace	C-0019 C-0119								
1081	Wishing You A Yummy Christmas	109754Ⓢ	523801Ⓓ							
1082	Wishing You A Yummy Christmas	455814								
1083	Wishing You Grrr-eatness	109479								
1084	Wishing You Roads Of Happiness *Our First Christmas Together	520780				521558Ⓓ *525324Ⓓ				
1085	Wishing You The Sweetest Christmas	530166Ⓓ	530204Ⓓ	530174Ⓓ		530190Ⓓ 530212Ⓓ		530182Ⓓ		
1086	Wishing You Were Here				526916					
1087	With This Ring I...	104019								
1088	Worship The Lord	100064								
1089	Worship The Lord	102229								

Ⓢ = Suspended   Ⓔ = Limited Edition   Ⓡ = Retired   ② = Two Year Collectible   Ⓓ = Dated Annual   Ⓐ = Annual

* Searchable in original Title

177

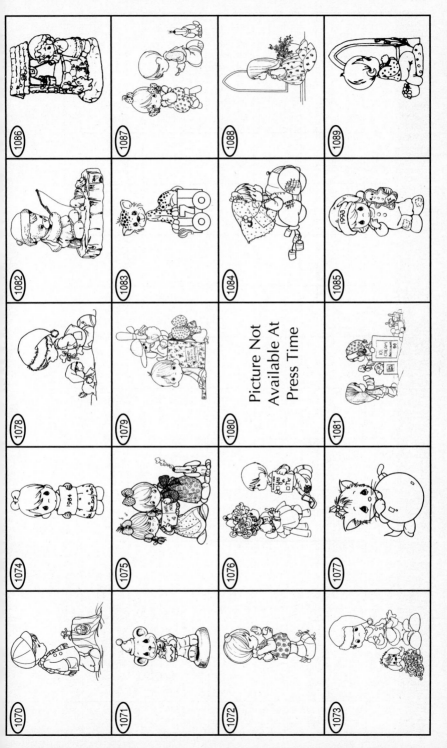

1086

1087

1088

1089

1082

1083

1084

1085

1078

1079

1080 — Picture Not Available At Press Time

1081

1074

1075

1076

1077

1070

1071

1072

1073

AC#	TITLE	FIG	PLATE	BELL	MUSIC	ORN	DOLL	THMBL	FRAME	OTHER
1090	YEA, THOUGH I WALK THROUGH THE VALLEY OF THE SHADOW OF DEATH...	523356Ⓛ								
1091	YER A PEL-I-CAN COUNT ON	BC-942								
1092	YIELD NOT TO TEMPTATION	521310Ⓢ								
1093	YOU ALWAYS STAND BEHIND ME	492140								
1094	YOU ARE A BLESSING TO ME	PM-902								
1095	YOU ARE A DUCHESS TO ME (HOLLAND)	456373								
1096	YOU ARE A LIFESAVER TO ME	204854								
1097	YOU ARE ALWAYS IN MY HEART					530972Ⓓ				
1098	YOU ARE ALWAYS ON MY MIND	306967								
1099	YOU ARE ALWAYS THERE FOR ME	163600								
1100	YOU ARE ALWAYS THERE FOR ME	163627								
1101	YOU ARE ALWAYS THERE FOR ME	163597								
1102	YOU ARE ALWAYS THERE FOR ME	163619								
1103	YOU ARE ALWAYS THERE FOR ME	163635								
1104	YOU ARE MY AMOUR (FRANCE)	456918								
1105	YOU ARE MY FAVORITE STAR	527378Ⓡ								
1106	YOU ARE MY GIFT COME TRUE					520276Ⓓ				
1107	YOU ARE MY HAPPINESS	526185Ⓐ								
1108	YOU ARE MY MAIN EVENT	115231Ⓐ								
1109	YOU ARE MY NUMBER ONE	520829								

Ⓢ = Suspended   Ⓛ = Limited Edition   Ⓡ = Retired   Ⓒ = Two Year Collectible   Ⓓ = Dated Annual   Ⓐ = A...

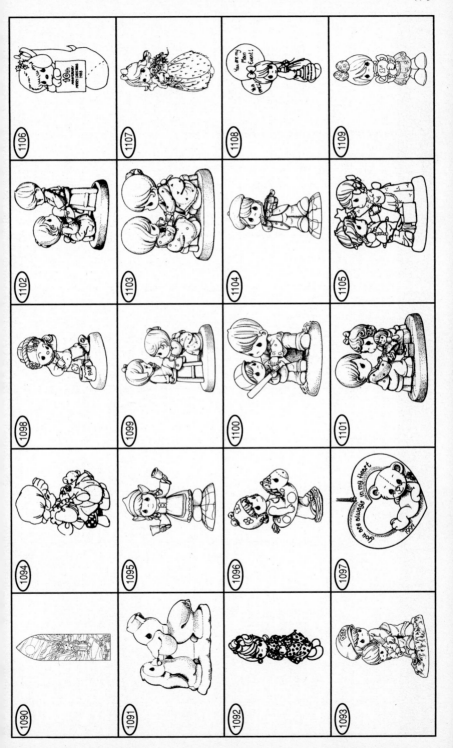

AC#	TITLE	FIG	PLATE	BELL	MUSIC	ORN	DOLL	THMBL	FRAME	OTHER
1110	You Are My Once In A Lifetime	531030								
1111	You Are Such A Purr-Fect Friend	524395								
		526010Ⓛ								
1112	You Are The End Of My Rainbow	C-0114								
		C-0014								
1113	You Are The End Of My Rainbow					PM-041				
1114	You Are The Rose Of His Creation	531243Ⓛ								
1115	You Are The Type I Love	523542								
1116	You Can Always Bring A Friend	527122Ⓐ								
1117	You Can Always Count On Me	526827Ⓐ								
1118	You Can Always Count On Me	487953								
1119	You Can Always Fudge A Little During The Season	455792								
1120	You Can Fly	12335Ⓢ								
1121	You Can't Beat The Red, White And Blue (United States)	456411								
1122	You Can't Run Away From God	E-0525Ⓡ								
1123	You Can't Take It With You	488321								
1124	You Count	488372								
1125	You Deserve A Halo–Thank You	531693Ⓡ								
1126	You Deserve An Ovation	520578								
1127	You Fill The Pages Of My Life & Precious Moments Last Forever										PMB034 Book & Figurine
1128	You Have Mastered The Art Of Caring	456276Ⓐ								

Ⓢ = Suspended   Ⓛ = Limited Edition   Ⓡ = Retired   ② = Two Year Collectible   Ⓓ = Dated Annual   Ⓐ = Annual

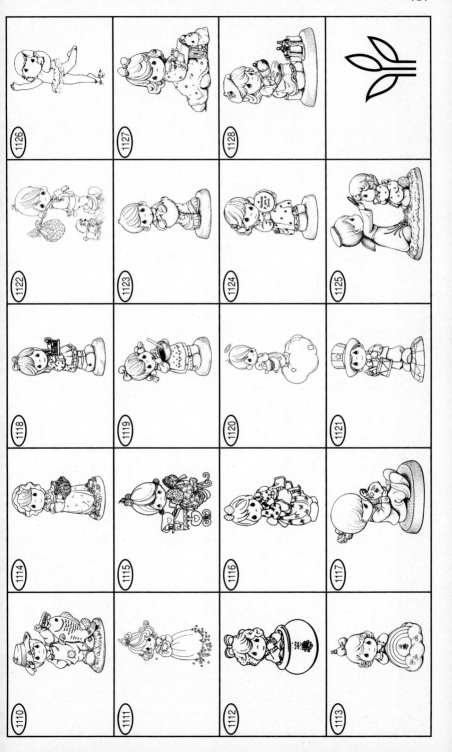

AC#	TITLE	FIG	PLATE	BELL	MUSIC	ORN	DOLL	THMBL	FRAME	OTHER
1129	You Have Such A Special Way Of Caring Each And Every Day	320706								
1130	You Have Touched So Many Hearts	E-2821⑤ 523283⑥ 527661⑤			112577⑤ 422282②	112356®	427527②			
1131	You Have Touched So Many Hearts	261084								
1132	You Have Touched So Many Hearts	272485								
1133	You Just Can't Replace A Good Friendship	488054								
1134	You Just Cannot Chuck A Good Friendship	PM-882								
1135	You Make My Spirit Soar	139564								
1136	You Make Such A Lovely Pair	531588④								
1137	You Make The World A Sweeter Place	139521								
1138	You Set My Heart Ablaze	320625								
1139	You Suit Me To A Tee	526193								
1140	You Will Always Be A Treasure To Me	PM-971								
1141	You Will Always Be A Winner To Me (Boy)	272612								
1142	You Will Always Be A Winner To Me (Girl)	283460								
1143	You Will Always Be My Choice	PM-891								
1144	You Will Always Be Our Hero	136271④								
1145	You're As Pretty As A Christmas Tree	530425①	530409①	604216①		530387① 530395①				
1146	You're As Pretty As A Picture	C-0116 C-0016								
1147	You're First In My Heart	BC-962								

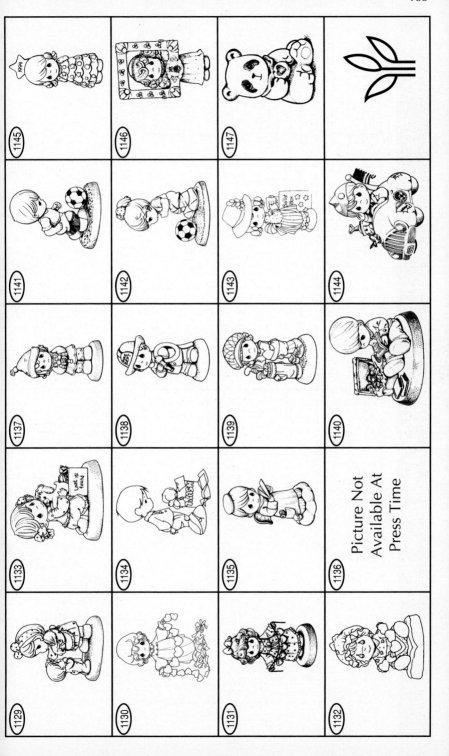

183

1129

1130

1131

1132

1133

1134

1135

1136 Picture Not Available At Press Time

1137

1138

1139

1140

1141

1142

1143

1144

1145

1146

1147

AC#	TITLE	FIG	PLATE	BELL	MUSIC	ORN	DOLL	THMBL	FRAME	OTHER
1148	You're Forever In My Heart	139548								
1149	You're Just As Sweet As Pie	307017								
1150	You're Just Perfect In My Book	320560								
1151	You're Just Too Sweet To Be Scary	183849								
1152	You're My Honey Bee	487929								
1153	You're My Number One Friend	530026Ⓐ								
1154	You're One In A Million To Me	PM-951								
1155	You're The Berry Best	139513								
1156	You're The Sweetest Cookie In The Batch	C-0115								
		C-0015								
1157	You're Worth Your Weight In Gold	E-9282Ⓢ								
		E-9282BⓈ								
1158	Your Love Is So Uplifting	520675Ⓑ								
1159	Your Precious Spirit Comes Shining Through	212563Ⓓ								
		212563AⒹ								
		212563BⒹ								

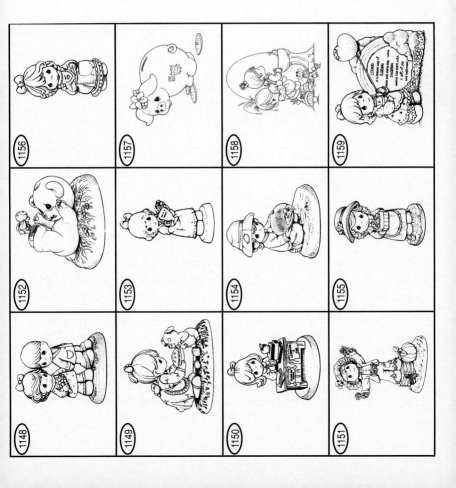

GREENBOOK Listings are in Enesco Item Number order.

Enesco Item Numbers can be found on the understamp of most pieces produced from 1982 to the present.

If you don't know the Enesco Item Number, but you do know the Inspirational Title, use the alphabetical ARTCHART™ to obtain the Enesco Item Number.

Sugar Town, Two By Two and Sammy's Circus pieces are included in the Listings. Collectors' Club and Birthday Club pieces are included at the end of the Listings in their own separate sections.

The parts of a Listing are illustrated on the sample Listing below.

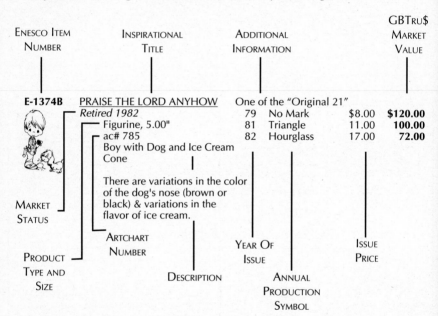

ENESCO ITEM NUMBER	INSPIRATIONAL TITLE	ADDITIONAL INFORMATION				GBTRU$ MARKET VALUE

E-1374B   PRAISE THE LORD ANYHOW   One of the "Original 21"

Retired 1982

		79	No Mark	$8.00	**$120.00**

Figurine, 5.00"   81 Triangle 11.00 **100.00**

ac# 785   82 Hourglass 17.00 **72.00**

Boy with Dog and Ice Cream Cone

There are variations in the color of the dog's nose (brown or black) & variations in the flavor of ice cream.

MARKET STATUS

ARTCHART NUMBER

PRODUCT TYPE AND SIZE

DESCRIPTION

YEAR OF ISSUE

ANNUAL PRODUCTION SYMBOL

ISSUE PRICE

- The **Enesco Item Number** appears in brochures, catalogs, ads, and on the understamp of most pieces produced from 1982 to the present. It is a quick and *absolute* means of identification.

- The GREENBOOK lists the **Year Of Issue** for each change in Annual Production Symbol. A very common error made by collectors is to mistake the copyright date for the year of issue because the copyright date appears on the understamp written out as ©19XX. **In other words, in order to determine what year your piece was produced, you must refer to the Annual Production Symbol, not the © date.**

HOW TO READ & USE GREENBOOK LISTINGS

- The GREENBOOK lists the **Issue Price** (Suggested Retail Price) for each piece when it was first introduced and for each year the Annual Production Symbol is/was changed.

- The **Size** in inches indicates the diameter of plates and the height of figurines.

- **Market Status**: Enesco periodically Retires and Suspends individual pieces. In addition, an item can be limited in other ways, including: 1) A Specific Number (for example a Limited Edition of 15,000); 2) By Year (Annual or Dated Annual); 3) Two Year Collectible (Available for two years); 4) Available to Club Members Only (Members Only); 5) By Event. "Ongoing" indicates the piece, in the current Annual Production Symbol, is generally available from retailers at Suggested Retail Price.

- **Annual Production Symbol**: Since mid-1981, Enesco has indicated when Precious Moments collectibles were produced by including an Annual Production Symbol as part of the understamp. Pieces produced prior to mid-1981 have no Annual Production Symbol and are termed "No Marks."

  The GREENBOOK defines "No Mark" as prior to mid-1981.

  There are also "Unmarked" PRECIOUS MOMENTS collectibles. It was not until 1984 that some product types such as plates and ornaments were marked with an Annual Production Symbol. The GREENBOOK terms 1981, 1982, and 1983 pieces that fall into this category as "Unmarked." HINT: Most "Unmarked" pieces (vs. "No Mark") will have the Enesco Item Number on the understamp, but not an Annual Production Symbol.

  An "Unmarked" piece can also be a production error. Some pieces simply miss getting marked!

  Yet another category is "Not Marked." Little Moments are not marked.

  The next page outlines and illustrates the different Annual and Special Production Symbols and their meanings.

- The **GREENBOOK TRUMARKET VALUE** reflects the current primary and secondary market prices for each piece. Because there are so many factors based on individual judgements, and because prices can vary from one section of the country to another, **GREENBOOK TRUMARKET VALUES are never an absolute number.** Use them as a benchmark.
  (An "NE" = The Value is **N**ot **E**stablished.)

ANNUAL PRODUCTION SYMBOLS:

PRIOR TO
1981   "No Mark"

1981	Triangle	Symbol of the Triune - God, the Father, Son, & Holy Spirit.
1982	Hourglass	Represents the time we have on earth to serve the Lord.
1983	Fish	Earliest symbol used by believers of the early apostolic church.
1984	Cross	Symbol of Christianity recognized worldwide.
1985	Dove	Symbol of love and peace.
1986	Olive Branch	Symbol of peace & understanding.
1987	Cedar Tree	Symbol of strength, beauty, and preservation.
1988	Flower	Represents God's love toward His children.
1989	Bow & Arrow	Represents the power of the Bible.
1990	Flame	For those who have gone through the fire of life & found comfort in believing.
1991	Vessel	A reminder of God's love which flows through the vessel of life.
1992	G-Clef	Symbolizes the harmony of God's love.
1993	Butterfly	Represents the rebirth of man who comes from darkness into the light.

1994	Trumpet		Represents Precious Moments as a voice to our nation with a message of loving, caring and sharing. The trumpet is the battle cry to war and the heralder of victory.
1995	Ship		Ships, which are mentioned many times in Scripture symbolically portrayed a message of hope. For those in earlier times who depended on ships for transportation and provisions, seeing a ship was assurance that friends, family and help were on their way.
1996	Heart		Symbol of love.
1997	Sword		From Hebrews 4:12 For the word of God is quick and powerful and sharper than any two edged sword.
1998	Eyeglasses		Chosen by Sam Butcher to symbolize that it has been "20 Years And The Vision's Still The Same."
1999	Star		From Matthew 2:2 "Where is He who has been born King of the Jews? For we have seen His star in the East and have come to worship Him."

SPECIAL PRODUCTION SYMBOLS:

---	Diamond		Appeared on one piece only -#103004, "We Belong To The Lord," the Damien-Dutton figurine.
---	Easter Seal		Appears on figurines benefiting the National Easter Seal Society.
---	Rosebud		Appeared on one figurine only -#525049, "Good Friends Are Forever," a Special Events figurine.
1991	'91 Flag		'91 & '92 Flag appeared on all "Bless Those Who Serve Their Country" figurines.
1992	'92 Flag		

WEBSITE ADDRESSES

Enesco	www.enesco.com
Precious Moments Chapel	www.preciousmoments.com
Precious Moments Collectible Treasures	www.preciousmom.com
GREENBOOK	www.greenbooks.com
GREENBOOK Guides on CD-Rom	www.greenbooksoftware.com

Listings

GREENBOOK LISTINGS

The GREENBOOK LISTINGS are where specific factual information as well as GREENBOOK TRUMARKET VALUES for each collectible can be found.

GREENBOOK LISTINGS are in Enesco Item Number order. Enesco Item Numbers can be found on the understamp of most pieces produced from 1982 to the present. If you don't know the Enesco Item Number, but you do know the Inspirational Title, use the alphabetical ARTCHART section to obtain the Enesco Item Number.

Collectors' Club and Birthday Club pieces are at the end in their own separate sections starting on page 390 and page 401, respectively.

None	**HOW CAN THREE WORK TOGETHER EXCEPT THEY AGREE**				
	Created in Honor of the 20th Anniversary				
Picture Not	*Limited Edition 20*	98	Eyeglasses	N/A	**NE**
Available At	Figurine,				
Press Time	ac# 451				
	Sam, Fujioka-san and Gene				
	Collaborating on the				
	"Original 21"				

20th Anniversary Logo on understamp. Individually Numbered 1 - 20. Signed by Master Sculptor Yasuhei Fujioka-san, artist Sam Butcher and Enesco Chairman & CEO Gene Freedman. Each have received a figurine and the remaining 17 are/were available for collectors. One is/was available by raffle or auction at each of the Hometown Celebrations. Proceeds raised from the figurines benefit Second Harvest, the nation's largest charitable hunger relief organization. As we go to press, winning bids on 12 of the figurines have ranged from $1,200 to $7,685.13, with the average being $4,381.

None	**GOD LOVETH A CHEERFUL GIVER**	Gift to Club Members joining			
	by 6/30/98				
Picture Not	*Gift*	98	Eyeglasses	$Gift	**$25.00**
Available At	Limoges Box, 3.00"				
Press Time	ac# 337				
	Girl with Puppies				

E-0501	**SHARING OUR SEASON TOGETHER**				
	Suspended 1986	83	Fish	$50.00	**$170.00**
	Figurine, 4.90"	84	Cross	50.00	**150.00**
	ac# 852	85	Dove	50.00	**145.00**
	Boy Pushing Girl on Sled	86	Olive Branch	50.00	**140.00**

E-0502	**JESUS IS THE LIGHT THAT SHINES**				
	Suspended 1986	83	Fish	$22.50	**$70.00**
	Figurine, 5.25"	84	Cross	23.00	**65.00**
	ac# 528	85	Dove	23.00	**60.00**
	Boy with Candle & Mouse	86	Olive Branch	23.00	**55.00**

E-0503	**BLESSINGS FROM MY HOUSE TO YOURS**				
	Suspended 1986	83	Fish	$27.00	**$85.00**
	Figurine, 5.80"	84	Cross	27.00	**80.00**
	ac# 167	85	Dove	27.00	**78.00**
	Girl in Snow Looking at	86	Olive Branch	27.00	**75.00**
	Birdhouse				

E-0504	**CHRISTMASTIME IS FOR SHARING**				
	Retired 1990	83	Fish	$37.00	**$110.00**
	Figurine, 5.25"	84	Cross	37.00	**95.00**
	ac# 206	85	Dove	37.00	**88.00**
	Boy Giving Teddy to a Poor	86	Olive Branch	37.00	**85.00**
	Boy	87	Cedar Tree	40.00	**78.00**
		88	Flower	40.00	**72.00**
		89	Bow & Arrow	47.50	**70.00**
		90	Flame	50.00	**68.00**

E-0505	**CHRISTMASTIME IS FOR SHARING**	Series: "Joy Of Christmas"–2nd Issue			
	Dated Annual 1983	83	Unmarked	$40.00	**$75.00**
	Plate, 8.50"				
	ac# 206				
	Boy Giving Teddy to a Poor				
	Boy				

1983

E-0506	SURROUNDED WITH JOY				
	Retired 1989	83	Fish	$21.00	**$90.00**
	Figurine, 4.15"	84	Cross	21.00	**78.00**
	ac# 901	85	Dove	21.00	**75.00**
	Boy with Wreath	86	Olive Branch	21.00	**72.00**
		87	Cedar Tree	23.00	**70.00**
		88	Flower	23.00	**68.00**
		89	Bow & Arrow	27.50	**67.00**
E-0507	GOD SENT HIS SON				
	Suspended 1987	83	Fish	$32.50	**$98.00**
	Figurine, 5.50"	84	Cross	32.50	**85.00**
	ac# 341	85	Dove	32.50	**80.00**
	Girl Looking into Manger	86	Olive Branch	32.50	**75.00**
		87	Cedar Tree	37.00	**72.00**
E-0508	PREPARE YE THE WAY OEC'HE LORD	Set of 6			
	Suspended 1986	83	Fish	$75.00	**$160.00**
	Figurine, 5.75"	84	Cross	75.00	**150.00**
	ac# 792	85	Dove	75.00	**140.00**
	Angels Preparing Manger	86	Olive Branch	75.00	**130.00**
E-0509	BRINGING GOD'S BLESSING TO YOU				
	Suspended 1987	83	Fish	$35.00	**$90.00**
	Figurine, 5.50"	84	Cross	35.00	**80.00**
	ac# 175	85	Dove	35.00	**75.00**
	Girl Angel Pushing Jesus in	86	Olive Branch	35.00	**70.00**
	Buggy	87	Cedar Tree	38.50	**68.00**
E-0511	TUBBY'S FIRST CHRISTMAS	Nativity Addition			
	Suspended 1993	83	Fish	$12.00	**$50.00**
	Figurine, 3.25"	84	Cross	12.00	**45.00**
	ac# 1026	85	Dove	12.00	**40.00**
	Rooster & Bird on Pig	86	Olive Branch	12.00	**38.00**
		87	Cedar Tree	13.50	**38.00**
		88	Flower	13.50	**35.00**
		89	Bow & Arrow	15.00	**35.00**
		90	Flame	16.50	**35.00**
		91	Vessel	16.50	**32.00**
		92	G-Clef	16.50	**32.00**
		93	Butterfly	16.50	**32.00**
E-0512	IT'S A PERFECT BOY	Nativity Addition			
	Suspended 1990	83	Fish	$18.50	**$72.00**
	Figurine, 4.75"	84	Cross	18.50	**65.00**
	ac# 510	85	Dove	18.50	**62.00**
	Boy Angel with Red Cross	86	Olive Branch	18.50	**60.00**
	Bag	87	Cedar Tree	21.00	**58.00**
		88	Flower	21.00	**57.00**
		89	Bow & Arrow	25.00	**55.00**
		90	Flame	27.50	**54.00**
E-0513	SURROUND US WITH JOY				
	Dated Annual 1983	83	Fish	$9.00	**$62.00**
	Ornament, 3.00"				
	ac# 901				
	Boy with Wreath				

E-0514 — MOTHER SEW DEAR
Ongoing
Ornament, 3.00"
ac# 698
Mother Needlepointing

*Also exists with a stamped
ink Cross. GBTru$ is $32.00.

Year	Symbol		
83	Fish	$9.00	**$34.00**
84	Cross*	10.00	**25.00**
85	Dove	10.00	**22.00**
86	Olive Branch	10.00	**22.00**
87	Cedar Tree	11.00	**20.00**
88	Flower	11.00	**20.00**
89	Bow & Arrow	13.50	**20.00**
90	Flame	15.00	**20.00**
91	Vessel	15.00	**19.00**
92	G-Clef	15.00	**19.00**
93	Butterfly	15.00	**19.00**
94	Trumpet	16.00	**18.50**
95	Ship	17.00	**18.50**
96	Heart	18.50	**18.50**
97	Sword	18.50	**18.50**
98	Eyeglasses	18.50	**18.50**
99	Star	18.50	**18.50**

E-0515 — TO A SPECIAL DAD
Suspended 1988
Ornament, 3.00"
ac# 1002
Boy in Dad's Duds

*Also exists with a stamped
ink Cross. GBTru$ is $60.00.

Year	Symbol		
83	Fish	$9.00	**$58.00**
84	Cross*	10.00	**55.00**
85	Dove	10.00	**52.00**
86	Olive Branch	10.00	**50.00**
87	Cedar Tree	11.00	**48.00**
88	Flower	11.00	**46.00**

E-0516 — THE PURR-FECT GRANDMA
Ongoing
Ornament, 3.00"
ac# 963
Grandma in Rocker

*Also exists with a stamped
ink Cross. GBTru$ is $50.00.

Year	Symbol		
83	Fish	$9.00	**$37.00**
84	Cross*	10.00	**26.00**
85	Dove	10.00	**24.00**
86	Olive Branch	10.00	**22.00**
87	Cedar Tree	11.00	**22.00**
88	Flower	11.00	**20.00**
89	Bow & Arrow	13.50	**20.00**
90	Flame	15.00	**19.00**
91	Vessel	15.00	**19.00**
92	G-Clef	15.00	**19.00**
93	Butterfly	15.00	**19.00**
94	Trumpet	16.00	**18.50**
95	Ship	17.00	**18.50**
96	Heart	18.50	**18.50**
97	Sword	18.50	**18.50**
98	Eyeglasses	18.50	**18.50**
99	Star	18.50	**18.50**

E-0517 — THE PERFECT GRANDPA
Suspended 1990
Ornament, 3.00"
ac# 962
Grandpa in Rocking Chair

*Also exists with a stamped
ink Cross. GBTru$ is $48.00.

Year	Symbol		
83	Fish	$9.00	**$45.00**
84	Cross*	10.00	**40.00**
85	Dove	10.00	**38.00**
86	Olive Branch	10.00	**36.00**
87	Cedar Tree	11.00	**35.00**
88	Flower	11.00	**32.00**
89	Bow & Arrow	13.50	**30.00**
90	Flame	15.00	**28.00**

E-0518 — BLESSED ARE THE PURE IN HEART
Dated Annual 1983
Ornament, 2.00"
ac# 162
Baby in Cradle

Year	Symbol		
83	Fish	$9.00	**$40.00**

E-0519	SHARING OUR SEASON TOGETHER		Tune: Winter Wonderland		
	Retired 1986	83	Fish	$70.00	**$160.00**
	Musical, 6.00"	84	Cross	70.00	**150.00**
	ac# 852	85	Dove	70.00	**145.00**
	Boy Pushing Girl on Sled	86	Olive Branch	70.00	**138.00**

E-0520	WEE THREE KINGS		Tune: We Three Kings		
	Suspended 1986	83	Fish	$60.00	**$140.00**
	Musical, 7.00"	84	Cross	60.00	**130.00**
	ac# 1053	85	Dove	60.00	**125.00**
	Three Kings	86	Olive Branch	60.00	**118.00**

E-0521	BLESSED ARE THE PURE IN HEART				
	Suspended 1987	83	Fish	$18.00	**$52.00**
	Frame, 4.50"	84	Cross	19.00	**45.00**
	ac# 162	85	Dove	19.00	**42.00**
	Baby in Cradle	86	Olive Branch	19.00	**40.00**
		87	Cedar Tree	21.00	**38.00**

E-0522	SURROUNDED WITH JOY				
	Dated Annual 1983	83	Unmarked	$18.00	**$65.00**
	Bell, 5.15"				
	ac# 901				
	Boy with Wreath				

E-0523	ONWARD CHRISTIAN SOLDIERS				
	Ongoing	*	Unmarked	$24.00	**$225.00**
	Figurine, 6.25"	83	Fish**	24.00	**65.00**
	ac# 745	84	Cross	24.00	**50.00**
	Knight in Armor	85	Dove	24.00	**45.00**
		86	Olive Branch	24.00	**42.00**
	*Though very rare, Unmarked	87	Cedar Tree	27.00	**42.00**
	pieces could have been	88	Flower	30.00	**40.00**
	produced in any of the years	89	Bow & Arrow	33.00	**40.00**
	of production. Consider Fish	90	Flame	35.00	**40.00**
	as the First Mark.**Also exists	91	Vessel	35.00	**38.00**
	with a decal Fish. GBTru$ is	92	G-Clef	35.00	**38.00**
	$100.00.	93	Butterfly	35.00	**38.00**
		94	Trumpet	35.00	**37.50**
		95	Ship	35.00	**37.50**
		96	Heart	37.50	**37.50**
		97	Sword	37.50	**37.50**
		98	Eyeglasses	37.50	**37.50**
		99	Star	37.50	**37.50**

E-0525	YOU CAN'T RUN AWAY FROM GOD				
	Retired 1989	83	Hourglass	$28.50	**$175.00**
	Figurine, 5.15"	83	Fish*	28.50	**100.00**
	ac# 1122	84	Cross	28.50	**90.00**
	Boy and Dog Running Away	85	Dove	28.50	**85.00**
		86	Olive Branch	28.50	**84.00**
	*Also exists with a decal Fish.	87	Cedar Tree	32.50	**82.00**
	GBTru$ is $110.00.	88	Flower	35.00	**80.00**
		89	Bow & Arrow	38.50	**79.00**

E-0526 | HE UPHOLDETH THOSE WHO CALL

Suspended 1985

		*	Unmarked	$28.50	**$135.00**
Figurine, 5.15"		83	Fish**	28.50	**90.00**
ac# 409		84	Cross	35.00	**90.00**
Angel Catching Skater		85	Dove	35.00	**85.00**

*Unmarked pieces could have been produced in any of the years of production. Consider Fish as the First Mark. **Also exists with a removable inked Fish. GBTru$ is $120.00. Fall 1986 GOODNEWSLETTER announced Sam had wanted this piece to be titled "He Upholdeth Those Who Fall" and went on to say if/when the piece was brought back from Suspension the title would be changed to "...Fall." From that point on, in much of their written literature, Enesco began referring to the suspended figurine as "...Fall." This has confused many collectors. Thinking the understamp should say "...Fall," they presume their "...Call" piece is an error or variation.

E-0530 | HIS EYE IS ON THE SPARROW

Retired 1987

	83	Fish	$28.50	**$120.00**
Figurine, 5.25"	84	Cross	28.50	**110.00**
ac# 428	85	Dove	28.50	**100.00**
Girl with Bird in Hand	86	Olive Branch	28.50	**98.00**
	87	Cedar Tree	32.50	**95.00**

E-0531 | O COME ALL YE FAITHFUL

Suspended 1986

	83	Fish	$9.00	**$60.00**
Ornament, 3.25"	84	Cross	10.00	**50.00**
ac# 727	85	Dove	10.00	**48.00**
Boy Caroller	86	Olive Branch	10.00	**47.00**

E-0532 | LET HEAVEN AND NATURE SING

Retired 1986

	83	Fish	$9.00	**$50.00**
Ornament, 3.10"	84	Cross	10.00	**45.00**
ac# 562	85	Dove	10.00	**42.00**
Angel with Book and Songbird	86	Olive Branch	10.00	**40.00**

E-0533 | TELL ME THE STORY OF JESUS

Suspended 1988

	83	Fish	$9.00	**$60.00**
Ornament, 3.00"	84	Cross	10.00	**50.00**
ac# 917	85	Dove	10.00	**48.00**
Girl with Doll Reading Book	86	Olive Branch	10.00	**47.00**
	87	Cedar Tree	11.00	**47.00**
	88	Flower	12.50	**47.00**

E-0534 | TO THEE WITH LOVE

Retired 1989

	83	Fish	$9.00	**$55.00**
Ornament, 3.25"	84	Cross	10.00	**45.00**
ac# 1017	85	Dove	10.00	**42.00**
Girl with Box of Kittens	86	Olive Branch	10.00	**40.00**
	87	Cedar Tree*	11.00	**39.00**
*There are Cedar Tree pieces	88	Flower	12.50	**35.00**
w/two hooks from the	89	Bow & Arrow	13.50	**34.00**
Retailers Wreath, #111465.				

E-0535 | LOVE IS PATIENT

Suspended 1986

	83	Fish	$9.00	**$60.00**
Ornament, 2.75"	84	Cross	10.00	**57.00**
ac# 610	85	Dove	10.00	**50.00**
Boy with Slate	86	Olive Branch	10.00	**48.00**

E-0536 LOVE IS PATIENT

Suspended 1986		83	Fish	$9.00	**$70.00**
Ornament, 3.10"		84	Cross	10.00	**60.00**
ac# 611		85	Dove	10.00	**58.00**
Girl with Slate		86	Olive Branch	10.00	**58.00**

E-0537 JESUS IS THE LIGHT THAT SHINES

Suspended 1985		83	Fish	$9.00	**$70.00**
Ornament, 3.00"		84	Cross	10.00	**62.00**
ac# 528		85	Dove	10.00	**60.00**
Boy in Night Cap with Candle					

E-0538 WEE THREE KINGS   Series: "Christmas Collection"–3rd Issue   Individually Numbered

Limited Edition 15,000		83	Unmarked	$40.00	**$40.00**
Plate, 8.50"			Dove		**40.00**
ac# 1053			Olive Branch		**40.00**
Three Kings					

E-0539 KATIE LYNNE

Suspended 1988		83	Unmarked	$150.00	**$185.00**
Doll, 16.00"		83	Fish	150.00	**175.00**
ac# 554		84	Cross	165.00	**175.00**
Baby Collector's Doll		85	Dove	165.00	**175.00**
		86	Olive Branch	165.00	**175.00**
		87	Cedar Tree	175.00	**175.00**
		88	Flower	175.00	**175.00**

E-1372B JESUS LOVES ME   One of the "Original 21"

Retired 1998		79	No Mark	$7.00	**$120.00**
Figurine, 4.50"		81	Triangle	10.00	**70.00**
ac# 531		82	Hourglass	15.00	**50.00**
Boy with Teddy		83	Fish	15.00	**40.00**
		84	Cross	17.00	**35.00**
		85	Dove	17.00	**32.00**
		86	Olive Branch	17.00	**32.00**
		87	Cedar Tree	19.00	**30.00**
		88	Flower	21.00	**30.00**
		89	Bow & Arrow	23.00	**30.00**
		90	Flame	25.00	**28.00**
		91	Vessel	25.00	**28.00**
		92	G-Clef	25.00	**28.00**
		93	Butterfly	25.00	**28.00**
		94	Trumpet	25.00	**27.50**
		95	Ship	27.50	**27.50**
		96	Heart	27.50	**27.50**
		97	Sword	27.50	**27.50**
		98	Eyeglasses	27.50	**27.50**

E-1372G   JESUS LOVES ME   One of the "Original 21"

Ongoing
Figurine, 4.50"
ac# 532
Girl with Bunny

79	No Mark	$7.00	**$130.00**
81	Triangle	10.00	**75.00**
82	Hourglass	15.00	**50.00**
83	Fish	15.00	**48.00**
84	Cross	17.00	**45.00**
85	Dove	17.00	**36.00**
86	Olive Branch	17.00	**30.00**
87	Cedar Tree	19.00	**30.00**
88	Flower	21.00	**30.00**
89	Bow & Arrow	23.00	**28.00**
90	Flame	25.00	**28.00**
91	Vessel	25.00	**28.00**
92	G-Clef	25.00	**28.00**
93	Butterfly	25.00	**28.00**
94	Trumpet	25.00	**27.50**
95	Ship	27.50	**27.50**
96	Heart	27.50	**27.50**
97	Sword	27.50	**27.50**
98	Eyeglasses	27.50	**27.50**
99	Star	27.50	**27.50**

E-1373B   SMILE, GOD LOVES YOU   One of the "Original 21"

Retired 1984
Figurine, 4.50"
ac# 875
Boy with Black* Eye

*There is a "Brown Eye" variation which is actually a very pale black eye.

79	No Mark	$7.00	**$110.00**
81	Triangle	12.00	**65.00**
82	Hourglass	15.00	**60.00**
83	Fish	15.00	**55.00**
84	Cross	17.00	**50.00**

E-1373G   JESUS IS THE LIGHT   One of the "Original 21"

Retired 1988
Figurine, 4.50"
ac# 527
Girl with Doll and Candle

79	No Mark	$7.00	**$135.00**
81	Triangle	10.00	**65.00**
82	Hourglass	15.00	**55.00**
83	Fish	15.00	**45.00**
84	Cross	17.00	**40.00**
85	Dove	17.00	**40.00**
86	Olive Branch	17.00	**40.00**
87	Cedar Tree	19.00	**40.00**
88	Flower	21.00	**40.00**

E-1374B   PRAISE THE LORD ANYHOW   One of the "Original 21"

Retired 1982
Figurine, 5.00"
ac# 785
Boy with Dog and Ice Cream Cone

79	No Mark	$8.00	**$120.00**
81	Triangle	11.00	**100.00**
82	Hourglass	17.00	**72.00**

There are variations in the color of the dog's nose (brown or black) & variations in the flavor of ice cream.

E-1374G	MAKE A JOYFUL NOISE One of the "Original 21"				
	Ongoing	79	No Mark	$8.00	**$150.00**
	Figurine, 4.75"	81	Triangle	13.00	**75.00**
	ac# 644	82	Hourglass	17.00	**55.00**
	Girl with Goose	83	Fish	17.00	**42.00**
		84	Cross	19.00	**40.00**
		85	Dove	19.00	**40.00**
		86	Olive Branch	19.00	**38.00**
		87	Cedar Tree	21.00	**38.00**
		88	Flower	23.00	**35.00**
		89	Bow & Arrow	25.00	**35.00**
		90	Flame	27.50	**35.00**
		91	Vessel	27.50	**33.00**
		92	G-Clef	27.50	**33.00**
		93	Butterfly	30.00	**33.00**
		94	Trumpet	30.00	**32.50**
		95	Ship	30.00	**32.50**
		96	Heart	32.50	**32.50**
		97	Sword	32.50	**32.50**
		98	Eyeglasses	32.50	**32.50**
		99	Star	32.50	**32.50**
E-1375A	LOVE LIFTED ME One of the "Original 21"				
	Retired 1993	79	No Mark	$11.00	**$170.00**
	Figurine, 5.00"	81	Triangle	17.00	**110.00**
	ac# 620	82	Hourglass	21.00	**90.00**
	Boy & Girl on Seesaw	83	Fish	21.00	**85.00**
		84	Cross	22.50	**80.00**
		85	Dove	22.50	**80.00**
		86	Olive Branch	22.50	**78.00**
		87	Cedar Tree	25.00	**78.00**
		88	Flower	30.00	**75.00**
		89	Bow & Arrow	33.00	**75.00**
		90	Flame	35.00	**72.00**
		91	Vessel	35.00	**70.00**
		92	G-Clef	35.00	**68.00**
		93	Butterfly	37.50	**65.00**
E-1375B	PRAYER CHANGES THINGS One of the "Original 21"				
	Suspended 1984	79	No Mark	$11.00	**$230.00**
	Figurine, 5.00"	81	Triangle	17.00	**160.00**
	ac# 787	82	Hourglass	21.00	**155.00**
	Boy & Girl with Bluebirds on	83	Fish	21.00	**150.00**
	Shovel	84	Cross	22.50	**140.00**
E-1376	LOVE ONE ANOTHER One of the "Original 21"				
	Ongoing	79	No Mark	$10.00	**$135.00**
	Figurine, 4.75"	81	Triangle	16.00	**72.00**
	ac# 625	82	Hourglass	21.00	**55.00**
	Boy & Girl Sitting on Stump	83	Fish	21.00	**50.00**
		84	Cross	22.50	**48.00**
		85	Dove	22.50	**46.00**
		86	Olive Branch	22.50	**45.00**
		87	Cedar Tree	25.00	**45.00**
		88	Flower	30.00	**45.00**
		89	Bow & Arrow	33.00	**44.00**
		90	Flame	35.00	**42.00**
		91	Vessel	35.00	**40.00**
		92	G-Clef	35.00	**40.00**
		93	Butterfly	37.50	**40.00**
		94	Trumpet	37.50	**40.00**
		95	Ship	40.00	**40.00**
		96	Heart	40.00	**40.00**
		97	Sword	40.00	**40.00**
		98	Eyeglasses	40.00	**40.00**
		99	Star	40.00	**40.00**

E-1377A — HE LEADETH ME One of the "Original 21"

Suspended 1984 / Retired 1998	79	No Mark*	$9.00	**$130.00**
Figurine, 4.75"	81	Triangle	15.00	**105.00**
ac# 403	82	Hourglass	19.00	**95.00**
Boy Leading Lamb	83	Fish	19.00	**90.00**
	84	Cross	20.00	**90.00**

*Classic Variation: The incorrect Inspirational Title, "He Careth For You," is on the understamp decal of some No Mark pieces. This is one of the most difficult to find of all the classic variations. The few known sales are in the $350.00 range. Re-introduced in 1998 with a color change as E-1377R–November 19 on QVC & November 21 at DSRs and Century Circle Retailers. See E-1377R below.

E-1377B — HE CARETH FOR YOU One of the "Original 21"

Suspended 1984	79	No Mark*	$9.00	**$140.00**
Figurine, 4.00"	81	Triangle	15.00	**115.00**
ac# 393	82	Hourglass	19.00	**100.00**
Boy Helping Lamb	83	Fish	19.00	**98.00**
	84	Cross	20.00	**95.00**

*Classic Variation: The incorrect Inspirational Title, "He Leadeth Me" is on the understamp decal of some No Mark pieces. This is a more difficult variation to find than the variation on E-1377A. Known sale at $600.00.

E-1377R — HE LEADETH ME Turn Back The Clock Celebration II

Retired 1998	98	Eyeglasses	$9.00*	**NE**
Figurine, 4.75"				
ac# 403				
Shepherd Leading Lamb				

Brought back with a color change for 11/21/98 Turn Back the Clock Event. Will immediately retire after the event. *SRP is original issue price of $9.00 with the purchase of a full size figurine.

E-1378 — GOD LOVETH A CHEERFUL GIVER One of the "Original 21"

Retired 1981	79	No Mark	$15.00	**$1050.00**
Figurine, 5.15"				
ac# 337				
Girl with Puppies				

E-1379A — LOVE IS KIND One of the "Original 21"

Suspended 1984 / Retired 1998	79	No Mark	$8.00	**$135.00**
Figurine, 4.50"	81	Triangle	13.00	**105.00**
ac# 606	82	Hourglass	17.00	**96.00**
Boy with Turtle	83	Fish	17.00	**88.00**
	84	Cross	19.00	**85.00**

Re-introduced in 1998 as E-1379R. See E-1379R below.

E-1379B — GOD UNDERSTANDS One of the "Original 21"

Suspended 1984	79	No Mark	$8.00	**$125.00**
Figurine, 5.00"	81	Triangle	13.00	**95.00**
ac# 343	82	Hourglass	17.00	**90.00**
Boy with Report Card	83	Fish	17.00	**85.00**
	84	Cross	19.00	**80.00**

E-1379R — LOVE IS KIND Turn Back The Clock Event Celebration Exclusive–6/6/98

Retired 1998	98	Eyeglasses	$8.00	**NE**
Figurine, 4.00"				
ac# 606				
Boy with Turtle				

Piece retired immediately after event. Color change for re-introduction. Precious Moments 20th Anniversary understamp.

E-1380B	O, HOW I LOVE JESUS	One of the "Original 21"				
	Retired 1984		79	No Mark	$8.00	**$145.00**
	Figurine, 4.75"		81	Triangle	13.00	**115.00**
	ac# 729		82	Hourglass	17.00	**98.00**
	Native American Boy		83	Fish	17.00	**95.00**
			84	Cross	19.00	**88.00**

E-1380G	HIS BURDEN IS LIGHT	One of the "Original 21"				
	Retired 1984		79	No Mark	$8.00	**$160.00**
	Figurine, 4.75"		81	Triangle	13.00	**125.00**
	ac# 427		82	Hourglass	17.00	**110.00**
	Native American Girl		83	Fish	17.00	**98.00**
			84	Cross	19.00	**90.00**

E-1381	JESUS IS THE ANSWER	One of the "Original 21"				
	Suspended 1984 / Retired 1996		79	No Mark	$11.50	**$170.00**
	Figurine, 4.50"		81	Triangle	19.00	**145.00**
	ac# 525		82	Hourglass	21.00	**135.00**
	Boy Patching World		83	Fish	21.00	**130.00**
			84	Cross	22.50	**120.00**

E-1381 was re-sculptured and re-introduced in April 1992 as E-1381R.
E-1381R was subsequently retired in 1996. By definition, GREENBOOK
considers E-1381 to be retired as well. See next listing,

E-1381R	JESUS IS THE ANSWER					
	Retired 1996		92	G-Clef	$55.00	**$75.00**
			93	Butterfly	55.00	**68.00**
	Figurine, 4.50"		94	Trumpet	55.00	**65.00**
	ac# 526		95	Ship	55.00	**62.00**
	Boy Holding Stethoscope to		96	Heart	55.00	**60.00**
	a Bandaged World					

In this re-sculptured figurine the globe reflected boundary changes &
new nations that emerged as a result of political changes around the
world.

E-2010	WE HAVE SEEN HIS STAR	One of the "Original 21"				
	Suspended 1984		79	No Mark	$8.00	**$120.00**
	Figurine, 5.50"		81	Triangle	13.00	**140.00**
	ac# 1044		82	Hourglass	17.00	**90.00**
	Boy Holding Lamb		83	Fish	17.00	**85.00**
			84	Cross	19.00	**80.00**

E-2011	COME LET US ADORE HIM	One of the "Original 21"				
	Retired 1981		79	No Mark	$10.00	**$285.00**
	Figurine, 5.00"					
	ac# 220					
	Boy with Manger Baby					

E-2012	JESUS IS BORN	One of the "Original 21"				
	Suspended 1984		79	No Mark	$12.00	**$145.00**
	Figurine, 6.25"		81	Triangle	19.00	**165.00**
	ac# 521		82	Hourglass	22.50	**115.00**
	Boy & Girl Playing Angels		83	Fish	22.50	**100.00**
			84	Cross	25.00	**98.00**

E-2013	UNTO US A CHILD IS BORN	One of the "Original 21"				
	Suspended 1984		79	No Mark	$12.00	**$135.00**
	Figurine, 4.75"		81	Triangle	19.00	**155.00**
	ac# 1029		82	Hourglass	22.50	**95.00**
	Boy & Girl Reading Book		83	Fish	22.50	**92.00**
			84	Cross	22.50	**90.00**

E-2343 JOY TO THE WORLD
Suspended 1988
Ornament, 2.00"
ac# 538
Boy Angel Playing Trumpet

82	Unmarked	$9.00	**$60.00**
84	Cross	10.00	**55.00**
85	Dove	10.00	**50.00**
86	Olive Branch	10.00	**45.00**
87	Cedar Tree	11.00	**40.00**
88	Flower	12.50	**38.00**

E-2344 JOY TO THE WORLD   Set of 2
Suspended 1985
Candle Climber, 2.50"
ac# 538
Boy Angel Playing Trumpet

82	Unmarked	$20.00	**$118.00**
84	Cross	20.00	**98.00**
85	Dove	22.50	**92.00**

E-2345 MAY YOUR CHRISTMAS BE COZY
Suspended 1984
Figurine, 4.25"
ac# 672
Boy in Pajamas with Teddy

82	Hourglass	$23.00	**$85.00**
83	Fish	23.00	**78.00**
84	Cross	25.00	**75.00**

E-2346 LET HEAVEN AND NATURE SING   Tune: Joy To The World
Suspended 1989
Musical, 6.00"
ac# 562
Angel with Friends Carolling

*Unmarked pieces could
have been produced in any of
the years of production.
Consider Hourglass as the
First Mark.

*	Unmarked	$50.00	**$170.00**
82	Hourglass	50.00	**150.00**
83	Fish	55.00	**135.00**
84	Cross	60.00	**130.00**
85	Dove	60.00	**125.00**
86	Olive Branch	60.00	**120.00**
87	Cedar Tree	65.00	**118.00**
88	Flower	70.00	**115.00**
89	Bow & Arrow	75.00	**110.00**

E-2347 LET HEAVEN AND NATURE SING   Series: "Christmas Collection"–2nd
Issue   Individually Numbered
Limited Edition 15,000
Plate, 8.50"
ac# 562
Angel with Friends Carolling

82	Unmarked	$40.00	**$45.00**
	Cross		**40.00**
	Dove		**40.00**
	Olive Branch		**40.00**

E-2348 MAY YOUR CHRISTMAS BE WARM
Suspended 1988
Figurine, 4.75"
ac# 676
Boy Next to a Potbelly Stove

82	Hourglass	$30.00	**$140.00**
83	Fish	30.00	**130.00**
84	Cross	33.00	**125.00**
85	Dove	33.00	**120.00**
86	Olive Branch	33.00	**115.00**
87	Cedar Tree	37.00	**100.00**
88	Flower	37.00	**98.00**

E-2349 TELL ME THE STORY OF JESUS
Suspended 1985
Figurine, 5.00"
ac# 917
Girl with Doll Reading Book

82	Hourglass	$30.00	**$110.00**
83	Fish	30.00	**100.00**
84	Cross	33.00	**98.00**
85	Dove	33.00	**95.00**

E-2350 DROPPING IN FOR CHRISTMAS
Suspended 1984
Figurine, 5.15"
ac# 250
Boy Ice Skater in Santa Cap

82	Hourglass	$18.00	**$85.00**
83	Fish	18.00	**80.00**
84	Cross	18.00	**75.00**

E-2351	HOLY SMOKES				
	Retired 1987	82	Hourglass	$27.00	**$135.00**
	Figurine, 5.75"	83	Fish	27.00	**120.00**
	ac# 438	84	Cross	30.00	**115.00**
	Two Angels with Candles	85	Dove	30.00	**110.00**
		86	Olive Branch	30.00	**105.00**
		87	Cedar Tree	33.50	**100.00**

E-2352	O COME ALL YE FAITHFUL	Tune: O Come All Ye Faithful			
	Suspended 1984	82	Unmarked	$45.00	**$180.00**
	Musical, 7.25"	82	Hourglass	45.00	**150.00**
	ac# 727	83	Fish	45.00	**145.00**
	Boy Carolling by Lamp Post	84	Cross	50.00	**140.00**

E-2353	O COME ALL YE FAITHFUL				
	Retired 1986	82	Hourglass	$27.50	**$105.00**
	Figurine, 6.25"	83	Fish	27.50	**85.00**
	ac# 727	84	Cross	30.00	**82.00**
	Boy Carolling by Lamp Post	85	Dove	30.00	**80.00**
		86	Olive Branch	30.00	**78.00**

E-2355	I'LL PLAY MY DRUM FOR HIM	Tune: Little Drummer Boy			
	Suspended 1984	82	Hourglass	$45.00	**$205.00**
	Musical, 6.75"	83	Fish	45.00	**192.00**
	ac# 485	84	Cross	50.00	**190.00**
	Drummer Boy at Manger				

E-2356	I'LL PLAY MY DRUM FOR HIM				
	Suspended 1985	82	Hourglass	$30.00	**$115.00**
	Figurine, 5.50"	83	Fish	30.00	**82.00**
	ac# 485	84	Cross	33.00	**75.00**
	Drummer Boy at Manger	85	Dove	33.00	**70.00**

E-2357	I'LL PLAY MY DRUM FOR HIM	Series: "Joy Of Christmas"–1st Issue			
	Dated Annual 1982	82	Unmarked	$40.00	**$72.00**
	Plate, 8.50"				
	ac# 485				
	Drummer Boy at Manger				

E-2358	I'LL PLAY MY DRUM FOR HIM				
	Dated* Annual 1982	82	Unmarked	$17.00	**$60.00**
	Bell, 5.75"				
	ac# 485				
	Drummer Boy				

*Prototypes were dated, actual production wasn't.

E-2359	I'LL PLAY MY DRUM FOR HIM				
	Dated Annual 1982	82	Hourglass	$9.00	**$86.00**
	Ornament, 3.25"				
	ac# 485				
	Drummer Boy				

E-2360 I'LL PLAY MY DRUM FOR HIM   Nativity Addition

Ongoing
Figurine, 5.00"
ac# 485
Drummer Boy

Year	Mark	Price	GBTru
82	Hourglass	$16.00	**$48.00**
83	Fish	16.00	**40.00**
84	Cross	17.00	**38.00**
85	Dove	17.00	**35.00**
86	Olive Branch	17.00	**32.00**
87	Cedar Tree	19.00	**30.00**
88	Flower	19.00	**30.00**
89	Bow & Arrow	23.00	**28.00**
90	Flame	25.00	**28.00**
91	Vessel	25.00	**28.00**
92	G-Clef	25.00	**28.00**
93	Butterfly	25.00	**27.50**
94	Trumpet	25.00	**27.50**
95	Ship	25.00	**27.50**
96	Heart	27.50	**27.50**
97	Sword	27.50	**27.50**
98	Eyeglasses	27.50	**27.50**
99	Star	27.50	**27.50**

E-2361 CHRISTMAS JOY FROM HEAD TO TOE

Suspended 1986
Figurine, 5.50"
ac# 204
Girl with Stocking

Year	Mark	Price	GBTru
82	Hourglass	$25.00	**$80.00**
83	Fish	25.00	**72.00**
84	Cross	27.50	**70.00**
85	Dove	27.50	**68.00**
86	Olive Branch	27.50	**65.00**

E-2362 BABY'S FIRST CHRISTMAS

Suspended 1988
Ornament, 3.50"
ac# 89
Baby Girl in Christmas
Stocking

Year	Mark	Price	GBTru
82	Unmarked*	$9.00	**$50.00**
84	Cross	10.00	**45.00**
85	Dove	10.00	**42.00**
86	Olive Branch	10.00	**40.00**
87	Cedar Tree	10.00	**38.00**
88	Flower	11.00	**35.00**

*Classic Variation: Unmarked pieces exist in four variations: 1) Straight hair and no caption, 2) Curly hair and no caption, 3) Straight hair with the caption, "Baby's First Christmas," and, 4) Curly hair with the caption, "Baby's First Christmas." Subsequent pieces (Cross through Flower) were curly hair with the caption. The straight hair, with or without the caption, is considered the variation. The GBTru$ for an Unmarked "Straight Hair" ornament is $65.00. See page 414.

E-2363 CAMEL   Nativity Addition

Ongoing
Figurine, 4.00"
ac# 186
Camel

Year	Mark	Price	GBTru
82	Hourglass	$20.00	**$50.00**
83	Fish	20.00	**42.00**
84	Cross	22.50	**40.00**
85	Dove	22.50	**38.00**
86	Olive Branch	22.50	**35.00**
87	Cedar Tree	25.00	**35.00**
88	Flower	25.00	**35.00**
89	Bow & Arrow	30.00	**33.00**
90	Flame	32.50	**33.00**
91	Vessel	32.50	**33.00**
92	G-Clef	32.50	**33.00**
93	Butterfly	32.50	**32.50**
94	Trumpet	32.50	**32.50**
95	Ship	32.50	**32.50**
96	Heart	32.50	**32.50**
97	Sword	32.50	**32.50**
98	Eyeglasses	32.50	**32.50**
99	Star	32.50	**32.50**

E-2364	GOAT Nativity Addition	82	Unmarked	$10.00	**$65.00**
	Suspended 1989	83	Fish	10.00	**62.00**
	Figurine, 3.00"	84	Cross	11.00	**60.00**
	ac# 305	85	Dove	11.00	**58.00**
	Goat	86	Olive Branch	11.00	**55.00**
		87	Cedar Tree	12.00	**55.00**
		88	Flower	12.00	**50.00**
		89	Bow & Arrow	15.00	**48.00**

E-2365	THE FIRST NOEL Nativity Addition				
	Suspended 1984	82	Unmarked	$16.00	**$80.00**
	Figurine, 4.50"	82	Hourglass	16.00	**70.00**
	ac# 928	83	Fish	16.00	**65.00**
	Boy Angel with Candle	84	Cross	17.00	**60.00**

E-2366	THE FIRST NOEL Nativity Addition				
	Suspended 1984	82	Unmarked	$16.00	**$80.00**
	Figurine, 4.50"	82	Hourglass	16.00	**70.00**
	ac# 929	83	Fish	16.00	**65.00**
	Girl Angel Praying	84	Cross	17.00	**60.00**

E-2367	THE FIRST NOEL				
	Suspended 1984	82	Hourglass	$9.00	**$70.00**
	Ornament, 3.10"	83	Fish	9.00	**65.00**
	ac# 928	84	Cross	10.00	**62.00**
	Boy Angel with Candle				

E-2368	THE FIRST NOEL				
	Retired 1984	82	Hourglass	$9.00	**$70.00**
	Ornament, 3.00"	83	Fish	9.00	**50.00**
	ac# 929	84	Cross	10.00	**30.00**
	Girl Angel Praying				

E-2369	DROPPING IN FOR CHRISTMAS				
	Retired 1986	82	Unmarked	$9.00	**$60.00**
	Ornament, 3.50"	82	Hourglass	9.00	**52.00**
	ac# 250	83	Fish	9.00	**50.00**
	Boy Ice Skater in Santa Cap	84	Cross	10.00	**48.00**
		85	Dove	10.00	**47.00**
		86	Olive Branch	10.00	**42.00**

E-2371	UNICORN				
	Retired 1988	82	Unmarked	$10.00	**$60.00**
	Ornament, 3.00"	84	Cross	10.00	**52.00**
	ac# 1028	85	Dove	11.00	**50.00**
	Unicorn	86	Olive Branch	11.00	**48.00**
		87	Cedar Tree	12.00	**48.00**
		88	Flower	13.00	**45.00**

E-2372	BABY'S FIRST CHRISTMAS				
	Suspended 1985	82	Unmarked*	$9.00	**$40.00**
	Ornament, 2.75"	84	Cross	10.00	**39.00**
	ac# 90	85	Dove	10.00	**38.00**
	Boy Holding Block				

*Exists with and without caption, "Baby's First Christmas," in Unmarked version. Caption piece is rarer, add $10.00 to GBTru$.

E-2374	BUNDLES OF JOY				
	Retired 1993	82	Hourglass	$27.50	**$125.00**
	Figurine, 6.75"	83	Fish	27.50	**95.00**
	ac# 180	84	Cross	30.00	**92.00**
	Girl with Presents	85	Dove	30.00	**90.00**
		86	Olive Branch	30.00	**88.00**
		87	Cedar Tree	33.50	**85.00**
		88	Flower	33.50	**85.00**
		89	Bow & Arrow	40.00	**82.00**
		90	Flame	45.00	**82.00**
		91	Vessel	45.00	**80.00**
		92	G-Clef	45.00	**78.00**
		93	Butterfly	45.00	**75.00**

E-2375	DROPPING OVER FOR CHRISTMAS				
	Retired 1991	82	Hourglass	$30.00	**$125.00**
	Figurine, 5.15"	83	Fish	30.00	**95.00**
	ac# 252	84	Cross	33.00	**90.00**
	Girl with Pie	85	Dove	33.00	**90.00**
		86	Olive Branch	33.00	**85.00**
		87	Cedar Tree	37.00	**85.00**
		88	Flower	37.00	**82.00**
		89	Bow & Arrow	42.50	**82.00**
		90	Flame	45.00	**80.00**
		91	Vessel	45.00	**78.00**

E-2376	DROPPING OVER FOR CHRISTMAS				
	Retired 1985	82	Hourglass	$9.00	**$55.00**
	Ornament, 3.00"	83	Fish	9.00	**45.00**
	ac# 252	84	Cross	10.00	**40.00**
	Girl with Pie	85	Dove	10.00	**38.00**

E-2377	OUR FIRST CHRISTMAS TOGETHER				
	Suspended 1985	82	Hourglass	$35.00	**$100.00**
	Figurine, 5.15"	83	Fish	35.00	**90.00**
	ac# 750	84	Cross	37.50	**88.00**
	Girl Knitting Tie for Boy	85	Dove	37.50	**82.00**

E-2378	OUR FIRST CHRISTMAS TOGETHER				
	Suspended 1985	82	Unmarked	$30.00	**$40.00**
	Plate, 7.00"	84	Cross	30.00	**35.00**
	ac# 750	85	Dove	30.00	**30.00**
	Girl Knitting Tie for Boy				

E-2381	MOUSE WITH CHEESE				
	Suspended 1984	82	Hourglass	$9.00	**$120.00**
	Ornament, 2.50"	83	Fish	9.00	**115.00**
	ac# 699	84	Cross	10.00	**110.00**
	Mouse with Cheese				

E-2385	OUR FIRST CHRISTMAS TOGETHER				
	Suspended 1991	82	Hourglass	$10.00	**$52.00**
	Ornament, 4.00"	83	Fish	10.00	**44.00**
	ac# 942	84	Cross	10.00	**42.00**
	Bride and Groom	85	Dove	11.00	**38.00**
		86	Olive Branch	11.00	**36.00**
		87	Cedar Tree	12.00	**35.00**
		88	Flower	13.00	**34.00**
		89	Bow & Arrow	15.00	**30.00**
		90	Flame	15.00	**28.00**
		91	Vessel	15.00	**25.00**

E-2386	CAMEL, DONKEY, AND COW	Set of 3			
Suspended 1984	*	Unmarked	$25.00	**$95.00**
Ornament, 2.25"	82	Hourglass	25.00	**84.00**
ac# 187	83	Fish	25.00	**80.00**
Camel	84	Cross	27.50	**78.00**

*Unmarked pieces could have been produced in any of the years of production. Mixed sets of Unmarked/Hourglass are common. Take lower GBTru$.

E-2387	HOUSE SET AND PALM TREE	Mini Nativity Addition	Set of 3		
Ongoing	82	Hourglass*	$45.00	**$125.00**
Figurine, 3.00"	83	Fish	45.00	**95.00**
ac# 449	84	Cross	50.00	**90.00**
Mini Houses and Palm Tree	85	Dove	50.00	**85.00**
	86	Olive Branch	50.00	**82.00**
*Some Hourglass sets were	87	Cedar Tree	55.00	**82.00**
shipped with the pink house	88	Flower	55.00	**80.00**
having No Mark. Add $50.00	89	Bow & Arrow	65.00	**80.00**
to GBTru$.	90	Flame	70.00	**80.00**
	91	Vessel	70.00	**78.00**
	92	G-Clef	70.00	**78.00**
	93	Butterfly	70.00	**78.00**
	94	Trumpet	75.00	**75.00**
	95	Ship	75.00	**75.00**
	96	Heart	75.00	**75.00**
	97	Sword	75.00	**75.00**
	98	Eyeglasses	75.00	**75.00**
	99	Star	75.00	**75.00**

E-2395	COME LET US ADORE HIM	Mini Nativity	Set of 11		
Ongoing	82	Hourglass*	$80.00	**$170.00**
Figurine, 3.50"	83	Fish	80.00	**150.00**
ac# 221	84	Cross	90.00	**148.00**
Mini Nativity Set	85	Dove	90.00	**145.00**
	86	Olive Branch	90.00	**145.00**
*Classic Variation: Termed	87	Cedar Tree	90.00	**142.00**
the "Turban Nativity," the	88	Flower	95.00	**142.00**
shepherd holding a lamb was	89	Bow & Arrow	110.00	**140.00**
replaced in some Hourglass	90	Flame	120.00	**140.00**
sets with a shepherd wearing	91	Vessel	120.00	**140.00**
a turban. "Turban Boy"	92	G-Clef	120.00	**140.00**
shepherds were also shipped	93	Butterfly	120.00	**140.00**
individually to retailers as	94	Trumpet	125.00	**140.00**
replacement pieces, so	95	Ship	130.00	**140.00**
collectors were sometimes	96	Heart	140.00	**140.00**
able to add the "Turban Boy"	97	Sword	140.00	**140.00**
as a twelfth piece to this	98	Eyeglasses	140.00	**140.00**
eleven piece mini Nativity	99	Star	140.00	**140.00**

Set. The GBTru$ for the "Turban Nativity" is $225.00. The GBTru$ for the individual "Turban Boy" piece is $90.00 (Add $90 to the GBTru$ of the 11 piece set if a "Turban Boy"" has been added as a 12th piece.) See page 415.

E-2800	COME LET US ADORE HIM	Nativity	Set of 9		
Discontinued	80	No Mark	$60.00	**$185.00**
Figurine, 4.75"	81	Triangle	70.00	**160.00**
ac# 221	82	Hourglass	80.00	**145.00**
Nativity Set	83	Fish	80.00	**140.00**
	84	Cross	90.00	**135.00**
	85	Dove	90.00	**130.00**

This set was re-sculptured, the new version is #104000. Mixed sets of Triangle/Hourglass & Hourglass/Fish are common. Take lower GBTru$.

E-2801	JESUS IS BORN			
Suspended 1984	80	No Mark	$37.50	**$350.00**
Figurine, 5.75"	81	Triangle	45.00	**325.00**
ac# 522	82	Hourglass	50.00	**300.00**
Angels in Chariot	83	Fish	50.00	**295.00**
	84	Cross	55.00	**290.00**

E-2802	CHRISTMAS IS A TIME TO SHARE			
Suspended 1984	80	No Mark	$20.00	**$110.00**
Figurine, 5.00"	81	Triangle	22.50	**85.00**
ac# 202	82	Hourglass	25.00	**80.00**
Boy Giving Toy Lamb to	83	Fish	25.00	**78.00**
Baby Jesus	84	Cross	27.50	**75.00**
	*	Dove		**70.00**

*Piece was Suspended in 1984 yet exists in the 1985 Dove Annual Production Symbol.

E-2803	CROWN HIM LORD OF ALL			
Suspended 1984	80	No Mark	$20.00	**$105.00**
Figurine, 4.50"	81	Triangle	22.50	**90.00**
ac# 230	82	Hourglass	25.00	**85.00**
Boy Holding Crown at	83	Fish	25.00	**80.00**
Manger	84	Cross	27.50	**75.00**
	*	Dove		**74.00**

*Piece was Suspended in 1984 yet exists in the 1985 Dove Annual Production Symbol.

E-2804	PEACE ON EARTH			
Suspended 1984	80	No Mark	$20.00	**$155.00**
Figurine, 6.00"	81	Triangle	22.50	**138.00**
ac# 769	82	Hourglass	25.00	**132.00**
Boy Angel on Globe with	83	Fish	25.00	**125.00**
Teddy	84	Cross	27.50	**118.00**

E-2805	WISHING YOU A SEASON FILLED WITH JOY			
Retired 1985	80	No Mark	$20.00	**$115.00**
Figurine, 4.25"	81	Triangle	22.50	**105.00**
ac# 1078	82	Hourglass	25.00	**95.00**
Boy in Santa Cap with Dog	83	Fish	25.00	**85.00**
	84	Cross	27.50	**75.00**
No Mark thru Cross have only	85	Dove	27.50	**65.00**
one dog's eye painted. Dove			
exists w/both one & two eyes			
painted.			

E-2806	CHRISTMAS IS A TIME TO SHARE	Tune: Away In A Manger		
Retired 1984	80	No Mark	$35.00	**$180.00**
Musical, 6.00"	81	Triangle	35.00	**162.00**
ac# 202	82	Hourglass	40.00	**160.00**
Boy Giving Toy Lamb to	83	Fish	45.00	**158.00**
Baby Jesus	84	Cross	50.00	**155.00**

E-2807	CROWN HIM LORD OF ALL	Tune: O Come All Ye Faithful		
Suspended 1984	80	No Mark	$35.00	**$130.00**
Musical, 5.50"	81	Triangle	40.00	**110.00**
ac# 230	82	Hourglass	45.00	**100.00**
Boy Holding Crown at	83	Fish	45.00	**96.00**
Manger	84	Cross	50.00	**92.00**

E-2808	UNTO US A CHILD IS BORN	Tune: Jesus Loves Me		
Suspended 1984	80	No Mark	$35.00	**$140.00**
Musical, 5.75"	81	Triangle	40.00	**115.00**
ac# 1029	82	Hourglass	45.00	**105.00**
Boy & Girl Reading Book	83	Fish	45.00	**100.00**
	84	Cross	50.00	**95.00**

E-2809	JESUS IS BORN Tune: Hark! The Herald Angels Sing				
	Suspended 1985	80	No Mark	$35.00	**$170.00**
	Musical, 7.00"	81	Triangle	45.00	**150.00**
	ac# 521	82	Hourglass	45.00	**145.00**
	Boy & Girl Playing Angels	83	Fish	45.00	**140.00**
		84	Cross	50.00	**135.00**
		85	Dove	50.00	**130.00**

E-2810	COME LET US ADORE HIM Tune: Joy To The World				
	Suspended 1993	80	No Mark	$45.00	**$155.00**
	Musical, 6.50"	81	Triangle	45.00	**130.00**
	ac# 221	82	Hourglass	60.00	**125.00**
	Nativity Scene	83	Fish	60.00	**120.00**
		84	Cross	65.00	**115.00**
		85	Dove	65.00	**112.00**
		86	Olive Branch	65.00	**110.00**
		87	Cedar Tree	70.00	**110.00**
		88	Flower	70.00	**110.00**
		89	Bow & Arrow	80.00	**110.00**
		90	Flame	85.00	**100.00**
		91	Vessel	85.00	**100.00**
		92	G-Clef	85.00	**100.00**
		93	Butterfly	100.00	**100.00**

E-2821	YOU HAVE TOUCHED SO MANY HEARTS				
	Suspended 1996	84	Fish	$25.00	**$75.00**
	Figurine, 5.50"	84	Cross	25.00	**65.00**
	ac# 1130	85	Dove	25.00	**62.00**
	Girl with String of Hearts	86	Olive Branch	25.00	**55.00**
		87	Cedar Tree	27.50	**52.00**
		88	Flower	30.00	**50.00**
		89	Bow & Arrow	33.00	**48.00**
		90	Flame	35.00	**47.00**
		91	Vessel	35.00	**46.00**
		92	G-Clef	35.00	**45.00**
		93	Butterfly	35.00	**44.00**
		94	Trumpet	37.50	**42.00**
		95	Ship	37.50	**41.00**
		96	Heart	37.50	**40.00**

E-2822	THIS IS YOUR DAY TO SHINE				
	Retired 1988	84	Fish	$37.50	**$155.00**
	Figurine, 6.00"	84	Cross	37.50	**110.00**
	ac# 986	85	Dove	37.50	**98.00**
	Girl Polishing Table	86	Olive Branch	37.50	**95.00**
		87	Cedar Tree	40.00	**90.00**
		88	Flower	40.00	**89.00**

E-2823	TO GOD BE THE GLORY				
	Suspended 1987	84	Fish	$40.00	**$120.00**
	Figurine, 5.50"	84	Cross	40.00	**90.00**
	ac# 1009	85	Dove	40.00	**85.00**
	Boy Holding Picture Frame	86	Olive Branch	40.00	**82.00**
		87	Cedar Tree	45.00	**80.00**

E-2824 — TO A VERY SPECIAL MOM

Ongoing
Figurine, 5.75"
ac# 1004
Girl with Floppy Hat

Year	Mark	Price	Value
84	Cross	$27.50	**$62.00**
85	Dove	27.50	**52.00**
86	Olive Branch	27.50	**50.00**
87	Cedar Tree	30.00	**48.00**
88	Flower	32.50	**45.00**
89	Bow & Arrow	35.00	**42.00**
90	Flame	37.50	**40.00**
91	Vessel	37.50	**40.00**
92	G-Clef	37.50	**40.00**
93	Butterfly	37.50	**40.00**
94	Trumpet	37.50	**40.00**
95	Ship	37.50	**40.00**
96	Heart	40.00	**40.00**
97	Sword	40.00	**40.00**
98	Eyeglasses	40.00	**40.00**
99	Star	40.00	**40.00**

E-2825 — TO A VERY SPECIAL SISTER

Ongoing
Figurine, 5.50"
ac# 1006
Girl Putting Bows in Sister's Hair

Year	Mark	Price	Value
84	Cross	$37.50	**$75.00**
85	Dove	37.50	**60.00**
86	Olive Branch	37.50	**58.00**
87	Cedar Tree	40.00	**55.00**
88	Flower	40.00	**55.00**
89	Bow & Arrow	45.00	**52.00**
90	Flame	50.00	**52.00**
91	Vessel	50.00	**50.00**
92	G-Clef	50.00	**50.00**
93	Butterfly	50.00	**50.00**
94	Trumpet	50.00	**50.00**
95	Ship	50.00	**50.00**
96	Heart	50.00	**50.00**
97	Sword	50.00	**50.00**
98	Eyeglasses	50.00	**50.00**
99	Star	50.00	**50.00**

E-2826 — MAY YOUR BIRTHDAY BE A BLESSING

Suspended 1986
Figurine, 5.25"
ac# 665
Girl at Table with Dolls

Year	Mark	Price	Value
84	Fish	$37.50	**$112.00**
84	Cross	37.50	**95.00**
85	Dove	37.50	**85.00**
86	Olive Branch	37.50	**82.00**

E-2827 — I GET A KICK OUT OF YOU

Suspended 1986
Figurine, 4.75"
ac# 463
Girl with Bucket on Head

Year	Mark	Price	Value
84	Fish	$50.00	**$205.00**
84	Cross	50.00	**195.00**
85	Dove	50.00	**185.00**
86	Olive Branch	50.00	**175.00**

E-2828 PRECIOUS MEMORIES

Ongoing
Figurine, 5.50"
ac# 789
Girl at Trunk with Wedding
Gown

Year	Mark	Issue Price	Current Value
84	Fish	$45.00	**$115.00**
84	Cross	45.00	**82.00**
85	Dove	45.00	**75.00**
86	Olive Branch	45.00	**68.00**
87	Cedar Tree	50.00	**65.00**
88	Flower	50.00	**65.00**
89	Bow & Arrow	55.00	**65.00**
90	Flame	60.00	**65.00**
91	Vessel	60.00	**65.00**
92	G-Clef	60.00	**65.00**
93	Butterfly	65.00	**65.00**
94	Trumpet	65.00	**65.00**
95	Ship	65.00	**65.00**
96	Heart	65.00	**65.00**
97	Sword	65.00	**65.00**
98	Eyeglasses	65.00	**65.00**
99	Star	65.00	**65.00**

E-2829 I'M SENDING YOU A WHITE CHRISTMAS

Ongoing
Figurine, 5.00"
ac# 495
Girl Mailing Snowball

Year	Mark	Issue Price	Current Value
84	Cross	$37.50	**$80.00**
85	Dove	37.50	**65.00**
86	Olive Branch	37.50	**60.00**
87	Cedar Tree	40.00	**60.00**
88	Flower	45.00	**60.00**
89	Bow & Arrow	47.50	**60.00**
90	Flame	50.00	**60.00**
91	Vessel	50.00	**60.00**
92	G-Clef	50.00	**60.00**
93	Butterfly	50.00	**60.00**
94	Trumpet	50.00	**60.00**
95	Ship	55.00	**60.00**
96	Heart	60.00	**60.00**
97	Sword	60.00	**60.00**
98	Eyeglasses	60.00	**60.00**
99	Star	60.00	**60.00**

E-2831 BRIDESMAID   Series: "Bridal"–1st Issue

Ongoing
Figurine, 4.25"
ac# 172
Bridesmaid

Year	Mark	Issue Price	Current Value
84	Cross	$13.50	**$35.00**
85	Dove	13.50	**29.00**
86	Olive Branch	13.50	**28.00**
87	Cedar Tree	15.00	**27.00**
88	Flower	16.00	**26.00**
89	Bow & Arrrow	17.50	**25.00**
90	Flame	19.50	**25.00**
91	Vessel	19.50	**25.00**
92	G-Clef	19.50	**25.00**
93	Butterfly	20.00	**25.00**
94	Trumpet	22.50	**25.00**
95	Ship	22.50	**25.00**
96	Heart	25.00	**25.00**
97	Sword	25.00	**25.00**
98	Eyeglasses	25.00	**25.00**
99	Star	25.00	**25.00**

E-2832 GOD BLESS THE BRIDE

Ongoing	84	Cross	$35.00	**$60.00**
Figurine, 5.50"	85	Dove	35.00	**55.00**
ac# 312	86	Olive Branch	35.00	**52.00**
Bride with Flower Girl	87	Cedar Tree	38.50	**52.00**
	88	Flower	40.00	**50.00**
	89	Bow & Arrow	45.00	**50.00**
	90	Flame	50.00	**50.00**
	91	Vessel	50.00	**50.00**
	92	G-Clef	50.00	**50.00**
	93	Butterfly	50.00	**50.00**
	94	Trumpet	50.00	**50.00**
	95	Ship	50.00	**50.00**
	96	Heart	50.00	**50.00**
	97	Sword	50.00	**50.00**
	98	Eyeglasses	50.00	**50.00**
	99	Star	50.00	**50.00**

E-2833 RINGBEARER   Series: "Bridal"–4th Issue

Ongoing	85	Dove	$11.00	**$28.00**
Figurine, 3.00"	86	Olive Branch	11.00	**22.00**
ac# 810	87	Cedar Tree	12.00	**20.00**
Ringbearer	88	Flower	13.00	**18.00**
	89	Bow & Arrow	15.00	**18.00**
	90	Flame	16.50	**18.00**
	91	Vessel	16.50	**18.00**
	92	G-Clef	16.50	**18.00**
	93	Butterfly	16.50	**18.00**
	94	Trumpet	17.00	**17.50**
	95	Ship	17.00	**17.50**
	96	Heart	17.50	**17.50**
	97	Sword	17.50	**17.50**
	98	Eyeglasses	17.50	**17.50**
	99	Star	17.50	**17.50**

E-2834 SHARING OUR JOY TOGETHER

Suspended 1991	86	Olive Branch	$31.00	**$65.00**
Figurine, 5.50"	87	Cedar Tree	35.00	**55.00**
ac# 851	88	Flower	36.00	**52.00**
Bridesmaid	89	Bow & Arrow	38.50	**50.00**
	90	Flame	40.00	**48.00**
	91	Vessel	40.00	**45.00**

E-2835 FLOWER GIRL   Series: "Bridal"–3rd Issue

Ongoing	85	Dove	$11.00	**$32.00**
Figurine, 3.00"	86	Olive Branch	11.00	**25.00**
ac# 279	87	Cedar Tree	12.00	**24.00**
Flower Girl	88	Flower	13.00	**22.00**
	89	Bow & Arrow	15.00	**22.00**
	90	Flame	16.50	**20.00**
	91	Vessel	16.50	**20.00**
	92	G-Clef	16.50	**18.00**
	93	Butterfly	16.50	**18.00**
	94	Trumpet	17.00	**18.00**
	95	Ship	17.00	**17.50**
	96	Heart	17.50	**17.50**
	97	Sword	17.50	**17.50**
	98	Eyeglasses	17.50	**17.50**
	99	Star	17.50	**17.50**

E-2836 GROOMSMAN   Series: "Bridal"–2nd Issue

Ongoing

Figurine, 4.25"

ac# 361

Groomsman with Frog

84	Cross	$13.50	**$35.00**
85	Dove	13.50	**29.00**
86	Olive Branch	13.50	**28.00**
87	Cedar Tree	13.50	**27.00**
88	Flower	16.00	**26.00**
89	Bow & Arrow	17.50	**25.00**
90	Flame	19.50	**25.00**
91	Vessel	19.50	**25.00**
92	G-Clef	19.50	**25.00**
93	Butterfly	20.00	**25.00**
94	Trumpet	22.50	**25.00**
95	Ship	22.50	**25.00**
96	Heart	25.00	**25.00**
97	Sword	25.00	**25.00**
98	Eyeglasses	25.00	**25.00**
99	Star	25.00	**25.00**

E-2837 GROOM   Series: "Bridal"–6th Issue

Ongoing

Figurine, 4.50"

ac# 360

Groom

*Termed the "No Hands Groom," during the first year of production (Olive Branch) this piece was produced with no hands. The mold was changed for the subsequent years (Cedar Tree to present) to show the boy's hands. See page 415.

86	Olive Branch*	$15.00	**$38.00**
87	Cedar Tree	17.00	**29.00**
88	Flower	18.00	**28.00**
89	Bow & Arrow	20.00	**27.00**
90	Flame	22.50	**26.00**
91	Vessel	22.50	**25.00**
92	G-Clef	22.50	**25.00**
93	Butterfly	25.00	**25.00**
94	Trumpet	25.00	**25.00**
95	Ship	25.00	**25.00**
96	Heart	25.00	**25.00**
97	Sword	25.00	**25.00**
98	Eyeglasses	25.00	**25.00**
99	Star	25.00	**25.00**

E-2838 THIS IS THE DAY WHICH THE LORD HATH MADE   Series: "Bridal"–8th & Final Issue

Annual 1987

Figurine, 5.25"

ac# 985

Complete Wedding Party

87	Cedar Tree	$175.00	**$225.00**

E-2840 BABY'S FIRST STEP   Series: "Baby's First"–1st Issue

Suspended 1988

Figurine, 5.25"

ac# 121

Angel Carrying Baby

84	Cross	$35.00	**$105.00**
85	Dove	35.00	**95.00**
86	Olive Branch	35.00	**90.00**
87	Cedar Tree	38.50	**88.00**
88	Flower	40.00	**85.00**

E-2841 BABY'S FIRST PICTURE   Series: "Baby's First"–2nd Issue

Retired 1986

Figurine, 5.00"

ac# 120

Angel Taking Baby's Picture

84	Cross	$45.00	**$175.00**
85	Dove	45.00	**165.00**
86	Olive Branch	45.00	**155.00**

E-2845 JUNIOR BRIDESMAID   Series: "Bridal"–5th Issue

Ongoing
Figurine, 3.75"
ac# 548
Junior Bridesmaid

86	Olive Branch	$12.50	**$28.00**
87	Cedar Tree	14.00	**25.00**
88	Flower	15.00	**24.00**
89	Bow & Arrow	17.00	**23.00**
90	Flame	18.50	**23.00**
91	Vessel	18.50	**23.00**
92	G-Clef	18.50	**23.00**
93	Butterfly	18.50	**23.00**
94	Trumpet	20.00	**22.50**
95	Ship	20.00	**22.50**
96	Heart	22.50	**22.50**
97	Sword	22.50	**22.50**
98	Eyeglasses	22.50	**22.50**
99	Star	22.50	**22.50**

E-2846 BRIDE   Series: "Bridal"–7th Issue

Ongoing
Figurine, 4.75"
ac# 171
Bride

87	Cedar Tree	$18.00	**$30.00**
88	Flower	22.50	**26.00**
89	Bow & Arrow	25.00	**25.00**
90	Flame	25.00	**25.00**
91	Vessel	25.00	**25.00**
92	G-Clef	25.00	**25.00**
93	Butterfly	25.00	**25.00**
94	Trumpet	25.00	**25.00**
95	Ship	25.00	**25.00**
96	Heart	25.00	**25.00**
97	Sword	25.00	**25.00**
98	Eyeglasses	25.00	**25.00**
99	Star	25.00	**25.00**

E-2847 LOVE IS KIND   Series: "Inspired Thoughts"–4th Issue

Individually Numbered
Limited Edition 15,000
Plate, 8.50"
ac# 607
Boy Pushing Girl on Swing

84	Unmarked	$40.00	**$45.00**
	Cross		**40.00**

E-2848 LOVING THY NEIGHBOR   Series: "Mother's Love"–4th Issue

Individually Numbered
Limited Edition 15,000
Plate, 8.50"
ac# 637
Mother Wrapping Bread

84	Cross	$40.00	**$40.00**

E-2850 MOTHER SEW DEAR

Retired 1985
Doll, 16.00"
ac# 698
Mother Needlepointing

84	Unmarked	$350.00	**$350.00**
84	Cross	350.00	**350.00**
85	Dove	350.00	**350.00**

E-2851 KRISTY

Suspended 1989
Doll, 12.00"
ac# 557
Baby Collector Doll

84	Cross	$150.00	**$175.00**
85	Dove	150.00	**170.00**
86	Olive Branch	150.00	**170.00**
87	Cedar Tree	160.00	**170.00**
88	Flower	160.00	**170.00**
89	Bow & Arrow	170.00	**170.00**

E-2852 | BABY FIGURINES Set of 6 / (Divide by 6 for an "each" value)

	Set Discontinued 1987 /	84	Cross	$72.00	**$228.00**
	Pieces Suspended 1996	85	Dove	72.00	**198.00**
	Figurine, 3.50"	86	Olive Branch	72.00	**192.00**
	ac# 86	87	Cedar Tree	81.00	**180.00**
	Baby Figurines				

In 1987, individual Enesco Item #s were assigned for each figurine in this set of 6. See the following E-2852/A, /B, /C, /D, /E and /F. Note Cedar Tree pieces exist both as a set and as individual pieces with the A through F suffix.

E-2852/A | BABY FIGURINE

Suspended 1996
Figurine, 3.75"
ac# 80
Baby Boy Standing

87	Cedar Tree	$13.50	**$32.00**
88	Flower	14.00	**31.00**
89	Bow & Arrow	15.00	**31.00**
90	Flame	16.50	**30.00**
91	Vessel	16.50	**30.00**
92	G-Clef	16.50	**28.00**
93	Butterfly	16.50	**28.00**
94	Trumpet	17.50	**27.00**
95	Ship	17.50	**27.00**
96	Heart	18.50	**27.00**

E-2852/B | BABY FIGURINE

Suspended 1996
Figurine, 3.75"
ac# 81
Baby Girl with Bow in Hair

87	Cedar Tree	$13.50	**$33.00**
88	Flower	14.00	**31.00**
89	Bow & Arrow	15.00	**31.00**
90	Flame	16.50	**30.00**
91	Vessel	16.50	**30.00**
92	G-Clef	16.50	**28.00**
93	Butterfly	16.50	**28.00**
94	Trumpet	17.50	**27.00**
95	Ship	17.50	**27.00**
96	Heart	18.50	**27.00**

E-2852/C | BABY FIGURINE

Suspended 1996
Figurine, 3.00"
ac# 82
Baby Boy Sitting

87	Cedar Tree	$13.50	**$32.00**
88	Flower	14.00	**31.00**
89	Bow & Arrow	15.00	**31.00**
90	Flame	16.50	**30.00**
91	Vessel	16.50	**30.00**
92	G-Clef	16.50	**28.00**
93	Butterfly	16.50	**28.00**
94	Trumpet	17.50	**27.00**
95	Ship	17.50	**27.00**
96	Heart	18.50	**27.00**

E-2852/D | BABY FIGURINE

Suspended 1996
Figurine, 3.25"
ac# 83
Baby Girl Clapping Hands

87	Cedar Tree	$13.50	**$34.00**
88	Flower	14.00	**32.00**
89	Bow & Arrow	15.00	**31.00**
90	Flame	16.50	**31.00**
91	Vessel	16.50	**30.00**
92	G-Clef	16.50	**30.00**
93	Butterfly	16.50	**29.00**
94	Trumpet	17.50	**29.00**
95	Ship	17.50	**28.00**
96	Heart	18.50	**28.00**

E-2852/E   <u>BABY FIGURINE</u>

Suspended 1996
Figurine, 2.75"
ac# 84
Baby Boy Crawling

87	Cedar Tree	$13.50	**$32.00**
88	Flower	14.00	**31.00**
89	Bow & Arrow	15.00	**31.00**
90	Flame	16.50	**30.00**
91	Vessel	16.50	**30.00**
92	G-Clef	16.50	**28.00**
93	Butterfly	16.50	**28.00**
94	Trumpet	17.50	**27.00**
95	Ship	17.50	**27.00**
96	Heart	18.50	**27.00**

E-2852/F   <u>BABY FIGURINE</u>

Suspended 1996
Figurine, 2.50"
ac# 85
Baby Girl Lying Down

87	Cedar Tree	$13.50	**$34.00**
88	Flower	14.00	**33.00**
89	Bow & Arrow	15.00	**33.00**
90	Flame	16.50	**32.00**
91	Vessel	16.50	**32.00**
92	G-Clef	16.50	**31.00**
93	Butterfly	16.50	**31.00**
94	Trumpet	17.50	**30.00**
95	Ship	17.50	**30.00**
96	Heart	18.50	**30.00**

E-2853   <u>GOD BLESSED OUR YEARS TOGETHER WITH SO MUCH LOVE & HAPPINESS</u>

Ongoing
Figurine, 5.50"
ac# 324
Happy Anniversary Couple

84	Cross	$35.00	**$62.00**
85	Dove	35.00	**58.00**
86	Olive Branch	35.00	**57.00**
87	Cedar Tree	38.50	**56.00**
88	Flower	40.00	**55.00**
89	Bow & Arrow	45.00	**54.00**
90	Flame	50.00	**53.00**
91	Vessel	50.00	**52.00**
92	G-Clef	50.00	**50.00**
93	Butterfly	50.00	**50.00**
94	Trumpet	50.00	**50.00**
95	Ship	50.00	**50.00**
96	Heart	50.00	**50.00**
97	Sword	50.00	**50.00**
98	Eyeglasses	50.00	**50.00**
99	Star	50.00	**50.00**

E-2854   <u>GOD BLESSED OUR YEAR* TOGETHER WITH SO MUCH LOVE & HAPPINESS</u>

Ongoing
Figurine, 5.50"
ac# 323
First Anniversary Couple

*GBTru$ for "Year<u>s</u>" Error is $75.00.

84	Cross	$35.00	**$65.00**
85	Dove	35.00	**58.00**
86	Olive Branch	35.00	**57.00**
87	Cedar Tree	38.50	**55.00**
88	Flower	40.00	**54.00**
89	Bow & Arrow	45.00	**53.00**
90	Flame	50.00	**52.00**
91	Vessel	50.00	**50.00**
92	G-Clef	50.00	**50.00**
93	Butterfly	50.00	**50.00**
94	Trumpet	50.00	**50.00**
95	Ship	50.00	**50.00**
96	Heart	50.00	**50.00**
97	Sword	50.00	**50.00**
98	Eyeglasses	50.00	**50.00**
99	Star	50.00	**50.00**

E-2855 GOD BLESSED OUR YEARS TOGETHER WITH SO MUCH LOVE & HAPPINESS

Suspended 1996
Figurine, 5.50"
ac# 325
5th Anniversary Couple

84	Cross	$35.00	**$75.00**
85	Dove	35.00	**70.00**
86	Olive Branch	35.00	**68.00**
87	Cedar Tree	38.50	**68.00**
88	Flower	40.00	**65.00**
89	Bow & Arrow	45.00	**65.00**
90	Flame	50.00	**65.00**
91	Vessel	50.00	**65.00**
92	G-Clef	50.00	**62.00**
93	Butterfly	50.00	**62.00**
94	Trumpet	50.00	**62.00**
95	Ship	50.00	**60.00**
96	Heart	50.00	**60.00**

E-2856 GOD BLESSED OUR YEARS TOGETHER WITH SO MUCH LOVE & HAPPINESS

Suspended 1996
Figurine, 5.50"
ac# 326
10th Anniversary Couple

84	Cross	$35.00	**$78.00**
85	Dove	35.00	**75.00**
86	Olive Branch	35.00	**74.00**
87	Cedar Tree	38.50	**73.00**
88	Flower	40.00	**72.00**
89	Bow & Arrow	45.00	**71.00**
90	Flame	50.00	**70.00**
91	Vessel	50.00	**70.00**
92	G-Clef	50.00	**69.00**
93	Butterfly	50.00	**69.00**
94	Trumpet	50.00	**69.00**
95	Ship	50.00	**68.00**
96	Heart	50.00	**67.00**

E-2857 GOD BLESSED OUR YEARS TOGETHER WITH SO MUCH LOVE & HAPPINESS

Ongoing
Figurine, 5.50"
ac# 327
25th Anniversary Couple

84	Cross	$35.00	**$65.00**
85	Dove	35.00	**58.00**
86	Olive Branch	35.00	**55.00**
87	Cedar Tree	38.50	**52.00**
88	Flower	40.00	**52.00**
89	Bow & Arrow	45.00	**50.00**
90	Flame	50.00	**50.00**
91	Vessel	50.00	**50.00**
92	G-Clef	50.00	**50.00**
93	Butterfly	50.00	**50.00**
94	Trumpet	50.00	**50.00**
95	Ship	50.00	**50.00**
96	Heart	50.00	**50.00**
97	Sword	50.00	**50.00**
98	Eyeglasses	50.00	**50.00**
99	Star	50.00	**50.00**

E-2859 GOD BLESSED OUR YEARS TOGETHER WITH SO MUCH LOVE & HAPPINESS

Suspended 1996
Figurine, 5.50"
ac# 328
40th Anniversary Couple

84	Cross	$35.00	**$80.00**
85	Dove	35.00	**79.00**
86	Olive Branch	35.00	**78.00**
87	Cedar Tree	38.50	**77.00**
88	Flower	40.00	**76.00**
89	Bow & Arrow	45.00	**75.00**
90	Flame	50.00	**74.00**
91	Vessel	50.00	**73.00**
92	G-Clef	50.00	**72.00**
93	Butterfly	50.00	**71.00**
94	Trumpet	50.00	**70.00**
95	Ship	50.00	**68.00**
96	Heart	50.00	**67.00**

E-2860 — GOD BLESSED OUR YEARS TOGETHER WITH SO MUCH LOVE & HAPPINESS

Ongoing
Figurine, 5.50"
ac# 329
50th Anniversary Couple

Year	Mark	Price	Value
84	Cross	$35.00	**$78.00**
85	Dove	35.00	**75.00**
86	Olive Branch	35.00	**74.00**
87	Cedar Tree	38.50	**73.00**
88	Flower	40.00	**72.00**
89	Bow & Arrow	45.00	**70.00**
90	Flame	50.00	**69.00**
91	Vessel	50.00	**68.00**
92	G-Clef	50.00	**67.00**
93	Butterfly	50.00	**65.00**
94	Trumpet	50.00	**64.00**
95	Ship	50.00	**62.00**
96	Heart	50.00	**60.00**
97	Sword	50.00	**50.00**
98	Eyeglasses	50.00	**50.00**
99	Star	50.00	**50.00**

E-3104 — BLESSED ARE THE PURE IN HEART

Suspended 1991
Figurine, 2.75"
ac# 162
Baby in Cradle

*Unmarked pieces also exist, i.e. they have no mark but do have the Enesco Item # on the understamp.

Year	Mark	Price	Value
80	No Mark*	$9.00	**$57.00**
81	Triangle	10.50	**48.00**
82	Hourglass	12.00	**47.00**
83	Fish	12.00	**45.00**
84	Cross	13.50	**44.00**
85	Dove	13.50	**42.00**
86	Olive Branch	13.50	**41.00**
87	Cedar Tree	16.00	**40.00**
88	Flower	16.00	**39.00**
89	Bow & Arrow	17.50	**40.00**
90	Flame	19.00	**37.00**
91	Vessel	19.00	**37.00**

E-3105 — HE WATCHES OVER US ALL

Suspended 1984
Figurine, 5.25"
ac# 411
Boy on Crutches with Bible

Year	Mark	Price	Value
80	No Mark	$11.00	**$78.00**
81	Triangle	11.00	**70.00**
82	Hourglass	15.00	**68.00**
83	Fish	15.00	**67.00**
84	Cross	17.00	**65.00**

E-3106 — MOTHER SEW DEAR

Ongoing
Figurine, 5.00"
ac# 698
Mother Needlepointing

Year	Mark	Price	Value
80	No Mark	$13.00	**$80.00**
81	Triangle	13.00	**55.00**
82	Hourglass	16.00	**45.00**
83	Fish	16.00	**42.00**
84	Cross	17.00	**40.00**
85	Dove	17.00	**39.00**
86	Olive Branch	17.00	**38.00**
87	Cedar Tree	21.00	**36.00**
88	Flower	22.50	**35.00**
89	Bow & Arrow	25.00	**35.00**
90	Flame	27.50	**33.00**
91	Vessel	27.50	**33.00**
92	G-Clef	27.50	**32.50**
93	Butterfly	30.00	**32.50**
94	Trumpet	30.00	**32.50**
95	Ship	30.00	**32.50**
96	Heart	32.50	**32.50**
97	Sword	32.50	**32.50**
98	Eyeglasses	32.50	**32.50**
99	Star	32.50	**32.50**

E-3107	BLESSED ARE THE PEACEMAKERS				
	Retired 1985	80	No Mark	$13.00	**$125.00**
	Figurine, 5.25"	81	Triangle	15.00	**105.00**
	ac# 160	82	Hourglass	17.00	**85.00**
	Boy Holding Cat & Dog	83	Fish	17.00	**80.00**
		84	Cross	19.00	**75.00**
		85	Dove	19.00	**70.00**

E-3108	THE HAND THAT ROCKS THE FUTURE				
	Suspended 1984	80	No Mark	$13.00	**$100.00**
	Figurine, 4.50"	81	Triangle	15.00	**85.00**
	ac# 937	82	Hourglass	17.00	**80.00**
	Girl Rocking Cradle	83	Fish	17.00	**78.00**
		84	Cross	19.00	**75.00**

E-3109	THE PURR-FECT GRANDMA				
	Ongoing	80	No Mark	$13.00	**$75.00**
	Figurine, 4.75"	81	Triangle	15.00	**55.00**
	ac# 963	82	Hourglass	17.00	**45.00**
	Grandma in Rocker	83	Fish	17.00	**42.00**
		84	Cross	19.00	**40.00**
		85	Dove	19.00	**38.00**
		86	Olive Branch	19.00	**35.00**
		87	Cedar Tree	21.00	**33.00**
		88	Flower	23.00	**33.00**
		89	Bow & Arrow	25.00	**33.00**
		90	Flame	27.50	**33.00**
		91	Vessel	27.50	**32.50**
		92	G-Clef	27.50	**32.50**
		93	Butterfly	30.00	**32.50**
		94	Trumpet	30.00	**32.50**
		95	Ship	30.00	**32.50**
		96	Heart	32.50	**32.50**
		97	Sword	32.50	**32.50**
		98	Eyeglasses	32.50	**32.50**
		99	Star	32.50	**32.50**

E-3110B	LOVING IS SHARING				
	Retired 1993	80	No Mark	$13.00	**$140.00**
	Figurine, 4.50"	81	Triangle	15.00	**105.00**
	ac# 635	82	Hourglass	17.00	**100.00**
	Boy Sharing with Puppy	83	Fish	17.00	**88.00**
		84	Cross	19.00	**80.00**
		85	Dove	19.00	**78.00**
		86	Olive Branch	19.00	**75.00**
		87	Cedar Tree	21.00	**74.00**
		88	Flower	24.00	**73.00**
		89	Bow & Arrow	27.50	**72.00**
		90	Flame	30.00	**72.00**
		91	Vessel	30.00	**72.00**
		92	G-Clef	30.00	**70.00**
		93	Butterfly	30.00	**70.00**

E-3110G LOVING IS SHARING

Ongoing
Figurine, 4.50"
ac# 636
Girl Sharing with Puppy

80	No Mark	$13.00	**$105.00**
81	Triangle	15.00	**55.00**
82	Hourglass	17.00	**45.00**
83	Fish	17.00	**38.00**
84	Cross	19.00	**38.00**
85	Dove	19.00	**38.00**
86	Olive Branch	19.00	**35.00**
87	Cedar Tree	21.00	**35.00**
88	Flower	24.00	**33.00**
89	Bow & Arrow	27.50	**33.00**
90	Flame	30.00	**33.00**
91	Vessel	30.00	**33.00**
92	G-Clef	30.00	**33.00**
93	Butterfly	30.00	**32.50**
94	Trumpet	30.00	**32.50**
95	Ship	30.00	**32.50**
96	Heart	32.50	**32.50**
97	Sword	32.50	**32.50**
98	Eyeglasses	32.50	**32.50**
99	Star	32.50	**32.50**

E-3111 BE NOT WEARY IN WELL DOING

Retired 1985
Figurine, 4.00"
ac# 124
Girl Helper

80	No Mark*	$14.00	**$130.00**
81	Triangle	16.00	**110.00**
82	Hourglass	18.00	**90.00**
83	Fish	18.00	**88.00**
84	Cross	19.00	**85.00**
85	Dove	19.00	**80.00**

*Classic Variation. Figurines exist in No Mark versions with an error in the Inspirational Title on the understamp decal. Instead of "Be Not Weary <u>In</u> Well Doing," they read "Be Not Weary <u>And</u> Well Doing." The black and white boxes in which the pieces were shipped also have the incorrect title on the label. The GBTru$ for "...And Well Doing" is $200.00. See page 407.

E-3112 GOD'S SPEED

Retired 1983
Figurine, 4.75"
ac# 350
Boy Jogging with Dog

80	No Mark	$14.00	**$120.00**
81	Triangle	16.00	**85.00**
82	Hourglass	18.00	**65.00**
83	Fish	18.00	**60.00**

Exists in a double mark Triangle/Hourglass. GBTru$ is $225.00.

E-3113 THOU ART MINE

Ongoing
Figurine, 5.00"
ac# 992
Boy with Girl Writing in Sand

80	No Mark	$16.00	**$90.00**
81	Triangle	19.00	**65.00**
82	Hourglass	22.50	**55.00**
83	Fish	22.50	**50.00**
84	Cross	25.00	**45.00**
85	Dove	25.00	**44.00**
86	Olive Branch	25.00	**43.00**
87	Cedar Tree	27.50	**42.00**
88	Flower	30.00	**42.00**
89	Bow & Arrow	33.00	**40.00**
90	Flame	35.00	**40.00**
91	Vessel	35.00	**40.00**
92	G-Clef	35.00	**40.00**
93	Butterfly	37.50	**40.00**
94	Trumpet	37.50	**40.00**
95	Ship	40.00	**40.00**
96	Heart	40.00	**40.00**
97	Sword	40.00	**40.00**
98	Eyeglasses	40.00	**40.00**
99	Star	40.00	**40.00**

E-3114 THE LORD BLESS YOU AND KEEP YOU

Ongoing
Figurine, 5.00"
ac# 942
Bride and Groom

80	No Mark	$16.00	**$85.00**
81	Triangle	19.00	**65.00**
82	Hourglass	22.50	**58.00**
83	Fish	22.50	**55.00**
84	Cross	25.00	**54.00**
85	Dove	25.00	**53.00**
86	Olive Branch	25.00	**52.00**
87	Cedar Tree	27.50	**50.00**
88	Flower	32.50	**50.00**
89	Bow & Arrow	37.50	**50.00**
90	Flame	37.50	**50.00**
91	Vessel	37.50	**50.00**
92	G-Clef	37.50	**50.00**
93	Butterfly	40.00	**50.00**
94	Trumpet	40.00	**50.00**
95	Ship	45.00	**50.00**
96	Heart	50.00	**50.00**
97	Sword	50.00	**50.00**
98	Eyeglasses	50.00	**50.00**
99	Star	50.00	**50.00**

E-3115 BUT LOVE GOES ON FOREVER

Ongoing
Figurine, 5.25"
ac# 184
Boy & Girl Angels on Cloud

80	No Mark	$16.50	**$105.00**
81	Triangle	19.00	**65.00**
82	Hourglass	22.50	**55.00**
83	Fish	22.50	**52.00**
84	Cross	25.00	**50.00**
85	Dove	25.00	**45.00**
86	Olive Branch	25.00	**40.00**
87	Cedar Tree	27.50	**40.00**
88	Flower	30.00	**40.00**
89	Bow & Arrow	33.00	**40.00**
90	Flame	35.00	**40.00**
91	Vessel	35.00	**40.00**
92	G-Clef	35.00	**40.00**
93	Butterfly	35.00	**40.00**
94	Trumpet	35.00	**40.00**
95	Ship	37.50	**40.00**
96	Heart	40.00	**40.00**
97	Sword	40.00	**40.00**
98	Eyeglasses	40.00	**40.00**
99	Star	40.00	**40.00**

E-3116 THEE I LOVE

Retired 1994
Figurine, 6.00"
ac# 970
Boy Carving Tree for Girl

80	No Mark	$16.50	**$145.00**
81	Triangle	19.00	**100.00**
82	Hourglass	22.50	**85.00**
83	Fish	22.50	**82.00**
84	Cross	25.00	**80.00**
85	Dove	25.00	**79.00**
86	Olive Branch	25.00	**78.00**
87	Cedar Tree	27.50	**77.00**
88	Flower	32.50	**76.00**
89	Bow & Arrow	36.00	**75.00**
90	Flame	37.50	**75.00**
91	Vessel	37.50	**75.00**
92	G-Clef	37.50	**72.00**
93	Butterfly	40.00	**72.00**
94	Trumpet	40.00	**72.00**

E-3117 — WALKING BY FAITH
Ongoing
Figurine, 7.25"
ac# 1034
Boy Pulling Wagon with Girl

80	No Mark	$35.00	**$130.00**
81	Triangle	40.00	**100.00**
82	Hourglass	45.00	**90.00**
83	Fish	45.00	**88.00**
84	Cross	50.00	**85.00**
85	Dove	50.00	**80.00**
86	Olive Branch	50.00	**79.00**
87	Cedar Tree	55.00	**78.00**
88	Flower	60.00	**77.00**
89	Bow & Arrow	67.50	**76.00**
90	Flame	70.00	**75.00**
91	Vessel	70.00	**75.00**
92	G-Clef	70.00	**75.00**
93	Butterfly	75.00	**75.00**
94	Trumpet	75.00	**75.00**
95	Ship	75.00	**75.00**
96	Heart	75.00	**75.00**
97	Sword	75.00	**75.00**
98	Eyeglasses	75.00	**75.00**
99	Star	75.00	**75.00**

E-3118 — EGGS OVER EASY
Retired 1983
Figurine, 5.00"
ac# 257
Girl with Frypan

80	No Mark	$12.00	**$125.00**
81	Triangle	14.00	**100.00**
82	Hourglass	15.00	**90.00**
83	Fish	15.00	**80.00**

E-3119 — IT'S WHAT'S INSIDE THAT COUNTS
Suspended 1984
Figurine, 5.25"
ac# 515
Boy with Books

80	No Mark	$13.00	**$125.00**
81	Triangle	15.00	**100.00**
82	Hourglass	17.00	**95.00**
83	Fish	17.00	**90.00**
84	Cross	19.00	**89.00**

E-3120 — TO THEE WITH LOVE
Suspended 1986
Figurine, 5.75"
ac# 1017
Girl with Box of Kittens

*Piece was Suspended in 1986 yet exists in the 1987 Cedar Tree Annual Production Symbol.

80	No Mark	$13.00	**$90.00**
81	Triangle	15.00	**75.00**
82	Hourglass	17.00	**65.00**
83	Fish	17.00	**64.00**
84	Cross	19.00	**63.00**
85	Dove	19.00	**62.00**
86	Olive Branch	19.00	**61.00**
*	Cedar Tree		**60.00**

E-4720 — THE LORD BLESS YOU AND KEEP YOU
Suspended 1987
Figurine, 5.25"
ac# 943
Boy Graduate

81	No Mark	$14.00	**$40.00**
81	Triangle	14.00	**38.00**
82	Hourglass	17.00	**35.00**
83	Fish	17.00	**34.00**
84	Cross	19.00	**33.00**
85	Dove	19.00	**32.00**
86	Olive Branch	19.00	**31.00**
87	Cedar Tree	22.50	**30.00**

E-4721	THE LORD BLESS YOU AND KEEP YOU				
	Ongoing	81	No Mark	$14.00	**$70.00**
	Figurine, 5.25"	81	Triangle	14.00	**50.00**
	ac# 944	82	Hourglass	17.00	**45.00**
	Girl Graduate	83	Fish	17.00	**42.00**
		84	Cross	19.00	**40.00**
		85	Dove	19.00	**39.00**
		86	Olive Branch	19.00	**38.00**
		87	Cedar Tree	22.50	**37.00**
		88	Flower	24.00	**36.00**
		89	Bow & Arrow	27.00	**35.00**
		90	Flame	30.00	**35.00**
		91	Vessel	30.00	**35.00**
		92	G-Clef	30.00	**35.00**
		93	Butterfly	30.00	**35.00**
		94	Trumpet	30.00	**35.00**
		95	Ship	32.50	**35.00**
		96	Heart	35.00	**35.00**
		97	Sword	35.00	**35.00**
		98	Eyeglasses	35.00	**35.00**
		99	Star	35.00	**35.00**
E-4722	LOVE CANNOT BREAK A TRUE FRIENDSHIP				
	Suspended 1985	81	No Mark	$22.50	**$145.00**
	Figurine, 5.00"	81	Triangle	22.50	**120.00**
	ac# 601	82	Hourglass	25.00	**110.00**
	Girl with Piggy Bank	83	Fish	25.00	**105.00**
		84	Cross	27.50	**100.00**
		85	Dove	27.50	**98.00**
E-4723	PEACE AMID THE STORM				
	Suspended 1984	81	No Mark	$22.50	**$100.00**
	Figurine, 4.75"	81	Triangle	22.50	**90.00**
	ac# 768	82	Hourglass	25.00	**85.00**
	Boy Reading Holy Bible	83	Fish	25.00	**82.00**
		84	Cross	27.50	**80.00**
E-4724	REJOICING WITH YOU				
	Ongoing	81	No Mark*	$25.00	**$105.00**
	Figurine, 5.25"	81	Triangle*	25.00	**75.00**
	ac# 805	82	Hourglass	27.50	**68.00**
	Christening	83	Fish	27.50	**65.00**
		84	Cross	30.00	**64.00**
	*Classic Variation: "No E" or	85	Dove	30.00	**62.00**
	"Bibl Error." During the first	86	Olive Branch	30.00	**61.00**
	years of production the "e"	87	Cedar Tree	33.50	**60.00**
	was missing from the word	88	Flower	37.50	**58.00**
	Bible. Some Hourglass & Fish	89	Bow & Arrow	40.00	**55.00**
	pieces also have this	90	Flame	45.00	**55.00**
	variation. See page 407.	91	Vessel	45.00	**55.00**
		92	G-Clef	45.00	**55.00**
		93	Butterfly	50.00	**55.00**
		94	Trumpet	50.00	**55.00**
		95	Ship	50.00	**55.00**
		96	Heart	55.00	**55.00**
		97	Sword	55.00	**55.00**
		98	Eyeglasses	55.00	**55.00**
		99	Star	55.00	**55.00**
E-4725	PEACE ON EARTH				
	Suspended 1984	81	No Mark	$25.00	**$105.00**
	Figurine, 5.25"	81	Triangle	25.00	**78.00**
	ac# 770	82	Hourglass	27.50	**74.00**
	Choir Boys with Bandages	83	Fish	27.50	**72.00**
		84	Cross	30.00	**70.00**

E-4726	PEACE ON EARTH Tune: Jesus Loves Me				
	Suspended 1984	81	No Mark	$45.00	**$150.00**
	Musical, 6.25"	81	Triangle	45.00	**125.00**
	ac# 770	82	Hourglass	45.00	**120.00**
	Choir Boys with Bandages	83	Fish	45.00	**115.00**
		84	Cross	50.00	**112.00**

E-5200	BEAR YE ONE ANOTHER'S BURDENS				
	Suspended 1984	81	No Mark	$20.00	**$110.00**
	Figurine, 4.74"	81	Triangle	20.00	**100.00**
	ac# 126	82	Hourglass	22.50	**85.00**
	Sad Boy with Teddy	83	Fish	22.50	**80.00**
		84	Cross	25.00	**78.00**

E-5201	LOVE LIFTED ME				
	Suspended 1984	81	No Mark	$25.00	**$105.00**
	Figurine, 5.50"	81	Triangle	25.00	**85.00**
	ac# 621	82	Hourglass	30.00	**80.00**
	Boy Helping Friend	83	Fish	30.00	**78.00**
		84	Cross	33.00	**75.00**

E-5202	THANK YOU FOR COMING TO MY ADE				
	Suspended 1984	81	No Mark	$22.50	**$150.00**
	Figurine, 5.50"	81	Triangle	22.50	**125.00**
	ac# 920	82	Hourglass	27.50	**115.00**
	Lemonade Stand	83	Fish	27.50	**112.00**
		84	Cross	30.00	**108.00**

E-5203	LET NOT THE SUN GO DOWN UPON YOUR WRATH				
	Suspended 1984	81	No Mark	$22.50	**$180.00**
	Figurine, 6.75"	81	Triangle	22.50	**160.00**
	ac# 564	82	Hourglass	27.50	**156.00**
	Boy with Dog on Stairs	83	Fish	30.00	**146.00**
		84	Cross	30.00	**140.00**

E-5204	THE HAND THAT ROCKS THE FUTURE Tune: Mozart's Lullaby				
	Ongoing	81	No Mark	$30.00	**$100.00**
	Musical, 5.50"	81	Triangle	30.00	**85.00**
	ac# 937	82	Hourglass	35.00	**75.00**
	Girl Rocking Cradle	83	Fish	35.00	**72.00**
		84	Cross	37.50	**70.00**
		85	Dove	37.50	**64.00**
		86	Olive Branch	37.50	**63.00**
		87	Cedar Tree	40.00	**62.00**
		88	Flower	45.00	**61.00**
		89	Bow & Arrow	50.00	**60.00**
		90	Flame	55.00	**60.00**
		91	Vessel	55.00	**60.00**
		92	G-Clef	55.00	**60.00**
		93	Butterfly	60.00	**60.00**
		94	Trumpet	60.00	**60.00**
		95	Ship	60.00	**60.00**
		96	Heart	60.00	**60.00**
		97	Sword	60.00	**60.00**
		98	Eyeglasses	60.00	**60.00**
		99	Star	60.00	**60.00**

E-5205	MY GUARDIAN ANGEL Tune: Brahms' Lullaby				
	Suspended 1985	81	No Mark	$22.50	**$118.00**
	Musical, 5.50"	84	Cross	27.50	**90.00**
	ac# 184	85	Dove	27.50	**88.00**
	Boy Angel on Cloud				

E-5206	MY GUARDIAN ANGEL Tune: Brahms' Lullaby				
	Suspended 1988	81	No Mark	$22.50	**$110.00**
	Musical, 5.50"	84	Cross	27.50	**90.00**
	ac# 184	85	Dove	27.50	**85.00**
	Girl Angel on Cloud	86	Olive Branch	27.50	**84.00**
		87	Cedar Tree	30.00	**82.00**
		88	Flower	33.00	**80.00**
E-5207	MY GUARDIAN ANGELS				
	Suspended 1984	81	No Mark	$30.00	**$252.00**
	Night Light, 3.50"	84	Cross	37.50	**175.00**
	ac# 184				
	Boy & Girl Angels on Cloud				
E-5208	JESUS LOVES ME				
	Suspended 1985	81	No Mark	$15.00	**$52.00**
	Bell, 5.75"	84	Cross	19.00	**48.00**
	ac# 531	85	Dove	19.00	**42.00**
	Boy with Teddy				
E-5209	JESUS LOVES ME				
	Suspended 1985	81	No Mark	$15.00	**$58.00**
	Bell, 5.75"	84	Cross	19.00	**54.00**
	ac# 532	85	Dove	19.00	**48.00**
	Girl with Bunny				
E-5210	PRAYER CHANGES THINGS				
	Suspended 1984	81	No Mark	$15.00	**$50.00**
	Bell, 5.75"	84	Cross	19.00	**45.00**
	ac# 922				
	Girl Praying				
E-5211	GOD UNDERSTANDS				
	Retired 1984	81	No Mark	$15.00	**$50.00**
	Bell, 5.75"	84	Cross	19.00	**45.00**
	ac# 343				
	Boy with Report Card				
E-5212	TO A SPECIAL DAD				
	Ongoing	81	No Mark	$20.00	**$75.00**
	Figurine, 5.50"	81	Triangle	20.00	**55.00**
	ac# 1002	82	Hourglass	22.50	**48.00**
	Boy in Dad's Duds with Dog	83	Fish	22.50	**45.00**
		84	Cross	25.00	**39.00**
		85	Dove	25.00	**38.00**
		86	Olive Branch	25.00	**37.00**
		87	Cedar Tree	27.50	**36.00**
		88	Flower	30.00	**35.00**
		89	Bow & Arrow	33.00	**35.00**
		90	Flame	35.00	**35.00**
		91	Vessel	35.00	**35.00**
		92	G-Clef	35.00	**35.00**
		93	Butterfly	35.00	**35.00**
		94	Trumpet	35.00	**35.00**
		95	Ship	35.00	**35.00**
		96	Heart	35.00	**35.00**
		97	Sword	35.00	**35.00**
		98	Eyeglasses	35.00	**35.00**
		99	Star	35.00	**35.00**

E-5213 GOD IS LOVE

Suspended 1989
Figurine, 5.00"
ac# 332
Girl with Goose in Lap

This piece was re-sculptured in 1985.

81	No Mark	$17.00	**$115.00**
81	Triangle	17.00	**85.00**
82	Hourglass	20.00	**74.00**
83	Fish	20.00	**68.00**
84	Cross	22.50	**64.00**
85	Dove	22.50	**62.00**
86	Olive Branch	22.50	**60.00**
87	Cedar Tree	25.00	**58.00**
88	Flower	27.00	**55.00**
89	Bow & Arrow	30.00	**52.00**

E-5214 PRAYER CHANGES THINGS

Suspended 1984
Figurine, 5.15"
ac# 788
Boy & Girl Praying at Table with Bible

81	No Mark	$35.00	*
81	Triangle	35.00	*
82	Hourglass	35.00	*
83	Fish	35.00	**105.00**
84	Cross	37.50	**100.00**
**	Dove		**90.00**

*Classic Variation: "Backwards Bible." The first production of this figurine had the words "Holy Bible" inscribed on the back cover. Pieces with this error exist in No Mark and Triangle versions. Reportedly, No Mark and Triangle pieces also exist where the title is correctly placed, but these may be considered extremely rare. The majority of Hourglass pieces have the correctly placed title. GBTru$ Prices are as follows: Backwards No Mark $168.00, Backwards Triangle $160.00, Backwards Hourglass $140.00, and correct Hourglass $120.00. **Piece was Suspended in 1984 yet exists in the 1995 Dove Annual Production Symbol. See page 408.

E-5215 LOVE ONE ANOTHER Series: "Inspired Thoughts"–1st Issue

Individually Numbered
Limited Edition 15,000
Plate, 8.50"
ac# 625
Boy & Girl Sitting on Stump

81	Unmarked	$40.00	**$50.00**

E-5216 THE LORD BLESS YOU AND KEEP YOU

Suspended 1987
Plate, 7.00"
ac# 942
Bride and Groom

81	Unmarked	$30.00	**$40.00**
84	Cross	30.00	**35.00**
85	Dove	30.00	**35.00**
86	Olive Branch	30.00	**35.00**
87	Cedar Tree	35.00	**35.00**

E-5217 MOTHER SEW DEAR Series: "Mother's Love"–1st Issue

Individually Numbered
Limited Edition 15,000
Plate, 8.50"
ac# 698
Mother Needlepointing

81	Unmarked	$40.00	**$50.00**

E-5376 MAY YOUR CHRISTMAS BE BLESSED

Suspended 1986
Figurine, 5.75"
ac# 671
Girl with Long Hair & Bible

84	Cross	$37.50	**$75.00**
85	Dove	37.50	**65.00**
86	Olive Branch	37.50	**62.00**

E-5377 LOVE IS KIND

Retired 1987
Figurine, 4.00"
ac# 608
Girl with Mouse

84	Cross	$27.50	**$90.00**
85	Dove	27.50	**80.00**
86	Olive Branch	27.50	**78.00**
87	Cedar Tree	27.50	**75.00**

E-5378	JOY TO THE WORLD	Nativity Addition				
	Suspended 1989		84	Cross	$18.00	**$62.00**
	Figurine, 4.00"		85	Dove	18.00	**60.00**
	ac# 539		86	Olive Branch	18.00	**58.00**
	Boy Playing Harp		87	Cedar Tree	20.00	**55.00**
			88	Flower	20.00	**54.00**
			89	Bow & Arrow	25.00	**52.00**

E-5379	ISN'T HE PRECIOUS	Nativity Addition				
	Ongoing					
	Figurine, 5.00"		84	Cross	$20.00	**$45.00**
	ac# 503		85	Dove	20.00	**35.00**
	Girl with Broom		86	Olive Branch	20.00	**35.00**
			87	Cedar Tree	22.50	**33.00**
	With the opening of a new		88	Flower	22.50	**33.00**
	production facility in Indonesia,		89	Bow & Arrow	27.50	**32.50**
	numerous pieces of whiteware		90	Flame	30.00	**32.50**
	(unpainted figurines) were		91	Vessel	30.00	**32.50**
	inadvertently shipped to		92	G-Clef	30.00	**32.50**
	retailers. The few known sales		93	Butterfly	30.00	**32.50**
	of this piece range from		94	Trumpet	30.00	**32.50**
	$400.00 to $650.00.		95	Ship	30.00	**32.50**
	See page 408.		96	Heart	32.50	**32.50**
			97	Sword	32.50	**32.50**
			98	Eyeglasses	32.50	**32.50**
			99	Star	32.50	**32.50**

E-5380	A MONARCH IS BORN					
	Suspended 1986		84	Cross	$33.00	**$88.00**
	Figurine, 5.00"		85	Dove	33.00	**84.00**
	ac# 11		86	Olive Branch	33.00	**80.00**
	Boy with Butterfly at Manger					

E-5381	HIS NAME IS JESUS					
	Suspended 1987		84	Cross	$45.00	**$120.00**
	Figurine, 5.00"		85	Dove	45.00	**110.00**
	ac# 432		86	Olive Branch	45.00	**100.00**
	Boys at Manger		87	Cedar Tree	50.00	**98.00**

E-5382	FOR GOD SO LOVED THE WORLD	Nativity	Set of 4			
	Suspended 1986		84	Cross	$70.00	**$138.00**
	Figurine, 5.00"		85	Dove	70.00	**120.00**
	ac# 283		86	Olive Branch	70.00	**118.00**
	Deluxe 4 Piece Nativity					

E-5383	WISHING YOU A MERRY CHRISTMAS					
	Dated Annual 1984		84	Cross	$17.00	**$45.00**
	Figurine, 4.75"					
	ac# 1074					
	Girl with Songbook					

E-5384 · I'LL PLAY MY DRUM FOR HIM · Mini Nativity Addition

Ongoing		84	Cross	$10.00	**$35.00**
Figurine, 3.50"		85	Dove	10.00	**25.00**
ac# 485		86	Olive Branch	10.00	**24.00**
Drummer Boy		87	Cedar Tree	11.00	**22.00**
		88	Flower	12.50	**20.00**
		89	Bow & Arrow	13.50	**19.00**
		90	Flame	15.00	**19.00**
		91	Vessel	15.00	**18.50**
		92	G-Clef	15.00	**18.50**
		93	Butterfly	15.00	**18.50**
		94	Trumpet	16.00	**18.50**
		95	Ship	16.00	**18.50**
		96	Heart	18.50	**18.50**
		97	Sword	18.50	**18.50**
		98	Eyeglasses	18.50	**18.50**
		99	Star	18.50	**18.50**

E-5385 · OH WORSHIP THE LORD · Mini Nativity Addition

Suspended 1986	84	Cross	$10.00	**$55.00**
Figurine, 3.25"	85	Dove	10.00	**45.00**
ac# 736	86	Olive Branch	10.00	**42.00**
Boy Angel with Candle				

E-5386 · OH WORSHIP THE LORD · Mini Nativity Addition

Suspended 1986	84	Cross	$10.00	**$65.00**
Figurine, 3.25"	85	Dove	10.00	**55.00**
ac# 737	86	Olive Branch	10.00	**45.00**
Girl Angel Praying				

E-5387 · WISHING YOU A MERRY CHRISTMAS

Dated Annual 1984	84	Cross	$10.00	**$36.00**
Ornament, 3.00"				
ac# 1074				
Girl with Songbook				

E-5388 · JOY TO THE WORLD

Retired 1987	84	Cross	$10.00	**$45.00**
Ornament, 2.50"	85	Dove	10.00	**42.00**
ac# 539	86	Olive Branch	10.00	**39.00**
Boy Playing Harp	87	Cedar Tree	11.00	**37.00**

E-5389 · PEACE ON EARTH

Suspended 1986	84	Cross	$10.00	**$38.00**
Ornament, 3.00"	85	Dove	10.00	**37.00**
ac# 772	86	Olive Branch	10.00	**36.00**
Boy in Choir				

E-5390 · MAY GOD BLESS YOU WITH A PERFECT SEASON

Suspended 1989	84	Cross	$10.00	**$33.00**
Ornament, 3.00"	85	Dove	10.00	**26.00**
ac# 660	86	Olive Branch	10.00	**25.00**
Girl in Scarf and Hat	87	Cedar Tree	10.00	**24.00**
	88	Flower	11.00	**23.00**
	89	Bow & Arrow	13.50	**22.00**

E-5391 — LOVE IS KIND
Suspended 1989
Ornament, 2.50"
ac# 609
Girl with Gift

84	Cross	$10.00	**$35.00**
85	Dove	10.00	**28.00**
86	Olive Branch	10.00	**27.00**
87	Cedar Tree	10.00	**26.00**
88	Flower	11.00	**25.00**
89	Bow & Arrow	13.50	**24.00**

E-5392 — BLESSED ARE THE PURE IN HEART
Dated Annual 1984
Ornament, 2.00"
ac# 162
Baby in Cradle

84	Cross	$10.00	**$36.00**

E-5393 — WISHING YOU A MERRY CHRISTMAS
Dated Annual 1984
Bell, 5.75"
ac# 1074
Girl with Songbook

84	Cross	$19.00	**$40.00**

E-5394 — WISHING YOU A MERRY CHRISTMAS   Tune: We Wish You A Merry Christmas
Suspended 1986
Musical, 6.50"
ac# 1075
Carollers with Puppy

84	Cross	$55.00	**$120.00**
85	Dove	55.00	**110.00**
86	Olive Branch	55.00	**105.00**

E-5395 — UNTO US A CHILD IS BORN   Series: "Christmas Collection"–
4th Issue   Individually Numbered
Limited Edition 15,000
Plate, 8.50"
ac# 1030
Shepherds and Lambs on Hillside

84	Unmarked	$40.00	**$45.00**
	Cross		**40.00**

E-5396 — THE WONDER OF CHRISTMAS   Series: "Joy Of Christmas"–3rd Issue
Dated Annual 1984
Plate, 8.50"
ac# 969
Boy Pulling Girl and Tree on Sled

84	Cross	$40.00	**$50.00**

E-5397 — TIMMY
Suspended 1991
Doll, 10.00"
ac# 999
Boy Jogger

84	Cross	$125.00	**$160.00**
85	Dove	125.00	**150.00**
86	Olive Branch	125.00	**150.00**
87	Cedar Tree	135.00	**150.00**
88	Flower	135.00	**150.00**
89	Bow & Arrow	145.00	**150.00**
90	Flame	150.00	**150.00**
91	Vessel	150.00	**150.00**

E-5619 — COME LET US ADORE HIM
Suspended 1985
Figurine, 2.00"
ac# 222
Manger Child

81	No Mark	$10.00	**$45.00**
81	Triangle	10.00	**38.00**
82	Hourglass	10.50	**35.00**
83	Fish	10.50	**33.00**
84	Cross	11.00	**32.00**
85	Dove	11.00	**30.00**

E-5620	WE HAVE SEEN HIS STAR				
	Suspended 1985	81	No Mark	$15.00	**$52.00**
	Bell, 5.50"	84	Cross	15.00	**48.00**
	ac# 1044	85	Dove	19.00	**47.00**
	Boy Holding Lamb				

E-5621	DONKEY Nativity Addition				
	Ongoing	81	Unmarked	$6.00	**$34.00**
	Figurine, 2.75"	84	Cross	9.00	**25.00**
	ac# 244	85	Dove	9.00	**22.00**
	Donkey	86	Olive Branch	9.00	**20.00**
		87	Cedar Tree	11.00	**18.00**
		88	Flower	11.00	**16.00**
		89	Bow & Arrow	12.00	**15.00**
		90	Flame	13.50	**15.00**
		91	Vessel	13.50	**15.00**
		92	G-Clef	13.50	**15.00**
		93	Butterfly	13.50	**15.00**
		94	Trumpet	15.00	**15.00**
		95	Ship	15.00	**15.00**
		96	Heart	15.00	**15.00**
		97	Sword	15.00	**15.00**
		98	Eyeglasses	15.00	**15.00**
		99	Star	15.00	**15.00**

E-5622	LET THE HEAVENS REJOICE				
	Dated Annual 1981	81	Unmarked	$15.00	**$220.00**
	Bell, 5.75"				
	ac# 565				
	Praying Angel Boy				

E-5623	JESUS IS BORN				
	Suspended 1984	81	Unmarked	$15.00	**$50.00**
	Bell, 5.75"	84	Cross	19.00	**40.00**
	ac# 523				
	Shepherd				

E-5624	THEY FOLLOWED THE STAR Nativity Addition Set of 3				
	Ongoing	*	Unmarked	$130.00	**$275.00**
	Figurine, 8.75"	81	Triangle	130.00	**245.00**
	ac# 979	82	Hourglass	150.00	**240.00**
	3 Kings on Camels	83	Fish	150.00	**235.00**
		84	Cross	165.00	**230.00**
	*Unmarked pieces could	85	Dove	165.00	**225.00**
	have been produced in any of	86	Olive Branch	165.00	**225.00**
	the years of production.	87	Cedar Tree	175.00	**225.00**
	Consider Triangle as the First	88	Flower	175.00	**225.00**
	Mark. Mixed sets of Triangle/	89	Bow & Arrow	190.00	**225.00**
	Hourglass & Hourglass/Fish	90	Flame	200.00	**225.00**
	are common. Take lower	91	Vessel	200.00	**225.00**
	GBTru$.	92	G-Clef	200.00	**225.00**
		93	Butterfly	225.00	**225.00**
		94	Trumpet	225.00	**225.00**
		95	Ship	225.00	**225.00**
		96	Heart	225.00	**225.00**
		97	Sword	225.00	**225.00**
		98	Eyeglasses	225.00	**225.00**
		99	Star	225.00	**225.00**

E-5627 | BUT LOVE GOES ON FOREVER
Suspended 1985
Ornament, 3.00"
ac# 184
Boy Angel on Cloud

*	Unmarked	$6.00	**$88.00**
81	Triangle	6.00	**95.00**
82	Hourglass	6.00	**80.00**
83	Fish	9.00	**75.00**
84	Cross	10.00	**70.00**
85	Dove	10.00	**65.00**

*Unmarked pieces could have been produced in any of the years of production. Consider Triangle as the First Mark.

E-5628 | BUT LOVE GOES ON FOREVER
Suspended 1985
Ornament, 3.00"
ac# 184
Girl Angel on Cloud

*	Unmarked	$6.00	**$115.00**
81	Triangle	6.00	**120.00**
82	Hourglass	6.00	**110.00**
83	Fish	9.00	**100.00**
84	Cross	10.00	**90.00**
85	Dove	10.00	**90.00**

*Unmarked pieces could have been produced in any of the years of production. Consider Triangle as the First Mark.

E-5629 | LET THE HEAVENS REJOICE
Dated Annual 1981
Ornament, 3.10"
ac# 565
Praying Angel Boy

81	Triangle	$6.00	**$240.00**

Some ornaments are without the patch on the angel. The GBTru$ is $285.00.

E-5630 | UNTO US A CHILD IS BORN
Suspended 1985
Ornament, 3.25"
ac# 523
Shepherd

81	No Mark	$6.00	**$70.00**
81	Triangle	6.00	**60.00**
82	Hourglass	6.00	**58.00**
83	Fish	9.00	**55.00**
84	Cross	10.00	**53.00**
85	Dove	10.00	**52.00**

E-5631 | BABY'S FIRST CHRISTMAS
Suspended 1985
Ornament, 3.00"
ac# 531
Boy with Teddy

*	Unmarked	$6.00	**$68.00**
81	Triangle	6.00	**64.00**
82	Hourglass	6.50	**55.00**
83	Fish	9.00	**50.00**
84	Cross	10.00	**49.00**
85	Dove	10.00	**48.00**

*Unmarked pieces could have been produced in any of the years of production. Consider Triangle as the First Mark.

E-5632 | BABY'S FIRST CHRISTMAS
Suspended 1985
Ornament, 3.00"
ac# 532
Girl with Bunny

*	Unmarked	$6.00	**$65.00**
81	Triangle	6.00	**62.00**
82	Hourglass	6.50	**55.00**
83	Fish	9.00	**53.00**
84	Cross	10.00	**50.00**
85	Dove	10.00	**49.00**

*Unmarked pieces could have been produced in any of the years of production. Consider Triangle as the First Mark.

E-5633 | COME LET US ADORE HIM   Set of 4
Suspended 1984
Ornament, 2.50"
ac# 221
Jesus, Mary, Joseph & Lamb

*	Unmarked	$22.00	**$145.00**
81	Triangle	22.00	**140.00**
82	Hourglass	25.00	**125.00**
83	Fish	31.50	**120.00**
84	Cross	31.50	**115.00**

*Unmarked pieces could have been produced in any of the years of production. Consider Triangle as the First Mark. Mixed sets of Triangle/Hourglass & Hourglass/Fish are common. Take lower GBTru$.

E-5634 <u>WEE THREE KINGS</u> Set of 3

Suspended 1984	*	Unmarked	$19.00	**$150.00**
Ornament, 3.50"	81	Triangle	19.00	**154.00**
ac# 1053	82	Hourglass	19.00	**138.00**
Three Kings	83	Fish	25.00	**125.00**
	84	Cross	27.50	**120.00**

*Unmarked pieces could have been produced in any of the years of production. Consider Triangle as the First Mark. Mixed sets of Triangle/Hourglass & Hourglass/Fish are common. Take lower GBTru$.

E-5635 <u>WEE THREE KINGS</u> Nativity Addition Set of 3

Ongoing	*	Unmarked	$40.00	**$160.00**
Figurine, 5.50"	81	Triangle	40.00	**128.00**
ac# 1053	82	Hourglass	50.00	**95.00**
Three Kings	83	Fish	50.00	**90.00**
	84	Cross	55.00	**85.00**
*Although scarce, Unmarked	85	Dove	55.00	**80.00**
pieces could have been	86	Olive Branch	55.00	**78.00**
produced in any of the years	87	Cedar Tree	60.00	**76.00**
of production. Consider	88	Flower	60.00	**75.00**
Triangle as the First Mark.	89	Bow & Arrow	70.00	**75.00**
	90	Flame	75.00	**75.00**
	91	Vessel	75.00	**75.00**
	92	G-Clef	75.00	**75.00**
	93	Butterfly	75.00	**75.00**
	94	Trumpet	75.00	**75.00**
	95	Ship	75.00	**75.00**
	96	Heart	75.00	**75.00**
	97	Sword	75.00	**75.00**
	98	Eyeglasses	75.00	**75.00**
	99	Star	75.00	**75.00**

E-5636 <u>REJOICE O EARTH</u> Nativity Addition

Ongoing	*	Unmarked	$15.00	**$78.00**
Figurine, 5.00"	81	Triangle	15.00	**65.00**
ac# 803	82	Hourglass	19.00	**50.00**
Angel with Trumpet	83	Fish	19.00	**45.00**
	84	Cross	20.00	**40.00**
*Unmarked pieces could	85	Dove	20.00	**35.00**
have been produced in any of	86	Olive Branch	20.00	**33.00**
the years of production.	87	Cedar Tree	22.50	**33.00**
Consider Triangle as the First	88	Flower	22.50	**33.00**
Mark.	89	Bow & Arrow	27.50	**33.00**
	90	Flame	30.00	**32.50**
	91	Vessel	30.00	**32.50**
	92	G-Clef	30.00	**32.50**
	93	Butterfly	30.00	**32.50**
	94	Trumpet	30.00	**32.50**
	95	Ship	30.00	**32.50**
	96	Heart	32.50	**32.50**
	97	Sword	32.50	**32.50**
	98	Eyeglasses	32.50	**32.50**
	99	Star	32.50	**32.50**

E-5637 THE HEAVENLY LIGHT   Nativity Addition

Ongoing
Figurine, 4.85"
ac# 938
Angel with Flashlight

*Unmarked pieces could have been produced in any of the years of production. Consider Triangle as the First Mark.

*	Unmarked	$15.00	**$76.00**
81	Triangle	15.00	**65.00**
82	Hourglass	17.00	**57.00**
83	Fish	17.00	**48.00**
84	Cross	19.00	**45.00**
85	Dove	19.00	**35.00**
86	Olive Branch	19.00	**34.00**
87	Cedar Tree	21.00	**33.00**
88	Flower	21.00	**33.00**
89	Bow & Arrow	25.00	**33.00**
90	Flame	27.50	**33.00**
91	Vessel	27.50	**32.50**
92	G-Clef	27.50	**32.50**
93	Butterfly	27.50	**32.50**
94	Trumpet	27.50	**32.50**
95	Ship	30.00	**32.50**
96	Heart	32.50	**32.50**
97	Sword	32.50	**32.50**
98	Eyeglasses	32.50	**32.50**
99	Star	32.50	**32.50**

E-5638 COW   Nativity Addition

Ongoing
Figurine, 3.50"
ac# 229
Cow with Bell

84	Unmarked	$16.00	**$50.00**
84	Cross	21.00	**45.00**
85	Dove	21.00	**36.00**
86	Olive Branch	22.50	**35.00**
87	Cedar Tree	22.50	**34.00**
88	Flower	27.50	**33.00**
89	Bow & Arrow	30.00	**33.00**
90	Flame	32.50	**33.00**
91	Vessel	32.50	**32.50**
92	G-Clef	32.50	**32.50**
93	Butterfly	32.50	**32.50**
94	Trumpet	32.50	**32.50**
95	Ship	32.50	**32.50**
96	Heart	32.50	**32.50**
97	Sword	32.50	**32.50**
98	Eyeglasses	32.50	**32.50**
99	Star	32.50	**32.50**

E-5639 ISN'T HE WONDERFUL   Nativity Addition

Suspended 1985
Figurine, 4.75"
ac# 504
Boy Angel Praying with Harp

*	Unmarked	$12.00	**$75.00**
81	Triangle	12.00	**70.00**
82	Hourglass	15.00	**62.00**
83	Fish	15.00	**60.00**
84	Cross	17.00	**58.00**
85	Dove	17.00	**52.00**

*Unmarked pieces could have been produced in any of the years of production. Consider Triangle as the First Mark.

E-5640 ISN'T HE WONDERFUL   Nativity Addition

Suspended 1985
Figurine, 4.75"
ac# 505
Girl Angel Praying with Harp

*	Unmarked	$12.00	**$80.00**
81	Triangle	12.00	**80.00**
82	Hourglass	15.00	**68.00**
83	Fish	15.00	**65.00**
84	Cross	17.00	**60.00**
85	Dove	17.00	**52.00**

*Unmarked pieces could have been produced in any of the years of production. Consider Triangle as the First Mark.

E-5641 THE FOLLOWED THE STAR   Nativity Addition

Suspended 1985		*	Unmarked	$75.00	**$230.00**
	Figurine, 6.00"	81	Triangle	75.00	**250.00**
	ac# 980	82	Hourglass	90.00	**205.00**
	"Follow Me" Angel with	83	Fish	90.00	**200.00**
	Three Kings	84	Cross	100.00	**195.00**
		85	Dove	100.00	**185.00**

*Unmarked pieces could have been produced in any of the years of production. Consider Triangle as the First Mark.

E-5642 SILENT KNIGHT   Tune: Silent Night

Suspended 1985		*	Unmarked	$45.00	**$475.00**
	Musical, 6.25"	81	Triangle	45.00	**450.00**
	ac# 864	82	Hourglass	55.00	**425.00**
	Boy Angel & Knight	83	Fish	55.00	**415.00**
		84	Cross	60.00	**400.00**
		85	Dove	60.00	**390.00**

*Unmarked pieces could have been produced in any of the years of production. Consider Triangle as the First Mark. Exists in a double mark Triangle/Hourglass.

E-5644 TWO SECTION WALL   Nativity Addition   Set of 2

Ongoing		*	Unmarked	$60.00	**$160.00**
	Figurine, 6.00"	81	Triangle	60.00	**150.00**
	ac# 1027	82	Hourglass	80.00	**140.00**
	Two Section Wall	83	Fish	80.00	**135.00**
		84	Cross	90.00	**125.00**
	*Unmarked pieces could	85	Dove	90.00	**124.00**
	have been produced in any of	86	Olive Branch	90.00	**123.00**
	the years of production.	87	Cedar Tree	100.00	**122.00**
	Consider Triangle as the First	88	Flower	100.00	**120.00**
	Mark.	89	Bow & Arrow	110.00	**120.00**
		90	Flame	120.00	**120.00**
		91	Vessel	120.00	**120.00**
		92	G-Clef	120.00	**120.00**
		93	Butterfly	120.00	**120.00**
		94	Trumpet	120.00	**120.00**
		95	Ship	120.00	**120.00**
		96	Heart	120.00	**120.00**
		97	Sword	120.00	**120.00**
		98	Eyeglasses	120.00	**120.00**
		99	Star	120.00	**120.00**

E-5645 REJOICE O EARTH   Tune: Joy To The World

Retired 1988		81	Unmarked	$35.00	**$130.00**
	Musical, 6.25"	84	Cross	45.00	**115.00**
	ac# 803	85	Dove	45.00	**110.00**
	Angel with Trumpet	86	Olive Branch	45.00	**105.00**
		87	Cedar Tree	50.00	**100.00**
		88	Flower	50.00	**95.00**

E-5646 COME LET US ADORE HIM   Series: "Christmas Collection"–
1st Issue   Individually Numbered

Limited Edition 15,000		81	Unmarked	$40.00	**$42.00**
	Plate, 8.50"				
	ac# 221				
	Nativity Scene				

E-6118 BUT LOVE GOES ON FOREVER   Set of 2

Suspended 1988		81	Unmarked	$14.00	**$110.00**
	Candle Climber, 2.50"	84	Cross	20.00	**100.00**
	ac# 184	85	Dove	20.00	**95.00**
	Angels on Clouds	86	Olive Branch	20.00	**92.00**
		87	Cedar Tree	22.50	**90.00**
		88	Flower	25.00	**85.00**

E-6120	WE HAVE SEEN HIS STAR				
	Retired 1984	81	No Mark	$6.00	**$75.00**
	Ornament, 3.00"	81	Triangle	6.00	**65.00**
	ac# 1044	82	Hourglass	6.00	**54.00**
	Boy Holding Lamb	83	Fish	9.00	**50.00**
		84	Cross	10.00	**45.00**

E-6214B	MIKEY				
	Suspended 1985	81	Unmarked	$150.00	**$230.00**
	Doll, 16.50"	83	Fish	175.00	**200.00**
	ac# 687	84	Cross	200.00	**200.00**
	Mikey	85	Dove	200.00	**200.00**

E-6214G	DEBBIE				
	Suspended 1985	81	Unmarked	$150.00	**$260.00**
	Doll, 16.50"	83	Fish	175.00	**245.00**
	ac# 237	84	Cross	200.00	**242.00**
	Debbie	85	Dove	200.00	**240.00**

E-6613	GOD SENDS THE GIFT OF HIS LOVE				
	Suspended 1987	84	Cross	$22.50	**$70.00**
	Figurine, 5.75"	85	Dove	22.50	**65.00**
	ac# 339	86	Olive Branch	22.50	**64.00**
	Girl with Present	87	Cedar Tree	22.50	**62.00**

E-6901	COLLECTION PLAQUE				
	Suspended 1986	82	Hourglass	$19.00	**$110.00**
	Plaque, 3.50"	83	Fish	19.00	**65.00**
	ac# 184	84	Cross	20.00	**62.00**
	Boy Angel on Cloud	85	Dove	20.00	**58.00**
		86	Olive Branch	20.00	**57.00**
	Exists in a double mark Hourglass/Fish.				

E-7153	GOD IS LOVE, DEAR VALENTINE				
	Suspended 1986	82	Triangle	$16.00	**$58.00**
	Figurine, 5.50"	82	Hourglass	16.00	**32.00**
	ac# 333	83	Fish	16.00	**28.00**
	Boy Holding Heart	84	Cross	17.00	**25.00**
		85	Dove	17.00	**24.00**
		86	Olive Branch	17.00	**23.00**

E-7154	GOD IS LOVE, DEAR VALENTINE				
	Suspended 1986	82	Triangle	$16.00	**$58.00**
	Figurine, 5.50"	82	Hourglass	16.00	**32.00**
	ac# 334	83	Fish	16.00	**28.00**
	Girl Holding Heart	84	Cross	17.00	**25.00**
		85	Dove	17.00	**24.00**
		86	Olive Branch	17.00	**23.00**

E-7155	THANKING HIM FOR YOU				
	Suspended 1984	82	Hourglass	$16.00	**$60.00**
	Figurine, 5.50"	83	Fish	16.00	**58.00**
	ac# 922	84	Cross	17.00	**54.00**
	Girl Praying				

E-7156	I BELIEVE IN MIRACLES				
	Suspended 1985 / Retired 1992	82	Hourglass	$17.00	**$100.00**
	Figurine, 4.25"	83	Fish	17.00	**88.00**
	ac# 455	84	Cross	19.00	**82.00**
	Boy Holding Chick	85	Dove	19.00	**80.00**
	Suspended in 1985, re-introduced in 1987, retired in 1992. See next listing and page 409.				

236

E-7156R

I BELIEVE IN MIRACLES
Retired 1992
Figurine, 4.50"
ac# 456
Boy Holding Bluebird

87	Cedar Tree	$22.50	**$72.00**
88	Flower	22.50	**68.00**
89	Bow & Arrow	25.00	**65.00**
90	Flame	27.50	**63.00**
91	Vessel	27.50	**60.00**

First introduced in 1982 as E-7156, the original version of this figurine had the boy holding a yellow chick. E-7156 was suspended in 1985, and in 1987 was re-sculptured and returned to production as E-7156R. Among the changes made was the addition of the incised "Sam B" on the base of the figurine, and a change in the color of the chick–from yellow to blue. The re-sculptured piece is also considerably larger than the original version. During the early part of production in 1987 (Cedar Tree), the molds from the suspended piece, E-7156, were pulled and used along with the molds for the new re-introduced piece, E-7156R. Shipments of figurines crafted from the old suspended mold but with the new blue painting of the chick were made before the error was discovered. These pieces are the rare version. All rare versions have the Cedar Tree Symbol. The GBTru$ for the rare version is $200.00. See page 409.

E-7157

THERE IS JOY IN SERVING JESUS
Retired 1986
Figurine, 5.50"
ac# 972
Waitress Carrying Food

82	Hourglass	$17.00	**$68.00**
83	Fish	17.00	**62.00**
84	Cross	19.00	**59.00**
85	Dove	19.00	**55.00**
86	Olive Branch	19.00	**52.00**

E-7158

LOVE BEARETH ALL THINGS
Ongoing
Figurine, 5.15"
ac# 599
Nurse Giving Shot to Bear

82	Hourglass	$25.00	**$72.00**
83	Fish	25.00	**55.00**
84	Cross	27.50	**50.00**
85	Dove	27.50	**48.00**
86	Olive Branch	27.50	**45.00**
87	Cedar Tree	30.00	**45.00**
88	Flower	32.50	**45.00**
89	Bow & Arrow	36.00	**45.00**
90	Flame	37.50	**45.00**
91	Vessel	37.50	**45.00**
92	G-Clef	37.50	**45.00**
93	Butterfly	37.50	**45.00**
94	Trumpet	40.00	**45.00**
95	Ship	40.00	**45.00**
96	Heart	45.00	**45.00**
97	Sword	45.00	**45.00**
98	Eyeglasses	45.00	**45.00**
99	Star	45.00	**45.00**

E-7159

LORD GIVE ME PATIENCE
Suspended 1985
Figurine, 5.50"
ac# 581
Bandaged Boy by Sign

82	Hourglass	$25.00	**$68.00**
83	Fish	25.00	**62.00**
84	Cross	27.50	**60.00**
85	Dove	27.50	**55.00**

E-7160

THE PERFECT GRANDPA
Suspended 1986
Figurine, 5.00"
ac# 962
Grandpa in Rocking Chair

82	Hourglass	$25.00	**$82.00**
83	Fish	25.00	**75.00**
84	Cross	27.50	**70.00**
85	Dove	27.50	**68.00**
86	Olive Branch	27.50	**65.00**

E-7161	HIS SHEEP AM I				
	Suspended 1984	*	Unmarked	$25.00	**$120.00**
	Figurine, 5.25"	82	Hourglass	25.00	**75.00**
	ac# 434	83	Fish	25.00	**72.00**
	Shepherd Painting Lamb	84	Cross	27.50	**70.00**

*Unmarked pieces could have been produced in any of the years of production. Consider Hourglass as the First Mark.

E-7162	LOVE IS SHARING				
	Suspended 1984	82	Hourglass	$25.00	**$170.00**
	Figurine, 4.75"	83	Fish	25.00	**160.00**
	ac# 613	84	Cross	27.50	**148.00**
	Girl at School Desk				

E-7163	GOD IS WATCHING OVER YOU				
	Suspended 1984	82	Hourglass	$27.50	**$110.00**
	Figurine, 5.25"	83	Fish	27.50	**95.00**
	ac# 336	84	Cross	30.00	**90.00**
	Boy with Ice Bag on Head				

E-7164	BLESS THIS HOUSE				
	Suspended 1984	82	Hourglass	$45.00	**$250.00**
	Figurine, 5.50"	83	Fish	45.00	**215.00**
	ac# 143	84	Cross	50.00	**198.00**
	Boy & Girl Painting Dog House				

E-7165	LET THE WHOLE WORLD KNOW				
	Suspended 1987	*	Unmarked	$45.00	**$165.00**
	Figurine, 6.00"	82	Hourglass	45.00	**140.00**
	ac# 566	83	Fish	45.00	**128.00**
	Boy & Girl in Baptism	84	Cross	50.00	**120.00**
	Bucket	85	Dove	50.00	**115.00**
		86	Olive Branch	50.00	**110.00**
		87	Cedar Tree	50.00	**100.00**

*Unmarked pieces could have been produced in any of the years of production. Consider Hourglass as the First Mark.

E-7166	THE LORD BLESS YOU AND KEEP YOU				
	Suspended 1993	82	Hourglass	$22.50	**$68.00**
	Frame, 5.50"	83	Fish	22.50	**60.00**
	ac# 942	84	Cross	25.00	**55.00**
	Bride and Groom	85	Dove	25.00	**53.00**
		86	Olive Branch	25.00	**52.00**
		87	Cedar Tree	25.00	**51.00**
		88	Flower	27.50	**50.00**
		89	Bow & Arrow	30.00	**49.00**
		90	Flame	32.50	**48.00**
		91	Vessel	32.50	**47.00**
		92	G-Clef	32.50	**46.00**
		93	Butterfly	32.50	**45.00**

E-7167	THE LORD BLESS YOU AND KEEP YOU				
	Suspended 1985	82	Hourglass	$22.50	**$64.00**
	Box, 5.00"	83	Fish	22.50	**60.00**
	ac# 942	84	Cross	25.00	**55.00**
	Bride and Groom	85	Dove	25.00	**52.00**

E-7168	MY GUARDIAN ANGEL				
	Suspended 1984	82	Hourglass	$18.00	**$68.00**
	Frame, 5.50"	83	Fish	18.00	**64.00**
	ac# 702	84	Cross	19.00	**62.00**
	Boy Angel				

E-7169	MY GUARDIAN ANGEL				
	Suspended 1984	82	Hourglass	$18.00	**$70.00**
	Frame, 5.50"	83	Fish	18.00	**62.00**
	ac# 703	84	Cross	19.00	**60.00**
	Girl Angel				

E-7170	JESUS LOVES ME				
	Suspended 1985	82	Hourglass	$17.00	**$65.00**
	Frame, 4.25"	83	Fish	17.00	**60.00**
	ac# 531	84	Cross	19.00	**58.00**
	Boy with Teddy	85	Dove	19.00	**55.00**

E-7171	JESUS LOVES ME				
	Suspended 1985	82	Hourglass	$17.00	**$70.00**
	Frame, 4.25"	83	Fish	17.00	**67.00**
	ac# 532	84	Cross	19.00	**65.00**
	Girl with Bunny	85	Dove	19.00	**64.00**

E-7172	REJOICING WITH YOU				
	Suspended 1985	82	Unmarked	$30.00	**$35.00**
	Plate, 7.25"	84	Cross	30.00	**30.00**
	ac# 805	85	Dove	30.00	**30.00**
	Christening				

E-7173	THE PURR-FECT GRANDMA	Series: "Mother's Love"–2nd Issue			
	Individually Numbered				
	Limited Edition 15,000	82	Unmarked	$40.00	**$40.00**
	Plate, 8.50"				
	ac# 963				
	Grandma in Rocker				

E-7174	MAKE A JOYFUL NOISE	Series: "Inspired Thoughts"–2nd Issue			
	Individually Numbered				
	Limited Edition 15,000	82	Unmarked	$40.00	**$42.00**
	Plate, 8.50"		Cross		**40.00**
	ac# 644				
	Girl with Goose				

E-7175	THE LORD BLESS YOU AND KEEP YOU				
	Suspended 1985	82	Unmarked	$17.00	**$40.00**
	Bell, 5.75"	84	Cross	19.00	**38.00**
	ac# 943	85	Dove	19.00	**35.00**
	Boy Graduate				

E-7176	THE LORD BLESS YOU AND KEEP YOU				
	Suspended 1985	82	Unmarked	$17.00	**$65.00**
	Bell, 5.75"	84	Cross	19.00	**58.00**
	ac# 944	85	Dove	19.00	**55.00**
	Girl Graduate				

E-7177	THE LORD BLESS YOU AND KEEP YOU				
	Suspended 1987	82	Hourglass	$18.00	**$52.00**
	Frame, 5.50"	83	Fish	18.00	**48.00**
	ac# 943	84	Cross	19.00	**46.00**
	Boy Graduate	85	Dove	19.00	**45.00**
		86	Olive Branch	19.00	**44.00**
		87	Cedar Tree	20.00	**43.00**

E-7178	THE LORD BLESS YOU AND KEEP YOU				
	Suspended 1987	82	Hourglass	$18.00	**$80.00**
	Frame, 5.25"	83	Fish	18.00	**78.00**
	ac# 944	84	Cross	19.00	**75.00**
	Girl Graduate	85	Dove	19.00	**70.00**
		86	Olive Branch	19.00	**68.00**
		87	Cedar Tree	20.00	**65.00**

E-7179	THE LORD BLESS YOU AND KEEP YOU				
	Suspended 1993	82	Unmarked	$22.50	**$67.00**
	Bell, 5.50"	84	Cross	25.00	**60.00**
	ac# 942	85	Dove	25.00	**58.00**
	Bride and Groom	86	Olive Branch	25.00	**56.00**
		87	Cedar Tree	25.00	**55.00**
		88	Flower	30.00	**53.00**
		89	Bow & Arrow	33.00	**52.00**
		90	Flame	35.00	**51.00**
		91	Vessel	35.00	**50.00**
		92	G-Clef	35.00	**49.00**
		93	Butterfly	35.00	**48.00**

E-7180	THE LORD BLESS YOU AND KEEP YOU		Tune: Wedding March		
	Ongoing	82	No Mark	$55.00	**$105.00**
	Musical, 6.00"	84	Cross	55.00	**90.00**
	ac# 942	85	Dove	60.00	**88.00**
	Bride and Groom on Cake	86	Olive Branch	60.00	**85.00**
		87	Cedar Tree	60.00	**85.00**
		88	Flower	70.00	**85.00**
		89	Bow & Arrow	75.00	**85.00**
		90	Flame	80.00	**85.00**
		91	Vessel	80.00	**85.00**
		92	G-Clef	80.00	**85.00**
		93	Butterfly	85.00	**85.00**
		94	Trumpet	85.00	**85.00**
		95	Ship	85.00	**85.00**
		96	Heart	85.00	**85.00**
		97	Sword	85.00	**85.00**
		98	Eyeglasses	85.00	**85.00**
		99	Star	85.00	**85.00**

E-7181	MOTHER SEW DEAR				
	Suspended 1988	82	Unmarked	$17.00	**$46.00**
	Bell, 5.50"	84	Cross	19.00	**38.00**
	ac# 698	85	Dove	19.00	**37.00**
	Mother Needlepointing	86	Olive Branch	19.00	**36.00**
		87	Cedar Tree	20.00	**35.00**
		88	Flower	22.50	**33.00**

E-7182 | MOTHER SEW DEAR | Tune: You Light Up My Life

Ongoing
Musical, 6.25"
ac# 698
Mother Needlepointing

	82	Unmarked	$35.00	**$100.00**
	84	Cross	37.50	**70.00**
	85	Dove	37.50	**65.00**
	86	Olive Branch	37.50	**65.00**
	87	Cedar Tree	37.50	**65.00**
	88	Flower	45.00	**65.00**
	89	Bow & Arrow	50.00	**65.00**
	90	Flame	55.00	**65.00**
	91	Vessel	55.00	**65.00**
	92	G-Clef	55.00	**65.00**
	93	Butterfly	60.00	**65.00**
	94	Trumpet	60.00	**65.00**
	95	Ship	60.00	**65.00**
	96	Heart	65.00	**65.00**
	97	Sword	65.00	**65.00**
	98	Eyeglasses	65.00	**65.00**
	99	Star	65.00	**65.00**

E-7183 — THE PURR-FECT GRANDMA

Suspended 1988
Bell, 5.50"
ac# 963
Grandma in Rocker

*Also exists with inked Cross. GBTru$ is $72.00.

82	Unmarked	$17.00	**$54.00**
84	Cross*	19.00	**42.00**
85	Dove	19.00	**40.00**
86	Olive Branch	19.00	**38.00**
87	Cedar Tree	20.00	**37.00**
88	Flower	22.50	**36.00**

E-7184 — THE PURR-FECT GRANDMA | Tune: Always In My Heart

Suspended 1993
Musical, 6.00"
ac# 963
Grandma in Rocker

82	Unmarked	$35.00	**$98.00**
84	Cross	37.50	**90.00**
85	Dove	37.50	**80.00**
86	Olive Branch	37.50	**75.00**
87	Cedar Tree	37.50	**72.00**
88	Flower	45.00	**70.00**
89	Bow & Arrow	50.00	**68.00**
90	Flame	55.00	**65.00**
91	Vessel	55.00	**62.00**
92	G-Clef	55.00	**60.00**
93	Butterfly	60.00	**58.00**

E-7185 — LOVE IS SHARING | Tune: School Days

Retired 1985
Musical, 5.75"
ac# 613
Girl at School Desk

82	Hourglass	$40.00	**$175.00**
83	Fish	40.00	**162.00**
84	Cross	45.00	**158.00**
85	Dove	45.00	**155.00**

E-7186 — LET THE WHOLE WORLD KNOW | Tune: What A Friend We Have In Jesus

Suspended 1986
Musical, 6.25"
ac# 566
Boy & Girl in Baptism
Bucket

82	Unmarked	$60.00	**$155.00**
82	Hourglass	60.00	**136.00**
83	Fish	60.00	**125.00**
84	Cross	65.00	**120.00**
85	Dove	65.00	**118.00**
86	Olive Branch	65.00	**115.00**

E-7241 — MOTHER SEW DEAR

Suspended 1986
Frame, 5.50"
ac# 698
Mother Needlepointing

82	Hourglass	$18.00	**$55.00**
83	Fish	18.00	**52.00**
84	Cross	19.00	**42.00**
85	Dove	19.00	**38.00**
86	Olive Branch	19.00	**35.00**

E-7242	THE PURR-FECT GRANDMA				
	Suspended 1988	82	Hourglass	$18.00	**$54.00**
	Frame, 5.50"	83	Fish	18.00	**50.00**
	ac# 963	84	Cross	19.00	**48.00**
	Grandma in Rocker	85	Dove	19.00	**46.00**
		86	Olive Branch	19.00	**45.00**
		87	Cedar Tree	20.00	**44.00**
		88	Flower	22.50	**42.00**

E-7267B	CUBBY Individually Numbered on Foot / Certificate of Authenticity				
	Limited Edition 5,000	82	Unmarked	$200.00	**$400.00**
	Doll, 18.00"				
	ac# 232				
	Groom Doll				

E-7267G	TAMMY Individually Numbered on Foot / Certificate of Authenticity				
	Limited Edition 5,000	82	Unmarked	$300.00	**$525.00**
	Doll, 18.00"				
	ac# 911				
	Bride Doll				

E-7350	RETAILER'S DOME Gift to Centers / Figurine under Dome				
	Special Gift	84	Cross	$Gift	**$825.00**
	Figurine, 9.00"		(w/o dome)		**675.00**
	ac# 184				
	Kids on Cloud under Dome				

E-9251	LOVE IS PATIENT				
	Suspended 1985	83	Fish	$35.00	**$90.00**
	Figurine, 5.00"	84	Cross*	35.00	**82.00**
	ac# 612	85	Dove	35.00	**78.00**
	Boy Holding Blackboard with Teacher				

*Also exists with decal Cross. GBTru$ is $105.00.

E-9252	FORGIVING IS FORGETTING				
	Suspended 1989	83	Fish	$37.50	**$95.00**
	Figurine, 5.75"	84	Cross	37.50	**84.00**
	ac# 286	85	Dove	37.50	**82.00**
	Boy & Girl with Bandage	86	Olive Branch	37.50	**78.00**
		87	Cedar Tree	37.50	**75.00**
		88	Flower	42.50	**70.00**
		89	Bow & Arrow	47.50	**68.00**

E-9253	THE END IS IN SIGHT				
	Suspended 1985	*	Unmarked	$25.00	**$140.00**
	Figurine, 5.25"	83	Hourglass	25.00	**80.00**
	ac# 925	83	Fish	25.00	**78.00**
	Boy with Dog Ripping Pants	84	Cross	25.00	**75.00**
		85	Dove	25.00	**72.00**

*Unmarked pieces could have been produced in any of the years of production, however it is known many were released in the first year of production.

E-9254   PRAISE THE LORD ANYHOW
Retired 1994

Figurine, 4.75"
ac# 786
Girl at Typewriter

*Classic Variation: "Inked Fish." During 1983, the Fish appeared as part of the understamp decal on many pieces. Pieces were also produced that did not have a Fish at all–incised or decal. When this occurred we can only theorize an attempt was made to correct it by actually drawing the Fish on the bottom of the piece. This inked symbol can be washed off, creating an unmarked piece. The GBTru$ for the "Erasable Inked Fish" is $182.00. See page 409.

83	Hourglass	$35.00	**$120.00**
83	Fish*	35.00	**95.00**
84	Cross	35.00	**91.00**
85	Dove	35.00	**90.00**
86	Olive Branch	35.00	**89.00**
87	Cedar Tree	38.50	**86.00**
88	Flower	40.00	**84.00**
89	Bow & Arrow	47.50	**82.00**
90	Flame	50.00	**80.00**
91	Vessel	50.00	**75.00**
92	G-Clef	50.00	**72.00**
93	Butterfly	50.00	**70.00**
94	Trumpet	55.00	**65.00**

E-9255   BLESS YOU TWO
Ongoing

Figurine, 5.25"
ac# 150
Groom Carrying Bride

83	Fish	$21.00	**$55.00**
84	Cross	21.00	**48.00**
85	Dove	21.00	**45.00**
86	Olive Branch	21.00	**45.00**
87	Cedar Tree	23.00	**45.00**
88	Flower	25.00	**45.00**
89	Bow & Arrow	30.00	**45.00**
90	Flame	32.50	**45.00**
91	Vessel	32.50	**45.00**
92	G-Clef	32.50	**45.00**
93	Butterfly	35.00	**45.00**
94	Trumpet	37.50	**45.00**
95	Ship	40.00	**45.00**
96	Heart	45.00	**45.00**
97	Sword	45.00	**45.00**
98	Eyeglasses	45.00	**45.00**
99	Star	45.00	**45.00**

E-9256   THE HAND THAT ROCKS THE FUTURE   Series: "Mother's Love"–3rd Issue
Individually Numbered
Limited Edition 15,000

Plate, 8.50"
ac# 937
Girl Rocking Cradle

83	Unmarked	$40.00	**$42.00**
84	Cross		**40.00**

E-9257   I BELIEVE IN MIRACLES   Series: "Inspired Thoughts"–3rd Issue
Individually Numbered
Limited Edition 15,000

Plate, 8.50"
ac# 455
Boy Holding Chick

83	Unmarked	$40.00	**$42.00**
	Cross		**40.00**

E-9258 — WE ARE GOD'S WORKMANSHIP

Ongoing
Figurine, 5.25"
ac# 1039
Bonnet Girl with Butterfly

Year	Symbol	Price	Value
83	Hourglass	$19.00	**$58.00**
83	Fish	19.00	**45.00**
84	Cross	19.00	**38.00**
85	Dove	19.00	**37.00**
86	Olive Branch	19.00	**35.00**
87	Cedar Tree	21.00	**35.00**
88	Flower	22.50	**35.00**
89	Bow & Arrow	25.00	**35.00**
90	Flame	27.50	**35.00**
91	Vessel	27.50	**35.00**
92	G-Clef	27.50	**35.00**
93	Butterfly	30.00	**35.00**
94	Trumpet	30.00	**35.00**
95	Ship	32.50	**35.00**
96	Heart	35.00	**35.00**
97	Sword	35.00	**35.00**
98	Eyeglasses	35.00	**35.00**
99	Star	35.00	**35.00**

E-9259 — WE'RE IN IT TOGETHER

Suspended 1990
Figurine, 3.75"
ac# 1048
Boy with Piggy

Year	Symbol	Price	Value
83	Hourglass	$24.00	**$98.00**
83	Fish	24.00	**95.00**
84	Cross	24.00	**88.00**
85	Dove	24.00	**87.00**
86	Olive Branch	24.00	**80.00**
87	Cedar Tree	27.00	**75.00**
88	Flower	30.00	**70.00**
89	Bow & Arrow	33.00	**65.00**
90	Flame	35.00	**60.00**

E-9260 — GOD'S PROMISES ARE SURE   Series: "Heavenly Halos"

Suspended 1987
Figurine, 5.50"
ac# 348
Boy Angel Winding Rainbow

Year	Symbol	Price	Value
83	Fish*	$30.00	**$80.00**
84	Cross	30.00	**75.00**
85	Dove	30.00	**74.00**
86	Olive Branch	30.00	**72.00**
87	Cedar Tree	33.50	**70.00**

*Also exists with a stamped Fish.

E-9261 — SEEK YE THE LORD

Suspended 1986
Figurine, 4.75"
ac# 829
Boy Graduate with Scroll

Year	Symbol	Price	Value
83	Fish*	$21.00	**$52.00**
84	Cross	21.00	**50.00**
85	Dove	21.00	**48.00**
86	Olive Branch	21.00	**45.00**

*Most figurines with the Fish Annual Production Symbol do not have the "h" in the word "he" in the inscription on the graduate's scroll capitalized. See page 410.

E-9262 — SEEK YE THE LORD

Suspended 1986
Figurine, 4.75"
ac# 830
Girl Graduate with Scroll

Year	Symbol	Price	Value
83	Fish*	$21.00	**$70.00**
84	Cross	21.00	**64.00**
85	Dove	21.00	**60.00**
86	Olive Branch	21.00	**55.00**

*Most figurines with the Fish Annual Production Symbol do not have the "h" in the word "he" in the inscription on the graduate's scroll capitalized. See page 410.

E-9263 — HOW CAN TWO WALK TOGETHER EXCEPT THEY AGREE

Suspended 1985
Figurine, 5.25"
ac# 452
Boy and Girl in Horse Costume

Year	Symbol	Price	Value
83	Hourglass	$35.00	**$180.00**
83	Fish	35.00	**152.00**
84	Cross	35.00	**140.00**
85	Dove	35.00	**130.00**

E-9265

PRESS ON
Ongoing
Figurine, 5.75"
ac# 793
Girl Ironing Clothes

83	Hourglass	$40.00	**$90.00**
83	Fish	40.00	**80.00**
84	Cross	40.00	**70.00**
85	Dove	40.00	**68.00**
86	Olive Branch	40.00	**65.00**
87	Cedar Tree	45.00	**65.00**
88	Flower	45.00	**65.00**
89	Bow & Arrow	50.00	**65.00**
90	Flame	55.00	**65.00**
91	Vessel	55.00	**65.00**
92	G-Clef	55.00	**65.00**
93	Butterfly	60.00	**65.00**
94	Trumpet	60.00	**65.00**
95	Ship	60.00	**65.00**
96	Heart	65.00	**65.00**
97	Sword	65.00	**65.00**
98	Eyeglasses	65.00	**65.00**
99	Star	65.00	**65.00**

E-9266

I'M FALLING FOR SOMEBUNNY
Suspended 1988
Box, 3.00"
ac# 489
Lamb and Bunny

Some understamp decals
have the title "Somebunny
Cares."

83	Unmarked	$13.50	**$50.00**
83	Fish	13.50	**48.00**
84	Cross	16.00	**44.00**
85	Dove	16.00	**42.00**
86	Olive Branch	16.00	**40.00**
87	Cedar Tree	16.00	**38.00**
88	Flower	18.50	**35.00**

E-9266

OUR LOVE IS HEAVEN SCENT
Suspended 1988
Box, 3.00"
ac# 489
Lamb and Skunk

Some understamp decals
have the title "Somebunny
Cares."

83	Unmarked	$13.50	**$52.00**
83	Fish	13.50	**50.00**
84	Cross	16.00	**45.00**
85	Dove	16.00	**42.00**
86	Olive Branch	16.00	**40.00**
87	Cedar Tree	16.00	**39.00**
88	Flower	18.50	**38.00**

E-9267

ANIMAL COLLECTION   Set of 6 / (Divide by 6 for an "each" value)
Suspended 1991
Figurine, 2.50"
ac# 64
Animals

83	Unmarked	$39.00	**$160.00**
83	Fish	39.00	**156.00**
84	Cross	45.00	**150.00**
85	Dove	45.00	**144.00**
86	Olive Branch	45.00	**138.00**
87	Cedar Tree	48.00	**132.00**

Note: The Animal Collection was shipped to retailers in sets of 6,
consequently they do not have individual boxes. In 1988, individual
Enesco Item #s were assigned for each figurine in the set of 6. Some
Cedar Tree Annual Symbol pieces have the A - F suffix.

E-9267/A

ANIMAL COLLECTION A
Suspended 1991
Figurine, 2.50"
ac# 65
Teddy Bear

88	Flower	$8.50	**$21.00**
89	Bow & Arrow	10.00	**20.00**
90	Flame	11.00	**20.00**
91	Vessel	11.00	**19.00**

E-9267/B

ANIMAL COLLECTION B
Suspended 1991
Figurine, 3.00"
ac# 66
Dog with Slippers

88	Flower	$8.50	**$20.00**
89	Bow & Arrow	10.00	**19.00**
90	Flame	11.00	**19.00**
91	Vessel	11.00	**18.00**

E-9267/C	ANIMAL COLLECTION C				
	Suspended 1991	88	Flower	$8.50	**$21.00**
	Figurine, 2.60"	89	Bow & Arrow	10.00	**20.00**
	ac# 67	90	Flame	11.00	**20.00**
	Bunny with Carrot	91	Vessel	11.00	**19.00**

E-9267/D	ANIMAL COLLECTION D				
	Suspended 1991	88	Flower	$8.50	**$21.00**
	Figurine, 2.40"	89	Bow & Arrow	10.00	**20.00**
	ac# 68	90	Flame	11.00	**20.00**
	Cat with Bow Tie	91	Vessel	11.00	**19.00**

E-9267/E	ANIMAL COLLECTION E				
	Suspended 1991	88	Flower	$8.50	**$21.00**
	Figurine, 2.60"	89	Bow & Arrow	10.00	**20.00**
	ac# 69	90	Flame	11.00	**20.00**
	Lamb with Bird on Back	91	Vessel	11.00	**19.00**

E-9267/F	ANIMAL COLLECTION F				
	Suspended 1991	88	Flower	$8.50	**$21.00**
	Figurine, 2.10"	89	Bow & Arrow	10.00	**20.00**
	ac# 70	90	Flame	11.00	**20.00**
	Pig with Patches	91	Vessel	11.00	**19.00**

E-9268	NOBODY'S PERFECT!				
	Retired 1990	83	Hourglass*	$21.00	**$88.00**
	Figurine, 7.00"	83	Fish	21.00	**82.00**
	ac# 721	84	Cross	21.00	**78.00**
	Boy with Dunce Cap	85	Dove	21.00	**76.00**
		86	Olive Branch	21.00	**75.00**
	*Classic Variation: "Smiling	87	Cedar Tree	23.00	**72.00**
	Dunce." The first Hourglass	88	Flower	24.00	**70.00**
	pieces produced are known	89	Bow & Arrow	27.00	**68.00**
	as "Smiling Dunces" or	90	Flame	30.00	**65.00**
	"Smiley" and appeared with a				
	smile. An "O" shaped mouth				
	is the normal piece. The				
	GBTru$ for "Smiley" is				
	$525.00. See page 410.				

E-9273	LET LOVE REIGN				
	Retired 1987	83	Hourglass*	$27.50	**$250.00**
	Figurine, 5.25"	83	Fish	27.50	**80.00**
	ac# 563	84	Cross	27.50	**75.00**
	Girl with Chicks in Umbrella	85	Dove	27.50	**74.00**
		86	Olive Branch	27.50	**73.00**
	*Extremely rare, consider Fish	87	Cedar Tree	30.00	**70.00**
	as first Annual Production				
	Symbol.				

E-9274	TASTE AND SEE THAT THE LORD IS GOOD	Series: "Heavenly Halos"			
	Retired 1986	83	Fish	$22.50	**$80.00**
	Figurine, 6.25"	84	Cross	22.50	**72.00**
	ac# 913	85	Dove	22.50	**70.00**
	Girl Angel Preparing Food	86	Olive Branch	22.50	**68.00**

E-9275 JESUS LOVES ME
Suspended 1984

	83	Unmarked	$30.00	**$40.00**
	84	Cross	30.00	**35.00**

Plate, 7.25"
ac# 531
Boy with Teddy

E-9276 JESUS LOVES ME
Suspended 1984

	83	Unmarked	$30.00	**$40.00**
	84	Cross	30.00	**35.00**

Plate, 7.25"
ac# 532
Girl with Bunny

E-9278 JESUS LOVES ME
Ongoing
Figurine, 3.00"
ac# 531
Boy with Teddy

	83	Hourglass	$9.00	**$40.00**
	83	Fish	9.00	**30.00**
	84	Cross	10.00	**23.00**
	85	Dove	10.00	**21.00**
	86	Olive Branch	10.00	**20.00**
	87	Cedar Tree	10.00	**20.00**
	88	Flower	12.50	**19.00**
	89	Bow & Arrow	13.50	**18.00**
	90	Flame	15.00	**18.00**
	91	Vessel	15.00	**18.00**
	92	G-Clef	15.00	**18.00**
	93	Butterfly	15.00	**17.50**
	94	Trumpet	16.00	**17.50**
	95	Ship	17.00	**17.50**
	96	Heart	17.50	**17.50**
	97	Sword	17.50	**17.50**
	98	Eyeglasses	17.50	**17.50**
	99	Star	17.50	**17.50**

E-9279 JESUS LOVES ME
Ongoing
Figurine, 3.00"
ac# 532
Girl with Bunny

	83	Hourglass	$9.00	**$38.00**
	83	Fish	9.00	**32.00**
	84	Cross	10.00	**30.00**
	85	Dove	10.00	**28.00**
	86	Olive Branch	10.00	**25.00**
	87	Cedar Tree	10.00	**22.00**
	88	Flower	12.50	**20.00**
	89	Bow & Arrow	13.50	**20.00**
	90	Flame	15.00	**18.00**
	91	Vessel	15.00	**18.00**
	92	G-Clef	15.00	**18.00**
	93	Butterfly	15.00	**17.50**
	94	Trumpet	16.00	**17.50**
	95	Ship	17.00	**17.50**
	96	Heart	17.50	**17.50**
	97	Sword	17.50	**17.50**
	98	Eyeglasses	17.50	**17.50**
	99	Star	17.50	**17.50**

E-9280 JESUS LOVES ME
Suspended 1985
Box, 5.00"
ac# 531
Boy with Teddy

	83	Hourglass	$17.50	**$55.00**
	83	Fish	17.50	**50.00**
	84	Cross	19.00	**48.00**
	85	Dove	19.00	**45.00**

E-9281	JESUS LOVES ME				
	Suspended 1985	83	Hourglass	$17.50	**$68.00**
	Box, 5.00"	83	Fish	17.50	**65.00**
	ac# 532	84	Cross	19.00	**63.00**
	Girl with Bunny	85	Dove	19.00	**58.00**

E-9282	TO SOMEBUNNY SPECIAL				
	Suspended 1990	*	Unmarked	$8.00	**$45.00**
	Figurine, 3.00"	83	Fish	8.00	**40.00**
	ac# 1014	84	Cross	9.00	**38.00**
	Bunny on Heart Base	85	Dove	9.00	**36.00**
		86	Olive Branch	9.00	**35.00**
		87	Cedar Tree	10.00	**34.00**

*Unmarked pieces could have been produced in any of the years of production. Consider Fish as the First Mark. Letter "A" suffix added to Item Number in 1988. See next listing.

E-9282A	TO SOMEBUNNY SPECIAL				
	Suspended 1990	88	Flower	$10.50	**$33.00**
	Figurine, 3.00"	89	Bow & Arrow	12.00	**32.00**
	ac# 1014	90	Flame	13.50	**31.00**
	Bunny on Heart Base				

E-9282	YOU'RE WORTH YOUR WEIGHT IN GOLD				
	Suspended 1990	*	Unmarked	$8.00	**$45.00**
	Figurine, 2.50"	83	Fish	8.00	**40.00**
	ac# 1157	84	Cross	9.00	**38.00**
	Pig with Patches on Base	85	Dove	9.00	**37.00**
		86	Olive Branch	9.00	**36.00**
		87	Cedar Tree	10.00	**35.00**

*Unmarked pieces could have been produced in any of the years of production. Consider Fish as the First Mark. Letter "B" suffix added to Item Number in 1988. See next listing.

E-9282B	YOU'RE WORTH YOUR WEIGHT IN GOLD				
	Suspended 1990	88	Flower	$10.50	**34.00**
	Figurine, 2.50"	89	Bow & Arrow	12.00	**33.00**
	ac# 1157	90	Flame	13.50	**32.00**
	Pig with Patches on Base				

E-9282	ESPECIALLY FOR EWE				
	Suspended 1990	*	Unmarked	$8.00	**$45.00**
	Figurine, 3.00"	83	Fish	8.00	**40.00**
	ac# 262	84	Cross	9.00	**37.00**
	Lamb with Bird	85	Dove	9.00	**36.00**
		86	Olive Branch	9.00	**35.00**
		87	Cedar Tree	10.00	**34.00**

*Unmarked pieces could have been produced in any of the years of production. Consider Fish as the First Mark. The original title for this figurine was "Loving Ewe." Letter "C" suffix added to Item Number in 1988. See next listing.

E-9282C	ESPECIALLY FOR EWE				
	Suspended 1990	88	Flower	$10.50	**$33.00**
	Figurine, 3.00"	89	Bow & Arrow	12.00	**32.00**
	ac# 262	90	Flame	13.50	**30.00**
	Lamb with Bird				

E-9283/A — FOREVER FRIENDS

Suspended 1984
Box, 4.25"
ac# 285
Dog

83	Hourglass	$15.00	**$85.00**
83	Fish	15.00	**70.00**
84	Cross	17.00	**68.00**
*	Dove		**65.00**

*Piece was Suspended in 1984 yet exists in the 1995 Dove Annual Production Symbol.

E-9283/B — FOREVER FRIENDS

Suspended 1984
Box, 4.10"
ac# 285
Cat

83	Hourglass*	$15.00	**$115.00**
83	Fish	15.00	**98.00**
84	Cross	17.00	**88.00**

*Also exists with a decal Hourglass. GBTru$ is $135.00.

E-9285 — IF GOD BE FOR US, WHO CAN BE AGAINST US

Suspended 1985
Figurine, 5.85"
ac# 498
Boy at Pulpit

83	Fish	$27.50	**$95.00**
84	Cross	27.50	**76.00**
85	Dove	27.50	**70.00**

E-9287 — PEACE ON EARTH

Suspended 1986
Figurine, 5.25"
ac# 771
Girl with Lion & Lamb

83	Fish	$37.50	**$185.00**
84	Cross	37.50	**175.00**
85	Dove	37.50	**165.00**
86	Olive Branch	37.50	**150.00**

Re-introduced in 1997 as E-9287R. See next listing.

E-9287R — AND A CHILD SHALL LEAD THEM

Ongoing
Figurine, 5.25"
ac# 57
Child with Lion and Lamb

97	Heart	$50.00	**$53.00**
97	Sword	50.00	**50.00**
98	Eyeglasses	50.00	**50.00**
99	Star	50.00	**50.00**

Re-designed and brought back from Suspension, original title was "Peace On Earth."

E-9288 — SENDING YOU A RAINBOW   Series: "Heavenly Halos"

Suspended 1986
Figurine, 5.50"
ac# 833
Girl Angel with Sprinkler

83	Fish	$22.50	**$100.00**
84	Cross	22.50	**94.00**
85	Dove	22.50	**90.00**
86	Olive Branch	22.50	**84.00**

E-9289 — TRUST IN THE LORD   Series: "Heavenly Halos"

Suspended 1987
Figurine, 5.90"
ac# 1024
Boy Angel Taking Flying
Lessons

83	Fish	$20.00	**$85.00**
84	Cross	21.00	**75.00**
85	Dove	21.00	**68.00**
86	Olive Branch	21.00	**65.00**
87	Cedar Tree	23.00	**64.00**

12009 — LOVE COVERS ALL

Suspended 1991
Figurine, 4.50"
ac# 602
Girl Making Heart Quilt

85	Cross	$27.50	**$78.00**
85	Dove	27.50	**75.00**
86	Olive Branch	27.50	**72.00**
87	Cedar Tree	30.00	**70.00**
88	Flower	32.50	**68.00**
89	Bow & Arrow	35.00	**65.00**
90	Flame	37.50	**62.00**
91	Vessel	37.50	**60.00**

12017	LOVING YOU				
	Suspended 1987	85	Cross	$19.00	**$58.00**
	Frame, 4.50"	85	Dove	19.00	**54.00**
	ac# 333	86	Olive Branch	19.00	**52.00**
	Boy Holding Heart	87	Cedar Tree	20.00	**50.00**

12025	LOVING YOU				
	Suspended 1987	85	Cross	$19.00	**$62.00**
	Frame, 4.50"	85	Dove	19.00	**58.00**
	ac# 334	86	Olive Branch	19.00	**55.00**
	Girl Holding Heart	87	Cedar Tree	20.00	**50.00**

12033	GOD'S PRECIOUS GIFT				
	Suspended 1987	85	Dove	$19.00	**$105.00**
	Frame, 4.50"	86	Olive Branch	19.00	**90.00**
	ac# 345	87	Cedar Tree	20.00	**85.00**
	Baby Boy				

12041	GOD'S PRECIOUS GIFT				
	Suspended 1992	85	Dove	$19.00	**$65.00**
	Frame, 4.50"	86	Olive Branch	19.00	**58.00**
	ac# 346	87	Cedar Tree	19.00	**55.00**
	Baby Girl	88	Flower	22.50	**52.00**
		89	Bow & Arrow	25.00	**50.00**
		90	Flame	27.50	**48.00**
		91	Vessel	27.50	**45.00**
		92	G-Clef	27.50	**42.00**

12068	THE VOICE OF SPRING Series: "The Four Seasons"–1st Issue				
	Annual 1985	85	Cross	$30.00	**$285.00**
	Figurine, 6.40"		Dove		**255.00**
	ac# 968				
	Girl with Bible				

12076	SUMMER'S JOY Series: "The Four Seasons"–2nd Issue				
	Annual 1985	85	Cross	$30.00	**$105.00**
	Figurine, 6.40"		Dove		**95.00**
	ac# 898				
	Girl with Ducklings				

12084	AUTUMN'S PRAISE Series: "The Four Seasons"–3rd Issue				
	Annual 1986	86	Dove	$30.00	**$75.00**
	Figurine, 6.40"		Olive Branch		**55.00**
	ac# 79				
	Girl in Field of Flowers				

12092	WINTER'S SONG Series: "The Four Seasons"–4th Issue				
	Annual 1986	86	Dove	$30.00	**$135.00**
	Figurine, 6.40"		Olive Branch		**115.00**
	ac# 1064				
	Girl in Snow with Birds				

12106 THE VOICE OF SPRING   Series: "The Four Seasons"–1st Issue

Annual 1985	85	Cross	$40.00	**$100.00**
Plate, 8.50"		Dove		**90.00**
ac# 968				
Girl with Bible				

12114 SUMMER'S JOY   Series: "The Four Seasons"–2nd Issue

Annual 1985	85	Cross	$40.00	**$85.00**
Plate, 8.50"		Dove		**75.00**
ac# 898				
Girl with Ducklings				

12122 AUTUMN'S PRAISE   Series: "The Four Seasons"–3rd Issue

Annual 1986	86	Olive Branch	$40.00	**$40.00**
Plate, 8.50"				
ac# 79				
Girl in Field of Flowers				

12130 WINTER'S SONG   Series: "The Four Seasons"–4th Issue

Annual 1986	86	Dove	$40.00	**$42.00**
Plate, 8.50"		Olive Branch		**40.00**
ac# 1064				
Girl in Snow with Birds				

12149 PART OF ME WANTS TO BE GOOD

Suspended 1989	85	Cross	$19.00	**$88.00**
Figurine, 5.10"	85	Dove	19.00	**85.00**
ac# 767	86	Olive Branch	19.00	**84.00**
Angel Boy in Devil Suit	87	Cedar Tree	21.00	**83.00**
	88	Flower	22.50	**80.00**
	89	Bow & Arrow	25.00	**79.00**

12157 THIS IS THE DAY (WHICH) THE LORD HAS MADE

Suspended 1990	87	Olive Branch	$20.00	**$110.00**
Figurine, 5.00"	87	Cedar Tree	22.50	**76.00**
ac# 984	88	Flower	24.00	**75.00**
Birthday Boy	89	Bow & Arrow	27.00	**74.00**
	90	Flame	30.00	**72.00**

12165 LORD, KEEP MY LIFE IN TUNE   Series: "Rejoice In The Lord" Band
Tune: Amazing Grace / Set of 2

Suspended 1989	85	Dove	$37.50	**$150.00**
Musical, 4.50"	86	Olive Branch	37.50	**145.00**
ac# 592	87	Cedar Tree	40.00	**140.00**
Boy Playing Piano	88	Flower	45.00	**138.00**
	89	Bow & Arrow	50.00	**135.00**

12173 THERE'S A SONG IN MY HEART   Series: "Rejoice In The Lord" Band

Suspended 1990	85	Dove	$11.00	**$58.00**
Figurine, 3.50"	86	Olive Branch	11.00	**55.00**
ac# 977	87	Cedar Tree	12.00	**54.00**
Girl Playing Triangle	88	Flower	13.00	**53.00**
	89	Bow & Arrow	15.00	**52.00**
	90	Flame	16.50	**48.00**

12203 GET INTO THE HABIT OF PRAYER

Suspended 1986	85	Cross	$19.00	**$46.00**
Figurine, 5.10"	85	Dove	19.00	**40.00**
ac# 302	86	Olive Branch	19.00	**35.00**
Nun				

12211 BABY'S FIRST HAIRCUT   Series: "Baby's First"–3rd Issue

Suspended 1987	85	Dove	$32.50	**$185.00**
Figurine, 4.50"	86	Olive Branch	32.50	**165.00**
ac# 117	87	Cedar Tree	32.50	**155.00**
Angel Cutting Baby's Hair				

12238 CLOWN FIGURINES   Set of 4 / (Divide by 4 for an "each" value)

Suspended 1996	85	Dove	$54.00	**$168.00**
Figurine, 4.25"	86	Olive Branch	54.00	**160.00**
ac# 213	87	Cedar Tree	54.00	**148.00**
Mini Clowns				

Classic Variation. "CLOWNS" was misspelled "CROWNS" on the understamp decal of some sets. The GBTru$ for the set of four figurines with the "CROWNS" title error is $240.00. In 1987, individual Enesco Item #s were assigned to each figurine in the set of 4. See page 411.

12238/A CLOWN FIGURINE

Suspended 1996	87	Cedar Tree	$16.00	**$35.00**
Figurine, 3.00"	88	Flower	16.00	**33.00**
ac# 209	89	Bow & Arrow	17.50	**33.00**
Boy Balancing Ball	90	Flame	19.00	**33.00**
	91	Vessel	19.00	**31.00**
	92	G-Clef	19.00	**30.00**
	93	Butterfly	20.00	**29.00**
	94	Trumpet	20.00	**29.00**
	95	Ship	20.00	**29.00**
	96	Heart	20.00	**29.00**

12238/B CLOWN FIGURINE

Suspended 1996	87	Cedar Tree	$16.00	**$37.00**
Figurine, 4.40"	88	Flower	16.00	**35.00**
ac# 210	89	Bow & Arrow	17.50	**35.00**
Girl Holding Balloon	90	Flame	19.00	**35.00**
	91	Vessel	19.00	**33.00**
	92	G-Clef	19.00	**33.00**
	93	Butterfly	20.00	**32.00**
	94	Trumpet	20.00	**32.00**
	95	Ship	20.00	**32.00**
	96	Heart	20.00	**32.00**

12238/C CLOWN FIGURINE

Suspended 1996	87	Cedar Tree	$16.00	**$35.00**
Figurine, 3.75"	88	Flower	16.00	**33.00**
ac# 211	89	Bow & Arrow	17.50	**33.00**
Boy Bending over Ball	90	Flame	19.00	**33.00**
	91	Vessel	19.00	**31.00**
	92	G-Clef	19.00	**30.00**
	93	Butterfly	20.00	**29.00**
	94	Trumpet	20.00	**29.00**
	95	Ship	20.00	**29.00**
	96	Heart	20.00	**29.00**

12238/D CLOWN FIGURINE

Suspended 1996	87	Cedar Tree	$16.00	**$37.00**
Figurine, 3.75"	88	Flower	16.00	**35.00**
ac# 212	89	Bow & Arrow	17.50	**35.00**
Girl with Flower Pot	90	Flame	19.00	**35.00**
	91	Vessel	19.00	**33.00**
	92	G-Clef	19.00	**33.00**
	93	Butterfly	20.00	**32.00**
	94	Trumpet	20.00	**32.00**
	95	Ship	20.00	**32.00**
	96	Heart	20.00	**32.00**

12246 <u>PRECIOUS MOMENTS LAST FOREVER</u>   Sharing Season Gift

Annual 1984		84	Cross	$10.00	**$105.00**

Medallion, 3.25"
ac# 184
Medallion

Gift to Club Members for signing up new members to the Club.

12254 <u>LOVE COVERS ALL</u>

Suspended 1990
Thimble, 2.25"
ac# 602
Girl Making Heart Quilt

Year	Mark	Price	Value
85	Dove	$5.50	**$20.00**
86	Olive Branch	5.50	**17.00**
87	Cedar Tree	6.00	**16.00**
88	Flower	7.00	**15.00**
89	Bow & Arrow	8.00	**14.00**
90	Flame	8.00	**13.00**

12262 <u>I GET A BANG OUT OF YOU</u>   Series: "Clown"–1st Issue

Retired 1997
Figurine, 6.60"
ac# 462
Clown Holding Balloons

Year	Mark	Price	Value
85	Dove	$30.00	**$80.00**
86	Olive Branch	30.00	**75.00**
87	Cedar Tree	33.50	**74.00**
88	Flower	35.00	**73.00**
89	Bow & Arrow	40.00	**72.00**
90	Flame	45.00	**71.00**
91	Vessel	45.00	**70.00**
92	G-Clef	45.00	**69.00**
93	Butterfly	45.00	**68.00**
94	Trumpet	45.00	**67.00**
95	Ship	45.00	**66.00**
96	Heart	45.00	**65.00**
97	Sword	45.00	**64.00**

12270 <u>LORD KEEP ME ON THE BALL</u>   Series: "Clown"–4th Issue

Suspended 1998
Figurine, 7.00"
ac# 590
Clown Sitting on Ball

Year	Mark	Price	Value
86	Olive Branch	$30.00	**$68.00**
87	Cedar Tree	33.50	**55.00**
88	Flower	35.00	**52.00**
89	Bow & Arrow	40.00	**50.00**
90	Flame	45.00	**50.00**
91	Vessel	45.00	**50.00**
92	G-Clef	45.00	**45.00**
93	Butterfly	45.00	**45.00**
94	Trumpet	45.00	**45.00**
95	Ship	45.00	**45.00**
96	Heart	45.00	**45.00**
97	Sword	45.00	**45.00**
98	Eyeglasses	45.00	**45.00**

12297 <u>IT IS BETTER TO GIVE THAN TO RECEIVE</u>

Suspended 1987
Figurine, 5.25"
ac# 506
Policeman Writing Ticket

Year	Mark	Price	Value
85	Dove	$19.00	**$178.00**
86	Olive Branch	19.00	**165.00**
87	Cedar Tree	21.00	**160.00**

12300	LOVE NEVER FAILS				
	Ongoing	85	Dove	$25.00	**$62.00**
	Figurine, 5.50"	86	Olive Branch	25.00	**50.00**
	ac# 623	87	Cedar Tree	27.50	**48.00**
	Teacher at Desk with Report	88	Flower	30.00	**45.00**
	Card	89	Bow & Arrow	33.00	**42.00**
		90	Flame	35.00	**42.00**
		91	Vessel	35.00	**40.00**
		92	G-Clef	35.00	**40.00**
		93	Butterfly	37.50	**40.00**
		94	Trumpet	37.50	**40.00**
		95	Ship	37.50	**40.00**
		96	Heart	40.00	**40.00**
		97	Sword	40.00	**40.00**
		98	Eyeglasses	40.00	**40.00**
		99	Star	40.00	**40.00**
12319	GOD BLESS OUR HOME				
	Retired 1998	85	Dove	$40.00	**$78.00**
	Figurine, 4.40"	86	Olive Branch	40.00	**72.00**
	ac# 309	87	Cedar Tree	45.00	**70.00**
	Boy & Girl Building	88	Flower	45.00	**68.00**
	Sandcastle	89	Bow & Arrow	50.00	**68.00**
		90	Flame	55.00	**65.00**
		91	Vessel	55.00	**65.00**
		92	G-Clef	55.00	**65.00**
		93	Butterfly	60.00	**65.00**
		94	Trumpet	60.00	**65.00**
		95	Ship	60.00	**65.00**
		96	Heart	65.00	**65.00**
		97	Sword	65.00	**65.00**
		98	Eyeglasses	65.00	**65.00**
12335	YOU CAN FLY				
	Suspended 1988	86	Olive Branch	$25.00	**$68.00**
	Figurine, 5.50"	87	Cedar Tree	27.50	**65.00**
	ac# 1120	88	Flower	30.00	**62.00**
	Boy Angel on Cloud				
12343	JESUS IS COMING SOON				
	Suspended 1986	85	Dove	$22.50	**$55.00**
	Figurine, 4.75"	86	Olive Branch	22.50	**45.00**
	ac# 524				
	Mary Knitting Booties				
12351	HALO, AND MERRY CHRISTMAS				
	Suspended 1988	85	Dove	$40.00	**$218.00**
	Figurine, 6.10"	86	Olive Branch	40.00	**180.00**
	ac# 365	87	Cedar Tree	40.00	**175.00**
	Angels Making Snowman	88	Flower	45.00	**170.00**
12378	HAPPINESS IS THE LORD	Series: "Rejoice In The Lord" Band			
	Suspended 1990	85	Dove	$15.00	**$52.00**
	Figurine, 4.75"	86	Olive Branch	15.00	**50.00**
	ac# 372	87	Cedar Tree	17.00	**48.00**
	Boy Playing Banjo	88	Flower	18.00	**46.00**
		89	Bow & Arrow	20.00	**45.00**
		90	Flame	22.50	**44.00**

12386 LORD GIVE ME A SONG   Series: "Rejoice In The Lord" Band

Suspended 1990	85	Dove	$15.00	**$54.00**
Figurine, 4.90"	86	Olive Branch	15.00	**48.00**
ac# 580	87	Cedar Tree	17.00	**47.00**
Girl Playing Harmonica	88	Flower	18.00	**46.00**
	89	Bow & Arrow	20.00	**45.00**
	90	Flame	22.50	**44.00**

12394 HE IS MY SONG   Series: "Rejoice In The Lord" Band

Suspended 1990	85	Dove	$17.50	**$50.00**
Figurine, 4.50"	86	Olive Branch	17.50	**45.00**
ac# 399	87	Cedar Tree	20.00	**42.00**
Boy Playing Trumpet with	88	Flower	22.50	**40.00**
Dog	89	Bow & Arrow	25.00	**38.00**
	90	Flame	27.50	**36.00**

12408 WE SAW A STAR   Set of 3 / Tune: Joy To The World

Suspended 1987	85	Dove	$50.00	**$130.00**
Musical, 4.75"	86	Olive Branch	50.00	**120.00**
ac# 1046	87	Cedar Tree	55.00	**115.00**
Two Angels Sawing Star				

12416 HAVE A HEAVENLY CHRISTMAS

Suspended 1998	85	Dove	$12.00	**$30.00**
Ornament, 2.60"	86	Olive Branch	12.00	**25.00**
ac# 389	87	Cedar Tree*	13.50	**24.00**
Boy in Airplane	88	Flower	14.00	**23.00**
	89	Bow & Arrow	15.00	**22.00**
*There are Cedar Tree pieces	90	Flame	16.00	**20.00**
with two hooks from the	91	Vessel	16.00	**20.00**
Retailer's Wreath, #111465.	92	G-Clef	16.00	**20.00**
There are also some	93	Butterfly	16.00	**20.00**
ornaments, again from the	94	Trumpet	17.50	**20.00**
Retailer's Wreath, that have	95	Ship	18.50	**20.00**
the inscription "Heaven	96	Heart	20.00	**20.00**
Bound" upside-down. Re-	97	Sword	20.00	**20.00**
introduced in 1998 as 12416R,				
the Care-A-Van Exclusive, Have				
A Heavenly Journey. See next				
listing and page 412.				

12416R HAVE A HEAVENLY JOURNEY   Care-A-Van Exclusive

Dated Annual 1998	98	Eyeglasses	$25.00	**$25.00**
Figurine, 3.25"				
ac# 389				
Boy in Airplane				

12424 AARON

Suspended 1986	85	Dove	$135.00	**$140.00**
Doll, 12.00"	86	Olive Branch	135.00	**135.00**
ac# 27				
Boy Angel				

12432 BETHANY

Suspended 1986	85	Dove	$135.00	**$148.00**
Doll, 12.00"	86	Olive Branch	135.00	**145.00**
ac# 131				
Girl Angel				

12440	GOD BLESS OUR YEARS TOGETHER 5th Anniversary Club Commemmorative				
	Member Only	85	Dove	$175.00	**$300.00**
	Figurine, 5.50"				
	ac# 311				
	Mom, Dad, Kids, Cake w/5 Candles				

12459	WADDLE I DO WITHOUT YOU Series: "Clown"–2nd Issue				
	Retired 1989	85	Dove	$30.00	**$105.00**
	Figurine, 5.50"	86	Olive Branch	30.00	**90.00**
	ac# 1032	87	Cedar Tree	30.00	**88.00**
	Girl Clown with Basket &	88	Flower	30.00	**86.00**
	Goose	89	Bow & Arrow	40.00	**85.00**

12467	THE LORD WILL CARRY YOU THROUGH Series: "Clown"–3rd Issue				
	Retired 1988	86	Olive Branch	$30.00	**$88.00**
	Figurine, 5.75"	87	Cedar Tree	33.50	**85.00**
	ac# 957	88	Flower	30.00	**83.00**
	Clown with Dog in Mud				

12475	P.D.				
	Suspended 1986	85	Unmarked	$50.00	**$65.00**
	Doll, 7.00"	85	Dove	50.00	**60.00**
	ac# 764	86	Olive Branch	50.00	**55.00**
	Baby Boy				

12483	TRISH				
	Suspended 1986	85	Unmarked	$50.00	**$72.00**
	Doll, 7.00"	85	Dove	50.00	**70.00**
	ac# 1022	86	Olive Branch	50.00	**68.00**
	Baby Girl				

12491	ANGIE, THE ANGEL OF MERCY Individually Numbered				
	Limited Edition 12,500	87	Cedar Tree	$160.00	**$300.00**
	Doll, 12.00"				
	ac# 62				
	Nurse				

12580	LORD KEEP MY LIFE IN TUNE Series: "Rejoice In The Lord" Band Tune: I'd Like To Teach The World To Sing / Set of 2				
	Suspended 1990	87	Olive Branch	$37.50	**$275.00**
	Musical, 4.00"	87	Cedar Tree	40.00	**255.00**
	ac# 593	88	Flower	45.00	**250.00**
	Girl with Piano	89	Bow & Arrow	50.00	**245.00**
		90	Flame	55.00	**240.00**

13293 **MOTHER SEW DEAR**

Ongoing
Thimble, 2.25"
ac# 698
Mother Needlepointing

85	Dove	$5.50	**$15.00**
86	Olive Branch	5.50	**12.00**
87	Cedar Tree	6.00	**11.00**
88	Flower	7.00	**10.00**
89	Bow & Arrow	8.00	**10.00**
90	Flame	8.00	**9.00**
91	Vessel	8.00	**8.00**
92	G-Clef	8.00	**8.00**
93	Butterfly	8.00	**8.00**
94	Trumpet	8.00	**8.00**
95	Ship	8.00	**8.00**
96	Heart	8.00	**8.00**
97	Sword	8.00	**8.00**
98	Eyeglasses	8.00	**8.00**
99	Star	8.00	**8.00**

13307 **THE PURR-FECT GRANDMA**

Ongoing
Thimble, 2.25"
ac# 963
Grandma in Rocker

85	Dove	$5.50	**$18.00**
86	Olive Branch	5.50	**16.00**
87	Cedar Tree	6.00	**15.00**
88	Flower	7.00	**14.00**
89	Bow & Arrow	8.00	**13.00**
90	Flame	8.00	**12.00**
91	Vessel	8.00	**12.00**
92	G-Clef	8.00	**10.00**
93	Butterfly	8.00	**10.00**
94	Trumpet	8.00	**8.00**
95	Ship	8.00	**8.00**
96	Heart	8.00	**8.00**
97	Sword	8.00	**8.00**
98	Eyeglasses	8.00	**8.00**
99	Star	8.00	**8.00**

15237 **TELL ME THE STORY OF JESUS** Series: "Joy Of Christmas"–4th Issue

Dated Annual 1985
Plate, 8.50"
ac# 917
Girl with Doll Reading Book

85	Dove	$40.00	**$90.00**

15482 **MAY YOUR CHRISTMAS BE DELIGHTFUL**

Suspended 1994
Figurine, 5.00"
ac# 673
Boy Tangled in Christmas
Lights

85	Dove	$25.00	**$65.00**
86	Olive Branch	25.00	**62.00**
87	Cedar Tree	27.50	**60.00**
88	Flower	30.00	**59.00**
89	Bow & Arrow	33.00	**58.00**
90	Flame	35.00	**57.00**
91	Vessel	35.00	**55.00**
92	G-Clef	35.00	**53.00**
93	Butterfly	35.00	**52.00**
94	Trumpet	35.00	**50.00**

15490	HONK IF YOU LOVE JESUS	Nativity Addition	Set of 2			
	Ongoing	85	Dove		$13.00	**$32.00**
	Figurine, 3.25"	86	Olive Branch		13.00	**28.00**
	ac# 441	87	Cedar Tree		15.00	**25.00**
	Mother Goose in Bonnet	88	Flower		15.00	**24.00**
	with Babies	89	Bow & Arrow		17.50	**22.00**
		90	Flame		19.00	**20.00**
		91	Vessel		19.00	**20.00**
		92	G-Clef		19.00	**20.00**
		93	Butterfly		19.00	**20.00**
		94	Trumpet		20.00	**20.00**
		95	Ship		20.00	**20.00**
		96	Heart		20.00	**20.00**
		97	Sword		20.00	**20.00**
		98	Eyeglasses		20.00	**20.00**
		99	Star		20.00	**20.00**

15504	GOD SENT YOU JUST IN TIME	Tune: We Wish You A Merry Christmas			
	Retired 1989	85	Dove	$45.00	**$120.00**
	Musical, 6.25"	86	Olive Branch	45.00	**110.00**
	ac# 342	87	Cedar Tree	50.00	**105.00**
	Clown with Jack-in-the-Box	88	Flower	55.00	**102.00**
		89	Bow & Arrow	60.00	**100.00**

15539	BABY'S FIRST CHRISTMAS				
	Dated Annual 1985	85	Dove	$13.00	**$38.00**
	Figurine, 3.00"				
	ac# 91				
	Baby Boy with Bottle				

15547	BABY'S FIRST CHRISTMAS				
	Dated Annual 1985	85	Dove	$13.00	**$38.00**
	Figurine, 3.00"				
	ac# 92				
	Baby Girl with Bottle				

15768	GOD SENT HIS LOVE				
	Dated Annual 1985	85	Dove	$10.00	**$25.00**
	Ornament, 3.00"				
	ac# 340				
	Boy Holding Heart				

15776	MAY YOU HAVE THE SWEETEST CHRISTMAS	Series: "Family Christmas Scene"			
	Suspended 1992	85	Dove	$17.00	**$60.00**
	Figurine, 4.90"	86	Olive Branch	17.00	**55.00**
	ac# 664	87	Cedar Tree	19.00	**53.00**
	Mother with Cookie Sheet	88	Flower	19.00	**52.00**
		89	Bow & Arrow	23.00	**50.00**
		90	Flame	25.00	**48.00**
		91	Vessel	25.00	**47.00**
		92	G-Clef	25.00	**45.00**

15784	THE STORY OF GOD'S LOVE	Series: "Family Christmas Scene"			
	Suspended 1992	85	Dove	$22.50	**$60.00**
	Figurine, 4.00"	86	Olive Branch	22.50	**58.00**
	ac# 965	87	Cedar Tree	25.00	**57.00**
	Father Reading Bible	88	Flower	25.00	**56.00**
		89	Bow & Arrow	32.50	**55.00**
		90	Flame	35.00	**54.00**
		91	Vessel	35.00	**53.00**
		92	G-Clef	35.00	**52.00**

258

15792 — <u>TELL ME A STORY</u>   Series: "Family Christmas Scene"

Suspended 1992
Figurine, 2.00"
ac# 916
Boy Sitting Listening to Story

Unmarked pieces are known
to exist.

85	Dove	$10.00	**$35.00**
86	Olive Branch	10.00	**34.00**
87	Cedar Tree	11.00	**33.00**
88	Flower	11.00	**32.00**
89	Bow & Arrow	13.50	**31.00**
90	Flame	15.00	**30.00**
91	Vessel	15.00	**29.00**
92	G-Clef	15.00	**28.00**

15806 — <u>GOD GAVE HIS BEST</u>   Series: "Family Christmas Scene"

Suspended 1992
Figurine, 3.50"
ac# 331
Girl with Ornament

85	Dove	$13.00	**$50.00**
86	Olive Branch	13.00	**45.00**
87	Cedar Tree	15.00	**42.00**
88	Flower	15.00	**40.00**
89	Bow & Arrow	17.50	**38.00**
90	Flame	19.00	**36.00**
91	Vessel	19.00	**34.00**
92	G-Clef	19.00	**32.00**

15814 — <u>SILENT NIGHT</u>   Series: "Family Christmas Scene"   Tune: Silent Night

Suspended 1992
Musical, 5.60"
ac# 865
Christmas Tree

85	Dove	$37.50	**$105.00**
86	Olive Branch	37.50	**100.00**
87	Cedar Tree	40.00	**95.00**
88	Flower	40.00	**93.00**
89	Bow & Arrow	50.00	**90.00**
90	Flame	55.00	**87.00**
91	Vessel	55.00	**86.00**
92	G-Clef	55.00	**85.00**

15822 — <u>MAY YOUR CHRISTMAS BE HAPPY</u>

Suspended 1989
Ornament, 3.25"
ac# 210
Girl Clown with Balloon

85	Dove	$10.00	**$45.00**
86	Olive Branch	10.00	**43.00**
87	Cedar Tree	11.00	**42.00**
88	Flower	12.50	**40.00**
89	Bow & Arrow	13.50	**38.00**

15830 — <u>HAPPINESS IS THE LORD</u>

Suspended 1989
Ornament, 2.10"
ac# 211
Boy Clown with Ball

85	Dove	$10.00	**$32.00**
86	Olive Branch	10.00	**31.00**
87	Cedar Tree	11.00	**30.00**
88	Flower	12.50	**29.00**
89	Bow & Arrow	13.50	**28.00**

15849 — <u>MAY YOUR CHRISTMAS BE DELIGHTFUL</u>

Suspended 1993
Ornament, 3.00"
ac# 673
Boy Tangled in Christmas
Lights

85	Dove	$10.00	**$38.00**
86	Olive Branch	10.00	**34.00**
87	Cedar Tree	11.00	**33.00**
88	Flower	12.50	**32.00**
89	Bow & Arrow	13.50	**31.00**
90	Flame	15.00	**30.00**
91	Vessel	15.00	**29.00**
92	G-Clef	15.00	**28.00**
93	Butterfly	15.00	**27.00**

15857 — <u>HONK IF YOU LOVE JESUS</u>

Suspended 1993
Ornament, 3.60"
ac# 441
Mother Goose in Bonnet

85	Dove	$10.00	**$36.00**
86	Olive Branch	10.00	**35.00**
87	Cedar Tree	11.00	**34.00**
88	Flower	12.50	**33.00**
89	Bow & Arrow	13.50	**32.00**
90	Flame	15.00	**31.00**
91	Vessel	15.00	**30.00**
92	G-Clef	15.00	**29.00**
93	Butterfly	15.00	**27.00**

15865	GOD SENT HIS LOVE				
	Dated Annual 1985	85	Dove	$5.50	**$60.00**
	Thimble, 2.20"				
	ac# 340				
	Boy Holding Heart				

15873	GOD SENT HIS LOVE				
	Dated Annual 1985	85	Dove	$19.00	**$40.00**
	Bell, 5.40"				
	ac# 340				
	Boy Holding Heart				

15881	GOD SENT HIS LOVE				
	Dated Annual 1985	85	Dove	$17.00	**$45.00**
	Figurine, 4.50"				
	ac# 340				
	Boy Holding Heart				

15903	BABY'S FIRST CHRISTMAS				
	Dated Annual 1985	85	Dove	$10.00	**$48.00**
	Ornament, 2.40"				
	ac# 91				
	Baby Boy with Bottle				

15911	BABY'S FIRST CHRISTMAS				
	Dated Annual 1985	85	Dove	$10.00	**$44.00**
	Ornament, 2.40"				
	ac# 92				
	Baby Girl with Bottle				

15938   MAY YOUR BIRTHDAY BE WARM   Series: "Birthday Circus Train"

Ongoing — Figurine, 2.75" — ac# 669 — Teddy on Caboose – "For Baby"

Year	Mark	Issue	Value
86	Dove	$10.00	**$40.00**
86	Olive Branch	10.00	**25.00**
87	Cedar Tree	11.00	**22.00**
88	Flower	12.00	**18.00**
89	Bow & Arrow	13.50	**15.00**
90	Flame	15.00	**15.00**
91	Vessel	15.00	**15.00**
92	G-Clef	15.00	**15.00**
93	Butterfly	15.00	**15.00**
94	Trumpet	15.00	**15.00**
95	Ship	15.00	**15.00**
96	Heart	15.00	**15.00**
97	Sword	15.00	**15.00**
98	Eyeglasses	15.00	**15.00**
99	Star	15.00	**15.00**

260

15946	HAPPY BIRTHDAY LITTLE LAMB	Series: "Birthday Circus Train"		
Ongoing		86	Dove	$10.00	**$42.00**
Figurine, 3.00"		86	Olive Branch	10.00	**28.00**
ac# 378		87	Cedar Tree	11.00	**22.00**
Lamb–Age 1		88	Flower	12.00	**20.00**
		89	Bow & Arrow	13.50	**18.00**
		90	Flame	15.00	**17.00**
		91	Vessel	15.00	**16.00**
		92	G-Clef	15.00	**15.00**
		93	Butterfly	15.00	**15.00**
		94	Trumpet	15.00	**15.00**
		95	Ship	15.00	**15.00**
		96	Heart	15.00	**15.00**
		97	Sword	15.00	**15.00**
		98	Eyeglasses	15.00	**15.00**
		99	Star	15.00	**15.00**

15954	HEAVEN BLESS YOUR SPECIAL DAY	Series: "Birthday Circus Train"		
Ongoing		86	Dove	$11.00	**$38.00**
Figurine, 3.50"		86	Olive Branch	11.00	**28.00**
ac# 417		87	Cedar Tree	12.00	**25.00**
Pig–Age 3		88	Flower	13.50	**20.00**
		89	Bow & Arrow	15.00	**18.00**
		90	Flame	16.50	**18.00**
		91	Vessel	16.50	**18.00**
		92	G-Clef	16.50	**18.00**
		93	Butterfly	16.50	**18.00**
		94	Trumpet	16.50	**17.50**
		95	Ship	17.50	**17.50**
		96	Heart	17.50	**17.50**
		97	Sword	17.50	**17.50**
		98	Eyeglasses	17.50	**17.50**
		99	Star	17.50	**17.50**

15962	GOD BLESS YOU ON YOUR BIRTHDAY	Series: "Birthday Circus Train"		
Ongoing		86	Dove	$11.00	**$45.00**
Figurine, 3.75"		86	Olive Branch	11.00	**30.00**
ac# 320		87	Cedar Tree	12.00	**28.00**
Seal–Age 2		88	Flower	13.50	**25.00**
		89	Bow & Arrow	15.00	**22.00**
		90	Flame	16.50	**20.00**
		91	Vessel	16.50	**20.00**
		92	G-Clef	16.50	**18.00**
		93	Butterfly	16.50	**18.00**
		94	Trumpet	16.50	**17.50**
		95	Ship	17.50	**17.50**
		96	Heart	17.50	**17.50**
		97	Sword	17.50	**17.50**
		98	Eyeglasses	17.50	**17.50**
		99	Star	17.50	**17.50**

15970	MAY YOUR BIRTHDAY BE GIGANTIC	Series: "Birthday Circus Train"		
Ongoing		86	Dove	$12.50	**$42.00**
Figurine, 3.50"		86	Olive Branch	12.50	**28.00**
ac# 667		87	Cedar Tree	14.00	**25.00**
Elephant–Age 4		88	Flower	15.00	**22.00**
		89	Bow & Arrow	17.00	**20.00**
		90	Flame	18.50	**20.00**
		91	Vessel	18.50	**20.00**
		92	G-Clef	18.50	**20.00**
		93	Butterfly	18.50	**20.00**
		94	Trumpet	18.50	**20.00**
		95	Ship	20.00	**20.00**
		96	Heart	20.00	**20.00**
		97	Sword	20.00	**20.00**
		98	Eyeglasses	20.00	**20.00**
		99	Star	20.00	**20.00**

15989 — THIS DAY IS SOMETHING TO ROAR ABOUT — Series: "Birthday Circus Train"

Ongoing
Figurine, 4.00"
ac# 983
Lion–Age 5

Year	Mark		
86	Dove	$13.50	**$35.00**
86	Olive Branch	13.50	**25.00**
87	Cedar Tree	15.00	**24.00**
88	Flower	17.50	**23.00**
89	Bow & Arrow	20.00	**23.00**
90	Flame	20.00	**23.00**
91	Vessel	20.00	**23.00**
92	G-Clef	20.00	**22.50**
93	Butterfly	20.00	**22.50**
94	Trumpet	20.00	**22.50**
95	Ship	22.50	**22.50**
96	Heart	22.50	**22.50**
97	Sword	22.50	**22.50**
98	Eyeglasses	22.50	**22.50**
99	Star	22.50	**22.50**

15997 — KEEP LOOKING UP — Series: "Birthday Circus Train"

Ongoing
Figurine, 5.50"
ac# 556
Giraffe–Age 6

Year	Mark		
86	Dove	$13.50	**$40.00**
86	Olive Branch	13.50	**30.00**
87	Cedar Tree	15.00	**25.00**
88	Flower	17.50	**24.00**
89	Bow & Arrow	20.00	**23.00**
90	Flame	20.00	**23.00**
91	Vessel	20.00	**23.00**
92	G-Clef	20.00	**22.50**
93	Butterfly	20.00	**22.50**
94	Trumpet	20.00	**22.50**
95	Ship	22.50	**22.50**
96	Heart	22.50	**22.50**
97	Sword	22.50	**22.50**
98	Eyeglasses	22.50	**22.50**
99	Star	22.50	**22.50**

16004 — BLESS THE DAYS OF OUR YOUTH — Series: "Birthday Circus Train"

Ongoing
Figurine, 5.25"
ac# 142
Clown with Pull Rope

Year	Mark		
86	Dove	$15.00	**$40.00**
86	Olive Branch	15.00	**30.00**
87	Cedar Tree	17.00	**25.00**
88	Flower	19.50	**23.00**
89	Bow & Arrow	22.50	**23.00**
90	Flame	22.50	**23.00**
91	Vessel	22.50	**23.00**
92	G-Clef	22.50	**22.50**
93	Butterfly	22.50	**22.50**
94	Trumpet	22.50	**22.50**
95	Ship	22.50	**22.50**
96	Heart	22.50	**22.50**
97	Sword	22.50	**22.50**
98	Eyeglasses	22.50	**22.50**
99	Star	22.50	**22.50**

16012 — BABY'S FIRST TRIP — Series: "Baby's First"–4th Issue

Suspended 1989
Figurine, 5.00"
ac# 122
Angel Pushing Buggy

Year	Mark		
86	Olive Branch	$32.50	**$300.00**
87	Cedar Tree	37.00	**285.00**
88	Flower	40.00	**280.00**
89	Bow & Arrow	45.00	**275.00**

16020 — GOD BLESS YOU WITH RAINBOWS

Suspended 1989
Night Light, 5.00"
ac# 322
Angel behind Rainbow

Year	Mark		
86	Dove	$45.00	**$115.00**
86	Olive Branch	45.00	**110.00**
87	Cedar Tree	50.00	**100.00**
88	Flower	52.50	**95.00**
89	Bow & Arrow	57.50	**92.00**

100021 — TO MY FAVORITE PAW

TO MY FAVORITE PAW
Suspended 1988
Figurine, 3.50"
ac# 1012
Boy Sitting with Teddy

	86	Dove	$22.50	**$95.00**
	86	Olive Branch	22.50	**68.00**
	87	Cedar Tree	25.00	**65.00**
	88	Flower	27.00	**60.00**

100048 — TO MY DEER FRIEND

TO MY DEER FRIEND
Ongoing
Figurine, 5.75"
ac# 1010
Girl with Flowers and Deer

	87	Olive Branch	$33.00	**$105.00**
	87	Cedar Tree	37.00	**65.00**
	88	Flower	40.00	**55.00**
	89	Bow & Arrow	45.00	**52.00**
	90	Flame	50.00	**50.00**
	91	Vessel	50.00	**50.00**
	92	G-Clef	50.00	**50.00**
	93	Butterfly	50.00	**50.00**
	94	Trumpet	50.00	**50.00**
	95	Ship	50.00	**50.00**
	96	Heart	50.00	**50.00**
	97	Sword	50.00	**50.00**
	98	Eyeglasses	50.00	**50.00**
	99	Star	50.00	**50.00**

100056 — SENDING MY LOVE

<u>SENDING MY LOVE</u>
Suspended 1991
Figurine, 5.75"
ac# 831
Boy with Bow & Arrow on
Cloud

	86	Dove	$22.50	**$75.00**
	86	Olive Branch	22.50	**68.00**
	87	Cedar Tree	25.00	**65.00**
	88	Flower	27.00	**64.00**
	89	Bow & Arrow	30.00	**63.00**
	90	Flame	32.50	**62.00**
	91	Vessel	32.50	**60.00**

100064 — WORSHIP THE LORD

<u>WORSHIP THE LORD</u>
Ongoing
Figurine, 5.25"
ac# 1088
Girl Kneeling at Church
Window

	86	Dove	$24.00	**$55.00**
	86	Olive Branch	24.00	**48.00**
	87	Cedar Tree	24.00	**45.00**
	88	Flower	30.00	**42.00**
	89	Bow & Arrow	33.00	**40.00**
	90	Flame	35.00	**40.00**
	91	Vessel	35.00	**40.00**
	92	G-Clef	35.00	**40.00**
	93	Butterfly	35.00	**40.00**
	94	Trumpet	35.00	**40.00**
	95	Ship	37.50	**40.00**
	96	Heart	40.00	**40.00**
	97	Sword	40.00	**40.00**
	98	Eyeglasses	40.00	**40.00**
	99	Star	40.00	**40.00**

100072 — TO MY FOREVER FRIEND

<u>TO MY FOREVER FRIEND</u>
Ongoing
Figurine, 5.50"
ac# 1013
Two Girls with Flowers

	86	Dove	$33.00	**$135.00**
	86	Olive Branch	33.00	**70.00**
	87	Cedar Tree	33.00	**60.00**
	88	Flower	40.00	**58.00**
	89	Bow & Arrow	45.00	**55.00**
	90	Flame	50.00	**55.00**
	91	Vessel	50.00	**55.00**
	92	G-Clef	50.00	**55.00**
	93	Butterfly	50.00	**55.00**
	94	Trumpet	50.00	**55.00**
	95	Ship	50.00	**55.00**
	96	Heart	55.00	**55.00**
	97	Sword	55.00	**55.00**
	98	Eyeglasses	55.00	**55.00**
	99	Star	55.00	**55.00**

100080 HE'S THE HEALER OF BROKEN HEARTS

Ongoing		87	Olive Branch	$33.00	**$62.00**
Figurine, 5.50"		87	Cedar Tree	37.00	**55.00**
ac# 413		88	Flower	40.00	**52.00**
Girl & Boy with Bandaged		89	Bow & Arrow	45.00	**51.00**
Heart		90	Flame	50.00	**50.00**
		91	Vessel	50.00	**50.00**
		92	G-Clef	50.00	**50.00**
		93	Butterfly	50.00	**50.00**
		94	Trumpet	50.00	**50.00**
		95	Ship	50.00	**50.00**
		96	Heart	50.00	**50.00**
		97	Sword	50.00	**50.00**
		98	Eyeglasses	50.00	**50.00**
		99	Star	50.00	**50.00**

100102 MAKE ME A BLESSING

Retired 1990		87	Olive Branch	$35.00	**$135.00**
Figurine, 5.50"		87	Cedar Tree	38.50	**94.00**
ac# 646		88	Flower	40.00	**88.00**
Girl with Sick Bear		89	Bow & Arrow	45.00	**82.00**
		90	Flame	50.00	**78.00**

100110 LORD I'M COMING HOME

Ongoing		86	Dove	$22.50	**$105.00**
Figurine, 5.00"		86	Olive Branch	22.50	**55.00**
ac# 586		87	Cedar Tree	25.00	**40.00**
Baseball Player with Bat		88	Flower	27.00	**39.00**
		89	Bow & Arrow	30.00	**38.00**
		90	Flame	32.50	**35.00**
		91	Vessel	32.50	**35.00**
		92	G-Clef	32.50	**35.00**
		93	Butterfly	35.00	**35.00**
		94	Trumpet	35.00	**35.00**
		95	Ship	35.00	**35.00**
		96	Heart	35.00	**35.00**
		97	Sword	35.00	**35.00**
		98	Eyeglasses	35.00	**35.00**
		99	Star	35.00	**35.00**

100129 LORD KEEP ME ON MY TOES

Retired 1988		86	Dove	$22.50	**$105.00**
Figurine, 5.75"		86	Olive Branch	22.50	**95.00**
ac# 588		87	Cedar Tree	25.00	**88.00**
Ballerina		88	Flower	27.00	**85.00**

100137 THE JOY OF THE LORD IS MY STRENGTH

Ongoing		86	Dove	$35.00	**$125.00**
Figurine, 5.40"		86	Olive Branch	35.00	**75.00**
ac# 939		87	Cedar Tree	35.00	**65.00**
Mother with Babies		88	Flower	40.00	**60.00**
		89	Bow & Arrow	47.50	**55.00**
		90	Flame	50.00	**55.00**
		91	Vessel	50.00	**55.00**
		92	G-Clef	50.00	**55.00**
		93	Butterfly	50.00	**55.00**
		94	Trumpet	50.00	**55.00**
		95	Ship	50.00	**55.00**
		96	Heart	55.00	**55.00**
		97	Sword	55.00	**55.00**
		98	Eyeglasses	55.00	**55.00**
		99	Star	55.00	**55.00**

100145 GOD BLESS THE DAY WE FOUND YOU

Suspended 1990	86	Olive Branch	$40.00	**$120.00**
Figurine, 5.50"	87	Cedar Tree	40.00	**110.00**
ac# 313	88	Flower	47.50	**105.00**
Mom & Dad with Adopted	89	Bow & Arrow	50.00	**100.00**
Daughter	90	Flame	55.00	**95.00**

Re-introduced in 1995 as 100145R. See next listing.

100145R GOD BLESS THE DAY WE FOUND YOU

Ongoing	95	Trumpet	$60.00	**$65.00**
Figurine, 5.50"	95	Ship	60.00	**60.00**
ac# 316	96	Heart	60.00	**60.00**
Mom & Dad with Adopted	97	Sword	60.00	**60.00**
Daughter	98	Eyeglasses	60.00	**60.00**
	99	Star	60.00	**60.00**

Re-designed and brought back from Suspension with original title.

100153 GOD BLESS THE DAY WE FOUND YOU

Suspended 1990	86	Olive Branch	$40.00	**$115.00**
Figurine, 5.50"	87	Cedar Tree	40.00	**110.00**
ac# 314	88	Flower	47.50	**105.00**
Mom & Dad with Adopted	89	Bow & Arrow	50.00	**100.00**
Son	90	Flame	55.00	**92.00**

Re-introduced in 1995 as 100153R. See next listing.

100153R GOD BLESS THE DAY WE FOUND YOU

Ongoing	95	Trumpet	$60.00	**$62.00**
Figurine, 5.50"	95	Ship	60.00	**60.00**
ac# 315	96	Heart	60.00	**60.00**
Mom & Dad with Adopted	97	Sword	60.00	**60.00**
Son	98	Eyeglasses	60.00	**60.00**
	99	Star	60.00	**60.00**

Re-designed and brought back from Suspension with original title.

100161 SERVING THE LORD

Suspended 1990	86	Dove	$19.00	**$82.00**
Figurine, 5.00"	86	Olive Branch	19.00	**75.00**
ac# 842	87	Cedar Tree	21.00	**68.00**
Tennis Girl	88	Flower	22.50	**65.00**
	89	Bow & Arrow	25.00	**62.00**
	90	Flame	27.50	**60.00**

100188 I'M A POSSIBILITY

Retired 1993	86	Olive Branch	$22.00	**$85.00**
Figurine, 5.25"	87	Cedar Tree	25.00	**78.00**
ac# 486	88	Flower	27.00	**76.00**
Boy with Football	89	Bow & Arrow	30.00	**75.00**
	90	Flame	32.50	**74.00**
	91	Vessel	32.50	**72.00**
	92	G-Clef	32.50	**70.00**
	93	Butterfly	35.00	**68.00**

100196 THE SPIRIT IS WILLING BUT THE FLESH IS WEAK

Retired 1991	87	Cedar Tree	$19.00	**$84.00**
Figurine, 5.50"	88	Flower	24.00	**82.00**
ac# 964	89	Bow & Arrow	27.00	**78.00**
Girl on Scale	90	Flame	30.00	**74.00**
	91	Vessel	30.00	**69.00**

100226 THE LORD GIVETH AND THE LORD TAKETH AWAY

Retired 1995
Figurine, 5.25"
ac# 948
Girl with Cat & Bird Cage

87	Cedar Tree	$33.50	**$85.00**
88	Flower	36.00	**80.00**
89	Bow & Arrow	38.50	**79.00**
90	Flame	40.00	**78.00**
91	Vessel	40.00	**77.00**
92	G-Clef	40.00	**76.00**
93	Butterfly	40.00	**75.00**
94	Trumpet	40.00	**74.00**
95	Ship	40.00	**73.00**

100250 FRIENDS NEVER DRIFT APART

Ongoing
Figurine, 4.25"
ac# 292
Kids in Boat

86	Dove	$35.00	**$82.00**
86	Olive Branch	35.00	**68.00**
87	Cedar Tree	38.50	**65.00**
88	Flower	42.50	**62.00**
89	Bow & Arrow	47.50	**60.00**
90	Flame	50.00	**60.00**
91	Vessel	50.00	**60.00**
92	G-Clef	50.00	**60.00**
93	Butterfly	50.00	**60.00**
94	Trumpet	55.00	**60.00**
95	Ship	55.00	**60.00**
96	Heart	60.00	**60.00**
97	Sword	60.00	**60.00**
98	Eyeglasses	60.00	**60.00**
99	Star	60.00	**60.00**

100269 HELP LORD, I'M IN A SPOT

Retired 1989
Figurine, 5.25"
ac# 423
Boy Standing in Ink Spot

86	Olive Branch	$18.50	**$75.00**
87	Cedar Tree	21.00	**74.00**
88	Flower	22.50	**72.00**
89	Bow & Arrow	25.00	**70.00**

100277 HE CLEANSED MY SOUL

Ongoing
Figurine, 4.90"
ac# 394
Girl in Old Bathtub

86	Dove	$24.00	**$65.00**
86	Olive Branch	24.00	**48.00**
87	Cedar Tree	27.00	**45.00**
88	Flower	30.00	**42.00**
89	Bow & Arrow	33.00	**40.00**
90	Flame	35.00	**40.00**
91	Vessel	35.00	**40.00**
92	G-Clef	35.00	**40.00**
93	Butterfly	35.00	**40.00**
94	Trumpet	37.50	**40.00**
95	Ship	37.50	**40.00**
96	Heart	40.00	**40.00**
97	Sword	40.00	**40.00**
98	Eyeglasses	40.00	**40.00**
99	Star	40.00	**40.00**

100285 HEAVEN BLESS YOU   Tune: Brahms' Lullaby

Suspended 1993
Musical, 5.00"
ac# 415
Baby with Bunny & Turtle

86	Dove	$45.00	**$125.00**
86	Olive Branch	45.00	**95.00**
87	Cedar Tree	50.00	**92.00**
88	Flower	52.50	**90.00**
89	Bow & Arrow	57.50	**88.00**
90	Flame	60.00	**87.00**
91	Vessel	60.00	**85.00**
92	G-Clef	60.00	**82.00**
93	Butterfly	60.00	**80.00**

100293 SERVING THE LORD
Suspended 1990
    Figurine, 5.25"
    ac# 843
    Tennis Boy

86	Dove	$19.00	**$62.00**
86	Olive Branch	19.00	**58.00**
87	Cedar Tree	21.00	**50.00**
88	Flower	22.50	**48.00**
89	Bow & Arrow	25.00	**45.00**
90	Flame	27.50	**40.00**

100455 BONG BONG   Individually Numbered on Foot / Certificate of Authenticity
Limited Edition 12,000
    Doll, 13.00"
    ac# 170
    Boy Clown

86	Olive Branch	$150.00	**$265.00**

100463 CANDY   Individually Numbered on Foot / Certificate of Authenticity
Limited Edition 12,000
    Doll, 13.00"
    ac# 191
    Girl Clown

86	Olive Branch	$150.00	**$300.00**

100498 GOD BLESS OUR FAMILY
Ongoing
    Figurine, 5.50"
    ac# 307
    Parents of the Groom

87	Cedar Tree	$35.00	**$65.00**
88	Flower	40.00	**60.00**
89	Bow & Arrow	45.00	**57.00**
90	Flame	50.00	**55.00**
91	Vessel	50.00	**53.00**
92	G-Clef	50.00	**52.00**
93	Butterfly	50.00	**50.00**
94	Trumpet	50.00	**50.00**
95	Ship	50.00	**50.00**
96	Heart	50.00	**50.00**
97	Sword	50.00	**50.00**
98	Eyeglasses	50.00	**50.00**
99	Star	50.00	**50.00**

100501 GOD BLESS OUR FAMILY
Ongoing
    Figurine, 5.50"
    ac# 308
    Parents of the Bride

87	Cedar Tree	$35.00	**$65.00**
88	Flower	40.00	**60.00**
89	Bow & Arrow	45.00	**58.00**
90	Flame	50.00	**55.00**
91	Vessel	50.00	**53.00**
92	G-Clef	50.00	**52.00**
93	Butterfly	50.00	**51.00**
94	Trumpet	50.00	**50.00**
95	Ship	50.00	**50.00**
96	Heart	50.00	**50.00**
97	Sword	50.00	**50.00**
98	Eyeglasses	50.00	**50.00**
99	Star	50.00	**50.00**

100528 SCENT FROM ABOVE
Retired 1991
    Figurine, 5.25"
    ac# 824
    Girl with Skunk

87	Olive Branch	$19.00	**$78.00**
87	Cedar Tree	21.00	**74.00**
88	Flower	23.00	**68.00**
89	Bow & Arrow	25.00	**65.00**
90	Flame	27.50	**62.00**
91	Vessel	27.50	**60.00**

100536 I PICKED A SPECIAL MOM
Annual 1987
    Figurine, 5.50"
    ac# 471
    Boy with His Gardening
    Mother

87	Olive Branch	$37.50	**$85.00**
	Cedar Tree		**75.00**

100544	BROTHERLY LOVE			
	Suspended 1989	86	Olive Branch	$37.00	**$105.00**
	Figurine, 4.50"	87	Cedar Tree	40.00	**92.00**
	ac# 179	88	Flower	42.50	**90.00**
	Pilgrim & Native American with Turkey	89	Bow & Arrow	47.50	**88.00**

100625	GOD IS LOVE, DEAR VALENTINE			
	Suspended 1989	86	Dove	$5.50	**$25.00**
	Thimble, 2.25"	86	Olive Branch	5.50	**18.00**
	ac# 334	87	Cedar Tree	6.00	**17.00**
	Girl Holding Heart	88	Flower	7.00	**16.00**
		89	Bow & Arrow	8.00	**15.00**

100633	THE LORD BLESS YOU AND KEEP YOU			
	Suspended 1991	86	Dove	$5.50	**$22.00**
	Thimble, 2.25"	86	Olive Branch	5.50	**20.00**
	ac# 171	87	Cedar Tree	6.00	**19.00**
	Bride	88	Flower	7.00	**18.00**
		89	Bow & Arrow	8.00	**17.00**
		90	Flame	8.00	**16.00**
		91	Vessel	8.00	**15.00**

100641	FOUR SEASONS THIMBLES Set of 4			
	Annual 1986	86	Dove	$20.00	**$150.00**
	Thimble, 2.00"		Olive Branch		**90.00**
	ac# 968				
	Four Seasons Thimbles				

100668	CLOWN THIMBLES Set of 2			
	Suspended 1988	86	Olive Branch	$11.00	**$40.00**
	Thimble, 2.00"	87	Cedar Tree	12.00	**38.00**
	ac# 213	88	Flower	14.00	**35.00**
	Clowns				

101702	OUR FIRST CHRISTMAS TOGETHER Tune: We Wish You A Merry Christmas			
	Retired 1992	86	Olive Branch	$50.00	**$120.00**
	Musical, 5.50"	87	Cedar Tree	55.00	**115.00**
	ac# 751	88	Flower	55.00	**110.00**
	Boy and Girl in Package	89	Bow & Arrow	67.50	**105.00**
		90	Flame	70.00	**100.00**
		91	Vessel	70.00	**95.00**
		92	G-Clef	70.00	**90.00**

101826	NO TEARS PAST THE GATE			
	Ongoing	87	Cedar Tree	$40.00	**$95.00**
	Figurine, 6.25"	88	Flower	47.50	**80.00**
	ac# 718	89	Bow & Arrow	55.00	**78.00**
	Girl at Gate	90	Flame	60.00	**75.00**
		91	Vessel	60.00	**72.00**
		92	G-Clef	60.00	**70.00**
		93	Butterfly	65.00	**70.00**
		94	Trumpet	65.00	**70.00**
		95	Ship	70.00	**70.00**
		96	Heart	70.00	**70.00**
		97	Sword	70.00	**70.00**
		98	Eyeglasses	70.00	**70.00**
		99	Star	70.00	**70.00**

101834   **I'M SENDING YOU A WHITE CHRISTMAS**   Series: "Christmas Love"–1st Issue

Dated Annual 1986   86   Olive Branch $45.00   **$65.00**
     Plate, 8.50"
     ac# 495
     Girl Mailing Snowball

101842   SMILE ALONG THE WAY

Retired 1991	87	Olive Branch	$30.00	**$195.00**
Figurine, 6.75"	87	Cedar Tree	33.50	**170.00**
ac# 874	88	Flower	35.00	**168.00**
Clown Doing Handstand	89	Bow & Arrow	40.00	**165.00**
	90	Flame	45.00	**160.00**
	91	Vessel	45.00	**155.00**

101850   LORD, HELP US KEEP OUR ACT TOGETHER

Retired 1992	87	Olive Branch	$35.00	**$148.00**
Figurine, 7.00"	87	Cedar Tree	38.50	**135.00**
ac# 585	88	Flower	40.00	**125.00**
Clowns on Unicycle	89	Bow & Arrow	45.00	**120.00**
	90	Flame	50.00	**115.00**
	91	Vessel	50.00	**105.00**

102229   WORSHIP THE LORD

Ongoing

Figurine, 5.50"	86	Dove	$24.00	**$52.00**
ac# 1089	86	Olive Branch	24.00	**40.00**
Boy Kneeling at Church	87	Cedar Tree	27.00	**40.00**
Window	88	Flower	30.00	**40.00**
	89	Bow & Arrow	33.00	**40.00**
Some of these figurines have	90	Flame	35.00	**40.00**
the title, "O Worship The	91	Vessel	35.00	**40.00**
Lord."	92	G-Clef	35.00	**40.00**
	93	Butterfly	35.00	**40.00**
	94	Trumpet	35.00	**40.00**
	95	Ship	37.50	**40.00**
	96	Heart	40.00	**40.00**
	97	Sword	40.00	**40.00**
	98	Eyeglasses	40.00	**40.00**
	99	Star	40.00	**40.00**

102253   CONNIE   Individually Numbered

Limited Edition 7,500   86   Olive Branch $160.00   **$275.00**
     Doll, 12.00"
     ac# 228
     Doll with Stand

102261   SHEPHERD OF LOVE   Mini Nativity Addition

Ongoing	86	Olive Branch	$10.00	**$28.00**
Figurine, 3.25"	87	Cedar Tree	10.00	**22.00**
ac# 858	88	Flower	12.50	**20.00**
Angel with Black Lamb	89	Bow & Arrow	13.50	**19.00**
	90	Flame	15.00	**19.00**
	91	Vessel	15.00	**18.50**
	92	G-Clef	15.00	**18.50**
	93	Butterfly	15.00	**18.50**
	94	Trumpet	16.00	**18.50**
	95	Ship	16.00	**18.50**
	96	Heart	18.50	**18.50**
	97	Sword	18.50	**18.50**
	98	Eyeglasses	18.50	**18.50**
	99	Star	18.50	**18.50**

102288	SHEPHERD OF LOVE				
	Suspended 1993	86	Olive Branch	$10.00	**$36.00**
	Ornament, 3.25"	87	Cedar Tree	11.00	**34.00**
	ac# 858	88	Flower	12.50	**32.00**
	Angel with Black Lamb	89	Bow & Arrow	13.50	**31.00**
		90	Flame	15.00	**30.00**
		91	Vessel	15.00	**28.00**
		92	G-Clef	15.00	**26.00**
		93	Butterfly	15.00	**25.00**

102296	MINI ANIMAL FIGURINES Mini Nativity Addition Set of 3				
	Suspended 1992	86	Olive Branch	$13.50	**$40.00**
	Figurine, 1.75"	87	Cedar Tree	15.00	**38.00**
	ac# 688	88	Flower	15.00	**36.00**
	Black Sheep, Bunny and	89	Bow & Arrow	17.50	**35.00**
	Turtle	90	Flame	19.00	**34.00**
		91	Vessel	19.00	**33.00**
		92	G-Clef	19.00	**32.00**

102318	WISHING YOU A COZY CHRISTMAS				
	Dated Annual 1986	86	Olive Branch	$20.00	**$38.00**
	Bell, 5.50"				
	ac# 1069				
	Girl with Muff				

102326	WISHING YOU A COZY CHRISTMAS				
	Dated Annual 1986	86	Olive Branch	$10.00	**$40.00**
	Ornament, 3.00"				
	ac# 1069				
	Girl with Muff				

102334	WISHING YOU A COZY CHRISTMAS				
	Dated Annual 1986	86	Olive Branch	$5.50	**$24.00**
	Thimble, 2.25"				
	ac# 1069				
	Girl with Muff				

102342	WISHING YOU A COZY CHRISTMAS				
	Dated Annual 1986	86	Olive Branch	$18.00	**$48.00**
	Figurine, 4.75"				
	ac# 1069				
	Girl with Muff				

102350	OUR FIRST CHRISTMAS TOGETHER				
	Dated Annual 1986	86	Olive Branch	$10.00	**$35.00**
	Ornament, 2.75"				
	ac# 751				
	Boy and Girl in Package				

102369	WEDDING ARCH				
	Suspended 1992	86	Olive Branch	$22.50	**$65.00**
	Figurine, 7.75"	87	Cedar Tree	25.00	**58.00**
	ac# 1052	88	Flower	25.00	**55.00**
	Bridal Arch	89	Bow & Arrow	27.50	**50.00**
		90	Flame	30.00	**48.00**
		91	Vessel	30.00	**45.00**
		92	G-Clef	30.00	**40.00**

102377 TRUST AND OBEY

Ongoing
Ornament, 3.00"
ac# 506
Policeman Writing Ticket

86	Olive Branch	$10.00	**$22.00**
87	Cedar Tree	11.00	**20.00**
88	Flower	12.50	**19.00**
89	Bow & Arrow	13.50	**19.00**
90	Flame	15.00	**19.00**
91	Vessel	15.00	**19.00**
92	G-Clef	15.00	**18.50**
93	Butterfly	15.00	**18.50**
94	Trumpet	16.00	**18.50**
95	Ship	17.00	**18.50**
96	Heart	18.50	**18.50**
97	Sword	18.50	**18.50**
98	Eyeglasses	18.50	**18.50**
99	Star	18.50	**18.50**

102385 LOVE RESCUED ME

Ongoing
Ornament, 3.00"
ac# 628
Fireman Holding Puppy

86	Olive Branch	$10.00	**$25.00**
87	Cedar Tree	11.00	**20.00**
88	Flower	12.50	**19.00**
89	Bow & Arrow	13.50	**19.00**
90	Flame	15.00	**19.00**
91	Vessel	15.00	**18.50**
92	G-Clef	15.00	**18.50**
93	Butterfly	15.00	**18.50**
94	Trumpet	16.00	**18.50**
95	Ship	17.00	**18.50**
96	Heart	18.50	**18.50**
97	Sword	18.50	**18.50**
98	Eyeglasses	18.50	**18.50**
99	Star	18.50	**18.50**

102393 LOVE RESCUED ME

Ongoing
Figurine, 5.50"
ac# 628
Fireman Holding Puppy

86	Olive Branch	$22.50	**$55.00**
87	Cedar Tree	25.00	**45.00**
88	Flower	27.00	**42.00**
89	Bow & Arrow	30.00	**40.00**
90	Flame	32.50	**38.00**
91	Vessel	32.50	**38.00**
92	G-Clef	32.50	**38.00**
93	Butterfly	35.00	**38.00**
94	Trumpet	35.00	**38.00**
95	Ship	37.50	**37.50**
96	Heart	37.50	**37.50**
97	Sword	37.50	**37.50**
98	Eyeglasses	37.50	**37.50**
99	Star	37.50	**37.50**

102407 ANGEL OF MERCY

Ongoing
Ornament, 3.00"
ac# 59
Nurse with Potted Plant

86	Olive Branch	$10.00	**$28.00**
87	Cedar Tree	11.00	**22.00**
88	Flower	12.50	**20.00**
89	Bow & Arrow	13.50	**19.00**
90	Flame	15.00	**18.50**
91	Vessel	15.00	**18.50**
92	G-Clef	15.00	**18.50**
93	Butterfly	15.00	**18.50**
94	Trumpet	16.00	**18.50**
95	Ship	17.00	**18.50**
96	Heart	18.50	**18.50**
97	Sword	18.50	**18.50**
98	Eyeglasses	18.50	**18.50**
99	Star	18.50	**18.50**

102415 IT'S A PERFECT BOY
Suspended 1989
    Ornament, 3.00"
    ac# 510
    Boy Angel with Red Cross
    Bag

86	Olive Branch	$10.00	**$32.00**
87	Cedar Tree	11.00	**30.00**
88	Flower	12.50	**28.00**
89	Bow & Arrow	13.50	**27.00**

102423 LORD KEEP ME ON MY TOES
Retired 1990
    Ornament, 3.50"
    ac# 588
    Ballerina

86	Olive Branch	$10.00	**$45.00**
87	Cedar Tree*	11.00	**43.00**
88	Flower	12.50	**42.00**
89	Bow & Arrow	13.50	**41.00**
90	Flame	15.00	**40.00**

*There are Cedar Tree pieces with two hooks from the Retailers Wreath, #111465.

102431 SERVE WITH A SMILE
Suspended 1988
    Ornament, 3.25"
    ac# 843
    Tennis Boy

86	Olive Branch	$10.00	**$28.00**
87	Cedar Tree	11.00	**25.00**
88	Flower	12.50	**20.00**

102458 SERVE WITH A SMILE
Suspended 1988
    Ornament, 3.25"
    ac# 842
    Tennis Girl

86	Olive Branch	$10.00	**$36.00**
87	Cedar Tree	11.00	**32.00**
88	Flower	12.50	**30.00**

102466 REINDEER   Birthday Collection
Dated Annual 1986
    Ornament, 3.25"
    ac# 801
    Reindeer and Teddy Bear

| 86 | Olive Branch | $11.00 | **$185.00** |

102474 ROCKING HORSE
Suspended 1991
    Ornament, 2.50"
    ac# 812
    Rocking Horse

    *There are Cedar Tree pieces
    with two hooks from the
    Retailers Wreath, #111465.

86	Olive Branch	$10.00	**$36.00**
87	Cedar Tree*	11.00	**34.00**
88	Flower	12.50	**33.00**
89	Bow & Arrow	13.50	**32.00**
90	Flame	15.00	**31.00**
91	Vessel	15.00	**30.00**

102482 ANGEL OF MERCY
Ongoing
    Figurine, 5.50"
    ac# 59
    Nurse with Potted Plant

86	Olive Branch	$20.00	**$55.00**
87	Cedar Tree	22.50	**40.00**
88	Flower	24.00	**38.00**
89	Bow & Arrow	27.00	**35.00**
90	Flame	30.00	**33.00**
91	Vessel	30.00	**33.00**
92	G-Clef	30.00	**33.00**
93	Butterfly	30.00	**32.50**
94	Trumpet	30.00	**32.50**
95	Ship	30.00	**32.50**
96	Heart	32.50	**32.50**
97	Sword	32.50	**32.50**
98	Eyeglasses	32.50	**32.50**
99	Star	32.50	**32.50**

102490	SHARING OUR CHRISTMAS TOGETHER				
	Suspended 1988	86	Olive Branch	$37.00	**$90.00**
	Figurine, 5.25"	87	Cedar Tree	40.00	**85.00**
	ac# 849	88	Flower	45.00	**80.00**
	Husband & Wife w/Cookies				
	& Pup				

102504	BABY'S FIRST CHRISTMAS				
	Dated Annual 1986	86	Olive Branch	$10.00	**$30.00**
	Ornament, 2.75"				
	ac# 93				
	Girl with Candy Cane				

102512	BABY'S FIRST CHRISTMAS				
	Dated Annual 1986	86	Olive Branch	$10.00	**$28.00**
	Ornament, 2.75"				
	ac# 94				
	Boy with Candy Cane				

102520	LET'S KEEP IN TOUCH Tune: Be A Clown				
	Ongoing	86	Olive Branch	$65.00	**$115.00**
	Musical, 7.00"	87	Cedar Tree	70.00	**95.00**
	ac# 569	88	Flower	75.00	**94.00**
	Clown on Elephant	89	Bow & Arrow	80.00	**92.00**
		90	Flame	85.00	**90.00**
		91	Vessel	85.00	**90.00**
		92	G-Clef	85.00	**90.00**
		93	Butterfly	90.00	**90.00**
		94	Trumpet	90.00	**90.00**
		95	Ship	90.00	**90.00**
		96	Heart	90.00	**90.00**
		97	Sword	90.00	**90.00**
		98	Eyeglasses	90.00	**90.00**
		99	Star	90.00	**90.00**

102903	WE ARE ALL PRECIOUS IN HIS SIGHT				
	Annual 1987	87	Cedar Tree	$30.00	**$78.00**
	Figurine, 7.10"				
	ac# 1038				
	Girl with Pearl				

The announcement that "some" figurines were missing the title on the understamp was made in the Fall 1987 GOODNEWSLETTER. However figurines with the title appear to be nonexistent. Because of the statement in the GOODNEWSLETTER, all who own the piece without the title, and, again, to our knowledge, that's everyone, are under the mistaken impression they own a variation.

102938	GOD BLESS AMERICA				
	Annual 1986	86	Olive Branch	$30.00	**$75.00**
	Figurine, 5.50"				
	ac# 306				
	Uncle Sam Holding Bible				
	with Dog				

102954	MY PEACE I GIVE UNTO THEE Series: "Christmas Love"–2nd Issue				
	Dated Annual 1987	87	Cedar Tree	$45.00	**$80.00**
	Plate, 8.50"				
	ac# 773				
	Children around Lamppost				

102962 IT'S THE BIRTHDAY OF A KING   Nativity Addition

Suspended 1989
Figurine, 5.50"
ac# 514
Boy Angel with Birthday Cake

Year	Mark	Issue	Value
86	Olive Branch	$19.00	**$57.00**
87	Cedar Tree	19.00	**55.00**
88	Flower	21.00	**52.00**
89	Bow & Arrow	25.00	**50.00**

102970 I WOULD BE SUNK WITHOUT YOU

Ongoing
Figurine, 3.25"
ac# 478
Baby Boy in Tub

Year	Mark	Issue	Value
87	Cedar Tree	$15.00	**$28.00**
88	Flower	16.00	**24.00**
89	Bow & Arrow	17.50	**22.00**
90	Flame	19.00	**22.00**
91	Vessel	19.00	**20.00**
92	G-Clef	19.00	**20.00**
93	Butterfly	19.00	**20.00**
94	Trumpet	19.00	**20.00**
95	Ship	20.00	**20.00**
96	Heart	20.00	**20.00**
97	Sword	20.00	**20.00**
98	Eyeglasses	20.00	**20.00**
99	Star	20.00	**20.00**

103004 WE BELONG TO THE LORD   Damien-Dutton Piece

Special Piece
Figurine, 4.90"
ac# 1041
Shepherd & Lambs Figurine w/Leather Bound Bible

Year	Mark	Issue	Value
86	Diamond	$50.00	**$230.00**
	(w/o Bible)		**215.00**

103497 MY LOVE WILL NEVER LET YOU GO

Ongoing
Figurine, 5.50"
ac# 709
Boy with Hat and Fish

Year	Mark	Issue	Value
87	Cedar Tree	$25.00	**$48.00**
88	Flower	30.00	**42.00**
89	Bow & Arrow	33.00	**40.00**
90	Flame	35.00	**38.00**
91	Vessel	35.00	**38.00**
92	G-Clef	35.00	**38.00**
93	Butterfly	35.00	**38.00**
94	Trumpet	35.00	**37.50**
95	Ship	37.50	**37.50**
96	Heart	37.50	**37.50**
97	Sword	37.50	**37.50**
98	Eyeglasses	37.50	**37.50**
99	Star	37.50	**37.50**

103632 I BELIEVE IN THE OLD RUGGED CROSS

Ongoing
Figurine, 5.25"
ac# 458
Girl Holding Cross

Year	Mark	Issue	Value
86	Dove	$25.00	**$55.00**
86	Olive Branch	25.00	**42.00**
87	Cedar Tree	27.50	**40.00**
88	Flower	30.00	**38.00**
89	Bow & Arrow	33.00	**36.00**
90	Flame	35.00	**35.00**
91	Vessel	35.00	**35.00**
92	G-Clef	35.00	**35.00**
93	Butterfly	35.00	**35.00**
94	Trumpet	35.00	**35.00**
95	Ship	35.00	**35.00**
96	Heart	35.00	**35.00**
97	Sword	35.00	**35.00**
98	Eyeglasses	35.00	**35.00**
99	Star	35.00	**35.00**

104000	COME LET US ADORE HIM	Nativity	Set of 9		
	Ongoing	86	Olive Branch	$95.00	**$140.00**
	Figurine, 4.75"	87	Cedar Tree	95.00	**140.00**
	ac# 223	88	Flower	100.00	**140.00**
	Nativity Set with Cassette	89	Bow & Arrow	110.00	**140.00**
		90	Flame	110.00	**140.00**
	Redesigned E-2800.	91	Vessel	110.00	**140.00**
		92	G-Clef	110.00	**140.00**
		93	Butterfly	120.00	**140.00**
		94	Trumpet	125.00	**140.00**
		95	Ship	130.00	**140.00**
		96	Heart	140.00	**140.00**
		97	Sword	140.00	**140.00**
		98	Eyeglasses	140.00	**140.00**
		99	Star	140.00	**140.00**

104019	WITH THIS RING I...				
	Ongoing	87	Cedar Tree	$40.00	**$80.00**
	Figurine, 5.00"	88	Flower	45.00	**70.00**
	ac# 1087	89	Bow & Arrow	50.00	**68.00**
	Boy Giving Girl Ring	90	Flame	55.00	**65.00**
		91	Vessel	55.00	**65.00**
		92	G-Clef	55.00	**65.00**
		93	Butterfly	60.00	**65.00**
		94	Trumpet	60.00	**65.00**
		95	Ship	65.00	**65.00**
		96	Heart	65.00	**65.00**
		97	Sword	65.00	**65.00**
		98	Eyeglasses	65.00	**65.00**
		99	Star	65.00	**65.00**

104027	LOVE IS THE GLUE THAT MENDS				
	Suspended 1990	87	Cedar Tree	$33.50	**$72.00**
	Figurine, 4.00"	88	Flower	36.00	**65.00**
	ac# 616	89	Bow & Arrow	38.50	**64.00**
	Boy Mending Hobby Horse	90	Flame	40.00	**62.00**

104035	CHEERS TO THE LEADER				
	Retired 1997	87	Cedar Tree	$22.50	**$88.00**
	Figurine, 5.25"	88	Flower	24.00	**80.00**
	ac# 200	89	Bow & Arrow	27.00	**75.00**
	Girl Cheerleader	90	Flame	30.00	**73.00**
		91	Vessel	30.00	**72.00**
		92	G-Clef	30.00	**70.00**
		93	Butterfly	30.00	**69.00**
		94	Trumpet	30.00	**68.00**
		95	Ship	30.00	**65.00**
		96	Heart	32.50	**62.00**
		97	Sword	32.50	**60.00**

104396	HAPPY DAYS ARE HERE AGAIN				
	Suspended 1990	87	Cedar Tree	$25.00	**$82.00**
	Figurine, 5.25"	88	Flower	27.00	**78.00**
	ac# 380	89	Bow & Arrow	30.00	**75.00**
	Girl Clown with Books	90	Flame	32.50	**74.00**

104418	FRIENDS TO THE END	Birthday Collection			
	Suspended 1993	88	Unmarked	$15.00	**$60.00**
	Figurine, 2.50"	88	Flower	17.00	**45.00**
	ac# 294	89	Bow & Arrow	17.00	**42.00**
	Rhino with Bird	90	Flame	18.50	**40.00**
		91	Vessel	18.50	**38.00**
		92	G-Clef	18.50	**35.00**
		93	Butterfly	18.50	**32.00**

104515   <u>BEAR THE GOOD NEWS OF CHRISTMAS</u>   Birthday Collection

Dated Annual 1987	87	Cedar Tree	$11.00	**$20.00**
Ornament, 2.10"				
ac# 125				
Teddy Bear in Cup on Skis				

104523   <u>"DEALERS ONLY" NATIVITY</u>   Nativity   Set of 9

Dealers Only Promotional Pieces	86	Olive Branch	$400.00	**$550.00**
Figurine, 9.00"				
ac# 235				
Nativity with Backdrop / Video				

104531   <u>JESUS LOVES ME</u>   Easter Seal / Lily Understamp / Individually Numbered

Limited Edition 1,000	88	Cedar Tree	$500.00	**$1645.00**
Figurine, 9.00"				
ac# 532				
Girl with Bunny				

104817   <u>A TUB FULL OF LOVE</u>

Suspended 1998	87	Cedar Tree	$22.50	**$40.00**
Figurine, 3.75"	88	Flower	24.00	**35.00**
ac# 22	89	Bow & Arrow	27.50	**33.00**
Baby Boy in Wood Tub	90	Flame	30.00	**33.00**
	91	Vessel	30.00	**33.00**
	92	G-Clef	30.00	**32.50**
	93	Butterfly	30.00	**32.50**
	94	Trumpet	30.00	**32.50**
	95	Ship	30.00	**32.50**
	96	Heart	32.50	**32.50**
	97	Sword	32.50	**32.50**
	98	Eyeglasses	32.50	**32.50**

104825   <u>SITTING PRETTY</u>

Suspended 1990	87	Cedar Tree	$22.50	**$68.00**
Figurine, 5.50"	88	Flower	24.00	**60.00**
ac# 868	89	Bow & Arrow	27.00	**55.00**
Girl Angel on Stool	90	Flame	30.00	**52.00**
	*	Vessel		**50.00**

*Piece was Suspended in 1990 yet exists in the 1991 Vessel Annual Production Symbol.

105635   <u>HAVE I GOT NEWS FOR YOU</u>   Nativity Addition

Suspended 1991	87	Cedar Tree	$22.50	**$60.00**
Figurine, 4.75"	88	Flower	22.50	**58.00**
ac# 390	89	Bow & Arrow	27.50	**55.00**
Boy Reading Scroll	90	Flame	30.00	**52.00**
	91	Vessel	30.00	**50.00**

105643   <u>SOMETHING'S MISSING WHEN YOU'RE NOT AROUND</u>

Suspended 1991	88	Flower	$32.50	**$85.00**
Figurine, 5.50"	89	Bow & Arrow	36.00	**82.00**
ac# 886	90	Flame	37.50	**80.00**
Girl Holding Doll with Dog	91	Vessel	37.50	**78.00**

105813   <u>TO TELL THE TOOTH YOU'RE SPECIAL</u>

Suspended 1990	87	Cedar Tree	$38.50	**$225.00**
Figurine, 5.00"	88	Flower	42.50	**215.00**
ac# 1015	89	Bow & Arrow	47.50	**210.00**
Dentist and Patient w/Pulled Tooth	90	Flame	50.00	**205.00**

105821 HALLELUJAH COUNTRY

Ongoing
Figurine, 5.50"
ac# 362
Cowboy on Fence with
Guritar

*Extremely rare, consider
Flower as first Annual
Production Symbol.

			$*
88	Cedar Tree	$35.00	**$***
88	Flower	35.00	**68.00**
89	Bow & Arrow	40.00	**55.00**
90	Flame	45.00	**52.00**
91	Vessel	45.00	**48.00**
92	G-Clef	45.00	**45.00**
93	Butterfly	45.00	**45.00**
94	Trumpet	45.00	**45.00**
95	Ship	45.00	**45.00**
96	Heart	45.00	**45.00**
97	Sword	45.00	**45.00**
98	Eyeglasses	45.00	**45.00**
99	Star	45.00	**45.00**

105945 SHOWERS OF BLESSINGS Birthday Collection

Retired 1993
Figurine, 3.25"
ac# 863
Elephant Showering Mouse

87	Cedar Tree	$16.00	**$55.00**
88	Flower	18.50	**45.00**
89	Bow & Arrow	20.00	**44.00**
90	Flame	20.00	**42.00**
91	Vessel	20.00	**41.00**
92	G-Clef	20.00	**40.00**
93	Butterfly	20.00	**39.00**

105953 BRIGHTEN SOMEONE'S DAY Birthday Collection

Suspended 1993
Figurine, 2.50"
ac# 173
Skunk & Mouse

88	Cedar Tree	$12.50	**$45.00**
88	Flower	12.50	**39.00**
89	Bow & Arrow	13.50	**38.00**
90	Flame	15.00	**37.00**
91	Vessel	15.00	**35.00**
92	G-Clef	15.00	**34.00**
93	Butterfly	15.00	**32.00**

106151 WE'RE PULLING FOR YOU

Suspended 1991
Figurine, 5.00"
ac# 1049
Boy with Donkey

87	Cedar Tree	$40.00	**$84.00**
88	Flower	45.00	**70.00**
89	Bow & Arrow	50.00	**65.00**
90	Flame	55.00	**60.00**
91	Vessel	55.00	**58.00**

106194 GOD BLESS YOU GRADUATE

Ongoing
Figurine, 5.00"
ac# 319
Boy Graduate

86	Olive Branch	$20.00	**$55.00**
87	Cedar Tree	22.50	**38.00**
88	Flower	24.00	**37.00**
89	Bow & Arrow	27.00	**36.00**
90	Flame	30.00	**35.00**
91	Vessel	30.00	**35.00**
92	G-Clef	30.00	**35.00**
93	Butterfly	30.00	**35.00**
94	Trumpet	30.00	**35.00**
95	Ship	32.50	**35.00**
96	Heart	35.00	**35.00**
97	Sword	35.00	**35.00**
98	Eyeglasses	35.00	**35.00**
99	Star	35.00	**35.00**

106208 — CONGRATULATIONS, PRINCESS

Ongoing
Figurine, 5.50"
ac# 226
Girl Graduate

Year	Mark	Price	Value
86	Olive Branch	$20.00	**$65.00**
87	Cedar Tree	22.50	**38.00**
88	Flower	24.00	**37.00**
89	Bow & Arrow	27.00	**35.00**
90	Flame	30.00	**35.00**
91	Vessel	30.00	**35.00**
92	G-Clef	30.00	**35.00**
93	Butterfly	30.00	**35.00**
94	Trumpet	30.00	**35.00**
95	Ship	32.50	**35.00**
96	Heart	35.00	**35.00**
97	Sword	35.00	**35.00**
98	Eyeglasses	35.00	**35.00**
99	Star	35.00	**35.00**

106216 — LORD HELP ME MAKE THE GRADE

Suspended 1990
Figurine, 5.00"
ac# 582
Schoolboy Clown

Year	Mark	Price	Value
87	Cedar Tree	$25.00	**$55.00**
88	Flower	27.00	**52.00**
89	Bow & Arrow	30.00	**50.00**
90	Flame	32.50	**48.00**

106755 — HEAVEN BLESS YOUR TOGETHERNESS

Ongoing
Figurine, 5.50"
ac# 418
Groom Popping out of Trunk / Bride

Year	Mark	Price	Value
88	Cedar Tree	$65.00	**$100.00**
88	Flower	65.00	**92.00**
89	Bow & Arrow	75.00	**90.00**
90	Flame	80.00	**90.00**
91	Vessel	80.00	**90.00**
92	G-Clef	80.00	**90.00**
93	Butterfly	90.00	**90.00**
94	Trumpet	90.00	**90.00**
95	Ship	90.00	**90.00**
96	Heart	90.00	**90.00**
97	Sword	90.00	**90.00**
98	Eyeglasses	90.00	**90.00**
99	Star	90.00	**90.00**

106763 — PRECIOUS MEMORIES

Ongoing
Figurine, 4.50"
ac# 790
Couple on Couch Looking at Wedding Album

Year	Mark	Price	Value
88	Cedar Tree	$37.50	**$75.00**
88	Flower	37.50	**60.00**
89	Bow & Arrow	45.00	**58.00**
90	Flame	50.00	**55.00**
91	Vessel	50.00	**52.00**
92	G-Clef	50.00	**50.00**
93	Butterfly	50.00	**50.00**
94	Trumpet	50.00	**50.00**
95	Ship	50.00	**50.00**
96	Heart	50.00	**50.00**
97	Sword	50.00	**50.00**
98	Eyeglasses	50.00	**50.00**
99	Star	50.00	**50.00**

106798 — PUPPY LOVE IS FROM ABOVE

Retired 1995
Figurine, 5.50"
ac# 797
Anniversary Couple with Dog

Year	Mark	Price	Value
88	Cedar Tree	$45.00	**$98.00**
88	Flower	45.00	**94.00**
89	Bow & Arrow	50.00	**90.00**
90	Flame	55.00	**89.00**
91	Vessel	55.00	**88.00**
92	G-Clef	55.00	**85.00**
93	Butterfly	55.00	**82.00**
94	Trumpet	55.00	**80.00**
95	Ship	55.00	**78.00**

106836   HAPPY BIRTHDAY POPPY

Suspended 1993
Figurine, 5.50"
ac# 379
Girl Holding Poppy Plant

88	Cedar Tree	$27.50	**$72.00**
88	Flower	27.50	**68.00**
89	Bow & Arrow	31.50	**67.00**
90	Flame	33.50	**65.00**
91	Vessel	33.50	**64.00**
92	G-Clef	33.50	**63.00**
93	Butterfly	35.00	**62.00**

106844   SEW IN LOVE

Retired 1997
Figurine, 5.50"
ac# 844
Girl Sewing Boy's Pants

88	Cedar Tree	$45.00	**$95.00**
88	Flower	45.00	**90.00**
89	Bow & Arrow	50.00	**89.00**
90	Flame	55.00	**85.00**
91	Vessel	55.00	**84.00**
92	G-Clef	55.00	**83.00**
93	Butterfly	55.00	**82.00**
94	Trumpet	55.00	**81.00**
95	Ship	55.00	**80.00**
96	Heart	55.00	**77.00**
97	Sword	55.00	**75.00**

107999   HE WALKS WITH ME   Easter Seal Commemorative / Lily Understamp

Annual 1987
Figurine, 5.50"
ac# 410
Girl on Crutches

87	Olive Branch	$25.00	**$100.00**
	Cedar Tree		**45.00**

108243   THEY FOLLOWED THE STAR   Mini Nativity Addition   Set of 3

Ongoing
Figurine, 6.50"
ac# 979
3 Kings on Camels

87	Cedar Tree	$75.00	**$135.00**
88	Flower	75.00	**120.00**
89	Bow & Arrow	95.00	**120.00**
90	Flame	100.00	**120.00**
91	Vessel	100.00	**120.00**
92	G-Clef	100.00	**120.00**
93	Butterfly	110.00	**120.00**
94	Trumpet	110.00	**120.00**
95	Ship	120.00	**120.00**
96	Heart	120.00	**120.00**
97	Sword	120.00	**120.00**
98	Eyeglasses	120.00	**120.00**
99	Star	120.00	**120.00**

109231   THE GREATEST GIFT IS A FRIEND

Ongoing
Figurine, 4.25"
ac# 935
Baby Boy Sitting by Dog

87	Cedar Tree	$30.00	**$55.00**
88	Flower	32.50	**48.00**
89	Bow & Arrow	36.00	**45.00**
90	Flame	37.50	**42.00**
91	Vessel	37.50	**40.00**
92	G-Clef	37.50	**40.00**
93	Butterfly	37.50	**40.00**
94	Trumpet	37.50	**40.00**
95	Ship	37.50	**40.00**
96	Heart	40.00	**40.00**
97	Sword	40.00	**40.00**
98	Eyeglasses	40.00	**40.00**
99	Star	40.00	**40.00**

109401   BABY'S FIRST CHRISTMAS

Dated Annual 1987
Ornament, 3.25"
ac# 95
Girl on Rocking Horse

87	Cedar Tree	$12.00	**$40.00**

109428 **BABY'S FIRST CHRISTMAS**
Dated Annual 1987
    Ornament, 3.25"
    ac# 96
    Boy on Rocking Horse

87	Cedar Tree	$12.00	**$40.00**

109460 **ISN'T EIGHT JUST GREAT**   Series: "Birthday Circus Train"
Ongoing
    Figurine, 4.50"
    ac# 502
    Ostrich–Age 8

88	Cedar Tree	$18.50	**$34.00**
88	Flower	18.50	**30.00**
89	Bow & Arrow	20.00	**28.00**
90	Flame	22.50	**25.00**
91	Vessel	22.50	**23.00**
92	G-Clef	22.50	**23.00**
93	Butterfly	22.50	**22.50**
94	Trumpet	22.50	**22.50**
95	Ship	22.50	**22.50**
96	Heart	22.50	**22.50**
97	Sword	22.50	**22.50**
98	Eyeglasses	22.50	**22.50**
99	Star	22.50	**22.50**

109479 **WISHING YOU GRRR-EATNESS**   Series: "Birthday Circus Train"
Ongoing
    Figurine, 4.25"
    ac# 1083
    Leopard–Age 7

88	Cedar Tree	$18.50	**$32.00**
88	Flower	18.50	**26.00**
89	Bow & Arrow	20.00	**25.00**
90	Flame	22.50	**24.00**
91	Vessel	22.50	**23.00**
92	G-Clef	22.50	**23.00**
93	Butterfly	22.50	**22.50**
94	Trumpet	22.50	**22.50**
95	Ship	22.50	**22.50**
96	Heart	22.50	**22.50**
97	Sword	22.50	**22.50**
98	Eyeglasses	22.50	**22.50**
99	Star	22.50	**22.50**

109487 **BELIEVE THE IMPOSSIBLE**
Suspended 1991
    Figurine, 5.50"
    ac# 130
    Boy with Barbells

88	Cedar Tree	$35.00	**$95.00**
88	Flower	35.00	**75.00**
89	Bow & Arrow	40.00	**70.00**
90	Flame	45.00	**68.00**
91	Vessel	45.00	**65.00**

109584 **HAPPINESS DIVINE**
Retired 1992
    Figurine, 5.50"
    ac# 369
    Clown Angel with Flowers

88	Flower	$25.00	**$82.00**
89	Bow & Arrow	27.50	**75.00**
90	Flame	30.00	**70.00**
91	Vessel	30.00	**68.00**
92	G-Clef	30.00	**65.00**

109746 **PEACE ON EARTH**   Tune: Hark! The Herald Angels Sing
Suspended 1993
    Musical, 6.50"
    ac# 773
    Kids with Pup, Kitten and
    Bird

88	Flower	$100.00	**$145.00**
89	Bow & Arrow	110.00	**140.00**
90	Flame	120.00	**130.00**
91	Vessel	120.00	**129.00**
92	G-Clef	120.00	**128.00**
93	Butterfly	130.00	**125.00**

109754 — WISHING YOU A YUMMY CHRISTMAS

Suspended 1994	87	Cedar Tree	$35.00	**$65.00**
Figurine, 5.00"	88	Flower	35.00	**62.00**
ac# 1081	89	Bow & Arrow	42.50	**58.00**
Girl with Ice Cream	90	Flame	45.00	**55.00**
	91	Vessel	45.00	**52.00**
	92	G-Clef	45.00	**50.00**
	93	Butterfly	50.00	**49.00**
	94	Trumpet	50.00	**48.00**

109762 — WE GATHER TOGETHER TO ASK THE LORD'S BLESSING   Set of 6

Retired 1995	87	Cedar Tree	$130.00	**$345.00**
Figurine, 5.00"	88	Flower	130.00	**320.00**
ac# 1042	89	Bow & Arrow	145.00	**315.00**
Family Thanksgiving Set	90	Flame	150.00	**312.00**
	91	Vessel	150.00	**310.00**
	92	G-Clef	150.00	**305.00**
	93	Butterfly	150.00	**300.00**
	94	Trumpet	150.00	**295.00**
	95	Ship	150.00	**285.00**

109770 — LOVE IS THE BEST GIFT OF ALL

Dated Annual 1987	87	Cedar Tree	$11.00	**$40.00**
Ornament, 2.75"				
ac# 615				
Girl with Package & Doll				

109800 — MEOWIE CHRISTMAS

Ongoing	88	Flower	$30.00	**$50.00**
Figurine, 4.50"	89	Bow & Arrow	33.00	**42.00**
ac# 683	90	Flame	35.00	**40.00**
Girl with Kitten	91	Vessel	35.00	**38.00**
	92	G-Clef	35.00	**35.00**
	93	Butterfly	35.00	**35.00**
	94	Trumpet	35.00	**35.00**
	95	Ship	35.00	**35.00**
	96	Heart	35.00	**35.00**
	97	Sword	35.00	**35.00**
	98	Eyeglasses	35.00	**35.00**
	99	Star	35.00	**35.00**

109819 — OH WHAT FUN IT IS TO RIDE

Ongoing	87	Cedar Tree	$85.00	**$130.00**
Figurine, 6.25"	88	Flower	85.00	**120.00**
ac# 735	89	Bow & Arrow	100.00	**118.00**
Grandma on Sled	90	Flame	110.00	**115.00**
	91	Vessel	110.00	**110.00**
	92	G-Clef	110.00	**110.00**
	93	Butterfly	110.00	**110.00**
	94	Trumpet	110.00	**110.00**
	95	Ship	110.00	**110.00**
	96	Heart	110.00	**110.00**
	97	Sword	110.00	**110.00**
	98	Eyeglasses	110.00	**110.00**
	99	Star	110.00	**110.00**

109835 — LOVE IS THE BEST GIFT OF ALL

Dated Annual 1987	87	Cedar Tree	$22.50	**$45.00**
Bell, 5.75"				
ac# 615				
Girl with Package & Doll				

109843 · LOVE IS THE BEST GIFT OF ALL

Dated Annual 1987	87	Cedar Tree	$6.00	**$35.00**
Thimble, 2.25"				
ac# 615				
Girl with Package & Doll				

109886 · WISHING YOU A HAPPY EASTER

Ongoing	88	Cedar Tree	$23.00	**$45.00**
Figurine, 5.50"	88	Flower	23.00	**38.00**
ac# 1072	89	Bow & Arrow	25.00	**36.00**
Girl Holding Bunny	90	Flame	27.50	**35.00**
	91	Vessel	27.50	**35.00**
	92	G-Clef	27.50	**35.00**
	93	Butterfly	30.00	**35.00**
	94	Trumpet	30.00	**35.00**
	95	Ship	32.50	**35.00**
	96	Heart	35.00	**35.00**
	97	Sword	35.00	**35.00**
	98	Eyeglasses	35.00	**35.00**
	99	Star	35.00	**35.00**

109924 · WISHING YOU A BASKET FULL OF BLESSINGS

Ongoing	88	Cedar Tree	$23.00	**$45.00**
Figurine, 5.50"	88	Flower	23.00	**37.00**
ac# 1066	89	Bow & Arrow	25.00	**35.00**
Boy Holding Basket	90	Flame	27.50	**35.00**
	91	Vessel	27.50	**35.00**
	92	G-Clef	27.50	**35.00**
	93	Butterfly	30.00	**35.00**
	94	Trumpet	30.00	**35.00**
	95	Ship	32.50	**35.00**
	96	Heart	35.00	**35.00**
	97	Sword	35.00	**35.00**
	98	Eyeglasses	35.00	**35.00**
	99	Star	35.00	**35.00**

109967 · SENDING YOU MY LOVE

Ongoing	88	Cedar Tree	$35.00	**$65.00**
Figurine, 5.00"	88	Flower	35.00	**52.00**
ac# 835	89	Bow & Arrow	40.00	**50.00**
Girl with Hearts in Cloud	90	Flame	45.00	**47.00**
	91	Vessel	45.00	**45.00**
	92	G-Clef	45.00	**45.00**
	93	Butterfly	45.00	**45.00**
	94	Trumpet	45.00	**45.00**
	95	Ship	45.00	**45.00**
	96	Heart	45.00	**45.00**
	97	Sword	45.00	**45.00**
	98	Eyeglasses	45.00	**45.00**
	99	Star	45.00	**45.00**

109975 · MOMMY, I LOVE YOU

Ongoing	88	Cedar Tree	$22.50	**$40.00**
Figurine, 5.50"	88	Flower	22.50	**35.00**
ac# 694	89	Bow & Arrow	25.00	**32.00**
Boy with Flower	90	Flame	27.50	**30.00**
	91	Vessel	27.50	**30.00**
	92	G-Clef	27.50	**30.00**
	93	Butterfly	27.50	**30.00**
	94	Trumpet	27.50	**30.00**
	95	Ship	30.00	**30.00**
	96	Heart	30.00	**30.00**
	97	Sword	30.00	**30.00**
	98	Eyeglasses	30.00	**30.00**
	99	Star	30.00	**30.00**

109983   <u>JANUARY GIRL</u>   Series: "Calendar Girl"

Ongoing	88	Cedar Tree	$37.50	**$52.00**
Figurine, 5.50"	88	Flower	37.50	**48.00**
ac# 518	89	Bow & Arrow	42.50	**45.00**
Girl Pushing Doll in Sleigh	90	Flame	45.00	**45.00**
	91	Vessel	45.00	**45.00**
	92	G-Clef	45.00	**45.00**
	93	Butterfly	45.00	**45.00**
	94	Trumpet	45.00	**45.00**
	95	Ship	45.00	**45.00**
	96	Heart	45.00	**45.00**
	97	Sword	45.00	**45.00**
	98	Eyeglasses	45.00	**45.00**
	99	Star	45.00	**45.00**

109991   <u>FEBRUARY GIRL</u>   Series: "Calendar Girl"

Ongoing	88	Cedar Tree	$27.50	**$50.00**
Figurine, 5.25"	88	Flower	27.50	**40.00**
ac# 271	89	Bow & Arrow	31.50	**39.00**
Girl Looking at Plant Peeking	90	Flame	33.50	**38.00**
thru Snow	91	Vessel	33.50	**38.00**
	92	G-Clef	33.50	**38.00**
	93	Butterfly	35.00	**37.50**
	94	Trumpet	35.00	**37.50**
	95	Ship	37.50	**37.50**
	96	Heart	37.50	**37.50**
	97	Sword	37.50	**37.50**
	98	Eyeglasses	37.50	**37.50**
	99	Star	37.50	**37.50**

110019   <u>MARCH GIRL</u>   Series: "Calendar Girl"

Ongoing	88	Cedar Tree	$27.50	**$55.00**
Figurine, 5.00"	88	Flower	27.50	**42.00**
ac# 653	89	Bow & Arrow	31.50	**40.00**
Girl with Kite	90	Flame	33.50	**38.00**
	91	Vessel	33.50	**38.00**
	92	G-Clef	33.50	**38.00**
	93	Butterfly	35.00	**38.00**
	94	Trumpet	35.00	**37.50**
	95	Ship	37.50	**37.50**
	96	Heart	37.50	**37.50**
	97	Sword	37.50	**37.50**
	98	Eyeglasses	37.50	**37.50**
	99	Star	37.50	**37.50**

110027   <u>APRIL GIRL</u>   Series: "Calendar Girl"

Ongoing	88	Cedar Tree	$30.00	**$110.00**
Figurine, 6.00"	88	Flower	30.00	**50.00**
ac# 73	89	Bow & Arrow	33.00	**42.00**
Girl with Umbrella	90	Flame	35.00	**40.00**
	91	Vessel	35.00	**40.00**
	92	G-Clef	35.00	**40.00**
	93	Butterfly	35.00	**40.00**
	94	Trumpet	35.00	**40.00**
	95	Ship	37.50	**40.00**
	96	Heart	40.00	**40.00**
	97	Sword	40.00	**40.00**
	98	Eyeglasses	40.00	**40.00**
	99	Star	40.00	**40.00**

110035 MAY GIRL Series: "Calendar Girl"

Ongoing		88	Cedar Tree	$25.00	**$140.00**
Figurine, 5.75"		88	Flower	25.00	**38.00**
ac# 659		89	Bow & Arrow	27.50	**37.00**
Girl with Potted Plant		90	Flame	30.00	**35.00**
		91	Vessel	30.00	**35.00**
		92	G-Clef	30.00	**35.00**
		93	Butterfly	35.00	**35.00**
		94	Trumpet	35.00	**35.00**
		95	Ship	35.00	**35.00**
		96	Heart	35.00	**35.00**
		97	Sword	35.00	**35.00**
		98	Eyeglasses	35.00	**35.00**
		99	Star	35.00	**35.00**

110043 JUNE GIRL Series: "Calendar Girl"

Ongoing		88	Cedar Tree	$40.00	**$168.00**
Figurine, 5.50"		88	Flower	40.00	**52.00**
ac# 547		89	Bow & Arrow	45.00	**50.00**
Girl Dressing Up as Bride		90	Flame	50.00	**50.00**
		91	Vessel	50.00	**50.00**
		92	G-Clef	50.00	**50.00**
		93	Butterfly	50.00	**50.00**
		94	Trumpet	50.00	**50.00**
		95	Ship	50.00	**50.00**
		96	Heart	50.00	**50.00**
		97	Sword	50.00	**50.00**
		98	Eyeglasses	50.00	**50.00**
		99	Star	50.00	**50.00**

110051 JULY GIRL Series: "Calendar Girl"

Ongoing		88	Flower	$35.00	**$50.00**
Figurine, 5.50"		89	Bow & Arrow	40.00	**45.00**
ac# 544		90	Flame	45.00	**45.00**
Girl with Puppy in Basket		91	Vessel	45.00	**45.00**
		92	G-Clef	45.00	**45.00**
		93	Butterfly	45.00	**45.00**
		94	Trumpet	45.00	**45.00**
		95	Ship	45.00	**45.00**
		96	Heart	45.00	**45.00**
		97	Sword	45.00	**45.00**
		98	Eyeglasses	45.00	**45.00**
		99	Star	45.00	**45.00**

110078 AUGUST GIRL Series: "Calendar Girl"

Ongoing		88	Flower	$40.00	**$65.00**
Figurine, 4.00"		89	Bow & Arrow	45.00	**57.00**
ac# 75		90	Flame	50.00	**55.00**
Girl in Pool		91	Vessel	50.00	**53.00**
		92	G-Clef	50.00	**50.00**
		93	Butterfly	50.00	**50.00**
		94	Trumpet	50.00	**50.00**
		95	Ship	50.00	**50.00**
		96	Heart	50.00	**50.00**
		97	Sword	50.00	**50.00**
		98	Eyeglasses	50.00	**50.00**
		99	Star	50.00	**50.00**

110086 SEPTEMBER GIRL   Series: "Calendar Girl"

Ongoing
Figurine, 5.75"
ac# 839
Girl Balancing Books

88	Flower	$27.50	**$45.00**
89	Bow & Arrow	31.50	**42.00**
90	Flame	33.50	**38.00**
91	Vessel	33.50	**38.00**
92	G-Clef	33.50	**38.00**
93	Butterfly	35.00	**37.50**
94	Trumpet	35.00	**37.50**
95	Ship	37.50	**37.50**
96	Heart	37.50	**37.50**
97	Sword	37.50	**37.50**
98	Eyeglasses	37.50	**37.50**
99	Star	37.50	**37.50**

110094 OCTOBER GIRL   Series: "Calendar Girl"

Ongoing
Figurine, 5.50"
ac# 731
Girl with Pumpkins

88	Flower	$35.00	**$52.00**
89	Bow & Arrow	40.00	**48.00**
90	Flame	45.00	**45.00**
91	Vessel	45.00	**45.00**
92	G-Clef	45.00	**45.00**
93	Butterfly	45.00	**45.00**
94	Trumpet	45.00	**45.00**
95	Ship	45.00	**45.00**
96	Heart	45.00	**45.00**
97	Sword	45.00	**45.00**
98	Eyeglasses	45.00	**45.00**
99	Star	45.00	**45.00**

110108 NOVEMBER GIRL   Series: "Calendar Girl"

Ongoing
Figurine, 5.50"
ac# 725
Girl in Pilgrim Suit

88	Flower	$32.50	**$52.00**
89	Bow & Arrow	35.00	**42.00**
90	Flame	37.50	**40.00**
91	Vessel	37.50	**38.00**
92	G-Clef	37.50	**38.00**
93	Butterfly	37.50	**37.50**
94	Trumpet	37.50	**37.50**
95	Ship	37.50	**37.50**
96	Heart	37.50	**37.50**
97	Sword	37.50	**37.50**
98	Eyeglasses	37.50	**37.50**
99	Star	37.50	**37.50**

110116 DECEMBER GIRL   Series: "Calendar Girl"

Ongoing
Figurine, 5.50"
ac# 239
Girl with Christmas Candle

88	Flower	$27.50	**$45.00**
89	Bow & Arrow	31.50	**40.00**
90	Flame	33.50	**38.00**
91	Vessel	33.50	**35.00**
92	G-Clef	33.50	**35.00**
93	Butterfly	35.00	**35.00**
94	Trumpet	35.00	**35.00**
95	Ship	35.00	**35.00**
96	Heart	35.00	**35.00**
97	Sword	35.00	**35.00**
98	Eyeglasses	35.00	**35.00**
99	Star	35.00	**35.00**

110930 LOVE IS THE BEST GIFT OF ALL

Dated Annual 1987
Figurine, 5.25"
ac# 615
Girl with Package & Doll

87	Cedar Tree	$22.50	**$42.00**

111120   <u>I'M A POSSIBILITY</u>

Suspended 1990	87	Cedar Tree*	$11.00	**$38.00**
Ornament, 3.25"	88	Flower	12.50	**35.00**
ac# 486	89	Bow & Arrow	13.50	**32.00**
Boy with Football	90	Flame	15.00	**30.00**

*There are Cedar Tree pieces with two hooks from the Retailers Wreath, #111465.

111155   <u>FAITH TAKES THE PLUNGE</u>

Ongoing	88	Cedar Tree*	$27.50	**$55.00**
Figurine, 5.50"	88	Flower*	27.50	**35.00**
ac# 269	89	Bow & Arrow	31.50	**35.00**
Girl with Plunger	90	Flame	33.50	**35.00**
	91	Vessel	33.50	**35.00**
*At some point during the	92	G-Clef	33.50	**35.00**
1988 production, the	93	Butterfly	35.00	**35.00**
expression on the face was	94	Trumpet	35.00	**35.00**
changed from a smile to a	95	Ship	35.00	**35.00**
"determined frown." The	96	Heart	35.00	**35.00**
smiling piece is often referred	97	Sword	35.00	**35.00**
to as the "Smiling Plunger."	98	Eyeglasses	35.00	**35.00**
GBTru$ are smiling with Cedar	99	Star	35.00	**35.00**

Tree (all Cedar Tree are smiling) Annual Production Symbol–$55.00 and smiling with the Flower Annual Production Symbol–$50.00. See page 411.

111163   <u>'TIS THE SEASON</u>

Suspended 1996	88	Flower	$27.50	**$64.00**
Figurine, 5.50"	89	Bow & Arrow	31.50	**60.00**
ac# 1001	90	Flame	33.50	**58.00**
Girl Adding Seasoning	91	Vessel	33.50	**55.00**
	92	G-Clef	33.50	**52.00**
	93	Butterfly	35.00	**51.00**
	94	Trumpet	35.00	**50.00**
	95	Ship	35.00	**48.00**
	96	Heart	35.00	**45.00**

111333   <u>O COME LET US ADORE HIM</u>   Nativity   Set of 4

Suspended 1991	87	Cedar Tree	$200.00	**$250.00**
Figurine, 9.00"	88	Flower	200.00	**225.00**
ac# 728	89	Bow & Arrow	220.00	**225.00**
Large Nativity	90	Flame	220.00	**225.00**
	91	Vessel	220.00	**225.00**

111465   <u>RETAILER'S WREATH</u>

Promotional Item	87	Cedar Tree	$150.00	**$219.00**
Wreath, 16.00"				
ac# 806				
Christmas Wreath				

On some wreaths, the "Have A Heavenly Christmas" ornament has the inscription "Heaven Bound" upside-down. The GBTru$ for the wreath with the upside-down "Heaven Bound" ornament is $285.00.

112143 <u>MOMMY, I LOVE YOU</u>

Ongoing
Figurine, 5.75"
ac# 695
Girl with Flower

88	Cedar Tree	$22.50	**$42.00**
88	Flower	22.50	**38.00**
89	Bow & Arrow	25.00	**35.00**
90	Flame	27.50	**32.00**
91	Vessel	27.50	**30.00**
92	G-Clef	27.50	**30.00**
93	Butterfly	27.50	**30.00**
94	Trumpet	27.50	**30.00**
95	Ship	30.00	**30.00**
96	Heart	30.00	**30.00**
97	Sword	30.00	**30.00**
98	Eyeglasses	30.00	**30.00**
99	Star	30.00	**30.00**

112313 <u>A TUB FULL OF LOVE</u>

Ongoing
Figurine, 3.50"
ac# 23
Baby Girl in Wood Tub

87	Cedar Tree	$22.50	**$44.00**
88	Flower	22.50	**38.00**
89	Bow & Arrow	27.50	**35.00**
90	Flame	30.00	**33.00**
91	Vessel	30.00	**33.00**
92	G-Clef	30.00	**32.50**
93	Butterfly	30.00	**32.50**
94	Trumpet	30.00	**32.50**
95	Ship	30.00	**32.50**
96	Heart	32.50	**32.50**
97	Sword	32.50	**32.50**
98	Eyeglasses	32.50	**32.50**
99	Star	32.50	**32.50**

112348 <u>RETAILER'S WREATH BELL</u>

Promotional Item
Bell, 3.25"
ac# 807
Retailer's Wreath Bell

87	Cedar Tree	NA	**$62.00**

This is the bell from the Retailer's Wreath, #111465. It has its own Enesco Item #.

112356 <u>YOU HAVE TOUCHED SO MANY HEARTS</u>

Retired 1997
Ornament, 3.25"
ac# 1130
Girl with String of Hearts

*There are Cedar Tree pieces with two hooks from the Retailers Wreath, #111465

87	Cedar Tree*	$11.00	**$42.00**
88	Flower	12.50	**40.00**
89	Bow & Arrow	13.50	**32.00**
90	Flame	15.00	**32.00**
91	Vessel	15.00	**30.00**
92	G-Clef	15.00	**30.00**
93	Butterfly	15.00	**29.00**
94	Trumpet	16.00	**29.00**
95	Ship	17.00	**28.00**
96	Heart	18.50	**28.00**

112364 <u>WADDLE I DO WITHOUT YOU</u>

Ongoing
Ornament, 3.50"
ac# 1032
Girl Clown with Basket & Goose

87	Cedar Tree	$11.00	**$28.00**
88	Flower	12.50	**22.00**
89	Bow & Arrow	13.50	**20.00**
90	Flame	15.00	**19.00**
91	Vessel	15.00	**19.00**
92	G-Clef	15.00	**18.50**
93	Butterfly	15.00	**18.50**
94	Trumpet	16.00	**18.50**
95	Ship	17.00	**18.50**
96	Heart	18.50	**18.50**
97	Sword	18.50	**18.50**
98	Eyeglasses	18.50	**18.50**
99	Star	18.50	**18.50**

112372 I'M SENDING YOU A WHITE CHRISTMAS

Suspended 1992
Ornament, 3.00"
ac# 495
Girl Mailing Snowball

*There are Cedar Tree pieces with two hooks from the Retailers Wreath, #111465.

87	Cedar Tree*	$11.00	**$36.00**
88	Flower	12.50	**34.00**
89	Bow & Arrow	13.50	**32.00**
90	Flame	15.00	**30.00**
91	Vessel	15.00	**29.00**
92	G-Clef	15.00	**28.00**

112380 HE CLEANSED MY SOUL

Ongoing
Ornament, 2.75"
ac# 394
Girl in Old Bathtub

*There are Cedar Tree pieces with two hooks from the Retailers Wreath, #111465.

87	Cedar Tree*	$12.00	**$30.00**
88	Flower	13.00	**25.00**
89	Bow & Arrow	15.00	**22.00**
90	Flame	15.00	**21.00**
91	Vessel	15.00	**20.00**
92	G-Clef	15.00	**19.00**
93	Butterfly	15.00	**18.50**
94	Trumpet	16.00	**18.50**
95	Ship	17.00	**18.50**
96	Heart	18.50	**18.50**
97	Sword	18.50	**18.50**
98	Eyeglasses	18.50	**18.50**
99	Star	18.50	**18.50**

112399 OUR FIRST CHRISTMAS TOGETHER

Dated Annual 1987
Ornament, 2.75"
ac# 751
Boy and Girl in Package

87	Cedar Tree	$11.00	**$35.00**

112402 I'M SENDING YOU A WHITE CHRISTMAS   Tune: White Christmas

Retired 1993
Musical, 6.00"
ac# 495
Girl Mailing Snowball

87	Cedar Tree	$55.00	**$135.00**
88	Flower	55.00	**125.00**
89	Bow & Arrow	67.50	**122.00**
90	Flame	70.00	**120.00**
91	Vessel	70.00	**115.00**
92	G-Clef	70.00	**112.00**
93	Butterfly	75.00	**110.00**

112577 YOU HAVE TOUCHED SO MANY HEARTS   Tune: Everybody Loves Somebody

Suspended 1996
Musical, 6.50"
ac# 1130
Girl with String of Hearts

88	Cedar Tree	$50.00	**$110.00**
88	Flower	50.00	**108.00**
89	Bow & Arrow	55.00	**105.00**
90	Flame	60.00	**100.00**
91	Vessel	60.00	**96.00**
92	G-Clef	60.00	**95.00**
93	Butterfly	60.00	**92.00**
94	Trumpet	60.00	**90.00**
95	Ship	60.00	**85.00**
96	Heart	65.00	**80.00**

113956 TO MY FOREVER FRIEND

Ongoing
Ornament, 3.00"
ac# 1013
Two Girls with Flowers

88	Flower	$16.00	**$35.00**
89	Bow & Arrow	17.50	**28.00**
90	Flame	17.50	**25.00**
91	Vessel	17.50	**22.00**
92	G-Clef	17.50	**20.00**
93	Butterfly	17.50	**20.00**
94	Trumpet	17.50	**20.00**
95	Ship	18.50	**20.00**
96	Heart	20.00	**20.00**
97	Sword	20.00	**20.00**
98	Eyeglasses	20.00	**20.00**
99	Star	20.00	**20.00**

113964 SMILE ALONG THE WAY

Suspended 1993
Ornament, 3.50"
ac# 874
Clown Doing Handstand

88	Flower	$15.00	**$38.00**
89	Bow & Arrow	17.00	**35.00**
90	Flame	17.50	**32.00**
91	Vessel	17.50	**30.00**
92	G-Clef	17.50	**28.00**
93	Butterfly	17.50	**25.00**

113972 GOD SENT YOU JUST IN TIME

Suspended 1991
Ornament, 3.00"
ac# 342
Clown with Jack-in-the-Box

88	Flower	$13.50	**$38.00**
89	Bow & Arrow	15.00	**37.00**
90	Flame	15.00	**35.00**
91	Vessel	15.00	**33.00**

113980 REJOICE O EARTH

Retired 1991
Ornament, 3.00"
ac# 803
Angel with Trumpet

88	Flower	$13.50	**$45.00**
89	Bow & Arrow	15.00	**42.00**
90	Flame	15.00	**40.00**
91	Vessel	15.00	**37.00**

113999 CHEERS TO THE LEADER

Suspended 1991
Ornament, 3.00"
ac# 200
Girl Cheerleader

88	Flower	$13.50	**$37.00**
89	Bow & Arrow	15.00	**35.00**
90	Flame	15.00	**34.00**
91	Vessel	15.00	**33.00**

114006 MY LOVE WILL NEVER LET YOU GO

Suspended 1991
Ornament, 3.25"
ac# 709
Boy with Hat and Fish

88	Flower	$13.50	**$38.00**
89	Bow & Arrow	15.00	**35.00**
90	Flame	15.00	**33.00**
91	Vessel	15.00	**30.00**

114014 THIS TOO SHALL PASS

Ongoing
Figurine, 5.50"
ac# 989
Boy with Broken Heart

88	Cedar Tree	$23.00	**$40.00**
88	Flower	23.00	**35.00**
89	Bow & Arrow	25.00	**32.00**
90	Flame	27.50	**30.00**
91	Vessel	27.50	**30.00**
92	G-Clef	27.50	**30.00**
93	Butterfly	30.00	**30.00**
94	Trumpet	30.00	**30.00**
95	Ship	30.00	**30.00**
96	Heart	30.00	**30.00**
97	Sword	30.00	**30.00**
98	Eyeglasses	30.00	**30.00**
99	Star	30.00	**30.00**

114022 THE GOOD LORD HAS BLESSED US TENFOLD 10th Anniversary
Commemorative

Annual 1988
Figurine, 5.75"
ac# 933
Couple with Dogs and
Puppies

88	Cedar Tree	$90.00	**$250.00**
	Flower		**240.00**

115231 YOU ARE MY MAIN EVENT Special Event

	Annual 1988	88	Cedar Tree	$30.00	**$60.00**
	Figurine, 6.50"		Flower		**55.00**
	ac# 1108				
	Girl Holding Balloons and				
	Bag				

The balloon strings on this piece are metal wires covered with colored paper. The first Cedar Tree pieces produced had pink strings–the rest of the production (balance of Cedar Tree and all of Flower) had white strings. "Pink Strings" is the coveted piece. The GBTru$ for "Pink Strings" is $82.00.

115274 SOME BUNNY'S SLEEPING Nativity Addition

Suspended 1996	88	Flower	$15.00	**$42.00**
Figurine, 2.75"	89	Bow & Arrow	17.00	**38.00**
ac# 880	90	Flame	18.50	**36.00**
Bunnies	91	Vessel	18.50	**35.00**
	92	G-Clef	18.50	**32.00**
	93	Butterfly	18.50	**30.00**
	94	Trumpet	18.50	**29.00**
	95	Ship	18.50	**27.00**
	96	Heart	18.50	**25.00**

115282 BABY'S FIRST CHRISTMAS

Dated Annual 1988	88	Flower	$15.00	**$20.00**
Ornament, 2.25"				
ac# 97				
Boy in Sleigh				

115290 OUR FIRST CHRISTMAS TOGETHER

Suspended 1991	88	Flower	$50.00	**$84.00**
Figurine, 5.50"	89	Bow & Arrow	55.00	**72.00**
ac# 752	90	Flame	60.00	**70.00**
Couple with Gifts	91	Vessel	60.00	**68.00**

115304 TIME TO WISH YOU A MERRY CHRISTMAS

Dated Annual 1988	88	Flower	$25.00	**$40.00**
Bell, 6.00"				
ac# 998				
Girl with Clock and Mouse				

115312 TIME TO WISH YOU A MERRY CHRISTMAS

Dated Annual 1988	88	Flower	$7.00	**$50.00**
Thimble, 2.00"				
ac# 998				
Girl with Clock and Mouse				

115320 TIME TO WISH YOU A MERRY CHRISTMAS

Dated Annual 1988	88	Flower	$13.00	**$40.00**
Ornament, 3.00"				
ac# 998				
Girl with Clock and Mouse				

115339 TIME TO WISH YOU A MERRY CHRISTMAS

Dated Annual 1988	88	Flower	$24.00	**$42.00**
Figurine, 5.00"				
ac# 998				
Girl with Clock and Mouse				

115479 — BLESSED ARE THEY THAT OVERCOME   Easter Seal Commemorative

Annual 1988   88   Cedar Tree $27.50   **$35.00**
Figurine, 5.50"   Flower   30.00
ac# 164
Boy on Crutches at Finish
Line

Easter Seal Lily missing on all decals.

127019 — LOVE BLOOMS ETERNAL   Series: "Dated Cross"–1st Issue

Dated Annual 1995   95   Trumpet $35.00   **$40.00**
Figurine, 6.00"   Ship   35.00
ac# 600
Girl Kneeling by Cross

127809 — CONGRATULATIONS, YOU EARNED YOUR STRIPES   Two By Two

Ongoing   95   Ship $15.00   **$20.00**
Figurine, 2.00"   96   Heart   15.00   **15.00**
ac# 227   97   Sword   15.00   **15.00**
Boy & Girl Zebras   98   Eyeglasses   15.00   **15.00**
                                                    99   Star   15.00   **15.00**

127817 — A PERFECT DISPLAY OF 15 HAPPY YEARS

Member Only   95   Ship $100.00   **$150.00**
Figurine, 6.75"
ac# 12
Girl Next to Showcase
Holding Miniature Pieces

128295A — AN EVENT SHOWERED WITH LOVE   Regional Event—Wisconsin /
Approximately 1,000 Distributed
Dated Annual 1994   94   Trumpet $30.00   **$100.00**
Ornament, 3.25"
ac# 55
Girl with Umbrella

128295C — AN EVENT SHOWERED WITH LOVE   Regional Event—Texas /
Approximately 1,000 Distributed
Dated Annual 1994   94   Trumpet $30.00   **$100.00**
Ornament, 3.25"
ac# 55
Girl with Umbrella

128295D — AN EVENT SHOWERED WITH LOVE   Regional Event—California /
Approximately 1,500 Distributed
Dated Annual 1994   94   Trumpet $30.00   **$98.00**
Ornament, 3.25"
ac# 55
Girl with Umbrella

128309 — DREAMS REALLY DO COME TRUE

Ongoing   95   Trumpet $37.50   **$40.00**
Figurine, 4.75"   95   Ship   37.50   **38.00**
ac# 249   96   Heart   37.50   **37.50**
Girl on Rainbow   97   Sword   37.50   **37.50**
                                                    98   Eyeglasses   37.50   **37.50**
                                                    99   Star   37.50   **37.50**

128686 ANOTHER YEAR AND MORE GREY HARES

Ongoing
Figurine, 2.25"
ac# 71
Three Bunnies with Birthday
Cake

95	Trumpet	$17.50	**$25.00**
95	Ship	17.50	**19.00**
96	Heart	18.50	**18.50**
97	Sword	18.50	**18.50**
98	Eyeglasses	18.50	**18.50**
99	Star	18.50	**18.50**

128694 HAPPY HULA DAYS

Ongoing
Figurine, 4.75"
ac# 382
Girl in Grass Skirt

95	Ship	$30.00	**$35.00**
96	Heart	32.50	**32.50**
97	Sword	32.50	**32.50**
98	Eyeglasses	32.50	**32.50**
99	Star	32.50	**32.50**

128708 OWL BE HOME FOR CHRISTMAS   Birthday Collection

Dated Annual 1996
Ornament, 2.50"
ac# 763
Owl in Stocking Cap on
Bough

96	Heart	$18.50	**$25.00**

129097 LOVE VOWS TO ALWAYS BLOOM   Series: "To Have And To Hold"

Ongoing
Figurine, 6.50"
ac# 629
Newlyweds

96	Ship	$70.00	**$72.00**
96	Heart	70.00	**70.00**
97	Sword	70.00	**70.00**
98	Eyeglasses	70.00	**70.00**
99	Star	70.00	**70.00**

129100 I GIVE YOU MY LOVE FOREVER TRUE

Ongoing
Figurine, 6.75"
ac# 464
Bride & Groom

95	Trumpet	$70.00	**$80.00**
95	Ship	70.00	**72.00**
96	Heart	70.00	**70.00**
97	Sword	70.00	**70.00**
98	Eyeglasses	70.00	**70.00**
99	Star	70.00	**70.00**

129151 HE HATH MADE EVERYTHING BEAUTIFUL IN HIS TIME   Series: "Mother's Day"–2nd Issue

Dated Annual 1995
Plate, 8.50"
ac# 397
Girl Watches Butterfly on
Tulips

95	Ship	$50.00	**$50.00**

129259 GRANDPA'S ISLAND   Chapel Exclusive

Ongoing
Figurine, 5.25"
ac# 359
Girl Reaches to Bird / Castle
Turret / Bunnies Watch

95	Ship	$100.00	**$125.00**
96	Heart	100.00	**100.00**

129267 LIGHTING THE WAY TO A HAPPY HOLIDAY   Chapel Exclusive

Ongoing
Figurine, 4.75"
ac# 578
Boy Angel w/Candle and
Teddy Bear

95	Ship	$30.00	**$42.00**
96	Heart	30.00	**30.00**

129275 LIGHTING THE WAY TO A HAPPY HOLIDAY   Chapel Exclusive

Ongoing
Ornament, 3.25"
ac# 578
Boy Angel w/Candle and
Teddy Bear

95	Ship	$20.00	**$28.00**
96	Heart	20.00	**20.00**
97	Sword	20.00	**20.00**

129488 | LOVE LETTERS IN THE SAND
Ongoing		97	Heart	$35.00	**$42.00**
Figurine, 4.00"		97	Sword	35.00	**35.00**
ac# 619		98	Eyeglasses	35.00	**35.00**
Child Traces "God Loves You" in Sand		99	Star	35.00	**35.00**

135992 | HEAVEN MUST HAVE SENT YOU Chapel Exclusive
Ongoing		96	Unmarked	$45.00	**$52.00**
Figurine, 5.25"		97	Sword	45.00	**45.00**
ac# 419					
Child Kisses Angel on the Avenue of Angels					

Concrete angel is unpainted.

136190 | AGE 1 Series: "Growing In Grace"
Ongoing		95	Ship	$25.00	**$30.00**
Figurine, 3.00"		96	Heart	25.00	**25.00**
ac# 29		97	Sword	25.00	**25.00**
Baby with Cake		98	Eyeglasses	25.00	**25.00**
		99	Star	25.00	**25.00**

136204 | IT'S A GIRL Series: "Growing In Grace"
Ongoing		95	Ship	$22.50	**$28.00**
Figurine, 3.50"		96	Heart	22.50	**22.50**
ac# 509		97	Sword	22.50	**22.50**
Infant Angel with Birth		98	Eyeglasses	22.50	**22.50**
Announcement		99	Star	22.50	**22.50**

136212 | AGE 2 Series: "Growing In Grace"
Ongoing		95	Ship	$25.00	**$30.00**
Figurine, 3.00"		96	Heart	25.00	**25.00**
ac# 36		97	Sword	25.00	**25.00**
Girl with Blocks		98	Eyeglasses	25.00	**25.00**
		99	Star	25.00	**25.00**

136220 | AGE 3 Series: "Growing In Grace"
Ongoing		95	Ship	$25.00	**$30.00**
Figurine, 3.00"		96	Heart	25.00	**25.00**
ac# 37		97	Sword	25.00	**25.00**
Girl with Flowers		98	Eyeglasses	25.00	**25.00**
		99	Star	25.00	**25.00**

136239 | AGE 4 Series: "Growing In Grace"
Ongoing		95	Ship	$27.50	**$33.00**
Figurine, 4.00"		96	Heart	27.50	**27.50**
ac# 38		97	Sword	27.50	**27.50**
Girl with Doll		98	Eyeglasses	27.50	**27.50**
		99	Star	27.50	**27.50**

136247 | AGE 5 Series: "Growing In Grace"
Ongoing		95	Ship	$27.50	**$33.00**
Figurine, 4.00"		96	Heart	27.50	**27.50**
ac# 39		97	Sword	27.50	**27.50**
Girl with Lunch Box		98	Eyeglasses	27.50	**27.50**
		99	Star	27.50	**27.50**

136255 | AGE 6 Series: "Growing In Grace"
Ongoing		95	Ship	$30.00	**$35.00**
Figurine, 4.00"		96	Heart	30.00	**30.00**
ac# 40		97	Sword	30.00	**30.00**
Girl on Bicycle		98	Eyeglasses	30.00	**30.00**
		99	Star	30.00	**30.00**

136263	SWEET SIXTEEN / AGE 16 Series: "Growing In Grace"				
	Ongoing	95	Ship	$45.00	**$52.00**
	Figurine, 6.50"	96	Heart	45.00	**45.00**
	ac# 904	97	Sword	45.00	**45.00**
	Girl Holding Sixteen Roses	98	Eyeglasses	45.00	**45.00**
		99	Star	45.00	**45.00**

136271	YOU WILL ALWAYS BE OUR HERO 50th Anniversary WWII				
	Commemorative				
	Annual 1995	95	Trumpet	$40.00	**$52.00**
	Figurine, 4.50"		Ship		**46.00**
	ac# 1144				
	Soldier in Auto w/Sailor /				
	Pup / American Flag				

139475	LOVE MAKES THE WORLD GO 'ROUND Century Circle Exclusive /				
	Individually Numbered				
	Limited Edition 15,000	95	Ship	$200.00	**$365.00**
	Figurine, 9.00"				
	ac# 622				
	Carousel				

139491	WHERE WOULD I BE WITHOUT YOU Little Moments				
	Ongoing	97	Not Marked	$20.00	**$20.00**
	Figurine, 3.25"	98		20.00	**20.00**
	ac# 1061	99		20.00	**20.00**
	Girl Sitting and Thinking				

139505	ALL THINGS GROW WITH LOVE Little Moments				
	Ongoing	97	Not Marked	$20.00	**$20.00**
	Figurine, 4.00"	98		20.00	**20.00**
	ac# 47	99		20.00	**20.00**
	Girl Holding Newborn Baby				

139513	YOU'RE THE BERRY BEST Little Moments				
	Ongoing	97	Not Marked	$20.00	**$20.00**
	Figurine, 3.00"	98		20.00	**20.00**
	ac# 1155	99		20.00	**20.00**
	Girl with Basket of Berries				

139521	YOU MAKE THE WORLD A SWEETER PLACE Little Moments				
	Ongoing	97	Not Marked	$20.00	**$20.00**
	Figurine, 4.00"	98		20.00	**20.00**
	ac# 1137	99		20.00	**20.00**
	Clown				

139548	YOU'RE FOREVER IN MY HEART Little Moments				
	Ongoing	97	Not Marked	$25.00	**$25.00**
	Figurine, 3.75"	98		25.00	**25.00**
	ac# 1148	99		25.00	**25.00**
	Boy & Girl w/Bouquet, Hold				
	Hands				

139556	BIRTHDAY WISHES WITH HUGS AND KISSES Little Moments				
	Ongoing	97	Not Marked	$20.00	**$20.00**
	Figurine, 3.75"	98		20.00	**20.00**
	ac# 136	99		20.00	**20.00**
	Girl Wearing a Crown Holds				
	a Birthday Cake				

139564 — YOU MAKE MY SPIRIT SOAR — Little Moments

Ongoing	97	Not Marked	$20.00	**$20.00**
Figurine, 3.75"	98		20.00	**20.00**
ac# 1135	99		20.00	**20.00**
Angel Creates a Paper Airplane				

142654 — HE COVERS THE EARTH WITH HIS BEAUTY

Dated Annual 1995	95	Ship	$30.00	**$35.00**
Figurine, 4.75"				
ac# 396				
Girl Trims Snowflake				

142662 — HE COVERS THE EARTH WITH HIS BEAUTY

Dated Annual 1995	95	Ship	$17.00	**$32.00**
Ornament, 3.00"				
ac# 396				
Girl Trims Snowflake				

142670 — HE COVERS THE EARTH WITH HIS BEAUTY

Dated Annual 1995	95	Ship	$50.00	**$60.00**
Plate, 8.25"				
ac# 396				
Girl Trims Snowflake				

142689 — HE COVERS THE EARTH WITH HIS BEAUTY

Dated Annual 1995	95	Ship	$30.00	**$40.00**
Ornament, 3.25"				
ac# 396				
Girl Trims Snowflake				

142700 — OUR FIRST CHRISTMAS TOGETHER

Dated Annual 1995	95	Ship	$18.50	**$28.00**
Ornament, 2.75"				
ac# 755				
Two Birds on Heart Wreath				

142719 — BABY'S FIRST CHRISTMAS

Dated Annual 1995	95	Ship	$17.50	**$30.00**
Ornament, 3.00"				
ac# 108				
Girl Sits on Star				

142727 — BABY'S FIRST CHRISTMAS

Dated Annual 1995	95	Ship	$17.50	**$30.00**
Ornament, 3.00"				
ac# 107				
Boy Sits on Star				

142735 — COME LET US ADORE HIM — Nativity — Three Piece Nativity Starter Set with

Booklet	95	Ship	$50.00	**$52.00**
Ongoing	96	Heart	50.00	**50.00**
Figurine, 4.25"	97	Sword	50.00	**50.00**
ac# 224	98	Eyeglasses	50.00	**50.00**
The Holy Family	99	Star	50.00	**50.00**

142743 COME LET US ADORE HIM Mini Nativity   Three Piece Mini Nativity

Starter Set with Booklet	95	Ship	$35.00	**$38.00**
Ongoing	96	Heart	35.00	**35.00**
Figurine, 2.75"	97	Sword	35.00	**35.00**
ac# 224	98	Eyeglasses	35.00	**35.00**
The Holy Family	99	Star	35.00	**35.00**

142751 MAKING A TRAIL TO BETHLEHEM   Nativity Addition

Retired 1998	95	Ship	$30.00	**$35.00**
Figurine, 5.00"	96	Heart	32.50	**32.50**
ac# 648	97	Sword	32.50	**32.50**
Boy on Hobby Horse	98	Eyeglasses	32.50	**32.50**

150061 SAILABRATION   Cruise Piece

Dated Annual 1995	95	Trumpet	$Gift	**$600.00**
Figurine, 3.25"				
ac# 814				
Sailor Boy on Life Preserver				

150088 I'LL GIVE HIM MY HEART

Ongoing	95	Ship	$40.00	**$45.00**
Figurine, 5.25"	96	Heart	45.00	**45.00**
ac# 482	97	Sword	45.00	**45.00**
Shepherd Boy Gives Heart	98	Eyeglasses	45.00	**45.00**
Gift to Baby Jesus	99	Star	45.00	**45.00**

150096 SOOT YOURSELF TO A MERRY CHRISTMAS

Ongoing	95	Ship	$35.00	**$37.00**
Figurine, 5.75"	96	Heart	35.00	**35.00**
ac# 888	97	Sword	35.00	**35.00**
Chimney Cleaner Boy with	98	Eyeglasses	35.00	**35.00**
Brush	99	Star	35.00	**35.00**

150118 MAKING SPIRITS BRIGHT

Ongoing	95	Ship	$37.50	**$40.00**
Figurine, 5.50"	96	Heart	37.50	**37.50**
ac# 649	97	Sword	37.50	**37.50**
Girl Carries Candle	98	Eyeglasses	37.50	**37.50**
	99	Star	37.50	**37.50**

150126 JOY FROM HEAD TO MISTLETOE

Ongoing	95	Ship	$17.00	**$22.00**
Ornament, 3.50"	96	Heart	18.50	**18.50**
ac# 536	97	Sword	18.50	**18.50**
Girl Carries Sprig of	98	Eyeglasses	18.50	**18.50**
Mistletoe	99	Star	18.50	**18.50**

150134 MERRY CHRISMOOSE   Holiday Preview Event

Dated Annual 1995	95	Ship	$17.00	**$25.00**
Ornament, 2.75"				
ac# 684				
Moose with Decorated				
Antlers				

150142 YOU'RE "A" NUMBER ONE IN MY BOOK, TEACHER

Ongoing	95	Ship	$17.00	**$22.00**
Ornament, 3.25"	96	Heart	18.50	**18.50**
ac# 623	97	Sword	18.50	**18.50**
Teacher and Report Card	98	Eyeglasses	18.50	**18.50**
	99	Star	18.50	**18.50**

150150 TRAIN STATION NIGHT LIGHT Sugar Town Lighted

Retired 1997	95	Ship	$100.00 **$125.00**
Night Light, 6.50"	96	Heart	100.00 **110.00**
ac# 1020	97	Sword	100.00 **110.00**
Ticket Booth & Waiting Room			

150169 SAM Sugar Town

Annual 1995	95	Ship	$20.00 **$45.00**
Figurine, 3.25"			
ac# 815			
Sam as Train Conductor			
Sign has passenger list of 18.			

150177 RAILROAD CROSSING SIGN Sugar Town

Retired 1997	95	Ship	$12.00 **$20.00**
Figurine, 4.25"	96	Heart	12.00 **17.00**
ac# 800	97	Sword	12.00 **17.00**
Sign Placed Where Tracks Cross Road			

150185 LUGGAGE CART Sugar Town

Retired 1997	95	Ship	$13.00 **$23.00**
Figurine, 2.00"	96	Heart	13.00 **17.00**
ac# 641	97	Sword	13.00 **17.00**
Cart Carries Suitcase and Kitten			

150207 BUS STOP SIGN Sugar Town

Retired 1997	95	Ship	$8.50 **$18.00**
Figurine, 3.25"	96	Heart	8.50 **15.00**
ac# 183	97	Sword	8.50 **12.00**
Pink Bow on Bus Sign			

150215 FIRE HYDRANT Sugar Town

Retired 1997	95	Ship	$5.00 **$12.00**
Figurine, 1.25"	96	Heart	5.00 **8.00**
ac# 275	97	Sword	5.00 **7.00**
Pink Fire Hydrant w/Heart on Side			

150223 BIRD BATH Sugar Town

Retired 1997	95	Ship	$8.50 **$18.00**
Figurine, 2.00"	96	Heart	8.50 **15.00**
ac# 133	97	Sword	8.50 **12.00**
Bird Sits on Snow Filled Bird Bath			

150231 CHRISTMAS PERSONALIZATION

Out Of Production	95	Ship	$19.95 **$85.00***
Ornament, 2.25"			
ac# 205			
Girl with Gift outside House			

*Never personalized. Samples are selling for the GBTru$ of $85.00. Issued in a Sugar Town box.

150312 — EVEN THE HEAVENS SHALL PRAISE HIM   Century Circle Exclusive
Limited Edition 15,000   98 Eyeglasses $125.00 **$125.00**
   Figurine, 6.75"
   ac# 263
   Girl Angel Plays Harp as
   Kitten Listens

150320 — JOY TO THE WORLD
Ongoing   95 Ship $20.00 **$22.00**
   Ornament, 4.00"   96 Heart   20.00   **20.00**
   ac# 540   97 Sword   20.00   **20.00**
   Winged Angel Blows a Horn   98 Eyeglasses   20.00   **20.00**
                                   99 Star   20.00   **20.00**

152277 — HE LOVES ME   Easter Seal / Lily Understamp / Individually Numbered
Limited Edition 2,000   96 Ship $500.00 **$550.00**
   Figurine, 9.00"
   ac# 406
   Girl Pulls Flower Petals

153338 — JOY TO THE WORLD
Ongoing   96 Heart $20.00 **$22.00**
   Ornament, 4.00"   97 Sword   20.00   **20.00**
   ac# 541   98 Eyeglasses   20.00   **20.00**
   Winged Angel Plays Flute   99 Star   20.00   **20.00**

160334 — AN EVENT FILLED WITH SUNSHINE AND SMILES   Regional Event—Illinois
Dated Annual 1995   95 Ship $35.00 **$70.00**
   Ornament, 3.25"
   ac# 53
   Girl with Sunflower Garland

160334A — AN EVENT FILLED WITH SUNSHINE AND SMILES   Regional Event—Ohio
Dated Annual 1995   95 Ship $35.00 **$75.00**
   Ornament, 3.25"
   ac# 53
   Girl with Sunflower Garland

160334B — AN EVENT FILLED WITH SUNSHINE AND SMILES   Regional Event—
California
Dated Annual 1995   95 Ship $35.00 **$75.00**
   Ornament, 3.25"
   ac# 53
   Girl with Sunflower Garland

160334C — AN EVENT FILLED WITH SUNSHINE AND SMILES   Regional Event—New
Jersey
Dated Annual 1995   95 Ship $35.00 **$75.00**
   Ornament, 3.25"
   ac# 53
   Girl with Sunflower Garland

160334D — AN EVENT FILLED WITH SUNSHINE AND SMILES   Regional Event—
Missouri
Dated Annual 1995   95 Ship $35.00 **$75.00**
   Ornament, 3.25"
   ac# 53
   Girl with Sunflower Garland

160334E — AN EVENT FILLED WITH SUNSHINE AND SMILES — Regional Event—
Maryland
Dated Annual 1995 — 95 — Ship — $35.00 — **$80.00**
Ornament, 3.25"
ac# 53
Girl with Sunflower Garland

160334F — AN EVENT FILLED WITH SUNSHINE AND SMILES — Regional Event—Florida
Dated Annual 1995 — 95 — Ship — $35.00 — **$60.00**
Ornament, 3.25"
ac# 53
Girl with Sunflower Garland

160334G — AN EVENT FILLED WITH SUNSHINE AND SMILES — Regional Event—Ohio
Dated Annual 1995 — 95 — Ship — $35.00 — **$75.00**
Ornament, 3.25"
ac# 53
Girl with Sunflower Garland

160334H — AN EVENT FILLED WITH SUNSHINE AND SMILES — Regional Event—Canada
Dated Annual 1995 — 95 — Ship — $35.00 — **$100.00**
Ornament, 3.25"
ac# 53
Girl with Sunflower Garland

163597 — YOU ARE ALWAYS THERE FOR ME
Ongoing
Figurine, 4.25"
ac# 1101
Father Bandages Daughter's
Doll's Foot

97	Heart	$50.00	**$53.00**
97	Sword	50.00	**50.00**
98	Eyeglasses	50.00	**50.00**
99	Star	50.00	**50.00**

163600 — YOU ARE ALWAYS THERE FOR ME
Ongoing
Figurine, 6.25"
ac# 1099
Mother Bandages Daughter's
Knee & Kisses Owie

96	Ship	$50.00	**$53.00**
96	Heart	50.00	**50.00**
97	Sword	50.00	**50.00**
98	Eyeglasses	50.00	**50.00**
99	Star	50.00	**50.00**

163619 — YOU ARE ALWAYS THERE FOR ME
Ongoing
Figurine, 6.25"
ac# 1102
Mother Bandages Son's Knee
& Kisses Owie

97	Heart	$50.00	**$53.00**
97	Sword	50.00	**50.00**
98	Eyeglasses	50.00	**50.00**
99	Star	50.00	**50.00**

163627 — YOU ARE ALWAYS THERE FOR ME
Ongoing
Figurine, 4.25"
ac# 1100
Father & Son

96	Ship	$50.00	**$52.00**
96	Heart	50.00	**50.00**
97	Sword	50.00	**50.00**
98	Eyeglasses	50.00	**50.00**
99	Star	50.00	**50.00**

163635 — YOU ARE ALWAYS THERE FOR ME
Ongoing
Figurine, 4.75"
ac# 1103
Two Sisters

96	Heart	$50.00	**$50.00**
97	Sword	50.00	**50.00**
98	Eyeglasses	50.00	**50.00**
99	Star	50.00	**50.00**

163651G	BABY GIRL PERSONALIZED			
	Ongoing	98		$32.50	**$32.50**
	Figurine, 5.25"	99		32.50	**32.50**
	ac# 87				
	Stork with Baby in Pink				
	Blanket				
	Initially introduced in 1996 @ $24.95 but never produced.				

163651B	BABY BOY PERSONALIZED			
	Ongoing	98		$32.50	**$32.50**
	Figurine, 5.25"	99		32.50	**32.50**
	ac# 87				
	Stork with Baby in Blue				
	Blanket				
	Initially introduced in 1996 @ $24.95 but never produced.				

163686	BIRTHDAY PERSONALIZED			
	Ongoing	98		$42.50	**$42.50**
	Figurine, 6.00"	99		42.50	**42.50**
	ac# 135				
	Girl in Birthday Hat with				
	Cake				
	Initially introduced in 1996 @ $37.50 but never produced.				

163694	I'D GOAT ANYWHERE WITH YOU Two By Two			
	Ongoing	96	Ship	$10.00	**$15.00**
	Figurine, 2.00"	96	Heart	10.00	**10.00**
	ac# 479	97	Sword	10.00	**10.00**
	Girl & Boy Goats	98	Eyeglasses	10.00	**10.00**
		99	Star	10.00	**10.00**

163708	JENNIFER Sammy's Circus Set of 2			
	Suspended 1996	96	Ship	$20.00	**$40.00**
	Figurine, 3.00"	96	Heart	20.00	**35.00**
	ac# 519				
	Girl Clown & Teddy Bear				

163716	OF ALL THE MOTHERS I HAVE KNOWN, THERE'S NONE AS PRECIOUS AS MY OWN Series: "Mother's Day "–3rd Issue			
	Dated Annual 1996	96	Heart	$37.50	**$40.00**
	Plate, 5.75"				
	ac# 732				
	Mother with Spring Flowers				
	Bouquet				

163732	STANDING IN THE PRESENCE OF THE LORD Series: "Dated Cross"–2nd Issue			
	Dated Annual 1996	96	Ship	$37.50	**$40.00**
	Figurine, 5.75"		Heart		**40.00**
	ac# 891				
	Girl Points to Garland				
	Draped Cross				

163740	AGE 7 Series: "Growing In Grace"			
	Ongoing	96	Ship	$32.50	**$35.00**
	Figurine, 4.75"	96	Heart	32.50	**32.50**
	ac# 41	97	Sword	32.50	**32.50**
	Girl Gives Tonic to Sick	98	Eyeglasses	32.50	**32.50**
	Kitten	99	Star	32.50	**32.50**

163759 <u>AGE 8</u>   Series: "Growing In Grace"

Ongoing		96	Ship	$32.50	**$35.00**
Figurine, 3.75"		96	Heart	32.50	**32.50**
ac# 42		97	Sword	32.50	**32.50**
Girl Plays Marbles with Pup		98	Eyeglasses	32.50	**32.50**
		99	Star	32.50	**32.50**

163767 <u>TAKE IT TO THE LORD IN PRAYER</u>

Ongoing		96	Ship	$30.00	**$33.00**
Figurine, 4.00"		96	Heart	30.00	**30.00**
ac# 908		97	Sword	30.00	**30.00**
Praying Girl		98	Eyeglasses	30.00	**30.00**
		99	Star	30.00	**30.00**

163775 <u>THE SUN IS ALWAYS SHINING SOMEWHERE</u>

Ongoing		96	Ship	$37.50	**$38.00**
Figurine, 4.50"		96	Heart	37.50	**37.50**
ac# 966		97	Sword	37.50	**37.50**
Girl Puts Umbrella Down to		98	Eyeglasses	37.50	**37.50**
Look at Sun		99	Star	37.50	**37.50**

163783 <u>A YEAR OF BLESSINGS</u>   Series: "To Have And To Hold"

Ongoing		96	Ship	$70.00	**$75.00**
Figurine, 6.50"		96	Heart	70.00	**70.00**
ac# 26		97	Sword	70.00	**70.00**
Couple Hold 1st Anniversary		98	Eyeglasses	70.00	**70.00**
Cake		99	Star	70.00	**70.00**

163791 <u>EACH HOUR IS PRECIOUS WITH YOU</u>   Series: "To Have And To Hold"

Ongoing		96	Ship	$70.00	**$75.00**
Figurine, 6.50"		96	Heart	70.00	**70.00**
ac# 255		97	Sword	70.00	**70.00**
Couple Hold 5th Anniver-		98	Eyeglasses	70.00	**70.00**
sary Clock		99	Star	70.00	**70.00**

163805 <u>TEN YEARS HEART TO HEART</u>   Series: "To Have And To Hold"

Ongoing		96	Ship	$70.00	**$75.00**
Figurine, 6.50"		96	Heart	70.00	**70.00**
ac# 919		97	Sword	70.00	**70.00**
Couple Hold 10th Anniver-		98	Eyeglasses	70.00	**70.00**
sary Heart		99	Star	70.00	**70.00**

163813 <u>A SILVER CELEBRATION TO SHARE</u>   Series: "To Have And To Hold"

Ongoing		96	Ship	$70.00	**$75.00**
Figurine, 6.50"		96	Heart	70.00	**70.00**
ac# 17		97	Sword	70.00	**70.00**
Couple Hold 25th Anniver-		98	Eyeglasses	70.00	**70.00**
sary Plate		99	Star	70.00	**70.00**

163821 <u>SHARING THE GIFT OF FORTY PRECIOUS YEARS</u>   Series: "To Have And To Hold"

Ongoing		96	Ship	$70.00	**$75.00**
Figurine, 6.50"		96	Heart	70.00	**70.00**
ac# 854		97	Sword	70.00	**70.00**
Couple Hold 40th Anniver-		98	Eyeglasses	70.00	**70.00**
sary Gift		99	Star	70.00	**70.00**

163848 <u>PRECIOUS MOMENTS TO REMEMBER</u>   Series: "To Have And To Hold"

Ongoing					
Figurine, 6.50"		96	Ship	$70.00	**$75.00**
ac# 791		96	Heart	70.00	**70.00**
Couple Hold 50th Anniver-		97	Sword	70.00	**70.00**
sary Album		98	Eyeglasses	70.00	**70.00**
		99	Star	70.00	**70.00**

163856 SOWING SEEDS OF KINDNESS   Series: "Growing In God's Garden Of Love"–1st Issue, aka Garden Angels

Ongoing
Figurine, 4.50"
ac# 889
Praying Angel with Bag of Seeds

96	Ship	$37.50	**$40.00**
96	Heart	37.50	**37.50**
97	Sword	37.50	**37.50**
98	Eyeglasses	37.50	**37.50**
99	Star	37.50	**37.50**

163864 HALLELUJAH HOEDOWN   Spring Celebration Event

Annual 1996
Figurine, ——
ac# 364
Girl with Guitar

96	Ship	$32.50	**$95.00**
	Heart		**58.00**

163872 HIS PRESENCE IS FELT IN THE CHAPEL   Chapel Exclusive

Ongoing
Figurine, 3.00"
ac# 433
Chapel as a Manger for Baby Jesus

96	Unmarked	$25.00	**$25.00**

163880 HIS PRESENCE IS FELT IN THE CHAPEL   Chapel Exclusive

Suspended 1997
Ornament, 2.25"
ac# 433
Chapel as a Manger for Baby Jesus

96	Unmarked	$17.50	**$25.00**

163899 IT MAY BE GREENER, BUT IT'S JUST AS HARD TO CUT

Ongoing
Figurine, 5.00"
ac# 508
Boy Looks over Fence at Grass

96	Ship	$37.50	**$40.00**
96	Heart	37.50	**37.50**
97	Sword	37.50	**37.50**
98	Eyeglasses	37.50	**37.50**
99	Star	37.50	**37.50**

175277 GOD'S LOVE IS REFLECTED IN YOU   Century Circle Exclusive / Individually Numbered

Limited Edition 15,000
Figurine, 4.50"
ac# 344
Girl at Vanity

96	Heart	$150.00	**$225.00**

176958 SOME PLANT, SOME WATER, BUT GOD GIVETH THE INCREASE   Series: "Growing In God's Garden Of Love"–2nd Issue, aka Garden Angels

Ongoing
Figurine, 6.13"
ac# 881
Winged Girl Angel Waters Buds

96	Heart	$37.50	**$37.50**
97	Sword	37.50	**37.50**
98	Eyeglasses	37.50	**37.50**
99	Star	37.50	**37.50**

177083 A PERFECT DISPLAY OF 15 HAPPY YEARS   Convention Piece

Convention Gift
Medallion, 3.50"
ac# 12
Girl Holds a Figurine

95	Ship	$Gift	**$400.00**

177091 PEACE ON EARTH   Century Circle Exclusive

Limited Edition 15,000
Ornament, 3.50"
ac# 774
Angel in Filigree Heart

95	Unmarked	$25.00	**$32.00**

183342	**PEACE ON EARTH...ANYWAY**					
	Dated Annual 1996	96	Heart		$32.50	**$35.00**
	Figurine, 5.00"					
	ac# 775					
	Tin-foil Halo Angel					

183350	**PEACE ON EARTH...ANYWAY**					
	Dated Annual 1996	96	Heart		$30.00	**$38.00**
	Ornament, 3.50"					
	ac# 775					
	Tin-foil Halo Angel					

183369	**PEACE ON EARTH...ANYWAY**					
	Dated Annual 1996	96	Heart		$18.50	**$30.00**
	Ornament, 3.50"					
	ac# 775					
	Tin-foil Halo Angel					

183377	**PEACE ON EARTH...ANYWAY**					
	Dated Annual 1996	96	Heart		$50.00	**$50.00**
	Plate, 8.50"					
	ac# 775					
	Tin-foil Halo Angel					

183776	**ANGELS ON EARTH**					
	Ongoing	96	Heart		$40.00	**$40.00**
	Figurine, 4.00"	97	Sword		40.00	**40.00**
	ac# 60	98	Eyeglasses		40.00	**40.00**
	Boy Makes Snow Angel	99	Star		40.00	**40.00**

183792	**SNOWBUNNY LOVES YOU LIKE I DO**					
	Ongoing	96	Heart		$18.50	**$20.00**
	Figurine, 3.75"	97	Sword		18.50	**18.50**
	ac# 878	98	Eyeglasses		18.50	**18.50**
	Bunny Perched on Snowball	99	Star		18.50	**18.50**

183814 S	**THE MOST PRECIOUS GIFT OF ALL** Catalog Early Release / Special					
	Understamp	96	Heart		$37.50	**$50.00**
	Annual 1996					
	Figurine, 5.25"					
	ac# 960					
	Girl Holds Heart Family					
	Ornament					

The "S" suffix does not appear on the box or understamp of the figurine.

183814	**THE MOST PRECIOUS GIFT OF ALL**					
	Ongoing	97	Sword		$37.50	**$37.50**
	Figurine, 5.25"	98	Eyeglasses		37.50	**37.50**
	ac# 960	99	Star		37.50	**37.50**
	Girl Holds Heart Family					
	Ornament					

183830	SING IN EXCELSIS DEO				
	Ongoing	96	Heart	$125.00	**$125.00**
	Tree Topper, 8.75"	97	Sword	125.00	**125.00**
	ac# 866	98	Eyeglasses	125.00	**125.00**
	Winged Angel Plays Trumpet	99	Star	125.00	**125.00**
	Voluntary				

183849	YOU'RE JUST TOO SWEET TO BE SCARY				
	Ongoing	97	Sword	$55.00	**$58.00**
	Figurine, 6.25"	98	Eyeglasses	55.00	**55.00**
	ac# 1151	99	Star	55.00	**55.00**
	Boy Dressed as Scarecrow				
	Stands atop Box				

183857	COLOR YOUR WORLD WITH THANKSGIVING				
	Retired 1998	96	Heart	$50.00	**$75.00**
	Figurine, 6.00"	97	Sword	50.00	**70.00**
	ac# 219	98	Eyeglasses	50.00	**65.00**
	Elf & Bunny Paint Fall Colors				

183865	AGE 9 Series: "Growing In Grace"				
	Ongoing	96	Heart	$30.00	**$30.00**
	Figurine, 5.50"	97	Sword	30.00	**30.00**
	ac# 43	98	Eyeglasses	30.00	**30.00**
	Girl Shows Bird Her Pearl	99	Star	30.00	**30.00**
	Bracelet				

183873	AGE 10 Series: "Growing In Grace"				
	Ongoing	96	Heart	$37.50	**$38.00**
	Figurine, 5.25"	97	Sword	37.50	**37.50**
	ac# 30	98	Eyeglasses	37.50	**37.50**
	Girl Holds Bowling Ball	99	Star	37.50	**37.50**
	Near Pin Setup				

183881	GOD'S PRECIOUS GIFT White on White				
	Ongoing	96	Heart	$20.00	**$25.00**
	Ornament, 3.00"	97	Sword	20.00	**20.00**
	ac# 347	98	Eyeglasses	20.00	**20.00**
	The Holy Family	99	Star	20.00	**20.00**
	Called "White on White," this piece is all white.				

183903	WHEN THE SKATING'S RUFF, TRY PRAYER				
	Ongoing	96	Heart	$18.50	**$20.00**
	Ornament, 3.50"	97	Sword	18.50	**18.50**
	ac# 1060	98	Eyeglasses	18.50	**18.50**
	Pup in Ice Skate	99	Star	18.50	**18.50**

183911	OUR FIRST CHRISTMAS TOGETHER				
	Dated Annual 1996	96	Heart	$22.50	**$28.00**
	Ornament, 3.25"				
	ac# 756				
	Couple Share Skis				

183938	BABY'S FIRST CHRISTMAS (GIRL)				
	Dated Annual 1996	96	Heart	$17.50	**$25.00**
	Ornament, 3.25"				
	ac# 114				
	Baby Girl in Christmas				
	Stocking				

183946	BABY'S FIRST CHRISTMAS (BOY)					
	Dated Annual 1996	96	Heart		$17.50	**$25.00**
	Ornament, 3.25"					
	ac# 110					
	Baby Boy in Christmas					
	Stocking					

183954	SHEPHERD WITH LAMBS	Nativity Addition	Set of 3			
	Ongoing	96	Heart		$40.00	**$40.00**
	Figurine, 1.25"	97	Sword		40.00	**40.00**
	ac# 859	98	Eyeglasses		40.00	**40.00**
	Shepherd with Lambs	99	Star		40.00	**40.00**

183962	SHEPHERD WITH LAMBS	Nativity Addition	Set of 3			
	Ongoing	97	Sword		$40.00	**$40.00**
	Figurine, 1.50"	98	Eyeglasses		40.00	**40.00**
	ac# 860	99	Star		40.00	**40.00**
	Shepherd Carries a Lamb / 2					
	Lambs Close by					

184004	MAKING A TRAIL TO BETHLEHEM	Mini Nativity Addition				
	Ongoing	96	Heart		$18.50	**$18.50**
	Figurine, 3.25"	97	Sword		18.50	**18.50**
	ac# 648	98	Eyeglasses		18.50	**18.50**
	Boy on Hobby Horse	99	Star		18.50	**18.50**

184012	ALL SING HIS PRAISES	Nativity Addition				
	Ongoing	96	Heart		$32.50	**$32.50**
	Figurine, 4.50"	97	Sword		32.50	**32.50**
	ac# 46	98	Eyeglasses		32.50	**32.50**
	Girl with Bird Cage	99	Star		32.50	**32.50**

184020	SKATING SIGN	Sugar Town				
	Annual 1996	96	Heart		$15.00	**$35.00**
	Figurine, 3.25"					
	ac# 870					
	Snow Covered Sign with					
	Birds					

Sign reads: "Ice Skating, 1:00 - 7:00, All 22 Residents Welcome."

184039	LIGHTED TREE	Sugar Town	Lighted			
	Retired 1997	96	Heart		$45.00	**$75.00**
	Night Light, 6.50"	97	Sword		45.00	**62.00**
	ac# 577					
	Trimmed Tree with Star					
	Topper					

184047	SKATING POND	Sugar Town				
	Retired 1997	96	Heart		$40.00	**$55.00**
	Figurine, 1.25"	97	Sword		40.00	**$50.00**
	ac# 869					
	Frozen Ice Skating Pond					

184055	MAZIE	Sugar Town				
	Retired 1997	96	Heart		$18.50	**$32.00**
	Figurine, 3.50"	97	Sword		18.50	**30.00**
	ac# 681					
	Girl Skating					

184063	COCOA Sugar Town				
	Retired 1997	96	Heart	$7.50	**$15.00**
	Figurine, 0.75"	97	Sword	7.50	**12.00**
	ac# 215				
	Pup Slides along Ice on Belly				

184071	LEROY Sugar Town				
	Retired 1997	96	Heart	$18.50	**$25.00**
	Figurine, 3.25"	97	Sword	18.50	**22.00**
	ac# 561				
	Boy Carries Hockey Stick & Skates				

184098	HANK AND SHARON Sugar Town				
	Retired 1997	96	Heart	$25.00	**$33.00**
	Figurine, 3.25"	97	Sword	25.00	**30.00**
	ac# 368				
	Boy and Girl Skating Together				

184101	TRAIN STATION ORNAMENT Sugar Town				
	Annual 1996	96	Heart	$18.50	**$25.00**
	Ornament, 2.50"				
	ac# 1021				
	Conductor Stands on Platform				

May be lighted by placing a miniature Christmas light into opening on bottom.

184136	FLAG POLE Sugar Town				
	Retired 1997	96	Heart	$15.00	**$20.00**
	Figurine, 4.50"	97	Sword	15.00	**18.00**
	ac# 277				
	Kitten on Fence next to Sugar Town Flag				

184144	HOT COCOA STAND Sugar Town				
	Retired 1997	96	Heart	$15.00	**$20.00**
	Figurine, 3.00"	97	Sword	15.00	**18.00**
	ac# 447				
	Cocoa Carafe, Mugs, Cookies atop Barrel				

184152	BONFIRE Sugar Town				
	Retired 1997	96	Heart	$10.00	**$17.00**
	Figurine, 1.50"	97	Sword	10.00	**15.00**
	ac# 169				
	Bunnies Warm Their Tails at Bonfire				

184209	LOVE MAKES THE WORLD GO 'ROUND Century Circle Event				
	Annual 1996	96	Heart	$22.50	**$42.00**
	Ornament, 4.00"				
	ac# 622				
	Girl on a Carousel House				

184217   <u>MAY THE SUN ALWAYS SHINE ON YOU</u>   Century Circle Event

Annual 1996	96	Heart	$37.50	**$60.00**

Figurine, 4.75"
ac# 662
Girl Holds a String of
Sunshine Faces

184268   <u>A BOUQUET FROM GOD'S GARDEN OF LOVE</u>   Series: "Growing In God's Garden Of Love"–3rd Issue, aka Garden Angels

Ongoing	97	Heart	$37.50	**$38.00**
Figurine, 5.75"	97	Sword	37.50	**37.50**
ac# 6	98	Eyeglasses	37.50	**37.50**
Girl Holds a Bouquet of	99	Star	37.50	**37.50**
Flowers				

192341   <u>WARMING HUT NIGHT LIGHT</u>   Sugar Town   Lighted

Retired 1997	96	Heart	$60.00	**$68.00**
Night Light, 5.50"	97	Sword	60.00	**62.00**

ac# 1035
Pond-side Hut for Warming
Hands & Toes

192368   <u>GIVE ABILITY A CHANCE</u>   Easter Seal Commemorative / Lily Understamp

Annual 1997	97	Heart	$30.00	**$32.00**

Figurine, 5.50"
ac# 304
Boy in Wheel Chair Plays
Basketball

192376   <u>LOVE IS UNIVERSAL</u>   Easter Seal / Lily Understamp / Individually Numbered

Limited Edition 2,000	97	Heart	$500.00	**$500.00**

Figurine, 9.00"
ac# 618
Girl Signs Love

204854   <u>YOU ARE A LIFESAVER TO ME</u>

Ongoing	97	Heart	$35.00	**$35.00**
Figurine, 5.25"	97	Sword	35.00	**35.00**
ac# 1096	98	Eyeglasses	35.00	**35.00**
Girl in Horse Flotation Ring	99	Star	35.00	**35.00**

204862   <u>THE LORD IS OUR CHIEF INSPIRATION</u>   Chapel Exclusive

Ongoing	96	Unmarked	$45.00	**$55.00**
Figurine, 6.25"	97	Sword	45.00	**45.00**

ac# 952
Native American Boy in
Headdress

204870   <u>THE LORD IS OUR CHIEF INSPIRATION</u>   Chapel Exclusive

Annual 1996	96	Unmarked	$250.00	**$275.00**
Figurine, 10.25"	97	Sword	250.00	**250.00**

ac# 952
Native American Boy in
Headdress

204889   <u>COLEENIA</u>   Chapel Exclusive

Ongoing	96	Unmarked	$32.50	**$40.00**
Figurine, 5.75"	97	Sword	32.50	**32.50**

ac# 216
Girl with Clown Doll

212520 — THE MOST PRECIOUS GIFT OF THEM ALL   Catalog Exclusive
Annual 1996   96   Heart $20.00   **$35.00**
  Ornament, 5.25"
  ac# 960
  Girl Holds Heart Family
  Ornament

212547 — THIS WORLD IS NOT MY HOME (I'M JUST A PASSIN' THRU)   Chapel
Exclusive   Honors Albert E. Brumley
Ongoing   97   Unmarked $85.00   **$85.00**
  Figurine, 5.00"
  ac# 990
  Angel in Packed up Car

  Gospel cassette tape is included, performed by Al Brumley, Jr.

212563 — YOUR PRECIOUS SPIRIT COMES SHINING THROUGH   Regional Event—
Knoxville
Dated Annual 1996   96   Heart $35.00   **$125.00**
  Figurine, 3.75"
  ac# 1159
  Girl Flies Heart-Shaped Kite

212563A — YOUR PRECIOUS SPIRIT COMES SHINING THROUGH   Regional Event—
Indianapolis
Dated Annual 1996   96   Heart $35.00   **$125.00**
  Figurine, 3.75"
  ac# 1159
  Girl Flies Heart-Shaped Kite

212563B — YOUR PRECIOUS SPIRIT COMES SHINING THROUGH   Regional Event—
Minneapolis
Dated Annual 1996   96   Heart $35.00   **$120.00**
  Figurine, 3.75"
  ac# 1159
  Girl Flies Heart-Shaped Kite

213616 — SHEPHERD WITH SHEEP   Mini Nativity Addition   Set of 2
Ongoing   97   Sword $22.50   **$22.50**
  Figurine, ——   98   Eyeglasses   22.50   **22.50**
  ac# 861   99   Star   22.50   **22.50**
  Boy Carries Lamb as Another
  Stands Next to Him

213624 — WEE THREE KINGS   Mini Nativity Addition   Set of 3
Ongoing   96   Heart $55.00   **$55.00**
  Figurine, 3.50"   97   Sword   55.00   **55.00**
  ac# 1053   98   Eyeglasses   55.00   **55.00**
  Three Kings   99   Star   55.00   **55.00**

260916 — LEAD ME TO CALVARY   Series: "Dated Cross"–3rd Issue
Dated Annual 1997   97   Heart $37.50   **$40.00**
  Figurine, 6.00"
  ac# 559
  Girl w/Lamb beside Cross

260924 — AGE 11   Series: "Growing In Grace"
Ongoing   97   Heart $37.50   **$40.00**
  Figurine, 5.00"   97   Sword   37.50   **37.50**
  ac# 31   98   Eyeglasses   37.50   **37.50**
  11 Flavors Ice Cream Girl &   99   Star   37.50   **37.50**
  Pup

260932	AGE 12 Series: "Growing In Grace"				
	Ongoing	97	Heart	$37.50	**$40.00**
	Figurine, 5.50"	97	Sword	37.50	**37.50**
	ac# 32	98	Eyeglasses	37.50	**37.50**
	Girl with Hungry Pup	99	Star	37.50	**37.50**

260940	FROM THE TIME I SPOTTED YOU I KNEW (KNOW)* WE'D BE FRIENDS Birthday Collection				
	Ongoing	97	Heart*	$20.00	**$100.00**
	Figurine, 2.00"	97	Sword*	20.00	**20.00**
	ac# 299	98	Eyeglasses	20.00	**20.00**
	Monkey Paints Heart & Spots / Sleeping Cat	99	Star	20.00	**20.00**

*The "Know" error occurred on all Heart Marks and the first production run of Sword Marks.

261068	FRIENDS FROM THE VERY BEGINNING				
	Ongoing	97	Heart	$50.00	**$53.00**
	Figurine, 4.75"	97	Sword	50.00	**50.00**
	ac# 291	98	Eyeglasses	50.00	**50.00**
	Girl Sits Next to a Dinosaur	99	Star	50.00	**50.00**

261084	YOU HAVE TOUCHED SO MANY HEARTS				
	Ongoing	97	Heart	$37.50	**$38.00**
	Figurine, 6.00"	97	Sword	37.50	**37.50**
	ac# 1131	98	Eyeglasses	37.50	**37.50**
	Girl Holds String of Hearts	99	Star	37.50	**37.50**

261106	HOGS AND KISSES Country Lane Collection				
	Ongoing	99	Eyeglasses	$50.00	**$50.00**
	Figurine, 5.00"	99	Star	50.00	**50.00**
	ac# 435				
	Girl Kisses Pig Pal				

261106S	HOGS AND KISSES				
	Limited Edition 1,500	98	Unmarked	$Gift	**NE**
	Figurine, 5.00"				
	ac# 435				
	Girl Kisses Pig Pal				

Gift to all registered attendees of the Fourth Annual Licensee Show and Swap 'N Sell Weekend at the Chapel, July 31 - August 1, 1998. Special Chapel Understamp.

261122	LETTUCE PRAY				
	Ongoing	97	Heart	$17.50	**$25.00**
	Figurine, 2.75"	97	Sword	17.50	**17.50**
	ac# 572	98	Eyeglasses	17.50	**17.50**
	Mouse in Salad Bowl	99	Star	17.50	**17.50**

261130	HAVE YOU ANY ROOM FOR JESUS				
	Ongoing	97	Heart*	$35.00	**$40.00**
	Figurine, 5.75"	97	Sword	35.00	**35.00**
	ac# 392	98	Eyeglasses	35.00	**35.00**
	Girls w/Calendar Filled w/ Activities	99	Star	35.00	**35.00**

*Error in spelling on activity list: "Biowling" on some Heart Marks– GBTru$ is $150.00.

261149	SAY I DO					
	Ongoing	97	Heart	$55.00	**$55.00**
	Figurine, 4.75"	97	Sword	55.00	**55.00**
	ac# 822	98	Eyeglasses	55.00	**55.00**
	Boy Proposes to Sweetheart	99	Star	55.00	**55.00**

261157	WE ALL HAVE OUR BAD HAIR DAYS				
	Ongoing	97	Heart	$35.00	**$35.00**
	Figurine, 5.25"	97	Sword	35.00	**35.00**
	ac# 1037	98	Eyeglasses	35.00	**35.00**
	Girl Halfway through a Haircut	99	Star	35.00	**35.00**

261173	BLESS YOUR LITTLE TUTU Little Moments				
	Ongoing	97	Not Marked	$20.00	**$20.00**
	Figurine, 3.75"	98		20.00	**20.00**
	ac# 151	99		20.00	**20.00**
	Ballerina				

261203	BIRTHSTONE JANUARY Little Moments				
	Ongoing	96	Not Marked	$20.00	**$20.00**
	Figurine, 3.75"	97		20.00	**20.00**
	ac# 139	98		20.00	**20.00**
	Angel w/Golden Halo	99		20.00	**20.00**
	Displays Birthstone				

261211	BIRTHSTONE MAY Little Moments				
	Ongoing	96	Not Marked	$20.00	**$20.00**
	Figurine, 3.75"	97		20.00	**20.00**
	ac# 139	98		20.00	**20.00**
	Angel w/Golden Halo	99		20.00	**20.00**
	Displays Birthstone				

261238	BIRTHSTONE SEPTEMBER Little Moments				
	Ongoing	96	Not Marked	$20.00	**$20.00**
	Figurine, 3.75"	97		20.00	**20.00**
	ac# 139	98		20.00	**20.00**
	Angel w/Golden Halo	99		20.00	**20.00**
	Displays Birthstone				

261246	BIRTHSTONE FEBRUARY Little Moments				
	Ongoing	96	Not Marked	$20.00	**$20.00**
	Figurine, 3.75"	97		20.00	**20.00**
	ac# 138	98		20.00	**20.00**
	Angel w/Golden Halo	99		20.00	**20.00**
	Displays Birthstone				

261254	BIRTHSTONE JUNE Little Moments				
	Ongoing	96	Not Marked	$20.00	**$20.00**
	Figurine, 3.75"	97		20.00	**20.00**
	ac# 138	98		20.00	**20.00**
	Angel w/Golden Halo	99		20.00	**20.00**
	Displays Birthstone				

261262	BIRTHSTONE OCTOBER Little Moments				
	Ongoing	96	Not Marked	$20.00	**$20.00**
	Figurine, 3.75"	97		20.00	**20.00**
	ac# 138	98		20.00	**20.00**
	Angel w/Golden Halo	99		20.00	**20.00**
	Displays Birthstone				

261270	BIRTHSTONE MARCH	Little Moments				
	Ongoing		96	Not Marked	$20.00	**$20.00**
	Figurine, 3.75"		97		20.00	**20.00**
	ac# 140		98		20.00	**20.00**
	Angel w/Golden Halo		99		20.00	**20.00**
	Displays Birthstone					

261289	BIRTHSTONE JULY	Little Moments				
	Ongoing		96	Not Marked	$20.00	**$20.00**
	Figurine, 3.75"		97		20.00	**20.00**
	ac# 140		98		20.00	**20.00**
	Angel w/Golden Halo		99		20.00	**20.00**
	Displays Birthstone					

261297	BIRTHSTONE NOVEMBER	Little Moments				
	Ongoing		96	Not Marked	$20.00	**$20.00**
	Figurine, 3.75"		97		20.00	**20.00**
	ac# 140		98		20.00	**20.00**
	Angel w/Golden Halo		99		20.00	**20.00**
	Displays Birthstone					

261300	BIRTHSTONE APRIL	Little Moments				
	Ongoing		96	Not Marked	$20.00	**$20.00**
	Figurine, 3.75"		97		20.00	**20.00**
	ac# 137		98		20.00	**20.00**
	Angel w/Golden Halo		99		20.00	**20.00**
	Displays Birthstone					

261319	BIRTHSTONE AUGUST	Little Moments				
	Ongoing		96	Not Marked	$20.00	**$20.00**
	Figurine, 3.75"		97		20.00	**20.00**
	ac# 137		98		20.00	**20.00**
	Angel w/Golden Halo		99		20.00	**20.00**
	Displays Birthstone					

261327	BIRTHSTONE DECEMBER	Little Moments				
	Ongoing		96	Not Marked	$20.00	**$20.00**
	Figurine, 3.75"		97		20.00	**20.00**
	ac# 137		98		20.00	**20.00**
	Angel w/Golden Halo		99		20.00	**20.00**
	Displays Birthstone					

261351	WE'RE SO HOPPY YOU'RE HERE	Spring Celebration Event				
	Annual 1997		97	Sword	$32.50	**$35.00**
	Figurine, 4.25"					
	ac# 1050					
	Girl w/Picnic Basket Sees					
	Bunny under Corner of					
	Blanket					

261378	HAPPINESS TO THE CORE	Catalog Exclusive				
	Annual 1997		97	Heart	$37.50	**$50.00**
	Figurine, 5.75"			Sword		**48.00**
	ac# 373					
	Girl w/Apples, Mouse					
	Munches on a Core					

261556	BLESSED ARE THOU AMONGST WOMEN	1998 Fall Show Exclusive				
	Figurine, 9.50"		99	Star	$175.00	**$175.00**
	ac# 165					
	Mary and Baby Jesus on					
	Cloud-Shaped Base					

261564	THE LORD IS THE HOPE OF OUR FUTURE				
	Ongoing	97	Heart	$40.00	**$42.00**
	Figurine, 6.25"	97	Sword	40.00	**40.00**
	ac# 953	98	Eyeglasses	40.00	**40.00**
	Grad Girl	99	Star	40.00	**40.00**

261599	IN GOD'S BEAUTIFUL GARDEN OF LOVE	Century Circle Exclusive			
	Annual 1997	97	Sword	$50.00	**$60.00**
	Ornament, 5.00"				
	ac# 499				
	Girl w/Bouquet within Metal				
	Scrolled Archway				

261602	CROWN HIM LORD OF ALL	Chapel Exclusive			
	Ongoing	97	Unmarked	$35.00	**$35.00**
	Figurine, 2.25"				
	ac# 231				
	Baby Jesus Rests in Crown/				
	Gold Trim/Rhinestones				

261610	CROWN HIM LORD OF ALL	Chapel Exclusive			
	Ongoing	97	Unmarked	$25.00	**$25.00**
	Ornament, 1.75"				
	ac# 231				
	Baby Jesus Rests in Crown/				
	Gold Trim/Rhinestones				

261629	IN GOD'S BEAUTIFUL GARDEN OF LOVE	Century Circle Exclusive			
	Limited Edition 15,000	97	Sword	$150.00	**$160.00**
	Figurine,				
	ac# 499				
	Girl w/Bouquet within				
	Gilded Arch of Flower Vines				

266841	SWEET SIXTEEN BY PRECIOUS MOMENTS	Convention Piece			
	Convention Gift	96	Heart	$Gift	**$425.00**
	Ornament, 3.50"				
	ac# 749				
	Girl in Poodle Skirt				

270741	A FESTIVAL OF PRECIOUS MOMENTS	Regional Event—San Jose			
	Dated Annual 1997	97	Sword	$30.00	**$78.00**
	Figurine, 3.50"				
	ac# 7				
	Buccaneer Costumed Boy				
	Holds Proclamation Banner				
	& Bluebird				

270741A	A FESTIVAL OF PRECIOUS MOMENTS	Regional Event—Cleveland			
	Dated Annual 1997	97	Sword	$30.00	**$75.00**
	Figurine, 3.50"				
	ac# 7				
	Buccaneer Costumed Boy				
	Holds Proclamation Banner				
	& Bluebird				

270741B	A FESTIVAL OF PRECIOUS MOMENTS	Regional Event—Houston			
	Dated Annual 1997	97	Sword	$30.00	**$82.00**
	Figurine, 3.50"				
	ac# 7				
	Buccaneer Costumed Boy				
	Holds Proclamation Banner				
	& Bluebird				

270741C A FESTIVAL OF PRECIOUS MOMENTS   Regional Event—Philadelphia
Dated Annual 1997   97 Sword $30.00   **$78.00**
Figurine, 3.50"
ac# 7
Buccaneer Costumed Boy
Holds Proclamation Banner
& Bluebird

271586 SEEDS OF LOVE FROM THE CHAPEL   Chapel Exclusive
Ongoing   97 Unmarked $30.00   **$40.00**
Figurine, 5.00"   98 Eyeglasses 30.00   **30.00**
ac# 827
Angel Spreads Bird Seed
While a Bluebird Rests on
His Head

272422 GOOD FRIENDS ARE FOREVER   Baby Classics
Ongoing   97 Heart $30.00   **$30.00**
Figurine, 3.50"   97 Sword   30.00   **30.00**
ac# 355   98 Eyeglasses 30.00   **30.00**
Baby Girls Smelling Flowers 99 Star   30.00   **30.00**

272434 WE ARE GOD'S WORKMANSHIP   Baby Classics
Ongoing   97 Heart $25.00   **$25.00**
Figurine, 3.50"   97 Sword   25.00   **25.00**
ac# 1040   98 Eyeglasses 25.00   **25.00**
Baby Girl with Butterfly   99 Star   25.00   **25.00**

272450 MAKE A JOYFUL NOISE   Baby Classics
Ongoing   97 Heart $30.00   **$30.00**
Figurine, 3.75"   97 Sword   30.00   **30.00**
ac# 645   98 Eyeglasses 30.00   **30.00**
Baby Girl with Goose   99 Star   30.00   **30.00**

272469 I BELIEVE IN MIRACLES   Baby Classics
Ongoing   97 Heart $25.00   **$25.00**
Figurine, 3.25"   97 Sword   25.00   **25.00**
ac# 457   98 Eyeglasses 25.00   **25.00**
Baby Boy with Chick   99 Star   25.00   **25.00**

272477 GOD LOVETH A CHEERFUL GIVER   Baby Classics
Ongoing   97 Heart $25.00   **$25.00**
Figurine, 3.75"   97 Sword   25.00   **25.00**
ac# 338   98 Eyeglasses 25.00   **25.00**
Baby Girl with Puppies   99 Star   25.00   **25.00**

272485 YOU HAVE TOUCHED SO MANY HEARTS   Baby Classics
Ongoing   97 Heart $25.00   **$25.00**
Figurine, 3.50"   97 Sword   25.00   **25.00**
ac# 1132   98 Eyeglasses 25.00   **25.00**
Baby Girl w/String of Hearts 99 Star   25.00   **25.00**

272493 LOVE IS SHARING   Baby Classics
Ongoing   97 Heart $25.00   **$25.00**
Figurine, 3.25"   97 Sword   25.00   **25.00**
ac# 614   98 Eyeglasses 25.00   **25.00**
Baby Boy Eating Ice Cream   99 Star   25.00   **25.00**
with Puppy

272507   LOVE ONE ANOTHER   Baby Classics

Ongoing	97	Heart	$30.00	**$30.00**
Figurine, 3.75"	97	Sword	30.00	**30.00**
ac# 626	98	Eyeglasses	30.00	**30.00**
Baby Couple with Seedling	99	Star	30.00	**30.00**

272523   HAPPY BIRTHDAY JESUS

Ongoing	97	Sword	$35.00	**$35.00**
Figurine, 5.50"	98	Eyeglasses	35.00	**35.00**
ac# 377	99	Star	35.00	**35.00**
Girl Carries Birthday Cake				

272531   SHARING THE LIGHT OF LOVE

Ongoing	97	Sword	$35.00	**$35.00**
Figurine, 5.25"	98	Eyeglasses	35.00	**35.00**
ac# 856	99	Star	35.00	**35.00**
Girl Carries Lit Candle for				
Children's Service				

272558   I THINK YOU'RE JUST DIVINE

Ongoing	97	Sword	$40.00	**$40.00**
Figurine, 4.25"	98	Eyeglasses	40.00	**40.00**
ac# 475	99	Star	40.00	**40.00**
Angel Completes Portrait of				
Cow with Halo				

Known as "Holy Cow." First production has the logo missing from the understamp.

272566   JOY TO THE WORLD

Ongoing	97	Sword	$20.00	**$20.00**
Ornament, 3.25"	98	Eyeglasses	20.00	**20.00**
ac# 542	99	Star	20.00	**20.00**
Winged Angel with Harp				

272582   ENHANCEMENT SET FOR LARGE NATIVITY   Nativity Addition   Set of 4

Ongoing	97	Sword	$60.00	**$60.00**
Figurine,	98	Eyeglasses	60.00	**60.00**
ac# 260	99	Star	60.00	**60.00**
Baby Food, Bottle of Milk;				
Straw Bedding; Palm Tree w/				
Napping Pup; Palm Tree				

272590   I'M DREAMING OF A WHITE CHRISTMAS

Ongoing	97	Sword	$25.00	**$25.00**
Figurine, 2.50"	98	Eyeglasses	25.00	**25.00**
ac# 488	99	Star	25.00	**25.00**
Mouse Asleep in a Match				
Box				

272612   YOU WILL ALWAYS BE A WINNER TO ME (BOY)   Little Moments

Ongoing	97	Not Marked	$20.00	**$20.00**
Figurine, 3.50"	98		20.00	**20.00**
ac# 1141	99		20.00	**20.00**
Boy Soccer Player				

272639	IT'S RUFF TO ALWAYS BE CHEERY	Little Moments			
	Ongoing	97	Not Marked	$20.00	**$20.00**
	Figurine, 3.25"	98		20.00	**20.00**
	ac# 512	99		20.00	**20.00**
	Cheerleader with Puppy				

272647	AGE 13 Series: "Growing In Grace"				
	Ongoing	97	Sword	$40.00	**$40.00**
	Figurine, 4.50"	98	Eyeglasses	40.00	**40.00**
	ac# 33	99	Star	40.00	**40.00**
	Girl Watches Turtle Race to Finish Line				

272655	AGE 14 Series: "Growing In Grace"				
	Ongoing	97	Sword	$35.00	**$35.00**
	Figurine, 4.75"	98	Eyeglasses	35.00	**35.00**
	ac# 34	99	Star	35.00	**35.00**
	Girl Holds Diary w/Notes of Special Memories				

272663	AGE 15 Series: "Growing In Grace"–Final Issue				
	Ongoing	97	Sword	$40.00	**$40.00**
	Figurine, 5.75"	98	Eyeglasses	40.00	**40.00**
	ac# 35	99	Star	40.00	**40.00**
	Pup Checks that Girl Has His Name on Guest List				

272671	CANE YOU JOIN US FOR A MERRY CHRISTMAS				
	Dated Annual 1997	97	Sword	$30.00	**$32.00**
	Figurine, 5.00"				
	ac# 192				
	Girl Carries Candy Cane Heart Wreath				

272698	CANE YOU JOIN US FOR A MERRY CHRISTMAS				
	Dated Annual 1997	97	Sword	$18.50	**$28.00**
	Ornament, 3.50"				
	ac# 192				
	Girl Carries Candy Cane Heart Wreath				

272701	CANE YOU JOIN US FOR A MERRY CHRISTMAS				
	Dated Annual 1997	97	Sword	$50.00	**$50.00**
	Plate, 8.50"				
	ac# 192				
	Girl Carries Candy Cane Heart Wreath				

272728	CANE YOU JOIN US FOR A MERRY CHRISTMAS				
	Dated Annual 1997	97	Sword	$30.00	**$30.00**
	Ornament, 4.00"				
	ac# 192				
	Girl Carries Candy Cane Heart Wreath				

272736	OUR FIRST CHRISTMAS TOGETHER				
	Dated Annual 1997	97	Sword	$20.00	**$25.00**
	Ornament, 3.25"				
	ac# 757				
	Boy and Girl Ride Candy Train Engine				

272744   <u>BABY'S FIRST CHRISTMAS (GIRL)</u>
Dated Annual 1997   97   Sword $18.50   **$22.00**
Ornament, 3.50"
ac# 115
Baby Seated in Flowerpot

272752   <u>BABY'S FIRST CHRISTMAS (BOY)</u>
Dated Annual 1997   97   Sword $18.50   **$22.00**
Ornament, 3.25"
ac# 111
Baby Seated in Flowerpot

272760   <u>SLOW DOWN FOR THE HOLIDAYS</u>   Birthday Collection
Dated Annual 1997   97   Sword $18.50   **$25.00**
Ornament, 2.50"
ac# 873
Snail in Santa Claus Hat

272787   <u>AND YOU SHALL SEE A STAR</u>   Nativity Addition
Ongoing   97   Sword $32.50   **$32.50**
Figurine, 4.50"   98   Eyeglasses   32.50   **32.50**
ac# 58   99   Star   32.50   **32.50**
Boy Angel Carries 'Follow
Me' Signboards

272795   <u>LIGHTED SCHOOL HOUSE</u>   Sugar Town   Lighted
Retired 1997   97   Sword $80.00   **$100.00**
Night Light, 6.75"
ac# 576
One-Room Schoolhouse w/
American* Flag by Entry

*Also exists with a Canadian flag for shipments to Canada. GBTru$ for
piece with Canadian flag is $120.00.

272809   <u>CHUCK</u>   Sugar Town
Dated Annual 1997   97   Sword $22.50   **$30.00**
Figurine, 3.25"
ac# 207
Boy Stands next to School
Event Board

272817   <u>AUNT CLEO</u>   Sugar Town
Retired 1997   97   Sword $18.50   **$21.00**
Figurine, 3.25"
ac# 77
Town Teacher Carries Book
Gift to Students

272825   <u>AUNT BULAH AND UNCLE SAM</u>   Sugar Town
Retired 1997   97   Sword $22.50   **$24.00**
Figurine, 3.25"
ac# 76
Couple Carry Baked Goods
to School Sale

272833 HEATHER Sugar Town
Retired 1997   97   Sword $20.00   **$22.00**
Figurine, 3.00"
ac# 414
Student Sitting at Bustop w/
Books and Cupcake

272841 MERRY-GO-ROUND Sugar Town
Retired 1997   97   Sword $20.00   **$20.00**
Figurine, 2.25"
ac# 686
Pup and Kitten Play by
Schoolyard Merry-go-round

272892 PUPPIES WITH SLED
Ongoing   97   Sword $18.50   **$22.00**
Ornament, 1.75"   98   Eyeglasses   18.50   **18.50**
ac# 795   99   Star   18.50   **18.50**
One Puppy Pushes Another
Pup on Sled

272906 BIKE RACK Sugar Town
Retired 1997   97   Sword $15.00   **$15.00**
Figurine, 2.00"
ac# 132
Pipe Bike Stand Holds
Student's Bike

272914 GARBAGE CAN Sugar Town
Retired 1997   97   Sword $20.00   **$20.00**
Figurine, 2.75"
ac# 300
Cats Read '10 Days Till
Christmas' Sign in Trash/Bird
Watches

272949 PACK YOUR TRUNK FOR THE HOLIDAYS Holiday Preview Event
Dated Annual 1997   97   Sword $20.00   **$25.00**
Ornament, 2.25"
ac# 765
Elephant with Poinsettia
Perched on its Head

272957 S MY LOVE WILL KEEP YOU WARM Catalog Early Release
Annual 1997   97   Sword $37.50   **$40.00**
Figurine, 5.25"
ac# 707
Girl Knits Christmas Stocking

The "S" suffix does not appear on the box or understamp of the figurine.

272957 MY LOVE WILL KEEP YOU WARM
Ongoing   98   Eyeglasses $37.50   **$37.50**
Figurine, 5.50"   99   Star   37.50   **37.50**
ac# 708
Girl Knitting Stocking

272965 MY LOVE WILL KEEP YOU WARM Syndicated Catalog Exclusive
Annual 1997   97   Sword $20.00   **$22.00**
Ornament, 5.25"
ac# 707
Knitted Stocking Filled w/
Gifts & Picture of Girl
Knitting

272981	LOVE GROWS HERE	Easter Seal / Lily Understamp / Individually Numbered		
	Limited Edition 2,000	98 Sword	$500.00	**$500.00**
	Figurine, 9.00"			
	ac# 603			
	Girl Holds Potted Tree with			
	2 Perched Birds			

273007	CARGO CAR	Sugar Town		
	Dated Annual 1997	97 Sword	$27.50	**$29.00**
	Train, 13.00"			
	ac# 193			
	Train Car			

279323	ANIMAL ADDITIONS	Mini Nativity Addition	Set of 3	
	Ongoing	97 Sword	$30.00	**$30.00**
	Figurine	98 Eyeglasses	30.00	**30.00**
	ac# 63	99 Star	30.00	**30.00**
	Camel, Donkey and Cow			

283428	LIGHTED INN	Nativity Addition	Lighted	
	Ongoing	97 Sword	$100.00	**$100.00**
	Night Light, 8.00"	98 Eyeglasses	100.00	**100.00**
	ac# 575	99 Star	100.00	**100.00**
	Village Inn with "No			
	Vacancy" Sign			

283436	MINI-NATIVITY WALL	Mini Nativity Addition		
	Ongoing	97 Sword	$40.00	**$40.00**
	Figurine, 6.25"	98 Eyeglasses	40.00	**40.00**
	ac# 689	99 Star	40.00	**40.00**
	Lamb Stands in Doorway of			
	Stone Wall / Bird Watches			

283444	FOR AN ANGEL YOU'RE SO DOWN TO EARTH	Mini Nativity Addition		
	Ongoing	97 Sword	$17.50	**$17.50**
	Figurine, 2.50"	98 Eyeglasses	17.50	**17.50**
	ac# 282	99 Star	17.50	**17.50**
	Seated Angel Holds Flowers			

283460	YOU WILL ALWAYS BE A WINNER TO ME (GIRL)	Little Moments		
	Ongoing	97 Not Marked	$20.00	**$20.00**
	Figurine, 3.75"	98	20.00	**20.00**
	ac# 1142	99	20.00	**20.00**
	Girl Soccer Player			

291293	CATS WITH KITTEN	Mini Nativity Addition		
	Ongoing	97 Sword	$18.50	**$18.50**
	Figurine, 1.50"	98 Eyeglasses	18.50	**18.50**
	ac# 195	99 Star	18.50	**18.50**
	Kitten Naps under Bench			
	Watched by Cats and Bird			

292753	WISHING WELL	Nativity Addition		
	Ongoing	97 Sword	$30.00	**$30.00**
	Figurine, 4.00"	98 Eyeglasses	30.00	**30.00**
	ac# 1065	99 Star	30.00	**30.00**
	Kitten and Mouse Kiss by			
	Well			

318

306835 — HE SHALL COVER YOU WITH HIS WINGS   Series: "Dated Cross"–4th Issue

Dated Annual 1998 — 98   Sword $40.00   **$40.00**
Figurine, 5.75" — Eyeglasses   **40.00**
ac# 408
Girl Holds Bird While
Standing by Cross

306843 — 20 YEARS AND THE VISION'S STILL THE SAME   Commemorates 20th
Anniversary of Precious Moments
Annual 1998 — 98   Sword/Eyeglasses*$55.00   **$55.00**
Figurine, 5.25" — 98   Eyeglasses   55.00   **55.00**
ac# 5
Girl and Kitten Take Eye Test
Given by Boy Optometrist
and Mouse

306916 — FRIENDSHIP HITS THE SPOT   Baby Classics

Ongoing — 98   Sword $30.00   **$30.00**
Figurine, 3.50" — 98   Eyeglasses   30.00   **30.00**
ac# 298 — 99   Star   30.00   **30.00**
Girl Pours Cup of Tea for
Friend

306932 — LOVING YOU DEAR VALENTINE   Baby Classics

Ongoing — 98   Sword $25.00   **$25.00**
Figurine, 3.25" — 98   Eyeglasses   25.00   **25.00**
ac# 640 — 99   Star   25.00   **25.00**
Boy Draws Heart on Card

306940 — HE CLEANSED MY SOUL   Baby Classics

Ongoing — 98   Sword $25.00   **$25.00**
Figurine, 3.00" — 98   Eyeglasses   25.00   **25.00**
ac# 395 — 99   Star   25.00   **25.00**
Girl Reads Bible Scripture
While in Bathtub

306959 — FOR THE SWEETEST TU-LIPS IN TOWN

Ongoing — 98   Sword $30.00   **$30.00**
Figurine, 5.25" — 98   Eyeglasses   30.00   **30.00**
ac# 284 — 99   Star   30.00   **30.00**
Boy Holds Tulip Bouquet
Behind his Back

306967 — YOU ARE ALWAYS ON MY MIND

Ongoing — 98   Sword $37.50   **$40.00**
Figurine, 5.25" — 98   Eyeglasses   37.50   **37.50**
ac# 1098 — 99   Star   37.50   **37.50**
Clown Paints Word YOU
onto Forehead

306991 — MISSUM YOU

Ongoing — 98   Sword $45.00   **$48.00**
Figurine, 5.75" — 98   Eyeglasses   45.00   **45.00**
ac# 690 — 99   Star   45.00   **45.00**
Native American Boy Shoots
Arrow into Tree Trunk
Between Bunny's Ears

307009 — CHARITY BEGINS IN THE HEART   Series: "Always Victorian"–1st Issue

Retired June 1998 — 98   Sword $50.00   **$50.00**
Figurine, 7.25" — 98   Eyeglasses   50.00   **50.00**
ac# 199
Victorian Girl with Seeds

307017   <u>YOU'RE JUST AS SWEET AS PIE</u>   Country Lane Collection

Ongoing
Figurine, 5.00"
ac# 1149
Girl Shares Aroma of Freshly
Baked Pie with Pig

98	Eyeglasses	$45.00	**$45.00**
99	Star	45.00	**45.00**

307025   <u>OH TASTE AND SEE THAT THE LORD IS GOOD</u>   Country Lane Collection

Ongoing
Figurine, 5.50"
ac# 734
Girl at Produce Stand

98	Eyeglasses	$55.00	**$55.00**
99	Star	55.00	**55.00**

307033   <u>FORK OVER THOSE BLESSINGS</u>   Country Lane Collection

Ongoing
Figurine, 5.25"
ac# 287
Boy with Pitchfork

98	Eyeglasses	$50.00	**$50.00**
99	Star	50.00	**50.00**

307041   <u>NOBODY LIKES TO BE DUMPED</u>   Country Lane Collection

Ongoing
Figurine, 4.75"
ac# 720
Boy Tumbles Girl out of
Wheelbarrow

98	Eyeglasses	$65.00	**$65.00**
99	Star	65.00	**65.00**

307068   <u>I'LL NEVER TIRE OF YOU</u>   Country Lane Collection

Ongoing
Figurine, 4.50"
ac# 484
Dog Pushing Boy in Tire

98	Eyeglasses	$50.00	**$50.00**
99	Star	50.00	**50.00**

307076   <u>PEAS PASS THE CARROTS</u>   Country Lane Collection

Ongoing
Figurine, 4.00"
ac# 777
Kitten Checks to See What
Girl Is Eating, Hoping to Share

98	Eyeglasses	$45.00	**$45.00**
99	Star	45.00	**45.00**

307084   <u>BRINGING IN THE SHEAVES</u>   Country Lane Collection   Tune: Bringing In
The Sheaves

Limited Edition 12,000
Musical, 6.00"
ac# 176
Boy Drives a Tractor as
Nesting Hen Rides atop

98	Sword	$90.00	**NE**
98	Eyeglasses	90.00	**$250.00**

Only offered to retailers who attended the January 1998 Gift Show, 6 or
less each. 3 pieces are known to exist with Sword, consider Eyeglasses
as First Mark.

312444   <u>HOLIDAY WISHES, SWEETIE PIE</u>   Little Moments   Set of 2

Annual 1997
Figurine, 3.00"
ac# 437
Girl Holding Pie Plus a Free
Miniature Cinnamon
Potpourri Pie

97	Not Marked	$20.00	**$22.00**

Gift boxed together.

320560 YOU'RE JUST PERFECT IN MY BOOK Little Moments
Ongoing — 98 — Not Marked — $25.00 — **$25.00**
Figurine, 3.50" — 99 — — 25.00 — **25.00**
ac# 1150
Girl Teacher Seated at Desk

320579 LOVING IS CARING Little Moments
Ongoing — 98 — Not Marked — $20.00 — **$20.00**
Figurine, 3.50" — 99 — — 20.00 — **20.00**
ac# 633
Girl Health Care Provider

320595 LOVING IS CARING Little Moments
Ongoing — 98 — Not Marked — $20.00 — **$20.00**
Figurine, 3.50" — 99 — — 20.00 — **20.00**
ac# 634
Boy Doctor

320625 YOU SET MY HEART ABLAZE Little Moments
Ongoing — 98 — Not Marked — $20.00 — **$20.00**
Figurine, 3.50" — 99 — — 20.00 — **20.00**
ac# 1138
Boy Firefighter with Hose

320668 JUST THE FACTS... YOU'RE TERRIFIC Little Moments
Ongoing — 98 — Not Marked — $20.00 — **$20.00**
Figurine, 3.50" — 99 — — 20.00 — **20.00**
ac# 552
Policeman Issuing a Ticket

320706 YOU HAVE SUCH A SPECIAL WAY OF CARING EACH AND EVERY DAY Little Moments
Ongoing — 98 — Not Marked — $25.00 — **$25.00**
Figurine, 3.75" — 99 — — 25.00 — **25.00**
ac# 1129
Girl Caregiver w/Children

320714 WHAT WOULD I DO WITHOUT YOU Little Moments
Ongoing — 98 — Not Marked — $25.00 — **$25.00**
Figurine, 3.50" — 99 — — 25.00 — **25.00**
ac# 1059
Girl Secretary Carries Coffee
Mug / Pup Watches

325309 ONLY ONE LIFE TO OFFER
Ongoing — 98 — Sword — $35.00 — **$35.00**
Figurine, 4.00" — 98 — Eyeglasses — 35.00 — **35.00**
ac# 744 — 99 — Star — 35.00 — **35.00**
Boy Sits in Offering Plate

325325 THE GOOD LORD WILL ALWAYS UPHOLD US
Ongoing — 98 — Sword — $50.00 — **$50.00**
Figurine, 6.25" — 98 — Eyeglasses — 50.00 — **50.00**
ac# 934 — 99 — Star — 50.00 — **50.00**
Angel Stands on Stool to
Work Marionette Strings

325368	THERE ARE TWO SIDES TO EVERY STORY				
	Ongoing	98	Sword	$15.00	**$18.00**
	Figurine, 2.25"	98	Eyeglasses	15.00	**15.00**
	ac# 971	99	Star	15.00	**15.00**
	Bunnies Share Bedtime Story Book				

325457	LIFE CAN BE A JUNGLE	10/31/98 Jungle Jamboree DSR Event Piece			
	Annual 1998	98	Eyeglasses	$37.50	**$37.50**
	Figurine, 5.25"				
	ac# 573				
	Boy Holds up Binoculars as Monkey Holds onto His Shoulders				

325465	MOM YOU ALWAYS MAKE OUR HOUSE A HOME		Catalog Exclusive		
	Annual 1998	98	Sword	$37.50	**$40.00**
	Figurine, 5.25"		Eyeglasses		**38.00**
	ac# 691				
	Girl Holds Birdhouse with Resident Bird				

325473	MOM, YOU'RE MY SPECIAL-TEA	Mother's Day 1999			
	Retiring May 9, 1999	99	Star	$25.00	**$25.00**
	Figurine, 4.50"				
	ac# 692				
	Girl Holding a Tray with Teapot and Cup				

Early Release to retailers attending Fall 1998 Enesco Show.

325481	HOME IS WHERE THE HEART IS	1998 Catalog Exclusive			
	Annual 1998	98	Sword	$37.50	**$37.50**
	Figurine, 5.75"	98	Eyeglasses	37.50	**37.50**
	ac# 440				
	Girl with Heart-Shaped Wreath with Image of Home				

325503	MARVELOUS GRACE	Century Circle Event			
	Annual 1998	98	Eyeglasses	$50.00	**$50.00**
	Figurine, 5.25"				
	ac# 656				
	Ballerina in Long Gown				

325511	OUR FUTURE IS LOOKING MUCH BRIGHTER	Cruise Piece			
	Dated Annual 1998	98	Eyeglasses	$Gift	**$450.00**
	Figurine, 3.25"				
	ac# 761				
	Pirate in Treasure Chest Uses Spyglass to Look Around				

325538	WELL, BLOW ME DOWN IT'S YER BIRTHDAY				
	Ongoing	98	Sword	$50.00	**$52.00**
	Figurine, 4.50"	98	Eyeglasses	50.00	**50.00**
	ac# 1054	99	Star	50.00	**50.00**
	Mouse Holds onto Candle on Birthday Cake as Boy Prepares to Blow it out				

335533	JANUARY	98	Eyeglasses	$25.00	**$25.00**
	Ongoing	99	Star	25.00	**25.00**
	Limoges Box, 3.00"				
	ac# 517				
	Girl Holds Flower				

335541	FEBRUARY				
Picture Not	*Ongoing*	98	Eyeglasses	$25.00	**$25.00**
Available At	Limoges Box, 3.00"	99	Star	25.00	**25.00**
Press Time	ac# 270				
	Girl in Bonnet Holding				
	Hands in Prayer				

335568	MARCH				
Picture Not	*Ongoing*	98	Eyeglasses	$25.00	**$25.00**
Available At	Limoges Box, 3.00"	99	Star	25.00	**25.00**
Press Time	ac# 652				
	Girl in Bonnet Holds Basket				

335576	APRIL				
	Ongoing	98	Eyeglasses	$25.00	**$25.00**
	Limoges Box, 3.00"	99	Star	25.00	**25.00**
	ac# 72				
	Girl in Spring Hat with				
	Bouquet of Spring Flowers				

335584	MAY				
	Ongoing	98	Eyeglasses	$25.00	**$25.00**
	Limoges Box, 3.00"	99	Star	25.00	**25.00**
	ac# 657				
	Girl at Birdbath				

335592	JUNE				
	Ongoing	98	Eyeglasses	$25.00	**$25.00**
	Limoges Box, 3.00"	99	Star	25.00	**25.00**
	ac# 546				
	Girl Holding Shell				

335606	JULY				
	Ongoing	98	Eyeglasses	$25.00	**$25.00**
	Limoges Box, 3.00"	99	Star	25.00	**25.00**
	ac# 543				
	Girl with Swan				

335614	AUGUST				
Picture Not	*Ongoing*	98	Eyeglasses	$25.00	**$25.00**
Available At	Limoges Box, 3.00"	99	Star	25.00	**25.00**
Press Time	ac# 74				
	Girl Scatters Dandelion Seed				
	Puff				

335622	SEPTEMBER				
	Ongoing	98	Eyeglasses	$25.00	**$25.00**
	Limoges Box, 3.00"	99	Star	25.00	**25.00**
	ac# 838				
	Girl Holding Flower				

335657	OCTOBER				
Picture Not	*Ongoing*	98	Eyeglasses	$25.00	**$25.00**
Available At	Limoges Box, 3.00"	99	Star	25.00	**25.00**
Press Time	ac# 730				
	Girl Holds Bouquet of Fall				
	Flowers				

335665 Picture Not Available At Press Time	NOVEMBER *Ongoing* Limoges Box, 3.00" ac# 724 Girl with Hands Behind Her Back		98 99	Eyeglasses Star	$25.00 25.00	**$25.00** **25.00**
335673	DECEMBER *Ongoing* Limoges Box, 3.00" ac# 238 Girl Carries Lit Candle		98 99	Eyeglasses Star	$25.00 25.00	**$25.00** **25.00**
354406	A PRAYER WARRIOR'S FAITH CAN MOVE MOUNTAINS *Ongoing* Figurine, 5.00" ac# 14 Native American Woman Praying	Chapel Exclusive	98	Unmarked	$45.00	**$45.00**
354414	A PRAYER WARRIOR'S FAITH CAN MOVE MOUNTAINS *Annual 1998* Figurine, 9.00" ac# 14 Native American Woman Praying	Chapel Exclusive	98	Unmarked	$250.00	**$250.00**
384844 Picture Not Available At Press Time	FOUNTAIN OF ANGELS Chapel Exclusive *Ongoing* Figurine, 5.75" ac# 288 Girl Angel Riding a Fish		98	Unmarked	$45.00	**$45.00**
384887	MANY YEARS OF BLESSING YOU Commemorates Kirlin Hallmark 50th Anniversary *Limited Time Release* 1998* Figurine, —— ac# 651 Dale Kirlin Presents Flower Bouquet to Marian Kirlin		98	Sword Eyeglasses	$60.00	**$60.00** **60.00**

*Limited Time Release (2/15/98 to 4/1/98) to 61 retailers. Remainders subsequently available to retailers who attended October 1998 Enesco Show.

408735	THE VOICE OF SPRING Series: "The Four Seasons" Jack-in-the-Box / Tune: April Love *Two Year Collectible* Musical, 13.00" ac# 968 Spring Girl		90 91	Flame Vessel	$200.00 200.00	**$200.00** **200.00**
408743	SUMMER'S JOY Series: "The Four Seasons" Jack-in-the-Box / Tune: You Are My Sunshine *Two Year Collectible* Musical, 13.00" ac# 898 Girl with Ducklings		90 91	Flame Vessel	$200.00 200.00	**$200.00** **200.00**

408751 AUTUMN'S PRAISE   Series: "The Four Seasons"   Jack-in-the-Box / Tune: Autumn Leaves

Two Year Collectible	90	Flame	$200.00	**$200.00**
Musical, 13.00"	91	Vessel	200.00	**200.00**
ac# 79				
Autumn Girl				

408778 WINTER'S SONG   Series: "The Four Seasons"   Jack-in-the-Box / Tune: Thru The Eyes Of Love

Two Year Collectible	90	Flame	$200.00	**$200.00**
Musical, 13.00"	91	Vessel	200.00	**200.00**
ac# 1064				
Winter Girl				

408786 THE VOICE OF SPRING   Series: "The Four Seasons"

Two Year Collectible	90	Flame	$150.00	**$150.00**
Doll, 15.00"	91	Vessel	150.00	**150.00**
ac# 968				
Spring Girl				

408794 SUMMER'S JOY   Series: "The Four Seasons"

Two Year Collectible	90	Flame	$150.00	**$150.00**
Doll, 15.00"	91	Vessel	150.00	**150.00**
ac# 898				
Girl with Ducklings				

408808 AUTUMN'S PRAISE   Series: "The Four Seasons"

Two Year Collectible	90	Flame	$150.00	**$150.00**
Doll, 15.00"	91	Vessel	150.00	**150.00**
ac# 79				
Autumn Girl				

408816 WINTER'S SONG   Series: "The Four Seasons"

Two Year Collectible	90	Flame	$150.00	**$150.00**
Doll, 15.00"	91	Vessel	150.00	**150.00**
ac# 1064				
Winter Girl				

417777 MAY YOU HAVE AN OLD FASHIONED CHRISTMAS   Jack-in-the-Box / Tune: Have Yourself A Merry Little Christmas

Two Year Collectible	91	Flame	$200.00	**$200.00**
Musical, 12.00"	91	Vessel	200.00	**200.00**
ac# 663	92	G-Clef	200.00	**200.00**
Christmas Girl in Plaid Dress				

417785 MAY YOU HAVE AN OLD FASHIONED CHRISTMAS

Two Year Collectible	91	Flame	$150.00	**$150.00**
Doll, 12.00"	92	Vessel	150.00	**150.00**
ac# 663	92	G-Clef	150.00	**150.00**
Christmas Girl in Plaid Dress				

422282 YOU HAVE TOUCHED SO MANY HEARTS   Jack-in-the-Box / Tune: Everybody Loves Somebody

Two Year Collectible	91	Flame	$175.00	**$175.00**
Musical, 12.00"	91	Vessel	175.00	**175.00**
ac# 1130	92	G-Clef	175.00	**175.00**
Girl with String of Hearts				

427527   <u>YOU HAVE TOUCHED SO MANY HEARTS</u>

	Two Year Collectible	91	Flame	$90.00	**$90.00**
	Doll, 12.00"	91	Vessel	90.00	**90.00**
	ac# 1130	92	G-Clef	90.00	**90.00**
	Girl with String of Hearts				

429570   <u>THE EYES OF THE LORD ARE UPON YOU</u>   Tune: Brahms' Lullaby / Motion

Musical Doll

	Suspended 1994	91	Flame	$65.00	**$70.00**
	Musical, 10.00"	91	Vessel	65.00	**65.00**
	ac# 926	92	G-Clef	65.00	**65.00**
	Baby Boy on Pillow	93	Butterfly	65.00	**65.00**
		94	Trumpet	65.00	**65.00**

429589   <u>THE EYES OF THE LORD ARE UPON YOU</u>   Tune: Brahms' Lullaby / Motion

Musical Doll

	Suspended 1994	91	Flame	$65.00	**$70.00**
	Musical, 10.00"	91	Vessel	65.00	**65.00**
	ac# 927	92	G-Clef	65.00	**65.00**
	Baby Girl on Pillow	93	Butterfly	65.00	**65.00**
		94	Trumpet	65.00	**65.00**

451312   <u>20 YEARS AND THE VISION'S STILL THE SAME</u>   Commemorates 20th

Anniversary of Precious Moments

	Annual 1998	98	Eyeglasses	$22.50	**$22.50**
	Ornament, 3.25"				
	ac# 5				
	Boy Optometrist Checks				
	Message of Loving, Caring				
	and Sharing for Perfect				
	Vision				

453722   <u>FEED MY LAMBS</u>   Chapel Exclusive   Shepherd Of The Hills Exclusive

	Ongoing	98	Unmarked	$67.50	**$67.50**
	Figurine, 6.00"				
	ac# 272				
	Shepherd Shares Scriptures				
	with Boy and Girl as Lamb				
	Listens				

455601   <u>I'M SENDING YOU A MERRY CHRISTMAS</u>

	Dated Annual 1998	98	Eyeglasses	$30.00	**$30.00**
	Figurine, 4.75"				
	ac# 494				
	Elf with an Air Mail Letter to				
	Santa				

455628   <u>I'M SENDING YOU A MERRY CHRISTMAS</u>

	Dated Annual 1998	98	Eyeglasses	$18.50	**$18.50**
	Ornament, 3.25"				
	ac# 494				
	Elf with an Air Mail Letter to				
	Santa				

455636   <u>OUR FIRST CHRISTMAS TOGETHER</u>

	Dated Annual 1998	98	Eyeglasses	$25.00	**$25.00**
	Ornament, 2.25"				
	ac# 758				
	Couple Share Ride in				
	Airplane				

455644 BABY'S FIRST CHRISTMAS - (GIRL)

Dated Annual 1998   98   Eyeglasses $18.50   **$18.50**
Ornament, 3.25"
ac# 116
Baby Girl Holding Blanket
and Sucking Thumb Sits on
Block

455652 BABY'S FIRST CHRISTMAS - (BOY)

Dated Annual 1998   98   Eyeglasses $18.50   **$18.50**
Ornament, 3.25"
ac# 112
Baby Boy Holding Blanket
and Sucking Thumb Sits on
Block

455660 I'LL BE DOG-GED IT'S THAT SEASON AGAIN

Dated Annual 1998   98   Eyeglasses $18.50   **$18.50**
Ornament, 2.75"
ac# 481
St. Bernard in Santa Hat
Carries Keg of Cocoa

455687 MORNIN' PUMPKIN

Ongoing   98   Eyeglasses $45.00   **$45.00**
Figurine, 4.50"   99   Star   45.00   **45.00**
ac# 697
Kitten Peeks out of Heart-
Shaped Cutout that Girl
Carved in Pumpkin

455695 PRAISE GOD FROM WHOM ALL BLESSINGS FLOW

Ongoing   98   Eyeglasses $40.00   **$40.00**
Figurine, 5.25"   99   Star   40.00   **40.00**
ac# 783
Girl Says Thankful Prayer by
a Cornucopia of Fall Harvest
Food

455733 PRAISE THE LORD AND DOSIE-DO

Ongoing   98   Eyeglasses $50.00   **$50.00**
Figurine, 5.50"   99   Star   50.00   **50.00**
ac# 784
Boy and Girl Square
Dancing

455768 PEAS ON EARTH

Ongoing   98   Eyeglasses $32.50   **$32.50**
Figurine, 4.50"   99   Star   32.50   **32.50**
ac# 776
Girl in Santa Cap with
Upside Down Can of Peas

455776 I'M JUST NUTTY ABOUT THE HOLIDAYS

Ongoing   98   Eyeglasses $17.50   **$17.50**
Ornament, 2.50"   99   Star   17.50   **17.50**
ac# 491
Squirrel Holding Acorn Gift

455784 ALASKA ONCE MORE, HOW'S YER CHRISTMAS?

Ongoing   98   Eyeglasses $35.00   **$35.00**
Figurine, 3.50"   99   Star   35.00   **35.00**
ac# 44
Eskimo and Penguin Share
Holiday Stories

455792 YOU CAN ALWAYS FUDGE A LITTLE DURING THE SEASON
Ongoing 98 Eyeglasses $35.00 **$35.00**
Figurine, 5.50" 99 Star 35.00 **35.00**
ac# 1119
Girl Licks Fudge out of Bowl

455814 WISHING YOU A YUMMY CHRISTMAS
Ongoing 98 Eyeglasses $30.00 **$30.00**
Figurine, 3.50" 99 Star 30.00 **30.00**
ac# 1082
Ice Fishing Teddy Bear
Catches a Fish

455822 I SAW MOMMY KISSING SANTA CLAUS
Ongoing 98 Eyeglasses $65.00 **$65.00**
Figurine, 5.50" 99 Star 65.00 **65.00**
ac# 472
Boy Sees His Mommy
Kissing "Santa" Dad

455849 TIME FOR A HOLY HOLIDAY
Ongoing 98 Eyeglasses $35.00 **$35.00**
Figurine, 5.25" 99 Star 35.00 **35.00**
ac# 996
Angel Holding Wreath Clock

455873 HAVE A COZY COUNTRY CHRISTMAS
Ongoing 98 Eyeglasses $50.00 **$50.00**
Figurine, 5.50" 99 Star 50.00 **50.00**
ac# 388
Girl Decorating Christmas
Tree with Santa Hat and
Scarf

455903 FRIENDS ARE FOREVER, SEW BEE IT
Ongoing 98 Flame $60.00 **$60.00**
Figurine, 5.50" 99 Star 60.00 **60.00**
ac# 290
Girls in a Quilting Bee

455938 I NOW PRONOUNCE YOU MAN AND WIFE
Ongoing 98 Eyeglasses $30.00 **$30.00**
Figurine, 4.75" 99 Star 30.00 **30.00**
ac# 468
Pastor Presiding at Wedding

455954 THE LIGHT OF THE WORLD IS JESUS   Nativity Addition
Ongoing 98 Eyeglasses $30.00 **$30.00**
Figurine, 4.50" 99 Star 30.00 **30.00**
ac# 941
Inn Keeper

455962 HANG ON TO THAT HOLIDAY FEELING   Mini Nativity Addition
Ongoing 98 Eyeglasses $17.50 **$17.50**
Figurine, 3.25" 99 Star 17.50 **17.50**
ac# 367
Angel Holding Peace Star
over Her Head

455970 — **FLIGHT INTO EGYPT** Complements Large Nativity Set of 2
Annual* 1998   98   Eyeglasses $75.00   **$75.00**
Figurine, 6.00"
ac# 278
Joseph Leads Donkey
Carrying Mary and Baby
Jesus

*Only offered to retailers who attended the 1998 Spring Fling Show.

455989 — **MY TRUE LOVE GAVE TO ME** Series: "12 Days Of Christmas"–Day 1
Annual 1998   98   Eyeglasses $20.00   **$20.00**
Ornament, 2.75"
ac# 712
Girls Opens Gift to Find
Partridge and Pear

455997 — **WE'RE TWO OF A KIND** Series: "12 Days Of Christmas"–Day 2
Annual 1998   98   Eyeglasses $20.00   **$20.00**
Ornament, 3.25"
ac# 1051
Seated Girl Holds Two Turtle
Doves

456004 — **SAYING "OUI" TO OUR LOVE** Series: "12 Days Of Christmas"–Day 3
Annual 1998   98   Eyeglasses $20.00   **$20.00**
Ornament, 3.25"
ac# 823
Boy Stands with Three
French Hens

456012 — **RINGING IN THE SEASON** Series: "12 Days Of Christmas"–Day 4
Annual 1998   98   Eyeglasses $20.00   **$20.00**
Ornament, 3.00"
ac# 811
Girl with Four Calling Birds

456217 — **SUGAR TOWN POST OFFICE 7* PIECE COLLECTOR SET** Sugar Town
*Set of 8
Annual 1998   98   Eyeglasses $250.00   **$250.00**
Figurine
ac# 896
Lighted Post Office

Also includes little girl with goose, young girl with string of lights,
young girl pushing sleigh of pups, boy sharing snow cone with pup,
mailman delivering cards and gifts in van, little girl posting a snowball
at mailbox.

456225 — **GOD LOVETH A CHEERFUL GIVER** Loving, Caring & Sharing Contest 20th
Anniversary Piece
Limited Edition 20   98   Eyeglasses   NA   **NE**
Figurine, 9.00"
ac# 337
Girl with Puppies

456268 — **HOW CAN TWO WORK TOGETHER EXCEPT THEY AGREE** Care-A-Van
Exclusive
Annual 1998   98   Eyeglasses $25.00   **$25.00**
Ornament, 3.25"
ac# 453
Sam and Fujioka-san
Working Together on the
"Original 21"

456276 YOU HAVE MASTERED THE ART OF CARING   Fall Syndicated Catalog
Early Release
Annual 1998   98   Eyeglasses $40.00   **$40.00**
    Figurine, 4.50"
    ac# 1128
    Girl Painting Ornaments

456314 HEAVEN BLESS YOU EASTER SEAL   Easter Seal Commemorative / Lily
Understamp
Annual 1999   99   Eyeglasses $35.00   **$35.00**
    Figurine, 4.75"   99   Star   35.00   **35.00**
    ac# 416
    Boy Angel Adjusts Bunny
    Ears Headband on Baby Seal

456373 YOU ARE A DUCHESS TO ME (HOLLAND)   Little Moments
Ongoing   98   Not Marked $20.00   **$20.00**
    Figurine, 3.75"   99   20.00   **20.00**
    ac# 1095
    Dutch Girl with Bells

456381 LIFE IS A FIESTA (SPAIN)   Little Moments
Ongoing   98   Not Marked $20.00   **$20.00**
    Figurine, 3.75"   99   20.00   **20.00**
    ac# 574
    Spanish Flamenco Dancer

456403 DON'T ROME TOO FAR FROM HOME (ITALY)   Little Moments
Ongoing   98   Not Marked $20.00   **$20.00**
    Figurine, 3.50"   99   20.00   **20.00**
    ac# 243
    Boy Singing Song

456411 YOU CAN'T BEAT THE RED, WHITE AND BLUE (UNITED STATES)   Little
Moments
Ongoing   98   Not Marked $20.00   **$20.00**
    Figurine, 3.75"   99   20.00   **20.00**
    ac# 1121
    Boy as "Uncle Sam" Plays
    Drum

456446 LOVE'S RUSSIAN INTO MY HEART (RUSSIA)   Little Moments
Ongoing   98   Not Marked $20.00   **$20.00**
    Figurine, 3.75"   99   20.00   **20.00**
    ac# 630
    Boy Doing Traditional
    Russian Dance

456454 HOLA, AMIGO (MEXICO)   Little Moments
Ongoing   98   Not Marked $20.00   **$20.00**
    Figurine, 3.75"   99   20.00   **20.00**
    ac# 436
    Boy Plays a Guitar

456462 AFRI-CAN BE THERE FOR YOU, I WILL BE (KENYA)   Little Moments
Ongoing   98   Not Marked $20.00   **$20.00**
    Figurine, 3.75"   99   20.00   **20.00**
    ac# 28
    Boy Plays Traditional African
    Drum

456470 I'D TRAVEL THE HIGHLANDS TO BE WITH YOU (SCOTLAND) Little Moments

Ongoing		98	Not Marked	$20.00	**$20.00**
	Figurine, 3.75"	99		20.00	**20.00**
	ac# 480				
	Scottish Bagpiper Boy				

456896 SURE WOULD LOVE TO SQUEEZE YOU (GERMANY) Little Moments

Ongoing		98	Not Marked	$20.00	**$20.00**
	Figurine, 3.75"	99		20.00	**20.00**
	ac# 899				
	Boy Playing An Accordion				

456918 YOU ARE MY AMOUR (FRANCE) Little Moments

Ongoing		98	Not Marked	$20.00	**$20.00**
	Figurine, 3.75"	99		20.00	**20.00**
	ac# 1104				
	Boy Playing a Violin				

456926 OUR FRIENDSHIP IS ALWAYS IN BLOOM (JAPAN) Little Moments

Ongoing		98	Not Marked	$20.00	**$20.00**
	Figurine, 3.75"	99		20.00	**20.00**
	ac# 759				
	Girl Wears Traditional Kimono				

456934 MY LOVE WILL STAND GUARD OVER YOU (ENGLAND) Little Moments

Ongoing		98	Not Marked	$20.00	**$20.00**
	Figurine, 4.00"	99		20.00	**20.00**
	ac# 710				
	Boy Dressed as Buckingham Palace Guardsman				

469327 I'M SENDING YOU A MERRY CHRISTMAS

Dated Annual 1998		98	Eyeglasses	$50.00	**$50.00**
	Plate, 8.25"				
	ac# 494				
	Elf with Letter to Santa				

470279 MAY YOUR CHRISTMAS BE WARM - BABY Series: "Birthday Circus Train"

Ongoing		98	Eyeglasses	$15.00	**$15.00**
	Ornament, 2.50"	99	Star	15.00	**15.00**
	ac# 669				
	Teddy on Sled - Baby				

475068 WE ARE ALL PRECIOUS IN HIS SIGHT Easter Seal / Lily Understamp / Individually Numbered

Limited Edition 2,500		99	Eyeglasses	$500.00	**$500.00**
	Figurine, 9.00"				
	ac# 1038				
	Girl with Pearl				

475084 EVEN THE HEAVENS SHALL PRAISE HIM Century Circle Exclusive

Annual 1998		98	Eyeglasses	$30.00	**$30.00**
	Ornament, 4.50"				
	ac# 264				
	Girl with Harp				

Picture Not Available At Press Time

475092 TOY MAKER Chapel Exclusive Memorial to Pat Carson's father
Picture Not Available At Press Time *Ongoing* 98 Unmarked $40.00 **$40.00**
Figurine, 5.25"
ac# 1018
Boy Surrounded with Toys He Made

475106 TOY MAKER Chapel Exclusive Memorial to Pat Carson's father
Picture Not Available At Press Time *Ongoing* 98 Unmarked $20.00 **$20.00**
Ornament, 3.25"
ac# 1019
Boy Surrounded with Toys He Made

482242S LOVE IS THE KEY Avon Exclusive Piece / In Honor Of 20th Anniversary Celebration
Picture Not Available At Press Time Figurine $30.00 **$30.00**
ac# 617
Girl Holding Key

487902 MY UNIVERSE IS YOU
Ongoing 99 Eyeglasses $45.00 **$45.00**
Figurine, 4.50" 99 Star 45.00 **45.00**
ac# 713
Girl Looking Through Telescope at Star Held by Bird

487910 BELIEVE IT OR KNOT I LUV YOU
Ongoing 99 Eyeglasses $35.00 **$35.00**
Figurine, 4.25" 99 Star 35.00 **35.00**
ac# 129
Girl Tying Knot in Rope as Kitten Sits on Rope Coil

487929 YOU'RE MY HONEY BEE
Ongoing 99 Eyeglasses $20.00 **$20.00**
Figurine, 2.75" 99 Star 20.00 **20.00**
ac# 1152
Baby Teddy Bear and Bumblebee

487953 YOU CAN ALWAYS COUNT ON ME
Ongoing 99 Eyeglasses $35.00 **$35.00**
Figurine, 5.75" 99 Star 35.00 **35.00**
ac# 1118
Girl Counts Using an Abacus

487988 WHAT BETTER TO GIVE THAN YOURSELF
Ongoing 99 Eyeglasses $30.00 **$30.00**
Figurine, 5.75" 99 Star 30.00 **30.00**
ac# 1056
Girl Wrapped in Ribbon Sash and Bow

488003 TAKE YOUR TIME IT'S YOUR BIRTHDAY Series: "Birthday Circus Train"
Ongoing 99 Eyeglasses $25.00 **$25.00**
Figurine, 5.25" 99 Star 25.00 **25.00**
ac# 910
Turtle Carries Gift on its Shell - Age 11

332

488046	MOM, YOU'VE GIVEN ME SO MUCH					
	Ongoing	99	Eyeglasses	$35.00	**$35.00**
	Figurine, 5.00"	99	Star	35.00	**35.00**
	ac# 693				
	Mom with Stack of Gifts				

488054	YOU JUST CAN'T REPLACE A GOOD FRIENDSHIP					
	Ongoing	99	Eyeglasses	$35.00	**$35.00**
	Figurine, 4.25"	99	Star	35.00	**35.00**
	ac# 1133				
	Girl Lifts Puppy out of Lost-N-found Box				

488178	CONFIRMED IN THE LORD					
	Ongoing	99	Eyeglasses	$30.00	**$30.00**
	Figurine, 5.50"	99	Star	30.00	**30.00**
	ac# 225				
	Confirmation Girl Holding Bible				

488240	A VERY SPECIAL BOND					
	Ongoing	99	Eyeglasses	$70.00	**$70.00**
	Figurine, 6.00"	99	Star	70.00	**70.00**
	ac# 25				
	Adult Daughter with Her Mother				

488259	HOPE IS REVEALED THROUGH GOD'S WORD Series: "Victorian"–2nd Issue					
	Annual	98	Eyeglasses	$70.00	**$70.00**
	Figurine, 7.25"				
	ac# 442				
	Young Woman with Open Parasol Extends Her Hand to God				

488321	YOU CAN'T TAKE IT WITH YOU					
	Ongoing	99	Eyeglasses	$25.00	**$25.00**
	Figurine, 4.75"	99	Star	25.00	**25.00**
	ac# 1123				
	Boy Holding Large Piggy Bank				

488356	ALWAYS LISTEN TO YOUR HEART					
Picture Not Available At Press Time	*Ongoing*	99	Eyeglasses	$25.00	**$25.00**
	Figurine, 4.75"	99	Star	25.00	**25.00**
	ac# 49				
	Girl Holds Stethoscope to Hear Her Heartbeat				

488372	YOU COUNT					
	Ongoing	99	Eyeglasses	$25.00	**$25.00**
	Figurine, 4.50"	99	Star	25.00	**25.00**
	ac# 1124				
	Girl with Embroidery Hoop				

488380	JESUS LOVES ME "Original 21" Covered Boxes					
Picture Not Available At Press Time	*Ongoing*	98	Eyeglasses	$25.00	**$25.00**
	Limoges Box, 3.00"	99	Star	25.00	**25.00**
	ac# 532				
	Girl with Bunny				

488399	JESUS LOVES ME "Original 21" Covered Boxes				
Picture Not Available At Press Time	*Ongoing* Limoges Box, 3.00" ac# 531 Boy with Teddy Bear	98 99	Eyeglasses Star	$25.00 25.00	**$25.00** **25.00**

488402	MAKE A JOYFUL NOISE "Original 21" Covered Boxes				
	Ongoing Limoges Box, 3.00" ac# 644 Girl with Goose	98 99	Eyeglasses Star	$25.00 25.00	**$25.00** **25.00**

488410	LOVE ONE ANOTHER "Original 21" Covered Boxes				
	Ongoing Limoges Box, 3.00" ac# 625 Boy and Girl Sitting on Stump	98 99	Eyeglasses Star	$25.00 25.00	**$25.00** **25.00**

488429	HIS BURDEN IS LIGHT "Original 21" Covered Boxes				
	Ongoing Limoges Box, 3.00" ac# 427 Native American with Papoose	98 99	Eyeglasses Star	$25.00 25.00	**$25.00** **25.00**

488437	JESUS IS THE LIGHT "Original 21" Covered Boxes				
	Ongoing Limoges Box, 3.00" ac# 527 Girl with Candle and Doll	98 99	Eyeglasses Star	$25.00 25.00	**$25.00** **25.00**

492140	YOU ALWAYS STAND BEHIND ME				
	Ongoing Figurine, 5.50" ac# 1093 Young Boy Receives a Golf Lesson from Dad	99 99	Eyeglasses Star	$50.00 50.00	**$50.00** **50.00**

520233	OUR FIRST CHRISTMAS TOGETHER				
	Dated Annual 1988 Ornament, 2.50" ac# 751 Boy and Girl in Package	88	Flower	$13.00	**$20.00**

520241	BABY'S FIRST CHRISTMAS				
	Dated Annual 1988 Ornament, 2.25" ac# 98 Girl in Sleigh	88	Flower	$15.00	**$20.00**

520268   REJOICE O EARTH   Mini Nativity Addition

Ongoing
Figurine, 3.00"
ac# 803
Angel with Trumpet

88	Flower	$13.00	**$30.00**
89	Bow & Arrow	15.00	**25.00**
90	Flame	15.00	**22.00**
91	Vessel	15.00	**22.00**
92	G-Clef	15.00	**22.00**
93	Butterfly	15.00	**20.00**
94	Trumpet	16.00	**20.00**
95	Ship	17.00	**20.00**
96	Heart	18.50	**18.50**
97	Sword	18.50	**18.50**
98	Eyeglasses	18.50	**18.50**
99	Star	18.50	**18.50**

520276   YOU ARE MY GIFT COME TRUE   10th Anniversary Commemorative

Dated Annual 1988
Ornament, 2.50"
ac# 1106
Puppy in Sock

88	Flower	$12.50	**$20.00**

520284   MERRY CHRISTMAS, DEER   Series: "Christmas Love"–3rd Issue

Dated Annual 1988
Plate, 8.25"
ac# 685
Girl Decorating Reindeer

88	Flower	$50.00	**$60.00**

520292   HANG ON FOR THE HOLLY DAYS   Birthday Collection

Dated Annual 1988
Ornament, 3.50"
ac# 366
Kitten Hanging on to Wreath

88	Flower	$13.00	**$30.00**

520322   MAKE A JOYFUL NOISE   Easter Seal / Lily Understamp / Individually Numbered

Limited Edition 1,500
Figurine, 9.00"
ac# 644
Girl with Goose

89	Bow & Arrow	$500.00	**$745.00**

520357   JESUS THE SAVIOR IS BORN   Nativity Addition

Suspended 1993
Figurine, 4.50"
ac# 533
Angel with Newspaper & Dog

88	Flower	$25.00	**$65.00**
89	Bow & Arrow	30.00	**55.00**
90	Flame	32.50	**50.00**
91	Vessel	32.50	**48.00**
92	G-Clef	32.50	**46.00**
93	Butterfly	32.50	**45.00**

520403   HIPPO HOLIDAYS   Birthday Collection

Dated Annual 1995
Ornament, 2.75"
ac# 426
Hippo Wears Garland Belt

95	Ship	$17.00	**$25.00**

520411   I'M NUTS ABOUT YOU   Birthday Collection

Dated Annual 1992
Ornament, 2.50"
ac# 492
Squirrel Decorating Tree atop Log Filled w/Nuts

92	G-Clef	$16.00	**$20.00**

520438 SNO-BUNNY FALLS FOR YOU LIKE I DO   Birthday Collection
Dated Annual 1991   91   Vessel $15.00   **$30.00**
  Ornament, 3.25"
  ac# 877
  Rabbit on Skates

520454 HAPPY HOLI-DAZE
Ongoing   98   Eyeglasses $17.50   **$17.50**
  Ornament, 2.50"   99   Star   17.50   **17.50**
  ac# 381
  Snowball Bulls Eye to Teddy
  Bear

520462 CHRISTMAS IS RUFF WITHOUT YOU   Birthday Collection
Dated Annual 1989   89   Bow & Arrow $13.00   **$35.00**
  Ornament, 2.75"
  ac# 203
  Puppy Resting on Elbow

520470 TAKE A BOW 'CUZ YOU'RE MY CHRISTMAS STAR   Holiday Preview Event
Annual 1994   94   Trumpet $16.00   **$25.00**
  Ornament, 2.75"
  ac# 906
  Pup in Hat & Scarf Carries
  Holly Sprig

520489 SLOW DOWN AND ENJOY THE HOLIDAYS   Birthday Collection
Dated Annual 1993   93   Butterfly $16.00   **$25.00**
  Ornament, 2.50"
  ac# 872
  Reindeer Turtle Carrying Gift

520497 WISHING YOU A PURR-FECT HOLIDAY   Birthday Collection
Dated Annual 1990   90   Flame $15.00   **$30.00**
  Ornament, 2.75"
  ac# 1077
  Kitten with Ornament

520535 THE LORD TURNED MY LIFE AROUND
Suspended 1996   92   G-Clef $35.00   **$60.00**
  Figurine, 5.75"   93   Butterfly   35.00   **58.00**
  ac# 956   94   Trumpet   35.00   **55.00**
  Ballerina on Pointe (Red   95   Ship   35.00   **52.00**
  Tutu)   96   Heart   37.50   **50.00**

520543 IN THE SPOTLIGHT OF HIS GRACE
Suspended 1996   91   Vessel $35.00   **$65.00**
  Figurine, 5.75"   92   G-Clef   35.00   **60.00**
  ac# 501   93   Butterfly   35.00   **55.00**
  Ballerina on Pointe (Pink   94   Trumpet   35.00   **52.00**
  Tutu)   95   Ship   35.00   **50.00**
                       96   Heart   37.50   **48.00**

520551 — LORD, TURN MY LIFE AROUND

Suspended 1996
Figurine, 5.75"
ac# 598
Ballerina (Blue Tutu)

Year	Mark	Price	Value
90	Bow & Arrow	$35.00	**$70.00**
90	Flame	35.00	**65.00**
91	Vessel	35.00	**62.00**
92	G-Clef	35.00	**60.00**
93	Butterfly	35.00	**58.00**
94	Trumpet	35.00	**55.00**
95	Ship	35.00	**53.00**
96	Heart	37.50	**50.00**

520578 — YOU DESERVE AN OVATION

Ongoing
Figurine, 5.75"
ac# 1126
Ballerina on Pointe (Purple Tutu)

Year	Mark	Price	Value
92	G-Clef	$35.00	**$45.00**
93	Butterfly	35.00	**38.00**
94	Trumpet	35.00	**37.50**
95	Ship	35.00	**37.50**
96	Heart	37.50	**37.50**
97	Sword	37.50	**37.50**
98	Eyeglasses	37.50	**37.50**
99	Star	37.50	**37.50**

520624 — MY HEART IS EXPOSED WITH LOVE

Ongoing
Figurine, 5.25"
ac# 705
Nurse X-raying

Year	Mark	Price	Value
89	Flower	$45.00	**$78.00**
89	Bow & Arrow	45.00	**60.00**
90	Flame	50.00	**60.00**
91	Vessel	50.00	**60.00**
92	G-Clef	50.00	**60.00**
93	Butterfly	50.00	**60.00**
94	Trumpet	50.00	**60.00**
95	Ship	55.00	**60.00**
96	Heart	60.00	**60.00**
97	Sword	60.00	**60.00**
98	Eyeglasses	60.00	**60.00**
99	Star	60.00	**60.00**

520632 — A FRIEND IS SOMEONE WHO CARES

Retired 1995
Figurine, 4.25"
ac# 8
Mouse Wiping Clown's Tears

Year	Mark	Price	Value
89	Flower	$30.00	**$90.00**
89	Bow & Arrow	30.00	**85.00**
90	Flame	32.50	**82.00**
91	Vessel	32.50	**80.00**
92	G-Clef	32.50	**78.00**
93	Butterfly	32.50	**75.00**
94	Trumpet	35.00	**72.00**
95	Ship	35.00	**70.00**

520640 — I'M SO GLAD YOU FLUTTERED INTO MY LIFE

Retired 1991
Figurine, 5.75"
ac# 497
Angel with Butterfly's Net

Year	Mark	Price	Value
89	Flower	$40.00	**$325.00**
89	Bow & Arrow	40.00	**260.00**
90	Flame	45.00	**240.00**
91	Vessel	45.00	**225.00**

520659 — WISHING YOU A HAPPY BEAR HUG — Birthday Collection

Suspended 1996
Figurine, 5.00"
ac# 1071
Bear Carries Cake with Mouse Popping out

Year	Mark	Price	Value
95	Trumpet	$27.50	**$45.00**
95	Ship	27.50	**42.00**
96	Heart	27.50	**40.00**

520667 — EGGSPECIALLY FOR YOU

Ongoing
Figurine, 4.75"
ac# 258
Girl with Hen & Easter Egg

89	Flower	$45.00	**$65.00**
89	Bow & Arrow	45.00	**55.00**
90	Flame	50.00	**52.00**
91	Vessel	50.00	**50.00**
92	G-Clef	50.00	**50.00**
93	Butterfly	50.00	**50.00**
94	Trumpet	50.00	**50.00**
95	Ship	50.00	**50.00**
96	Heart	50.00	**50.00**
97	Sword	50.00	**50.00**
98	Eyeglasses	50.00	**50.00**
99	Star	50.00	**50.00**

520675 — YOUR LOVE IS SO UPLIFTING

Retired 1998
Figurine, 6.50"
ac# 1158
Boy Holding Girl at Fountain

89	Flower	$60.00	**$110.00**
89	Bow & Arrow	60.00	**105.00**
90	Flame	65.00	**100.00**
91	Vessel	65.00	**98.00**
92	G-Clef	65.00	**96.00**
93	Butterfly	75.00	**95.00**
94	Trumpet	75.00	**94.00**
95	Ship	75.00	**90.00**
96	Heart	75.00	**85.00**
97	Sword	75.00	**82.00**
98	Eyeglasses	75.00	**75.00**

520683 — SENDING YOU SHOWERS OF BLESSINGS

Retired 1992
Figurine, 5.50"
ac# 837
Boy with Newspaper over Head

89	Flower	$32.50	**$85.00**
89	Bow & Arrow	32.50	**78.00**
90	Flame	35.00	**75.00**
91	Vessel	35.00	**72.00**
92	G-Clef	35.00	**70.00**

520691 — LORD, KEEP MY LIFE IN BALANCE   Tune: Music Box Dancer

Suspended 1993
Musical, 7.00"
ac# 591
Ballerina at Barre

91	Vessel	$60.00	**$95.00**
92	G-Clef	60.00	**85.00**
93	Butterfly	65.00	**80.00**

520705 — BABY'S FIRST PET   Series: "Baby's First"–5th Issue

Suspended 1994
Figurine, 5.25"
ac# 119
Boy with Baby Feeding Dog

89	Flower	$45.00	**$85.00**
89	Bow & Arrow	45.00	**82.00**
90	Flame	50.00	**80.00**
91	Vessel	50.00	**78.00**
92	G-Clef	50.00	**75.00**
93	Butterfly	50.00	**72.00**
94	Trumpet	50.00	**70.00**

520721 — JUST A LINE TO WISH YOU A HAPPY DAY

Suspended 1996
Figurine, 6.50"
ac# 550
Dog Pulling Boy's Fishing Line

89	Flower	$65.00	**$115.00**
89	Bow & Arrow	65.00	**105.00**
90	Flame	70.00	**102.00**
91	Vessel	70.00	**100.00**
92	G-Clef	70.00	**100.00**
93	Butterfly	75.00	**98.00**
94	Trumpet	75.00	**98.00**
95	Ship	75.00	**95.00**
96	Heart	75.00	**93.00**

520748   <u>FRIENDSHIP HITS THE SPOT</u>

Ongoing
Figurine, 5.25"
ac# 297
Two Girls Having Tea

*Misspelled "Friendship" on
boxes and figurines in
Trumpet and Ship Marks.

89	Flower	$55.00	**$90.00**
89	Bow & Arrow	55.00	**78.00**
90	Flame	60.00	**75.00**
91	Vessel	60.00	**72.00**
92	G-Clef	60.00	**70.00**
93	Butterfly	65.00	**70.00**
94	Trumpet*	65.00	**70.00**
95	Ship*	65.00	**70.00**
96	Heart	70.00	**70.00**
97	Sword	70.00	**70.00**
98	Eyeglasses	70.00	**70.00**
99	Star	70.00	**70.00**

520756   <u>JESUS IS THE ONLY WAY</u>

Suspended 1993
Figurine, 6.00"
ac# 529
Boy at Crossroads

89	Flower	$40.00	**$75.00**
89	Bow & Arrow	40.00	**74.00**
90	Flame	45.00	**73.00**
91	Vessel	45.00	**72.00**
92	G-Clef	45.00	**70.00**
93	Butterfly	45.00	**68.00**

520764   <u>PUPPY LOVE</u>

Retiring 2/14/99
Figurine, 2.10"
ac# 796
Two Puppies

Enesco has announced this
piece will be retiring
Valentine's Day 1999.

89	Flower	$12.50	**$28.00**
89	Bow & Arrow	12.50	**22.00**
90	Flame	13.50	**20.00**
91	Vessel	13.50	**18.00**
92	G-Clef	13.50	**18.00**
93	Butterfly	15.00	**18.00**
94	Trumpet	16.00	**17.50**
95	Ship	17.00	**17.50**
96	Heart	17.50	**17.50**
97	Sword	17.50	**17.50**
98	Eyeglasses	17.50	**17.50**
99	Star	17.50	**17.50**

520772   <u>MANY MOONS IN SAME CANOE, BLESSUM YOU</u>

Retired 1990
Figurine, 5.00"
ac# 650
Native Americans in Canoe

89	Flower	$50.00	**$345.00**
89	Bow & Arrow	50.00	**330.00**
90	Flame	55.00	**320.00**

520780   <u>WISHING YOU ROADS OF HAPPINESS</u>

Ongoing
Figurine, 4.50"
ac# 1084
Bride and Groom in Car

89	Flower	$60.00	**$88.00**
89	Bow & Arrow	60.00	**80.00**
90	Flame	65.00	**78.00**
91	Vessel	65.00	**75.00**
92	G-Clef	65.00	**75.00**
93	Butterfly	70.00	**75.00**
94	Trumpet	75.00	**75.00**
95	Ship	75.00	**75.00**
96	Heart	75.00	**75.00**
97	Sword	75.00	**75.00**
98	Eyeglasses	75.00	**75.00**
99	Star	75.00	**75.00**

520799   <u>SOMEDAY MY LOVE</u>

Retired 1992
Figurine, 5.50"
ac# 884
Bride with Dress

89	Flower	$40.00	**$88.00**
89	Bow & Arrow	40.00	**80.00**
90	Flame	45.00	**75.00**
91	Vessel	45.00	**72.00**
92	G-Clef	45.00	**70.00**

520802   MY DAYS ARE BLUE WITHOUT YOU

Suspended 1991	89	Flower*	$65.00	**$120.00**
Figurine, 7.00"	89	Bow & Arrow*	65.00	**110.00**
ac# 701	90	Flame	70.00	**100.00**
Girl with Paint & Ladder	91	Vessel	70.00	**95.00**

*Exists with three variations of the mouth–smiling, frowning, and "O". Smiling is considered the variation. GBTru$ for Smiling with Flower is $130.00 & Smiling with Bow & Arrow is $125.00.

520810   WE NEED A GOOD FRIEND THROUGH THE RUFF TIMES

Suspended 1991	89	Flower	$35.00	**$65.00**
Figurine, 5.00"	89	Bow & Arrow	35.00	**60.00**
ac# 1045	90	Flame	37.50	**57.00**
Grandpa with Cane & Dog	91	Vessel	37.50	**55.00**

520829   YOU ARE MY NUMBER ONE

Ongoing	89	Flower	$25.00	**$45.00**
Figurine, 6.00"	89	Bow & Arrow	25.00	**40.00**
ac# 1109	90	Flame	27.50	**38.00**
Girl Holding Trophy	91	Vessel	27.50	**35.00**
	92	G-Clef	27.50	**35.00**
	93	Butterfly	30.00	**35.00**
	94	Trumpet	30.00	**35.00**
	95	Ship	32.50	**35.00**
	96	Heart	35.00	**35.00**
	97	Sword	35.00	**35.00**
	98	Eyeglasses	35.00	**35.00**
	99	Star	35.00	**35.00**

520837   THE LORD IS YOUR LIGHT TO HAPPINESS

Ongoing	89	Flower	$50.00	**$72.00**
Figurine, 4.75"	89	Bow & Arrow	50.00	**68.00**
ac# 955	90	Flame	55.00	**65.00**
Bridal Couple Lighting	91	Vessel	55.00	**65.00**
Candle	92	G-Clef	55.00	**65.00**
	93	Butterfly	60.00	**65.00**
	94	Trumpet	60.00	**65.00**
	95	Ship	65.00	**65.00**
	96	Heart	65.00	**65.00**
	97	Sword	65.00	**65.00**
	98	Eyeglasses	65.00	**65.00**
	99	Star	65.00	**65.00**

520845   WISHING YOU A PERFECT CHOICE

Ongoing	89	Flower	$55.00	**$80.00**
Figurine, 5.80"	89	Bow & Arrow	55.00	**70.00**
ac# 1076	90	Flame	60.00	**68.00**
Boy Proposing to Girl	91	Vessel	60.00	**65.00**
	92	G-Clef	60.00	**65.00**
	93	Butterfly	65.00	**65.00**
	94	Trumpet	65.00	**65.00**
	95	Ship	65.00	**65.00**
	96	Heart	65.00	**65.00**
	97	Sword	65.00	**65.00**
	98	Eyeglasses	65.00	**65.00**
	99	Star	65.00	**65.00**

520853   I BELONG TO THE LORD

Suspended 1991	89	Flower	$25.00	**$48.00**
Figurine, 5.10"	89	Bow & Arrow	25.00	**35.00**
ac# 459	90	Flame	27.50	**32.00**
Orphan Girl	91	Vessel	27.50	**30.00**

520861 SHARING BEGINS IN THE HEART Special Event
Annual 1989

Figurine, 5.75"	89	Flower	$25.00	**$80.00**
ac# 847		Bow & Arrow		**45.00**
Girl with Chalkboard				

520934 HEAVEN BLESS YOU
Ongoing

Figurine, 3.50"	90	Bow & Arrow	$35.00	**$128.00**
ac# 415	90	Flame	35.00	**48.00**
Baby with Bunny & Turtle	91	Vessel	35.00	**42.00**
	92	G-Clef	35.00	**38.00**
	93	Butterfly	35.00	**35.00**
	94	Trumpet	35.00	**35.00**
	95	Ship	35.00	**35.00**
	96	Heart	35.00	**35.00**
	97	Sword	35.00	**35.00**
	98	Eyeglasses	35.00	**35.00**
	99	Star	35.00	**35.00**

521000 THERE IS NO GREATER TREASURE THAN TO HAVE A FRIEND LIKE YOU
Ongoing

Figurine, 5.50"	93	G-Clef	$30.00	**$38.00**
ac# 973	93	Butterfly	30.00	**32.00**
Boy Swimmer Holding	94	Trumpet	30.00	**30.00**
Oyster with Pearl	95	Ship	30.00	**30.00**
	96	Heart	30.00	**30.00**
	97	Sword	30.00	**30.00**
	98	Eyeglasses	30.00	**30.00**
	99	Star	30.00	**30.00**

521043 TO MY FAVORITE FAN
Suspended 1993

Figurine, 2.50"	90	Bow & Arrow	$16.00	**$55.00**
ac# 1011	90	Flame	16.00	**40.00**
Gorilla and Parrot	91	Vessel	16.00	**38.00**
	92	G-Clef	16.00	**37.00**
	93	Butterfly	16.00	**35.00**

521078 MERRY CHRISTMAS, LITTLE LAMB Series: "Birthday Circus Train"
Ongoing

Ornament, 2.50"	98	Eyeglasses	$15.00	**$15.00**
ac# 378				
Lamb - Age 1				

521086 HEAVEN BLESS YOUR SPECIAL CHRISTMAS Series: "Birthday Circus Train"
Ongoing

Ornament, 2.50"	98	Eyeglasses	$15.00	**$15.00**
ac# 417				
Pig - Age 3				

521094 GOD BLESS YOU THIS CHRISTMAS Series: "Birthday Circus Train"
Ongoing

Ornament, 1.75"	98	Eyeglasses	$15.00	**$15.00**
ac# 320				
Seal - Age 2				

521108 MAY YOUR CHRISTMAS BE GIGANTIC Series: "Birthday Circus Train"
Ongoing

Ornament, 2.50"	98	Eyeglasses	$15.00	**$15.00**
ac# 667				
Elephant - Age 4				

521116 CHRISTMAS IS SOMETHING TO ROAR ABOUT   Series: "Birthday Circus Train"

Ongoing	98	Eyeglasses	$15.00	**$15.00**

Ornament, 2.75"
ac# 983
Lion - Age 5

521124 CHRISTMAS KEEPS LOOKING UP   Series: "Birthday Circus Train"

Ongoing	98	Eyeglasses	$15.00	**$15.00**

Ornament, 3.75"
ac# 556
Giraffe - Age 6

521175 HELLO WORLD!   Birthday Collection

Ongoing	89	Flower	$13.50	**$25.00**
Figurine, 3.25"	89	Bow & Arrow	13.50	**20.00**
ac# 422	90	Flame	15.00	**18.00**
Kangaroo with Baby	91	Vessel	15.00	**18.00**
	92	G-Clef	15.00	**18.00**
	93	Butterfly	15.00	**18.00**
	94	Trumpet	16.00	**17.50**
	95	Ship	17.00	**17.50**
	96	Heart	17.50	**17.50**
	97	Sword	17.50	**17.50**
	98	Eyeglasses	17.50	**17.50**
	99	Star	17.50	**17.50**

521183 THAT'S WHAT FRIENDS ARE FOR

Ongoing	90	Flame	$45.00	**$55.00**
Figurine, 6.00"	91	Vessel	45.00	**52.00**
ac# 923	92	G-Clef	45.00	**50.00**
Crying Girls Hugging	93	Butterfly	45.00	**50.00**
	94	Trumpet	45.00	**50.00**
	95	Ship	45.00	**50.00**
	96	Heart	50.00	**50.00**
	97	Sword	50.00	**50.00**
	98	Eyeglasses	50.00	**50.00**
	99	Star	50.00	**50.00**

521191 LORD, SPARE ME

Ongoing	97	Heart	$37.50	**$38.00**
Figurine, 5.25"	97	Sword	37.50	**37.50**
ac# 595	98	Eyeglasses	37.50	**37.50**
Boy Holds a Bowling Ball	99	Star	37.50	**37.50**

521205 HOPE YOU'RE UP AND ON THE TRAIL AGAIN

Suspended 1993	90	Bow & Arrow	$35.00	**$65.00**
Figurine, 5.50"	90	Flame	35.00	**60.00**
ac# 444	91	Vessel	35.00	**57.00**
Girl on Hobby Horse	92	G-Clef	35.00	**55.00**
	93	Butterfly	35.00	**52.00**

521213 THE FRUIT OF THE SPIRIT IS LOVE

Ongoing	93	Butterfly	$30.00	**$35.00**
Figurine, 6.00"	94	Trumpet	30.00	**33.00**
ac# 930	95	Ship	30.00	**32.50**
Girl Holding Bowl of Fruit	96	Heart	32.50	**32.50**
	97	Sword	32.50	**32.50**
	98	Eyeglasses	32.50	**32.50**
	99	Star	32.50	**32.50**

521221	ENTER HIS COURT WITH THANKSGIVING				
	Ongoing	96	Ship	$35.00	**$40.00**
	Figurine, 5.50"	96	Heart	35.00	**35.00**
	ac# 261	97	Sword	35.00	**35.00**
	Boy with Basketball	98	Eyeglasses	35.00	**35.00**
		99	Star	35.00	**35.00**

521272	TAKE HEED WHEN YOU STAND				
	*Suspended 1994**	91	Vessel	$55.00	**$78.00**
	Figurine, 6.00"	92	G-Clef	55.00	**75.00**
	ac# 907	93	Butterfly	55.00	**70.00**
	Boy on Rocking Horse	94	Trumpet	55.00	**65.00**

*Limited quantities offered to retailers attending Fall 1998 Enesco Show.

521280	HAPPY TRIP				
	Suspended 1994	90	Bow & Arrow	$35.00	**$80.00**
	Figurine, 5.75"	90	Flame	35.00	**65.00**
	ac# 384	91	Vessel	35.00	**62.00**
	Girl on Roller Skates	92	G-Clef	35.00	**60.00**
		93	Butterfly	35.00	**58.00**
		94	Trumpet	35.00	**55.00**

521299	HUG ONE ANOTHER				
	Retired 1995	91	Flame	$45.00	**$88.00**
	Figurine, 5.50"	91	Vessel	45.00	**81.00**
	ac# 454	92	G-Clef	45.00	**80.00**
	Girl and Boy Hugging	93	Butterfly	45.00	**79.00**
		94	Trumpet	50.00	**78.00**
		95	Ship	50.00	**75.00**

521302	MAY ALL YOUR CHRISTMASES BE WHITE				
	Suspended 1994	89	Bow & Arrow	$13.50	**$38.00**
	Ornament, 3.25"	90	Flame	15.00	**33.00**
	ac# 658	91	Vessel	15.00	**32.00**
	Girl Tying Snowball with	92	G-Clef	15.00	**31.00**
	Ribbon	93	Butterfly	15.00	**30.00**
		94	Trumpet	16.00	**29.00**

521310	YIELD NOT TO TEMPTATION				
	Suspended 1993	90	Bow & Arrow	$27.50	**$55.00**
	Figurine, 5.50"	90	Flame	27.50	**50.00**
	ac# 1092	91	Vessel	27.50	**48.00**
	Girl with Apple	92	G-Clef	27.50	**45.00**
		93	Butterfly	30.00	**42.00**

521329	HAVE I TOAD YOU LATELY THAT I LOVE YOU	Spring Catalog DSR Promo			
	Annual 1996	96	Ship	$30.00	**$45.00**
	Figurine, 5.75"		Heart		**40.00**
	ac# 391				
	Girl Holds a Toad				

521388	HEAVEN MUST HAVE SENT YOU				
	Ongoing	98	Sword	$60.00	**$60.00**
	Figurine, 4.25"	98	Eyeglasses	60.00	**60.00**
	ac# 420	99	Star	60.00	**60.00**
	Little Girl and Angel				

521396	FAITH IS A VICTORY				
	Retired 1993	90	Bow & Arrow	$25.00	**$160.00**
	Figurine, 5.50"	90	Flame	25.00	**150.00**
	ac# 267	91	Vessel	25.00	**145.00**
	Girl Wearing Boxing Gloves	92	G-Clef	25.00	**135.00**
		93	Butterfly	27.50	**130.00**

521418   <u>I'LL NEVER STOP LOVING YOU</u>

Retired 1996	90	Bow & Arrow	$37.50	**$90.00**
Figurine, 5.50"	90	Flame	37.50	**85.00**
ac# 483	91	Vessel	37.50	**82.00**
Girl with Letters Y O U	92	G-Clef	37.50	**80.00**
	93	Butterfly	37.50	**78.00**
	94	Trumpet	37.50	**75.00**
	95	Ship	37.50	**72.00**
	96	Heart	40.00	**70.00**

521434   <u>TO A VERY SPECIAL MOM AND DAD</u>

Suspended 1993	91	Vessel	$35.00	**$50.00**
Figurine, 5.75"	92	G-Clef	35.00	**45.00**
ac# 1005	93	Butterfly	35.00	**42.00**
Girl Holding Picture Frame				

521450   <u>LORD, HELP ME STICK TO MY JOB</u>

Retired 1997	90	Bow & Arrow	$30.00	**$68.00**
Figurine, 5.75"	90	Flame	30.00	**63.00**
ac# 583	91	Vessel	30.00	**62.00**
Girl with Account Books and	92	G-Clef	30.00	**61.00**
Glue	93	Butterfly	35.00	**60.00**
	94	Trumpet	35.00	**58.00**
	95	Ship	35.00	**57.00**
	96	Heart	35.00	**55.00**
	97	Sword	35.00	**54.00**

521477   <u>TELL IT TO JESUS</u>

Ongoing	89	Bow & Arrow	$35.00	**$57.00**
Figurine, 5.25"	90	Flame	37.50	**48.00**
ac# 915	91	Vessel	37.50	**45.00**
Girl on Telephone	92	G-Clef	37.50	**44.00**
	93	Butterfly	37.50	**42.00**
	94	Trumpet	37.50	**40.00**
	95	Ship	37.50	**40.00**
	96	Heart	40.00	**40.00**
	97	Sword	40.00	**40.00**
	98	Eyeglasses	40.00	**40.00**
	99	Star	40.00	**40.00**

521485   <u>THERE'S A LIGHT AT THE END OF THE TUNNEL</u>

Suspended 1996	91	Vessel	$55.00	**$85.00**
Figurine, 4.00"	92	G-Clef	55.00	**82.00**
ac# 976	93	Butterfly	55.00	**80.00**
Girl Peeking at Bunny thru	94	Trumpet	55.00	**78.00**
Log	95	Ship	55.00	**75.00**
	96	Heart	60.00	**73.00**

521493   <u>A SPECIAL DELIVERY</u>

Ongoing	91	Vessel	$30.00	**$38.00**
Figurine, 5.75"	92	G-Clef	30.00	**34.00**
ac# 20	93	Butterfly	30.00	**33.00**
Girl with Baby	94	Trumpet	30.00	**32.50**
	95	Ship	30.00	**32.50**
	96	Heart	32.50	**32.50**
	97	Sword	32.50	**32.50**
	98	Eyeglasses	32.50	**32.50**
	99	Star	32.50	**32.50**

521507 THE LIGHT OF THE WORLD IS JESUS Tune: White Christmas

Ongoing	89	Bow & Arrow	$60.00	**$85.00**
Musical, 7.00"	90	Flame	65.00	**75.00**
ac# 940	91	Vessel	65.00	**72.00**
Girl by Lamppost	92	G-Clef	65.00	**70.00**
	93	Butterfly	70.00	**70.00**
	94	Trumpet	70.00	**70.00**
	95	Ship	70.00	**70.00**
	96	Heart	70.00	**70.00**
	97	Sword	70.00	**70.00**
	98	Eyeglasses	70.00	**70.00**
	99	Star	70.00	**70.00**

521515 WATER-MELANCHOLY DAY WITHOUT YOU

Ongoing	98	Sword	$35.00	**$38.00**
Figurine, 4.50"	98	Eyeglasses	35.00	**35.00**
ac# 1036	99	Star	35.00	**35.00**
Boy and Bluebirds Share a				
Slice of Melon				

521558 OUR FIRST CHRISTMAS TOGETHER

Dated Annual 1989	89	Bow & Arrow	$17.50	**$37.00**
Ornament, 2.75"				
ac# 1084				
Bride and Groom in Car				

521566 GLIDE THROUGH THE HOLIDAYS

Retired 1992	90	Flame	$13.50	**$38.00**
Ornament, 3.50"	91	Vessel	13.50	**35.00**
ac# 384	92	G-Clef	13.50	**32.00**
Girl on Roller Skates				

521574 DASHING THROUGH THE SNOW

Suspended 1994	90	Flame	$15.00	**$35.00**
Ornament, 3.00"	91	Vessel	15.00	**33.00**
ac# 518	92	G-Clef	15.00	**32.00**
Girl Pushing Doll in Sleigh	93	Butterfly	15.00	**30.00**
	94	Trumpet	16.00	**29.00**

521590 DON'T LET THE HOLIDAYS GET YOU DOWN

Retired 1994	90	Flame	$15.00	**$42.00**
Ornament, 2.25"	91	Vessel	15.00	**38.00**
ac# 242	92	G-Clef	15.00	**36.00**
Boy with Christmas Tree	93	Butterfly	15.00	**35.00**
	94	Trumpet	16.00	**34.00**

521671 HOPE YOU'RE OVER THE HUMP Birthday Collection

Suspended 1996	93	Butterfly	$17.50	**$30.00**
Figurine, 3.00"	94	Trumpet	17.50	**28.00**
ac# 443	95	Ship	17.50	**25.00**
Monkey Riding on Camel's	96	Heart	18.50	**22.00**
Back				

521698 THUMB-BODY LOVES YOU

Suspended 1996	91	Flame	$55.00	**$90.00**
Figurine, 5.25"	91	Vessel	55.00	**80.00**
ac# 994	92	G-Clef	55.00	**78.00**
Girl Misses Nail, Hits Boy's	93	Butterfly	60.00	**75.00**
Thumb	94	Trumpet	60.00	**72.00**
	95	Ship	60.00	**70.00**
	96	Heart	60.00	**68.00**

521701 SHOOT FOR THE STARS AND YOU'LL NEVER STRIKE OUT   Boys & Girls

Clubs of America Commemorative

Ongoing	96	Heart	$60.00	**$65.00**
Figurine, 5.50"	97	Sword	60.00	**60.00**
ac# 862	98	Eyeglasses	60.00	**60.00**
Girl Baseball Player / Boy	99	Star	60.00	**60.00**
Basketball Player				

521728 MY LOVE BLOOMS FOR YOU

Ongoing	96	Ship	$50.00	**$55.00**
Figurine, 5.25"	96	Heart	50.00	**50.00**
ac# 706	97	Sword	50.00	**50.00**
Boy Gives Flower to Girl	98	Eyeglasses	50.00	**50.00**
	99	Star	50.00	**50.00**

521779 SWEEP ALL YOUR WORRIES AWAY

Retired 1996	90	Bow & Arrow	$40.00	**$130.00**
Figurine, 5.25"	90	Flame	40.00	**90.00**
ac# 903	91	Vessel	40.00	**85.00**
Girl Sweeping Dust under	92	G-Clef	40.00	**83.00**
Rug	93	Butterfly	40.00	**82.00**
	94	Trumpet	40.00	**80.00**
	95	Ship	40.00	**76.00**
	96	Heart	40.00	**74.00**

521817 GOOD FRIENDS ARE FOREVER   (Also see #525049)

Ongoing	90	Bow & Arrow	$50.00	**$70.00**
Figurine, 5.50"	90	Flame	50.00	**60.00**
ac# 354	91	Vessel	50.00	**58.00**
Girls with Flower	92	G-Clef	50.00	**55.00**
	93	Butterfly	50.00	**55.00**
	94	Trumpet	50.00	**55.00**
	95	Ship	55.00	**55.00**
	96	Heart	55.00	**55.00**
	97	Sword	55.00	**55.00**
	98	Eyeglasses	55.00	**55.00**
	99	Star	55.00	**55.00**

521825 MAY YOUR BIRTHDAY BE MAMMOTH   Series: "Birthday Circus Train"

Ongoing	92	G-Clef	$25.00	**$30.00**
Figurine, 4.12"	93	Butterfly	25.00	**26.00**
ac# 668	94	Trumpet	25.00	**25.00**
Whale Riding Wave	95	Ship	25.00	**25.00**
Wearing Sailor Hat (10)	96	Heart	25.00	**25.00**
	97	Sword	25.00	**25.00**
	98	Eyeglasses	25.00	**25.00**
	99	Star	25.00	**25.00**

521833 BEING NINE IS JUST DIVINE   Series: "Birthday Circus Train"

Ongoing	92	G-Clef	$25.00	**$30.00**
Figurine, 4.25"	93	Butterfly	25.00	**27.00**
ac# 128	94	Trumpet	25.00	**25.00**
Curly Maned Prancing Pony	95	Ship	25.00	**25.00**
(9)	96	Heart	25.00	**25.00**
	97	Sword	25.00	**25.00**
	98	Eyeglasses	25.00	**25.00**
	99	Star	25.00	**25.00**

521841 LOVE IS FROM ABOVE

Suspended 1996	90	Bow & Arrow	$45.00	**$80.00**
Figurine, 5.50"	90	Flame	45.00	**74.00**
ac# 605	91	Vessel	45.00	**72.00**
Boy Whispering to Girl	92	G-Clef	45.00	**70.00**
	93	Butterfly	45.00	**69.00**
	94	Trumpet	45.00	**68.00**
	95	Ship	45.00	**65.00**
	96	Heart	50.00	**60.00**

521868 THE GREATEST OF THESE IS LOVE

Suspended 1991
Figurine, 5.25"
ac# 936
Angel Holding Command-
ments

89	Bow & Arrow	$27.50	**$58.00**
90	Flame	30.00	**52.00**
91	Vessel	30.00	**50.00**

521884 PIZZA ON EARTH

Ongoing
Figurine, 4.25"
ac# 781
Boy Falls and Drops Pizza to
Pup's Delight

97	Sword	$55.00	**$55.00**
98	Eyeglasses	55.00	**55.00**
99	Star	55.00	**55.00**

521892 EASTER'S ON ITS WAY

Ongoing
Figurine, 5.25"
ac# 256
Boy Pulling Girl & Lily in
Wagon

90	Bow & Arrow	$60.00	**$80.00**
90	Flame	60.00	**68.00**
91	Vessel	60.00	**67.00**
92	G-Clef	60.00	**66.00**
93	Butterfly	60.00	**65.00**
94	Trumpet	65.00	**65.00**
95	Ship	65.00	**65.00**
96	Heart	65.00	**65.00**
97	Sword	65.00	**65.00**
98	Eyeglasses	65.00	**65.00**
99	Star	65.00	**65.00**

521906 HOPPY EASTER FRIEND

Ongoing
Figurine, 5.25"
ac# 446
Girl Collecting Eggs with
Frog's Help

91	Flame	$40.00	**$50.00**
91	Vessel	40.00	**45.00**
92	G-Clef	40.00	**42.00**
93	Butterfly	40.00	**40.00**
94	Trumpet	40.00	**40.00**
95	Ship	40.00	**40.00**
96	Heart	40.00	**40.00**
97	Sword	40.00	**40.00**
98	Eyeglasses	40.00	**40.00**
99	Star	40.00	**40.00**

521914 PERFECT HARMONY

Ongoing
Figurine, 6.50"
ac# 778
Boys & Puppies Caroling

94	Trumpet	$55.00	**$58.00**
95	Ship	55.00	**55.00**
96	Heart	55.00	**55.00**
97	Sword	55.00	**55.00**
98	Eyeglasses	55.00	**55.00**
99	Star	55.00	**55.00**

521922 SAFE IN THE ARMS OF JESUS   Child Evangelism Fellowship Piece

Ongoing
Figurine, 3.00"
ac# 813
Baby Asleep on Cloud
Watched by Angel Bird

93	G-Clef	$30.00	**$35.00**
93	Butterfly	30.00	**33.00**
94	Trumpet	30.00	**32.50**
95	Ship	30.00	**32.50**
96	Heart	32.50	**32.50**
97	Sword	32.50	**32.50**
98	Eyeglasses	32.50	**32.50**
99	Star	32.50	**32.50**

521949 WISHING YOU A COZY SEASON

Suspended 1993
Figurine, 5.25"
ac# 1070
Boy by Stump

89	Bow & Arrow	$42.50	**$68.00**
90	Flame	45.00	**66.00**
91	Vessel	45.00	**64.00**
92	G-Clef	45.00	**62.00**
93	Butterfly	45.00	**60.00**

521957   HIGH HOPES

Suspended 1993
Figurine, 5.25"
ac# 425
Boy with Kite

90	Bow & Arrow	$30.00	**$55.00**
90	Flame	30.00	**50.00**
91	Vessel	30.00	**45.00**
92	G-Clef	30.00	**42.00**
93	Butterfly	30.00	**40.00**

521965   TO A SPECIAL MUM

Ongoing
Figurine, 5.25"
ac# 1003
Boy Looking at Bee on
Flower Pot for Mom

91	Flame	$30.00	**$45.00**
91	Vessel	30.00	**40.00**
92	G-Clef	30.00	**35.00**
93	Butterfly	35.00	**35.00**
94	Trumpet	35.00	**35.00**
95	Ship	35.00	**35.00**
96	Heart	35.00	**35.00**
97	Sword	35.00	**35.00**
98	Eyeglasses	35.00	**35.00**
99	Star	35.00	**35.00**

521973   CAUGHT UP IN SWEET THOUGHTS OF YOU

Ongoing
Figurine, 5.75"
ac# 196
Boy Gets Tangled in Fishing
Line and Fish Lands on His
Head

99	Eyeglasses	$30.00	**$30.00**
99	Star	30.00	**30.00**

521981   MARCHING TO THE BEAT OF FREEDOM'S DRUM

Ongoing
Figurine, 5.50"
ac# 654
Marching Boy with Drum

96	Ship	$35.00	**$38.00**
96	Heart	35.00	**35.00**
97	Sword	35.00	**35.00**
98	Eyeglasses	35.00	**35.00**
99	Star	35.00	**35.00**

522015   TO THE APPLE OF GOD'S EYE

Ongoing
Figurine, 5.50"
ac# 1016
Boy Carrying Apple & Book

93	Butterfly	$32.50	**$35.00**
94	Trumpet	32.50	**35.00**
95	Ship	32.50	**35.00**
96	Heart	35.00	**35.00**
97	Sword	35.00	**35.00**
98	Eyeglasses	35.00	**35.00**
99	Star	35.00	**35.00**

522023   MAY YOUR LIFE BE BLESSED WITH TOUCHDOWNS

Retired 1998
Figurine, 4.25"
ac# 679
Boy Playing Football

89	Bow & Arrow	$45.00	**$60.00**
90	Flame	50.00	**52.00**
91	Vessel	50.00	**50.00**
92	G-Clef	50.00	**50.00**
93	Butterfly	50.00	**50.00**
94	Trumpet	50.00	**50.00**
95	Ship	50.00	**50.00**
96	Heart	50.00	**50.00**
97	Sword	50.00	**50.00**
98	Eyeglasses	50.00	**50.00**

522031   THANK YOU LORD FOR EVERYTHING

Suspended 1993
Figurine, 5.25"
ac# 921
Boy Having Dinner with
Turkey

89	Bow & Arrow	$60.00	**$95.00**
90	Flame	60.00	**90.00**
91	Vessel	60.00	**85.00**
92	G-Clef	60.00	**82.00**
93	Butterfly	60.00	**80.00**

522058 NOW I LAY ME DOWN TO SLEEP

Retired 1997		94	Trumpet	$30.00	**$52.00**
Figurine, 5.50"		95	Ship	30.00	**42.00**
ac# 726		96	Heart	30.00	**40.00**
Boy Carries Candle & Book to Bed		97	Sword	30.00	**38.00**

522082 MAY YOUR WORLD BE TRIMMED WITH JOY

Suspended 1996		91	Vessel	$55.00	**$85.00**
Figurine, 5.50"		92	G-Clef	55.00	**80.00**
ac# 680		93	Butterfly	55.00	**78.00**
Boy Decorating Globe		94	Trumpet	55.00	**73.00**
		95	Ship	55.00	**72.00**
		96	Heart	55.00	**70.00**

522090 THERE SHALL BE SHOWERS OF BLESSINGS

Ongoing		90	Bow & Arrow	$60.00	**$80.00**
Figurine, 5.50"		90	Flame	60.00	**75.00**
ac# 974		91	Vessel	60.00	**72.00**
Boy and Girl in Garden		92	G-Clef	60.00	**70.00**
		93	Butterfly	65.00	**70.00**
		94	Trumpet	70.00	**70.00**
		95	Ship	70.00	**70.00**
		96	Heart	70.00	**70.00**
		97	Sword	70.00	**70.00**
		98	Eyeglasses	70.00	**70.00**
		99	Star	70.00	**70.00**

522104 IT'S NO YOLK WHEN I SAY I LOVE YOU

Suspended 1994		92	Vessel	$60.00	**$95.00**
Figurine, 5.25"		92	G-Clef	60.00	**90.00**
ac# 511		93	Butterfly	60.00	**85.00**
Hens Laugh 'Cause Girl Drop'd Egg on Puppy's Head		94	Trumpet	65.00	**80.00**

522112 DON'T LET THE HOLIDAYS GET YOU DOWN

Retired 1993		89	Bow & Arrow	$42.50	**$100.00**
Figurine, 4.25"		90	Flame	45.00	**95.00**
ac# 242		91	Vessel	45.00	**90.00**
Boy with Christmas Tree		92	G-Clef	45.00	**88.00**
		93	Butterfly	45.00	**85.00**

522120 WISHING YOU A VERY SUCCESSFUL SEASON

Ongoing		89	Bow & Arrow	$60.00	**$80.00**
Figurine, 6.00"		90	Flame	65.00	**75.00**
ac# 1079		91	Vessel	65.00	**72.00**
Boy with Box, Puppy and		92	G-Clef	65.00	**70.00**
Bat		93	Butterfly	70.00	**70.00**
		94	Trumpet	70.00	**70.00**
		95	Ship	70.00	**70.00**
		96	Heart	70.00	**70.00**
		97	Sword	70.00	**70.00**
		98	Eyeglasses	70.00	**70.00**
		99	Star	70.00	**70.00**

522201 BON VOYAGE!

Suspended 1996		89	Bow & Arrow	$75.00	**$145.00**
Figurine, 6.50"		90	Flame	80.00	**140.00**
ac# 168		91	Vessel	80.00	**135.00**
Boy & Girl on Motorcycle		92	G-Clef	80.00	**130.00**
		93	Butterfly	90.00	**125.00**
		94	Trumpet	90.00	**120.00**
		95	Ship	90.00	**115.00**
		96	Heart	90.00	**110.00**

522244	DO NOT OPEN TILL CHRISTMAS	Tune: Toyland			
	Suspended 1994	92	G-Clef	$75.00	**$105.00**
	Musical, 6.50"	93	Butterfly	75.00	**95.00**
	ac# 240	94	Trumpet	75.00	**90.00**
	Boy Peeking into Opened				
	Christmas Present				
	Color variations on package–pink or green. No price variation.				

522252	HE IS THE STAR OF THE MORNING				
	Suspended 1993	89	Bow & Arrow	$55.00	**$88.00**
	Figurine, 6.00"	90	Flame	60.00	**85.00**
	ac# 402	91	Vessel	60.00	**80.00**
	Angel on Cloud with Manger	92	G-Clef	60.00	**78.00**
		93	Butterfly	60.00	**75.00**

522260	TO BE WITH YOU IS UPLIFTING	Birthday Collection			
	Retired 1994	89	Bow & Arrow	$20.00	**$55.00**
	Figurine, 4.25"	90	Flame	22.50	**50.00**
	ac# 1008	91	Vessel	22.50	**48.00**
	Giraffe with Baby Bear	92	G-Clef	22.50	**45.00**
		93	Butterfly	22.50	**42.00**
		94	Trumpet	22.50	**40.00**

522279	A REFLECTION OF HIS LOVE				
	Ongoing	91	Vessel	$50.00	**$60.00**
	Figurine, 5.50"	92	G-Clef	50.00	**55.00**
	ac# 16	93	Butterfly	50.00	**50.00**
	Girl & Bird at Bird Bath	94	Trumpet	50.00	**50.00**
		95	Ship	50.00	**50.00**
	Title originally announced as	96	Heart	50.00	**50.00**
	"God Has Sent You My	97	Sword	50.00	**50.00**
	Way."	98	Eyeglasses	50.00	**50.00**
		99	Star	50.00	**50.00**

522287	THINKING OF YOU IS WHAT I REALLY LIKE TO DO				
	Suspended 1996	90	Bow & Arrow	$30.00	**$62.00**
	Figurine, 4.50"	90	Flame	30.00	**57.00**
	ac# 981	91	Vessel	30.00	**56.00**
	Kneeling Girl with Bouquet	92	G-Clef	30.00	**55.00**
		93	Butterfly	30.00	**54.00**
		94	Trumpet	30.00	**53.00**
		95	Ship	30.00	**52.00**
		96	Heart	32.50	**50.00**

522317	MERRY CHRISTMAS, DEER				
	Retired 1997	89	Bow & Arrow	$50.00	**$95.00**
	Figurine, 5.50"	90	Flame	55.00	**88.00**
	ac# 685	91	Vessel	55.00	**85.00**
	Girl Decorating Reindeer	92	G-Clef	55.00	**80.00**
		93	Butterfly	60.00	**78.00**
		94	Trumpet	60.00	**76.00**
		95	Ship	60.00	**74.00**
		96	Heart	60.00	**72.00**
		97	Sword	60.00	**70.00**

522325	SOMEBODY CARES	Easter Seal Commemorative / Lily Understamp			
	Annual 1998	98	Sword	$40.00	**$40.00**
	Figurine, 5.50"				
	ac# 882				
	Monkey Comforts Clown				
	after Balloon Pops				

522333 SWEETER AS THE YEARS GO BY
Retired 1998
Figurine, 5.50"
ac# 905
Gentleman Sniffs Pie Held
by Lady

96	Heart	$60.00	**$70.00**
97	Sword	60.00	**60.00**
98	Eyeglasses	60.00	**60.00**

522376 HIS LOVE WILL SHINE ON YOU   Easter Seal Commemorative / Lily
Understamp
Annual 1989
Figurine, 5.75"
ac# 430
Girl Holding Easter Lily

89	Flower	$30.00	**$55.00**
	Bow & Arrow		**50.00**

522546 OH HOLY NIGHT
Dated Annual 1989
Figurine, 4.75"
ac# 733
Girl Playing Violin

89	Bow & Arrow	$25.00	**$45.00**

522554 OH HOLY NIGHT
Dated Annual 1989
Thimble, 2.25"
ac# 733
Girl Playing Violin

89	Bow & Arrow	$7.50	**$25.00**

522821 OH HOLY NIGHT
Dated Annual 1989
Bell, 5.50"
ac# 733
Girl Playing Violin

89	Bow & Arrow	$25.00	**$35.00**

522848 OH HOLY NIGHT
Dated Annual 1989
Ornament, 3.25"
ac# 733
Girl Playing Violin

89	Bow & Arrow	$13.50	**$30.00**

522856 HAVE A BEARY MERRY CHRISTMAS   Series: "Family Christmas Scene"
Suspended 1992
Figurine, 3.75"
ac# 386
Teddy in Rocker

89	Bow & Arrow	$15.00	**$45.00**
90	Flame	16.50	**40.00**
91	Vessel	16.50	**37.00**
92	G-Clef	16.50	**35.00**

522864 JUST A LINE TO SAY YOU'RE SPECIAL
Ongoing
Figurine, 5.00"
ac# 549
Napping Fisherman Enjoys
Retirement

95	Butterfly	$45.00	**$59.00**
95	Trumpet	45.00	**52.00**
95	Ship	45.00	**50.00**
96	Heart	50.00	**50.00**
97	Sword	50.00	**50.00**
98	Eyeglasses	50.00	**50.00**
99	Star	50.00	**50.00**

522872 ON MY WAY TO A PERFECT DAY
Ongoing
Figurine, 4.75"
ac# 739
Girl in Car

97	Heart	$45.00	**$48.00**
97	Sword	45.00	**45.00**
98	Eyeglasses	45.00	**45.00**
99	Star	45.00	**45.00**

522910	MAKE A JOYFUL NOISE				
	Suspended 1996	89	Bow & Arrow	$15.00	**$40.00**
	Ornament, 3.25"	90	Flame	15.00	**37.00**
	ac# 644	91	Vessel	15.00	**35.00**
	Girl with Goose	92	G-Clef	15.00	**33.00**
		93	Butterfly	15.00	**32.00**
		94	Trumpet	16.00	**30.00**
		95	Ship	17.00	**28.00**
		96	Heart	18.50	**25.00**
522929	LOVE ONE ANOTHER				
	Ongoing	89	Bow & Arrow	$17.50	**$25.00**
	Ornament, 3.50"	90	Flame	17.50	**22.00**
	ac# 625	91	Vessel	17.50	**20.00**
	Boy & Girl Sitting on Stump	92	G-Clef	17.50	**20.00**
		93	Butterfly	17.50	**20.00**
		94	Trumpet	17.50	**20.00**
		95	Ship	18.50	**20.00**
		96	Heart	20.00	**20.00**
		97	Sword	20.00	**20.00**
		98	Eyeglasses	20.00	**20.00**
		99	Star	20.00	**20.00**
522937	FRIENDS NEVER DRIFT APART				
	Retired 1995	90	Flame	$17.50	**$40.00**
	Ornament, 2.50"	91	Vessel	17.50	**38.00**
	ac# 292	92	G-Clef	17.50	**35.00**
	Kids in Boat	93	Butterfly	17.50	**34.00**
		94	Trumpet	17.50	**32.00**
		95	Ship	18.50	**30.00**
522945	OUR FIRST CHRISTMAS TOGETHER				
	Dated Annual 1991	91	Vessel	$17.50	**$25.00**
	Ornament, 3.00"				
	ac# 418				
	Groom Popping out of Trunk				
	/ Bride				
522953	I BELIEVE IN THE OLD RUGGED CROSS				
	Suspended 1994	89	Bow & Arrow	$15.00	**$40.00**
	Ornament, 3.50"	90	Flame	15.00	**37.00**
	ac# 458	91	Vessel	15.00	**36.00**
	Girl Holding Cross	92	G-Clef	15.00	**35.00**
		93	Butterfly	15.00	**33.00**
		94	Trumpet	16.00	**32.00**
522988	ISN'T HE PRECIOUS Mini Nativity Addition				
	Suspended 1993	89	Bow & Arrow	$15.00	**$36.00**
	Figurine, 3.75"	90	Flame	16.50	**32.00**
	ac# 503	91	Vessel	16.50	**30.00**
	Girl with Broom	92	G-Clef	16.50	**28.00**
		93	Butterfly	16.50	**27.00**
522996	SOME BUNNIES SLEEPING Mini Nativity Addition				
	Suspended 1993	90	Flame	$12.00	**$40.00**
	Figurine, 1.75"	91	Vessel	12.00	**38.00**
	ac# 880	92	G-Clef	12.00	**35.00**
	Bunnies	93	Butterfly	12.00	**30.00**
523003	MAY YOUR CHRISTMAS BE A HAPPY HOME Series: "Christmas Love"–4th Issue				
	Dated Annual 1989	89	Bow & Arrow	$50.00	**$50.00**
	Plate, 8.50"				
	ac# 670				
	Family Christmas Scene				

523011 THERE'S A CHRISTIAN WELCOME HERE   Chapel Exclusive

Suspended 1995	89	Unmarked	$45.00	**$95.00**
Figurine, 4.00"	91	Vessel	45.00	**68.00**
ac# 975	92	G-Clef	45.00	**63.00**
Angel outside Chapel	94	Trumpet	45.00	**59.00**
	95	Ship	45.00	**48.00**

Unmarked pieces of this figurine exist with and without an eyebrow on the angel boy (bangs cover where the second eyebrow would be). The GBTru$ for the "Without Eyebrow" piece is $120.00.

523038 HE IS MY INSPIRATION   Chapel Exclusive

Ongoing	91	Unmarked	$60.00	**$85.00**
Figurine, 5.00"	97	Sword	60.00	**60.00**
ac# 398				
Sam Butcher as Artist				
Painting / Animals				

523062 PEACE ON EARTH   Series: "Masterpiece Ornament"–1st Issue

Dated Annual 1989	89	Bow & Arrow	$25.00	**$68.00**
Ornament, 4.25"				
ac# 773				
Kids with Pup, Kitten and Bird				

523097 JESUS IS THE SWEETEST NAME I KNOW   Nativity Addition

Suspended 1993	89	Bow & Arrow	$22.50	**$48.00**
Figurine, 4.75"	90	Flame	25.00	**45.00**
ac# 530	91	Vessel	25.00	**42.00**
Angel with Baby Name Book	92	G-Clef	25.00	**40.00**
	93	Butterfly	25.00	**38.00**

523178 JOY ON ARRIVAL

Ongoing	91	Vessel	$50.00	**$60.00**
Figurine, 5.50"	92	G-Clef	50.00	**55.00**
ac# 537	93	Butterfly	50.00	**55.00**
Stork Delivering Baby to	94	Trumpet	50.00	**55.00**
Mother	95	Ship	50.00	**55.00**
	96	Heart	55.00	**55.00**
	97	Sword	55.00	**55.00**
	98	Eyeglasses	55.00	**55.00**
	99	Star	55.00	**55.00**

523194 BABY'S FIRST CHRISTMAS

Dated Annual 1989	89	Bow & Arrow	$15.00	**$30.00**
Ornament, 2.50"				
ac# 97				
Boy in Sleigh				

523208 BABY'S FIRST CHRISTMAS

Dated Annual 1989	89	Bow & Arrow	$15.00	**$32.00**
Ornament, 2.50"				
ac# 98				
Girl in Sleigh				

523224 HAPPY TRAILS IS TRUSTING JESUS

Suspended 1994	91	Vessel	$15.00	**$35.00**
Ornament, 3.25"	92	G-Clef	15.00	**30.00**
ac# 444	93	Butterfly	15.00	**28.00**
Girl on Hobby Horse	94	Trumpet	16.00	**25.00**

353

523283 YOU HAVE TOUCHED SO MANY HEARTS   Easter Seal / Lily Understamp /
Individually Numbered
Limited Edition 2,000   90   Bow & Arrow $500.00   **$620.00**
    Figurine, 9.00"
    ac# 1130
    Girl with String of Hearts

523291 BLESSED ARE THE MERCIFUL   Series: "Beatitude"–5th Issue   Chapel
Exclusive / Chapel Window Collection
Annual 1994   94   Trumpet $55.00   **$55.00**
    Wall Hanging, 6.50"
    ac# 156
    Lady Gives Donation to
    Handicapped Child

523305 HE LEADS ME BESIDE THE STILL WATERS   Chapel Exclusive / 23rd Psalm
Collection   Individually Numbered
Limited Edition 7,500   97   Sword $55.00   **$55.00**
    Figurine, 6.25"
    ac# 404
    Shepherd and Lamb Take
    Rest in Meadow

    2nd of 7 23rd Psalm Figurines.

523313 BLESSED ARE THE MEEK   Series: "Beatitude"–3rd Issue   Chapel Exclusive /
Chapel Window Collection
Annual 1993   93   Butterfly $55.00   **$55.00**
    Wall Hanging, 6.50"
    ac# 155
    Native American with Fawn

523321 BLESSED ARE THE ONES WHO HUNGER   Series: "Beatitude"–4th
Issue   Chapel Exclusive / Chapel Window Collection
Annual 1993   93   Butterfly $55.00   **$55.00**
    Wall Hanging, 6.50"
    ac# 158
    Girl Praying

523348 BLESSED ARE THE PEACEMAKERS   Series: "Beatitude"–7th & Final
Issue   Chapel Exclusive / Chapel Window Collection
Annual 1995   95   Trumpet $55.00   **$150.00**
    Wall Hanging, 6.50"   Ship   55.00   **55.00**
    ac# 161
    Girl Holds Dove in Hands

523356 YEA, THOUGH I WALK THROUGH THE VALLEY OF THE SHADOW OF
DEATH...   Chapel Exclusive / 23rd Psalm Collection   Individually Numbered
Limited Edition 7,500   98   Unmarked $55.00   **$55.00**
    Figurine, 6.25"
    ac# 1090
    Shepherd Carries Lamb
    through Narrow Rock
    Canyon

    4th of 7 23rd Psalm Figurines.

523364 HE RESTORETH MY SOUL...   Chapel Exclusive / 23rd Psalm
Collection   Individually Numbered
Limited Edition 7,500   98   Unmarked $55.00   **$55.00**
    Figurine, 6.25"
    ac# 407
    Shepherd Carries Lamb
    Along Pathway

    3rd of 7 23rd Psalm Figurines.

523372 THOU PREPAREST A TABLE BEFORE ME... Chapel Exclusive / 23rd Psalm
Collection   Individually Numbered
Limited Edition 7,500   98   Unmarked $55.00   **$55.00**
Figurine, 6.25"
ac# 993
Shepherd Prays at Table /
Lamb Stands at Side

5th of 7 23rd Psalm Figurines.

523380 BLESSED ARE THE ONES WHO MOURN   Series: "Beatitude"–2nd
Issue   Chapel Exclusive / Chapel Window Collection
Annual 1992   92   G-Clef $55.00   **$55.00**
Wall Hanging, 6.50"
ac# 159
Girl Crying over Spilled Milk
/ Kitten

523399 BLESSED ARE THE PURE IN HEART   Series: "Beatitude"–6th Issue   Chapel
Exclusive / Chapel Window Collection
Annual 1994   94   Trumpet $55.00   **$120.00**
Wall Hanging, 6.50"
ac# 163
Girl with Butterfly

523402 THE LORD IS MY SHEPHERD, I SHALL NOT WANT   Chapel Exclusive /
23rd Psalm Collection   Individually Numbered
Limited Edition 7,500   97   Sword $55.00   **$60.00**
Figurine, 6.25"
ac# 951
Shepherd with Lamb

1st of 7 23rd Psalm Figurines.

523410 SURELY GOODNESS AND MERCY SHALL FOLLOW ME...   Chapel
Exclusive / 23rd Psalm Collection   Individually Numbered
Limited Edition 7,500   98   Unmarked $55.00   **$55.00**
Figurine, 6.25"
ac# 900
Shepherd Plays Harp / Lamb
Nearby / Angel Sounds
Trumpet

7th of 7 23rd Psalm Figurines.

523429 THOU ANNOINTEST MY HEAD WITH OIL...   Chapel Exclusive / 23rd
Psalm Collection   Individually Numbered
Limited Edition 7,500   98   Eyeglasses $55.00   **$55.00**
Figurine, 6.25"
ac# 991
Shepherd Puts Oil on Lamb's
Head

6th of 7 23rd Psalm Figurines.

523437 BLESSED ARE THE HUMBLE   Series: "Beatitude"–1st Issue   Chapel
Exclusive / Chapel Window Collection
Annual 1992   92   G-Clef $55.00   **$65.00**
Wall Hanging, 6.50"
ac# 154
Princess Washing Servant's
Feet

523453 · THE GOOD LORD ALWAYS DELIVERS

Ongoing	90	Bow & Arrow	$27.50	**$40.00**
Figurine, 5.50"	90	Flame	27.50	**35.00**
ac# 932	91	Vessel	27.50	**30.00**
Mother-to-Be with Baby	92	G-Clef	27.50	**30.00**
Book	93	Butterfly	30.00	**30.00**
	94	Trumpet	30.00	**30.00**
	95	Ship	30.00	**30.00**
	96	Heart	30.00	**30.00**
	97	Sword	30.00	**30.00**
	98	Eyeglasses	30.00	**30.00**
	99	Star	30.00	**30.00**

523496 · THIS DAY HAS BEEN MADE IN HEAVEN

Ongoing	90	Bow & Arrow	$30.00	**$40.00**
Figurine, 5.50"	90	Flame	30.00	**35.00**
ac# 982	91	Vessel	30.00	**35.00**
Girl Holding Bible & Cross	92	G-Clef	30.00	**35.00**
	93	Butterfly	30.00	**35.00**
	94	Trumpet	30.00	**35.00**
	95	Ship	32.50	**35.00**
	96	Heart	35.00	**35.00**
	97	Sword	35.00	**35.00**
	98	Eyeglasses	35.00	**35.00**
	99	Star	35.00	**35.00**

523518 · GOD IS LOVE DEAR VALENTINE

Ongoing	90	Bow & Arrow	$27.50	**$38.00**
Figurine, 5.50"	90	Flame	27.50	**32.00**
ac# 335	91	Vessel	27.50	**30.00**
Girl Hiding Valentine	92	G-Clef	27.50	**30.00**
Behind her Back	93	Butterfly	30.00	**30.00**
	94	Trumpet	30.00	**30.00**
	95	Ship	30.00	**30.00**
	96	Heart	30.00	**30.00**
	97	Sword	30.00	**30.00**
	98	Eyeglasses	30.00	**30.00**
	99	Star	30.00	**30.00**

523526 · I'M A PRECIOUS MOMENTS FAN

Annual 1990	Special Event			
Figurine, 5.50"	90	Bow & Arrow	$30.00	**$48.00**
ac# 487		Flame		**45.00**
Girl with Fan				

523534 · I WILL CHERISH THE OLD RUGGED CROSS

Dated Annual 1991	91	Flame	$27.50	**$40.00**
Egg, 4.75"		Vessel		**39.00**
ac# 458				
Girl Holding Cross				

523542 · YOU ARE THE TYPE I LOVE

Ongoing	92	Vessel	$40.00	**$50.00**
Figurine, 5.40"	92	G-Clef	40.00	**46.00**
ac# 1115	93	Butterfly	40.00	**45.00**
Girl Typing Message on	94	Trumpet	40.00	**45.00**
Typewriter	95	Ship	40.00	**45.00**
	96	Heart	45.00	**45.00**
	97	Sword	45.00	**45.00**
	98	Eyeglasses	45.00	**45.00**
	99	Star	45.00	**45.00**

523550 HE IS OUR SHELTER FROM THE STORM   Boys & Girls Clubs Of America
Commemorative
Ongoing

	98	Sword	$75.00	**$78.00**
Figurine, 6.50"	98	Eyeglasses	75.00	**75.00**
ac# 401	99	Star	75.00	**75.00**

Girl & Boy Share Umbrella
w/Boys and Girls Club Logo

523593 THE LORD WILL PROVIDE
Annual 1993

	93	G-Clef	$40.00	**$68.00**
Figurine, 6.50"		Butterfly		**55.00**

ac# 958
Girl Carrying Seeds for
Flowers and Birds

523615 GOOD NEWS IS SO UPLIFTING
Ongoing

	91	Vessel	$60.00	**$75.00**
Figurine, 6.50"	92	G-Clef	60.00	**70.00**
ac# 356	93	Butterfly	60.00	**70.00**
Girl on Ladder by Mailboxes	94	Trumpet	65.00	**70.00**
	95	Ship	65.00	**70.00**
	96	Heart	70.00	**70.00**
	97	Sword	70.00	**70.00**
	98	Eyeglasses	70.00	**70.00**
	99	Star	70.00	**70.00**

523623 I'M SO GLAD THAT GOD BLESSED ME WITH A FRIEND LIKE YOU
Retired 1995

	93	G-Clef	$50.00	**$115.00**
Figurine, 5.50"	93	Butterfly	50.00	**93.00**
ac# 496	94	Trumpet	50.00	**85.00**
Girl Holding Kitten While	95	Ship	55.00	**80.00**
Friend Offers Milk				

523631 I WILL ALWAYS BE THINKING OF YOU
Retired 1996

	94	Butterfly	$45.00	**$80.00**
Figurine, 5.50"	94	Trumpet	45.00	**74.00**
ac# 476	95	Ship	45.00	**70.00**
Girl Stands by Gate & Holds	96	Heart	45.00	**65.00**
Flower				

523682 THIS DAY HAS BEEN MADE IN HEAVEN   Tune: Amazing Grace
Ongoing

	92	Vessel	$60.00	**$78.00**
Musical, 6.60"	92	G-Clef	60.00	**65.00**
ac# 982	93	Butterfly	60.00	**65.00**
Girl Holding Bible & Cross	94	Trumpet	60.00	**65.00**
	95	Ship	60.00	**65.00**
	96	Heart	65.00	**65.00**
	97	Sword	65.00	**65.00**
	98	Eyeglasses	65.00	**65.00**
	99	Star	65.00	**65.00**

523704 MAY YOUR CHRISTMAS BE A HAPPY HOME   Series: "Masterpiece
Ornament"–2nd Issue
Dated Annual 1990

Ornament, 4.50"	90	Flame	$27.50	**$30.00**
ac# 670				

Family Christmas Scene

Variation: GBTru for sitting boy with yellow (usual color is blue) shirt is
$50.00.

523739	TIME HEALS				
	Ongoing	90	Flame	$37.50	**$45.00**
	Figurine, 5.50"	91	Vessel	37.50	**40.00**
	ac# 997	92	G-Clef	37.50	**40.00**
	Nurse at Desk with Clock	93	Butterfly	37.50	**40.00**
		94	Trumpet	37.50	**40.00**
		95	Ship	37.50	**40.00**
		96	Heart	40.00	**40.00**
		97	Sword	40.00	**40.00**
		98	Eyeglasses	40.00	**40.00**
		99	Star	40.00	**40.00**
523747	BLESSINGS FROM ABOVE				
	Retired 1994	90	Flame	$45.00	**$110.00**
	Figurine, 6.50"	91	Vessel	45.00	**100.00**
	ac# 166	92	G-Clef	45.00	**95.00**
	Boy and Girl Kissing under	93	Butterfly	50.00	**93.00**
	Mistletoe	94	Trumpet	50.00	**90.00**
523755	JUST POPPIN' IN TO SAY HALO!				
	Ongoing	94	Trumpet	$45.00	**$50.00**
	Figurine, 6.25"	95	Ship	45.00	**45.00**
	ac# 551	96	Heart	45.00	**45.00**
	Girl Looking at Angel Jack-	97	Sword	45.00	**45.00**
	in-the-Box	98	Eyeglasses	45.00	**45.00**
		99	Star	45.00	**45.00**
523763	I CAN'T SPELL SUCCESS WITHOUT YOU				
	Suspended 1994	91	Flame	$40.00	**$150.00**
	Figurine, 5.00"	91	Vessel	40.00	**78.00**
	ac# 461	92	G-Clef	40.00	**75.00**
	Boy and Dog Using Blocks	93	Butterfly	40.00	**72.00**
	to Spell	94	Trumpet	45.00	**69.00**
523771	BABY'S FIRST CHRISTMAS				
	Dated Annual 1990	90	Flame	$15.00	**$25.00**
	Ornament, 2.75"				
	ac# 99				
	Baby Girl with Pie				
523798	BABY'S FIRST CHRISTMAS				
	Dated Annual 1990	90	Flame	$15.00	**$22.00**
	Ornament, 2.75"				
	ac# 100				
	Baby Boy with Pie				
523801	WISHING YOU A YUMMY CHRISTMAS	Series: "Christmas Blessings"–1st Issue			
	Dated Annual 1990	90	Flame	$50.00	**$65.00**
	Plate, 8.25"				
	ac# 1081				
	Boy and Girl at Ice Cream Stand				
523828	ONCE UPON A HOLY NIGHT				
	Dated Annual 1990	90	Flame	$25.00	**$38.00**
	Bell, 5.75"				
	ac# 741				
	Girl with Book and Candle				

523836 — ONCE UPON A HOLY NIGHT
Dated Annual 1990
Figurine, 5.50"
ac# 741
Girl with Book and Candle

90	Flame	$25.00	**$45.00**

523844 — ONCE UPON A HOLY NIGHT
Dated Annual 1990
Thimble, 1.50"
ac# 741
Girl with Book and Candle

90	Flame	$8.00	**$22.00**

523852 — ONCE UPON A HOLY NIGHT
Dated Annual 1990
Ornament, 3.25"
ac# 741
Girl with Book and Candle

90	Flame	$15.00	**$34.00**

523860 — BLESSINGS FROM ME TO THEE   Series: "Christmas Blessings"–2nd Issue
Dated Annual 1991
Plate, 8.50"
ac# 167
Girl at Birdhouse

1991

91	Vessel	$50.00	**$60.00**

523879 — WE ARE GOD'S WORKMANSHIP   Easter Seal / Lily Understamp / Individually Numbered
Limited Edition 2,000
Figurine, 9.00"
ac# 1039
Bonnet Girl with Butterfly

91	Flame	$500.00	**$700.00**

523941 — LOVE NEVER LEAVES A MOTHER'S ARMS
Ongoing
Figurine, 5.25"
ac# 624
Mother Rocks Baby

96	Ship	$40.00	**$43.00**
96	Heart	40.00	**40.00**
97	Sword	40.00	**40.00**
98	Eyeglasses	40.00	**40.00**
99	Star	40.00	**40.00**

524069 — BABY'S FIRST BIRTHDAY   Series: "Baby's First"–8th & Final Issue
Ongoing
Figurine, 3.50"
ac# 88
Baby Holding up One Finger
by Cake w/One Candle

93	G-Clef	$25.00	**$35.00**
93	Butterfly	25.00	**25.00**
94	Trumpet	25.00	**25.00**
95	Ship	25.00	**25.00**
96	Heart	25.00	**25.00**
97	Sword	25.00	**25.00**
98	Eyeglasses	25.00	**25.00**
99	Star	25.00	**25.00**

524077 — BABY'S FIRST MEAL   Series: "Baby's First"–6th Issue
Ongoing
Figurine, 5.25"
ac# 118
Baby in High Chair with
Cereal Bowl

91	Vessel	$35.00	**$45.00**
92	G-Clef	35.00	**40.00**
93	Butterfly	35.00	**40.00**
94	Trumpet	37.50	**40.00**
95	Ship	37.50	**40.00**
96	Heart	40.00	**40.00**
97	Sword	40.00	**40.00**
98	Eyeglasses	40.00	**40.00**
99	Star	40.00	**40.00**

524085	MY WARMEST THOUGHTS ARE YOU				
	Retired 1996	92	Vessel	$55.00	**$110.00**
	Figurine, 5.75"	92	G-Clef	55.00	**105.00**
	ac# 714	93	Butterfly	55.00	**102.00**
	Little Bird Watching Girl on	94	Trumpet	60.00	**100.00**
	Tree Swing	95	Ship	60.00	**98.00**
		96	Heart	60.00	**95.00**

524123	GOOD FRIENDS ARE FOR ALWAYS				
	Ongoing	91	Vessel	$27.50	**$40.00**
	Figurine, 5.50"	92	G-Clef	27.50	**35.00**
	ac# 353	93	Butterfly	30.00	**35.00**
	Girl in Snowsuit Holding	94	Trumpet	30.00	**35.00**
	Bunny	95	Ship	32.50	**35.00**
		96	Heart	35.00	**35.00**
		97	Sword	35.00	**35.00**
		98	Eyeglasses	35.00	**35.00**
		99	Star	35.00	**35.00**

524131	GOOD FRIENDS ARE FOR ALWAYS				
	Retired 1997	92	G-Clef	$15.00	**$35.00**
	Ornament, 3.50"	93	Butterfly	15.00	**30.00**
	ac# 353	94	Trumpet	16.00	**30.00**
	Girl in Snowsuit Holding	95	Ship	17.00	**30.00**
	Bunny	96	Heart	18.50	**30.00**
		97	Sword	18.50	**30.00**

524158	LORD, TEACH US TO PRAY	National Day Of Prayer			
	Annual 1994	94	Trumpet	$35.00	**$40.00**
	Figurine, 4.75"				
	ac# 597				
	Girl Kneels				

524166	MAY YOUR CHRISTMAS BE MERRY				
	Dated Annual 1991	91	Vessel	$27.50	**$35.00**
	Figurine, 5.25"				
	ac# 675				
	Girl Holding Bird				

524174	MAY YOUR CHRISTMAS BE MERRY				
	Dated Annual 1991	91	Vessel	$15.00	**$35.00**
	Ornament, 3.50"				
	ac# 675				
	Girl Holding Bird				

524182	MAY YOUR CHRISTMAS BE MERRY				
	Dated Annual 1991	91	Vessel	$25.00	**$38.00**
	Bell, 5.75"				
	ac# 675				
	Girl Holding Bird				

524190	MAY YOUR CHRISTMAS BE MERRY				
	Dated Annual 1991	91	Vessel	$8.00	**$22.00**
	Thimble, 2.25"				
	ac# 675				
	Girl Holding Bird				

524204 LOVE IS COLOR BLIND   Boys & Girls Clubs Of America Commemorative

Ongoing	99	Eyeglasses	$60.00	**$60.00**
Figurine, 6.00"	99	Star	60.00	**60.00**
ac# 604				
Boy and Girl Share a Scooter Ride				

524212 WALK IN THE SONSHINE

Ongoing	95	Ship	$35.00	**$37.00**
Figurine, 5.00"	96	Heart	35.00	**35.00**
ac# 1033	97	Sword	35.00	**35.00**
Walking Girl Looks to	98	Eyeglasses	35.00	**35.00**
Heaven w/Kitten at Side	99	Star	35.00	**35.00**

524263 HE LOVES ME

Annual 1991	91	Flame	$35.00	**$50.00**
Figurine, 6.25"		Vessel		**45.00**
ac# 405				
Girl Holding Flower				

524271 FRIENDSHIP GROWS WHEN YOU PLANT A SEED

Retired 1994	92	Vessel	$40.00	**$115.00**
Figurine, 4.10"	92	G-Clef	40.00	**85.00**
ac# 296	93	Butterfly	40.00	**80.00**
Girl in Sunbonnet Watering a Seedling	94	Trumpet	40.00	**75.00**

524298 MAY YOUR EVERY WISH COME TRUE

Ongoing	93	G-Clef	$50.00	**$65.00**
Figurine, 5.50"	93	Butterfly	50.00	**55.00**
ac# 677	94	Trumpet	50.00	**50.00**
Girl Blowing Cake w/	95	Ship	50.00	**50.00**
Candles to Edge of Table	96	Heart	50.00	**50.00**
	97	Sword	50.00	**50.00**
	98	Eyeglasses	50.00	**50.00**
	99	Star	50.00	**50.00**

524301 MAY YOUR BIRTHDAY BE A BLESSING

Ongoing	91	Flame	$30.00	**$55.00**
Figurine, 5.75"	91	Vessel	30.00	**40.00**
ac# 666	92	G-Clef	30.00	**35.00**
Girl with Cake and Candles	93	Butterfly	30.00	**35.00**
	94	Trumpet	30.00	**35.00**
	95	Ship	32.50	**35.00**
	96	Heart	35.00	**35.00**
	97	Sword	35.00	**35.00**
	98	Eyeglasses	35.00	**35.00**
	99	Star	35.00	**35.00**

524336 OUR FRIENDSHIP IS SODA-LICIOUS

Ongoing	93	G-Clef	$65.00	**$78.00**
Figurine, 6.00"	93	Butterfly	65.00	**72.00**
ac# 760	94	Trumpet	65.00	**70.00**
Girl & Boy Sharing an Ice	95	Ship	65.00	**70.00**
Cream Soda	96	Heart	70.00	**70.00**
	97	Sword	70.00	**70.00**
	98	Eyeglasses	70.00	**70.00**
	99	Star	70.00	**70.00**

524352 WHAT THE WORLD NEEDS NOW

Retired 1997
Figurine, 5.75"
ac# 1058
Girl Gazing at Globe Praying
for Peace & Love

92	Vessel	$50.00	**$75.00**
92	G-Clef	50.00	**73.00**
93	Butterfly	50.00	**72.00**
94	Trumpet	50.00	**70.00**
95	Ship	50.00	**68.00**
96	Heart	50.00	**67.00**
97	Sword	50.00	**65.00**

524360 SOMETHING PRECIOUS FROM ABOVE

Ongoing
Figurine, 6.00"
ac# 885
Girl Looks into Baby
Carriage

97	Heart	$50.00	**$53.00**
97	Sword	50.00	**50.00**
98	Eyeglasses	50.00	**50.00**
99	Star	50.00	**50.00**

524379 SO GLAD I PICKED YOU AS A FRIEND

Annual 1994
Figurine
ac# 879
Girl Standing by Flowerpot

94	Butterfly	$40.00	**$50.00**
	Trumpet		**45.00**

524387 TAKE TIME TO SMELL THE FLOWERS   Easter Seal Commemorative / Lily

Understamp
Annual 1995
Figurine, 6.00"
ac# 909
Girl Holds Basket of Flowers

95	Trumpet	$30.00	**$42.00**
	Ship		**38.00**

524395 YOU ARE SUCH A PURR-FECT FRIEND

Ongoing
Figurine, 6.00"
ac# 1111
Girl Holding Kitten in Her
Arms

93	G-Clef	$35.00	**$45.00**
93	Butterfly	35.00	**40.00**
94	Trumpet	35.00	**35.00**
95	Ship	35.00	**35.00**
96	Heart	35.00	**35.00**
97	Sword	35.00	**35.00**
98	Eyeglasses	35.00	**35.00**
99	Star	35.00	**35.00**

524425 MAY ONLY GOOD THINGS COME YOUR WAY

Ongoing
Figurine, 5.50"
ac# 661
Girl Holding Net for
Butterfly

91	Flame	$30.00	**$70.00**
91	Vessel	30.00	**45.00**
92	G-Clef	30.00	**38.00**
93	Butterfly	35.00	**38.00**
94	Trumpet	35.00	**37.50**
95	Ship	37.50	**37.50**
96	Heart	37.50	**37.50**
97	Sword	37.50	**37.50**
98	Eyeglasses	37.50	**37.50**
99	Star	37.50	**37.50**

524441 SEALED WITH A KISS

Retired 1996
Figurine, 5.50"
ac# 826
Bride & Groom Kissing over
Mailbox

93	G-Clef	$50.00	**$98.00**
93	Butterfly	50.00	**95.00**
94	Trumpet	50.00	**93.00**
95	Ship	55.00	**92.00**
96	Heart	60.00	**90.00**

524468 A SPECIAL CHIME FOR JESUS

Retired 1997
Figurine, 5.50"
ac# 19
Boy in PJ's with Toy Duck

93	Butterfly	$32.50	**$45.00**
94	Trumpet	32.50	**40.00**
95	Ship	32.50	**40.00**
96	Heart	32.50	**38.00**
97	Sword	32.50	**35.00**

524476   GOD CARED ENOUGH TO SEND HIS BEST

Retired 1996
Figurine, 7.00"
ac# 330
Girl Hangs Ornament on Tree

94	Trumpet	$50.00	**$90.00**
95	Ship	55.00	**85.00**
96	Heart	55.00	**82.00**

524484   NOT A CREATURE WAS STIRRING   Birthday Collection   Set of 2

Suspended 1994
Figurine, 2.75"
ac# 722
Mouse on Cheese and Kitten

90	Flame	$17.00	**$40.00**
91	Vessel	17.00	**37.00**
92	G-Clef	17.00	**35.00**
93	Butterfly	17.00	**33.00**
94	Trumpet	17.00	**32.00**

524492   CAN'T BE WITHOUT YOU   Birthday Collection

Ongoing
Figurine, 2.50"
ac# 188
Bird on Cage Door and Cat

91	Vessel	$16.00	**$22.00**
92	G-Clef	16.00	**18.00**
93	Butterfly	16.00	**18.00**
94	Trumpet	16.00	**17.50**
95	Ship	16.00	**17.50**
96	Heart	17.50	**17.50**
97	Sword	17.50	**17.50**
98	Eyeglasses	17.50	**17.50**
99	Star	17.50	**17.50**

524506   OINKY BIRTHDAY   Birthday Collection

Ongoing
Figurine, 2.50"
ac# 738
Pig Holds Wrapped Present

94	Butterfly	$13.50	**$18.00**
94	Trumpet	13.50	**15.00**
95	Ship	13.50	**15.00**
96	Heart	15.00	**15.00**
97	Sword	15.00	**15.00**
98	Eyeglasses	15.00	**15.00**
99	Star	15.00	**15.00**

524522   ALWAYS IN HIS CARE   Easter Seal Commemorative / Lily Understamp

Annual 1990
Figurine, 5.00"
ac# 48
Girl Looking at Chick in Egg

90	Bow & Arrow	$30.00	**$45.00**
	Flame		**40.00**

524875   HAPPY BIRTHDAY DEAR JESUS   Nativity Addition

Suspended 1993
Figurine, 2.25"
ac# 375
Teddy Bear in Package

90	Flame	$13.50	**$35.00**
91	Vessel	13.50	**32.00**
92	G-Clef	13.50	**30.00**
93	Butterfly	13.50	**28.00**

524883   CHRISTMAS FIREPLACE   Series: "Family Christmas Scene"

Suspended 1992
Figurine, 4.50"
ac# 201
Fireplace with Stockings

90	Flame	$37.50	**$62.00**
91	Vessel	37.50	**57.00**
92	G-Clef	37.50	**55.00**

524905   IT'S SO UPLIFTING TO HAVE A FRIEND LIKE YOU

Ongoing
Figurine, 6.00"
ac# 513
Girl on Skis Startled by Ski Jump

92	G-Clef	$40.00	**$50.00**
93	Butterfly	40.00	**48.00**
94	Trumpet	40.00	**45.00**
95	Ship	45.00	**45.00**
96	Heart	45.00	**45.00**
97	Sword	45.00	**45.00**
98	Eyeglasses	45.00	**45.00**
99	Star	45.00	**45.00**

524913	WE'RE GOING TO MISS YOU				
	Ongoing	90	Flame	$50.00	**$70.00**
	Figurine, 5.50"	91	Vessel	50.00	**55.00**
	ac# 1047	92	G-Clef	50.00	**55.00**
	Girl and Melting Snowman	93	Butterfly	50.00	**55.00**
		94	Trumpet	50.00	**55.00**
		95	Ship	50.00	**55.00**
		96	Heart	55.00	**55.00**
		97	Sword	55.00	**55.00**
		98	Eyeglasses	55.00	**55.00**
		99	Star	55.00	**55.00**

524921	ANGELS WE HAVE HEARD ON HIGH				
	Retired 1996				
	Figurine, 7.25"	91	Vessel	$60.00	**$92.00**
	ac# 61	92	G-Clef	60.00	**88.00**
	Two Angels on Stool Afraid	93	Butterfly	65.00	**85.00**
	of Mouse	94	Trumpet	65.00	**82.00**
		95	Ship	65.00	**80.00**
		96	Heart	70.00	**78.00**

525049	GOOD FRIENDS ARE FOREVER	Special Event / Rosebud Decal Understamp			
	Annual 1990	90	Bow & Arrow $——		**$625.00**
	Figurine, 5.50"				
	ac# 354				
	Girls with Flower				

Only collectors who attended a 1990 "Good Friends Are Forever" Special Event with a friend had the opportunity to be included in a drawing for this special Rosebud Decal Understamp figurine. Identical to 521817 with exception of Rosebud decal. One per Center. See page 413.

525057	BUNDLES OF JOY				
	Annual 1990	90	Flame	$15.00	**$30.00**
	Ornament, 3.25"				
	ac# 180				
	Girl with Presents				

525278	TUBBY'S FIRST CHRISTMAS	Mini Nativity Addition			
	Ongoing	92	G-Clef	$10.00	**$15.00**
	Figurine, 1.75"	93	Butterfly	10.00	**12.00**
	ac# 1026	94	Trumpet	10.00	**10.00**
	Rooster Sitting on Pig's Back	95	Ship	10.00	**10.00**
		96	Heart	10.00	**10.00**
		97	Sword	10.00	**10.00**
		98	Eyeglasses	10.00	**10.00**
		99	Star	10.00	**10.00**

525286	IT'S A PERFECT BOY	Mini Nativity Addition			
	Ongoing	91	Vessel	$16.50	**$25.00**
	Figurine, 3.50"	92	G-Clef	16.50	**18.50**
	ac# 510	93	Butterfly	16.50	**18.50**
	Boy Angel with Red Cross	94	Trumpet	17.00	**18.50**
	Bag	95	Ship	17.00	**18.50**
		96	Heart	18.50	**18.50**
		97	Sword	18.50	**18.50**
		98	Eyeglasses	18.50	**18.50**
		99	Star	18.50	**18.50**

525316	MAY YOUR FUTURE BE BLESSED				
	Ongoing	93	G-Clef	$35.00	**$45.00**
	Figurine, 6.00"	93	Butterfly	35.00	**40.00**
	ac# 678	94	Trumpet	35.00	**40.00**
	Girl at Her First Communion	95	Ship	37.50	**40.00**
		96	Heart	40.00	**40.00**
		97	Sword	40.00	**40.00**
		98	Eyeglasses	40.00	**40.00**
		99	Star	40.00	**40.00**

525324 OUR FIRST CHRISTMAS TOGETHER
Dated Annual 1990 — 90 Flame $17.50 **$28.00**
Ornament, 2.50"
ac# 1084
Bride and Groom in Car

525332 LORD KEEP ME ON MY TOES
Ongoing

Yr	Mark	Price	
92	G-Clef	$15.00	**$22.00**
93	Butterfly	15.00	**18.50**
94	Trumpet	16.00	**18.50**
95	Ship	17.00	**18.50**
96	Heart	18.50	**18.50**
97	Sword	18.50	**18.50**
98	Eyeglasses	18.50	**18.50**
99	Star	18.50	**18.50**

Ornament, 3.75"
ac# 589
Ballerina on Pointe

525898 RING THOSE CHRISTMAS BELLS
Retired 1996

Yr	Mark	Price	
92	G-Clef	$95.00	**$170.00**
93	Butterfly	95.00	**168.00**
94	Trumpet	95.00	**165.00**
95	Ship	100.00	**163.00**
96	Heart	100.00	**160.00**

Figurine, 6.25"
ac# 809
Angel Ringing Bell, Angel Playing, Bunny Covering Ears

525928 LET'S PUT THE PIECES TOGETHER
Ongoing

Yr	Mark	Price	
98	Sword	$60.00	**$60.00**
98	Eyeglasses	60.00	**60.00**
99	Star	60.00	**60.00**

Figurine, 4.75"
ac# 571
Boy & Girl Put Heart Jig-saw Puzzle Together

525960 WE ARE GOD'S WORKMANSHIP
Dated Annual 1992 — 92 Vessel $27.50 **$28.00**, G-Clef **24.00**
Egg, 4.10"
ac# 1039
Bonnet Girl with Butterfly

525979 GOING HOME   Phillip Butcher Memorial Figurine
Ongoing

Yr	Mark	Price	
92	Vessel	$60.00	**$75.00**
92	G-Clef	60.00	**62.00**
93	Butterfly	60.00	**60.00**
94	Trumpet	60.00	**60.00**
95	Ship	60.00	**60.00**
96	Heart	60.00	**60.00**
97	Sword	60.00	**60.00**
98	Eyeglasses	60.00	**60.00**
99	Star	60.00	**60.00**

Figurine, 4.60"
ac# 352
Angel Stopping to Take God's Child to Heaven

526010 YOU ARE SUCH A PURR-FECT FRIEND   Easter Seal / Lily Understamp /
Individually Numbered
Limited Edition 2,000 — 92 Vessel $500.00 **$620.00**, G-Clef **600.00**
Figurine, 9.00"
ac# 1111
Girl Holding Kitten in Her Arms

All are signed by Artist Sam Butcher, Enesco President Eugene Freedman, and Sculptor Fujioka-San. Benefits Easter Seal Society.

526037	A PRINCE OF A GUY	Catalog Early Release / Special Understamp			
	Ongoing	95	Ship	$35.00	**$40.00**
	Figurine, 4.50"	96	Heart	35.00	**35.00**
	ac# 15	97	Sword	35.00	**35.00**
	Boy w/Gold Crown Jeweled	98	Eyeglasses	35.00	**35.00**
	Sceptor	99	Star	35.00	**35.00**
	Special Understamp Denotes Early Release.				

526053	PRETTY AS A PRINCESS	Catalog Early Release			
	Ongoing	95	Ship	$35.00	**$40.00**
	Figurine, 5.00"	96	Heart	35.00	**35.00**
	ac# 794	97	Sword	35.00	**35.00**
	Girl w/Gold Crown Jeweled	98	Eyeglasses	35.00	**35.00**
	Ring	99	Star	35.00	**35.00**
	Released without Special Understamp.				

526061	THE PEARL OF GREAT PRICE	Century Circle Event			
	Annual 1997	97	Sword	$50.00	**$60.00**
	Figurine, 4.50"				
	ac# 961				
	Mermaid Sits in Shell / Holds				
	Oystershell w/Pearl				

526142	I WOULD BE LOST WITHOUT YOU				
	Ongoing	92	Vessel	$27.50	**$35.00**
	Figurine, 5.75"	92	G-Clef	27.50	**30.00**
	ac# 477	93	Butterfly	30.00	**30.00**
	Girl Checking Roadmap	94	Trumpet	30.00	**30.00**
		95	Ship	30.00	**30.00**
		96	Heart	30.00	**30.00**
		97	Sword	30.00	**30.00**
		98	Eyeglasses	30.00	**30.00**
		99	Star	30.00	**30.00**

526150	FRIENDS TO THE VERY END				
	Retired 1997	94	Butterfly	$40.00	**$70.00**
	Figurine, 4.50"	94	Trumpet	40.00	**68.00**
	ac# 295	95	Ship	40.00	**65.00**
	Duck Upset at Boy Plucking	96	Heart	45.00	**62.00**
	Tail Feathers	97	Sword	45.00	**60.00**

526185	YOU ARE MY HAPPINESS				
	Annual 1992	92	Vessel	$37.50	**$70.00**
	Figurine, 6.75"		G-Clef		**62.00**
	ac# 1107				
	Bluebird Sitting on Bouquet				
	of Roses Held by Girl				

526193	YOU SUIT ME TO A TEE				
	Ongoing	94	Trumpet	$35.00	**$36.00**
	Figurine, 5.50"	95	Ship	35.00	**35.00**
	ac# 1139	96	Heart	35.00	**35.00**
	Girl Chooses Club for a	97	Sword	35.00	**35.00**
	Round of Golf	98	Eyeglasses	35.00	**35.00**
		99	Star	35.00	**35.00**

526487	SHARING SWEET MOMENTS TOGETHER				
	Ongoing	94	Butterfly	$45.00	**$50.00**
	Figurine, 4.00"	94	Trumpet	45.00	**45.00**
	ac# 853	95	Ship	45.00	**45.00**
	Boy Eats Candy as Dog Licks	96	Heart	45.00	**45.00**
	His Face	97	Sword	45.00	**45.00**
		98	Eyeglasses	45.00	**45.00**
		99	Star	45.00	**45.00**

526568 — BLESS THOSE WHO SERVE THEIR COUNTRY–NAVY

Suspended 1992
Figurine, 5.50"
ac# 149
Boy in Sailor Suit & Hat w/ Duffel Bag

91	Unmarked	$32.50	**$165.00**
91	91 Flag	32.50	**150.00**
92	92 Flag	32.50	**125.00**

526576 — BLESS THOSE WHO SERVE THEIR COUNTRY–ARMY

Suspended 1992
Figurine, 5.50"
ac# 146
Boy in Dress Uniform w/ Duffel

91	91 Flag	$32.50	**$40.00**
92	92 Flag	32.50	**40.00**

526584 — BLESS THOSE WHO SERVE THEIR COUNTRY–AIR FORCE

Suspended 1992
Figurine, 5.50"
ac# 145
Boy in Dress Uniform

91	91 Flag	$32.50	**$60.00**
92	92 Flag	32.50	**60.00**

526827 — YOU CAN ALWAYS COUNT ON ME   Easter Seal Commemorative / Lily

Understamp
Annual 1996
Figurine, 4.25"
ac# 1117
Girl Puts Coin in Piggy Bank

96	Ship	$30.00	**$35.00**
	Heart		**32.00**

526835 — THE LORD IS WITH YOU

Ongoing
Figurine, 5.50"
ac# 954
Praying Angel

96	Ship	$27.50	**$30.00**
96	Heart	27.50	**27.50**
97	Sword	27.50	**27.50**
98	Eyeglasses	27.50	**27.50**
99	Star	27.50	**27.50**

526886 — HE'S GOT THE WHOLE WORLD IN HIS HANDS   Easter Seal / Lily

Understamp / Individually Numbered
Limited Edition 2,000
Figurine, 9.00"
ac# 412
Boy Angel Holds Globe

95	Trumpet	$500.00	**$575.00**
	Ship		**550.00**

526916 — WISHING YOU WERE HERE   Tune: When You Wish Upon A Star

Ongoing
Musical, 7.00"
ac# 1086
Girl Dropping Coin into Wishing Well

93	G-Clef	$100.00	**$135.00**
93	Butterfly	100.00	**105.00**
94	Trumpet	100.00	**100.00**
95	Ship	100.00	**100.00**
96	Heart	100.00	**100.00**
97	Sword	100.00	**100.00**
98	Eyeglasses	100.00	**100.00**
99	Star	100.00	**100.00**

526924 — HOW CAN I EVER FORGET YOU   Birthday Collection

Ongoing
Figurine, 3.00"
ac# 450
Elephant with Knot in Trunk

91	Vessel	$15.00	**$22.00**
92	G-Clef	15.00	**18.00**
93	Butterfly	15.00	**18.00**
94	Trumpet	16.00	**17.50**
95	Ship	17.00	**17.50**
96	Heart	17.50	**17.50**
97	Sword	17.50	**17.50**
98	Eyeglasses	17.50	**17.50**
99	Star	17.50	**17.50**

526940 | MAY YOUR CHRISTMAS BE MERRY   Series: "Masterpiece Ornament"–3rd
Issue

Dated Annual 1991	91	Vessel	$30.00	**$35.00**
Ornament, 4.25"				
ac# 675				
Girl Holding Bird				

526959 | WE HAVE COME FROM AFAR   Nativity Addition

Suspended 1994	91	Vessel	$17.50	**$30.00**
Figurine, 2.50"	92	G-Clef	17.50	**28.00**
ac# 1043	93	Butterfly	17.50	**25.00**
Penguins as 3 Kings	94	Trumpet	17.50	**20.00**

527084 | BABY'S FIRST CHRISTMAS

Dated Annual 1991	91	Vessel	$15.00	**$30.00**
Ornament, 2.50"				
ac# 101				
Boy with Drum				

527092 | BABY'S FIRST CHRISTMAS

Dated Annual 1991	91	Vessel	$15.00	**$30.00**
Ornament, 2.50"				
ac# 102				
Girl with Drum				

527106 | HE IS NOT HERE FOR HE IS RISEN AS HE SAID   Chapel Exclusive

Ongoing	93	Unmarked	$60.00	**$***
Figurine, 5.00"	94	Trumpet	60.00	**60.00**
ac# 400	95	Ship	60.00	**60.00**
Angel by Cave	96	Heart	60.00	**60.00**
	97	Sword	60.00	**60.00**

*Variation "Math" instead of "Matt." GBTru$ for piece with "Math"
error is $90.00. GBTru$ for piece with the correct "Matt" is $150.00.
(Note: The correct version in Unmarked is rarer than incorrect version.)

527114 | SHARING A GIFT OF LOVE   Easter Seal Commemorative / Lily Understamp

Annual 1991	91	Flame	$30.00	**$65.00**
Figurine, 5.75"		Vessel		**60.00**
ac# 846				
Girl Helping Bird to Fly				

527122 | YOU CAN ALWAYS BRING A FRIEND   Special Event

Annual 1991	91	Flame	$27.50	**$50.00**
Figurine, 5.75"		Vessel		**45.00**
ac# 1116				
Girl Holding Puppy				

527165 | THE GOOD LORD ALWAYS DELIVERS

Suspended 1993	91	Vessel	$15.00	**$32.00**
Ornament, 3.50"	92	G-Clef	15.00	**30.00**
ac# 932	93	Butterfly	15.00	**28.00**
Expectant Mother				

527173 — A UNIVERSAL LOVE   Easter Seal Commemorative / Lily Understamp

Annual 1992	92	Vessel	$32.50	**$105.00**
Figurine, 5.10"		G-Clef		**100.00**
ac# 24				
Seated Child Signing				
Message				

527211 — SHARE IN THE WARMTH OF CHRISTMAS

Ongoing	93	Butterfly	$15.00	**$22.00**
Ornament, 3.25"	94	Trumpet	16.00	**18.50**
ac# 239	95	Ship	17.00	**18.50**
Girl with Christmas Candle	96	Heart	18.50	**18.50**
	97	Sword	18.50	**18.50**
	98	Eyeglasses	18.50	**18.50**
	99	Star	18.50	**18.50**

527238 — BABY'S FIRST WORD   Series: "Baby's First"–7th Issue

Ongoing	92	G-Clef	$25.00	**$35.00**
Figurine, 4.50"	93	Butterfly	25.00	**26.00**
ac# 123	94	Trumpet	25.00	**25.00**
Baby/Footed Sleepers	95	Ship	25.00	**25.00**
Talking into a Microphone	96	Heart	25.00	**25.00**
	97	Sword	25.00	**25.00**
	98	Eyeglasses	25.00	**25.00**
	99	Star	25.00	**25.00**

527270 — LET'S BE FRIENDS   Birthday Collection

Retired 1996	92	Vessel	$15.00	**$35.00**
Figurine, 3.00"	92	G-Clef	15.00	**34.00**
ac# 568	93	Butterfly	15.00	**33.00**
Pup w/Bow & Pup w/Party	94	Trumpet	16.00	**32.00**
Hat Hugging Each Other	95	Ship	17.00	**31.00**
	96	Heart	17.50	**30.00**

527289 — BLESS THOSE WHO SERVE THEIR COUNTRY–GIRL SOLDIER

Suspended 1992	91	91 Flag	$32.50	**$48.00**
Figurine, 5.50"	92	92 Flag	32.50	**48.00**
ac# 147				
Girl Soldier in Dress				
Uniform				

527297 — BLESS THOSE WHO SERVE THEIR COUNTRY–AFRICAN-AMERICAN SOLDIER

Suspended 1992	91	91 Flag	$32.50	**$45.00**
Figurine, 5.50"	92	92 Flag	32.50	**45.00**
ac# 144				
African-American Soldier in				
Dress Uniform/Duffel				

527319 — AN EVENT WORTH WADING FOR   Special Event

Annual 1992	92	Vessel	$32.50	**$62.00**
Figurine, 5.12"		G-Clef		**58.00**
ac# 56				
Girl Wading to View Mother				
Duck w/Eggs				

527327 — ONWARD CHRISTMAS SOLDIERS

Ongoing	94	Trumpet	$16.00	**$20.00**
Ornament, 4.75"	95	Ship	16.00	**18.50**
ac# 746	96	Heart	18.50	**18.50**
Soldier Boy	97	Sword	18.50	**18.50**
	98	Eyeglasses	18.50	**18.50**
	99	Star	18.50	**18.50**

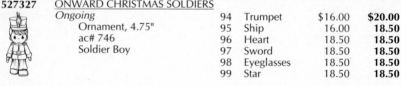

527335 BLESS-UM YOU
Retired 1998

	93	G-Clef	$35.00	**$40.00**
Figurine, 5.50"	93	Butterfly	35.00	**35.00**
ac# 153	94	Trumpet	35.00	**35.00**
Native American Girl	95	Ship	35.00	**35.00**
Raising Hand in Blessing	96	Heart	35.00	**35.00**
	97	Sword	35.00	**35.00**
	98	Eyeglasses	35.00	**35.00**

527343 HAPPY BIRDIE   Birthday Collection
Suspended 1996

	92	G-Clef	$16.00	**$30.00**
Figurine, 3.25"	93	Butterfly	16.00	**28.00**
ac# 374	94	Trumpet	16.00	**25.00**
Bird in Party Hat Blowing Lit	95	Ship	17.00	**22.00**
Candle on B/Day Cake	96	Heart	17.50	**20.00**

527378 YOU ARE MY FAVORITE STAR
Retired 1997

	92	G-Clef	$60.00	**$90.00**
Figurine, 5.50"	93	Butterfly	60.00	**85.00**
ac# 1105	94	Trumpet	60.00	**82.00**
Girl Placing Star on	95	Ship	60.00	**80.00**
Decorated Boy's Head	96	Heart	60.00	**78.00**
	97	Sword	60.00	**76.00**

527386 THIS LAND IS OUR LAND   500th Anniversary Voyage of Columbus
Commemorative
Member Only

Figurine, 9.50"	92	G-Clef	$350.00	**$375.00**
ac# 987				
Explorer & Animal Crew				
Sailing the High Seas in a				
Sail Boat				

527475 BABY'S FIRST CHRISTMAS (GIRL)
Dated Annual 1992

Ornament, 3.50"	92	G-Clef	$15.00	**$30.00**
ac# 113				
Girl Sitting on Upside-down				
Candy Cane				

527483 BABY'S FIRST CHRISTMAS (BOY)
Dated Annual 1992

Ornament, 3.50"	92	G-Clef	$15.00	**$29.00**
ac# 109				
Boy Sitting on Upside-down				
Candy Cane				

527521 BLESS THOSE WHO SERVE THEIR COUNTRY–MARINE
Suspended 1992

	91	91 Flag	$32.50	**$70.00**
Figurine, 5.50"	92	92 Flag	32.50	**70.00**
ac# 148				
Boy Marine in Full Dress				
Stands at Attention				

527556 BRING THE LITTLE ONES TO JESUS   Child Evangelism Fellowship
Ongoing

	92	Vessel	$90.00	**$115.00**
Figurine, 5.00"	92	G-Clef	90.00	**98.00**
ac# 174	93	Butterfly	90.00	**92.00**
Mother Reads Wordless	94	Trumpet	90.00	**90.00**
Book to Children	95	Ship	90.00	**90.00**
	96	Heart	90.00	**90.00**
	97	Sword	90.00	**90.00**
	98	Eyeglasses	90.00	**90.00**
	99	Star	90.00	**90.00**

527564 GOD BLESS THE USA

	Annual 1992	92	Vessel	$32.50	**$42.00**
	Figurine, 4.75"		G-Clef		**38.00**
	ac# 317				
	Uncle Sam Kneeling in Prayer				

National Day Of Prayer Figurine. Original 9" piece accepted by President Bush May 2, 1991 during National Day Of Prayer ceremonies.

527580 TIED UP FOR THE HOLIDAYS

	Suspended 1996	93	Butterfly	$40.00	**$60.00**
	Figurine, 6.00"	94	Trumpet	40.00	**55.00**
	ac# 995	95	Ship	40.00	**52.00**
	Dog Pulling Ribbon Tangling Girl with Gift	96	Heart	45.00	**50.00**

527599 BRINGING YOU A MERRY CHRISTMAS

	Retired 1995	93	Butterfly	$45.00	**$85.00**
	Figurine, 4.50"	94	Trumpet	45.00	**80.00**
	ac# 177	95	Ship	45.00	**75.00**
	Boy on Sled Watching Turtle with Gift				

527629 WISHING YOU A HO HO HO

	Ongoing	92	G-Clef	$40.00	**$50.00**
	Figurine, 5.75"	93	Butterfly	40.00	**45.00**
	ac# 1073	94	Trumpet	40.00	**45.00**
	Boy in Santa Suit Looking at	95	Ship	40.00	**45.00**
	Pup Holding Santa Whiskers	96	Heart	45.00	**45.00**
		97	Sword	45.00	**45.00**
		98	Eyeglasses	45.00	**45.00**
		99	Star	45.00	**45.00**

527661 YOU HAVE TOUCHED SO MANY HEARTS   Distinguished Service Retailers (DSRs) Exclusive

	Suspended 1996	91	Vessel	$35.00	**$37.50**
	Figurine, 5.50"	92	G-Clef	35.00	**37.50**
	ac# 1130	93	Butterfly	35.00	**37.50**
	Girl with String of Hearts	94	Trumpet	35.00	**37.50**
		95	Ship	37.50	**37.50**
		96	Heart	37.50	**37.50**

"Especially For You" version w/letter transfer kit so collectors may personalize figurine.

527688 BUT THE GREATEST OF THESE IS LOVE

	Dated Annual 1992	92	G-Clef	$27.50	**$35.00**
	Figurine, 5.50"				
	ac# 185				
	Girl Holding Her List to Santa Claus				

527696 BUT THE GREATEST OF THESE IS LOVE

	Dated Annual 1992	92	G-Clef	$15.00	**$45.00**
	Ornament, 4.00"				
	ac# 185				
	Girl Holding Her List to Santa Claus				

527718 BUT THE GREATEST OF THESE IS LOVE

	Dated Annual 1992	92	G-Clef	$8.00	**$20.00**
	Thimble, 2.50"				
	ac# 185				
	Girl Holding Her List to Santa Claus				

527726	BUT THE GREATEST OF THESE IS LOVE				
	Dated Annual 1992	92	G-Clef	$25.00	**$30.00**
	Bell, 6.50"				
	ac# 185				
	Girl Holding Her List to				
	Santa Claus				

527734	BUT THE GREATEST OF THESE IS LOVE Series: "Masterpiece Ornament"– 4th Issue				
	Dated Annual 1992	92	G-Clef	$30.00	**$40.00**
	Ornament, 4.00"				
	ac# 185				
	Girl Holding Her List to				
	Santa Claus				

527742	BUT THE GREATEST OF THESE IS LOVE Series: "Christmas Blessings"–3rd Issue				
	Dated Annual 1992	92	G-Clef	$50.00	**$50.00**
	Plate, 8.50"				
	ac# 185				
	Girl Holding Her List to				
	Santa Claus				

527750	WISHING YOU A COMFY CHRISTMAS Nativity Addition				
	Ongoing	92	G-Clef	$27.50	**$35.00**
	Figurine, 5.50"	93	Butterfly	27.50	**30.00**
	ac# 1068	94	Trumpet	27.50	**30.00**
	Angel Holding Favorite	95	Ship	30.00	**30.00**
	Patched Blanket	96	Heart	30.00	**30.00**
		97	Sword	30.00	**30.00**
		98	Eyeglasses	30.00	**30.00**
		99	Star	30.00	**30.00**

527769	I ONLY HAVE ARMS FOR YOU Birthday Collection				
	Retired 1998	93	G-Clef	$15.00	**$25.00**
	Figurine, 3.00"	93	Butterfly	15.00	**18.00**
	ac# 469	94	Trumpet	16.00	**17.50**
	Octopus and Fish Hugging	95	Ship	17.00	**17.50**
		96	Heart	17.50	**17.50**
		97	Sword	17.50	**17.50**
		98	Eyeglasses	17.50	**17.50**

527777	THIS LAND IS OUR LAND				
	Annual 1992	92	G-Clef	$35.00	**$40.00**
	Figurine, 4.88"				
	ac# 988				
	Explorer on One Knee				
	Holding Flag & Teddy				

528021	THERE'S A CHRISTIAN WELCOME HERE Chapel Exclusive				
	Ongoing	92	Unmarked	$22.50	**$35.00**
	Ornament, 2.00"	93	Butterfly	22.50	**22.50**
	ac# 975	96	Heart	22.50	**22.50**
	Angel outside Chapel	97	Sword	22.50	**22.50**

528064	FREE CHRISTMAS PUPPIES Sugar Town				
	Retired 1997	94	Trumpet	$12.50	**$16.00**
	Figurine, 2.50"	95	Ship	12.50	**12.50**
	ac# 289	96	Heart	12.50	**12.50**
	Pups in a Basket	97	Sword	12.50	**12.50**

528072 — NATIVITY CART   Nativity Addition

Ongoing
Figurine, 4.75"
ac# 717
Chicken in Farm Wagon w/
Gift- wrapped Egg

Year	Mark		
94	Trumpet	$18.50	**$20.00**
95	Ship	18.50	**18.50**
96	Heart	18.50	**18.50**
97	Sword	18.50	**18.50**
98	Eyeglasses	18.50	**18.50**
99	Star	18.50	**18.50**

528080 — FOLLOW YOUR HEART   Spring Celebration Event

Annual 1995
Figurine, 5.25"
ac# 281
Girl with Sign

95	Trumpet	$30.00	**$55.00**
	Ship		**45.00**

528099 — MARKIE   Sammy's Circus

Suspended 1996
Figurine, 4.75"
ac# 655
Girl Acrobat on Balance
Beam

94	Butterfly	$18.50	**$20.00**
94	Trumpet	18.50	**18.50**

528137 — HAVE I GOT NEWS FOR YOU   Mini Nativity Addition

Ongoing
Figurine, 4.25"
ac# 390
Boy Reading Scroll

94	Trumpet	$16.00	**$20.00**
95	Ship	17.00	**18.50**
96	Heart	18.50	**18.50**
97	Sword	18.50	**18.50**
98	Eyeglasses	18.50	**18.50**
99	Star	18.50	**18.50**

528196 — CIRCUS TENT   Sammy's Circus   Lighted

Suspended 1996
Night Light, 6.50"
ac# 208
Monkey Holds Balloons at
Tent Entrance

94	Butterfly	$90.00	**$100.00**
94	Trumpet	90.00	**90.00**

528218 — SENDING YOU A WHITE CHRISTMAS

Ongoing
Ornament, 4.50"
ac# 834
Girl Angel w/Basket of
Snowflakes

94	Trumpet	$16.00	**$20.00**
95	Ship	16.00	**18.50**
96	Heart	18.50	**18.50**
97	Sword	18.50	**18.50**
98	Eyeglasses	18.50	**18.50**
99	Star	18.50	**18.50**

528226 — BRINGING YOU A MERRY CHRISTMAS

Ongoing
Ornament, 4.50"
ac# 178
Boy Dressed as Santa w/Bag
of Toys

94	Trumpet	$16.00	**$20.00**
95	Ship	16.00	**18.50**
96	Heart	18.50	**18.50**
97	Sword	18.50	**18.50**
98	Eyeglasses	18.50	**18.50**
99	Star	18.50	**18.50**

528609 — SENDING MY LOVE YOUR WAY   Spring Catalog DSR Promo

Annual 1995
Figurine, 6.50"
ac# 832
Girl with Kite

95	Trumpet	$40.00	**$62.00**
	Ship		**60.00**

528617 — MAKE A JOYFUL NOISE

Dated Annual 1993
Egg, 4.75"
ac# 644
Girl with Goose

93	G-Clef	$27.50	**$35.00**
	Butterfly		**28.00**

528633 TO A VERY SPECIAL SISTER

Ongoing	94	Trumpet	$60.00	**$65.00**
Figurine, 4.75"	95	Ship	60.00	**60.00**
ac# 1007	96	Heart	60.00	**60.00**
Girls Receive Kittens from	97	Sword	60.00	**60.00**
Each Other	98	Eyeglasses	60.00	**60.00**
	99	Star	60.00	**60.00**

528668 SAMMY   Sugar Town

Retired 1997	93	Butterfly	$17.00	**$20.00**
Figurine, 3.00"	94	Trumpet	17.00	**17.00**
ac# 820	95	Ship	17.00	**17.00**
Boy Throwing Snowballs	96	Heart	17.00	**17.00**
	97	Sword	17.00	**17.00**

528684 EVERGREEN TREE   Sugar Town

Retired 1994	92	G-Clef	$15.00	**$35.00**
Figurine, 4.25"	93	Butterfly	15.00	**30.00**
ac# 265	94	Trumpet	15.00	**27.00**
Decorated Christmas Tree				

528846 IT'S SO UPLIFTING TO HAVE A FRIEND LIKE YOU

Ongoing	93	Butterfly	$16.00	**$22.00**
Ornament, 3.25"	94	Trumpet	16.00	**18.50**
ac# 513	95	Ship	17.00	**18.50**
Girl on Skis Startled by Ski	96	Heart	18.50	**18.50**
Jump	97	Sword	18.50	**18.50**
	98	Eyeglasses	18.50	**18.50**
	99	Star	18.50	**18.50**

528862 AMERICA, YOU'RE BEAUTIFUL   National Day Of Prayer

Annual 1993	93	G-Clef	$35.00	**$55.00**
Figurine, 5.50"		Butterfly		**45.00**
ac# 52				
Girl, as Statue of Liberty,				
Celebrates America				

528870 OUR FIRST CHRISTMAS TOGETHER

Dated Annual 1992	92	G-Clef	$17.50	**$30.00**
Ornament, 3.00"				
ac# 418				
Groom Popping out of Trunk / Bride				

529079 FRIENDS NEVER DRIFT APART   Cruise Piece

Dated Annual 1993	93	Butterfly	$Gift	**$675.00**
Medallion, 3.50"				
ac# 293				
Boy & Girl in Rowboat				

529087 15 YEARS, TWEET MUSIC TOGETHER   Cruise Piece

Dated Annual 1993	93	Butterfly	$Gift	**$65.00**
Medallion, 3.50"				
ac# 4				
Angel with Songbook				

*Medallion was also available at the Orlando FL show at a SRP of $10.00.

529095 | A REFLECTION OF HIS LOVE | Series: "Annual Eggs"–4th & Final Issue
| | *Dated Annual 1994* | 94 | Butterfly | $27.50 | **$32.00**
| | Egg, 4.25" | | Trumpet | | **28.00**
| | ac# 16 | | | |
| | Girl & Bird at Bird Bath | | | |

529168 | JORDAN Sammy's Circus Set of 2
| | *Suspended 1996* | 95 | Ship | $20.00 | **$23.00**
	Figurine, 3.00"			
	ac# 535			
	Lion Tamer w/Kitten Lion			

529176 | DUSTY Sammy's Circus
| | *Suspended 1996* | 94 | Butterfly | $22.50 | **$24.00**
| | Figurine, 3.50" | 94 | Trumpet | 22.50 | **23.00**
	ac# 254			
	Clown Prepares to Shoot			
	Teddy from Cannon			

529184 | KATIE Sammy's Circus
| | *Suspended 1996* | 94 | Butterfly | $17.00 | **$22.00**
| | Figurine, 3.50" | 94 | Trumpet | 17.00 | **18.00**
| | ac# 553 | | | |
| | Girl Clown Juggles Hearts | | | |

529192 | TIPPY Sammy's Circus
| | *Suspended 1996* | 94 | Butterfly | $12.00 | **$15.00**
| | Figurine, 3.00" | 94 | Trumpet | 12.00 | **12.00**
	ac# 1000			
	Pup Balances Ball & Mouse			
	with His Paws			

529206 | OUR FIRST CHRISTMAS TOGETHER
| | *Dated Annual 1994* | 94 | Trumpet | $18.50 | **$28.00**
	Ornament, 4.00"			
	ac# 754			
	Boy & Girl Sweethearts on			
	Reindeer			

529214 | COLLIN Sammy's Circus
| | *Suspended 1996* | 94 | Butterfly | $20.00 | **$25.00**
| | Figurine, 4.00" | 94 | Trumpet | 20.00 | **20.00**
| | ac# 218 | | | |
| | Boy Ringmaster with Drum | | | |

529222 | SAMMY Sammy's Circus
| | *Dated Annual 1994* | 94 | Butterfly | $20.00 | **$45.00**
| | Figurine, 3.00" | | Trumpet | | **30.00**
	ac# 821			
	Sam Hangs Circus Ad on			
	Fence			

529273 | MY TRUE LOVE GAVE TO ME
| | *Ongoing* | 96 | Heart | $40.00 | **$40.00**
| | Figurine, 4.50" | 97 | Sword | 40.00 | **40.00**
| | ac# 711 | 98 | Eyeglasses | 40.00 | **40.00**
| | Girl w/Partridge in a Pear | 99 | Star | 40.00 | **40.00**
| | Tree Gift | | | |

529435 DUSTY Sugar Town

Retired 1997
Figurine, 3.25"
ac# 253
Boy Carrying Christmas
Decorations

93	Butterfly	$17.00	**$30.00**
94	Trumpet	17.00	**20.00**
95	Ship	17.00	**20.00**
96	Heart	17.00	**17.00**
97	Sword	17.00	**17.00**

529443 SAM'S CAR Sugar Town

Retired 1997
Figurine, 3.50"
ac# 818
Car w/Tree on top/Pup Peeks
out Window

93	Butterfly	$22.50	**$25.00**
94	Trumpet	22.50	**22.50**
95	Ship	22.50	**22.50**
96	Heart	22.50	**22.50**
97	Sword	22.50	**22.50**

529486 AUNT RUTH & AUNT DOROTHY Sugar Town

Retired 1994
Figurine, 3.00"
ac# 78
Two Girls Singing Carols
from Songbook

92	G-Clef	$20.00	**$43.00**
93	Butterfly	20.00	**38.00**
94	Trumpet	20.00	**35.00**

529494 PHILIP Sugar Town

Retired 1994
Figurine, 3.00"
ac# 779
Boy Caroller w/Hat, Earmuffs
& Scarf

92	G-Clef	$17.00	**$30.00**
93	Butterfly	17.00	**28.00**
94	Trumpet	17.00	**26.00**

529508 NATIVITY Sugar Town

Retired 1994
Figurine, 2.00"
ac# 716
Crech with Holy Family

92	G-Clef	$20.00	**$55.00**
93	Butterfly	20.00	**48.00**
94	Trumpet	20.00	**46.00**

529516 GRANDFATHER Sugar Town

Retired 1994
Figurine, 2.50"
ac# 357
Preacher Kneels and Prays

92	G-Clef	$15.00	**$36.00**
93	Butterfly	15.00	**33.00**
94	Trumpet	15.00	**31.00**

529524 KATY LYNNE Sugar Town

Retired 1997
Figurine, 3.50"
ac# 555
Girl with Snowman

93	Butterfly	$20.00	**$25.00**
94	Trumpet	20.00	**22.00**
95	Ship	20.00	**20.00**
96	Heart	20.00	**20.00**
97	Sword	20.00	**20.00**

529540 PARK BENCH Sugar Town

Retired 1997
Figurine, 2.25"
ac# 766
Dog and Cat Sit on Bench

95	Ship	$13.00	**$17.00**
96	Heart	13.00	**13.00**
97	Sword	13.00	**13.00**

529559 LAMP POST Sugar Town

Retired 1997
Figurine, 5.25"
ac# 558
Lamp Post Decorated with
Bow

94	Trumpet	$8.00	**$10.00**
95	Ship	8.00	**8.00**
96	Heart	8.00	**8.00**
97	Sword	8.00	**8.00**

529567   <u>SAM BUTCHER</u>   Sugar Town

Dated Annual 1992   92   G-Clef $22.50   **$165.00**
     Figurine, 3.25"
     ac# 816
     Young Sam Painting Village
     Welcome Sign

Sign reads: "Established 1992. Population 5 and Growing."

529605   <u>HOUSE NIGHT LIGHT</u>   Sugar Town   Lighted

Retired 1997	93	Butterfly	$80.00	**$97.00**
Night Light, 5.00"	94	Trumpet	80.00	**85.00**
ac# 448	95	Ship	80.00	**85.00**
Celebrating Christmas at	96	Heart	85.00	**85.00**
Home	97	Sword	85.00	**85.00**

529621   <u>CHAPEL NIGHT LIGHT</u>   Sugar Town   Lighted

Retired 1994	92	G-Clef	$85.00	**$160.00**
Night Light, 8.00"	93	Butterfly	85.00	**150.00**
ac# 197	94	Trumpet	85.00	**140.00**
The Chapel Represents Sam				
Butcher's Faith & Commit-				
ment				

529648   <u>THE MAGIC STARTS WITH YOU</u>   Open House Event

Annual 1992   92   G-Clef $16.00   **$25.00**
     Ornament, 3.00"
     ac# 959
     Bunny Popping out of Top
     Hat/Girl in Magician's Cape

529680   <u>GATHER YOUR DREAMS</u>   Easter Seal / Lily Understamp / Individually
Numbered

Limited Edition 2,000	93	G-Clef	$500.00	**$600.00**
Figurine, 7.75"		Butterfly		**585.00**
ac# 301				
Girl Holding Bunnies in				
Apron				

529788   <u>STORK WITH BABY SAM</u>   Sugar Town

Annual 1994   94   Trumpet $22.50   **$48.00**
     Figurine, 4.50"
     ac# 892
     Stork Holds Sam & Birth
     Announcement / Town Sign

Sign reads: "It's a Boy. Population 13 + 1 and Growing."

529796   <u>FENCE</u>   Sugar Town

Retired 1997	93	Butterfly	$10.00	**$15.00**
Figurine, 2.00"	94	Trumpet	10.00	**10.00**
ac# 274	95	Ship	10.00	**10.00**
Bluebird Perched on Fence	96	Heart	10.00	**10.00**
	97	Sword	10.00	**10.00**

529818   <u>LEON AND EVELYN MAE</u>   Sugar Town

Retired 1997	94	Trumpet	$20.00	**$25.00**
Figurine, 4.75"	95	Ship	20.00	**20.00**
ac# 560	96	Heart	20.00	**20.00**
Sam's Parents Just Before His	97	Sword	20.00	**20.00**
Birth				

529826	JAN Sugar Town				
	Retired 1997	94	Trumpet	$17.00	**$20.00**
	Figurine, 4.75"	95	Ship	17.00	**17.00**
	ac# 516	96	Heart	17.00	**17.00**
	Girl Nurse	97	Sword	17.00	**17.00**

529842	SAM BUTCHER Sugar Town				
	Annual 1993	93	Butterfly	$22.50	**$70.00**
	Figurine, 3.25"				
	ac# 817				
	Young Sam Holding Candy				
	Cane by Town Sign				

Sign reads: "This Way to Sugar Town. Population 9 and Growing." Line art is from prototype, actual sign reads: "Sugar Avenue," not "Peppermint Lane."

529850	DR. SAM SUGAR Sugar Town				
	Retired 1997	94	Trumpet	$17.00	**$20.00**
	Figurine, 4.50"	95	Ship	17.00	**17.00**
	ac# 247	96	Heart	17.00	**17.00**
	Dr. Sugar Raises Hand in	97	Sword	17.00	**17.00**
	Greeting				

529869	DOCTOR'S OFFICE NIGHT LIGHT Sugar Town Lighted				
	Retired 1997	94	Trumpet	$80.00	**$90.00**
	Night Light, 7.00"	95	Ship	80.00	**85.00**
	ac# 241	96	Heart	85.00	**85.00**
	Office of Dr. Sugar	97	Sword	85.00	**85.00**

529931	HAPPINESS IS AT OUR FINGERTIPS Catalog Exclusive				
	Annual 1993	93	G-Clef	$35.00	**$90.00**
	Figurine, 5.50"		Butterfly		**70.00**
	ac# 370				
	Girl Reaching for Butterfly				

529966	RING OUT THE GOOD NEWS Nativity Addition				
	Retired 1997	93	G-Clef	$27.50	**$80.00**
	Figurine, 2.50"	93	Butterfly	27.50	**55.00**
	ac# 808	94	Trumpet	27.50	**50.00**
	Girl Holding a Doll &				
	Ringing a Bell				

529974	AN EVENT FOR ALL SEASONS Open House Event				
	Annual 1993	93	Butterfly	$15.00	**$25.00**
	Ornament, 3.00"				
	ac# 54				
	Girl Protecting Puppy inside				
	Slicker				

529982	MEMORIES ARE MADE OF THIS Special Event				
	Annual 1994	94	Butterfly	$30.00	**$45.00**
	Figurine, 5.00"		Trumpet		**42.00**
	ac# 682				
	Girl Blowing Bubbles				

530026	YOU'RE MY NUMBER ONE FRIEND	Easter Seal Commemorative / Lily		
	Understamp	93	G-Clef	$30.00	**$55.00**
	Annual 1993		Butterfly		**50.00**
	Figurine, 5.50"		Trumpet		**48.00**
	ac# 1153				
	Girl Wearing First Place				
	Award				

530042	NOAH, HIS WIFE & ARK	Two By Two	Lighted / Set of 3		
	Ongoing	93	Butterfly	$125.00	**$150.00**
	Night Light, 1.68–5.00"	94	Trumpet	125.00	**125.00**
	ac# 719	95	Ship	125.00	**125.00**
	Noah & Wife Welcome	96	Heart	125.00	**125.00**
	Animals to Ark	97	Sword	125.00	**125.00**
		98	Eyeglasses	125.00	**125.00**
		99	Star	125.00	**125.00**

530077	SHEEP	Two By Two			
	Ongoing	93	Butterfly	$10.00	**$15.00**
	Figurine, 1.68"	94	Trumpet	10.00	**10.00**
	ac# 857	95	Ship	10.00	**10.00**
	Girl & Boy Sheep	96	Heart	10.00	**10.00**
		97	Sword	10.00	**10.00**
		98	Eyeglasses	10.00	**10.00**
		99	Star	10.00	**10.00**

530085	PIGS	Two By Two			
	Ongoing	93	Butterfly	$12.00	**$18.00**
	Figurine, 3.25"	94	Trumpet	12.00	**12.00**
	ac# 780	95	Ship	12.00	**12.00**
	Girl & Boy Pigs	96	Heart	12.00	**12.00**
		97	Sword	12.00	**12.00**
		98	Eyeglasses	12.00	**12.00**
		99	Star	12.00	**12.00**

530115	GIRAFFES	Two By Two			
	Ongoing	93	Butterfly	$16.00	**$22.00**
	Figurine, 3.00"	94	Trumpet	16.00	**16.00**
	ac# 303	95	Ship	16.00	**16.00**
	Girl & Boy Giraffes	96	Heart	16.00	**16.00**
		97	Sword	16.00	**16.00**
		98	Eyeglasses	16.00	**16.00**
		99	Star	16.00	**16.00**

530123	BUNNIES	Two By Two			
	Ongoing	93	Butterfly	$9.00	**$15.00**
	Figurine, 1.38"	94	Trumpet	9.00	**9.00**
	ac# 181	95	Ship	9.00	**9.00**
	Girl & Boy Bunnies with	96	Heart	9.00	**9.00**
	Carrot	97	Sword	9.00	**9.00**
		98	Eyeglasses	9.00	**9.00**
		99	Star	9.00	**9.00**

530131	ELEPHANTS	Two By Two			
	Ongoing	93	Butterfly	$18.00	**$25.00**
	Figurine, 2.00"	94	Trumpet	18.00	**18.00**
	ac# 259	95	Ship	18.00	**18.00**
	Girl & Boy Elephants w/	96	Heart	18.00	**18.00**
	Trunks Entwined	97	Sword	18.00	**18.00**
		98	Eyeglasses	18.00	**18.00**
		99	Star	18.00	**18.00**

530158	AN EVENT FOR ALL SEASONS	Special Event			
	Annual 1993	93	G-Clef	$30.00	**$62.00**
	Figurine, 5.25"		Butterfly		**45.00**
	ac# 54				
	Girl Protecting Puppy inside				
	Slicker				

530166	WISHING YOU THE SWEETEST CHRISTMAS				
	Dated Annual 1993	93	Butterfly	$27.50	**$45.00**
	Figurine, 4.75"				
	ac# 1085				
	Girl in PJ's Holding Cookie				
	for Santa				

530174	WISHING YOU THE SWEETEST CHRISTMAS				
	Dated Annual 1993	93	Butterfly	$25.00	**$40.00**
	Bell, 5.75"				
	ac# 1085				
	Girl in PJ's Holding Cookie				
	for Santa				

530182	WISHING YOU THE SWEETEST CHRISTMAS				
	Dated Annual 1993	93	Butterfly	$8.00	**$20.00**
	Thimble, 2.25"				
	ac# 1085				
	Girl in PJ's Holding Cookie				
	for Santa				

530190	WISHING YOU THE SWEETEST CHRISTMAS Series: "Masterpiece Ornament"–5th Issue				
	Dated Annual 1993	93	Butterfly	$30.00	**$40.00**
	Ornament, 4.00"				
	ac# 1085				
	Girl in PJ's Holding Cookie				
	for Santa				

530204	WISHING YOU THE SWEETEST CHRISTMAS Series: "Christmas Blessings"–4th & Final Issue				
	Dated Annual 1993	93	Butterfly	$50.00	**$56.00**
	Plate, 8.50"				
	ac# 1085				
	Girl in PJ's Holding Cookie				
	for Santa				

530212	WISHING YOU THE SWEETEST CHRISTMAS				
	Dated Annual 1993	93	Butterfly	$15.00	**$35.00**
	Ornament, 3.25"				
	ac# 1085				
	Girl in PJ's Holding Cookie				
	for Santa				

530255	BABY'S FIRST CHRISTMAS				
	Dated Annual 1994	94	Trumpet	$16.00	**$30.00**
	Ornament, 3.00"				
	ac# 106				
	Baby Girl w/Doll Rides				
	Hobby Horse Deer				

530263	BABY'S FIRST CHRISTMAS				
	Dated Annual 1994	94	Trumpet	$16.00	**$30.00**
	Ornament, 3.00"				
	ac# 105				
	Baby Boy w/Teddy Rides				
	Hobby Horse Deer				

530387	YOU'RE AS PRETTY AS A CHRISTMAS TREE Series: "Masterpiece Ornament"–6th Issue				
	Dated Annual 1994	94	Trumpet	$30.00	**$40.00**
	Ornament, 5.25"				
	ac# 1145				
	Girl in Tree Outfit Holds Star				
	Aloft				

530395 YOU'RE AS PRETTY AS A CHRISTMAS TREE
Dated Annual 1994 94 Trumpet $16.00 **$35.00**
Ornament, 4.75"
ac# 1145
Girl in Tree Outfit Holds Star
Aloft

530409 YOU'RE AS PRETTY AS A CHRISTMAS TREE
Dated Annual 1994 94 Trumpet $50.00 **$54.00**
Plate, 9.50"
ac# 1145
Girl in Tree Outfit Holds Star
Aloft

530425 YOU'RE AS PRETTY AS A CHRISTMAS TREE
Dated Annual 1994 94 Trumpet $27.50 **$40.00**
Figurine, 6.75"
ac# 1145
Girl in Tree Outfit Holds Star
Aloft

530441 DR. SUGAR'S OFFICE ORNAMENT Sugar Town
Annual 1995 95 Ship $17.50 **$30.00**
Ornament, 3.50"
ac# 248
Dr. Sugar Waving by Office
Door

May be lighted by placing a miniature Christmas light into opening on bottom.

530468 SAM'S HOUSE ORNAMENT Sugar Town
Annual 1994 94 Trumpet $17.50 **$28.00**
Ornament, 3.00"
ac# 819
Sam Stands Outside His
House

May be lighted by placing a miniature Christmas light into opening on bottom.

530484 CHAPEL ORNAMENT Sugar Town
Annual 1993 93 Butterfly $17.50 **$35.00**
Ornament, 2.75"
ac# 198
Sam Waving Outside Chapel

May be lighted by placing a miniature Christmas light into opening on bottom.

530492 HAPPY BIRTHDAY JESUS Mini Nativity Addition
Ongoing

Figurine, 3.50"	93	Butterfly	$20.00	**$25.00**
ac# 376	94	Trumpet	20.00	**20.00**
Elephant	95	Ship	20.00	**20.00**
	96	Heart	20.00	**20.00**
	97	Sword	20.00	**20.00**
	98	Eyeglasses	20.00	**20.00**
	99	Star	20.00	**20.00**

530506 OUR FIRST CHRISTMAS TOGETHER
Dated Annual 1993 93 Butterfly $17.50 **$25.00**
Ornament, 2.50"
ac# 753
Boy and Girl in Sleigh

530697	SERENITY PRAYER GIRL					
	Ongoing	94	Butterfly	$35.00	**$40.00**	
	Figurine, 4.12"	94	Trumpet	35.00	**37.50**	
	ac# 841	95	Ship	35.00	**37.50**	
	Girl Kneels by Serenity	96	Heart	37.50	**37.50**	
	Prayer Plaque	97	Sword	37.50	**37.50**	
		98	Eyeglasses	37.50	**37.50**	
		99	Star	37.50	**37.50**	
530700	SERENITY PRAYER BOY					
	Ongoing	94	Butterfly	$35.00	**$40.00**	
	Figurine, 4.12"	94	Trumpet	35.00	**37.50**	
	ac# 840	95	Ship	35.00	**37.50**	
	Boy Kneels by Prayer Plaque	96	Heart	37.50	**37.50**	
		97	Sword	37.50	**37.50**	
		98	Eyeglasses	37.50	**37.50**	
		99	Star	37.50	**37.50**	
530786	15 HAPPY YEARS TOGETHER, WHAT A TWEET! 15th Anniversary Commemorative					
	Annual 1993	93	G-Clef	$100.00	**$160.00**	
	Figurine, 5.25"		Butterfly		**125.00**	
	ac# 2					
	Bunnies Listen as Angel					
	Leads Bluebird Choir					

Retailers received the piece with one walnut base, a display dome, brass plate and cloisonne 15 year logo Medallion; GBTru$ for G-Clef w/dome $270, Butterfly w/dome $250.

530840	15 YEARS, TWEET MUSIC TOGETHER 15th Anniversary Commemorative					
	Annual 1993	93	G-Clef	$15.00	**$25.00**	
	Ornament, 3.50"		Butterfly		**20.00**	
	ac# 3					
	Angel with Bluebird and					
	Songbook					
530859	BABY'S FIRST CHRISTMAS					
	Dated Annual 1993	93	Butterfly	$15.00	**$25.00**	
	Ornament, 3.25"					
	ac# 103					
	Boy in PJ's Wrapped in					
	Ribbon					
530867	BABY'S FIRST CHRISTMAS					
	Dated Annual 1993	93	Butterfly	$15.00	**$30.00**	
	Ornament, 3.25"					
	ac# 104					
	Girl in PJ's Wrapped in					
	Ribbon					
530913	WE HAVE COME FROM AFAR Mini Nativity Addition					
	Ongoing	95	Ship	$12.00	**$15.00**	
	Figurine, 1.50"	96	Heart	12.00	**12.00**	
	ac# 1043	97	Sword	12.00	**12.00**	
	Penguins as 3 Kings	98	Eyeglasses	12.00	**12.00**	
		99	Star	12.00	**12.00**	
530956	I ONLY HAVE ICE FOR YOU					
	Ongoing	95	Ship	$55.00	**$55.00**	
	Figurine, 4.50"	96	Heart	55.00	**55.00**	
	ac# 470	97	Sword	55.00	**55.00**	
	Seated Boy & Girl with Ice	98	Eyeglasses	55.00	**55.00**	
	Block	99	Star	55.00	**55.00**	

530964 — SOMETIMES YOU'RE NEXT TO IMPOSSIBLE

Ongoing
Figurine, 5.75"
ac# 887
Stubborn Boy and Girl

Year	Mark		
97	Heart	$50.00	**$53.00**
97	Sword	50.00	**50.00**
98	Eyeglasses	50.00	**50.00**
99	Star	50.00	**50.00**

530972 — YOU ARE ALWAYS IN MY HEART

Dated Annual 1994
Ornament, 4.00"
ac# 1097
Teddy Bear Rests on Heart

Year	Mark		
94	Trumpet	$16.00	**$22.00**

530999 — I STILL DO

Ongoing
Figurine, 5.75"
ac# 473
Girl Points to Finger w/
Wedding Ring

Year	Mark		
94	Butterfly	$30.00	**$50.00**
94	Trumpet	30.00	**32.00**
95	Ship	30.00	**30.00**
96	Heart	30.00	**30.00**
97	Sword	30.00	**30.00**
98	Eyeglasses	30.00	**30.00**
99	Star	30.00	**30.00**

531006 — I STILL DO

Ongoing
Figurine, 5.25"
ac# 474
Boy Points to Finger w/
Wedding Ring

Year	Mark		
94	Butterfly	$30.00	**$50.00**
94	Trumpet	30.00	**30.00**
95	Ship	30.00	**30.00**
96	Heart	30.00	**30.00**
97	Sword	30.00	**30.00**
98	Eyeglasses	30.00	**30.00**
99	Star	30.00	**30.00**

531014 — MY WORLD'S UPSIDE DOWN WITHOUT YOU

Ongoing
Figurine, 2.50"
ac# 715
Upside-down Turtle and
Tearful Bluebird

Year	Mark		
98	Sword	$15.00	**$18.00**
98	Eyeglasses	15.00	**15.00**
99	Star	15.00	**15.00**

531022 — POTTY TIME

Ongoing
Figurine, 4.50"
ac# 782
Boy on a Potty Chair

Year	Mark		
97	Heart	$25.00	**$28.00**
97	Sword	25.00	**25.00**
98	Eyeglasses	25.00	**25.00**
99	Star	25.00	**25.00**

531030 — YOU ARE MY ONCE IN A LIFETIME

Ongoing
Figurine, 5.25"
ac# 1110
Girl Holds up Prize-winning
#1 Fish

Year	Mark		
98	Sword	$45.00	**$45.00**
98	Eyeglasses	45.00	**45.00**
99	Star	45.00	**45.00**

531057 — I HAVEN'T SEEN MUCH OF YOU LATELY   Birthday Collection

Ongoing
Figurine, 2.75"
ac# 466
Hair Covers Pup's Eyes

Year	Mark		
96	Ship	$13.50	**$15.00**
96	Heart	13.50	**13.50**
97	Sword	13.50	**13.50**
98	Eyeglasses	13.50	**13.50**
99	Star	13.50	**13.50**

531065 WHAT THE WORLD NEEDS IS LOVE

Ongoing
Figurine, 5.50"
ac# 1057
Angel with World

95	Trumpet	$45.00	**$53.00**
95	Ship	45.00	**45.00**
96	Heart	45.00	**45.00**
97	Sword	45.00	**45.00**
98	Eyeglasses	45.00	**45.00**
99	Star	45.00	**45.00**

531073 MONEY'S NOT THE ONLY GREEN THING WORTH SAVING Spring

Catalog
Retired 1996
Figurine, 5.50"
ac# 696
Boy Sitting on Piggy Bank
Bandaging Tree

94	Trumpet	$50.00	**$85.00**
95	Ship	50.00	**80.00**
96	Heart	50.00	**78.00**

531111 IT IS NO SECRET WHAT GOD CAN DO Easter Seal Commemorative / Lily

Understamp
Annual 1994
Figurine, 4.62"
ac# 507
Girl Holds open Oyster to
Reveal Pearl inside

94	Butterfly	$30.00	**$50.00**
	Trumpet		**48.00**

531138 WHAT A DIFFERENCE YOU'VE MADE IN MY LIFE

Ongoing
Figurine, 3.25"
ac# 1055
Girl Paints Stripes on
Rocking Horse

96	Ship	$50.00	**$55.00**
96	Heart	50.00	**50.00**
97	Sword	50.00	**50.00**
98	Eyeglasses	50.00	**50.00**
99	Star	50.00	**50.00**

531146 VAYA CON DIOS (TO GO WITH GOD)

Ongoing
Figurine, 5.50"
ac# 1031
Hispanic Girl in Party Gown

95	Trumpet	$32.50	**$40.00**
95	Ship	35.00	**35.00**
96	Heart	35.00	**35.00**
97	Sword	35.00	**35.00**
98	Eyeglasses	35.00	**35.00**
99	Star	35.00	**35.00**

531162 BLESS YOUR SOUL

Ongoing
Figurine, 4.00"
ac# 152
Seated Girl with Hole in Sole
of Shoe

95	Trumpet	$25.00	**$42.00**
95	Ship	27.50	**32.00**
96	Heart	27.50	**27.50**
97	Sword	27.50	**27.50**
98	Eyeglasses	27.50	**27.50**
99	Star	27.50	**27.50**

531200 WISHING YOU A BEAR-IE MERRY CHRISTMAS Holiday Preview Event

Dated Annual 1996
Ornament, 2.50"
ac# 1067
Teddy Bear with Wrapped
Gift

96	Heart	$17.50	**$30.00**

531243 YOU ARE THE ROSE OF HIS CREATION Easter Seal / Lily Understamp /

Individually Numbered
Limited Edition 2,000
Figurine, 9.00"
ac# 1114
Girl in Bonnet & Long Dress

94	Butterfly	$500.00	**$550.00**
	Trumpet		**500.00**

531309   HIS LOVE WILL UPHOLD THE WORLD   Precious Moments Millennium
Piece   Early Release to Retailers Attending the Fall 1998 Show

Figurine	99	$150.00	**$150.00**
ac# 431			

Four Angels Clasp Hands
and Hold a Peace Banner to
Encircle the Earth

Early Release to retailers attending Fall 98 Shows. The angels are
designed to represent all people from all nations. Cloud-shaped base.

531359   BRING THE LITTLE ONES TO JESUS   Child Evangelism Fellowship

Dated Annual 1994	94	Butterfly	$50.00	**$55.00**
Plate, 8.50"		Trumpet		**50.00**
ac# 174				

Mother Reads Wordless
Book to Children

531375   LLAMAS   Two By Two

Ongoing	94	Trumpet	$15.00	**$20.00**
Figurine, 2.50"	95	Ship	15.00	**15.00**
ac# 579	96	Heart	15.00	**15.00**
Girl & Boy Llamas	97	Sword	15.00	**15.00**
	98	Eyeglasses	15.00	**15.00**
	99	Star	15.00	**15.00**

531588   YOU MAKE SUCH A LOVELY PAIR   GCC Fall Exclusive

Picture Not
Available At
Press Time

Annual 1998	98	Eyeglasses	$30.00	**$30.00**
Figurine, 5.75"				
ac# 1136				
Girl Holding Pear				

531634   WHO'S GONNA FILL YOUR SHOES?

Ongoing	97	Sword	$37.50	**$37.50**
Figurine, 6.25"	98	Eyeglasses	37.50	**37.50**
ac# 1063	99	Star	37.50	**37.50**
Girl Standing in Mom's				
Shoes				

531634S   WHO'S GONNA FILL YOUR SHOES?   Catalog Early Release / Special
Understamp

Annual 1996	96	Heart	$37.50	**$60.00**
Figurine, 6.25"				
ac# 1063				
Girl Standing in Mom's				
Shoes				

531677   SURROUNDED WITH JOY   Chapel Exclusive

Ongoing	93	Unmarked	$30.00	**$50.00**
Figurine, 5.00"	94	Trumpet	30.00	**30.00**
ac# 902	95	Ship	30.00	**30.00**
Girl with Wreath	97	Sword	30.00	**30.00**

531685   SURROUNDED WITH JOY   Chapel Exclusive

Ongoing	93	Unmarked	$17.50	**$32.00**
Ornament, 3.25"	94	Trumpet	17.50	**17.50**
ac# 902	95	Ship	17.50	**17.50**
Girl with Wreath	96	Heart	17.50	**17.50**
	97	Sword	17.50	**17.50**

531693 YOU DESERVE A HALO–THANK YOU

Retired 1998	96	Ship	$55.00	**$60.00**
Figurine, 5.50"	96	Heart	55.00	**58.00**
ac# 1125	97	Sword	55.00	**55.00**
Angel Places Halo on Little Girl	98	Eyeglasses	55.00	**55.00**

531707 THE LORD IS COUNTING ON YOU

Ongoing	94	Trumpet	$32.50	**$40.00**
Figurine, 5.50"	95	Ship	32.50	**35.00**
ac# 949	96	Heart	35.00	**35.00**
Girl Embroiders Phrase	97	Sword	35.00	**35.00**
	98	Eyeglasses	35.00	**35.00**
	99	Star	35.00	**35.00**

531766 THINKING OF YOU IS WHAT I REALLY LIKE TO DO   Series: "Mother's Day"–1st Issue

Dated Annual 1994	94	Butterfly	$50.00	**$55.00**
Plate, 8.50"		Trumpet		**50.00**
ac# 981				
Kneeling Girl with Bouquet				

531804 BUNNIES CAROLING   Sugar Town

Retired 1997	97	Sword	$10.00	**$10.00**
Figurine, 1.75"				
ac# 182				
Bunnies Singing Carols from Songbook				

531812 TAMMY AND DEBBIE   Sugar Town

Retired 1997	95	Ship	$22.50	**$25.00**
Figurine, 3.25"	96	Heart	22.50	**22.50**
ac# 912	97	Sword	22.50	**22.50**
Girls Carrying Gifts				

531847 MAILBOX   Sugar Town

Retired 1997	94	Trumpet	$5.00	**$6.00**
Figurine, 3.00"	95	Ship	5.00	**5.00**
ac# 643	96	Heart	5.00	**5.00**
House Curbside Mailbox	97	Sword	5.00	**5.00**

531871 DONNY   Sugar Town

Retired 1997	95	Ship	$22.50	**$25.00**
Figurine, 2.50"	96	Heart	22.50	**22.50**
ac# 245	97	Sword	22.50	**22.50**
Boy Pushes Logs on Sled				

531928 DEATH CAN'T KEEP HIM IN THE GROUND   Chapel Exclusive

Ongoing	94	Unmarked	$30.00	**$45.00**
Figurine, 5.00"	94	Trumpet	30.00	**30.00**
ac# 236	95	Ship	30.00	**30.00**
Angel Looking over a Lily	96	Heart	30.00	**30.00**
	97	Sword	30.00	**30.00**

531944 SHARING OUR CHRISTMAS TOGETHER

Ongoing	97	Sword	$35.00	**$35.00**
Figurine, 3.25"	98	Eyeglasses	35.00	**35.00**
ac# 850	99	Star	35.00	**35.00**
Pup Shares Bowl of Chow with Baby Holding Spoonful				

531952 DROPPING IN FOR THE HOLIDAYS

Retired 1998
Figurine, 6.00"
ac# 251
Angel Takes Rest in Egg Nog
Cup

94	Trumpet	$40.00	**$50.00**
95	Ship	40.00	**45.00**
96	Heart	45.00	**45.00**
97	Sword	45.00	**45.00**
98	Eyeglasses	45.00	**45.00**

The Pink Cup is found on Ship and Heart Marks. Blue Cup is found on Trumpet and Ship Marks. The rare and unusual is a Pink Cup with a Trumpet. No price variation.

531987 LORD SPEAK TO ME

Ongoing
Figurine, 5.00"
ac# 596
Girl Listening to Radio

99	Eyeglasses	$45.00	**$45.00**
99	Star	45.00	**45.00**

532002 HALLELUJAH FOR THE CROSS

Ongoing
Figurine, 5.50"
ac# 363
Boy with Lily & Cross

95	Trumpet	$35.00	**$37.00**
95	Ship	35.00	**35.00**
96	Heart	35.00	**35.00**
97	Sword	35.00	**35.00**
98	Eyeglasses	35.00	**35.00**
99	Star	35.00	**35.00**

532010 SENDING YOU OCEANS OF LOVE

Retired 1996
Figurine, 4.75"
ac# 836
Boy by Ocean with Note in Bottle

95	Trumpet	$35.00	**$65.00**
96	Heart	35.00	**60.00**

532037 I CAN'T BEAR TO LET YOU GO

Ongoing
Figurine, 5.25"
ac# 460
Cowgirl Lassos Bear with Rope

95	Trumpet	$50.00	**$58.00**
95	Ship	50.00	**50.00**
96	Heart	50.00	**50.00**
97	Sword	50.00	**50.00**
98	Eyeglasses	50.00	**50.00**
99	Star	50.00	**50.00**

532061 WHO'S GONNA FILL YOUR SHOES?

Ongoing
Figurine, 5.50"
ac# 1062
Boy Standing in Dad's Shoes

98	Sword	$37.50	**$40.00**
98	Eyeglasses	37.50	**37.50**
99	Star	37.50	**37.50**

Copper pennies in loafers.

532061'S' WHO'S GONNA FILL YOUR SHOES?   Catalog Early Release

Annual 1997
Figurine, 5.50"
ac# 1062
Boy Standing in Dad's Shoes

97	Ship	$37.50	**$40.00**

The "S" suffix does not appear on the box or understamp of the figurine. This piece does not have pennies in the loafers.

532088 A KING IS BORN   Chapel Exclusive

Retired 1995
Ornament, 3.00"
ac# 10
Baby Jesus in Manger

94	Unmarked	$17.50	**$40.00**

387

532096	LORD HELP ME TO STAY ON COURSE				
	Ongoing	95	Trumpet	$35.00	**$58.00**
	Figurine, 5.25"	95	Ship	35.00	**35.00**
	ac# 584	96	Heart	35.00	**35.00**
	Boy Golfer	97	Sword	35.00	**35.00**
		98	Eyeglasses	35.00	**35.00**
		99	Star	35.00	**35.00**

532118	THE LORD BLESS YOU AND KEEP YOU				
	Ongoing	94	Butterfly	$40.00	**$55.00**
	Figurine, 5.25"	94	Trumpet	40.00	**50.00**
	ac# 945	95	Ship	45.00	**50.00**
	African-American Bride &	96	Heart	50.00	**50.00**
	Groom	97	Sword	50.00	**50.00**
		98	Eyeglasses	50.00	**50.00**
		99	Star	50.00	**50.00**

532126	THE LORD BLESS YOU AND KEEP YOU				
	Ongoing	94	Butterfly	$30.00	**$40.00**
	Figurine, 5.25"	94	Trumpet	30.00	**35.00**
	ac# 946	95	Ship	32.50	**35.00**
	African-American Girl	96	Heart	35.00	**35.00**
	Graduate	97	Sword	35.00	**35.00**
		98	Eyeglasses	35.00	**35.00**
		99	Star	35.00	**35.00**

532134	THE LORD BLESS YOU AND KEEP YOU				
	Ongoing	94	Butterfly	$30.00	**$40.00**
	Figurine	94	Trumpet	30.00	**35.00**
	ac# 947	95	Ship	32.50	**35.00**
	African-American Boy	96	Heart	35.00	**35.00**
	Graduate	97	Sword	35.00	**35.00**
		98	Eyeglasses	35.00	**35.00**
		99	Star	35.00	**35.00**

532185	STREET SIGN Sugar Town				
	Retired 1997	95	Ship	$10.00	**$12.00**
	Figurine, 2.00"	96	Heart	10.00	**10.00**
	ac# 894	97	Sword	10.00	**10.00**
	Directional Street Sign				

532908	SUGAR TOWN SQUARE CLOCK Sugar Town				
	Retired 1997	94	Trumpet	$80.00	**$100.00**
	Figurine, 7.50"	95	Ship	80.00	**85.00**
	ac# 897	96	Heart	85.00	**85.00**
	Toy & Candy Stores w/Clock	97	Sword	85.00	**85.00**
	and Caroler				

Not dimensional like the buildings, works as stand-alone piece as well.

532916	LUKE 2:10 - 11				
	Ongoing	94	Trumpet	$35.00	**$38.00**
	Figurine, 4.50"	95	Ship	35.00	**37.50**
	ac# 642	96	Heart	37.50	**37.50**
	Shepherd / Lamb Kneels by	97	Sword	37.50	**37.50**
	Creche-shaped Manger	98	Eyeglasses	37.50	**37.50**
		99	Star	37.50	**37.50**

533149	CURVED SIDEWALK Sugar Town				
	Retired 1997	94	Trumpet	$10.00	**$13.00**
	Figurine, 7.25"	95	Ship	10.00	**10.00**
	ac# 233	96	Heart	10.00	**10.00**
	Curved Cobblestone Path	97	Sword	10.00	**10.00**

533157 — STRAIGHT SIDEWALK Sugar Town

Retired 1997
Figurine, 7.25"
ac# 893
Straight Cobblestone Path

Year	Mark		
94	Trumpet	$10.00	**$12.00**
95	Ship	10.00	**10.00**
96	Heart	10.00	**10.00**
97	Sword	10.00	**10.00**

533165 — SUGAR AND HER DOG HOUSE Sugar Town Set of 2

Retired 1997
Figurine, 3.00"
ac# 895
Dog with Dog House

94	Trumpet	$20.00	**$21.00**
95	Ship	20.00	**20.00**
96	Heart	20.00	**20.00**
97	Sword	20.00	**20.00**

533173 — SINGLE TREE Sugar Town

Retired 1997
Figurine, 4.25"
ac# 867
Decorated Evergreen Tree

94	Trumpet	$10.00	**$13.00**
95	Ship	10.00	**11.00**
96	Heart	10.00	**10.00**
97	Sword	10.00	**10.00**

533181 — DOUBLE TREE Sugar Town

Retired 1997
Figurine, 4.00"
ac# 246
Double Trees Decorated for Holidays

94	Trumpet	$10.00	**$14.00**
95	Ship	10.00	**11.00**
96	Heart	10.00	**11.00**
97	Sword	10.00	**10.00**

533203 — COBBLESTONE BRIDGE Sugar Town

Retired 1997
Figurine, 3.25"
ac# 214
Bunny Peeks from Cobblestone Bridge

94	Trumpet	$17.00	**$20.00**
95	Ship	17.00	**18.00**
96	Heart	17.00	**17.00**
97	Sword	17.00	**17.00**

549975 — LET'S KEEP OUR EYES ON THE GOAL Canadian Exclusive

Figurine,
ac# 570
Hockey Player with
Canadian Flag on Chest and
#99 on Back

		$37.50	**$37.50**

603171 — BISQUE ORNAMENT HOLDER

Ongoing
Ornament Holder, 6.00"
ac# 141
Angel Perches atop Open
Framed Window

94	Trumpet	$30.00	**$35.00**
95	Ship	30.00	**30.00**
96	Heart	30.00	**30.00**
97	Sword	30.00	**30.00**
98	Eyeglasses	30.00	**30.00**
99	Star	30.00	**30.00**

603503 — ON THE HILL OVERLOOKING THE QUIET BLUE STREAM Chapel Exclusive

Retired 1997
Figurine, 4.75"
ac# 740
Two Angels Standing Guard
over Poem

94	Unmarked*	$45.00	**$80.00**
96	Heart**	45.00	**55.00**

*Has 3 verses of poem.   **Has 4 verses of poem.

603864 NOTHING CAN DAMPEN THE SPIRIT OF CARING   Series: "Good
Samaritan"-1st Issue

Ongoing	94	Butterfly	$35.00	**$40.00**
Figurine, 5.12"	94	Trumpet	35.00	**35.00**
ac# 723	95	Ship	35.00	**35.00**
Boy Fills Sandbag as Pup	96	Heart	35.00	**35.00**
Holds Sack open	97	Sword	35.00	**35.00**
	98	Eyeglasses	35.00	**35.00**
	99	Star	35.00	**35.00**

604135 MAY YOUR CHRISTMAS BE DELIGHTFUL

Ongoing				
Figurine, 5.50"	97	Sword	$40.00	**$45.00**
ac# 674	98	Eyeglasses	40.00	**40.00**
Girl Wrapped up in Tree	99	Star	40.00	**40.00**
Light Cord				

604151 A KING IS BORN   Chapel Exclusive

Retired 1995	94	Unmarked	$25.00	**$75.00**
Figurine, 4.75"				
ac# 10				
Baby Jesus in Manger				

604208 A POPPY FOR YOU

Suspended 1998	94	Trumpet	$35.00	**$45.00**
Figurine, 5.75"	95	Ship	35.00	**35.00**
ac# 13	96	Heart	35.00	**35.00**
Girl Holds Poppy Honoring	97	Sword	35.00	**35.00**
Those Who Died in War	98	Eyeglasses	35.00	**35.00**

604216 YOU'RE AS PRETTY AS A CHRISTMAS TREE

Dated Annual 1994	94	Trumpet	$27.50	**$32.00**
Bell, 5.75"				
ac# 1145				
Girl in Tree Outfit Holds Star				
Aloft				

617334 REJOICE, O EARTH   Tune: Hark! The Herald Angels Sing

Annual 1990	90	Flame	$125.00	**$150.00**
Musical Tree Topper, 14.00"				
ac# 804				
Angel				

THE ENESCO PRECIOUS MOMENTS COLLECTORS CLUB
SYMBOLS OF CHARTER MEMBERSHIP

E-0001	BUT LOVE GOES ON FOREVER *Member Only* Figurine, 5.00" ac# 184 Boy & Girl Angels on Cloud	81	No Mark Triangle Hourglass	$15.00	**$180.00** **165.00** **160.00**
E-0102	BUT LOVE GOES ON FOREVER *Member Only* Plaque, 5.00" ac# 184 Boy & Girl Angels on Cloud	82	Unmarked Triangle Hourglass	$15.00	**$140.00** **85.00** **72.00**

*Note: "Precious Moments Last Forever" inscription on front of plaque confuses many because the Inspirational Title of this piece is "But Love Goes On Forever."

E-0103	LET US CALL THE CLUB TO ORDER *Member Only* Figurine, 5.75" ac# 567 Club Meeting	83	Hourglass Fish	$15.00	**$65.00** **60.00**
E-0104	JOIN IN ON THE BLESSINGS *Member Only* Figurine, 4.50" ac# 534 Girl with Dues Bank	84	Fish Cross	$17.50	**$62.00** **55.00**
E-0105	SEEK AND YE SHALL FIND *Member Only* Figurine, 5.25" ac# 828 Girl with Shopping Bag	85	Cross Dove	$17.50	**$55.00** **50.00**

Variation: 1985 Charter Member Inscription on some Cross Marks.

E-0106	BIRDS OF A FEATHER COLLECT TOGETHER *Member Only* Figurine, 5.75" ac# 134 Girl with Embroidery Hoop and Bird	86	Dove Olive Branch	$17.50	**$50.00** **48.00**
E-0107	SHARING IS UNIVERSAL *Member Only* Figurine, 5.00" ac# 848 Girl Sending Package to Friend	87	Olive Branch Cedar Tree	$17.50	**$50.00** **48.00**
E-0108	A GROWING LOVE *Member Only* Figurine, 4.50" ac# 9 Girl with Flowerpot and Sunflower	88	Cedar Tree Flower	$18.50	**$50.00** **45.00**

C-0109 | ALWAYS ROOM FOR ONE MORE
Member Only | 89 | Flower | $19.50 | **$50.00**
Figurine, 4.50" | | Bow & Arrow | | **45.00**
ac# 50
Girl with Puppies in Box

C-0110 | MY HAPPINESS
Member Only | 90 | Bow & Arrow | $21.00 | **$50.00**
Figurine, 4.50" | | Flame | | **42.00**
ac# 704
Girl at Table w/Figurine

C-0111 | SHARING THE GOOD NEWS TOGETHER
Member Only | 91 | Flame | $22.50 | **$50.00**
Figurine, 5.25" | | Vessel | | **42.00**
ac# 855
Girl at Mailbox with Club
Newsletter

C-0112 | THE CLUB THAT'S OUT OF THIS WORLD
Member Only | 92 | Vessel | $25.00 | **$48.00**
Figurine, 5.00" | | G-Clef | | **40.00**
ac# 924
Girl in Spacesuit Holding
Space Helmet

C-0113 | LOVING, CARING AND SHARING ALONG THE WAY
Member Only | 93 | G-Clef | $25.00 | **$50.00**
Figurine, 5.00" | | Butterfly | | **45.00**
ac# 632
Girl at Crossroads

C-0114 | YOU ARE THE END OF MY RAINBOW
Member Only | 94 | Butterfly | $26.00 | **$47.00**
Figurine, 5.00" | | Trumpet | | **40.00**
ac# 1112 | | Ship | | **39.00**
Girl in Pot of Gold

C-0115 | YOU'RE THE SWEETEST COOKIE IN THE BATCH
Member Only | 95 | Butterfly | $27.00 | **$48.00**
Figurine, 5.00" | | Trumpet | | **45.00**
ac# 1156 | | Ship | | **42.00**
Girl with Cookies

C-0116 | YOU'RE AS PRETTY AS A PICTURE
Member Only | 96 | Trumpet | $25.00 | **$40.00**
Figurine, 5.25" | | Ship | | **38.00**
ac# 1146 | | Heart | | **37.00**
Girl Holds up a Picture
Frame

C-0117 | A SPECIAL TOAST TO PRECIOUS MOMENTS
Member Only | 97 | Heart | $25.00 | **$40.00**
Figurine, 5.00" | | Sword | | **35.00**
ac# 21
Girl Holding Toaster

C-0118 — FOCUSING IN ON THOSE PRECIOUS MOMENTS
Member Only
Figurine, 4.75"
ac# 280
Child Holds Camera to Snap
Picture of Special Moment

| | | 98 | Sword | $28.00 | **NE** |
| | | | Eyeglasses | | NE |

C-0119 — WISHING YOU A WORLD OF PEACE
Member Only
Figurine, 5.25"
ac# 1080
Girl in Wagon Gazing at Star

Picture Not
Available At
Press Time

| | | 99 | Eyeglasses | $25.00 | **$25.00** |
| | | | Star | | 25.00 |

SYMBOLS OF MEMBERSHIP

E-0005 — SEEK AND YE SHALL FIND
Member Only
Figurine, 5.25"
ac# 828
Girl with Shopping Bag

| 85 | Cross | $17.50 | **$50.00** |
| | Dove | | 45.00 |

E-0006 — BIRDS OF A FEATHER COLLECT TOGETHER
Member Only
Figurine, 5.75"
ac# 134
Girl with Embroidery Hoop
and Bird

| 86 | Dove | $17.50 | **$45.00** |
| | Olive Branch | | 42.00 |

E-0007 — SHARING IS UNIVERSAL
Member Only
Figurine, 5.00"
ac# 848
Girl Sending Package to
Friend

| 87 | Olive Branch | $17.50 | **$45.00** |
| | Cedar Tree | | 42.00 |

E-0008 — A GROWING LOVE
Member Only
Figurine, 4.50"
ac# 9
Girl with Flowerpot and
Sunflower

| 88 | Cedar Tree | $18.50 | **$38.00** |
| | Flower | | 35.00 |

C-0009 — ALWAYS ROOM FOR ONE MORE
Member Only
Figurine, 4.50"
ac# 50
Girl with Puppies in Box

89	Flower	$19.50	**$40.00**
	Bow & Arrow		35.00
	Flame		34.00

C-0010 — MY HAPPINESS
Member Only
Figurine, 4.50"
ac# 704
Girl at Table w/Figurine

| 90 | Bow & Arrow | $21.00 | **$36.00** |
| | Flame | | 30.00 |

C-0011	SHARING THE GOOD NEWS TOGETHER				$22.50	**$37.00**
	Member Only	91	Flame			**35.00**
	Figurine, 5.25"		Vessel			
	ac# 855					
	Girl at Mailbox with Club Newsletter					

C-0012	THE CLUB THAT'S OUT OF THIS WORLD				$25.00	**$45.00**
	Member Only	92	Vessel			**35.00**
	Figurine, 5.00"		G-Clef			
	ac# 924					
	Girl in Spacesuit Holding Space Helmet					

C-0013	LOVING, CARING AND SHARING ALONG THE WAY				$25.00	**$42.00**
	Member Only	93	G-Clef			**37.00**
	Figurine, 5.00"		Butterfly			
	ac# 632					
	Girl at Crossroads					

C-0014	YOU ARE THE END OF MY RAINBOW				$26.00	**$35.00**
	Member Only	94	Butterfly			**30.00**
	Figurine, 5.00"		Trumpet			**32.00**
	ac# 1112		Ship			
	Girl in Pot of Gold					

C-0015	YOU'RE THE SWEETEST COOKIE IN THE BATCH				$27.00	**$30.00**
	Member Only	95	Trumpet			**27.00**
	Figurine, 5.00"		Ship			
	ac# 1156					
	Girl with Cookies					

C-0016	YOU'RE AS PRETTY AS A PICTURE				$25.00	**$29.00**
	Member Only	96	Ship			**25.00**
	Figurine, 5.25"		Heart			
	ac# 1146					
	Girl Holds up a Picture Frame					

C-0017	A SPECIAL TOAST TO PRECIOUS MOMENTS				$25.00	**$35.00**
	Member Only	97	Heart			**32.00**
	Figurine, 5.00"		Sword			
	ac# 21					
	Girl Holding Toaster					

C-0018	FOCUSING IN ON THOSE PRECIOUS MOMENTS				$28.00	**NE**
	Member Only	98	Sword			NE
	Figurine, 4.75"		Eyeglasses			
	ac# 280					
	Child Holds Camera to Snap Picture of Special Moment					

C-0019	WISHING YOU A WORLD OF PEACE				$25.00	**$25.00**
	Member Only	99	Eyeglasses			**25.00**
Picture Not	Figurine, 5.25"		Star			
Available At	ac# 1080					
Press Time	Girl in Wagon Gazing at Star					

E-0202 — BUT LOVE GOES ON FOREVER

Member Only
Plaque, 5.00"
ac# 184
Boy & Girl Angels on Cloud

	82	Unmarked	$15.00	**$122.00**
		Triangle		**75.00**
		Hourglass		**68.00**

*Note: "Precious Moments Last Forever" inscription on front of plaque confuses many because the Inspirational Title of this piece is "But Love Goes On Forever. "Termed the "Canadian Plaque Error," approximately 750 pieces of this 1982 Symbol Of Membership piece were produced in 1985 and shipped to Canada. These pieces are stamped "TAIWAN" and have a Dove Annual Production Symbol. The GBTru$ for the "Canadian Plaque Error" is $110.00.

E-0303 — LET US CALL THE CLUB TO ORDER

Member Only
Figurine, 5.75"
ac# 567
Club Meeting

	83	Hourglass	$15.00	**$60.00**
		Fish		**55.00**
		Cross		**50.00**

E-0404 — JOIN IN ON THE BLESSINGS

Member Only
Figurine, 4.50"
ac# 534
Girl with Dues Bank

	84	Hourglass	$17.50	**$111.00**
		Fish		**55.00**
		Cross		**50.00**

MEMBERSHIP PIECES

PMB034 — YOU FILL THE PAGES OF MY LIFE & PRECIOUS MOMENTS LAST FOREVER

Member Only
Book & Figurine, 4.00"
ac# 1127
Special Edition Book &
Figurine

	94	Trumpet	$67.50	**$73.00**

Available only to active Club Members who joined or renewed before 12/31/94. Order deadline was 4/30/95. Collector's Edition has color photo section and cover is the figurine. Stock number for figurine is #530980. Regular trade edition of book has plain cover–PMB94 @ $35.00.

PM-811 — HELLO LORD, IT'S ME AGAIN

Member Only
Figurine, 4.75"
ac# 421
Boy on Telephone

	81	Triangle	$25.00	**$425.00**
		Hourglass		**400.00**

PM-821 — SMILE, GOD LOVES YOU

Member Only
Figurine, 5.25"
ac# 876
Girl with Curlers

	82	Hourglass	$25.00	**$198.00**
		Fish		**180.00**

PM-822 — PUT ON A HAPPY FACE

Member Only
Figurine, 5.50"
ac# 799
Boy Clown Holding Mask

	83	Hourglass	$25.00	**$220.00**
		Fish		**198.00**
		Cross		**190.00**

PM-831	DAWN'S EARLY LIGHT				
	Member Only	83	Fish	$25.00	**$70.00**
	Figurine, 4.50"		Cross		**65.00**
	ac# 234				
	Girl Covering Kitten				

PM-841	GOD'S RAY OF MERCY				
	Member Only	84	Fish	$25.00	**$95.00**
	Figurine, 4.75"		Cross		**60.00**
	ac# 349		Dove		**55.00**
	Boy Angel with Flashlight				

PM-842	TRUST IN THE LORD TO THE FINISH				
	Member Only	84	Cross	$25.00	**$60.00**
	Figurine, 5.50"				
	ac# 1025				
	Boy with Racing Cup				

PM-851	THE LORD IS MY SHEPHERD				
	Member Only	85	Dove	$25.00	**$70.00**
	Figurine, 5.50"				
	ac# 950				
	Girl Holding Lamb				

PM-852	I LOVE TO TELL THE STORY				
	Member Only	85	Dove	$27.50	**$65.00**
	Figurine, 3.50"				
	ac# 467				
	Boy with Lamb and Book				

PM-861	GRANDMA'S PRAYER				
	Member Only	86	Dove	$25.00	**$90.00**
	Figurine, 4.50"		Olive Branch		**80.00**
	ac# 358		Cedar Tree		**75.00**
	Praying Grandma				

PM-862	I'M FOLLOWING JESUS				
	Member Only	86	Olive Branch	$25.00	**$80.00**
	Figurine, 4.25"				
	ac# 490				
	Boy in Car				

PM-871	FEED MY SHEEP				
	Member Only	87	Olive Branch	$25.00	**$92.00**
	Figurine, 4.75"		Cedar Tree		**65.00**
	ac# 273		Flower		**59.00**
	Girl Feeding Lamb				

PM-872	IN HIS TIME				
	Member Only	87	Cedar Tree	$25.00	**$58.00**
	Figurine, 4.10"		Flower		**55.00**
	ac# 500				
	Boy Waiting for Seed to Grow				

PM-873 LOVING YOU DEAR VALENTINE
Member Only
Figurine, 5.50" 87 Olive Branch $25.00 **$45.00**
ac# 638 Cedar Tree **42.00**
Boy Painting Valentine Flower **39.00**

PM-874 LOVING YOU DEAR VALENTINE
Member Only
Figurine, 5.25" 87 Olive Branch $25.00 **$49.00**
ac# 639 Cedar Tree **45.00**
Girl Drawing Valentine Flower **40.00**

PM-881 GOD BLESS YOU FOR TOUCHING MY LIFE
Member Only
Figurine, 4.75" 88 Cedar Tree $27.50 **$67.00**
ac# 318 Flower **55.00**
Girl Painting Butterfly Bow & Arrow **45.00**

PM-882 YOU JUST CANNOT CHUCK A GOOD FRIENDSHIP
Member Only
Figurine, 5.00" 88 Flower $27.50 **$54.00**
ac# 1134 Bow & Arrow **48.00**
Boy Rescuing Puppy from
Trash Can

PM-890 BEAUTITUDE ORNAMENT SERIES   Set of 7*
Member Only
Ornament, 5.50" 90 Unmarked $105.00 **$95.00**
ac# 127
Chapel Stained Glass
Window Replicas

*Set of 7 also individually numbered PM-190 through PM-790. For
individual titles see the QUIKREFERENCE SECTION.

PM-891 YOU WILL ALWAYS BE MY CHOICE
Member Only
Figurine, 4.75" 89 Bow & Arrow $27.50 **$45.00**
ac# 1143 Flame **42.00**
Girl with Ballot Box

PM-892 MOW POWER TO YA
Member Only
Figurine, 4.75" 89 Bow & Arrow $27.50 **$58.00**
ac# 700 Flame **52.00**
Boy Pushing Lawn Mower

PM-901 TEN YEARS AND STILL GOING STRONG
Member Only
Figurine, 3.75" 90 Flame $30.00 **$52.00**
ac# 918 Vessel **48.00**
Girl in Race Car

PM-902	YOU ARE A BLESSING TO ME	90	Flame	$27.50	**$58.00**
	Member Only		Vessel		55.00
	Figurine, 5.00"				
	ac# 1094				
	Girl Sewing Patch on Teddy Bear				

PM-911	ONE STEP AT A TIME	91	Vessel	$33.00	**$55.00**
	Member Only		G-Clef		50.00
	Figurine, 5.25"				
	ac# 742				
	Child Holding Mom's Hands Taking First Steps				

PM-912	LORD, KEEP ME IN TEEPEE TOP SHAPE	91	Vessel	$27.50	**$58.00**
	Member Only		G-Clef		55.00
	Figurine, 4.50"				
	ac# 587				
	Native American Boy Holding Can of Spinach				

PM-921	ONLY LOVE CAN MAKE A HOME	92	G-Clef	$30.00	**$60.00**
	Member Only		Butterfly		55.00
	Figurine, 4.25"				
	ac# 743				
	Mr. Webb Building Bird Home				

PM-922	SOWING THE SEEDS OF LOVE	92	G-Clef	$30.00	**$39.00**
	Member Only		Butterfly		30.00
	Figurine, 4.50"				
	ac# 890				
	Girl Kneeling & Praying by New Growing Flower				

PM-931	HIS LITTLE TREASURE	93	Butterfly	$30.00	**$48.00**
	Member Only		Trumpet		45.00
	Figurine, 4.25"				
	ac# 429				
	Girl Pointing to Sand Dollar				

PM-932	LOVING	93	Butterfly	$30.00	**$68.00**
	Member Only		Trumpet		65.00
	Figurine, 5.50"				
	ac# 631				
	Girl Hugs Teddy Bear				

PM-941	CARING	94	Trumpet	$35.00	**$55.00**
	Member Only		Ship		51.00
	Figurine				
	ac# 194				
	Girl Gives First Aid to Teddy				

PM-942	SHARING	94	Trumpet	$35.00	**$55.00**
	Member Only		Ship		50.00
	Figurine, 3.50"				
	ac# 845				
	Little Girl Shares Food with Her Teddy Bear				

PM-951 — YOU'RE ONE IN A MILLION TO ME
Member Only
Figurine, 4.50"
ac# 1154
Girl Panning for Gold
95 | Ship | $35.00 | **$35.00**

PM-952 — ALWAYS TAKE TIME TO PRAY
Member Only
Figurine, 4.75"
ac# 51
Girl Peeling Potatoes
95 | Ship | $35.00 | **$57.00**

PM-961 — TEACH US TO LOVE ONE ANOTHER   Sam Butcher honors Aunt Cleo
Member Only
Figurine, 4.75"
ac# 914
Teacher at Slate w/Loving,
Caring and Sharing
96 | Ship Heart | $40.00 | **$58.00** **50.00**

PM-962 — OUR CLUB IS SODA-LICIOUS
Member Only
Figurine, 5.75"
ac# 749
Girl in Poodle Skirt Carries
Ice Creme Soda
96 | Heart | $35.00 | **$58.00**

PM-971 — YOU WILL ALWAYS BE A TREASURE TO ME
Member Only
Figurine, 4.75"
ac# 1140
Boy Reading Bible by
Treasure Chest
97 | Heart Sword | $50.00 | **$55.00** **50.00**

PM-972 — BLESSED ARE THE MERCIFUL
Member Only
Figurine, 4.25"
ac# 157
Mouse on Stool Getting Tail
Bandaged
97 | Heart Sword | $40.00 | **$48.00** **45.00**

PM-981 — HAPPY TRAILS
Member Only
Figurine, 6.50"
ac# 383
Cowboy on Hobby Horse on
Wheels
98 | Eyeglasses Star | $50.00 | **$50.00** **50.00**

PM-982 — LORD PLEASE DON'T PUT ME ON HOLD
Member Only
Figurine, 5.25"
ac# 594
Girl on Pay Phone
98 | Eyeglasses Star | $40.00 | **$40.00** **40.00**

PM-983 — HOW CAN TWO WORK TOGETHER EXCEPT THEY AGREE
Member Only
Figurine, 6.00"
ac# 453
Sam and Fujioka-san
Working Together on the
"Original 21"
98 | Eyeglasses Star | $125.00 | **$125.00** **125.00**

PM-991	JUMPING FOR JOY					
	Member Only	99	Star		$30.00	**$30.00**
Picture Not	Figurine, 5.50"					
Available At	ac# 545					
Press Time	Girl with Jump Rope					

PM-992	GOD SPEED					
	Member Only	99	Star		$30.00	**$30.00**
Picture Not	Figurine, 5.25"					
Available At	ac# 351					
Press Time	Boy on Skateboard					

283541	REJOICE IN THE VICTORY	Precious Rewards Frequent Buyer Program			
	Member Only	97	Sword	$30.00	**$85.00**
	Figurine, 5.00"				
	ac# 802				
	Young Girl & Teddy				
	Acknowledge Bronze Medal				
	Award				

PRECIOUS REWARDS, Level 1: 300 points.

283584	GOD BLESS YOU WITH BOUQUETS OF VICTORY	Precious Rewards			
	Frequent Buyer Program	97	Sword	$50.00	**$117.00**
	Member Only				
	Figurine, 6.00"				
	ac# 321				
	Girl w/Silver Medal Holds				
	Bouquet & Pup Holds				
	Flower				

PRECIOUS REWARDS, Level 2: 500 points.

283592	FAITH IS THE VICTORY	Precious Rewards Frequent Buyer Program			
	Member Only	97	Sword	$75.00	**$135.00**
	Figurine, 6.50"				
	ac# 268				
	Girl w/Gold Medal Stands by				
	Balance Beam / Seal				
	Balances Ball on Nose				

PRECIOUS REWARDS, Level 3: 1000 points.

COMMEMORATIVE MEMBERSHIP PIECES

12440	GOD BLESS OUR YEARS TOGETHER	5th Anniversary Club			
	Commemmorative				
	Member Only	85	Dove	$175.00	**$300.00**
	Figurine, 5.50"				
	ac# 311				
	Mom, Dad, Kids, Cake w/5				
	Candles				

127817	A PERFECT DISPLAY OF 15 HAPPY YEARS				
	Member Only	95	Ship	$100.00	**$150.00**
	Figurine, 6.75"				
	ac# 12				
	Girl Next to Showcase				
	Holding Miniature Pieces				

527386	THIS LAND IS OUR LAND	500th Anniversary Voyage of Columbus				
	Commemorative					
	Member Only		92	G-Clef	$350.00	**$375.00**
	Figurine, 9.50"					
	ac# 987					
	Explorer & Animal Crew					
	Sailing the High Seas in a					
	Sail Boat					

SHARING SEASON ORNAMENTS
Gift to Club Members for signing up new members.

PM-037	SHARING THE GOOD NEWS TOGETHER				
	Member Only	91	Vessel	$17.50	**$60.00**
	Ornament, 3.25"				
	ac# 855				
	Girl at Mailbox with Club				
	Newsletter				

PM-038	THE CLUB THAT'S OUT OF THIS WORLD				
	Member Only	92	G-Clef	$17.50	**$65.00**
	Ornament, 3.00"				
	ac# 924				
	Girl in Spacesuit Holding				
	Space Helmet				

PM-864	BIRDS OF A FEATHER COLLECT TOGETHER				
	Member Only	86	Olive Branch	$12.50	**$150.00**
	Ornament, 2.25"				
	ac# 134				
	Girl with Embroidery Hoop				
	and Bird				

PM-904	MY HAPPINESS				
	Member Only	90	Flame	$15.00	**$70.00**
	Ornament, 3.00"				
	ac# 704				
	Girl at Table w/Figurine				

520349	A GROWING LOVE				
	Member Only	88	Flower	$15.00	**$67.00**
	Ornament, 2.80"				
	ac# 9				
	Girl with Flowerpot and				
	Sunflower				

522961	ALWAYS ROOM FOR ONE MORE				
	Member Only	89	Bow & Arrow	$15.00	**$94.00**
	Ornament, 2.80"				
	ac# 50				
	Girl with Puppies in Box				

MEMBERS ONLY ORNAMENTS

PM-040	LOVING, CARING AND SHARING				
	Member Only	93	Butterfly	$15.00	**$35.00**
	Ornament, 3.25"				
	ac# 632				
	Girl at Crossroads				

PM-041	YOU ARE THE END OF MY RAINBOW				
	Member Only	94	Trumpet	$15.00	**$30.00**
	Ornament, 2.50"				
	ac# 1113				
	Little Girl on a Cloud w/				
	Rainbow				

THE ENESCO PRECIOUS MOMENTS BIRTHDAY CLUB
SYMBOLS OF CHARTER MEMBERSHIP

B-0001	OUR CLUB CAN'T BE BEAT				
	Member Only	86	Dove	$10.00	**$90.00**
	Figurine, 3.50"		Olive Branch		**82.00**
	ac# 747		Cedar Tree		**80.00**
	Clown with Drum				

B-0102	A SMILE'S THE CYMBAL OF JOY				
	Member Only	87	Olive Branch	$10.00	**$80.00**
	Figurine, 4.50"		Cedar Tree		**70.00**
	ac# 18				
	Clown with Cymbals				

The first of these were shipped with a title error on the understamp decal–"A Smile's The Symbol Of Joy." The GBTru$ for the "Symbol Error" is $90.00. See page 413.

B-0103	THE SWEETEST CLUB AROUND				
	Member Only	88	Flower	$11.00	**$50.00**
	Figurine, 4.50"		Bow & Arrow		**45.00**
	ac# 967				
	Pippin Popping out of Cake				

B-0104	HAVE A BEARY SPECIAL BIRTHDAY				
	Member Only	89	Flower	$11.50	**$40.00**
	Figurine, 4.50"		Bow & Arrow		**35.00**
	ac# 387		Flame		**30.00**
	Teddy Bear with Balloon				

B-0105	OUR CLUB IS A TOUGH ACT TO FOLLOW				
	Member Only	90	Flame	$13.50	**$38.00**
	Figurine, 4.00"		Vessel		**35.00**
	ac# 748				
	Clown with Puppy Leaping				
	thru Drum				

B-0106	JEST TO LET YOU KNOW YOU'RE TOPS				
	Member Only	91	Vessel	$15.00	**$38.00**
	Figurine, 4.25"		G-Clef		**35.00**
	ac# 520				
	Jester Clown Popping out of				
	Box				

B-0107	ALL ABOARD FOR BIRTHDAY CLUB FUN				
	Member Only	92	G-Clef	$16.00	**$40.00**
	Figurine, 4.50"		Butterfly		**35.00**
	ac# 45				
	Engineer Riding Locomotive				

B-0108 HAPPINESS IS BELONGING
Member Only
    Figurine, 4.75"
    ac# 371
    Clown Carries Balloon

93   Butterfly $17.50   **$34.00**
       Trumpet   30.00

B-0109 CAN'T GET ENOUGH OF OUR CLUB
Member Only
    Figurine, 3.00"
    ac# 190
    Clown with Doll

94   Trumpet $17.50   **$35.00**
       Ship   34.00

B-0110 HOPPY BIRTHDAY
Member Only
    Figurine, 4.00"
    ac# 445
    Frog atop Birthday Cake

95   Ship $20.00   **$35.00**
       Heart   32.00

B-0111 SCOOTIN' BY JUST TO SAY HI
Member Only
    Figurine, 4.25"
    ac# 825
    Clown on Scooter

96   Heart $21.00   **$35.00**
       Sword   28.00

B-0112 THE FUN STARTS HERE
Member Only
    Figurine, 5.00"
    ac# 931
    Clown Juggles Hearts and
    Stars

97   Sword $22.50   **$28.00**

SYMBOLS OF MEMBERSHIP

B-0002 A SMILE'S THE CYMBAL OF JOY
Member Only
    Figurine, 4.50"
    ac# 18
    Clown with Cymbals

87   Olive Branch $10.00   **$70.00**
       Cedar Tree   65.00
       Flower   63.00

B-0003 THE SWEETEST CLUB AROUND
Member Only
    Figurine, 4.50"
    ac# 967
    Pippin Popping out of Cake

88   Flower $11.00   **$45.00**
       Bow & Arrow   43.00

B-0004 HAVE A BEARY SPECIAL BIRTHDAY
Member Only
    Figurine, 4.50"
    ac# 387
    Teddy Bear with Balloon

89   Bow & Arrow $11.50   **$35.00**
       Flame   30.00

B-0005 | OUR CLUB IS A TOUGH ACT TO FOLLOW
Member Only | 90 | Flame | $13.50 | **$35.00**
Figurine, 4.00" | | Vessel | | **32.00**
ac# 748
Clown with Puppy Leaping
thru Drum

B-0006 | JEST TO LET YOU KNOW YOU'RE TOPS
Member Only | 91 | Vessel | $15.00 | **$35.00**
Figurine, 4.25" | | G-Clef | | **32.00**
ac# 520
Jester Clown Popping out of
Box

B-0007 | ALL ABOARD FOR BIRTHDAY CLUB FUN
Member Only | 92 | G-Clef | $16.00 | **$35.00**
Figurine, 4.50" | | Butterfly | | **32.00**
ac# 45
Engineer Riding Locomotive

B-0008 | HAPPINESS IS BELONGING
Member Only | 93 | Butterfly | $17.50 | **$30.00**
Figurine, 4.75" | | Trumpet | | **29.00**
ac# 371
Clown Carries Balloon

B-0009 | CAN'T GET ENOUGH OF OUR CLUB
Member Only | 94 | Trumpet | $17.50 | **$30.00**
Figurine, 3.00" | | Ship | | **28.00**
ac# 190
Clown with Doll

B-0010 | HOPPY BIRTHDAY
Member Only | 95 | Ship | $20.00 | **$30.00**
Figurine, 4.00" | | Heart | | **28.00**
ac# 445
Frog atop Birthday Cake

B-0011 | SCOOTIN' BY JUST TO SAY HI
Member Only | 96 | Heart | $21.00 | **$32.00**
Figurine, 4.25" | | Sword | | **28.00**
ac# 825
Clown on Scooter

B-0012 | THE FUN STARTS HERE
Member Only | 97 | Sword | $22.50 | **$24.00**
Figurine, 5.00" | 98 | Star | | **22.50**
ac# 931
Clown Juggles Hearts and
Stars

BC-861	FISHING FOR FRIENDS		86	Olive Branch	$10.00	**$130.00**
	Member Only			Cedar Tree		**120.00**
	Figurine, 2.50"					
	ac# 276					
	Raccoon Holding Fish					

BC-871	HI SUGAR!		87	Cedar Tree	$11.00	**$100.00**
	Member Only			Flower		**90.00**
	Figurine, 2.60"			Bow & Arrow		**85.00**
	ac# 424					
	Mouse in Sugar Bowl					

BC-881	SOMEBUNNY CARES		88	Flower	$13.50	**$55.00**
	Member Only			Bow & Arrow		**50.00**
	Figurine, 3.00"					
	ac# 883					
	Bunny with Carrot					

BC-891	CAN'T BEE HIVE MYSELF WITHOUT YOU		89	Bow & Arrow	$13.50	**$50.00**
	Member Only			Flame		**48.00**
	Figurine, 2.50"			Vessel		**47.00**
	ac# 189					
	Teddy Bear with Bee and Bee Hive					

BC-901	COLLECTING MAKES GOOD SCENTS		90	Flame	$15.00	**$35.00**
	Member Only			Vessel		**32.00**
	Figurine, 2.50"					
	ac# 217					
	Skunk with Flowers					

BC-902	I'M NUTS OVER MY COLLECTION		90	Flame	$15.00	**$30.00**
	Member Only			Vessel		**28.00**
	Figurine, 2.50"					
	ac# 493					
	Squirrel with Nuts / Mesh Bag					

BC-911	LOVE PACIFIES		91	Vessel	$16.00	**$36.00**
	Member Only			G-Clef		**35.00**
	Figurine, 3.00"					
	ac# 627					
	Baby Monkey in Bonnet with Pacifer					

BC-912	TRUE BLUE FRIENDS		91	Vessel	$15.00	**$40.00**
	Member Only			G-Clef		**38.00**
	Figurine, 2.50"					
	ac# 1023					
	Puppy & Kitten Sharing Paint & Brush					

BC-921 | EVERY MAN'S HOUSE IS HIS CASTLE
Member Only | 92 | G-Clef | $16.50 | **$35.00**
Figurine, 2.50" | | Butterfly | | **33.00**
ac# 266 | | Trumpet | | **30.00**
Beaver Building Home

BC-922 | I GOT YOU UNDER MY SKIN
Member Only | 92 | G-Clef | $16.00 | **$35.00**
Figurine, 2.50" | | Butterfly | | **32.00**
ac# 465
Pup Wearing Fleece

BC-931 | PUT A LITTLE PUNCH IN YOUR BIRTHDAY
Member Only | 93 | Butterfly | $15.00 | **$20.00**
Figurine, 3.50" | | Trumpet | | **18.00**
ac# 798
Kangaroo Boxer

BC-932 | OWL ALWAYS BE YOUR FRIEND
Member Only | 93 | Butterfly | $16.00 | **$30.00**
Figurine, 3.00" | | Trumpet | | **28.00**
ac# 762
Two Owls Share Tree
Branch

BC-941 | GOD BLESS OUR HOME
Member Only | 94 | Trumpet | $16.00 | **$36.00**
Figurine, 3.50" | | Ship | | **32.00**
ac# 310
Mouse Naps on Turtle Shell

BC-942 | YER A PEL-I-CAN COUNT ON
Member Only | 94 | Trumpet | $16.00 | **$28.00**
Figurine | | Ship | | **25.00**
ac# 1091
Pelican & Penguin

BC-951 | MAKING A POINT TO SAY YOU'RE SPECIAL
Member Only | 95 | Ship | $15.00 | **$32.00**
Figurine, 2.75"
ac# 647
Porcupine

BC-952 | 10 WONDERFUL YEARS OF WISHES
Member Only | 95 | Ship | $50.00 | **$70.00**
Figurine, 2.75" | | Heart | | **65.00**
ac# 1
Birthday Clown

BC-961 | THERE'S A SPOT IN MY HEART FOR YOU
Member Only | 96 | Heart | $15.00 | **$24.00**
Figurine, 2.75"
ac# 978
Dalmatian Pup Pops out of a
Gift Box

BC-962

YOU'RE FIRST IN MY HEART
Member Only
  Figurine, 2.25"
  ac# 1147
  Panda Wears a #1 Locket

96	Heart	$15.00	**$24.00**
	Sword		**20.00**

BC-971

HARE'S TO THE BIRTHDAY CLUB
Member Only
  Figurine, 3.75"
  ac# 385
  Bunny Holds Cup Next to
  Flowerpot

| 97 | Sword | $16.00 | **$18.00** |

BC-972

HOLY TWEET
Member Only
  Figurine, 2.50"
  ac# 439
  Chick Holds open Umbrella
  with Holes

| 97 | Sword | $18.50 | **$18.50** |

BC-981

SLIDE INTO THE CELEBRATION   Commemorates the 20th Anniversary of
Precious Moments
Member Only
  Figurine, 4.75"
  ac# 871
  Skating Turtle Collides with
  Cake

| 98 | Eyeglasses | $15.00 | **$15.00** |
| | Star | 15.00 | **15.00** |

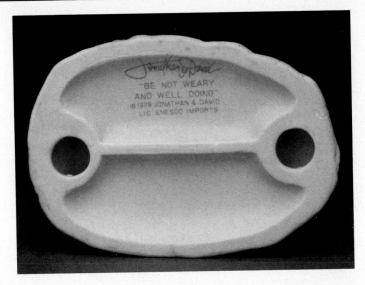

E-3111

Classic Variation. Figurines exist in No Mark versions with an error in the Inspirational Title on the understamp decal. Instead of "Be Not Weary In Well Doing," they read "Be Not Weary And Well Doing." The black and white boxes in which the pieces were shipped also have the incorrect title on the label.

E-4724

Classic Variation: "No E" or "Bibl Error." During the first years of production the "e" was missing from the word Bible. Some Hourglass & Fish pieces also have this variation.

E-5214

Classic Variation: "Backwards Bible." The first production of this figurine had the words "Holy Bible" inscribed on the back cover. Pieces with this error exist in No Mark and Triangle versions. Reportedly, No Mark and Triangle pieces also exist where the title is correctly placed, but these may be considered extremely rare. The majority of Hourglass pieces have the correctly placed title.

E-5379

With the opening of a new production facility in Indonesia, numerous pieces of whiteware (unpainted figurines) were inadvertently shipped to retailers.

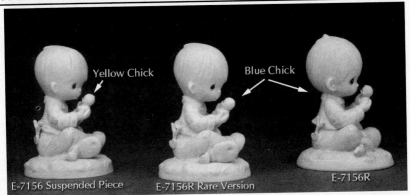

Yellow Chick

Blue Chick

E-7156 Suspended Piece   E-7156R Rare Version   E-7156R

E-7156R

First introduced in 1982 as E-7156, the original version of this figurine had the boy holding a yellow chick. E-7156 was suspended in 1985, and in 1987 was re-sculptured and returned to production as E-7156R. Among the changes made was the addition of the incised "Sam B" on the base of the figurine, and a change in the color of the chick–from yellow to blue. The re-sculptured piece is also considerably larger than the original version. During the early part of production in 1987 (Cedar Tree), the molds from the suspended piece, E-7156, were pulled and used along with the molds for the new re-introduced piece, E-7156R. Shipments of figurines crafted from the old suspended mold but with the new blue painting of the chick were made before the error was discovered. These pieces are the rare version. All rare versions have the Cedar Tree Symbol.

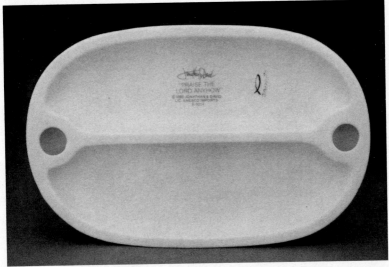

E-9254

Classic Variation: "Inked Fish." During 1983, the Fish appeared as part of the understamp decal on many pieces. Pieces were also produced that did not have a Fish at all–incised or decal. When this occurred we can only theorize an attempt was made to correct it by actually drawing the Fish on the bottom of the piece. This inked symbol can be washed off, creating an unmarked piece.

E-9261/E-9262
Most figurines with the Fish Annual Production Symbol do not have the "h" in the word "he" in the inscription on the graduate's scroll capitalized.

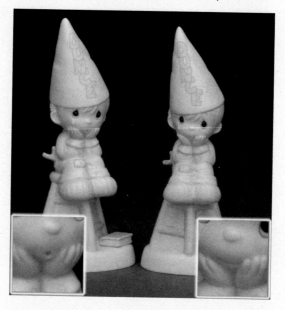

E-9268
Classic Variation: "Smiling Dunce." The first Hourglass pieces produced are known as "Smiling Dunces" or "Smiley" and appeared with a smile. An "O" shaped mouth is the normal piece.

111155

At some point during the 1988 production, the expression on the face was changed from a smile to a "determined frown." The smiling piece is often referred to as the "Smiling Plunger."

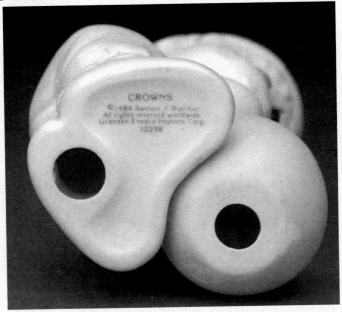

12238

Classic Variation. "CLOWNS" was misspelled "CROWNS" on the understamp decal of some sets.

12416

There are Cedar Tree pieces with two hooks from the Retailers Wreath, #111465. There are also some ornaments, again from the Retailer's Wreath, that have the inscription "Heaven Bound" upside-down.

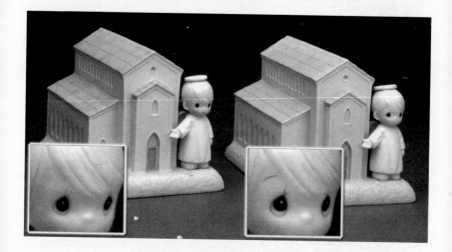

523011

Unmarked pieces of this figurine exist with and without an eyebrow on the angel boy (bangs cover where the second eyebrow would be).

525049

Only collectors who attended a 1990 "Good Friends Are Forever" Special Event with a friend had the opportunity to be included in a drawing for this special Rosebud Decal Understamp figurine. Identical to 521817 with exception of Rosebud decal. One per Center.

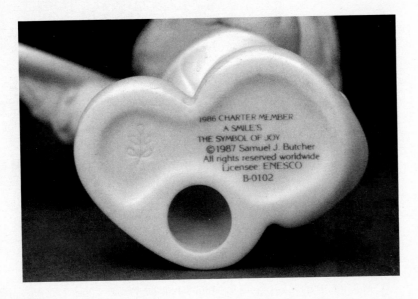

B-0102

The first of these were shipped with a title error on the understamp decal–"A Smile's The Symbol Of Joy."

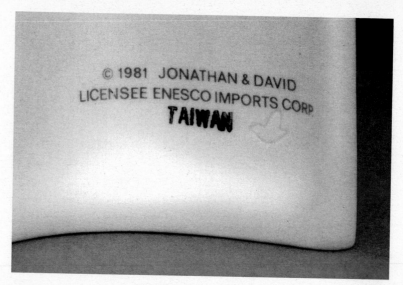

E-0202

Termed the "Canadian Plaque Error," approximately 750 pieces of this 1982 Symbol Of Membership piece were produced in 1985 and shipped to Canada. These pieces are stamped "TAIWAN" and have a Dove Annual Production Symbol.

E-2362

Classic Variation: Unmarked pieces exist in four variations: 1) Straight hair and no caption, 2) Curly hair and no caption, 3) Straight hair with the caption, "Baby's First Christmas," and, 4) Curly hair with the caption, "Baby's First Christmas." Subsequent pieces (Cross through Flower) were curly hair with the caption. The straight hair, with or without the caption, is considered the variation.

VARIATIONS

E-2395

Classic Variation: Termed the "Turban Nativity," the shepherd holding a lamb was replaced in some Hourglass sets with a shepherd wearing a turban. "Turban Boy" shepherds were also shipped individually to retailers as replacement pieces, so collectors were sometimes able to add the "Turban Boy" as a twelfth piece to this eleven piece mini Nativity Set.

E-2837

Termed the "No Hands Groom," during the first year of production (Olive Branch) this piece was produced with no hands. The mold was changed for the subsequent years (Cedar Tree to present) to show the boy's hands.